The Life of Horace Benedict De Saussure

Douglas W. Freshfield

Alpha Editions

This edition published in 2020

ISBN: 9789354189739 (Hardback)
ISBN: 9789354189975 (Paperback)

Design and Setting By
Alpha Editions
www.alphaedis.com
email - alphaedis@gmail.com

As per information held with us this book is in Public Domain.
This book is a reproduction of an important historical work. Alpha Editions uses the best technology to reproduce historical work in the same manner it was first published to preserve its original nature. Any marks or number seen are left intentionally to preserve its true form.

PREFACE

THE following pages represent an endeavour to fill an obvious gap in Alpine literature. After more than a century, Horace Benedict de Saussure still awaits his biographer. The fact has been proclaimed by two of his most distinguished successors in the University (formerly the Academy) of Geneva, the late Professor Ernest Naville and Professor Borgeaud. But their invitation has failed hitherto to call forth any local response. I had hoped that the pious task would be taken in hand by some Genevese man of letters, who, with all the advantage of local and technical knowledge, would do full justice to the part played in life by his illustrious fellow-citizen as a man of science and a mountain explorer, and would at the same time be able to appreciate the political services he endeavoured to render to the Republic in a tragical crisis in its history. It was this hope that first made me refrain when, as long ago as 1878, Ruskin—from boyhood an eager reader of the *Voyages dans les Alpes*—instigated by some articles on the lesser pioneers of the period I had contributed to the *Alpine Journal* (vol. ix.), proposed to me that I should write a life of de Saussure. In later years I found a more practical and conclusive obstacle to the acceptance of the tempting suggestion in the difficulty of collecting the material needful without researches among the family papers and public archives preserved at Geneva and Berne, which would have involved a prolonged stay in Switzerland.

This difficulty has recently been overcome by the kindness of Mr. H. F. Montagnier, an American gentleman known to his colleagues of the Alpine Club both as an assiduous climber and an accomplished student of the literature of mountain travel. Mr. Montagnier, finding himself resident in Switzerland and debarred from active service during the Great War, has at his own suggestion employed his leisure in ransacking public libraries and obtaining access to private collections in quest of material bearing on de Saussure's career, scientific, Alpine, political, and social. His efforts have been singularly successful. I have had brought under my eyes a mass of private correspondence, including letters between de Saussure and his scientific contemporaries, letters from and to his wife and nearest relations, and from his numerous friends in England and Paris. Mr. Montagnier has further had access to de Saussure's carefully kept journal of his Grand Tour of France, Holland, and England, as well as to the rough notebooks of many of his Alpine excursions, no account of which was included in the published *Voyages*. All this for the most part new material has been at my disposal. I have in addition made use, wherever possible, of the short biographical notices or eulogies of de Saussure contributed by his contemporaries Senebier, Cuvier, de Candolle, and more recently by Forbes, Wolf, Sainte-Beuve, Sayous, Töpffer, Favre, and Naville. Further, in order to realise to some extent the background against which de Saussure's figure must be set, I have turned over the pages of many local tracts and journals of the latter half of the eighteenth century and of some of the personal memoirs that throw light on the political and social state of Geneva during the most eventful period in its history: a period when not only Voltaire, Rousseau, and Bonnet, but visitors such as Madame d'Epinay and Grimm, Madame de Staël and Madame Necker, made it a centre of intellectual thought and activity. On the events of the succeeding years, when the internal quarrels of the Genevese reproduced on a small scale the miseries and crimes of the French Revolution, and finally wrecked their ancient Republic, several recently published volumes have thrown fresh light. They help to prove that throughout those political troubles de Saussure played a strenuous and persevering part— a part that has not as yet been adequately recognised by local historians. I have done my best to bring out the patriotic aims of his action, as it presents itself when closely studied in contemporary memoirs and documents from a point of view free from all party bias. I have also given some space to his energetic and persistent attitude as an educational reformer, a capacity in which he showed a breadth of outlook in advance of his time, and even, perhaps, of our own. In short, I have tried to deal with de Saussure's life as a whole; to present him not only in the two capacities in which his fame is best established as a geologist and Alpine explorer, but also as a member of society, a citizen and a philosopher—in the wider eighteenth-century acceptation of that word. It has been no slight task to examine, set in order, and select from the mass of manuscript material generously placed at my disposal. But it has been lightened to me by the pleasure I have had in following de Saussure as a traveller over ground every step of which has been familiar to me for more than half a century, and through valleys and villages, many of which, when I first knew them some sixty years ago, had lost comparatively little of the primitive character and charm vividly portrayed in the *Voyages*. It is a satisfaction to me to have been able in this volume to pay in part, and to the best of my ability, a debt which has been long owing to the memory of de Saussure, not only from the mountaineers who, having conquered the Alps and the 'inhospitable Caucasus,' are now wrestling with the Andes and the Himalaya, but from the great company of men and women who annually find rest and refreshment of body and soul in the mountains. I cannot hope to have surmounted all the difficulties that have faced me. But in so far as I may have succeeded in carrying out my intention, the credit will be largely due to the indefatigable aid I have received from Mr. Montagnier.

I have to thank several of my friends, and in particular Professor Bonney, Professor Garwood, and Dr. Mill, for their help with respect to the chapters devoted to de Saussure's scientific work and achievements. To the published works of the Rev. W. A. B. Coolidge and Dr. Dübi I have made frequent reference, and the latter has further aided me with his friendly advice. Mrs. Rathbone has kindly allowed me to reproduce the drawing of Mont Blanc made by Mr. E. T. Compton for her father, my old friend, the late C. E. Mathews.

Among the descendants of H. B. de Saussure and the members of old Genevese families who have been good enough to place at the disposal of my collaborator papers from their family archives, or otherwise to assist in the preparation of this volume, I desire specially to mention and thank :

> M. Horace de Saussure (a great-grandson), and other members of the de Saussure family in Geneva for allowing me to use the journals and papers of H. B. de Saussure in their possession.

M. F. Louis Perrot (a descendant through H. B. de Saussure's only daughter, Mme. Necker-de Saussure), for placing at my disposal letters of H. B. de Saussure to his wife, and miniatures.

Mme. Ferdinand de Saussure, for permission to reproduce several family portraits in the Townhouse in the Rue de la Cité, Geneva.

MM. Charles and Henry Turrettini (descendants), for permission to reproduce the portrait of Mme. Turrettini-Boissier, and the miniature of Mme. H. B. de Saussure.

M. H. Necker (a descendant through Mme. Necker-de Saussure), for permission to look over the family correspondence in his possession, and to inspect H. B. de Saussure's Greek diary.

Dr. Frédéric Rilliet, for allowing me the use of the papers of his ancestor, Marc Auguste Pictet, de Saussure's friend and successor.

Dr. H. Maillart-Gosse, for papers relating to the Col du Géant found among the MSS. of Henri Albert Gosse.

Professor Charles Borgeaud, of the University of Geneva, for unpublished material, suggestions, and advice.

M. Frédéric Gardy, Director of the University Library of Geneva, M. Théophile Dufour, Honorary Director of the Public Library of Geneva, and the Directors of various other libraries, for their unvarying courtesy.

MM. Paul Martin and Charles Roch, Archivist and Assistant-Archivist of the Republic and Canton of Geneva, for an immense amount of aid and advice in the task of reconstituting de Saussure's political career, verifying dates, etc., in the archives of Geneva.

M. Fernan Aubert, Keeper of the Manuscripts of the University Library in Geneva, for kindly advice and aid in connection with the splendid collection of manuscript material entrusted to his care.

Mlles. Danielle and Louise Plan, for much help in the difficult task of deciphering and copying the vast amount of unpublished material collected for this volume.

DOUGLAS W. FRESHFIELD.

September 1920.

CONTENTS

CHAP.		PAGE
I.	FORERUNNERS	1
II.	GENEVA IN THE EIGHTEENTH CENTURY	31
III.	YOUTH AND EARLY TRAVELS	47
IV.	THE GRAND TOUR (1768-69)	91
V.	ITALY	121
VI.	TEN YEARS' ALPINE TRAVEL (1774-84)	142
VII.	THE BUET	175
VIII.	MONT BLANC	197
IX.	THE COL DU GÉANT	242
X.	MONTE ROSA	262
XI.	DISCOURS PRÉLIMINAIRE, ETC.	286
XII.	POLITICS AT GENEVA	294
XIII.	EDUCATION AND THE RIVIERA (1772-81)	311
XIV.	POLITICS AND HOME LIFE (1781-92)	332
XV.	THE LAST YEARS	365
XVI.	BONNET AND HALLER	402
XVII.	DE SAUSSURE IN SCIENCE AND LITERATURE	421
	A NOTE ON THE METEOROLOGICAL WORK AND OBSERVATIONS ON DEEP TEMPERATURES OF H. B. DE SAUSSURE, BY DR. H. R. MILL	457
	LIST OF THE PRINCIPAL PUBLISHED WORKS AND SCIENTIFIC PAPERS OF H. B. DE SAUSSURE	467
	INDEX	469

ILLUSTRATIONS

H. B. DE SAUSSURE IN 1796	*Frontispiece*
Sketch by Saint-Ours.	
	Facing page
THE GROUNDS AT GENTHOD	21
From a photograph.	
GENEVA IN THE EIGHTEENTH CENTURY	32
From an old print.	
M. AND MME. NICOLAS DE SAUSSURE	49
From portraits.	
THE COURTYARD AT FRONTENEX	51
From a photograph.	
THE VILLA LULLIN AT GENTHOD	52
From a photograph.	
DR. TRONCHIN	58
From a portrait by Liotard.	
H. B. DE SAUSSURE AT 18	79
MME. H. B. DE SAUSSURE AS A GIRL	79
From miniatures.	
H. B. DE SAUSSURE ABOUT 1777	142
From a portrait by Jens Juel.	
MONT BLANC: SHOWING DE SAUSSURE'S ROUTE	197
From a drawing by E. T. Compton.	
THE ASCENT TO THE COL DU GÉANT	252
From a contemporary print.	
MLLE. ALBERTINE DE SAUSSURE	256
MME. TRONCHIN, MME. TURRETTINI	256
From miniatures.	

	Facing page
THE DESCENT FROM THE COL DU GÉANT	260
From a contemporary print.	
THE TOWNHOUSE FROM THE CORRATERIE . . .	336
From a photograph.	
STAIRCASE AND INNER COURT OF THE TOWNHOUSE .	346
From photographs.	
A PROCESSION IN GENEVA IN 1789	354
From a contemporary print.	
H. B. DE SAUSSURE	387
From a portrait by Saint-Ours.	
NICOLAS THÉODORE DE SAUSSURE	395
From a portrait.	
DOLOMIEU, AS SUCCESSOR TO DE SAUSSURE . .	439
From a sketch by Saint-Ours.	

MAPS

SKETCH-MAP OF DE SAUSSURE'S ALPINE TRAVELS .	*Inside front cover*
ROUTE-MAP OF MONT BLANC . . .	*Facing page* 225

CHAPTER I

FORERUNNERS

IN 1740, the date of Horace Benedict de Saussure's birth, a new period in European history was about to open. A few months later the disputed succession arising on the death of the Emperor Charles the Sixth was to involve the Continent in the confused Wars of the Spanish Succession. England under her Hanoverian kings could no longer hope to hold aloof from the quarrels of her neighbours, and Walpole's thirty years of inaction were drawing to their close. But the Swiss Cantons and the closely attached Republic of Geneva enjoyed the privilege of small States and were left outside the struggle, while for four years more England remained at peace with France. In 1740 young Englishmen of birth were still free to complete their education abroad, and to combine with the Grand Tour a course of lectures in the Protestant Academy on the shores of Lake Leman. There their studies were not so engrossing but that they found time to play Shakespeare to the Venerable Company of Pastors, and to reveal the existence of Mont Blanc and its glaciers to a world which for the moment found other things to think about.

The publication of Windham's and Martel's modest accounts of their visits to the glaciers of Savoy was the seed from which, after an interval of nearly twenty years, was to spring the career of de Saussure. The fact is emphasised by his contemporary, Senebier. But there were other local influences, and above all the general atmosphere of the time, which contributed towards converting a young Genevese patrician into the first scientific explorer of the Alps. The latter half of the eighteenth century was a period of movement, not only in politics, but in thought, in literature, and in science. It witnessed in every direction the break up of old barriers. Students came out of their libraries and sought knowledge and inspiration from direct contact with nature and with one another. Most of the leaders of that generation have long since been commemorated by competent writers. But of one of them, the subject of this volume, no adequate Life has hitherto appeared. The lack points to a strange remissness on the part of his fellow-citizens, for de Saussure is the greatest man of science Geneva can boast, and material was not lacking in the Public Library and private cabinets of the town.

De Saussure has two principal claims to our grateful remembrance. He took a leading part in raising Geology to its high place among the physical sciences; it is mainly to him we owe that we can count Alpine travel among the pleasures and consolations of life. These surely are services that called for an attempt to furnish some record of a career that has added largely to human knowledge and still more to human happiness. Yet in the words of his distinguished fellow-citizen, Professor Borgeaud, 'Horace Benedict de Saussure still awaits his biographer.'

To the general reader of to-day de Saussure is known, if known at all, as the conqueror of Mont Blanc. But even from this aspect the part he played in creating the modern taste for Alpine scenery and travel has been but imperfectly appreciated. It may help my readers to realise the change in the attitude of men towards mountains effected by the lad who, at the age of twenty, walked to Chamonix and offered a reward to the first climber of Mont Blanc, if, before telling the story of his life, I ask them to cast a glance backwards, and in so doing to pay a brief tribute to certain of the rare spirits who in earlier centuries found health and happiness on the heights. I shall dwell more particularly on the age immediately preceding de Saussure's own, the period before his personal influence had begun to make itself felt, the first sixty years of the eighteenth century, in which the outstanding figures are Rousseau and Voltaire in the Suisse Romande and Haller in German Switzerland.

In the consciousness of simple peoples all waste places, whether seas, deserts, or mountains, are apt to be objects of religious awe; they are regarded as portals to the unseen world. To the part played by mountains in the legendary dealings of Jehovah with his chosen people, the books of the Old Testament bear frequent witness,[1] and did space allow it would be easy to show a similar tendency among the nations of Farther Asia, the Chinese, Japanese, Tibetans, and Indians. But it is in ancient Greece, where primitive man, outgrowing his childhood with a rapidity unknown elsewhere, attained at a bound to a unique power of self-expression, that we recognise the best example of this primitive instinct in its highest development. The human mind abhors a void. It personifies the forces of nature, finding in solitudes a home for the supernatural; peopling the uninhabitable with creatures of its own fancy. The Greek enthroned the synod of the gods upon the broad heights and serried crags of Olympus; Pan held the wooded spurs of Parnassus; Apollo and the Muses its twin peaks. The woods and the streams were the haunt of a crowd of nymphs and fauns.

Races further advanced in civilisation are found to take a more practical and less poetical point of view. The characteristics that impress them most in mountains are that they are difficult, barren, inhospitable; our own ancestors summed up their feelings in a single word, 'horrid.'[2] This was the attitude habitually shown in Roman literature. Not that there was any dislike or indifference to all sorts of natural scenery in the days of Augustus, such as there was in those of Louis Quatorze. The Roman citizen was keenly interested in the features of the world he had conquered and had to administer. Latin poetry is as crowded with place-names as Milton's, and the singularly appropriate epithets as a rule attached to each local feature show close and sympathetic observation. But nature was valued chiefly as a background and in so far as it contributed to human enjoyment; it was shunned from the moment when it began to add to the toils or dangers of life. Virgil, Catullus, and the younger Pliny celebrated the Italian lakes or the Etrurian highlands; Horace his quiet nook in the hills behind Tibur; Ovid grew eloquent on the charms of his birthplace, Sulmo, the remote hill-town surrounded by running

[1] In the seventeenth century 'Bible Mountains' were made the subject of a long rhymed poem entitled 'Ein lustig ernsthaft poetisch Gastmal und Gespräch zweyer Bergen, nämlich des Niesens und Stockhorns' (Berne, 1606), by a worthy Swiss pastor named Rebmann.

[2] *Horridus* in Latin has a primary sense of 'bristling,' and is used of spears, or woods, or crags. Narrow gorges in the neighbourhood of the Italian lakes are locally known as *Orridi*.

brooks and green meadows in the heart of the tawny Apennine. As a foreign critic has laid down, *amœnitas*, pleasantness, is the keynote to Roman appreciation of scenery.[1] We have no description of the Passage of the Alps or of the Pyrenees from a picturesque point of view in Latin literature. Livy, Claudian, and Silius Italicus, when dealing with Alpine campaigns, emphasise only their disagreeable features.

In the days of the Empire, while the Roman Peace lasted and Roman roads, with their elaborate system of inns and posthouses, were kept in repair, the Alps were no very serious obstacle. They could be neglected, if not ignored. But when to the difficulties of broken tracks were added the dangers from Saracenic marauders or ordinary outlaws, they began to be looked on with extreme disfavour. In the tenth century an old English monk, who had doubtless suffered in crossing the Great St. Bernard on his way to Rome, wrote of 'the bitter blasts of glaciers and the Pennine army of evil spirits.' He used this quaint formula more than once as a malediction against any breaker of the covenants contained in the legal documents he was called on to draft.[2] It should be borne in mind that the mediaeval pilgrims to Rome generally crossed the passes at the worst possible season, before Easter, when the late avalanches are falling; at the moment of the year when spring is holding her first revel in the lowlands, and her fingers have not yet spread the brilliant flower-carpet of an Alpine summer over the higher pastures, where the brown bare slopes are still flecked with ugly patches of half-melting snow.

Thus the third or modern period, that of 'the love of the Alps,' was preceded by centuries during which the feeling for natural scenery was restricted within narrow bounds, and only such regions as could be put to human uses were brought within the reach of human sympathies. In the case of the High Alps, the discovery of such uses was very gradual. It came about mainly in this wise. As the years went on and the old order broke up, the Alpine valleys were found to contain retreats serviceable for the cure both of souls and bodies. The Church took the lead in familiarising men with mountains by showing that the solitudes

---

[1] Friedländer, *Darstellungen aus der Sittengeschichte Roms*, vol. ii.
[2] In some of the later documents a less-travelled scribe, puzzled by *Pennino*, substituted for it *pernici*.

they had dreaded as the haunts of demons might serve as refuges from the turmoil and wickedness of the outer world. She set up her houses not only on the outskirts, but in the very heart of the Alps—not only at Oropa, Novalesa, and Varallo, St. Gall and Einsiedeln, but also at Pesio, Chamonix, Engelberg, and Disentis, on the bleak crests of the St. Bernard and St. Gotthard and in the flowery wilderness of the Grande Chartreuse. The monks collected simples, they attended the sick, and thus the studies of botany and medicine went hand in hand. Glacier ice was found to be useful in fevers and 'most pertinacious toothache,' as well as to cool wine during the summer heats. The Alpine Baths sprang into repute. In the course of the sixteenth century fifty treatises dealing with twenty-one different resorts were published. Leonardo da Vinci (1452-1519) mentions the Baths of Bormio, and Conrad Gesner (1516-1565) visited them. The waters of St. Moritz were said to supersede the juice of the grape, a quality the innkeepers of the Engadine have, in recent years, been at no pains to advertise. To Pfäffers wounded warriors went to be healed; and it was reckoned a rival to the Swiss Baden as a scene of worldly dissipation. At the Baths of Loëche, as early as 1501, there was a large inn built by the Bishop of Sion, to which the patients were carried in panniers. Brigue, Tarasp, even remote spots such as the Baths of Masino, in a side glen of Val Tellina, Teniger Bad,[1] in the Bündner Oberland, had their votaries.

These facts have to be kept in mind in any attempt to ascertain the origin and growth of men's relations to the Alps. In the Middle Ages they were no longer traversed only in haste by princes and pilgrims and commercial travellers, to whom they were mainly important as an inconvenient impediment on the roads to Italy. By means of the Alpine monasteries and Baths men of leisure and of such scientific interests as were alive at the time were brought into daily contact with the great mountains. Hence there arose —it is true, in a relatively limited number of cases—among men of independent and active minds, a certain interest in the physical aspects and features of the Alps. It manifested itself differently according to the individual; the impulse might be

[1] Fifty years ago this Badhaus still retained its primitive simplicity. A series of wooden troughs resembling coffins so arranged as to fit into one another, head to feet, afforded opportunity for social bathing.

botanical, medical, or even artistic curiosity; it might spring from emotional feeling, or from a zest for climbing. It did not necessarily involve any love of mountain scenery, but it prepared the way for the growth of that sentiment. Juxtaposition revealed or created affinity. It would be easy to multiply instances of these exceptions to the temper of their age. But space forbids; moreover, the roll of early contributors to Alpine literature has been called over of late years by several distinguished writers, some of whom have also been members of the craft of mountaineers.

Foremost among the few forerunners to be mentioned here stands the name of Leonardo da Vinci. The world recognises him as a supreme artist. The literary or scientific critic knows him as one of the keenest observers, one of the widest and deepest thinkers of a great age, a Baconian before Bacon. Up to his day the scholastic mind had been a closed chamber. The Humanists remained in books. Physical science lives by original investigation and experiment, not in a library. In thought and method Leonardo was a modern; a mechanical inventor born out of his time; a philosopher who brushed aside all orthodox hindrances and recognised a universe with constantly receding limits.

Leonardo's marvellously varied activities are characteristically recorded, not in formal treatises, but in notebooks, sketches, and maps. The multitude of his ideas, his constant habit of verifying them by experiment, his passion for truth, stood in the way of any hasty theorising. A system, being, as he held, nothing else than the inclusion of particular truths in a higher and more comprehensive truth, could only be the result and crown of a life's work. In this respect, at least, we may recognise in him a kindred spirit to the author of the *Voyages dans les Alpes*, who left unwritten the volume which should have contained his 'Theory of the Earth.'

Leonardo's interest in the Alps was manifold. He abounds in practical notes that might serve for a modern guide-book. He reports that on the Grigna (the grey mountain opposite Cadenabbia above the Lecco branch of the Lake of Como) are 'the biggest bare cliffs' he knows; that Val Sassina (a glen behind it) is full of the 'cose fantastiche' he delights in; that there are waterfalls seven hundred feet high on the way up to the Splügen, which 'it is a pleasure to see'; that at the head of the Val Tellina there are Baths (at Bormio) and a group of snowy summits (the Ortler). He is not above chronicling for how many *soldi* a day you can get good living in the village inns, or how in the mountains behind Chiavenna the hunters pursue on hands and knees deer (probably chamois), bouquetin, and 'terrible bears.' He was, as his notes indicate,[1] once at Geneva, where he mentions the river Arve and the fair that was held in the suburb of St. Gervais at midsummer. It is possible that he may have been consulted on the project of new fortifications in hand about that date.

But by far the most interesting of his mountain excursions was the ascent of a mountain he calls Mon Boso. For long it remained unidentified, and it is to an Italian writer, Signor Uzielli, that we owe the solving of the riddle. For I cannot but hold that he has been successful where I and many others had gone astray. The Italian Ordnance maps show that this name is still in use for two of the tops of the lofty crest that stretches down from Monte Rosa and divides Val Sesia from Val de Lys and the Biellese.[2] Leonardo, it may be objected, describes his Mon Boso as part of the range that divides France from Italy, from the base of which flow four rivers (identified elsewhere as the Rhine, Rhône, Po, and Danube) to the four different points of the compass. But at that date divisions in political geography were vague. Germany was generally regarded as ending at the limits of the Swiss Cantons —that is, about the St. Gotthard. The Valais, under its Bishop, was connected more closely with Savoy than with the Empire. Again, with respect to the four rivers named, we have to remember that tributaries were often treated as sources, or rather that the particular source now recognised was not always that accepted by early geographers. Thus, for example, the Inn was reckoned the main stream of the Danube.

There seems good reason to believe that Leonardo touched a glacier. He reports finding in July ' a huge mass of ice formed

[1] The notes are numbered 300, 1030, 1031, 1057, 1060 in Dr. Paul Richter's *Literary Works of Leonardo da Vinci* (2nd vol., London, 1883). One of them is attached to a sketch. Dr. Richter's translations of notes 300 and 1060 stand in need of some correction.

[2] On a map of Lombardy published in 1749 ' M. Boso Rosa ' (*sic*) is printed north of the Val Sesia. This seems to indicate that the two names were either confused or used indifferently. Rosa (Ruize, Roesa = Glacier) may have been properly applied to the snows, Boso (Bosco ?) to the woods and pasturages below the snow level.

by layers of hail.' This phrase may, no doubt, possibly be taken to refer to a snowfield. But the words are much more applicable to a glacier. It seems to me probable, taking into account Leonardo's remarks about the dark hue of the sky and the brightness of the sunshine, that he may have climbed to a height of about ten thousand feet above Gressoney or Alagna, on the edge of one of the glaciers of Monte Rosa.

Leonardo found deeper sources of interest in Alpine scenery. These were not, as in the case of Petrarch, emotional; they were connected with physical rather than with psychical problems. He was a geologist before geology. He looked to the mountains, as no one did again for more than two hundred years, for a key to the story of our globe. He attributed valley formation largely to the action of rivers. He noted the distribution of rocks and the frequent correspondence of the strata on the opposite flanks of defiles. He recognised the true significance of fossils, and denied the possibility of their being the records of a universal deluge, which he boldly discredited. He realised that the plain of Lombardy had once been a gulf of the Adriatic. He no doubt invoked too frequently the agency of catastrophic floods, but in this delusion he was to have many followers in future generations, among them de Saussure himself. Finally, as an artist he was quick to note the manifold effects of distance and atmosphere displayed in mountain landscapes, the gathering of the storm clouds below the naked peaks, the sharp definition of the ridges on the skyline compared to the relative softness of the lower slopes, seen through a denser atmosphere.

In the early literature of the Alps no name is more worthy to be commemorated than that of Conrad Gesner of Zurich (1516-1565). In a relatively short life Gesner combined an amazing variety of intellectual activities; he was in his many-sidedness a typical figure of the Renaissance. Remembered to-day chiefly as a botanist, he was also the author of the standard work of the time on zoology. Cuvier described him as the creator of scientific botany and the founder of zoology, 'a prodigy of industry, of knowledge and sagacity.' Despite his labours in natural science, Gesner was also active as a humanist and a man of letters; he edited classics; he was the compiler of a universal catalogue of authors and a volume containing an account of one hundred and thirty languages, ancient and modern. He also practised as a doctor! But the trait that gives him a place here and endears him to all mountaineers is that he was the first man boldly to profess a love of climbing for its own sake, and to enjoy and depict in the modern spirit the incidents of Alpine travel.

Gesner died at the early age of forty-nine, before he had had time to write the book on mountains which he tells us he had in his mind. But it is clear from the letter written in 1541 to a friend on *The Admiration of Mountains*,[1] and from the preface to the account of his ascent of one of the summits of Pilatus in 1550, that the seed he sowed, if it took long to spread abroad and germinate,[2] did not fall altogether on stony ground. Passages from both have been of late frequently quoted, but they can hardly be quoted too often. Here is an extract from the former:

'I have determined, therefore,' writes Gesner to his friend, the most learned Avienus (his real name was Vogel), 'as long as God grants me life to climb every year several mountains, or at least one, in the flower-season, partly for the sake of botanical studies, partly for honest bodily exercise, and for my own satisfaction. For what, think you, must be the pleasure, what the delight a mind properly attuned feels when one gazes with admiration on the bulk of mountains and raises one's head among the clouds! The consciousness is in some vague way impressed by the stupendous heights [3] and is drawn to the contemplation of the Great Architect. Men of dull mind admire nothing, sleep at home, never go out into the Theatre of the World, hide in corners, like dormice, through the winter, never recognise that the human race was sent into the world in order that through its marvels it should learn to recognise some higher Power, the Supreme Being Himself. . . . Let them roll like pigs in their mud; let them lie stupefied by the pursuit of gain and illiberal studies. Students of philosophy endeavour to view with the eyes both of their souls and bodies the glories of this earthly Paradise, and amongst these they

---

[1] Printed as a preface to his *Libellus de Lacte*. See Coolidge's *J. Simler et les Origines de l'Alpinisme* for a full translation and comments.

[2] Simler, in the letter to the Bishop of Sion which introduces his *History of the Valais* (1574), paraphrases the former, and a hundred and thirty-four years later Scheuchzer started his *Itinera Alpina* (1708) with a long quotation from *The Admiration of Mountains*.

[3] Compare Tennyson's
'Some vague emotion of delight
In gazing up an Alpine height.'

count by no means least the lofty and broken ridges of the mountains, their inaccessible precipices, the vastness of the slopes that rise heavenward, the steep crags, the shady woods.'

In the Pilatus pamphlet [1] Gesner is equally emphatic. Here are a few sentences taken from several pages of a eulogy of mountaineering, wholly modern in the note they strike despite the trammels of a dead language to which Gesner succeeds in giving singular vivacity. In one sentence he celebrates the holiday humours often made a reproach by dyspeptic reviewers to the writers of Alpine articles. In the next he is anticipating Shelley's

'. . . deep music of the rolling world,
Kindling within the strings of the waved air
Æolian modulations.'

But let him speak for himself:

'The agreeable conversation of companions, their quips and jests, will give pleasure; then the delicious songs of the birds in the woods, and finally the very silence of the solitude. Here there can be no sounds to vex or harass the ears, no city riots or noise, no human strife. *Here in the deep and solemn silence on the topmost crests of the mountains you will seem to yourself almost to catch the music, if such there be, of the heavenly orbs.*[2]

'Let us conclude, therefore, that mountain walks, taken with friends, so long as the mind and body are capable of profiting by them, and the weather is suitable, afford the greatest possible enjoyment and the most delightful gratification to the senses. But there are no beds, feather mattresses, pillows! Oh you mollycoddle! (*mollem et effeminatum hominem*). Hay will serve for all; hay soft and fragrant, a heap of various grasses and fragrant flowers. Your sleep will be the healthier and more refreshing. You will have hay for a pillow to your head, for a mattress to your body, and you will even spread it over you for a coverlet.'

May we not claim Gesner as the spiritual father of all Alpine Clubs? What would we give for him to have lived to tell us the

[1] *Descriptio Montis Fracti*, 1551.

[2] Auditum suaves sociorum sermones, joci, facetiaeque, oblectabunt: et avicularum in silvis suavissimi cantus, et ipsum denique solitudinis silentium. Nihil hic auribus molestum esse potest, nihil importunum, nulli tumultus aut strepitus urbani, nullae hominum rixae. Hic in profundo et religioso quodam silentio ex praealtis montium jugis, ipsam fere coelestium, si quae est, orbium harmoniam exaudire tibi videberis.

story of ' the many and much loftier mountains [than Pilatus] in different parts of Switzerland which he had wandered amongst ' ?

We may note in passing that the legend of Pilatus supplies an excellent illustration of the gradual decay of superstition. When we first hear any mention of the mountain, it is to be told how the ghost of the Roman Proconsul is doomed to sit every Good Friday in his red robes of office on a rocky throne in the hollow below the peaks. The magistrates of Lucerne forbade under pain of imprisonment and fine any rash intrusion on a spirit who, if disturbed, might visit the countryside with storms and floods. At a later date we find special permits given to discreet professors and students to visit the locality ' for scientific purposes.' Finally, incredulous pleasure-seekers throw stones into the dark tarn beneath whose waters the unquiet ghost once lurked; Gesner botanises on its forbidden margin—and nobody is the worse.

Gesner was by no means solitary in his generation in his enthusiasm for mountain travel. Hear his friend, Benôit Marti, a Professor of Classics at Berne. In 1557 he wrote as follows of the view from his native city :

' These are the mountains which we love and delight in, when we gaze at them from the higher parts of our city and admire their mighty peaks and broken crags that threaten to fall at any moment. On them we watch the risings and settings of the sun and seek signs of the weather. In them we find food not only for our eyes and our minds, but also for our bellies ' ;

and he goes on to enumerate with equal enthusiasm the dairy products of the Oberland and the happy life of its population. This worthy man proceeds :

' Who, then, would not admire, love, willingly visit, explore, and climb places of this sort ? I assuredly should call those who are not attracted by them mushrooms ; stupid, dull fishes ; slow tortoises ' (*fungos ; stupidos, insulsos pisces ; lentasque chelonas*).

Having forcibly vented his scorn by these varied comparisons, he goes on :

' In truth, I cannot describe the sort of affection and natural love by which I am drawn to the mountains, so that I am never happier than on their crests, and there are no wanderings dearer to me than those among them. . . . They are the Theatre of the Lord, displaying monuments of past ages, such as precipices, rocks, peaks, chasms, and never-melting glaciers.'

The foregoing are only a selection from many equally enthusiastic outbursts.

Nor are their books the only evidence we have of the love of mountains in these scholars of the Renaissance. The mountains themselves bear, or once bore, records even more impressive. Most Swiss travellers have climbed to the picturesque old castle at Thun and seen, beyond the clear flood of the rushing Aar, the green heights of the outposts of the Alps, the Stockhorn and the Niesen. Our friend Marti, who scaled the former peak, records that he found on the summit 'tituli, rhythmi, et proverbia saxis inscripta unà cum imaginibus et nominibus auctorum. Inter alia cujusdam docti et montium amoenitate capti observare licebat illud :

"'Ο τῶν ὀρῶν ἔρως ἄριστος.'"

'Inscriptions, rhymes, and old saws carved on the rocks with the reflections (?) and names of their authors. Amongst others was noticeable this record of some scholar captivated by the mountain charm, "The love of mountains is best."' [1]

One more example may be taken from the sixteenth century. Josias Simler, a pupil and the biographer of Gesner, published in 1574 a Description of Valais and the Alps. In a dedicatory letter to the Bishop of Sion, which, after the fashion of the time, serves as an introduction to the dainty little volume, he paraphrases the passage I have quoted from his master's *Admiration of Mountains*. Simler furnishes a great deal of topographical and practical information, not only as to the high passes then in use, but also on the precautions taken in crossing them. His readers find themselves assisting at the birth of the craft of mountaineering above the snow level. Simler describes in detail the passage of the St. Théodule, mentioning the employment of guides and the rope, the alpenstock, crampons, hoops for use on the feet on soft snow, glass spectacles (*vitrea conspicilia*), precautions against

[1] For further details see Coolidge's *Josias Simler et les Origines de l'Alpinisme*, a vast volume full of specimens of and particulars relating to the early Alpine authors, and in particular to Conrad Gesner and Marti.

frost-bite. The rope and dark spectacles were not adopted, either at Chamonix or in the Oberland, until two hundred years later. On the other hand, the ice-axe was a Chamonix invention, a combination of the short axe used by crystal-hunters and the alpenstock.[1]

The following quotation may serve to show that even at Simler's date Alpine travellers with a taste for mountain scenery were not unknown. He writes:

'In the entire district, and particularly among the very lofty ranges by which the Valais is on all sides surrounded, wonders of nature offer themselves to our view and admiration. With my countrymen many of them have, through familiarity, lost their attraction; but foreigners are overcome at the mere sight of the Alps, and regard as marvels what we through habit pay no attention to.'

After the flood-tide of the Renaissance there was a notable reaction in Alpine literature. Religious wars and controversies ravaged Europe and distracted men's minds. The invention of printing proved far from an unmixed boon to the human intelligence. When the new impulse had spent its force, men's minds grew less active and less open to fresh, first-hand impressions. Swiss professors—students of philosophy, they called themselves— became more bookish, they took facts at second-hand from their shelves instead of from the direct observation of nature. For several generations there were no more Conrad Gesners.

The works published during the next hundred and fifty years paid relatively small attention to the mountain region. Their authors were more concerned with the towns than with the High Alps, with political and social statistics than with natural history. They had no difficulty in swallowing wonders—'miracles of nature'—or in accepting childish explanations of the physical problems that met their eyes. As late as Simler's day it was still held open to argument whether crystals such as were found in the Alpine crags might not be the result of intense and perpetual

[1] The cause of the distinction is obvious. Necessity is the mother of invention. Natives of the Upper Valais who wanted to get to Val d'Aosta had to cross a glacier pass: the peasants of Chamonix could go round Mont Blanc; but they needed a weapon to extract the crystals, the quest of which had developed into a local industry. (See Evelyn's *Diary*.)

frost.[1] Marc Lescarbot, a sceptical Frenchman who in 1618 visited Switzerland and borrowed largely from Simler in his poetical description of the Alps, attacked the vulgar belief in some very dull lines :

> ' Ecrivains qui couchez dans vos doctes esprits
> Le crystal être glace, où l'avez vous appris ?
> Si le crystal est tel, pourquoi dans les vallées
> Les Montagnes de glace en ce temps écroulées
> Fondent-elles au feu ? ' [2]

—and so on for several pages. But the superstition was too strong to be slain by so blunt a weapon as Lescarbot's verse.

In a volume known from its illustrator as Merian's *Topographia Helvetiae, Rhaetiae, et Vallesiae* (1642) we, for the first time, find the Grindelwald Glacier carefully described and depicted. About this date a certain number of Swiss students started in pursuit of a glacier theory and wrote more or less dull treatises. But it was not until the first decade of the eighteenth century that glacial problems were taken up seriously. The next landmark in Alpine literature is afforded by Johann Jakob Scheuchzer's voluminous works. The best known are *Beschreibung der Naturgeschichten des Schweitzerlands*, 1706-8, and the oddly named Ὀυρεσιφοίτης *Helveticus sive Itinera Alpina tria* (1708), republished and enlarged to four volumes in 1723. Scheuchzer (1672-1733) was by profession a doctor and by taste an energetic pedestrian. He was also a Fellow of the Royal Society. His rambles extended beyond the Bernese Oberland to Graubünden, Glarus, Uri, and the Valais. His thick volumes of Alpine travel present a strange combination of topography, legend, and fiction with a sprinkling of such scientific observation as was current in his day. He not only called attention to the marvels of the Alps—he added to them ! Yet Scheuchzer was an esteemed writer and obtained full recognition in the most learned circles. We owe to him some of the

---

[1] Strabo, bk. xi. ch. 6, describes how the natives of the Western Caucasus cross with the aid of snowshoes and toboggans its snows and glaciers. The phrase used is 'Τὰς χιόνας καὶ τοὺς κρυστάλλους.' This is the only reference to glaciers as distinct from snows that I remember in the classics. That in Greek the same word serves for both ice and crystal may have helped to create the subsequent confusion.

[2] *Tableau de la Suisse et autres alliés de la France et hautes Allemagnes*, par Marc Lescarbot, advocat en Parlement, 1618.

first efforts at barometrical determinations of Alpine heights, the first serious attempt to theorise about such subjects as glacier motion, ice-caves, periodical winds, and intermittent springs. Sir Isaac Newton accepted the dedication of one edition of his work to our Royal Society, and the Fellows of that illustrious body vied with one another in supplying funds for illustrations, to which their names were severally attached. In so doing they, perhaps unwittingly, lent their sanction to a feature that makes Scheuchzer's travels still sought after—a series of weird images of prodigious dragons sworn to have been seen, mostly after supper, by worthy and veracious peasants near their homes. These, however, were but an ornament to volumes which profess on their title-page to describe and illustrate 'whatever of rare and noteworthy in Nature, the Arts, or Antiquity is to be found in the Helvetic and Rhaetian Alps.' The subjects Scheuchzer most delights in—after dragons—are botany, Baths, pastoral industries, and milking utensils.

Scheuchzer was not the first to introduce the Alps and their glaciers to English men of science. In 1669 the Royal Society had received a brief communication from a Mr. Muraltus of Berne, 'Concerning the Icy and Crystalline Mountains of Helvetia called the Gletscher.' Four years later a 'worthy and obliging' Monsieur Justel of Paris sent a further and equally brief report, adding that there was such another mountain near Geneva, and thus indicating the existence of Mont Blanc.[1]

Writing in 1685, Gilbert Burnet, afterwards Bishop of Salisbury, in a letter to Robert Boyle, reported that 'one Hill not far from Geneva call'd Cursed, of which one-third is always covered with snow, is three miles in perpendicular height according to the observation of that incomparable mathematician and philosopher, Nicolas Fatio de Duillier.'[2] In 1709 the Bishop's son,

---

[1] See *Philosophical Transactions of the Royal Society*, vols. xlix and c. The reports are quoted in full in Coolidge's *The Alps in Nature and History*, and in *Alpine Journal*, vol. xiv. p. 319-20.

[2] N. F. de Duillier (1664-1753). There was much doubt and confusion as to the height of the Swiss peaks. The Schreckhorn and Finsteraarhorn were held the highest in the Oberland, but the St. Gotthard was thought by some to be still higher, and there was an old legend that Pizzo Stella in Graubünden was the highest of all. It figures conspicuously in the corner of Scheuchzer's four-sheet map of Switzerland (1712), a copy of which is hung in the Royal Geographical Society's House at Lowther Lodge.

William Burnet, sent to Sir Hans Sloane, the President of the Royal Society, a further description of the Grindelwald Glaciers, and even made an attempt to propound a glacier theory.

Scheuchzer had described his travels both in fluent Latin and in German. His successor, Gottlieb Sigmund Grüner, wrote only in German, in itself a significant fact. Unlike Scheuchzer, he was more of a compiler than a traveller. One of his contemporaries calls him a 'chamber philosopher,' and de Saussure mentions that his bad health and 'certain physical defects' compelled him to rely mainly on the reports of others. He employed a number of local correspondents, on whom he depended for his matter and his illustrations; as to the latter, the artists appear to have been far from conscientious.

Grüner was a practical book-maker and he wrote to meet a need which he was the first to recognise. There was, he saw, a public eager to read about the mountains and their natural wonders; a demand which the many editions of the old 'Délices de la Suisse' of the first half of the eighteenth century (1714 and later), dealing mainly with the towns and humanity, had failed to satisfy.[1] His own countrymen, and the foreign Milords and Barons who were now making pilgrimage to the Glaciers of Grindelwald and Chamonix, wanted something better. These visitors were yearly growing more numerous. The inn which the pastor had started at Grindelwald was a profitable concern, and as early as 1748 its goodwill had been transferred to a peasant landlord. The Duc de la Rochefoucauld had in 1762 followed Pococke and Windham to Chamonix. The 'Glaciers de Faucigny' could hardly be left out, though the only picture of them procurable was certainly not according to nature, and had subsequently to be apologised for. Grüner, in writing to Wyttenbach, attributes it to Nicolas Fatio, who must therefore be reckoned among the early visitors to Chamonix.

Grüner sets forth his purpose in a modest preface to the first edition of his work. He begins by asking those who know the

[1] It is true that the author of an edition of 1730 is at pains to argue that, despite obvious objections, mountains as affording pasturage, game, mines, good frontiers, and 'a thousand natural rarities and curiosities,' may claim to be counted among the attractions of his country. But he proceeds to give thirty-two pages to dragons and only a passing reference to glaciers, with a plate of the Lower Grindelwald Glacier.

FORERUNNERS

Alps for further contributions that may help to give his volumes greater completeness in future issues. He proposes first to describe the Alps in history and nature, and then to deal with the physical problems they suggest, and in doing so to aim at plain description rather than fine writing—at exactitude rather than novelty.

The late Professor Bernard Studer, a very competent critic, passes an impartial judgment on the *Eisgebirge*.[1]

'Grüner,' he writes, 'by his industry has done good service to Natural Science in Switzerland. But, since his information was mostly indirect, gathered from correspondence or by word of mouth, and his own knowledge in Physics and the Natural Sciences was superficial, no thorough treatment of his subject must be looked for. Still his was the first successful attempt to produce a comprehensive survey of the Swiss Alps.'

Studer goes on to praise Grüner's mineralogical chapters and to refer to his Theory of Glacier Motion, borrowed from two earlier authors, Hottinger and Altmann.[2] Grüner alleged that the advance of the ice was caused by its weight rather than, as had been suggested, by expansion due to summer warmth. Grüner's generalisations, when he went beyond local details, were apt to be unlucky; for instance, he imagined a continuous sea of ice extending from the Rheinwaldhorn to Mont Blanc. The topography of the Aar Glaciers was too much for him. Even nearer home he is badly at fault. The Susten Pass he describes as too steep for travellers with weak heads; the Wengern Alp as dangerous. Lack of method and critical power in the author result in his failure to weld his material so as to produce a satisfactory work. But such as they were, his volumes held the field. Their success encouraged Grüner to produce in 1778 (anony-

[1] *Physische Geographie der Schweiz*, B. Studer, Bern, Zurich, 1863. B. Studer was a friend of Professor Forbes, who dedicated to him his work on the Alps.

[2] J. H. Hottinger's tract is entitled *Montium Glacialium Helveticorum Descriptio. Ephemerid. Medicae, Physicae, Germanicae Academiae naturae curiosorum*, Decuriae iii., Annus nonus et decimus, Norimburgae, 1706.

J. G. Altmann, in 1751, published, at Zurich, a work with the ambitious title, *Versuch einer historischen und physischen Beschreibung der Helvetischen Eisberge*. The original portion of it consists of the description of a visit to Grindelwald, of which a recognisable engraving is supplied. He considers the glaciers to be the outflow of a central ice-sea. His ideas as to the structure of the ice and the conditions of its movement are very crude.

mously, with the false imprint 'London') a popular edition under a new title: *Reisen durch die merkwürdigsten Gegenden Helvetiens*, in two volumes. It was obviously aimed to catch the attention and serve the needs of the already rising tide of visitors to the glaciers.

In this aim Grüner was, on the whole, successful. His work had no rivals. The best tribute to its position is the fact that de Saussure set himself to learn German, in order to be able to read it.[1] In the first volume of the *Voyages* he refers to Grüner in characteristically generous terms:

'Many Swiss Naturalists or Geographers, Merian, Simler, Hottinger, Scheuchzer, and others, have dealt with glaciers. But no one has treated the subject more thoroughly than Monsieur G. S. Grüner. The descriptions which are the result of the author's own observations are very accurate and satisfactory, but as he was unable himself to visit so many mountains he has been obliged to avail himself of the help of others. . . . M. Grüner's third volume is a treatise on the origin, nature, and differences of glaciers. In this the author has exhausted his subject as far as a physical subject can be said to be exhaustible, and although his opinion may not be shared on all points by physical inquirers, it would be difficult, as a whole, to give a better account of the various phenomena presented by these frozen masses. . . . As to the engraving which pretends to represent the Glaciers of Faucigny, I do not know who sent it to Monsieur Grüner, but it is certain that it bears no resemblance whatever to its alleged subject.'

These words were published in 1779, the year following the appearance of the popular edition of Grüner's work, and also of his death. It is, I think, more than probable that the knowledge of the forthcoming appearance of the first volume of the *Voyages* incited Grüner to reissue his own book.

The typical specimens I have cited from what we may call pre-alpine literature must suffice for my present purpose. They may serve to show the nature of the material bearing on the study to which he proposed to devote his life which lay at de Saussure's hands, and also to indicate the trend of men's minds

[1] Grüner's work was not translated into French until 1770. Writing to Wyttenbach he describes the translation as very faulty. In 1774 he was proposing to publish a description of the Aletsch Glacier. De Saussure never mentions this greatest of Alpine ice-streams.

in the century and country in which he was born towards the natural sciences connected with the history of the earth.

We have seen how the enthusiasm of the old Renaissance scholars had died out in the denser atmosphere of the succeeding centuries, how their successors at Berne and Zurich had lived more in their libraries than on the mountains. The Reformation had, among its consequences, occupied men's minds with dogmatic disputes to the detriment of the natural sciences. Theology and dogma were doing their best to hinder the birth or check the growth of inconvenient rivals, the Logies that attempt to deal with ascertained facts. 'New Presbyter is but old priest writ large'— an ecclesiastical government naturally inclines to despotism, and Calvin's at Geneva was no exception to the rule. The control of the Venerable Company lay like a blight on many forms of independent mental activity. It was not until towards the close of the seventeenth century, when its tyranny had been relaxed, that the Republic produced any names that acquired in literature or physical science a more than local reputation. The chief agents in this great change, the admission of free inquiry and toleration in the place of dogma and persecution, were the Cartesian philosopher and magistrate, Jean Robert Chouet (1642-1731), and the liberal-minded pastor, Jean Alphonse Turrettini (1671-1737). Both were active champions of liberty, but of the two Turrettini was the more influential. His persuasive eloquence resounded in the pulpits of Geneva and was listened to with willing ears, and, if his dream of uniting the Protestant churches in a common bond remains still unfulfilled, he was successful in freeing his own city from the grosser forms of intellectual bondage in which it had been too long held. In the clerical oligarchy set up by Calvin he introduced the principle of individual liberty of mind of the English Puritans, and thus sowed the seeds which resulted in Rousseau and the Revolution of 1789.[1]

The results of this widening of the intellectual horizon were not, however, immediately manifest among the professors and the students of the Geneva Academy, at any rate in the field of physical research. Apart from his uncle Bonnet, it was to German Switzerland, to Albrecht von Haller and Grüner, that

[1] See Professor Borgeaud's review of Vallette's *J. J. Rousseau Genevois*, vol. viii. *Annales de la Société J. J. Rousseau, Genève.*

the young de Saussure had chiefly to look for encouragement and guidance in his special field of investigation.

It is not, I think, difficult to recognise further and adequate reasons for the relative backwardness of the Genevese in such branches of physical inquiry as related to their natural environment. The Swiss Cantons include many mountain districts united to the lowlands by administrative and other bonds which bring the dwellers in the towns into frequent contact with their neighbours of the highlands. But independent Geneva, enclosed in its narrow plot on the banks of the Rhône, was further encompassed by the domains of a dangerous neighbour, the Duke of Savoy. Its territory was less than a hundred square miles. Its inhabitants had no practical links with the country districts that lay beyond a short walk from their walls. Moreover, their social life and intellectual energies, so far as these had escaped from the rigid control of Calvinism, were profoundly influenced by those of the nation whose language they shared, their great neighbour France. And for a hundred years before the middle of the eighteenth century, French taste and intellect had turned their backs on natural scenery and research.

At this date the old towns of France had not yet grown into cities, they had no manufacturing suburbs, their inhabitants felt little longing to escape from their surroundings into a purer air. Persons of wealth and fashion, when they moved, took, as far as possible, their environment and atmosphere with them. Their country homes, if of recent date, were Palladian mansions with pillared porticoes and balustrades. When they were not conversing in salons, they were promenading on terraces and lawns, among elaborate parterres, and down interminable avenues. They were incapable of taking a rural walk or appreciating a woodland glade, unless, indeed, they had first dressed up as shepherds and shepherdesses. They had little indulgence for nature unadorned, except possibly in the form of a slender cascade. They preferred her made up and tricked out like a court lady by some gardener or architect. The feeling as to scenery reflected a hundred years earlier in the pages of Evelyn's Diary was still predominant up to the middle of the eighteenth century. For him the Forest of Fontainebleau was a confusion of 'hideous rocks' and 'gloomy precipices.' He was only happy in the walled gardens, among the

THE GROUNDS AT GENTHOD

paved walks, fountains, and 'perspectives,' of which he saw and described so many.

The generation of Louis Quinze lived physically and morally in an artificial world. Self-conscious, sentimental, engrossed in their own social relations, full of personal emotions, which, whether real or affected, they were at equal pains to cultivate, they had no eyes for the storm that was already looming on the near horizon.

It was from England that one of the earliest indications of the change of feeling that, if still inarticulate,[1] was already in the air, was to come. Formal gardening was among the first formalities to be called in question. Pope and Addison were active in the attack on an art the main object of which seemed to be to thwart and contradict nature at every turn. The founders of a new school, calling themselves landscape gardeners, responded to their appeal. Kent and 'Capability Brown,' followed by Repton, led the return to rusticity. They endeavoured to restore or improve nature, but on her own lines. They removed the marks of man's labour by turning fields into parks, hedgerows into ornamental clumps, boundary walls into sunk ha-has, and straight terraces into serpentine walks. The new taste soon extended to the Continent; the grounds of the Trianon remain as one of its more conspicuous examples. De Saussure, on the lake-shore at Genthod, imitated on a small scale the parks and gardens he had admired in Holland and Yorkshire, while a contemporary print shows that Bonnet's demesne on the hill above remained a specimen of the old style. Rousseau eagerly fell in with a change which fitted so well his mental attitude, and his description of Julie's garden at Clarens proves him a warm advocate of the English style as against French and Italian formality. We recognise that we are on the way to the mock ruins, artificial cascades, and shrubberies of the famous garden at Ermenonville.

Rousseau himself was doubtless a powerful agent in this peaceable revolution, but he was far from being its originator. Such changes are not the works of any one man. From age to age tastes differ and fashion alters, whether in art, architecture, or gardens. This absence of any permanent standard results partly

[1] See in Mr. Gosse's recent volume, *Some Diversions of a Man of Letters*, the chapter on 'The Message of the Wartons.'

from the differing material and social conditions of the times, partly from the desire, as old as Homer, of each generation to be better than, or at least other than its predecessor. I have dwelt on the revolution in gardening because it was a preliminary symptom of the far greater change that was to follow, the passion for wild scenery. But it was some time before the taste for artificial rusticity developed into a love of nature in her sterner moods, even in a region where she displays them so variously as on the shores of Lake Leman and in the highlands of Savoy. The Genevese still employed French architects to build them classical villas, and laid out formal frog-ponds in front of Mont Blanc!

How was the greater change brought about? How was it that first rural and pastoral and then mountain landscape grew into popular favour, that the romantic succeeded to the classical? I have already alluded, in speaking of landscape gardening, to the part played by Rousseau. Jean Jacques was one of the many voices which heralded a return to nature that was already more or less in the air. He was by far the most eloquent and vibrant among them. But as regards mountains, his appeal was not the first, and it had very definite limits. It had been preceded in Switzerland by another, larger in its scope, which at the time met with extraordinary success. Albrecht von Haller's poem on the Alps, first published at Berne in 1732, obtained at once a European reputation.[1] Haller, as I shall point out in a later chapter, was remarkable in many ways, but his supreme claim to the respect of all lovers of the Alps is that it was his influence that encouraged and inspired a young Genevese professor to make the mountains the study of his life. The conqueror of Mont Blanc looked up to the Bernese man of science as his beloved master. But if Haller was a primary agent and precursor in establishing a new relation between men and mountains, the founder of the cult was de Saussure. It was mainly through his practical example and his writings that the High Alps were brought within the scope of the new interest in natural scenery, that they won for themselves a place, grudgingly yielded at first, on men's lips as 'Beautiful Horrors,' and then came to be hailed by poets as the Palaces of Nature, and accepted by the European public as the Playground of

[1] *Versuch Schweizerischer Gedichte.* Bern, 1732.

Europe. De Saussure was the true author of our modern passion for Alpine scenery, as well as the first systematic Alpine explorer.

In making this claim I recognise that I am running counter to the common disposition to credit the creation of the love of the Alps to Rousseau, a tradition resting to a great extent on the authority of Chateaubriand, who disliked Rousseau and the Alps equally, and was delighted to couple them in his invective.

There were, no doubt, mental links between the author of the *Nouvelle Héloïse* and the climber of Mont Blanc in their common appreciation of the virtues of the Alpine peasantry; and in such phrases of de Saussure as ' Luxury and the love of money are the tomb of liberty ' we may seem to catch an echo of Rousseau's eloquence. But with respect to natural scenery, de Saussure's appreciation was independent of and very much wider in scope than that of the guest of Les Charmettes.

In an attempt to estimate the work of de Saussure it seems to me essential to reassert this fact, and it is the more essential since one so eminent, both as a critic and a climber, as Leslie Stephen has given his support to the popular tradition. In one of the opening chapters of *The Playground of Europe* (1871) he wrote as follows :

' If Rousseau were tried for the crime of setting up mountains as objects of human worship he would be convicted by any impartial jury. He was aided, it is true, by accomplices, none of whom were more conspicuous than de Saussure.'

Such a verdict, I venture to say, could only be returned by a jury which had not heard the competent witnesses, or had been wrongly charged from the Bench. Stephen goes on to call Rousseau ' The Columbus of the Alps, or the Luther of the new creed of Mountain Worship.' These comparisons are picturesque, but, I venture to think, unsustainable.

In appealing against them I shall call as witnesses critics of the highest rank. Lord Morley has put the case fairly enough. Rousseau's attitude towards nature, he tells us, was closely connected with his politics and philosophy; his praise of rustic or pastoral landscape was in great part inspired by his desire to contrast a complicated and corrupt civilisation with an idealised simple life. But in order to do this, writes Lord Morley, he did not have recourse to those aspects of nature 'which the poet of "Manfred" forced into an imputed sympathy with his own rebellion. Rousseau never moralised appalling landscapes; the Alpine wastes had no attraction for him.' Again, 'The humble heights of the Jura and the lovely points of the valley of Chambery sufficed to give him all the pleasure of which he was capable.'[1]

Sainte-Beuve has defined Rousseau's sphere of influence in the same sense with admirable clearness and more minuteness. There are, he points out,[2] three zones of Alpine scenery—the lowlands or foothills, ending at the limit of the walnuts; the middle zone, the region of mountain valleys, villages, and pine-forests; and the upper zone, that of the high summer pastures and the eternal snows. 'Jean Jacques'—I quote—'knew only the lowlands, the lakes, the gay cottages, and orchards. Les Charmettes remains his ideal. He never explored, or described in detail, even the middle zone. . . . The highest regions were in a sense the discovery and the conquest of the illustrious man of science, de Saussure.' The great French critic's verdict is definite and seems to me decisive. But it may be well to add the testimony of at least one local expert, Professor Philippe Godet of Neuchâtel, an eminent historian of the literature of Romance Switzerland, whose work has been crowned by the French Académie des Lettres.[3]

'Rousseau,' he writes, 'had made his mark as a man of letters and a describer of scenery, but in his description he had never risen above the middle zone of our country. With de Saussure, the point of view is enlarged—the High Alps become the central object of his studies; he creates Alpine literature; before him men talked about the sublime horrors of regions of which they knew nothing. From the date of the publication of his *Voyages* the horrors disappeared, the sublimity was better appreciated, descriptions in volumes inspired by the Alps became as numerous as the pictures of which their landscapes furnished the motives. By climbing Mont Blanc the Genevese

---

[1] *Life of Rousseau*, vol. ii. pp. 77-9.
[2] See article on Töpffer in his *Causeries du Lundi*, vol. viii.
[3] *Histoire Littéraire de la Suisse Française*, Paris, 1890.

writer opened a new path to the human spirit; a domain of which Science, Art, and Letters are still far from having exhausted the riches.'

Again the late M. Vallette, who, in his interesting volume, *Rousseau Genevois* (1911), is by no means disposed to minimise any claim that can fairly be put forward for his client, practically acquiesces in the view here suggested. He writes, 'To tell the truth, it is to the middle region of the mountains, among the buttresses of the Alpine giants, that St. Preux keeps. He preserved a respectful distance from the high rocky peaks which he esteems inaccessible, and the glaciers from which the crags separated him. Still he was here, too, a forerunner; he prepared and made ready the way for Bourrit and de Saussure.'

Contemporary testimony as to the local influence of de Saussure's example and teaching on his fellow-townsmen is afforded by Beckford, the creator of Font Hill. He visited Geneva in 1782, and on climbing the Salève found its crest frequented by holiday-makers, on whom he spends a page of mild sarcasm.

'The rage for natural history has so victoriously pervaded all ranks of people in the Republic that almost every day in the week sends forth some of its journeymen to ransack the neighbouring cliffs and transfix unhappy butterflies. Silversmiths and toymen, possessed by the spirit of Deluc's and de Saussure's lucubrations, throw away the light implements of their trade and sally forth with hammer and pickaxe to pound pebbles and knock at the door of every mountain for information. Instead of furbishing up teaspoons and sorting watchchains they talk of nothing but quartz and feldspath. One flourishes away on the durability of granite, whilst another treats calcareous rock with contempt; but, as human pleasures are seldom perfect, permanent acrimonious disputes too frequently interrupt the calm of the philosophic excursion. Squabbles arise about the genus of a coralite, or concerning the element which has borne the greatest part in the convulsion of nature. The advocate of water too often sneaks home to his wife with a tattered collar, whilst the partisan of fire and volcanoes lies vanquished in a puddle or is winding up the clue of his argument in a solitary ditch. I cannot help thinking so diffused a taste for fossils and petrifactions is of no very particular benefit to the artisans of Geneva, and that watches would go as well though their makers were less enlightened.'

Beside this may be put the testimony of Mademoiselle Rosalie de Constant, a friend of Mme. de Staël. Referring to the eighties of the eighteenth century, she wrote :

'It was only about this period that the gigantic nature by which we are surrounded began to be admired. Travellers from a distance came to Geneva in order to make the trip to Chamonix, which had only recently become known. Nothing can show more clearly the influence of fashion. It might seem that the great immovable mountains had only become noticeable since the observations and travels of Monsieur de Saussure.'[1]

A further and striking evidence of the growth during this decade of Alpine travel may be found in the long list of works and prints dealing with Switzerland appended to Ebel's guide-book (1793).

If we turn to the pages of the Alpine travellers who were Rousseau's contemporaries to ascertain to what extent they were influenced by his writings, we find that Bourrit's passion for the Alps took possession of him in 1757, some years before the publication of the *Nouvelle Héloïse*. The typical representative of the British tourist in Switzerland in Rousseau's and de Saussure's day was Archdeacon Coxe. Coxe, whose book went through several editions, and was translated into French by Ramond, the well-known Pyrenean traveller, expressly states that the object of his journey was to study the glaciers of which he had read so much. He adds a list of the authors he has consulted, which includes most of the principal works of the Swiss naturalists. To 'anecdotes of Haller' Coxe devotes a whole chapter. It was only at the end of his tour in 1776, when he reached Lausanne, that he borrowed a copy of the *Nouvelle Héloïse* from a circulating library and went over its sites. It must be obvious, I think, to any attentive reader of his work that the worthy Archdeacon was first led to the mountains by the reports about the glaciers, and that he was in no sense a pupil and follower of Rousseau.

Finally, let me turn to passages in Rousseau's own writings which have been cited in proof of his taste for mountain scenery.

[1] See *Rosalie de Constant, sa famille et ses amis,* par Mlle. Lucie Achard, Genève, 1902.

It is quite true that he professed in youth [1] a liking for 'torrents, rocks, firs, dark woods, mountains, rough up-and-down-hill roads with precipices at hand to make me tremble.' But read the context; the precipices he trembled at were those he could admire from a high road protected by a safe parapet, and the enjoyments he got from them were feeling dizzy and the puerile delight of dropping stones and watching them shiver before they reached the torrent below. He once penetrated as far as the Upper Valais. There he admired the cloud effects, enjoyed the qualities of the mountain air, and prophesied the air-cure. But he was far more interested in the Alpine peasantry than in the Alps themselves. There is nothing to prove that he ever noticed a snow-peak or admired a glacier. His descriptions of the details of the mountain landscape remain singularly vague and formless. So vague indeed are they that among the crowd of commentators on Rousseau's writings no one has yet ventured to identify the exact region of his rambles. Yet it seems to me a key is supplied by Bourrit in his *Description des Alpes Pennines et Rhétiennes* (1782). He tells us how, after visiting Val d'Anniviers, he wandered on to a group of villages where he met with hospitality similar to that which had previously been shown to Rousseau by their inhabitants. The villages he names, Oberemps, Unteremps, Unterbeck, and Eggen (Bourrit prints Equen), can all be found on the Siegfried Map—the two first above Turtmann, west of the Turtmann Thal, the others on the broad brows that overlook the Rhône valley between Turtmann and Visp.[2]

It is significant that, despite his many opportunities, Rousseau never cared to make a second pleasure trip to the mountains, or

---

[1] *Confessions*, part i. book iv., near end.

[2] At Geneva, where Rousseau's memory is still kept alive by a society named after him, students whose opinion carries just weight are inclined altogether to set aside the statement of Bourrit quoted above. The grounds, as I understand, alleged for this attitude are the lack of any direct evidence in Rousseau's writings as to the locality which afforded him material for the description of Alpine landscape and peasantry he puts into St. Preux's letter, and the habitual untrustworthiness of Bourrit.

It is, doubtless, true that the only positive evidence in the case is Bourrit's assertion. But in my opinion considerable indirect support for it may be derived both from known facts and from Rousseau's language. If we turn to the *Confessions* (part ii. book viii.) we learn, first, that the descriptions in the *Nouvelle Héloïse* were framed on his own experience; we learn further that Rousseau crossed the Simplon on his return from Venice in 1744, that the district he described was

to visit the glaciers. In 1754 he sailed round the Lake of Geneva with his friend, old Deluc, a radical watchmaker, and his two talented sons, and in the same year the young Delucs made the first of their excursions into the Alps of Savoy.[1] But it did not occur to Rousseau, though he boasts himself a stout pedestrian, to join his friends in any of their Alpine rambles. In all his life he never crossed any Alpine pass, except the Mont Cenis and Simplon on his way to and from Italy, and these only of necessity. Of their scenery he says nothing.

It may help me to emphasise Rousseau's point of view as I conceive it, if I compare it with that of some of his contemporaries in our own country. We find parallel instances of the period of transition in English literature. Take Cowper: to the English poet, we are told, 'everything he saw in the fields was an object of interest, he never in all his life let slip the opportunity of breathing fresh air and conversing with nature.' But when we look further into his letters it has to be admitted that the dweller in the fens found the scenery of Sussex oppressively mountainous! Still, he gave voice to a fresh tendency in the mind of his generation, he took the lead in setting an example of close and sympathetic natural observation. He was related to Wordsworth in the same sense that Rousseau was related to Byron and Shelley. Other contemporary writers show more or less trace of the coming change. Addison was but slightly touched by it, yet he anticipated Rousseau in appreciating to a certain extent the wilder aspects of the Lake of Geneva. He found the 'near prospect of the Alps from Thonon' affected his mind with an 'agreeable kind

---

in Haut Valais, and that no highway of traffic passed through it (*Nouvelle Héloïse*, part i. letter 23). Now the villages mentioned by Bourrit are within the limits of the Haut Valais, and they lie close to, but well off, the Simplon road. Another point worthy of note is that, being near the linguistic frontier, French is understood by at least a portion of their population, and to Rousseau—as well as to Bourrit—this would be of importance in any attempts at social intercourse. Further, I find in the *Jahrbuch* of the Schweizer Alpenklub (vol. lii. p. 97) a description of these villages and the primitive customs they still retain, that corresponds very exactly with Rousseau's.

[1] Byron, in his letters (April 9, 1817), alludes to the trip. At that date the elder son, J. A. Deluc, F.R.S., then a nonagenarian, was living at or near Windsor. Byron had heard from his sister that the old man, having had 'The Prisoner of Chillon' read to him, recalled his trip with Rousseau and recognised the correctness of the descriptions in the poem. See also the *Confessions* for an account of the voyage, part ii. book 8.

of horror.' Gray was far more seriously impressed. After a visit to Scotland in 1765 he bursts out, 'The mountains are ecstatic, and ought to be visited in pilgrimage once a year. None but these monstrous children of God know how to join so much beauty with so much horror.' But a quarter of a century earlier (in 1739) his letters to his mother and West show him to have been in love with 'cliffs, precipices, and torrents,' and if he shuddered on the Mont Cenis we must recollect that he crossed it in November, and even then, despite the wintry gloom, found 'something fine' in the scenery. Mr. Gosse, in his *Life of Gray*, tells us, 'In his youth he was the man who first looked on the sublimities of Alpine scenery with pleasure, and in old age he was to be the pioneer of Wordsworth in opening the eyes of Englishmen to the exquisite landscapes of Cumberland.'[1] Cowper and Gray were sensitive minds, leaders of their generation. But the attitude of a lady like Mrs. Thrale shows how much the old terror of rough places was giving way. She expresses herself as pleased with the Mont Cenis and delighted with the scenery of the ascent to the Brenner through the Trentino.

The love of mountains, which Conrad Gesner had planted in Switzerland and Haller had watered, was taking root; but it was de Saussure who spread it over Western Europe. Yet Rousseau must not be deprived of his due. To the sterner aspects of nature he was blind, to the voice of the mountains he shared the deafness of his generation. But in his appreciation of the sub-alpine region, the harmonious landscapes and delicious details of the Swiss lowlands, their lakes and lawns, their brown broad-roofed farms, their rich orchards and vineyards and narcissus meadows, he was a true pioneer. He inculcated and inspired a feeling which was capable of far wider application than he himself gave it. He helped to open men's eyes to the call of landscape, and in so doing he to some extent prepared their minds to take interest in and understand its more sublime forms. He was in this sense, but in this sense alone, a forerunner of de Saussure. Rousseau was the most eloquent of the many voices of the time that expressed a feeling already in the air, the sentimental regard for natural scenery, untouched by human needs and incidents.

[1] Gilpin's *Tours in the Lakes and Scotland* were visible signs of the same spirit of appreciation (*circa* 1780).

He was a preacher of the return to nature, but he was no prophet of the love of the Alps. His bust may be a most suitable adornment in a sub-alpine resort, it would be obviously out of place in any Alpine centre. It was de Saussure who led the nations to lift up their eyes to the eternal snows. Born and bred within a walk of the cliffs of the Salève, the rocky rampart the crest of which overshadows the homes and forms a playground for the holidays of the Genevese, and brought up in sight of the glaciers of Mont Blanc, he drew the inspiration of his life's work from the scenes familiar to his childhood.[1]

[1] The foregoing chapter makes, I need hardly say, no pretence to be a complete or even a general sketch of the early works more or less connected with mountains and their writers. Such sketches have been undertaken by very able hands—by Leslie Stephen in *The Playground of Europe*, by Sir Frederick Pollock in the Alpine volume of the Badminton series, by Mr. Coolidge in several of his scholarly and laborious works. (See *Josias Simler et les Origines de l'Alpinisme*, Grenoble, 1904.) Mr. Gribble's volume, *The Early Mountaineers*, 1899, contains some curious reprints.

CHAPTER II

GENEVA IN THE EIGHTEENTH CENTURY

In the preceding chapter an attempt has been made to indicate the attitude of European culture towards the Alps previous to the middle of the eighteenth century and de Saussure's travels. I have endeavoured to show by a few selected examples how far preceding generations had carried their investigations into the physical features of mountain structure and the phenomena of the glacier region, and what feelings the wilder forms of scenery—the waste places of the world—raised in their minds.

But any portrait of Horace Benedict de Saussure which exhibited him only as an Alpine traveller and a diligent pursuer of several branches of natural science would be sadly incomplete. From the age of twenty-two this versatile patrician was busy as a hard-working professor, an educational reformer, and a leader in social activities, while in middle life he found himself forced to take a prominent part in the stormy politics of the little Republic. It seems therefore desirable to supply here as a further setting to the story of his life some account of the scenes in which it was lived, of the local aspect and surroundings of Geneva a hundred and fifty years ago, and of the social and political conditions that prevailed among its inhabitants.

The point at which the Rhône issues from Lake Leman was indicated by nature for the site of an important town. An island [1] furnishes a convenient opportunity for bridging the impetuous river at the point where its translucent flood breaks out of the narrowing western horn of the great lake. A neighbouring height

[1] The present L'Ile, not the little sandbank now planted and connected by a bridge which stands out in the lake and has since 1835 been known as the Ile Rousseau.

on the southern bank offers a ready-made bridge-head, taken advantage of even in the earliest times. Here, before the Romans came and the passes of the Pennine Alps had been brought into frequent use, was the spot where tribes and traders, moving southwards from Central Europe and the Rhine towards Italy or Provence, would seek to cross the barrier of the Rhône. Here, at a later date, armies issuing from the defiles of the Western Alps might strike northwards for Central Gaul, or eastwards across the lowlands of Helvetia and past Aventicum to the Rhine. Caesar found Geneva 'the farthest town of the Allobroges and the nearest to the boundaries of the Helvetians'; he recognised its strategic importance and introduced its name into history.[1]

The Roman and Burgundian towns both kept exclusively to the high ground on the left bank of the Rhône. But under the rule of its bishops (1050-1535) the first walls, some of the towers of which still exist embedded in more modern buildings, took a wider circuit, and the streets and alleys began to stretch down to the lake and river-shore. Before the period with which we are concerned—the latter half of the eighteenth century—these limits had again been exceeded and Geneva had lost, externally at least, the mediaeval aspect still fortunately retained by several of the smaller towns in the low country between the Alps and the Jura. Its ancient towers and many-gated walls had been replaced by formidable bastions and broad grassy ramparts in the new style of military architecture which followed on the use of cannon. These fortifications, more adequate than the former walls to protect the citizens from any sudden attack on the part of their formidable neighbours, the Duke of Savoy or the French king, were planned and carried out early in the sixteenth century. They encircled both the city and St. Gervais, a considerable suburb, connected by bridges with the old town, that had grown up on the right bank of the Rhône, and in the sixteenth century was the seat of a famous fair. The lake-front was guarded by chains, and the river barricaded below the town with piles. In place of the many issues of the old walls the new ramparts were

---

[1] A long list of Roman inscriptions found in or near Geneva, given in Spon's *History of Geneva* (London, 1687), attests the early importance of the town. One of them, recording the death of C. Julius Caesar Longinus, a freedman of Julius Caesar, runs thus: 'Praeruptis montibus hùc tandem veni ut hic locus meos contegeret cineres.'

GENEVA IN THE EIGHTEENTH CENTURY

pierced by only three land gates, the Porte Neuve and the Port de Rive south of the Rhône, leading into Savoy, and the Porte de Cornavin in St. Gervais, leading to France and Switzerland. The business quarter lay on the lake or river-bank. If Geneva lacked the picturesque features of the old towns of the Swiss lowlands, its architecture had one characteristic of its own. In many of the streets of the lower town and round the market, the Place du Molard, broad overhanging penthouses, known as *dômes*, supported from the ground on huge wooden pillars, sheltered the walls and windows and gave a cover from rough weather to pedestrians similar to that afforded elsewhere by arcades. Many of these structures remained till the middle of the nineteenth century. At their base between the footway and the road nestled rows of tiny wooden stalls or booths. One main street, the Rue de la Cité, or Grand' Rue, and many narrow lanes, almost staircases, like those of Edinburgh, led up from the river-bank, the centre of the commercial quarter, to the upper town, the aristocratic quarter. Here were clustered the Town Hall with its inclined passage up which the bewigged councillors could be carried in their sedan chairs, the Arsenal, the Hospital, the Cathedral, and the 'Collège,' a public school, the buildings of which have been little altered. The external aspect of the public edifices was solid but plain; they reflected the austerity of the religion and life of their inhabitants. No gracious saints, no dancing figures, or grotesque troops of bears, presided over their fountains and their doorways. Eighteenth-century Geneva showed little sign of the *joie de vivre* of the Renaissance; it lacked both the homely humour of the Teutonic mind and the poetical imagination of Catholic legend.

Unlike the modern city, with its pretentious rows of open and wind-swept quays, old Geneva turned its back on its little port and the lake and the bleak north-easterly blasts which in winter blow over it. Its outlook lay towards the south-west and the sunshine. Early in the eighteenth century, as commercial and financial prosperity increased, the more wealthy citizens—bankers and merchants—began to erect fine houses. These were mostly in the classical style of architecture then in vogue in France—with some admixture of Italian features, such as internal courts and arcades, which might recall their old homes to refugees from Lucca or

Cremona.[1] As the visitor climbed the Rue de la Cité, which leads up from the bridges over the Rhône to the Cathedral, he had on his right near the beginning of the ascent a group of handsome houses that at the back enjoy a free view towards the Perte du Rhône. The largest of them was the Lullin mansion, de Saussure's town home. Higher up the street another row of stately edifices lines the ramparts, looking across the flat meadows of Plainpalais to the gap between the Salève and the Jura, through which runs the road to Annecy. On the top of the slope was the shady terrace of La Treille, where the wealth and fashion of Geneva took their afternoon stroll in face of the winter sunsets, or lounged in summer evenings on the long bench, set with its back to the view, and discussed local politics. Of these there was seldom any lack in a town which habitually did its best to deserve the title, given to it by Alexander von Humboldt, of 'a stormy Athens.'

Geneva in 1780 was relatively but a small city, not larger than many of the provincial towns of France. Its population, at the beginning of the century about twenty thousand, had according to an official census in 1781 risen to about twenty-five thousand. Its political affairs, however important in the eyes of its citizens, occupied therefore but a small place in the story of European politics. But it had an intellectual life and influence far beyond its material importance. Under Calvin it had become a city of refuge for all the more active spirits whom religious persecution had driven out of France or Italy, and the headquarters of an austere form of Protestantism. In the four months following the massacre of St. Bartholomew over sixteen hundred refugees, in the five weeks after the Revocation of the Edict of Nantes eight thousand, entered the town. Many of these immigrants permanently established themselves, not altogether to the satisfaction of the existing inhabitants, whose industries they invaded.

Before the eighteenth century the famous fairs which had made Geneva a mart for all Europe had been superseded; but the city had not lost its ancient industries, and it had added new ones. The chief of these, watchmaking, alone employed six thousand hands of both sexes. The cloth and shawl merchants

[1] The Reformation drove many families from Switzerland and Italy to Geneva. From Lucca came the Burlamaqui, Turrettini, Calandrini, and Diodati.

were prosperous, and several of them, turning bankers, had become the Rothschilds of the day and were ready to lend money even to princes. The citizens held investments in French securities the annual interest on which amounted in 1780, we are told, to sixteen millions of francs, and they had also large holdings in Holland and England.

The society of Geneva, if it fell far short of the brilliancy and extravagance of the Parisian *salons*, was very subject to their influence. With wealth had come more or less leisure and luxury; the upper classes were no longer content to submit to the sumptuary laws issued by a clerical committee. They assimilated to some extent the fashions of the French aristocracy and the mental atmosphere of the day. Their town mansions, though many and spacious, no longer sufficed them, and since the summer evenings were long and pleasant on the lake shores, and the city gates were regularly closed soon after sunset, they established country homes. Stately villas with terraced gardens replaced in the environs the homely granges of an earlier time. Their inmates must have seen Mont Blanc, but they took little notice of its distant snows.[1] De Saussure's contemporaries were not even sure on which side of Chamonix the 'Monts Maudits' stood. A party of Englishmen might set out to investigate certain strange masses of ice hanging from them, that were said to penetrate the forests and invade the meadows. But the Genevese were only vaguely interested in these disagreeable and baleful curiosities. They laughed at their visitors. It was like Englishmen, they said, to take trouble for such an object—but perhaps they were really looking for mines; there were known to be minerals worked near Sallanches. At any rate this was the view taken at the time by some of the Savoyard authorities, who were very suspicious of their foreign visitors. Modern mountaineers in remote districts have often found themselves subject to similar surmises. When in 1868 English

[1] De Saussure's grandson, the late M. Henri de Saussure, pointed out at a Conference of Alpine Clubs held at Geneva in 1879, that the eighteenth century has left in the country-houses of the environs of the city, a permanent record of its taste in scenery. He said:

'They most of them turn their backs to the view; fashion at that date preferred the picture formed by an artificial landscape ornamented with a geometrical frog-pond to the magnificent panorama of our Alps and our lake.'

climbers first visited the Caucasus no Russian official could believe that we climbed Kasbek and Elbruz without a commercial or a political purpose, and twenty years later the Prince of Suanetia invited me to develop gold mines under the shadow of Ushba.

The prosperity of Geneva was not confined to any single class, or even to the townspeople. The condition of the peasants in the rural districts of the Republic was a strong testimony to the efficiency of its government. The contrast between the Genevese territory and the neighbouring portions of Savoy is insisted on by every passing traveller—by no one more forcibly than the poet Gray.[1] I quote from one of his letters written the year before de Saussure's birth.

'To one that has passed through Savoy, as we did, nothing can be more striking than the contrast as soon as he approaches the town. Near the gates of Geneva runs the torrent Arve, which separates it from the King of Sardinia's dominions; on the other side of it lies a country naturally, indeed, fine and fertile; but you meet with nothing in it but meagre, ragged, barefooted peasants with their children in extreme misery and nastiness; and even of these no great numbers. You no sooner have crossed the stream I have mentioned than poverty is no more; not a beggar, hardly a discontented face to be seen; numerous and well-dressed people swarming on the ramparts, drums beating, soldiers, well clothed and armed, exercising, and folk with business in their looks hurrying to and fro, all contribute to make any person who is not blind sensible what a difference there is between the two governments that are the causes of one view and the other.'

With wealth came the call for luxury, and the natural result was frequent friction between the inhabitants and their paternal administration. From Calvin's day the government had taken on itself with an alacrity, if not an audacity, hardly equalled elsewhere, to decide what should be considered articles of luxury. In Geneva, however, the motive was not taxation, but prohibition. In 1646 the Senate, finding itself unequal to the task, determined to appoint a special tribunal, known thenceforth as the Chambre de la Réformation, competent to enact and enforce a code of sumptuary laws. Liberty in thinking was won at Geneva before liberty in dress. This egregious board survived, though with gradually diminishing powers, till 1770. No sentiment was too sacred, no

[1] Gray to his father, October 25, 1739.

details were too intimate or too small for these meticulous pastors. They revelled in the regulation of funerals and mourning; they forbade the use of monuments or inscribed tombstones; they rebuked a husband for wearing too long a scarf on his wife's death, a mother for putting on black for her infant. Ladies might not carry their watches pinned on their breasts. Gowns without waistbands were forbidden, 'since a mother of a family ought not to think of her dress,' nor might she go to church in shoes, which is 'too unbecoming.' The materials of the ladies' gowns must not be of extravagant richness, nor must they wear lace, except on their inner garments! The Chamber further made rules as to how many guests you might entertain, and how many courses you might offer them. Liveries were not allowed. Carriages might only be used for long country drives. Even a bride was expected to walk to church, nor might she receive, or give, wedding presents. Babies' christening robes must be simple. Finally, some wiseacre (or wit?) proposed that the Chamber 'should establish a standard costume both for men and women, *which should never be altered*'! Is it to be wondered at if, under such provocation, there were many fair recalcitrants? We are told of one petulant *demoiselle* who vented 'incoherent words' against the august tribunal. She was promptly fined fifty florins and costs, 'to be obtained by summary process.' It is pleasing to learn that a bold citizen was found with the good sense to retort by proposing that 'the Chamber of Reform be abolished, as useless.' His fate has not been recorded.

Happily, there is reason to believe that at the worst of times the critic of the Chamber I have just cited came near to expressing a fact, and it is clear that after the middle of the eighteenth century this petty tyranny had been greatly relaxed—at any rate for the upper classes. By a singular inconsistency, even in the period of the strictest control, the standard of luxury permissible was graduated according to social rank. The wives of the principal officers of State were allowed special privileges in the way of decorating their persons, doubtless a pleasing substitute for the share in their husbands' civil designations accorded ladies in countries east of the Rhine up to the present day. A print of 1789, commemorating a street procession held on one of the many reconciliations between the contending parties in the State, displays an exuberance and variety in the ladies' headgear which bears witness to their release from all restrictions.

By those who held to the old religion, Geneva was reckoned the anti-Rome long before Voltaire had established himself on its borders as an anti-Pope. Of this religious rancour, Lassels—a Catholic who travelled as tutor to young English gentlemen in the reign of James I., and produced a sort of embryo Handbook to Italy, a work which can still be read for the sake of some vigorous and picturesque touches—may serve as an instance:

'Geneva,' he writes, 'like a good sink at the bottom of three streets, is built at the bottom of Savoy, France, and Germany, and therefore fit to receive into it the corruption of the Apostates of the Roman Church.'[1]

It did not occur to the ingenious author of this somewhat crude comparison that he had put his finger on the main cause of the activity, both commercial and intellectual, of Geneva. The advantage as a mart given to the town by its natural position was supplemented by its convenience as a city of refuge. Here, as elsewhere, intolerance had its natural effect in transplanting men of independence and energy of mind to a spot where they could enjoy relative freedom. That which is strained out by persecution is apt to be not the dregs but the life-blood of civilisation. The city on the Rhône owes most of its famous names to the immigration provoked by the bigotry of its neighbours, France and Italy.[2]

To the intelligence of the Genevese of the eighteenth century and their relatively high standard of popular education many shrewd observers have borne witness. Of the general character of the citizens, of their pursuits and amusements, and their social habits we have a great deal of contemporary evidence. With a Parisian shopkeeper, Rousseau tells us, you could talk only of his trade; a Genevese watchmaker would discuss literature or philosophy. The ordinary citizen was serious and intelligent; fond of money, he regarded idleness as contemptible. But in conversation he was apt to be long-winded and disputative.

[1] *The Voyage of Italy*, R. Lassels, 1670. Lassels describes the government of Geneva as 'a kind of democracy, or rather a kind of aristocracy, a mingling of laymen and ministers.' The lake, he declares, is 'absolutely the fairest he has seen, fairer than either the Lake Major, the Lake of Como, the Lake of Zurich, the Lake of Wallenstadt, the Lake of Iseo, the Lake of Morat, or the Lake of Garda.'

[2] Some of the families of Italian origin have already been mentioned. The Tronchins, the de Candolles, the Jalaberts, and many others were French.

'While a Frenchman writes as he talks, these Genevese talk as they write; they lecture in place of conversing; they give one the impression that they always want to argue. . . . In short, their conversation is sustained, their speeches are harangues, and they gossip with a pulpit air. The Frenchman reads much, but nothing but new books, or rather he runs through them more to be able to say he has read them than for their own sake. The Genevese reads only good books—he reads them to digest them; he does not criticise them, but he knows them by heart. Women as well as men are given to books.[1] It needs all the good sense of the men, all the gaiety of the women, and all the talent both sexes have in common to overcome in the men a touch of pedantry and in the women of preciosity.'

The picture here drawn by Rousseau, himself by birth a Genevese, shows understanding and sympathy mixed with its criticism of his fellow-citizens. Voltaire, as might be expected, is far less appreciative. Established first at Les Délices, on the right bank of the Rhône close to the gates of Geneva, and afterwards a few miles off and outside its territory at Ferney, he amused himself by watching with a mischievous eye the doings of his neighbours, ready at any moment to make sport of their domestic troubles as far as he could venture to do so without risking his own convenience and social relations.

He took pleasure in, from time to time, shocking the serious circles of the Upper Town by some literary freak. He found it an agreeable diversion to distract the Venerable Company by casting doubts through the *Encyclopédie* on its orthodoxy, or to intervene with irritating comments in the strife between political parties. The squire of Ferney was always ready to mock in sprightly rhymes the sober lives and solemn diversions of the citizens :

'Noble cité, riche, fière et sournoise;
On y calcule et jamais on n'y rit :
L'art de Barême[2] est le seul qui fleurit;
On hait le bal, on hait la comédie;
Pour tout plaisir Genève psalmodie
Du bon David les antiques concerts,
Croyant que Dieu se plaît aux mauvais vers.'

---

[1] The Genevese ladies wrote as well as read. De Saussure's wife and sister both produced novels, which, however, never got beyond MSS. His daughter was a well-known writer, and her work on *L'Education Progressive* won the highest praise from Amiel. See p. 400.

[2] Barrême (*sic*) was an editor of Ready Reckoners.

By general consent, the great fault of Genevese society was its tendency to break up into small coteries. This began in childhood: a number of neighbours would arrange for their children to meet frequently at each other's houses, and the intimacies thus formed were apt to extend to after-life. About 1739 the lack of public amusements drove the men to form clubs or circles, to hire in winter a room where they could meet frequently to discuss politics and exchange the talk of the town, in summer a garden on the lake where they could spend the long evenings. In 1745 the Venerable Company of Pastors looked on these clubs with a pained disapproval. It complained to the Senate that there were too many of them—no less than fifty in the town, where, 'besides talking a great deal, perhaps too much, of politics and foreign affairs, it is certain that wine, gambling, the table, and loose conversation are the principal, if not only, attractions. Cards are played, even at the hour of the evening sermon.' The wives and daughters started in revenge similar, if less dissipated, assemblies. 'As the men are more susceptible than gallant, the women are more romantic than coquettish,' writes an observer. The impression left is of a society somewhat prim and decorous, taking itself seriously, and interested in serious subjects, in which the men who were not in business engaged in political administration, or literature, or learned pursuits; while the women were apt to be either genuine *femmes savantes*—interested in botany, like de Saussure's mother, or in education, like his daughter, or else full of domestic details and the home farm, like his wife. We find ourselves introduced to company that lacked the lightness in give-and-take, and also the mockery and frivolity of the *salons* on the Seine, that had for its centre not a corrupt court, but a more or less austere and puritanical group of about a hundred 'noble families of the first quality'—holders, present or past, of the higher offices in the State, who refused to intermarry or associate with the rest of the town.

Madame Récamier is at pains to summarise the intellectual bent of Genevese society:

'Observe them closely; all these Genevese of the old stock have acuteness, moderation, a certain reserve, a power of patient and exact analysis, more learning than effect, more substance than show, and when they converse it is with more detail than colour, the touch of the pencil rather than the brush. They excel in observing and describing mechanisms—organic, physical, or psychological—in extreme detail; they examine at length each object as through the microscope; they push patience to dullness; they are ingenious, but lacking in breadth of view.'[1]

In Mme. d'Epinay Geneva found a more appreciative guest. In 1758 she writes:

'I have made myself a society of people who would be sought after anywhere. I get up between five and seven, all my mornings are free. At midday I come down on my terrace, and, if the weather is fine, walk in the public garden. Women here can go anywhere on foot, alone, without footmen or maids. Even foreigners would be remarked and followed if they did otherwise. I like, and avail myself of, this liberty.

'I dine at one with M. Tronchin [the famous doctor] or at home. From two to six one pays or receives visits, at six all is dead in the town, and strangers find themselves in the most complete solitude, since the Genevese meet in their own sets. Each member holds an assembly in turn; they take tea in the English fashion, but they do not limit themselves to this beverage; there are plenty of cakes, coffee, and chocolate. The Assemblies, which are called Societies, are mixed, but girls are not admitted, they have their own Societies, where men and boys are only introduced when a member is married.

'In these Societies the diversions vary with the age and tastes of their members. There is a good deal of play, they occupy themselves with needlework, sometimes with music. Gambling seems to be the ruling passion with the women, and I am surprised, for I was told that they were all as cultivated as those I have met, who are really so.

'There are some "Societies" composed entirely of women. There are also assemblies of men, to which women are not admitted, which are called *Cercles*. But it is not true that the members smoke and get tipsy. These *Cercles* are held in rooms which are hired by subscription among a number of individuals of similar tastes. The members meet on a fixed day of the week, there is no eating or drink-

---

[1] 'Regardez-y bien; tous ces Genevois de la vieille souche ont finesse, modération, une certaine tempérance, l'analyse exacte, patiente, plus de savoir que d'effet, plus de fond que d'étalage et quand ils se produisent ils ont du dessin plutôt que de la couleur, le trait de poinçon plutôt que du pinceau. Ils excellent à observer, à décrire les mécanismes, organiques, physiques, psychologiques dans un parfait détail; ils regardent chaque pièce à la loupe et longtemps, ils poussent la patience jusqu'à la monotonie, ils sont ingénieux mais sans une grande portée.'—*Souvenirs de Mme. Récamier*, p. 135.

ing, but a supply of newspapers and endless political discussions. They exhaust themselves in guesses and discoveries about the plans of the Great Powers, and when the event does not correspond with the guesses of these gentlemen, they are no less satisfied of their sagacity in having recognised, if not what the State in question has done, at least what it ought to have done! After all, men are the same everywhere, with some trifling differences, for I know originals of this sort in Paris! Still, here they are more busy with their own affairs than with other people's. Nearly all the Genevese having their money invested in France, England, and Holland, they naturally take a particular interest in current events. But I have wandered a long way from what I was trying to say, which, if I remember right, was that at six o'clock I find myself alone, or nearly so. Ah well! It is the hour at which I should begin to live if I were here with my family and with you.

'To sum up, the manners and the mode of life of these men are more sympathetic and satisfactory to observe than easy to describe. Virtue, honesty, and above all, simplicity form the base of their politics. But these qualities are all besprinkled with a slight coating of pedantry, which, as far as I can judge, is essential to the maintenance of the simplicity which alone gives strength to their State.'

Madame de Staël, on the other hand, is a severe critic. She recognised in the Upper Town most of the characteristic defects of the aristocracy of a petty State: pride, exclusiveness, a strict conventional standard, lack of sentiment, and a seriousness habitually verging on dullness and sometimes ending in morbid religious melancholy. English visitors of the time noted that suicides were frequent even in the upper class.[1] We shall meet with two instances among de Saussure's near relatives. Lady Shelley, the wife of Sir John Shelley, visiting Geneva in 1816, records a

[1] Since Senebier points out that it was only in the cases of suicide and adultery that Calvin's code affixed any definite penalty, the prevalence of what was termed *délire mélancolique* must have been of long standing in Geneva. The Baron de Zurlauben's suggestion (in Laborde's volume) that the malady was introduced by English visitors may be summarily dismissed. Napoleon's Préfet du Léman in 1812 furnished his government with a curious report on its alleged origin. He attributed it to a combination of causes: the influence of Calvinism, the habit of political disputes, sedentary occupations combined with the intellectual strain of serious studies, and, above all, the oppressive scale of the local landscape and the cold, uncertain, and depressing climate! Dr. Moore in 1779 confirms in one respect the Préfet when he notes that 'it is not uncommon to find mechanics in the interval of their labours amusing themselves with the works of Locke, Montesquieu, Newton, and other productions of the same kind.'

remark of his son Théodore, 'Ah, Madame, nous apprenons de bonne heure le métier de nous ennuyer.'[1]

It is probable that to our countrymen and countrywomen the social atmosphere of the Upper Town proved more congenial than to visitors from the livelier *salons* on the Seine. At Geneva they found clubs where conversation was more like that at home, more solid, if less brilliant, than in the boudoirs of Paris, and where ladies were not so powerful and disturbing an influence. Rousseau asserts that English habits were the fashion at Geneva in his day; Sismondi describes it as a town where French was spoken and written, but where people read and thought in English. In 1773-74, under the auspices of Lord Stanhope, an 'English Club' was formed where debates, in which many of the leading citizens, including de Saussure, took part, were carried on in our language.

The criticisms quoted above apply, no doubt, to the general tone of Genevese society, modified in the leading families by frequent connection with Paris and London. But they are more or less borne out by the character of the literary output of Geneva up to the middle of the eighteenth century. This consists in the main of juridical and theological works, or party pamphlets. Of imagination we find little trace; of poetry there is a complete dearth apart from polemical rhymes. The glaciers of Savoy inspired no Genevese Shelley, or Coleridge, or Byron. The verses called forth by the earliest ascents of Mont Blanc were dull and lengthy squibs written by partisans anxious to assert the superior claims of Paccard, or Balmat, or de Saussure.

The aristocracy willingly undertook and, on the whole, faithfully carried out the public offices and duties of the State. But these were not incompatible with abundant leisure. In the absence, until Voltaire's day, of a theatre, social distractions were relatively few, and the upper class of both sexes found relaxation in their clubs and small social gatherings.

[1] Sir J. Shelley of Maresfield Park, Sussex. His wife's statement, though rashly endorsed by her grandson and editor, Mr. Edgcumbe, that 'he had the good fortune to accompany de Saussure in his remarkable ascent of Mont Blanc, is, it need hardly be said, a slip. Lady Shelley records that in 1787 her husband was at Geneva and had Pictet, de Saussure's friend and successor, for his tutor. Sir J. Shelley may possibly have been at Chamonix while de Saussure was staying there in 1787. Unnamed Englishmen are referred to in his and young Bourrit's diaries. See *The Diary of Frances Lady Shelley* (London, 1912).

The religious authorities, if exacting in matters of morals and venturesomely meddlesome in sumptuary concerns, left sufficient freedom in the more important domain of thought. In the eighteenth century, so long as a man did not want to go to mass, or declare himself an atheist, or fail to show a proper degree of respect and deference to the authorities, he might live and philosophise in peace. The language, though not free from provincialisms, was that of the nation foremost at the time in science and civilisation. Secondary education was regarded as one of the duties of the State, but only so far as the classes that provided the clergy and the magistracy were concerned. It was for these that the studies of the Academy were designed. The course of instruction for boys at the Collège, a public school, was deficient. But the Academy obtained a reputation which drew to it the youth of other nations, including our own. Our countrymen do not seem, as a rule, to have formally matriculated. They were 'coached' by a professor, attended lectures, and boarded together in what they termed 'a common room.'

No doubt the foreign students at the Academy were a valuable asset to the town. To Protestant parents and guardians Geneva, with its Calvinistic legislation, seemed to offer fewer dangers or distractions to youth than the capital cities of Europe. Dr. Moore, who travelled with the Duke of Hamilton, and visited with him the Mer de Glace in 1773,[1] recommended Geneva as preferable to any other place on the Continent for the education of an English lad. Here, he says, 'he may have a choice of men of eminence in every branch of literature to assist him in his studies. He will have constant opportunities of being in company with very ingenious people whose thoughts and conversation turn upon literary subjects. . . . It may also be numbered among the advantages of this place that there are few objects of dissipation and hardly any sources of amusement besides those derived from the natural beauties of the country and from an intimacy with a people by whose conversation a young man can hardly fail to improve.'

Apparently English youth found improving conversation without amusement somewhat monotonous. A singular instance of the exceptional tolerance shown to the band of our country-

[1] Moore's *View of Society and Manners in France, Switzerland, etc.* (London, 1779).

men who first explored Chamonix is recorded at length in the *Life of Benjamin Stillingfleet*, written by Archdeacon Coxe, the author of the work on Switzerland already referred to. Stillingfleet acted as tutor to young Mr. Windham of Felbrigg, who was one of the gay party; another was a Mr. Neville, who while at Eton had taken a prominent part in school theatricals. These young gentlemen actually persuaded the Venerable Company to let them build a temporary theatre holding three hundred people. They played to crowded audiences Shakespeare and pantomimes! Their natural style of acting was much admired. Mr. Hervey, who in 1768 became Earl of Bristol, took female parts, playing alternately as Lady Macbeth and Columbine, and was acclaimed as only second to the famous Parisian actress of the day, Mlle. Clairon. Most surprising of all, the players invited the Venerable Company, and offered free passes to the four Syndics, as well as to the English students at the Academy. The city of Calvin was obviously on the path of perdition! After this sidelight on the doings of 1741—even before the days of its arch-tempter Voltaire— we read with less surprise how, forty years later, Beckford, in 1782, returning at night from an excursion to the Salève, found the gates reopened to allow theatre-goers to get to their country homes. Beckford's reflections on this occasion, if forced and malicious, go some way to explain the fluid state of Genevese society immediately before the revolution.

'The Comédie,' he writes, 'is become of wonderful importance. The days of rigidity and plain living have completely gone by; the soft spirit of toleration, so eloquently insinuated by Voltaire, has removed all thorny fences, familiarised his numerous admirers with every innovation, and laughed scruples of every nature to scorn. Voltaire, indeed, may justly be styled the architect of that gay, well-ornamented bridge, by which free-thinking and immorality have been smuggled into the Republic under the mask of philosophy and liberality and sentiment. These monsters, like the Sin and Death of Milton, have made speedy and irreparable havoc. To facilitate their operations rose the genius of "Rentes viagères." At his bidding, tawdry villas, with their little pert groves of poplar and horse-chestnut, start up—his power enables Madame C. D., the bookseller's lady, to amuse the D. of G. with assemblies, sets Parisian cabriolets and English phaetons rolling from one faro table to another, and launches innumerable pleasure parties with banners and popguns on the lake, drumming and trumpeting away their time from morn till evening. I recollect, not many years past, how seldom the echoes of the mountains were profaned by such noises, and how rarely the drones of Geneva, if any there were in that once industrious city, had opportunities of displaying their idleness; but now Dissipation reigns triumphant, and to pay the tribute she exacts, every fool runs headlong to throw his scrapings into the voracious whirlpool of annuities; little caring, provided he feeds high and lolls in his carriage, what becomes of his posterity.'[1]

[1] *Travels in Italy, with Sketches of Spain and Portugal*, by the author of *Vathek*, 1834, vol. i.

CHAPTER III

YOUTH AND EARLY TRAVELS

Horace Benedict de Saussure was born at Conches, an estate on the bank of the Arve, near Geneva, on the 17th February 1740. His ancestors were among the many religious refugees who flocked from France and Italy to Geneva in the middle of the sixteenth century. Their name still survives in five villages in Lorraine which were at one time in the possession of the family. The most important of these 'Saulxures' lies near Remiremont in the pleasant, wooded heart of the Vosges among the valleys north-west of the Ballon d'Alsace. The family pedigree starts with one Mongin de Saussure 'Seigneur de Dompmartin et de Monteuil sous la ville d'Amance en Lorraine,' who was born in the fifteenth century and held the office of Grand Falconer in the Court of two successive Dukes of Lorraine, René II. and Antoine the Good. He was succeeded in this dignity by his son, Antoine de Saussure (1514-69). The great event of Antoine's life, which was to affect the fortune of his descendants, is thus recorded in the Genealogy of the family printed at Lausanne, 'chez David Gentil,' in 1671 :

'En l'an 1551 Dieu l'illumina de la connaissance de la pureté de S. Evangile. Au sujet duquel il fut arresté prisonnier par son Altesse de Lorraine et comparut pour ce fait à Nancy dans les Assises et Estats de la Noblesse de Lorraine. Et fut obligé ensuite de se retirer abandonnant tous ses biens fonds qui furent escheus au fisque du Prince. Il se retira dans la ville de Metz en l'an 1552 où Dieu le rendit l'un des premiers organes de sa grâce en la naissance de l'Église de Metz, avec un nommé Monsieur de Croppeville, Gentilhomme Picard. Ce que le rendit exilé de la dite ville par authorité du Magistrat. De là il alla avec la famille de douze enfants à Strasbourg et puis à Neufchastel en Suisse et depuis à Genève et enfin se rendit dans le Pays de Vaud sous la protection de leurs Excellences de Berne et s'arrêta dans la ville de Lausanne où il fut honoré et gratuitement favorisé de la Bourgeoisie de ladite ville en l'an 1556.'

It is recorded that Antoine's disgrace arose from a charge brought against him by Christine of Denmark, Duchess of Lorraine, of teaching heresy to her son, or, according to another account, to her husband. In Switzerland he became a friend of the leading Reformers, of Calvin at Geneva, Farel at Neuchâtel, and Viret at Lausanne.

Antoine de Saussure's grandson, Jean Baptiste (1576-1647), removed from Lausanne and settled at Geneva, where he married into another family of exiles, the Diodati of Lucca.[1]

Elie de Saussure, a son of Jean Baptiste, was in 1635 the first of the family to acquire the citizenship of Geneva. His grandson Théodore (1674-1750), the grandfather of Horace Benedict, became a member of the Senate in 1721, and one of the Syndics of the Republic in 1734. He was active in the service of the State, and his name appears frequently in the lists of officials of the time. He built the modest house at Frontenex, where he passed most of his days, and lived till 1750, ten years after his grandson's birth. Horace Benedict's father, Nicolas de Saussure, seems to have been contented to remain a country gentleman. He was elected in 1746 to the Council of Two Hundred, but declined to serve on the Senate. He had something of a scientific turn of mind, but his science was applied mainly to agriculture. It was, however, sufficient to obtain for him the honour of a respectful notice from Cuvier in the *Biographie Universelle*. His literary remains consist of tracts on *The Methods of Cultivation*, *The Failure of the Wheat Crops*, and *The Pruning of Vines*. His last effort, a treatise on *Le Feu, principe de la fécondité des plantes et de la fertilité de la terre*, was thought at the time to have some scientific value. His daughter-in-law describes Nicolas de Saussure at the age of seventy-three as always busy with his

---

[1] Daniel, a brother of Jean Baptiste de Saussure, established a branch of the family at Lausanne, members of which became, in due course, Town Councillors and Ministers of the Gospel, and played a prominent part in the social life of the Canton. About 1725 a César de Saussure wrote letters from England which have been published abroad and in this country. See *A Foreign View of England in the Reigns of George I. and George II.* (London, 1902). At a later date we find at least two de Saussures of this branch settled in England. The Vaudois branch is now extinct. Another member of the family emigrated to America and had two sons, one of whom was killed in the attack on Savannah in the War of Revolution, while the other became an Under-Secretary of State and signed the first dollar bill issued by the Treasury of the United States.

Monsieur and Madame Nicolas de Saussure

farming and an old system of physics, and but little interested in the stormy politics of the moment. Yet a few months before only his son's intervention had saved him from being held up as a hostage at the city gates and prevented from returning to his farm and his family. He died in 1792, at the age of eighty-three, predeceasing his son by only seven years. But there are few traces of any influence exercised by him on Horace Benedict's character and career. What correspondence between them has survived relates mainly to agricultural matters.

Nicolas de Saussure was fortunate in his marriage with Mlle. Renée de la Rive,[1] a member of a family of distinguished ability and considerable wealth, who brought him both happiness and an increase of fortune. During his father Théodore's lifetime Nicolas and his wife continued to live at Conches, a homely country-house situated in a bend of the Arve, some distance outside the town near the Savoyard frontier. It had come into the family through the marriage in 1683 of an Anne de Saussure to Andrew Hamilton, a 'gentilhomme écossais,' to whom it had belonged. Here, in the spring of 1740, Nicolas's son was born and named Horace Benedict, after his maternal grandfather. The chief authority for the events of de Saussure's early life, apart from the *Voyages*, private diaries and letters, and official documents, is a little volume by his friend Senebier.[2] Senebier was a man of many accomplishments, a pastor, a naturalist, the author of a literary history of Geneva and the keeper of the Town Library. But he wrote in a style—the style of Louis XVI.—which has been admirably characterised by Sainte-Beuve : ' It is essentially well-mannered, flowing, and gay ; it breathes a virtuous sentimentalism. Benevolence, desire for improvement, confidence, love of right, an optimism showy and quite amiable—these are its moral characteristics, and the mixture finds easy expression in a form that is elegant, but inclined to flatness and too sugary.' Senebier is of his age to a degree that is often distressing, and Sainte-Beuve's criticism exactly fits his flowing and flowery periods. De Candolle, who knew Senebier well, while speaking

[1] A Pierre Louis de la Rive was among the first oil painters to represent Mont Blanc on canvas. A picture painted in 1802, taken from Sécheron, is preserved in the Art Museum at Geneva. He also painted Mont Blanc from Sallanches.

[2] *Mémoire historique sur la Vie et les Ecrits de H. B. de Saussure*, par Jean Senebier, Geneva, ix. (1801).

of him with respect and affection as a man, fully confirms this opinion of him as an author. He writes: 'Arrived at Geneva, I made acquaintance with M. Senebier, who encouraged me in the wish to study the philosophy of plants, and gave me useful advice. He was a man of varied but superficial learning who had written a great many diffuse and ill-arranged books wanting in clearness of expression, without close argument, and in a wearisome style.' After describing Senebier's merits as a botanist and chemist, de Candolle goes on to bear testimony to his inexhaustible kindness, and concludes : ' I became sincerely attached to him. I kept up intimate relations with this worthy man until his death. I have had his bust placed in the Botanical Garden at Geneva, and I have always preserved for his memory a most tender recollection and sincere gratitude.' [1]

The worthy Librarian's effusiveness frequently palls on the modern reader, but we do not doubt him when he assures us that de Saussure's invalid mother was the centre of his home and the main formative influence in his character. She was, he writes, ' his best friend ; she taught him to endure hardships and privations, to sacrifice cheerfully pleasure to duty, and to possess the philosophic mind.' She is described as a woman of intellectual tastes who lived a more or less retired life in her quiet home at Frontenex, surrounded by flowers and animals. From the time of the birth of her first child she never enjoyed good health and was constantly confined to her sofa, and both her children seem to have inherited her constitution and tastes rather than those of the robust country gentleman who was their father.

Though by birth a citizen of Geneva, Horace Benedict was in no sense a town boy. Up to the age of twenty-five, until his marriage, his home was in the country, among fields and hedgerows and poplar avenues, with a wonderful landscape of lake and mountain always within reach. At the age of ten, on his grandfather's death, his parents moved to the family property at Frontenex, near the Thonon road. They had no home in the city.

To what extent his hero's career has been influenced by the surroundings of his childhood and early years must always be an interesting matter of inquiry to a biographer. De Saussure on

[1] *Mémoires et Souvenirs de A. P. de Candolle*, p. 47, Genève, Cherbuliez, 1862.

The Courtyard at Frontenex

the first page of his great work, the *Voyages*, has himself borne eloquent witness to the inspiration he drew from his environment. I quote the passage :

'Geneva by its situation seems made to inspire a taste for Natural History. Nature presents herself in her most brilliant aspect. She displays an infinity of divine features, a lake brimming with clear and azure waters, from which issues a beautiful river, surrounded by charming hills which form the foreground of an amphitheatre of mountains, crowned by the majestic summits of the Alps. These are themselves dominated by Mont Blanc, clothed in a mantle of ice and eternal snows reaching down to its foot, and presenting a surprising contrast between its frosts and the beautiful verdure which covers the hills and the lower ranges. This grand spectacle delights the eyes and inspires the keenest desire to study and explore its marvels.'

Before we pursue de Saussure's boyhood, the reader may, I trust, not be unwilling to join in a short pilgrimage to the three properties where de Saussure spent the best, if not the greatest, part of his life. They lie in different directions, respectively south, east, and north-east of the town.

The property at Conches, where de Saussure was born and where he passed his last years, was of some extent, and lay enclosed within a bend of the Arve, on its right bank, about two miles from the gates. The road leading to it, shaded by old oak-trees, passes between what were formerly open fields until the ground slopes somewhat sharply towards the river, the opposite bank of which is high, abrupt, and wooded. There seems reason to believe that the site of the old farmhouse was identical with that of a modern (or modernised) villa standing among meadows close to a picturesque weir. Near at hand an ancient barn and stable and some old garden walls indicate an earlier residence. There is little distant view, and in de Saussure's day Conches must have been a relatively remote and quiet retreat.

Frontenex, the principal de Saussure estate, lies some two miles east of Geneva. It still remains in the state in which it was in the eighteenth century, when the Duke of Gordon, Lord Palmerston, and other young Englishmen of rank and fashion, who were being educated at Geneva, were glad to come out and be entertained by the worthy old patrician, his clever son, and handsome daughter.

The buildings stand round three sides of a courtyard shaded by aged lime-trees; a homely dwelling, similar in character to an English manor-house, occupies two sides, and the old barns and outbuildings, still primitive in character, the third. The approach is under a walnut avenue, and some specimen conifers, probably planted by de Saussure or his father, are scattered about the meadows. Conches and Frontenex were examples of the old-fashioned Genevese pleasure farms.

Genthod, the mansion belonging to the Boissier sisters, where de Saussure, as he tells us, during many summers spent the happiest days of his life, was of a different type. It was the summer resort of a wealthy citizen. Situated four miles outside the town, on the north bank of the lake, and close to its shore, it stood at the spot whence the snows are seen to the greatest advantage. To the right of the Môle towers Mont Blanc, supported by the Mont Maudit and Mont Blanc de Tacul—'the staircase of Mont Blanc,' de Saussure tells us they were called at Geneva; more to the left the Aiguille du Géant and Grandes Jorasses are seen dwarfed by the noble pyramid of the Aiguille Verte. This was the view that for twenty years at once delighted and distracted de Saussure until he at last succeeded in setting foot on the great mountain. The snows are seen through green vistas that may remind the visitor of an English park. There can be little doubt that de Saussure and his wife on their return from their visit to our country did their best to imitate on a small scale the surroundings of the great Yorkshire houses they had so much admired. The chief features of the Genthod grounds are still a long horseshoe avenue and a picturesque private port a hundred yards from the house.

The Lullin villa both inside and out is a good specimen of a moderate-sized country-house in the formal French style. It shows a handsome façade decorated with family arms, and some of the sitting-rooms retain their original panelling. Near at hand, but detached, is a long, low out-building which contains sitting-rooms that served de Saussure for his scientific studies.

On the slope above, at a distance of a few hundred yards, stands a larger house of the same epoch and style which through his marriage with Mlle. de la Rive became Charles Bonnet's

The Villa Lutlin at Genthod

home. Old prints show that in the eighteenth century it had, in contrast to its neighbour, a formal garden of some extent, with terraces, obelisks, parterres, and specimens of the topiary art. This has been completely done away with by later owners.

As soon as he was old enough, at the age of six, the little Horace Benedict was sent to the Collège—the public school of the city—and at once won his first success by obtaining the Reading Prize. His biographer Senebier—always on literary stilts—celebrates this 'triumph' as 'the spark which lit in him the thirst for glory and led him to labour with so much ardour to merit it.' Surely a singularly unhappy flourish: for the conscious pursuit of glory is the last characteristic we shall recognise in the future career of a searcher after knowledge as modest and patient as he was earnest.

At school the boy began to show that he had ideas of his own; and, like most boys with ideas, he had also strong tastes, which to some extent interfered with his lessons. His country home, no doubt, helped to give him a zest for outdoor life. Long rambles and reading romances were his chief dissipations. But the child had the courage to place himself under discipline. He resolved to limit his country walks to one a week, and to put aside novels. In after years he could recall with pride that on his way home from school he had resisted the temptation to open the covers of the tempting volumes he was in the habit of bringing back for his mother.

Of his school life and teaching de Saussure retained no favourable recollections. In after years he gave the most convincing proof of his feeling by his refusal to send his own children to the Collège.

From school de Saussure, at the age of fourteen, passed on to the Academy, or, as we should call it, University. In his class, or in that above him, we find the names of the fathers of Sismondi, the historian, and de Candolle, the botanist, and of members of families subsequently connected with our own country, a Romilly, a Pasteur, a Thellusson, and a Marcet.

Before he was eighteen the boy in the weekly tramps that formed a welcome interlude to classwork had explored many of the lower mountains in the immediate neighbourhood of Geneva:

the Salève, the Voirons, and the heights of the Jura. On these excursions he was wont to collect for his mother, who loved and studied flowers, specimens of all the species of the mountain flora that came in his way. Already he had been bitten with the mountain passion. In the 'Discours Préliminaire' which introduces his *Voyages*, an autobiographical document of great interest, he recalls these early rambles :[1]

'I have had from childhood the most positive passion for the pleasures of the mountains. I still remember the sensation I felt when, for the first time, my hands touched the rocks of the Salève and my eyes enjoyed its points of view.'

As a rule, he tells us, he preferred solitary walks, since they left him more free to use his eyes. But he found companions for many of his youthful rambles in his contemporaries, Jean Louis Pictet (not to be confused with Marc Auguste Pictet, afterwards his great friend and successor in his professorship) and François Jalabert, the son of a well-known scientist. The former was an astronomer who visited Siberia in 1768 to observe the transit of Venus, while the latter was something of an artist. Both at a later date joined de Saussure in some of his more extensive Alpine expeditions.

These early excursions furnished many picturesque incidents which are pleasantly interspersed in the first volume of the *Voyages*. Here is a description of the deserted convent on Les Voirons (4856 feet) and its former inmates :

'A Madonna held in repute in the neighbourhood is the object of their worship and the motive of their sojourn in so wild and cold a locality. I saw one of these martyrs of superstition, a victim of rheumatism and subject to frightful torments. Heaven, weary of their sufferings, allowed their wretched dwellings to be burnt; they had the courage to pass one or two years in a vault the flames had spared, but at last gained permission to seek a milder climate, and the Madonna was transferred to Annecy. I always remember with a shudder the dark court which occupied the centre of the Convent—it was a real ice-cave, filled with melting snow, and formed in the middle of the building a reservoir of cold and damp that became more dangerous as the outer air grew hotter.' [*Voyages*, 275.]

[1] See pp. 286-91.

Of a visit to the Dôle, one of the highest ridges of the Jura near Geneva, de Saussure gives a pleasant account:

'To enjoy this view in all its brilliancy it ought to be seen as I once had the fortune to see it. A dense mist covered the lake, the hills which enclose it, and even the lower mountains. The top of the Dôle and the High Alps were the only summits which raised their heads above this vast cloud-carpet, the upper surface of which was illumined by a brilliant sun. The snowy Alps, lit both by its direct rays and by the light which the clouds threw back on them, showed themselves in all their splendour and were visible at prodigious distances. But my situation had something strange and terrible. I fancied myself alone on a rock in the middle of a stormy sea at a great distance from a continent fringed by a long reef of unapproachable rocks. Little by little the mists lifted, for a time enveloped me in their gloom, then, rising overhead, suddenly revealed the superb view of the lake and its shores, smiling, cultivated, and dotted with little towns and picturesque villages.

'On the top of the Dôle there is a considerable plain which forms a beautiful terrace covered with a carpet of grass. From time immemorial this terrace is on the two first Sundays in August the *rendez-vous* of all the youth of both sexes from the villages in the Pays de Vaud situated near the foot of the mountain. The shepherds of the neighbouring chalets set aside for these two days milk and cream, and prepare all the varieties of delicacies that they can compose out of their dairy produce.

'Here the holiday-makers enjoy the most varied pleasures; some engage in athletic games, others dance on the crisp and elastic turf, which bounds beneath the robust and heavy tread of these worthy Helvetians. Others, again, seek rest and variety on the brink of the precipice and enjoy the fine view before their eyes. One peasant points out the tower of his village, recognises the fields and orchards that surround it, and recalls to memory the chief events of his life. Another, who has travelled, names all the towns of the district, and indicates the direction of the Mont Cenis, the road to Rome, that city celebrated even for those who do not look to it for pardons and dispensations. The bolder prove their courage by walking on the edge of the cliffs on the Genevese side of the mountain. Others, less boastful and more gallant, display their skill in collecting the flowers which grow on the steep crags. They pluck the *Leontopodium*, remarkable for its cotton-like sheath, the *Senecio alpinus* with its circle of golden rays, the pansy of the Alps which has the scent of lilies, the *Satyrium nigrum* with the perfume of vanilla, while the echoes of the neighbouring hills resound with bursts of lively and uncontrolled laughter, the sure accompaniment of simple and innocent pleasures.

'But one day this mirth was checked by a fatal accident. A young couple married on the same morning had come, with all their wedding party, to the festival. To avoid for a moment the crowd, they had approached the edge of the mountain, when the bride's foot slipped, her husband tried to hold her, but was dragged over the precipice, and they both ended their lives together on their happiest day! A ruddy rock is pointed out which is reputed to be stained by their blood.' [*Voyages*, 355.]

I quote this passage in full, since it illustrates several sides of de Saussure's character—his feeling for nature, his early inclination for botany, and his sympathy, none the less real for being coloured in its expression by the sentiment of the day, for the simple life of country people. On another occasion he describes how he met a young girl from one of the villages on the Savoy shore of the Lake of Geneva, who, having been courted by a youth from Canton Fribourg, was starting off on a two days' tramp alone with her lover, in order to visit his home, and satisfy herself as to his means before accepting him. On this incident, as a proof both of the worldly prudence and the high moral standard of a peasantry who saw in it nothing compromising, de Saussure moralises sympathetically. It is in this direction far more than in connection with the appreciation of the scenery of the High Alps that any trace of Rousseau's influence can be detected in his pages. He is always quick to record any human traits that interest him, and he does not hesitate in the *Voyages* to wedge them in between solid blocks of geological detail.

Thus later in life he confesses to having filched some pears in passing an orchard in the Vallée de Montjoie, near St. Gervais, and having been delighted when the peasant woman to whom he offered payment replied: 'It is not for that I come; He who made the fruits did not make them for a single owner.' No better proof could be offered of the rarity of visitors in de Saussure's day! The indulgence that was extended to the pious pilgrim or rare wanderer could hardly hope to survive the inrush of the view-hunters and the visitors to the glaciers.

I must find space for one more passage, a description of the source of the Orbe in the Jura, that has attracted the admiration of literary critics:

'We went to see this source where it issues at the mills of Bonport, and found it well worthy of the visit of the curious traveller. A semi-circular cliff, about 220 feet high, composed of great horizontal layers, cut vertically, and broken by lines of pines which grow on the shelves formed by its protruding salients, closes to the west the vale of Vallorbes. Loftier mountains clad in forests form a circle open only where it allows the course of the Orbe, which rises at the very foot of this cliff. Its waters of a perfect purity flow with majestic calm over a bed carpeted with a beautiful green moss, *Fontinalis antipyretica*. Soon, however, the centre of the current, quickened by the steep slope, breaks in foam against the rock which occupies the middle of its channel, while the sides, less troubled and still flowing smoothly over their green bed, make the whiteness of the central stream more noticeable! Thus it glides out of sight, following the course of a deep glen clothed in pine-woods whose dark hue is rendered more striking by the brighter tone of the beeches that grow among them. Gazing at this source one understands how poets have been led to deify fountains, or to make them the homes of their divinities. The purity of the springs, the beautiful shades which surround them, the broken cliffs and dense forests which defend their access, this combination of charms, at once gentle and imposing, creates an impression difficult to express, and suggests the presence of a Being above humanity.

'Ah! had Petrarch discovered this source, and found here his Laura, how much would he have preferred it to that of Vaucluse, more abundant, perhaps, and swifter, but whose sterile rocks have neither the grandeur nor the rich setting which decorate ours.' [*Voyages*, 385.]

This passage has been selected by Ruskin, a lifelong admirer of de Saussure, for special eulogy. It loses, no doubt, in translation, yet I cannot rank it as high as others in de Saussure's works, less touched by the conventional classicism of his day.

The two remarkable men whose influence most affected de Saussure's early life and career must now be introduced to my readers. It was in 1756 that a sister of de Saussure's mother, Mlle. Jeanne Marie de la Rive, married Charles Bonnet, at that time one of the leading names in science and philosophy at Geneva and a man of European reputation. The relationship thus created was destined to be an enduring one. Fifty-four years afterwards

—in 1810—the uncle and nephew were coupled in the eulogy delivered by Cuvier at the Institut de France on those of its members who had died during the French Revolution, a period the orator described as 'the fatal epoch when all personal merit, all independent pre-eminence, was odious to authority.' After another half-century Sainte-Beuve was to write of them as 'the two names that form the true crown of this great literary and scientific century of Geneva.'

It was two years later that de Saussure first came in contact with Albrecht von Haller.[1] Their acquaintance was brought about in this wise. In 1758 Madame de Saussure's health gave renewed cause for anxiety. For three years she had been under the care of Théodore Tronchin, the most famous doctor of his time, and a notable character in the Geneva and Paris of his day. An old friend of the de Saussure family, and destined to be closely connected with Horace Benedict in after years, he calls for some notice here. Tronchin's father had lost his fortune by the collapse of Law and the South Sea Bubble. At the age of eighteen Théodore came to England, where Lord Bolingbroke, with whom there was some family connection, introduced him to Swift, Pope, and Addison—but not to a career. The youth went on to Holland, married a great-niece of John de Witte, and studied and successfully practised medicine for twenty-five years. When at the age of forty-five he set up in Geneva, Tronchin earned the cordial dislike of his colleagues by his contempt for the traditional treatment then in vogue. He ridiculed their antiquated 'systems,' he condemned their violent remedies, he called the medical science, as they practised it, 'the scourge of the human race,' he preached observing nature and helping it to cure itself. 'He,' wrote Grimm, 'treats not the sickness, but the sick man.' His favourite prescriptions were moderate diet, pure air, country life, riding—above all, out-of-door exercise. He recommended an Abbé to chop wood and an Abbesse to do her own room and polish the floor! He was an enthusiast for cold baths. 'As long as the Romans,' he wrote, 'after their exercise on the Campus Martius threw themselves into the Tiber they were the masters of the world; the hot baths of Agrippa and Nero turned them into slaves.' If he made enemies in his own profession, he had for his

[1] For a fuller notice of Bonnet and A. von Haller, see chapter xvi.

DR. TRONCHIN
By Liotard

friends the world of letters. To his lady patients who suffered from nerves Tronchin used very plain speaking, and they endured his scolding gladly. He became the fashion, and the arbiter of fashion. To take a morning walk in heelless shoes and a short dress was called 'tronchiner.' A bevy of fair ladies came from Paris to be under the physician *à la mode*; there were not enough houses or apartments in Geneva to hold them. Madame d'Epinay was delighted to dine constantly with her doctor; Grimm declared that all his patients became his friends. Voltaire rejoiced in his company and described him as six feet high, 'wise as Æsculapius, and beautiful as Apollo; no one talks better or more wittily.' Catherine, the Empress of Russia, tried to tempt him to St. Petersburg. In 1766 he left Geneva to become first physician to the Duke of Orleans at Paris, where he died fifteen years later at the age of seventy-four. His funeral was attended by a crowd of poor people whom he had benefited, and for whom he had reserved two hours a day for gratuitous consultations.

This paragon of a doctor was on the most intimate terms with the de Saussure family; but he could do nothing to restore Madame de Saussure's health. It is easy to realise the dilemma of her relatives, their anxiety for a more vigorous treatment in accordance with the traditions of the orthodox medicine of the day, and at the same time their reluctance to slight an old family friend. In these circumstances it no doubt seemed a good arrangement for Madame de Saussure to have recourse to the waters of Bex, where she would find her brother-in-law Bonnet's friend, 'The Great Haller,' close at hand in his château at Roche, and could profit informally by his medical advice. It was convenient that her son should go with her and exercise his taste for botanising in a new field, the Alps of Vaud. Bonnet, who was in constant correspondence with Haller, wrote to him warmly recommending his nephew. Haller, who had promised himself literary leisure in his retirement, seems to have soon found his country home dull, and readily welcomed the youth who was so keen on botany and so eager to be of use in collecting for him. The link between them resulted in a lifelong friendship and produced a voluminous correspondence, much of which is still preserved in the Public Library at Berne.

These two men, illustrious in their generation, were the chief formative influences in de Saussure's early manhood. Between them they gave a direction to his travels and encouragement to his scientific pursuits. In the course of a century and a half their fame has grown somewhat dim. I have therefore added in a supplementary chapter a brief sketch of their careers which may be of interest to some of my readers.

In the year 1759 de Saussure finished his course at the Academy in the philosophy class, and publicly delivered and printed, apparently as a qualification for his degree, *A Physical Discourse on Fire*,[1] a tract on the transmission of heat from the sun's rays. Senebier tells us that 'it was remarkable for precision of thought, clearness of style, and accuracy in excluding all hypothetical matter.' Amongst other details the student showed that dark objects are more quickly heated, an observation he was two years afterwards able to illustrate by the practice of Alpine peasants of spreading in spring black earth over their meadows to hasten the melting of the snow. About this date Haller's letters to him—Haller was always formal in his superscription—bear the title 'Avocat.' An explanation may be found in a passage in de Candolle's reminiscences. 'In 1796,' he writes, 'I quitted the School of Philosophy. As a matter of form and following a prevalent custom, I entered that of Law, firmly resolved never to be a jurisconsult, or lawyer, but hoping to gain some knowledge of affairs.' The custom is not confined to Geneva: many Englishmen read law and are called to the Bar with a similar motive.

De Saussure, now released for a time from his studies, found leisure for more extended rambles. He climbed the grassy cone of the Môle, a mountain which, rising conspicuously above Bonneville, forms a prominent object in all southward views from the neighbourhood of Geneva, and had served the English party of 1741 as a natural belvedere for Mont Blanc. These excursions excited his youthful energy to further enterprise. The call of the snows became most urgent. 'I burnt,' he writes, 'with desire for a nearer view of the High Alps, which from the summit of our mountains appear so majestic.'

The occasion came in the following year, 1760, a memorable

[1] *Dissertatio physica de igne.*

date in de Saussure's life, that of the first of his many visits to Chamonix.

There is no reason to think that the *Campus Munitus*[1] of old parchments, the once secluded dale lying immediately at the foot of the snows visible from the neighbourhood of Geneva, was uninhabited, or unknown, even in classical times. We have evidence in the shape of memorial inscriptions and a boundary stone of the permanent presence of Romans along its borders, on the sunny, vine-clad slopes of Passy, and on the wooded heights of the Forclaz above St. Gervais, which before the defile of Les Montets had been made passable, served as the chief means of access to the upper valley. From the end of the eleventh century its principal village, known as le Prieuré—the modern Chamonix—had been the seat of a religious house, many documents relating to which have been preserved and published.[2] It was dependent on the great Benedictine Abbey of St. Michel de la Cluse near Susa above the road to the Mont Cenis, to which the whole valley of Chamonix had been given by Count Aymon of Geneva by an Act of Donation dated 1091. As early as 1375 its Prior sent twelve baskets of what he described as most exquisite butter across the Great St. Bernard as an Easter offering to the Court of Savoy. In 1458 we find one of his successors in office engaged in contracting for a road wide enough for 'two-horse wine-carts, each capable of carrying three barrels,' being kept in repair between Servoz and the upper valley. Two centuries later the Prior of the day was more banefully employed in superintending the burning of poor women as alleged heretics and sorceresses, and in confiscating their goods to ecclesiastical uses. The belief in witchcraft was widespread in the Alpine region.

[1] It has been commonly assumed that the Latin form represents accurately the original name of the valley, '*le champ muni*,' and that this was a picturesque description of its situation enclosed by high mountains. It occurs to me that a primitive peasantry would be more likely to regard the singular feature of so large a cultivable expanse from its practical aspect. This undoubtedly imposed itself on its early visitors. For instance, Bordier, in his *Voyage Pittoresque*, writes as follows of 'the pleasant plain of Chamonix'—'C'est un ovale long de trois lieues d'étendue sur un quart de lieue de largeur d'un terrain excellent, parfaitement *uni*, tel qu'on n'en voit point aux environs de Genève.' Is not 'le champ uni' a plausible origin for the name ? In this case a curious analogy would exist with the old name of Zermatt, ' Praborgne, Praborno, or Praborny ' (Whymper, *Guidebook to Zermatt*).

[2] See *Histoire de la Vallée et du Prieuré de Chamonix de X[e] au XIVe siècle*, and *Documents relatifs au Prieuré et à la Vallée de Chamonix*, par MM. Perrin et Bonnefoy (Chambéry, 3 vols., 1879, 1883, and 1887).

During the thirteenth and fourteenth centuries, Bishops on their pastoral rounds occasionally penetrated this remote corner of their diocese. In 1606 the valley received an episcopal saint, St. François de Sales. Seventy-four years later another Bishop, Jean d'Arathon d'Alex, penetrated this corner of his diocese, and, we are told, successfully exorcised the glaciers, forcing them to retire 'half a quarter of a league.' But this exercise of episcopal authority was but a poor set-off for the executions and cruelties perpetrated in the name of religion. In the sixteenth century the Priory passed into the hands of the collegiate church of St. Jacques at Sallanches, and a period of disturbance followed. The Chamoniards on several occasions revolted against the exactions of their ecclesiastical lords. But it was not till 1786 that the Commune succeeded in buying out the Priory at the cost of 58,000 livres. Had the Chamoniards endured patiently for another year or two the Revolution would have relieved them for nothing.

The Reformation, in freeing Geneva from the rule of its Bishops, broke the links between the city and the highlands of Savoy.[1] There is no evidence that any of these ecclesiastical visitors noticed the splendour of Mont Blanc. The distinction of being the first to do so was left to a layman, a Treasury clerk from Grenoble, who visited on business what he was pleased to call 'ce pays affreux.' He seems to have been a shallow-witted person who lightened his official duties by amorous correspondence. Boileau, in his *Repas Ridicule*, alludes to him as a 'buffon plaisant,' 'un écrivain fort estimé par les provinciaux.' At Chamonix he displayed his ingenuity by making the glaciers serve him to turn an elaborate compliment in a love-letter—'Madame,' he wrote in May 1669:

'I see here five mountains which resemble you as if they were yourself . . . five mountains, Madame, made of pure ice from head to foot . . . for the rest, Madame, there is nothing so magnificent as these mountains.'[2]

Le Pays' premature—and probably fictitious—enthusiasm for the glaciers had no immediate consequences. Their chaste magnifi-

[1] The see of the diocese was transferred to Annecy after 1635.
[2] Les Nouvelles Œuvres de M. le Pays, *Amitiés, Amours, et Amourettes*, were published at Amsterdam in 1687. See vol. ii. p. 124.

YOUTH AND EARLY TRAVELS

cence remained for a century unsullied by any crowd of admirers. Chamonix was thought of at Geneva, as far as it was thought of at all, as a forbidding district inhabited by a peasantry of a more or less uncouth, if not dangerous, disposition, who made a precarious living by selling crystals,[1] butter, and honey, and telling strange tales of the 'frosty fairyland' which encompassed their home. The good citizens of Geneva no more looked on the glaciers of Savoy as an object for a holiday than the Russian officials at Kutais fifty years ago thought of pleasure-touring in Suanetia under the shadow of Tetnuld and Ushba.

The dwellers in the vale of Chamonix had been discovered to their cost by clerics and clerks. But, with few exceptions,[2] their visitors before 1760 had been bound on business; they had not gone beyond the chief village, or paid any particular attention to the strange features of the scenery. It was left to a party of our countrymen, most of them youths completing their education at Geneva, to furnish the world with the first detailed account of 'a visit to the Ice-Alps of Savoy.' The leaders of the expedition of eight Englishmen, which penetrated as far as the Montenvers, were Pococke, a well-known Eastern traveller, and Mr. Windham of Felbrigg. These adventurers were destined to be the forerunners of the host of 'visitors to the glaciers,' who a few years later disturbed Gibbon in his retreat at Lausanne.[3] In 1741 they were the first to reveal not only to the literary and scientific world of Europe, but also to the citizens of Geneva, that the glaciers of Grindelwald, already brought into notice by the scientists of Berne and the worthy Scheuchzer as 'miracles of nature,' had their rivals in Savoy. Windham's narrative has of late been often reprinted, condensed, and commented on, and need not be dealt with here in any detail.[3] But it is due to our countrymen to point out that their story has been unfairly criticised. Their claim to be discoverers has been

[1] Crystals are mentioned by Evelyn as one of the chief articles of commerce at Geneva.

[2] Amongst the exceptions before 1740 may be reckoned Fatio de Duillier, a Prince of Sulzbach in 1727, and soon after 1740 Firmin Abauzit.

[3] Archdeacon Coxe, in his *Life of Benjamin Stillingfleet*, mentions that Pococke and Windham were joint authors of the latter's letter, but were aided in its composition by the latter's tutor, Stillingfleet. The title of the rare tract is 'An Account of the Glaciers or Ice Alps of Savoy in two letters, one from an English gentleman to his friend at Geneva, the other from Peter Martel, engineer, to the said English gentleman,' 1744.

taken in far too literal a sense, while the more or less sarcastic comments made on their nervousness in going armed prove to be unreasonable. Contemporary records show that even twenty years later Savoy was infested with smugglers, tramps, and marauders to such an extent that the citizens of Geneva were in the habit of arming themselves before going a few miles into the environs. The doctor or the lawyer called to a sick-bed, the pedlar going the round with his wares, the landlord collecting his rents, did not set out without seeing to the priming of their pistols. In a letter dated 10th September 1761, de Saussure tells Haller the following story. Two German botanists had been recently murdered on the Salève. They had fallen victims to a band of 'Bohemians' who were lurking in the forests of Savoy. These marauders had been bold enough to enter villages and rob houses in broad daylight, until the Chamoniards turned out in force to 'hunt them down like wild beasts.' Fortunately for the Bohemians,[1] de Saussure writes, they escaped; for had they been caught they would have been slain without any form of trial. He concludes by lamenting that he may have for a time to give up his solitary rambles on the heights round Geneva.

Senebier, de Saussure's biographer, puts the case on the whole fairly enough: 'At Geneva,' he writes, 'in 1760 there was much talk of a journey made by some Englishmen to Chamonix; this

[1] De Saussure's first visit was, it may be noted, in the year before the murders, but he went to Chamonix again in 1761. 'Bohemian' was for a long time a common term for marauders in the Alps. Sebastian Munster, a professor at Basle, who published a Universal Cosmography in 1544, got into a scrape by asserting that the inhabitants of the Engadine were 'worse robbers than the Bohemians.' He had probably been taking a cure at St. Moritz, the waters of which were frequented from early times. It is amusing to learn that a solemn deputation was sent all the way from the valley to Basle to complain of the libel, with the result that due apology was offered and accepted. The disorders about 1760 were partly consequent on the Seven Years War, which was drawing towards its close. Troops of deserters and disbanded soldiers roamed the country and made the roads unsafe. Further evidence of the disturbed state of Faucigny at this period is found in a pleasant anecdote told by de Saussure himself of his reception at the Chartreuse of Le Reposoir. This lies in a secluded glen a few miles above Cluses, at the back of the Pointe Percée, a lion-like summit, the other side of which is a conspicuous object from the Baths of St. Gervais and stands prominent against the sunset in the view from the Grands Mulets. I give de Saussure's tale in his own words:

'I have stayed at this Convent, a convenient resort for a naturalist, two or three times, and always been well received by the Chartreux. My first visit,

district was then regarded as inaccessible; it was a fairyland, where imagination and credulity amused themselves in placing the most absurd and terrifying phenomena—it was the site of the "Montagnes Maudites."' Senebier goes on: 'De Saussure formed the project of visiting Les Montagnes Maudites. I know not which is most admirable, the courage of the youth who braves opinion and carries out his wish despite it, or the good sense of his parents who contemned popular nervousness and had sufficient confidence in the prudence of their son to authorise his journey.'

Adequate explanation of the comments on our countrymen's alleged timidity is not far to seek. They preferred tents to the wretched wine-shops which at that date were the only shelter at Chamonix; they carried arms, and Pococke, who had travelled in the Levant, seems to have put on an Arab dressing-gown, and, abetted by his companions, mystified the simple inhabitants of Sallanches by pretending to be an Oriental potentate. This harmless jest was quite enough to afford to the Chamoniards— 'nation gaie et railleuse,' as de Saussure called them—material for a tale which would be welcomed by their Genevese visitors, gossips by nature, and slightly annoyed that it should have been left to foreigners to reveal to the world wonders that had lain for centuries almost at their own gates—within, even at that date, a long day's journey. It was natural enough that they should take

however, gave them a great fright. At the time I was making a collection of Alpine birds. I carried a gun, my two servants who were with me had guns; the hunters who served me as guides were also armed. It was a Thursday; the Chartreux were enjoying the moment of recreation they term a *spaciment*—they were taking the air in a wood near the Convent. By chance we approached through the same wood, and the peaceable hosts of this solitude, seeing themselves suddenly surrounded by armed strangers, thought that their last day had come, or at least that we were about to pillage their Convent. In vain I tried to explain to them my objects in travel; curiosity seemed to them too feeble a motive to make anyone come to see mountains from their point of view gloomy and unattractive; and that all our armament was in order to kill little birds they looked on as a ridiculous and almost preposterous pretext. Notwithstanding, they invited us to enter the Convent and to refresh ourselves, being persuaded that in any case we should enter by force. It was only after having examined my scientific instruments and inspected us scrupulously that they persuaded themselves that we had no evil designs.' [*Voyages*, 284.]

The case, it may be noted, has points of resemblance with that of the English party, and indicates the general sense of insecurity in Savoy at this time. Even the unwarlike Bourrit took pistols with him when he went round Mont Blanc. It is true they were unloaded.

a mild and harmless revenge by making fun out of any eccentricities in the Englishmen they could lay hold of. It gave them something to laugh over at the afternoon tea-parties in the pleasant gardens on the shores of Lake Leman, while they glanced at the sunset on the snows they preferred to view from a discreet distance.[1]

Another glimpse of the supposed perils of a visit to the glaciers about this date is afforded by the high-spirited account of his own experiences given by de Saussure's friend, the young Duc de la Rochefoucauld d'Enville, afterwards a victim of the Revolution, who went to Chamonix in 1762. He does full justice to our countrymen, whom he imitated in taking arms. I quote a few lines:

'Mr. Windham, a young Englishman of about twenty, carried out successfully this arduous journey; it wanted an Englishman, or a knight-errant; he was an Englishman! It was worse than fighting with giants or winged dragons, sheep or windmills. It was a case of tramping through frightful regions by paths full of rocks fallen from the mountains, crossing streams, affronting the voracious insects with which the pothouses of Savoy are full; his courage carried him over all these obstacles. Since his time all the English who come to Geneva make this journey, and some Genevese, but no Frenchmen had yet attempted it.'[2]

The immediate motive of de Saussure's first visit to Chamonix in 1760 had been the desire to collect plants for Haller. In that year Haller mentions him along with the collectors from whom he hopes for great results, while Bonnet writes, 'My nephew glories in contributing to your botanical studies.' A few weeks later we hear that the pupil has 'created some new plants,' but later on he was apparently less successful, for Haller admonishes him gently as to his way of going to work. 'I fear, eager as you are, that on your excursions you walk a little too quickly; one ought to go as slowly

[1] In the year following Windham's visit (1742) Pierre Martel, an engineer living at Geneva, organised a party to repeat the trip of the Englishmen. He was better provided with instruments, and brought back some measurements and an attempt at a map. These he embodied in a narrative addressed to Windham, which is stated on the title-page to have been 'laid before the Royal Society.' It is not, however, included in any of its *Transactions*.

[2] See *Annuaire du Club Alpin Français*, 1893.

as possible, and above all on the alps to sit down from time to time, even to lie down, so as to get a close view of the growing plants. A league traversed thus slowly will bring you a better return than two hurried over.' In a later letter de Saussure alleges as an excuse for his slender booty, the relative poverty of the flora of the Chamonix valley.

De Saussure has given no separate account of this his first excursion to the snows, and his experiences have to be collected from different passages in the *Voyages*. At an age when walking for walking's sake is a pleasure to vigorous youth, he tramped alone all the fifty miles from Geneva. Up to Sallanches the road was excellent, for the rest of the way to the top of the defile of Les Montets there was only a rough cart-track hardly possible for wheels and liable to be interrupted by dangerous torrents.

But the young collector found more than compensation by the roadside :

'It is on these rocks,' he writes, 'that the first really Alpine plants one meets on the way to Chamonix grow. After the frosts and the occupations of winter have kept me for several months far from the High Alps, when I am at last able to return to them, the first Alpine plants, the moment that I recognise them, always give me a thrill of delight ; I feel then that I am in my element, in possession of the liveliest pleasures that the study of nature can give to its lovers. I rejoice to see again the *Rhododendron ferrugineum*, that charming bush whose ever-green branches are crowned by ruddy blossoms, the smell of which is as sweet as their colour is exquisite; the *Auricula* of the Alps, which in our garden has gained richer hues, but fails to preserve its delicate perfume, is spread over these rocks, with the *Astrantia alpina*, the *Saxifraga cotyledon*, and many others.' [*Voyages*, 508.]

De Saussure's first impression of the glaciers follows :

'On issuing from this wild and narrow defile [Les Montets] the traveller turns to the left, and enters the valley of Chamonix, the aspect of which is in contrast absolutely soft and smiling. The floor of the valley, which is in the form of a cradle with gently sloping sides, is covered with meadows between which the road passes, protected by low palings. The different glaciers which fall into the valley catch the eyes in succession. At first one notes only that of Taconnaz, which seems as if hanging on the steep slope of a narrow ravine, of which it occupies the bottom. But soon the eyes are drawn to the Glacier des Bossons, which is seen to descend from the summits neighbouring on Mont Blanc; its icy masses, wrought into the form of huge pyramids, produce an astonishing effect in the centre of the pine woods which they traverse and overtop. These majestic glaciers, separated by great forests, and crowned by granite crags of astounding height cut in the form of great obelisks and mixed with snow and ice, present one of the noblest and most singular spectacles it is possible to imagine. The fresh and pure air one breathes, so different from the close atmosphere of the basins of Sallanches and Servoz, the good cultivation of the soil, the pretty hamlets met with at every step, when seen on a fine day, give the impression of a new world, a sort of earthly paradise, enclosed by a kindly Deity in the circle of the mountains. The road, continuously good and easy,[1] allows the traveller to give himself up to delicious reveries and the pleasant, varied, and novel ideas which crowd on his brain.' [*Voyages*, 510.]

How are the 'Cursed Mountains' transformed in the eyes of the youth who was to lead Europe to do them homage! At the Prieuré there was no accommodation except in one or two rough *cabarets*, so that the young traveller found lodging with the curé, doubtless in the pleasant house that still stands to the right of the church as one looks up the village street. He undertook what since Pococke and Windham's day was the inevitable excursion, that which was afterwards described by a French tourist as 'le Mont Blanc jusqu'au Montenvers.' There he saw the 'Pierre des Anglais,' a shepherds' gite, under which local legend said—it appears falsely—that the English visitors had passed the night, but where, at any rate, they had lunched and drunk patriotic toasts, including the health of 'the Roi Georges'—a precedent the guides, no doubt pleased to share in the bottles opened, tried, we are told, to impose on travellers of other nationalities.[2] De Saussure, bolder than his predecessors, essayed the crossing of the glacier and visited the solitary shepherd who kept his flock on the scanty pasturage at the foot of the Aiguille du Dru. The old man asked for tobacco, which de Saussure could not supply, but he seemed to have no use for the coins offered him.

De Saussure on this occasion also climbed the Brévent, guided by Pierre Simon, whom for many years he constantly employed.

[1] This refers to the open valley above Les Houches as contrasted to the defile of Les Montets.
[2] Bordier, *Voyage Pittoresque aux Glacières de Savoie*, Genève, 1773.

This was probably the first ascent by a tourist. The most interesting fact connected with de Saussure's 1760 visit is that he issued a notice in each parish of the valley offering a handsome reward to the first man to climb Mont Blanc, and further promising to recompense any adventurers for time lost in searching for a way. The amount offered has not been recorded.

The young traveller's attention was not confined to the mountains, but extended also to their inhabitants. The human interest was always strong in de Saussure, whether in society or during his rambles. He tells us at the beginning of his chapter on the manners and customs of the Chamoniards that in his childhood the common folk at Geneva called the snowy mountains 'the Accursed Hills,' and believed that their eternal frosts—the snow and ice that grew in the place of forests on their mountain sides— were a punishment for the crimes committed by those who lived under them. Until the Savoy highlands became better known, this belief, absurd as it may seem, served as foundation for a distrust which obtained credit even among people who might have been expected to be above such prejudices. They had the excuse that their superstition was far from being singular; the Pyrenees have their Maladetta, and many similar cases might be cited. Waste places had to be peopled; and Christianity converted the classical fauns and nymphs either into demons and witches, or elves and fairies.

During de Saussure's life a great change came over Chamonix. Up to 1765 the curé's house had afforded the only decent lodging in the village. Twenty years later it boasted three large and good inns and eighteen hundred tourists a year to fill them. This influx of visitors to a certain extent corrupted the simplicity of the inhabitants, but, apart from petty tricks used to obtain engagement as guides, they were, we are told, honest, serviceable, and well content with their pay of five or six francs a day. The male population in summer was greatly reduced by the number who sought employment abroad not only in the large towns, but as cheesemakers in the French and Italian Alps. In this art they had acquired a reputation which has lasted to the present day, and it is by no means rare to find a Chamoniard employed in a chalet far from his own valley. Those who stayed at home were little given to field labour, which they left mostly to the women. Before the career of guides was open to them they resorted either to the search for crystals or to chamois-hunting, both highly dangerous pursuits in which many lives were lost. De Saussure tells several dramatic stories of the perils of the chase and the jealousy of the hunters of different districts. The charge of luring peasants to destruction which has sometimes been brought against mountaineers is obviously unsustainable, since the profession of guide is far less dangerous than the pursuits it has superseded. It is surprising to find as early as 1787 another charge—a less serious one—brought against the guides' employers. Tourists, a visitor alleges, anxious to make records—so long to the Montenvers, so many minutes in crossing the Mer de Glace—forced their laden guides to keep up an excessive pace, with the deplorable result that the guides, worn out by constant and excessive effort, became old men at forty. The same writer admits that many of the guides had already the fault of being too exacting, but points out that several may be found who retain the simplicity and disinterestedness of their fathers.[1]

There can be no doubt that the new form of employment created by the visitors to the glaciers was a great boon to a district which could not maintain its population. Unlike—as Bourrit points out—the independent peasant-farmers of the Bernese Oberland, who found sufficient sustenance in their fields and broad alps, the Chamoniards, shut up in their narrow valley and subject to the exactions of a religious community, were ready to welcome eagerly any new mode of wage-earning. The relative poverty of Chamonix was one cause of its school of guides attaining to a pre-eminence which was not seriously contested for many years by the men of Grindelwald and the Hasli Thal. Another was the quickness with which they picked up the icecraft called for in ascents of Mont Blanc. In my own early years Chamonix men were unrivalled on a difficult glacier. Icefalls locally deemed impracticable were a pastime to François Dévouassoud. Yet another qualification may be found in the wandering habit of the Savoyard peasantry. From very early days Chamoniards with their mules were ready to accompany travellers on extensive tours, and to act, as Ruskin's guide did, more or less as couriers.

[1] *Excursion dans les Mines du Haut Faucigny*, Berthoud van Berchem fils (Lausanne, 1787).

Bourrit reports that on one occasion when de Saussure was expected at Chamonix, a hunter who had gone out to secure a chamois as a present to him perished in the chase, and that de Saussure thereon behaved generously to his family. So great, Bourrit adds, was the respect felt for de Saussure in the valley, that the Chamoniards would habitually raise their hats in mentioning his name. Their famous visitor was by no means slow in returning the warm feelings entertained towards him by the comrades of his climbs. But at the same time he was very conscious of the weak points in the local character often brought out by the emergencies of travel. He records the devices by which on Mont Blanc his guides endeavoured to prevent him from camping on the snow, the sorry trick by which they sought to cut short his sojourn on the Col du Géant. But he has nothing but praise for his first guide, Pierre Simon, who died about 1780, and his successor, Marie Couttet. Of the former Bourrit has given us a picture :

'This guide is one of the best recommended of the valley, and he owes his reputation to M. de Saussure, who, recognising his good qualities, trained him in his various excursions. He is short of stature; his head buried in a large hat; small bright eyes, a short coat, heavy nailed shoes, and a spiked stick, a peculiar language as difficult to understand as to speak for everyone except his illustrious employer—such are his external qualities. What made me choose him was that he was experienced, prudent, courageous, and faithful.'[1]

The description will find an echo in the recollections of many more recent climbers. De Saussure's later guide, Marie Couttet, I picture as of the same type as his nephew, the guide of my own boyhood, Michel Alphonse Couttet, and his son, Ruskin's companion, Joseph Marie Couttet, so often mentioned in the pages of *Præterita*, tall, upright, with an almost military bearing, in disposition cautious, in conversation shrewd and sententious, on the road or in rough quarters full of devices for an employer's comfort, having for home a substantial house in the village. The Balmats of fifty years ago, one of whom was Sir Alfred Wills' guide, belonged to the same class. Balmat 'of Mont Blanc' was of another type, the peasant proprietors of the

[1] Bourrit's *Description des Aspects du Mont Blanc*, 1776.

outlying hamlets, who often either emigrated or sought to add to their scanty livelihood by crystal-hunting. De Saussure, though he employed him more than once, would seem never to have been on very cordial terms with him, or to have engaged him as his chief guide. The tradition in the de Saussure family, as reported by the late M. Henri de Saussure, is to the effect that Balmat did not work well with his fellows, amongst whom he was unpopular. Another of de Saussure's guides was Jean Louis Dévouassoud, 'dit le Professeur.' His nickname suggests that the well-known guide and explorer, François Dévouassoud, twice my companion in the Caucasus, may have inherited from him the fine manner and literary instincts that made him so delightful a companion to his many English employers. But I have not been able to trace the degree of relationship. François' monument [1] stands beside the church door at Chamonix, and may, I trust, long preserve and hand down the memory of a man who embodied the traditional qualities of a great guide, and combined with them those of an intrepid traveller and a never-failing friend.

De Saussure during this expedition made careful notes on the local methods of agriculture, and he is at pains to indicate a flaw in the communal system under which the pasturages and forests were administered. The peasant who owns no hayfields in the valley cannot feed cows in winter, and therefore gets no advantage from the common summer pasturage on the Alps. The 'wild hay' cut on ledges inaccessible to four-footed animals will not suffice by itself to maintain a single cow. The remedy de Saussure suggested was that the wealthier peasants who profit by the pasturages should pay a rent or tax to the commune, to be used as a poor-rate. Up to recent years the absence of any poor-law at Chamonix has been met by the custom among the villagers of taking turns to lodge for a period the aged and infirm, or orphans who have no family to support them.

[1] François Dévouassoud's monument, besides the names of some of his principal English friends, bears the following inscription: 'François Joseph Dévouassoud MDCCCXXXII-MDCCCCV Viro integro Comiti Amico Sodali jucundo dilecto desiderato Duci sagaci indomito per xl. annos spectato ne tantae Virtutis Memoria et Exemplum perderetur hunc Lapidem nonnulli ex Amicis quos saepe inter Alpium Juga et Caucasi Nives duxerat ponendum curaverunt.' It owes its Latin form to my late friends, Sir Richard Jebb and Mr. T. H. Rawlins, Vice-Provost of Eton. The latter was one of François' employers.

De Saussure points out the need of some winter occupation for the men. Wood-carving, he says, has never taken root in Savoy as in the Bernese Oberland. Many in the larger villages spend most of their time in drinking-shops, and gamble even for high stakes. In the more remote hamlets the evenings pass as in the play of the *Soirée Villageoise*. At nightfall everyone meets round the fire in the largest room, the women sew and card flax, or tell stories; the men make bowls and spoons or other such articles in wood, and the mistress of the house is at no expense beyond providing a jug of water and a bowl of apples cooked in the cinders to serve as supper.

'Their wits,' adds de Saussure, 'are keen and penetrating, their character is lively and given to mockery; they fasten with singular shrewdness on any eccentricities in strangers, and mimic them between themselves in the most amusing way. Nevertheless, they are capable of serious reflection. Many of them have attacked me on questions of religion or metaphysics, not so much on the points of difference between one religion and another as on general questions, in a way which showed that they had ideas of their own apart from those they had been brought up in.' [*Voyages*, 744.]

De Saussure proceeds to tell an affecting tale that has been already quoted more than once in connection with his travels:

'Nothing of the sort surprised me more than a woman of Argentière whose home I entered to ask for milk when coming down from the glacier in March 1764. The village had suffered from an epidemic of dysentery, which, some months previously, had carried off her father, her husband, and her brothers, so that she was left alone with three children in infancy. Her figure had something noble about it, and her countenance bore traces of a calm and deep sorrow which made it interesting. After she had given me the milk she asked who I was, and what I came for at that season. When she learned that I was Genevese, she said she could not believe that Protestants would be damned, that there were among us many honest people, and that God was too good and just to condemn us indiscriminately. Then after a moment's reflection, she added, shaking her head: "But what is very strange is that of so many who have gone, not one should have returned; I," she added with an accent of sorrow, "who have so deeply mourned my husband and my brothers, who have never ceased thinking of them, who every night implore them with the utmost earnestness to tell me where they are, and in what state—ah!

surely if they still exist somewhere they would not leave me in this uncertainty. But perhaps," she added, "I am not worthy of this privilege, perhaps the pure and innocent souls of these infants"—she looked at their cradles as she spoke—"enjoy their presence and the happiness which has been refused me."' [*Voyages*, 744.]

De Saussure goes on to moralise as follows :

'This curious mixture of sense and superstition, expressed forcibly in the energetic local dialect, had something most out of the common, something in the classic style, or rather in that of Shakespeare ; and her situation, her solitude, this frenzy of a soul distracted by grief, made on me an impression which will never be effaced from my memory.' [*Voyages*, 744.].

His holiday over, de Saussure returned to his home at Geneva and his academic career.

In 1761 he stood for the Chair of Mathematics. With this object he gave up for the moment the study of Physics and Natural Science, and 'crammed' geometry. He was, however, honourably defeated by a formidable rival, Louis Bertrand, who was to be his future opponent in the educational controversy, and at a later date to serve on the same committee with him in the revolutionary epoch. Bertrand was nine years older and already a member of the Academy of Sciences of Berlin. For the next twelve months de Saussure consoled himself by returning to the classics, and in particular to the Greek and Latin poets. Throughout his life, though primarily a man of science, he was a consistent supporter of the claim of the Humanities to a place in education, and we shall discover him reading and quoting Homer, taking Horace up Mont Blanc, and keeping an intimate journal in Greek. He found another congenial occupation in prosecuting his botanical studies. In 1762 he composed a treatise, *Sur l'Epiderme des Feuilles et des Pétales*, of which Cuvier afterwards wrote : 'This little work in itself gave him an honourable place among botanists.' He dedicated it to Haller, who contributed an appreciative preface.

De Saussure found time to attend Tronchin's lectures on Physiology. He also (in 1761) put in a second visit to Chamonix, of which we have few particulars. He relates incidentally in the *Voyages* a narrow escape he and his guide had from a stone avalanche which fell from the moraine of the glacier under the Aiguille du Midi.

In April 1762 another Professorship became vacant at the Academy, that of Philosophy. The title as understood at Geneva was a very comprehensive one. 'At this time,' writes a late Librarian of the Town Library at Geneva, 'Philosophy was held to include Psychology, Logic, Morals, and Divinity, and also the general principles of the Natural Sciences, with some acquaintance with the views of Bacon, Descartes, and Leibnitz.' The Venerable Company, the Pastors and Professors of the Academy, accordingly petitioned the Magnificent Council, which held Geneva under a wide-reaching control, that the Chair might be divided. Physical Science, they declared, was all the fashion, Rational Philosophy in great danger of being neglected. They talked, as clerical bodies are apt to talk, of 'the poison which spreads itself everywhere and threatens to infect the sources of public education.' But their proposal was obviously sound. It was clearly monstrous to call on a Professor of Physical Science to spend half his time in teaching metaphysics, while his own students were receiving instruction in the subjects on which he was an expert from a man who could have but slender qualifications for the task. It was equally unfortunate—and probably the Venerable Company resented it more—that a master in Metaphysics and Morals should be called on to devote his energies to other and more secular subjects.

The eloquence of the Pastors was fruitless; the conservative Senate resolved that there should be no change made at the coming election, but that it should be left open to consideration at a future date whether the steps proposed by the Venerable Company were desirable. This date did not arrive until 1823! Even then no satisfactory conclusion was reached.

In 1762 three candidates for the Professorship came forward. Each had to produce two theses, one on Philosophy and one on Natural Science. De Saussure was also able to adduce as a qualification his botanical tract. He now wrote on the 'Principal Causes of Errors arising from the Qualities of the Mind' and 'On Rainbows, Halos, and Parhelia.' His candidature had the influential support of 'The Great Haller,' and he was elected by a majority after a contest which is said 'to have done honour to the Academy.' His more formidable rival, François Mercier, had subsequently a creditable career as a Professor and Rector of the Academy.

On the 13th December two dignified representatives of the Venerable Company presented the young Professor of twenty-two for confirmation in his post to the Senate or Magnificent Council —a body composed of twenty-five grave and reverend signors, robed and capped with the flowing wigs to wear which was a privilege of the aristocracy. The usual picturesque formalities having been duly observed and the matter voted on both by acclamation and ballot, de Saussure was introduced and took the customary oath.

De Saussure's lectures have most of them perished, but fortunately enough material has been preserved among the papers of two of his pupils to enable us to form a fair idea of his philosophical position. Of his attitude towards physical inquiry, the *Voyages*, and above all the list of Agenda appended to their last volume, supply the best illustration. More will be said on these topics when we come to sum up his general character and position as an observer and philosopher.

De Saussure lectured in French on Physics one year, and the next in Latin on Metaphysics. For his Inaugural Discourse, delivered in October 1763, the Professor chose a subject of practical and perennial interest, one which he was twelve years later to develop more fully. He writes to Haller :

'On Friday I shall pronounce my Inaugural Discourse. I have taken as its subject "An Analysis of the Qualities necessary to form a Philosopher, and of the education to be given to children in order to foster or call forth such qualities." You will easily believe, Monsieur, that I am not going to sing the praises of the education in vogue with us and elsewhere, and that I do not insist on the study of Greek and Latin as the essential last touch in education.'

In this matter de Saussure, himself no mean scholar, shows a singularly impartial mind. But let us hope that, as regards children (*enfants* is the word used), philosophy was given a restricted interpretation by the Professor of twenty-three.

During 1762 de Saussure kept up a lively correspondence with Haller. The latter had, it appears, placed one of his sons in some commercial employ in Geneva. De Saussure bids him warn the youth to have nothing whatever to do with the German shopboys, who are in very bad repute owing to their conduct having been so disorderly that they have had to be publicly reprimanded. In April 1763 he writes to Haller a long memoir of twelve pages, entering in much medical detail into his mother's symptoms, and asking for a formal opinion. The patient, it seems, had again lost confidence in the favourite doctor of Geneva. No doubt she had many friends to suggest the expediency of taking other advice. Tronchin's treatment, which Madame de Saussure had been under for seven years, had been, her son writes, entirely palliative. Would not Haller come to her aid? If he thought badly of her case, would he be good enough to say so in a private note, and not in a formal opinion, so that the patient might not be alarmed. The whole letter bears witness to the affection and tender solicitude of a devoted son. Nothing, however, came of it, as Madame de Saussure was unable to make the journey to Berne which Haller suggested, and Tronchin was again called in.

His Professorship and his mother's health were not, however, de Saussure's only interests in the autumn of 1763. A still more absorbing one had come into his life. He was in love. The object of his affections was a girl of seventeen, Mlle. Albertine Amélie Boissier, the eldest of three sisters, who were the great heiresses of the city, and also, says Senebier, 'conspicuous in the society of Geneva by their charms both of mind and person.' Looking at the ages of the young ladies—the eldest was not yet eighteen—the worthy Senebier would appear to be here somewhat anticipating events. They were the only surviving children of Jean Jacques André Boissier, described to Haller by his future son-in-law as 'of a family not ancient, but wealthy and esteemed.' The Boissiers were prosperous bankers, and had a London house and English connections. Madame Boissier was the only daughter of a well-known professor and pastor, Ami Lullin (1695-1756), himself the son of a prosperous banker, Jean Antoine Lullin, whose wealth he had inherited. It was therefore to his wife's parents that de Saussure owed not only most of his means, but the townhouse, counted the finest in Geneva, in which he spent a great part of his life. It was built according to the designs of Abeille, a celebrated architect of his day, and completed in 1707. It now remains quite unaltered and is still in the possession of the family. A stone mansion of admirable proportions and dignified elevation, it occupies an excellent site fronting, but standing back from, the Rue de la Cité, the steep street that leads from the Rhône to the Upper Town. The entrance is through a lodge and courtyard. At the back a broad terrace overlooks the ramparts, the Corraterie, and the meadows of Plainpalais, and commands a view extending to the distant Jura and the Perte du Rhône. The corner of this terrace is occupied by a low pavilion used by de Saussure as a convenient laboratory and storehouse. According to tradition, Lullin never lived to cross his threshold or to climb his stately staircase. The story runs that the banker's coach broke down on his return from a long absence in Paris, and that in consequence he arrived so late that the city gates, always closed half an hour after sunset, were already shut. Forced to sleep at the inn outside the walls, he was suddenly taken ill and died before morning.

Mlle. Boissier's relatives desired that no formal engagement should take place till she was twenty. It was not till 1764 that de Saussure felt himself free to announce his approaching marriage to his friend at Roche. This is the description he gives of his betrothed in a letter to Haller:

'She has the most beautiful, tender, and generous disposition; devoted to her duty, she is made to render happy the man who appreciates her worth. Add a mind cultivated, sensitive, sympathetic, a gentle gaiety, a face in which all these qualities are expressed, a pleasing figure.'

We are able to put the young lady's portrait of herself beside that given by her lover. Here are two extracts from her private diary:

'I am fifteen and a half: I am plain, but not painfully so. Some people find an attraction in my air of gentleness and kindness. Am I clever? No: still I am not actually stupid. My excessive nervousness keeps me from talking as much as I might. I am rather disposed to languor than to too much vivacity. I do not care for fashionable society, and, to put it shortly, idleness is my favourite passion, and one I ought to try to conquer. It often interferes with my studies, to which, however, I am devoted. Finally, the best part of me is my heart, which will perhaps prove my misfortune. Its sensibility is so excessive, it agitates itself so often about nothing, that my reason

H.B. de Saussure
at 18

Mme. H.B. de Saussure
as a girl

from miniatures

really ought to control it. I trust, please God, I shall never love any object unworthy of my affection, but in those I love I disquiet myself over their faults and failings; there are, however, few for whom I feel this kind of affection, and I believe that I am quick in recognising objects worthy of it.'

Some three years later we find this discriminating young heiress reviewing her suitors and considering her settlement in life in a very independent spirit. It is evident that marriages at Geneva were not, as in France, wholly matters of family arrangement, and that those chiefly concerned enjoyed much liberty of choice:

'I have not,' writes Mlle. Boissier, 'seen anyone among the suitors brought forward this year who could induce me to change my state. All the same, my marriage has been constantly discussed: I am on the *tapis*, my friends send me congratulations. I shall be more crossexamined than ever next Monday, as the subject is a cavalier by whom some of my friends would have been pleased to be accorded the preference he has shown me—which I could do without. Mama (her grandmother) is very strongly in his favour. He is of high character and a savant, and I am surprised he has made so little progress in a heart so easily touched by merit as mine. I am very young, in no hurry, very happy, and little influenced by worldly considerations or the glamour of fashion.'

The diary concludes abruptly without any record of the final success of the savant in touching the heart of its writer.

Of de Saussure himself at this period we have a companion portrait from the pen of Gray's Swiss friend, Charles Victor de Bonstetten.

'At twenty-four de Saussure came out, so to speak, from the maternal lap to enter on the world. He was already—without knowing it—a great savant, witty, with a particular touch of naïveté which could not fail to please, and though he was not easily embarrassed, he almost invariably blushed when spoken to by a girl or a young woman.'

The fortunate couple had to wait for two and a half years. Meantime, they were able to meet, de Saussure writes, 'at least once a week,' yet the lover's impatience and nervousness rendered him, according to his biographer, 'stormy and restless.' Philosophy apparently not proving a sufficient anodyne for love, he turned for relief to logic, in which he gave a successful course of lectures. In March of the year 1764 he found a further distraction in a third excursion to Chamonix, where he saw the landscape under snow and studied the glaciers in a new aspect. He notes that in the valley the snow was so hard that laden mules did not break the surface, and so deep that the palings between the fields were buried. This, however, can only have been the case at the head of the valley, as at Chamonix there was only eighteen inches. De Saussure's remarks on the aspect of the scenery in its winter garb are interesting. He wrote :

'It was more wonderful than pleasing. The uniformity of white surfaces of enormous extent reaching from the tops of the mountains to the bottom of the valley, broken only by a few rocks where cliffs could not hold the snow, by forests of a dull grey hue, and by the Arve, which wound like a dark thread through the centre of the picture ; this combination, lit by the sun, had, in its grandeur and its dazzling purity, an element of death and infinite sadness. The glaciers, which so well ornament the landscape when their background is a beautiful green, made no effect in the middle of all this white, although when near at hand the ice-pyramids, whose sides remained bare, shone like emeralds under the fresh and white snow that capped their tops.' [*Voyages*, 730.]

De Saussure added that his excursion had proved to him three things—the formation of glaciers by the melting and refreezing of snow, their forward motion, and the permanence of the streams that issue from them.[1]

Three months later de Saussure gave an audience at the

[1] It may be convenient to take this opportunity to refer to recent observations as to the true origin of glacial streams in winter.

Up to the present time it has been generally believed that the winter outflow, the perfectly clear water issuing at that season from the foot of the glacier, is the result of a continuous melting of the ice caused by the warmth of the earth. It seems strange that the fountains which break out from under the snow on bare slopes in winter, when all else is frozen, did not suggest either to de Saussure or to any of his scientific successors that the permanence of the glacial streams might be due to similar sources in the bed of the glacier. This somewhat obvious fact was not recognised until, in 1904, I pointed it out in an address to the Geographical Section of the British Association at Cambridge. It was subsequently observed independently by Professor Collet, formerly director of the Service des Eaux of the Swiss Government, and now Professor of Geology in the University of Geneva. Professor Collet has verified my observation and placed the matter beyond doubt by a careful analysis of the waters issuing from the ice at different seasons of the year. (The Academy became a University under Napoleon.)

Academy the fruit of his experiences in his three first visits to Chamonix in a lecture entitled, 'A Description of the Glaciers of Savoy, and a Theory of their Formation.' In November he sent the MS. to Haller and asked for his advice as to whether it was worth publishing, but though Haller approved, publication seems to have been postponed. The material, no doubt, furnished the basis of the chapter 'Des Glaciers en général' subsequently inserted in the *Voyages*. We recognise in it the first signs of a shift in the direction of de Saussure's scientific aims. Henceforth, though by no means off with botany, geology, regarded as the key to the history of our planet, becomes the first object of his pursuit and study. His letters to Haller at this time indicate the change. He does his best to soften to the great botanist the fact that collecting rare plants has ceased to be his principal aim. He writes:

'I am very far from thinking of giving up botany; plants shall fail me before I will fail them. I meditate some *grandes courses* on the Alps for next summer. The active life of a mountain naturalist has a singular attraction for me. Plants, minerals, strange animals, seem to grow under one's feet. The more general physical phenomena are alone sufficient to attract observers. The purity of the air, the agreeable temperature, the beauty of the landscape, would be enough to induce me to frequent the mountains.'

His point of view is enlarging; a special study of mosses, he writes, may have to wait, and the flora of Chamonix, he repeats, is deplorably poor.

The following quotation from the anonymous journal of a visitor to Chamonix at this date (1764) bears witness to the reputation de Saussure had already attained.

'Professor de Saussure is not one of those who rely on the report of others. Young and eager to learn, laborious and acute, he has visited the district three times, twice in the summer, and lastly in March, not without much fatigue and risk. His eager curiosity has placed him in a position to satisfy ours, and we reap tranquilly the fruit of his labours.'[1]

De Saussure's marriage took place in the Chapel of the Hospital on the 12th May 1765. Mlle. Boissier's sister, Jeanne Françoise, was married at the same time and place to Jean

[1] Published by M. Henri Ferrand in the *Revue Alpine*, 1912, pp. 103-6.

Alphonse Turrettini, a member of an old family of Italian origin. De Saussure, by all accounts the most amiable of men in private life, entered warmly into the larger family circle now open to him. In the words of the sentimental Senebier, 'His expansive heart was not too narrow for the new relations which his marriage provided him; he cherished with tenderness the amiable sisters of his wife, who like her united bodily graces to the charms of the mind, education, and true virtue.' The relatively early deaths of his two brothers-in-law, combined with the fact that the country-house at Genthod remained the joint property and summer residence of the three sisters, led to the continuance of a singularly intimate and affectionate relationship of which we shall come across frequent indications in de Saussure's correspondence.

At this point de Saussure's biographer interpolates an anecdote suited to the sentiment of the day in order to illustrate his hero's kindness of heart. A few days after the wedding, news came to Geneva that his foster-brother had been arrested as a deserter at La Roche sur Foron in Faucigny, and was in danger of being shot; de Saussure at once rushed off to the spot and was successful in obtaining a commutation of the sentence. On this Senebier exclaims: 'A quoi serviraient le génie et le savoir s'ils flétrissaient la sensibilité ? Il est plus utile qu'on ne croit de peindre le cœur d'un observateur avant de raconter ses travaux.' The 'sensibility' of the biographer is somewhat of a trial to the modern reader, and would not, I fancy, have been congenial to his subject!

His marriage put de Saussure and his bride to a test in most cases incidental to that relationship in life in an unusually severe form. It was an anxious matter to marry a youth who had already avowed a passion for mountains, and a special devotion to the inaccessible Monts Maudits, who had even gone further, and plotted ways and means for conquering their snows. This ambition of de Saussure was, we are told by contemporaries, for years a constant source of uneasiness to his family. His wife in particular seems to have shown from the first, and never to have wholly overcome, a very natural anxiety. But his resolutions once formed were not easily set aside. He made up his mind, he tells us, to make every year an Alpine tour, and he did his best, while his health permitted, to carry out this intention. At this period he had Mont Blanc very much on the brain. Here is his confession in his own words :

'It became for me a sort of illness. My eyes could not encounter this mountain, which one sees from so many spots in our neighbourhood, without my being seized with a pang.' [*Voyages*, 2023.]

But if de Saussure was not to be diverted from the objects he had set before him, the survival of many of his letters of a later date enables us to appreciate with what tenderness he strove to soothe his wife's feelings. He writes :

'I should be in despair if I thought that you did not love me too much to look on my travels with indifference. Your affection makes, I must confess, the whole happiness of my life. I could wish—I swear to you—to make to it a complete sacrifice, but how can I renounce a vocation which absorbs me, and thus abandon my career in the middle ? I assure you that I have done all that is humanly in my power to shorten my journey without spoiling it. For there would be no lack of people to say, " Why did not he see that ? " " Why did not he do this ? " And how could I venture to reply to my critics, " It was in order sooner to rejoin my wife " ? '

Again he replies to some badinage on her part :

'I assure you I do not trouble myself much about *mes belles*. You, my children, my parents, are about the only objects that distract me from my philosophical contemplations. I include your sisters, to whom I am most sincerely attached.'

On a later occasion (in 1783), in reply to some protest on her part, he urges the claims of science in a lighter vein :

'In this Valle Leventina, which was new to me, I have made a number of observations of the greatest importance to me and quite beyond my hopes, but this is not what will interest you. You would like better—God pardon me—to see me as fat as a canon, asleep all day in the chimney corner after a good dinner, than to see me gain immortal fame by the most sublime discoveries at the cost of a few ounces of weight and several weeks of absence. If I make these journeys despite the uneasiness they cause you, it is because I regard it as an engagement of honour, that I feel myself bound to extend my knowledge on the subjects in question, and, as far as it depends on myself, to make my works perfect. I say to myself, " As an officer goes to the assault when it is sounded, as a merchant goes to the Fair on its day, so I ought to go to the mountains when I stand in need of observations." For how many years this feeling will last I cannot tell, but rest assured, my dear angel—I tell you this to remove the doubt you express in your letter—that when I have to give up you will not find me yawning in our daily life and sighing after the mountains. This long solitude does not give one a presentable figure. I see as I write my travelling coat hanging on its peg; it has the look of a clown, of a peasant, which makes me die of laughter: never would the elegant Minette confess herself the sister-in-law of a man who wore such a garment; yet under it is a heart that loves her and would assuredly make for her and her sisters far greater sacrifices than the wearers of the most fashionable waistcoats of Versailles.'

His wife was not alone in her remonstrances. At another moment Bonnet, the anxious uncle, is ready with a suitable caution. 'Take care of your health, above all, run no risks; you are now the head of a household, you are no longer your own property, you belong to your family, to your parents, and your friends. Never, then, put yourself in the case of becoming a martyr of natural science.'

The argument may sound familiar to modern mountaineers, to some of whom it has been addressed, possibly with more reason. Yet, despite her frequent remonstrances, Madame de Saussure does not seem to have been given any serious ground for complaint. Her husband's journeys in the Pennine or Bernese Alps seldom went beyond the limits of a few weeks, and on his longer tours she was, as a rule, his companion.

For the moment, however, it was physiological rather than Alpine studies that occupied the young husband's time. In September 1765, he is attacking deep problems. He writes to Bonnet:

'I find very great difficulties in fixing the exact limit of animal life. I recognise clearly the movements of a life which is in appearance spontaneous, but since it appears to pass by insensible degrees from this movement to true life, I trace the similarity but fail to fix the interval. I wish, however, to go as far as my powers can take me. The further I advance, the better I see that as you, sir, used to say, one must embrace little in order to grasp firmly.'

Here speaks the nephew of Bonnet. It was through his uncle that de Saussure was brought into correspondence and personal relations [1] with the celebrated naturalist, Spallanzani, who was prosecuting at Pavia his researches into the animalcules of infusoria and their modes of reproduction, and at a later date de Saussure made discoveries that led Spallanzani to congratulate Bonnet on there being another great naturalist in the world.

De Saussure was shortly to be occupied with a domestic and less abstruse problem. His first child, a daughter, was born in 1766, and christened Albertine Andrienne.[2] The young husband writes to inform Haller that he has become a father.

'You will easily understand, sensible as you are, monsieur, that this event has distracted me somewhat from my ordinary occupations. My distraction has been increased owing to my reading and observations having revealed to me a prodigious number of faults in the ordinary way of treating and dressing new-born infants, and I have been obliged to carry out myself, or at least to have carried out in my presence, all that was not according to custom!'

A man must be bold indeed to have the courage of his opinions in such circumstances, and de Saussure had to face a grandmother-in-law! This happy event was not the only interruption in his studies about this time. In October his father-in-law, M. Boissier, was found drowned in the Rhône. The evidence given at the inquest by Dr. Turton, a friend of the family, and afterwards physician to George III., who was at Geneva at the time, showed that he had committed suicide in an access of the acute melancholia for which, writing from Paris only two days before M. Boissier's death, Dr. Tronchin had advised change of scene as indispensable. The young couple were, no doubt, living with him at the time, in the great townhouse in the Rue de la Cité. De Saussure, writing to Haller, describes the calamity with much feeling:

'I have had the misfortune to lose my father-in-law by a violent death while still in the prime of his life. I was deeply attached to him; he was a man of intelligence, a wise counsellor, a good friend and father and citizen, who made the happiness of his family, who had

---

[1] De Saussure visited Spallanzani at Pavia in 1770. (See *post.*)

[2] By her marriage to Jacques Necker, a nephew of the statesman and a cousin of Madame de Staël, she became known in after life as Madame Necker-de Saussure. She inherited her father's tastes, assisted him at times by working out his observations, and followed in his footsteps in composing the work on education by which she is known to posterity. (See chap. xv.)

filled several public offices with distinction, and would have succeeded to others. I have had to console myself, my wife, who was in the deepest affliction, and her sisters, rendered orphans by this death. We have passed these last ten or twelve days in the saddest way. They seem to have lasted twelve months.'

He adds :

' I have observed on this occasion the great resource that crushed and deeply grieved souls find in religion. It is the surest channel through which consolation can be bestowed, it is from it alone that arguments can be drawn for submitting with patience and resignation to misfortune, and my detestation of those who endeavour to deprive men of this precious refuge has been redoubled.'

This is one of the few occasions on which de Saussure breaks his reserve on religious matters. His philosophical lectures, while giving little positive indication of the writer's doctrinal beliefs and sympathies, indicate a similar attitude of resolute opposition to the materialism of the day.

Meanwhile the young Professor's time was, we gather from his correspondence, fully occupied. In addition to the work of his double Professorship, he was, in 1766, called on to act as Secretary of the Venerable Company of Pastors, which, amongst other duties, practically controlled the Academy. His mind was further diverted, somewhat unwillingly perhaps, from his travels and his scientific studies by a prolonged political correspondence with his friend Haller. This will be better postponed to a subsequent chapter.

Marriage had naturally led to a sensible pause in de Saussure's visits to the mountains. The summer of 1765 was a blank in his Alpine record. In 1766 we read only of an ascent of the Môle, and a short excursion to Samoëns and Sixt. It was not till July 1767 that he resumed his serious travels by a tour of Mont Blanc with two friends, Jean Louis Pictet[1] and François Jalabert. Pictet was to provide a map, and Jalabert illustrations. The results were combined with those of earlier and later expeditions in the second volume of the *Voyages*. This journey, like all de Saussure's Alpine expeditions, was very carefully planned. He at first proposed to start from the Mont Cenis and traverse to Val

[1] Pictet the Siberian traveller, not de Saussure's pupil and successor in his Professorship.

d'Aosta, possibly by the Col d'Iseran, but gave this up for the tour of Mont Blanc. De Saussure was already ambitious to enlarge his article on glaciers and to make it the foundation of a work that might supplement or supersede Grüner's *Eisgebirge*, which touched but slightly on the glaciers of Savoy. But though he and his friend Lord Stanhope, then residing at Geneva, were both hard at work learning German, he could not yet read it easily. So he wrote to Haller in May 1767 to inquire if Grüner's treatment of his subject was adequate from the local and scientific points of view, and to ask for a German dictionary. In August he further inquired if good German would be of any use where 'the Swiss idiom' prevailed! The reply encouraged him to carry out both his projected tour and his literary undertaking.

In the middle of July he flew to the mountains, and left behind him the troubles and quarrels of Genevese politicians. It was his fourth visit to Chamonix. His programme is set out in a letter to Haller :

'I shall make experiments on heat and cold, on the weight of the atmosphere, on electricity, on the magnet, and on the modes of reproduction of animals, besides giving my greatest attention to natural history. I should like to bring back something to give you pleasure.'

He was still eager to collect and add to the alpine flora. But geology was now his main object. He writes to Haller : 'I am going to work for you and *myself*.'

De Saussure had not long to wait to study electric phenomena. The tour began with an ascent—de Saussure's third—of the Brévent. He writes to Haller from the chalets of Planpra, well known to modern tourists : 'It is with singular pleasure I give you news of a journey undertaken under your auspices.' He goes on to relate how, while on the top of the Brévent with his friends, his 'guides and domestics,' Pictet, on lifting a finger to point out one of the opposite peaks, heard a very lively whistling like that of an electric conductor (*aigrette*).

'We all, and then our guides and domestics, who thought it great fun, did the same, with a like result, hearing from time to time the crackle of little sparks which slightly pricked our fingers. M. Jalabert, who had a hat trimmed with gold lace, heard all round its edge a very distinct and almost alarming noise.'

Bonnet refers to this incident in a note to Haller:

'Our great Alpinier (*sic*)[1] has told you something of his trip to the glaciers. He had a narrow escape of being beatified—you will guess I refer to his electrification in the clouds. The adventure is unique, and could not have been foreseen.'

Most mountaineers nowadays have met with similar experiences.

De Saussure occupied a wet morning in the chalet in writing to his wife, who was then expecting her second child, born in the following October. His conscience was obviously a little uneasy at having left her in the circumstances, and he did his best to console her for his absence by a letter inspired by the fondest affection, in which he first pictures her occupied with her year-old baby and her thoughts of her husband, while the elders talk politics, and then describes his own surroundings:

'What a spectacle would present itself to my Albertine—how she would enjoy its surprising novelty! She would make fun of me; she would press the mosses I had already pressed and would repeat "*Hyposum siccatum*"! How she would laugh if she could see the three of us at this moment in a row on the straw of our chalet, making the most of the little light that comes through the gap left by a missing plank in our hovel, each writing on his knees to the person dearest to him. She would cast an eye on our three servants and four guides sitting round a fire built against the wall without any chimney. On this fire is a huge cauldron full of milk being boiled to make cheese; beside it stands a tall shepherd, continually stirring the milk with a big ladle and burying his naked white arms in the depths of the cauldron. Turning her head, she would see through a hole in the wall a huge mass of ice in the middle of a wood and a pasture covered with all sorts of flowers. What would strike her most by its oddity is a goat which, in its effort to find shelter from the rain, has climbed to the hole which serves us as a window and throws the shadow of its beard and horns across my paper.'

De Saussure, one notes, is careful to leave out, no doubt as too alarming, the adventure with lightning just recorded.

Before leaving Chamonix the travellers made an expedition to the Mer de Glace, and recognised that the interior of the chain

[1] This form, which has been superseded by Alpiniste, was doubtless formed by analogy to 'Crystallier,' used of the Chamonix crystal-seekers.

was a vast reservoir, with plateaux and valleys filled with snowfields which gave birth, both towards Savoy and Italy, to glaciers of every size and dimension. Above and around the snows towered apparently inaccessible granite peaks, split and torn by weather, from which blocks were continually falling.

From the point of view of botany de Saussure once more expresses his disappointment with Chamonix.

'The flora of the district,' he writes, 'is intolerably monotonous. I do not know whether it is the exposure, or the soil, or the neighbourhood of the glaciers, but it is always the same thing, and often nothing but bare rocks.'

He does not seem to have explored on this or on any of his later tours the sunward slopes under the Aiguille de Varens, where the flora, favoured by a limestone soil, is of exceptional beauty.

We note that the visitors to Savoy of the eighteenth century realised that the base of a great mountain is not the best point from which to appreciate its proportions. The aspects of Mont Blanc they most frequently admired and represented were those from the neighbourhood of Sallanches, which the modern tourist hurries past in a train. In this respect they showed more discrimination than their successors. But the spots from which the most perfect views of Mont Blanc may be gained have up to this day remained unknown and unvisited. From the alps above Passy and Servoz the great mountain is seen from top to base framed in the ravine of the Arve. Here nature has risen to the occasion by providing that rarity in the Alps, an exquisitely wooded foreground for a great snow mountain. Above the vineyards of Passy terraced lawns, smooth enough to serve as cricket-grounds, are watered by clear sparkling brooks and encircled by mossy groves of beech and ash. Higher still in the heart of this wilderness, and approached by tracks known to few, a solitary pool hides among the pinewoods and reflects in its still waters the crowning snows of Mont Blanc, completing a picture worthy of a great painter or poet. May it be long before these 'sedes discretae piorum' are invaded by the polluting multitude!

De Saussure now set out on his first tour of Mont Blanc. He dwells on the desolation and danger in bad weather of the Bonhomme, where one of his mules executed several somersaults on the brink of a precipice, fortunately without breaking the instruments it carried. The gloomy situation of the huts of Chapieu so much affected the Genevese servants who accompanied the party that they laid a plot to force him to give up the Col de la Seigne and go round by the Little St. Bernard. He admired the splendid view through the pine stems of the precipices of Mont Blanc as he passed the foot of the Brenva Glacier. At Courmayeur, where he found a good inn and bathing guests, he would have liked to spend more time, but his companions were impatient, an incident which led him to reflect on the advantages for a student of solitary travel. The party returned by the Great St. Bernard to Martigny and the Lake of Geneva.

Two months later, in October 1767, de Saussure's elder son, Nicolas Théodore, destined to be his father's companion and the sharer of his scientific tastes, was born.

CHAPTER IV

THE GRAND TOUR (1768-69)

IN 1768 de Saussure wisely determined that it was time both to escape from the political crisis at Geneva and to give the Alps a rest. He made up his mind to show his young wife the world, and himself to study men as well as mountains. Having obtained leave of absence from his duties at the Academy, he accordingly set out on February 3rd with his wife, the Turrettinis, and his unmarried sister-in-law (whom he constantly alludes to as 'the charming Minette') for Paris. The party lodged at the Hôtel de la Paix in the Rue Richelieu, where François Tronchin, a son of the doctor, had retained for them a sumptuous apartment full of tapestries and fine furniture with a vast *salon* hung with mirrors, of all of which he sent to Geneva a full and alluring inventory.[1]

Senebier in his *Life* gives the following summary of de Saussure's stay in Paris :

'From the moment of his arrival he devoted all his mornings to work : he followed the private courses of Petit, Rouelle, and Jussieu ;[2] he surprised those great men by the precision of his intellect and the originality of his views. Conchology was then the fashion ; de Saussure had not yet occupied himself with it, but he quickly became an expert, and pointed out to more than one amateur rare objects in his collection which he had not recognised.'

De Saussure was not content to use his time in Paris solely in gaining knowledge. He was curious to study the society of

[1] To be distinguished from François Tronchin, an amateur and collector who made himself useful to Voltaire in business matters. (See *Le Conseiller F. Tronchin et ses amis Voltaire, Diderot, Grimm*, par Henri Tronchin, Paris, 1895.)

[2] Pierre Petit (1728-1794), 'Géographe du Roi,' and student of physics ; G. F. Rouelle (1705-1770), Professor of Chemistry at the Jardin des Plantes ; B. de Jussieu (1699-1774), for many years ' démonstrateur ' at the Jardin du Roi— a leading botanist.

the great city, and (continues Senebier) 'in the evening in the gay world he had the same success he had had in the morning with the savants.'

De Saussure's own impressions of Paris, as recorded in his numerous letters and private journal, are more definite and vivid; they have also something of the cruelty of youth.

'In general,' he writes, 'I like the savants of Paris better than its *beaux esprits*; the latter are insupportably vain, have no respect for things human or divine, calumniate pitilessly all that is in the opposite camp, and exercise in conversation an intolerable despotism. The savants, on the other hand, at least those I have met, are as modest as it is possible to be—for Frenchmen! Both classes spend but little time in their studies, and are consequently shallow. Pleasure, female society, and, above all, the passion of frequenting and paying court to the great, absorb the best part of their time. Thus they have often the satisfaction of making discoveries owing to their ignorance of those that have been already made!'

The young Genevese Professor, it is clear, was by no means dazzled by the brilliancy of the glittering crust of Parisian life which twenty years later was to be shivered into fragments by the Great Revolution. The symptoms of the coming troubles did not altogether escape him. In the previous year (13th May 1767) he had written to Haller:

'There is all over Europe a fermentation which aims at liberty, but of which the sequel in many instances must be a redoubling of slavery. An imperfect philosophy produces aspirations to a liberty without limits; a more perfect philosophy, grounded on experience, will show that the tomb of liberty may be found in the cradle of democracy.'

One of de Saussure's most frequent haunts was the Jardin du Roi—of which Buffon had long been the Director—to which he went three times a week to study the plants. He writes to Bonnet:

'I see very often Bernard de Jussieu, the father of French botanists. He is the living image of the serenity and peace of soul that the assiduous study of nature ought to give to the philosopher. He enjoys the most perfect old age, all his senses intact, an incomparable memory, a sweetness, a gaiety, an unrivalled amenity of character adorn in him the deepest and widest learning. Without ever mixing himself in the intrigues of the Academy, he is loved and respected by all the academicians; always the same, always affable, always ready to instruct, he expresses his views with the noble assurance that springs from deep study and is far from either the insolence of pride, or the false pretence of an affected modesty. If he had your imagination, my dear uncle, he would be you.'

Next to Jussieu, de Saussure saw most of Buffon, who was then at the height of his reputation, the most celebrated man of science of his day. Nevertheless, in writing to his correspondents, the young Genevese ventured on very critical appreciations of the author of the *Epoques de la Nature*. To his mother he writes:

'It was the greatest pleasure for me to talk to him. He spoke coldly but politely of M. Bonnet, and I must confess in secret that to win his favour I let him see that I do not always agree with my dear uncle. M. de Buffon is tall and stout; he has a countenance at first sight dull and heavy, but which becomes animated and full of life and expression when he talks. He is polite and suffers contradiction patiently—a very rare quality here—and he knows how to discuss the most deep and learned matters without using long words. We have had several interesting conversations on general physics. He asked for an abstract of my experiments on the heat of the sun, which I gave him. He is bold in his speculations, but he sustains them with force and genius: his conversation instructs me and gives me enthusiasm and courage.'

At a later date de Saussure writes in a different tone:

'I have often had occasion to speak of M. de Buffon with members of the Academy. They do justice to the beauty of his style, but they think nothing of him as a man of science: they look on him neither as a physicist, nor a geometrician, nor a naturalist. His observations they account very inexact and his systems visionary. Perhaps jealousy enters into their judgment. M. de Buffon has, no doubt, excited it by his brilliancy: but it is certain his character also arouses hostility; he is severe in his criticisms, despotic in his opinions, and very exacting in his friendships. In youth he had a satirical disposition that made him very formidable.'

De Saussure, later in life, maintained this unfavourable view of Buffon's claims as a savant, characterising him as 'more of an orator than a naturalist.'

Here is another character:

'M. de Bomare, the author of the Dictionary,[1] if not a miracle like M. de Jussieu, is certainly the best man in the world. He is small, fat, pink and white, somewhat a victim to nerves; a grocer by trade, but his wife keeps the shop. He has a pretty cabinet of natural history, which one reaches through the shop (where Madame Bomare sells dried figs and raisins), is profound in mineralogy, but a little superficial in all the rest.'

To his mother de Saussure sent a lively social sketch:

'A pretty new opera has been brought out called *Les Moissonneurs*, in which there is a song that runs: "Argent, argent, maître du monde, tu règnes sur tous les états." It is here [in Paris] above all that one realises the truth of the song, and on this account the place is not very agreeable for folk like us who are crushed between the high nobility and the financiers. Rich young men like the Lullins [the Genevese bankers, relations of Madame de Saussure] or birds of passage like ourselves can face the situation, but people of moderate fortune (and I call moderate anything under 60,000 livres de rente), who came to settle here would suffer constant inconveniences, unless they were wise enough to live on exactly the same scale as those of similar fortune; but we Genevese who at home belong to the best set are apt to think ourselves made to hold our own with the best elsewhere, and have often occasion to regret it. The son of your neighbour, who could never have anticipated this, is beginning to realise it. He spent yesterday, as I do often, part of the afternoon at Mme. la Duchesse d'Enville's, who receives at that hour all that is most distinguished in the kingdom. He confessed to me that he felt so small that he grew almost ashamed of the room he took on his chair. These people combine with the greatest politeness a tone and manners which naturally, at first meeting, create an impression. As for me, I am pretty well seasoned. But enough moralising: still this is a place for moralising, and it is one of the principal gains of this kind of journey. One sees so many strange sights, so many originals of every sort, so many follies of every variety, that one is perforce drawn to reflection. Where do you think these reflections carry me? To you, my good mother, to the good education you gave me. I find continual occasion to apply the excellent lessons you gave me on the world and men, and then I regret that you are not planted invisibly on one of these gilded sofas to see what occupies me and to talk it over with me.'

[1] *A Dictionary of Natural History.* Valmont de Bomare was a considerable traveller, who visited most parts of Europe, Lapland, and Iceland in the employ of his Government, and made large collections.

Of his wife, de Saussure writes :

'My dear companion goes with me almost everywhere ; often she seizes things that escape me. Everyone is charmed to see a young wife accompany her husband on his travels, and share his occupations and his studies. She bears without any difficulty the fatigue and the little discomforts inseparable from travel ; always gay, always ready, she was destined to make my happiness.'

He recounts her social successes, her manners, free equally from timidity or affectation, her tact in talking always at the right moment and to the point. 'I wish,' he adds, 'some of our mincing coquettes could come here ; they would realise that their style is lower middle-class, and even the worse sort of that.'

Of the impression made by the three young Genevese ladies in the Paris *salons* we find an independent record in a letter written to de Saussure early in 1769 by the eloquent lawyer Loiseau de Mauléon, a friend of Voltaire, and remembered as the defender of the Calas.[1] The writer thanks de Saussure for sympathy on his mother's death, and then goes on to refer to the 'quatre amies de l'Hôtel de la Paix.' Translation would here take away the charm of the original French.

'Mes seules distractions sont de me rappeler cet extrême don de plaire que possède si parfaitement Madame Turrettin,[2] dont la beauté, l'esprit, la parole et la grâce sont tellement d'accord et font un tout si exquis que de ma vie je n'y ay vu femme plus aimable. Je n'oublieray jamais non plus ce caractère si noble, si distingué, si rare de Madame Tronchin.[3] Je le trouvois sur sa physionomie, sur son maintien, sur son silence même ; je l'admirois avec un respect tendre. Elle m'a laissé des traces qui ne s'anéantiront qu'avec moy. Sa destinée me sera toujours chère. Et si quelque chose pouvoit jamais adoucir l'amertume des maux que j'endure, dites luy, je vous prie, mon cher ami, que ce seroit le bonheur dont on m'assure que son nouvel établissement la fait jouir. Dites aussi, si vous le voulez bien, à votre respectable femme combien je suis touché de l'amitié qu'elle m'a montrée à son retour de Londres. J'ay souvent dit à Mademoiselle Tronchin [4] que je me reprochois de ne luy avoir pas assez fait voir les sentimens

---

[1] The *Nouvelle Biographie Universelle* states that de Mauléon died at the age of forty-three from depression caused by an unrequited love affair.

[2] The Genevese of this generation omitted the final 'i' in Italian names.

[3] Mlle. Boissier, 'Minette,' shortly after her return from Paris, married a son of the Procureur-Général, J. R. Tronchin.

[4] A daughter of Dr. Tronchin.

dont son mérite vray m'avoit pénétré. Ses lumières, ses vertus et son amour vous font le plus heureux des hommes. Gardez longtemps un si cher trésor.'

In addition to his family letters, de Saussure's intimate journal, written during his stay in Paris and Holland, has fortunately been preserved, and it shows that during the whole period he was assiduous in pursuing his scientific studies, visiting the savants of the day, and studying botany and horticulture at Choisy le Roi and at the Jardin du Roi with Coste, the chemical side of geology with Baume, and attending lectures by Valmont de Bomare. With the geologist Desmarets he talked over the basalts of Auvergne, the character of which was at that moment the subject of an acute controversy between Werner and the French geologists. If he was eager in the pursuit of knowledge the patrician Professor found plenty of time for pleasure, and the five young people went out a great deal. De Saussure's journal gives evidence both of his taste for society and his keen interest in character in both sexes, while the affectionate letters, still preserved, that he received in later years from several of his friends among the French aristocracy, both men and women, show that the young Genevese philosopher was at least as interesting as he was interested.

In Mlle. Tronchin, the daughter of the celebrated Dr. Tronchin, who had a fine apartment in the Petit Jardin of the Palais Royal, the party found a friend who knew the town and no doubt furnished them with many introductions. They frequented the *salon* of the Duchesse d'Enville and dined with the delightful young Duc de la Rochefoucauld, destined to be one of the victims of the Revolution, who had visited Geneva and Chamonix as early as 1762. They made the acquaintance of the Duc d'Harcourt, 'le meilleur homme du monde et de la vieille roche.' His brother the Marquis and his wife de Saussure describes as 'couple charmant, bonnes gens, simples et honnêtes.'

De Saussure reports at length the conversation at the d'Envilles' of the Abbé Galiani, 'an original who talked sensibly and cleverly on politics.'[1] He discussed liberty and tyranny.

[1] See Lord Morley's *Diderot*, vol. ii. p. 272: 'Galiani, the antiquary, the scholar, the politician, the incomparable mimic, the shrewdest, wittiest, and gayest of men after Voltaire.' He was the author of a work with the unpromising

He denied the existence of real liberty anywhere—either law or princes always restricted it, and according as the restrictions prevented people doing the things they wanted to, they thought themselves free or slaves. The man who did not like to be shut up by a *lettre de cachet* felt himself badly off in France; the man who wanted to keep a mistress found no liberty in Geneva. In England, of all European States, there was least freedom—less even than in Turkey. Tyranny was the result of a conspiracy of the more intelligent against the common herd; a single genius could not maintain a tyranny.

Another pleasant evening in famous company is thus recorded:

'Supped with Madame d'Epinay, who put us much at our ease with Messieurs Crommelin [the Genevese Resident in Paris] and Grimm; delighted with Madame d'Epinay, who is amiable and natural. M. Grimm has wit and experience; he attacks the Government of his country on privileges, exemptions, taxes, etc.'

Grimm would not take de Saussure to Baron Holbach's because 'attacks on religion formed there the only topic of conversation.' The Abbé Morellet, in his *Mémoires*, confirms this charge: 'On y disait des choses à faire cent fois tomber le tonnerre sur la maison, s'il tombait pour cela.'

Madame Necker, now at the height of her prosperity as the wife of the great banker and future Minister, at first affronted her compatriot by receiving him somewhat coldly, and he heartily vowed not to repeat the visit. 'Her head,' he writes, 'is turned; she frequents the great and the *beaux esprits*, she gives herself ridiculous airs, all the world laughs at her, and most of all Mlle. Clairon, to whom, nevertheless, she makes advances because she is in the height of the fashion.' It would seem as if Madame Necker was slow to open the doors of her *salon* to the three visitors from her own lake, while the young Genevese patrician probably resented any appearance of airs in the daughter of a Swiss minister, the Mlle. Curchod whom Gibbon had courted and then fled from. But a month later the coldness

title of *Dialogues on the Trade in Grain*. Voltaire vowed that 'Plato and Molière must have combined to produce a book that was as amusing as the best of romances and as instructive as the best of serious works.' Galiani was at one time a frequent correspondent of Madame Necker. (See also *Le Salon de Madame Necker* par le Comte d'Haussonville, Paris, 1888.)

had been removed. 'We see occasionally Madame Necker, who has at last invited our ladies. She has made great friends with me, and invites me constantly to dinner or supper, which I enjoy greatly, as she collects all the *beaux esprits*, the Encyclopædists, and the poets. The majority of these people would be no good as friends, but they are interesting to see and know.' In after years Madame Necker became closely connected with de Saussure by her nephew's marriage to his daughter, and both she and her husband proved themselves very good friends to him in the adversity of his later years.

The young party were frequent visitors to the Théâtre Français and the Comédie Italienne. De Saussure had a great liking for the theatre, possibly due in part to the scanty opportunities of enjoying it at Geneva! He surprises us in the *Voyages* by a suggestion in which, anticipating Byron's *Manfred*, he urges dramatic authors to find new scenes and subjects in the Alps. He even goes so far as to sketch a plot for a drama or opera. A 'crystallier' (the name given at Chamonix to those who made a living by seeking crystals among the glaciers) should risk his life in an attempt to reach a mass of crystal on the face of a precipice. He should be followed and rescued by the village maiden of his choice. De Saussure adds: 'The representation of these strange solitudes would enrich our theatrical scenery with an entire novelty; in a similar way, these savage landscapes, the rocks that fall, the avalanches of snow and ice, the storms and majestic echoes of the high mountains, might inspire in a great musician new and sublime ideas.' During their travels the young couple seldom missed a theatrical performance, even in a provincial town.

In Paris de Saussure renewed an agreeable acquaintance with the great tragic actress, Mlle. Clairon—the Sarah Bernhardt of her day—whom he had doubtless met previously at Ferney when she was a guest of Voltaire. His wife records going to see her play in a private house with two tickets she had given her husband—'a mark of the high favour in which he is with her'—and her enjoyment of the acting, although she was wedged in among a crowd of princesses and duchesses. De Saussure's frequent calls were rewarded by an inspection of the actress's 'cabinet' and choice library. 'A cabinet'—a collection of natural objects—shells, birds, fossils, seaweeds—it did not matter what—was at

THE GRAND TOUR (1768-69)

that date and for half a century later a fashionable ornament to the house of a gentleman or a lady of taste both in France and England. De Saussure had the further privilege of being admitted to the select party that met at supper on Wednesdays at Mlle. Clairon's house, where Marmontel led the conversation —not at all to de Saussure's satisfaction. He writes in his journal, 9th March :

'Marmontel talked a great deal; most of his stories were witty and in good taste, some, however, rather common, and all told too slowly. I recognised in him what I had been warned to expect in Parisian *beaux esprits*—a very arbitrary tone, a habit of speaking of his set as the only one to be called philosophic, and of despising and making odious insinuations against those who did not belong to it, attacking their manners and their integrity, and throwing doubt on their aims. It was thus he spoke of M. Mirabeau, the Abbé Troublet, M. le Batteux, M. Grimm, the Bishop of Mirepoix, and many others whose names I forget. He was, however, backed and applauded by all the company.'[1]

On 25th March the party went to St. Denis to view a Court function and procession on the anniversary of the death of the Dauphine. There they saw the Dauphin, the future Louis XVI., ' grand, pâle et maigre, mais avec une physionomie bonne et douce, un peu celle d'un Anglais,' and the whole Court defiling in full dress. De Saussure's ladies had to sit up all night with their coiffures arranged in order to be in time for the ceremony.

The party stayed in Paris for four months, from February to 10th June, when they parted, the Turrettinis taking back Mlle. Boissier to Geneva, while de Saussure and his wife started for Holland. They passed through Compiègne and Noyon, which interested them as the birthplace of Calvin, to St. Gobain, where they stayed three days in order to inspect the glass and chemical works of their friend M. Crommelin. From St. Gobain they drove by Ghent and Brussels. From Rotterdam they travelled in a canal boat to Leyden and by carriage to Amsterdam. There they were hospitably entertained by a wealthy Genevese of the name of Horngacher.

In a letter written to the ' charmante Minette,' his younger

---

[1] J. F. Marmontel (1723-1799), a prolific writer of plays and stories. His *Contes Moraux* had considerable success.

sister-in-law, shortly after his arrival in the Dutch capital, de Saussure summarises his first impressions of Holland and gives a pleasant picture of the relations of the gay young party, of which he, the eldest, was twenty-eight, that had just broken up:

'Here we are, my dear Minette, since Thursday evening, the 23rd of this month, in the great and famous city of Amsterdam. Your sister seems to accommodate herself to it very well, and, if it were not for the regret we both feel at being separated from you three, I believe we should manage to amuse ourselves. It is quite another thing to Paris; at Paris the beauty and the splendour is inside the houses, here it is outside. The city of Amsterdam and all Holland are beautiful beyond all anticipation and the most exaggerated ideas one could form of them; but it is all a spectacle for the eyes. Enter the houses, and your eyes will still be satisfied by the pictures, the carpets, and the porcelain, but you will find no gaiety, no amusements, no *Comédie Française*, hardly any conversation except about business. One must pass through Amsterdam and stay in Paris.

'Good-bye, my dear and good sister, love me as I love you—I cannot ask you for more. Give a thousand messages from me to Madame Turrettini. Despite our little skirmishes, I love her with all my heart; she has a witchery which makes all the world feel an irresistible tenderness for her; this malady seized me on our first acquaintance, and I do not expect ever to get over it. My greetings to our good brother Turrettini. I long eagerly for us all to meet again, but I fear that we shall never be so closely united as we were at Paris. Amuse yourself as well as you can, and above all think often of the best friend you have in the world.'

Minette followed faithfully one of her brother-in-law's injunctions. When the de Saussures returned to Geneva six months later, they found her married. Her wedded life was brief, and ended tragically in the suicide of her husband and the early deaths of both her children. But to the end of his life her affectionate relations with her brother-in-law remained unbroken. His letters home on his travels constantly contain messages to her and regrets that she is not at hand to discuss politics with him in his solitary inn. Madame de Saussure's interests, one gathers, were of a more domestic order.

Few of Madame Tronchin's letters have been preserved. But I have two before me written eighteen years later when she was spending the summer in the fashionable company of Spa. She protests that she is resisting the craze for gambling. ' I have to choose between the world and a regular life ; my wisdom prefers the last, the hours of play are too late, it lasts till five in the morning. It is not your sister-in-law who keeps it up.' She concludes, 'All I love most is at Genthod ; it is there that my eyes, my heart, and my tastes turn : you have a very large part, my best of friends.'

Minette, we recognise, despite the sadness of her married life, must have been the gayest, the most spirited of the three sisters, and a fast companion and ally to the brother-in-law, whose social and political interests she shared and entered into.

On the 11th July the de Saussures left Amsterdam for the Hague, where they remained a fortnight, returning to Amsterdam to visit Haarlem and North Holland before again travelling south to Rotterdam on the way to embark for England.

It is obvious from the diary that they saw Holland very thoroughly. Natural history cabinets and horticulture were the chief objects of de Saussure's study. But he also visited the museums and numerous private collections of pictures.

According to the sententious Senebier, he succeeded in gaining the esteem of the local savants, ' despite his vivacity, which contrasted so strongly with Dutch phlegm.' His own impressions of the country and its people are contained in a letter he wrote to Haller before embarking at Ostend. He finds ' the flat and learned Holland a country of fine gardens and heavy professors '; it is ' full of singular people who pursue in private and without any pretence either the fine arts, or rational philosophy, or natural history, and enjoy in silence and solitude the fruits of their studies and their labours.'

He proceeds to illustrate this general criticism by particular instances. First we have a sketch of the Biermanns, father and son, who kept a shop on the Keysersgracht at Amsterdam, where they sold seaweeds and fossils and published magnificently illustrated botanical works. They were ' living specimens of the old Dutch type, the father in a big wig, black as jet, talking nothing but Latin and surrounded by his huge folios, rough but with a friendly air, and really learned in the Batavian fashion ; the son bald and of mean appearance, clumsily modernised.' Then we hear of the Van der Meulens, ' the husband not even speaking Latin and no savant, but possessing a superb cabinet of natural history—seaweeds, minerals, butterflies, agates, monsters, human and animal, preserved in spirits of wine—a collection of extraordinary interest in the hands of an honest man, probably of little knowledge. One is tempted to think it luxury or ostentation, but the man is of such common appearance that you would not salute him if you met him in the street, and though he is very wealthy all about him is of the utmost simplicity. No, it is a singular taste for beautiful and rare objects, which he spends his life in arranging, admiring, and cataloguing. His wife also is quite common; the house is thoroughly Dutch. One is offered food and drink alternately every half-hour!'

Another individual sketch is M. Brawers, the owner of a large collection, including Chinese lacquer, porcelain, and a roomful of Italian pictures:

'A fine house, very ornate, but all in the Dutch taste; that is, dull, heavy, graceless, but, on the other hand, finished, solid, and very clean. The master of the house sits in his dressing-gown on the ground floor smoking his pipe, with a silver bowl holding a piece of smouldering peat, and receiving with an uncouth air the compliments on his cabinet of visitors as they arrive or leave. He has no taste, and puts by the side of the greatest masterpieces pictures of a protégé of his which are simply detestable.

'At supper-parties all the dishes are put on the table at once, and the guests sit at it till they leave. The breakfasts are charming, social, and easy, and last all the morning round a beautiful mahogany table, with rye bread, butter, cakes, venison, and the eternal tea.'

The Dutch gardens met with the travellers' unqualified approbation. At one house (M. Boreel's) near Amsterdam they admired superb pleached alleys, fish-ponds set in lawns and shaded by weeping willows, and, above all, the *bosquet anglais*, with winding paths and a variety of rare trees planted without any attempt at symmetry.

Among his Dutch hosts de Saussure does not seem to have made many lasting friends. But the pleasure of his visit was greatly increased by the hospitality he received from Genevese settled in the country. There were at that time not a few. The two Protestant States had many links; Geneva and Holland in the eighteenth century both held a high place in European finance, while the limited opportunities of the former sent its more adventurous sons to seek commercial success in larger fields, either in Holland or England.

De Saussure's health, at no time robust, suffered from the relaxing climate of the Low Countries in midsummer, and in the middle of August the travellers turned their thoughts towards England. With our country Geneva had even more ties than with Holland, and the moment was opportune. Great Britain had emerged successful from the vicissitudes of the Seven Years War (1755-62). The island-state was on the point of developing into a world commonwealth, she ruled already in India and Canada, and had not yet lost her American colonies. Europe looked up to her as the chief among its nations. The domestic troubles, the riots connected with Wilkes's prosecution, interested—they are often alluded to in letters from de Saussure's friends—but were not of a sort to affect foreign visitors. The de Saussures had, moreover, strong personal inducements to undertake the journey. They had relations established as bankers in London, old family friends, such as Dr. Turton, and close acquaintances, members of the English aristocracy, who had been guests at Frontenex or in the townhouse, on whose welcome they could count. Foremost among them was Lord Palmerston, the father of the statesman, a D.C.L. of Oxford, a traveller, a man of taste and fashion, a member of 'The Club,' an intimate friend of Reynolds, Garrick, and Gibbon. He visited Switzerland in 1763 and again in 1767. On the latter occasion he took with him William Pars, the artist of the Dilettanti Society, who made a drawing of the Mer de Glace, engraved with four other Alpine views by Woollett. There is nothing to show that de Saussure went to Chamonix with Lord Palmerston in 1767, but in subsequent years he made at least one Alpine tour in his company.

The ordinary route from Holland at that date was by Helvoetsluys and Harwich, but de Saussure was dissuaded from attempting it by his countryman Jalabert's [1] report of the terrors of the nineteen hours' passage. They found their friend at Rotterdam 'bien triste, bien lugubre, ne disant plus de bien de l'Angleterre, nous représentant tout comme hérissé de difficultés.' It is hard, perhaps, for islanders to realise the serious view taken by continental Europeans even to-day of the perils of the short Channel

[1] The friend who accompanied him to Chamonix in 1767.

passage. The sea anywhere is formidable to eyes and stomachs new to it. When Bernese guides are taken to the Caucasus it is not the risks of a strange mountain chain and wild people, but those of the Black Sea—a name of terror—that count most in their minds and alarm their families. De Saussure, writing to Bonnet, begs him not to tell his wife's grandmother, Madame Lullin, of their adventure till he can give the news that they are safe in England. In the end, to shorten the sea voyage, he hired a luxurious boat and sailed through the estuaries and among the islands to Flushing, and thence, after crossing the Scheldt, drove to Ostend.

The Straits of Dover proved quite as great an ordeal as had been anticipated, and de Saussure's journal gives a tragic description of physical sufferings so unfamiliar to the victim as to call from him for particular description. De Saussure is at pains to record that it was the downward roll that made him suffer most, and that he found temporary relief by accommodating his breathing to the movements of the vessel, drawing in his breath as it plunged. 'A lesson,' he remarks, 'for next time.'

In the circumstances it was surely brave of him to go on deck at 4 A.M. and view the scene.

'The vessel was now in mid-Channel. No land was in sight. The wind was always very strong. Heavens! how small did the packet that in the port had seemed so large, look now in the middle of this immense space. The sailors were lying down and perfectly still, for the steadiness of the breeze relieved them of their task. A profound silence prevailed everywhere; there were no sounds except the wind in the sails and the noise of the waves beating on the sides of the ship, or against one another. The whole surroundings gave to the vessel an air of abandonment which was vaguely sad and terrible. I admired the perfect evenness of the horizon, which one sees nowhere else so well, and——'

but we need follow no further. The poor passengers were kept three hours off Dover waiting to enter the harbour. On landing, de Saussure put on his best waistcoat and a red coat and went with his wife to the King's Head, a 'mediocre inn.' On the same afternoon they drove to Canterbury, arriving after dark, and leaving next morning at 5.30 A.M., much too shattered, apparently,

THE GRAND TOUR (1768-69)

even to look at the cathedral. I quote the account in the diary of the drive to London :

'The whole drive is very pretty; the roads, except in the towns, and above all in the tiresome Rochester, are not bad. One passes cultivated valleys, charming hills often wooded, beautiful, deliciously green meadows, pleasant country houses scattered here and there. A well-clothed, well-looking peasantry, and women with large hats, gave us a good impression of England. Still, the gloomy forebodings of our Joseph [their servant] on English coinage added to all the warnings we had been given in Holland; the effects of the movement of the vessel, which we still felt, and our general uncertainty as to our adventure, capped by the boredom of having our two servants in the carriage with us, took away a great deal from the pleasure of the journey.'

The first view of London surprised them by the crowd of steeples, in the centre of which rose the dome of St. Paul's, and the number of vessels, which seemed to form part of the city and added to its apparent size. They drove up Pall Mall, and, after being warmly received by their old friend Dr. Turton, sought rooms at ' The Gentleman's Hotel,' which, far from deserving its name, proved full of noxious insects.

For the next day or two I transcribe the entries in de Saussure's journal :

'*Friday, 15th August.*

' Rose early. Hairdresser who had been at Geneva. Breakfasted with Turton. Went with him to look for lodgings, to buy maps of London and England, to see Mr. Boissier [his cousin] at the Royal Exchange ; met Mr. Beauclerk, returned, took my wife to see lodgings, engaged those nearest Turton, very convenient, the landlady acting as cook, all for three guineas a week, dined there at once with Turton and young Fisher, very pleasant; after dinner went to the Opera to hear *La Buona Figliola*, actors heavy, but fine voices and excellent orchestra. Dances vigorous but wanting in grace. Saw for the first time Miss Harriet Blosset, with Mr. Banks,[1] her betrothed. Returned on foot from the opera with them and supped together. The eldest daughter, tall, decided, agreeable, a great musician, splendid voice, fond of society, polished. The second Miss Harriet, desperately in love with Mr. Banks, from whom she was to part next day—hitherto

---

[1] Sir Joseph Banks, afterwards president for many years of the Royal Society. His engagement to Miss Blosset is not referred to by his biographers.

a prudent coquette, but now only intent on pleasing her lover, and resolved to spend in the country all the time he is away. The youngest, a Methodist *dévote*, delighted to pass two or three years in the country with her sister and live out of the world. The mother, a good-natured little woman, talking politics. As Banks cannot speak a word of French, I could not judge of his abilities. [De Saussure apparently at this time could understand, but had great difficulty in speaking, English.] He seems to have a prodigious zest for natural history. I supped there with him and Dr. Solander, who is also starting with him for Isle St. George. They will work on natural history. They have an astronomer for the passage of Venus, a draughtsman, all the instruments, books, and appliances possible; after observing the passage they will endeavour to make discoveries in the Southern Ocean and return by the East Indies. Miss Blosset, not knowing that he was to start next day, was quite gay. Banks drank freely to hide his feelings. He promised to come and see me at Geneva and bring me some curios. We were charmed to have made acquaintance with this family, and I particularly to have seen before his departure a remarkable man.'

'16*th August*.

'Went with Turton to look for M. l'Espinasse in Greek Street. We did not find him, but found at the Museum Dr. Matey, friendly, playing the agreeable, a stout little man: he greeted me cordially and promised me the run of the Museum . . . dined with Turton and Pictet on a fine piece of venison sent by Mrs. Blosset, went afterwards with Miss Blosset to Ranelagh. I was much astonished at this fine circular hall, admirably lit, with a great column in the centre, boxes all round, good music with the best singers from the opera, a large company promenading, listening to the music, or sitting down and taking tea, some in the boxes and others at the tables round the column, numbers of pretty girls.'

'17*th August*.

'Rose early, studied English, visit from Lord Palmerston, who suggests we should go to York to see the races and return by Derbyshire. Called on the Misses Blosset, arranged for the theatre and ball, dined with Turton and the Misses Blosset and left my wife to dine alone and dress her hair at our lodgings. Went with Turton to the theatre to see *The Suspicious Husband*, in which, in honour of the King of Denmark, Garrick played Ranger, a part too young for him, but which he played as faithfully and agreeably as possible. The other actors also were very good. I enjoyed myself greatly. The short piece was a translation of *The Oracle* well played. The best actors from all the theatres had been collected in the King's honour. Garrick danced a quadrille with all the actors at the end of the principal piece. The pit encored him with noisy obstinacy. Fine theatre. Thence to supper with Mrs. Blosset and to the ball at the Redout with the eldest Miss Blosset. Ladies pay half a guinea, men a guinea. Fine room, fine company. Girls escorted by their " abbesses "; youths accost them in passing, everything well conducted, with a singular air of propriety. Talked to Lord Palmerston, who explained to me the customs and the company and gave me an excellent itinerary, with three letters of introduction of the most obliging character, one for Sir George Savile, M.P. for the county of York, one for Lord John Cavendish, M.P. for the town, and one for Lord Rockingham, the Lord-Lieutenant of the county. Returned to bed at 2 A.M. nervous lest my wife might be lost in her sedan chair.'

' 18*th August*.

'[The morning was spent in buying a carriage from M. l'Espinasse for twenty guineas and in inspecting various kinds of mathematical instruments.]

'Drove with Turton into the country with Lady Diana Bolingbroke,[1] wife of Mr. Beauclerk. . . . The estate Mr. Beauclerk inhabits is very pretty, there is a fine collection of exotic trees with a pleasant path winding among them, diversified with points of view, little ponds, shady and sunny spots. Dined with My Lady, who knows and understands French, but does not like speaking it. After dinner looked at some instruments with Mr. Beauclerk. He studies mathematics with his wife, and is a man of great attainments. He took me to drive in a cabriolet in Richmond Park close to his house, pretty landscapes : returned to tea and drove back at night to London, talking of highwaymen, but seeing none.'

' 19*th*.

'Went with my wife and Turton to breakfast with the Misses Blosset, met Mr. and Mrs. Earle, with whom we made a very pleasant acquaintance, he tall, a fine gentleman, she pale, thin, plain, affected by the death of a brother whom she had come to see, and found dead in London.[2]

---

[1] Topham Beauclerk was a man of taste and the owner of a great library. He is best remembered as the friend of Dr. Johnson. Lady Diana, a daughter of the Duke of Marlborough, had been divorced by her first husband, the second Lord Bolingbroke. She was an artist of some ability and much esteemed by Horace Walpole.

[2] Mrs. Earle was a Miss Bouchier and the heiress of Benningborough Hall, Yorkshire, where the de Saussure's subsequently stayed. She lived to be eighty.

'Mr. Earle gave me a good route to York and promised to meet us and entertain us at his home. Went with the ladies to hear the Musical Glasses of M. l'Espinasse; dined with Turton. Afterwards took Miss Harriet Blosset in my carriage to see the garden and the rosaries of Lyse, a gardener patronised by Mr. Banks, on the road to Richmond, walked about with her, collected many plants. The man seems a very good fellow, well-informed; his trees are very reasonably priced; he promised me a catalogue; the quantity he has is immense, most of them unknown in France. Thence, still with Miss Blosset, to see the insects of Mr. Banks, a superb collection beautifully arranged, insects pinned with the name underneath each, English and foreign, in drawers covered with glass and framed in cedarwood. Took tea with Mrs. Blosset, Miss Harriet, and her younger sister, the eldest had gone with my wife to the opera. I had a serious conversation with Miss Harriet. Her deep melancholy, her persuasion she should die, her firm resolve to live in the country to show her true love, make her very interesting.'

Here we take leave of Miss Harriet as far as de Saussure is concerned. He may have renewed his interesting acquaintance on his return to London in the autumn, but of that period no diary remains. In the official biographies of Banks the young lady plays no part. But in a privately printed memoir of the time, Lady Mary Coke's Journal, I find a footnote which throws a sad light on the end of her love story:

'*August* 11, 1771.—Mr. Morrice was exceedingly droll, according to custom, and said he hoped Mr. Banks, who, since his return, had desired Miss Blosset will excuse him marrying her, will pay for the materials of all the worked waistcoats she made for him during the time he was sailing round the world.'

On the 21st the most noteworthy event was a visit with Dr. Turton to a brother of the celebrated Wilkes, some three or four miles from London, where they found a 'famous painter' (the name is left blank—probably Sir Joshua Reynolds) and 'an author named Goldsmith,' ' un homme fort original, fort singulier, naturel, gai, vraiment comique dans ses idées et dans ses expressions.' Thence they all went to a house, 'a very fine bit of

eight, and, having lost both her sons, left her property to the boys' great friend at Eton, Mr. Henry Dawney, the grandfather of the present Lord Downe. Benningborough was sold in 1917 by the then owner, Colonel Dawney. Pictured in *Country Life*, it was advertised as having 'matured gardens.'

architecture, and full of the most beautiful pictures and marbles.' It was only to be visited with a permit from the owner, and it was a great favour of the painter to get them one. De Saussure mentions a portrait of Pope—which has enabled me (by the friendly aid of Mr. Austin Dobson) to identify the house as in all probability Caen Wood House, between Hampstead and Highgate, then the property of Lord Mansfield. The diary continues:

'22nd.

'To Tissot's shop, where I saw Graphometres he called theodolites, and other instruments, all very dear, but very good and well finished.

'Started in the afternoon for York. Four horses in the carriage, and our two servants on horseback, my wife but middlingly pleased to go, and I surprised, almost astounded, at this unforeseen and hastily undertaken journey.'

The journey proved less formidable than it had seemed in prospect. The first night was spent at Stevenage. At Stamford the host of the inn, forewarned by Mr. Earle, was waiting to take the travellers to Burghley, where they were received by domestics carrying silver staves, and, despite de Saussure's bad English, the housekeeper made herself very agreeable. They admired chiefly the pictures and the kitchen.[1] Next day, starting from Grantham, they reached York, having made the journey from London at the rate of seven and a half miles an hour. De Saussure is warm in praise of the roads :

'It is delightful to roll rapidly on such roads, seldom straight, through beautiful country, rich and well cultivated. The peasantry are better dressed than in France or Switzerland, but less well off; their cottages picturesque but wretched and white-washed.'

At York, after a first night in a crowded inn, they found lodgings, and were speedily introduced to the fine society collected for the races: Sir George Savile, Lord Rockingham, recently Prime Minister, and his wife, Lord Scarborough, Lord John Cavendish, and a host of others. The races, the horses and jockeys, the

[1] Gilpin, who visited Burghley in 1776, writes: 'We must not leave this grand house without looking into the kitchen, which is a noble room and decorated with the ensign memorial of hospitality, an immense carcase of beef, well painted.'
—*Observations relative chiefly to Picturesque Beauty made in the year 1776 in several parts of Great Britain, particularly the Highlands of Scotland.*

crowd, all had the charm of novelty for the Genevese travellers. At supper they feasted on the 'singuliers oiseaux qui viennent de la province de Lincoln et qui sont si peu sociables, mais excellents.' Apparently bitterns, which in those days were held a choice dish.

The York festival lasted a week. About noon the company went to the races. One day the de Saussures drove there in the carriage of Lady Rockingham, drawn by six horses and escorted by seven grooms in livery on horseback. Thence to the Assembly, for which they put on full dress on alternate days. De Saussure writes, 'Ce jour-ci les dames n'étaient pas habillées, elles le sont ou ne le sont pas, alternativement.' There were concerts and plays. One night a brilliant ball took place in 'the superb hall.' There was no lack of attention shown to the young Genevese couple. De Saussure had interesting conversations with the Whig statesman, Sir George Savile, on the government of England, and with the 'old and good' Archbishop, 'si honnête, si poli.' On the last evening the company broke up with many regrets and promises to meet again, and the de Saussures received numerous invitations to various parts of the kingdom. They went off at once to pay their first visit to an English country-house, that of their new acquaintance, Mr. Earle, ten miles north of York. They were fortunate in lighting on a very good specimen of the Queen Anne period. Benningborough Hall is a fine brick mansion, with a 'noble vestibule' and a dancing-room, which had remained untouched until the estate recently came into the market, a large garden going down to the river, a wooded park, and all the appurtenances of an English gentleman's place. 'Belle verdure de l'Angleterre, à laquelle aucun pays du monde n'est comparable,' is a note in de Saussure's journal. Their hosts were agreeable. 'At tea we talked of the human race and of all our acquaintances. Mr. Earle seemed to me a good judge of men, fine perceptions and shrewd and strong ideas; in general he is something of a pessimist, but he argues his case ably. His only fault seems to be a slight tendency to boast of himself and his country.' After a stay of two nights, Mr. Earle took his guests to view the sights of Yorkshire. They began with Castle Howard, where the magnificent gardens and hot-houses made a deep impression on the visitors. They admired also the house with its gallery of Italian paintings and drawings by Holbein of the Court of François Premier, which were shown by a 'concierge of a fine figure, very intelligent, and speaking Latin.'

The next object was Duncombe Park, built by Vanbrugh, the seat of the Earl of Feversham, where they were invited to lunch and stay to dinner, though they saw nothing of the owner, who with his ladies spied them from a balcony overlooking the vestibule. Here they admired a Titian 'Venus and Adonis,' 'almost too beautiful.' Through rain, which prevented their seeing much of the park, they drove on to Helmsley, where de Saussure notes, 'My farthest north, 54° 16".' Here they parted with their kind guide, with promises to meet again at Geneva. Between Helmsley and Thirsk they crossed the moors, the barrenness of which was noted. Their naked slopes reminded (we are surprised to hear) de Saussure of his own country: possibly he had in his mind the heights of the Jura. 'Sportsmen,' he relates, 'go and live on them in tents and pursue a kind of pheasant only to be found there.' Does he mean black game or grouse? Despite his early shooting parties round the Reposoir, ornithology does not seem to have been one of our philosopher's strong points.

The tourists next viewed Studley and Fountains Abbey. De Saussure, who shows far more enthusiasm for sylvan scenery, gardens, and classic summer-houses than for serious architecture, goes into ecstasies over the romantic ruins and the points of view. Here he encountered Mr. Pennant,[1] with a young companion from Harrogate; 'full of a poetical verve which these beauties inflamed, he escaped from time to time in order to write down the verses which came into his head, and groaned at being obliged to crush his genius by legal studies.'

They drove next to Hackfall and Mowbray Point. The impression it made on our travellers' eyes is remarkable:

'One discovers of a sudden and without any warning the most charming point of view that can be imagined—a little river winding through a deep glen, clothed in beautiful woods, broken only by bold crags which make a very fine contrast. The stream, which shows and

---

[1] This must have been the well-known author, naturalist, and traveller, whose *Tour in Scotland* Dr. Johnson warmly defended. This particular view is rapturously described by Pennant in a passage in his posthumous work, *A Tour from Alston Moor to Harrowgate* (sic) *and Brimham Crags*, 1904, cited in Murray's *Handbook to Yorkshire*. Who was the young poet?

previously, next received the travellers at Wentworth House, where they found agreeable feminine company. The size of the mansion impressed de Saussure. He repeats a *mot* of Sir George Savile, who, when Lady Rockingham hoped that the de Saussures would visit them if they lay on their road, had cried, ' Oh, the house is so large that if one end of it is not on your road, the other must be.' Before supper at 9.30 there were evening prayers in the chapel attached to the house, 'chose très édifiante,' de Saussure remarks. They saw Wentworth Castle before returning to Sheffield, where the walls of their inn were hung with specimens of Scarborough seaweed in place of pictures. The process of manufacture of Sheffield plate was inspected, and then they started for another great place, Chatsworth. Here they were received by Lord John Cavendish, and found Horace Walpole and his friend General Conway, ' both very unaffected and amiable.' They talked of Rousseau and his imaginary fears of being pursued in England and forbidden to leave the country, and how he had begged General Conway to give him leave to depart, offering in return to write nothing more about Hume. Horace Walpole, whom de Saussure speaks of as ' the author of the letter of the King of Prussia to Rousseau,' he thought somewhat Frenchified and affected. But General Conway proved a most pleasant companion. By his advice the de Saussures drove to Matlock, where they admired the scenery and visited a lead-mine. The marvels of Chatsworth surprised them; the house is described as ' a fairy palace in a beautiful wilderness.' Lord John Cavendish gave de Saussure further light on the humours of a parliamentary election; his own seat for York, he said, cost him £1000 a year, though his return was unopposed. Next day they drove on to the marble quarries at Bakewell and, over hills showing nothing but sheep and heather, to Castleton and the Peak Cavern, at that day one of the sights of England.

At Manchester, a market town of forty thousand inhabitants, but not yet a city, a cotton manufactory was visited and an excursion made on the Bridgewater Canal. De Saussure called on that strange collector, Sir Ashton Lever, who ruined himself in making a most heterogeneous museum, which subsequently, when shown at the Rotunda on the Surrey side, became one of the sights of London. He was then living at Allerington Hall, some six miles out of Manchester. 'A man of extraordinary vivacity, over forty, with the frame of individuals of great talents and strong passions, he has that manner and appearance; for the rest lively, pleasant, agreeable, serviceable, at least towards myself.'

At Buxton they found a good Bath-house and accommodation for visitors, and visited another cavern with stalactites, and a lead-mine belonging to the Duke of Devonshire near Eaton Hill, where de Saussure had to go down a great many awkward ladders and to crouch in low corridors. These subterranean excursions of her husband obviously bored Madame de Saussure, who was apt to be uneasy in his absence and impatient when his return was delayed.

Here, on the 15th September, the surviving portion of de Saussure's diary ends.[1] It is diffuse with respect to the many country seats, visits to which occupied a large part of the tour. The writer has an eye for detail in all things, and a very strong natural taste for sylvan landscapes and ornamental gardening. He admires the picturesque in English scenery, but prefers it as improved by man. The austere charm of the moors escapes him; like Cobbett, he looks with disfavour on sheep and heather. In mineral products, and in natural eccentricities such as caverns, he is much interested, looking at them not from the tourist point of view, but as possible sources of information for his History of the Earth.

The diary offers in one respect a singular illustration of how travel has been affected by the increase in travellers. In the eighteenth century a visitor to England could, on the strength of an introduction such as de Saussure's from Lord Palmerston, count on being admitted at once both to the literary circle of the capital and the great houses of the country. At each of the latter the travellers spent two or three days, and in her letters home Madame de Saussure dwells on the kindness with which they were everywhere received. She adds that most Englishmen spoke French, though the accomplishment was not so common among the women. Her husband 'loves England prodigiously.' She obviously repeats what we are told was his favourite phrase.

[1] The manuscript diary I have had access to ends abruptly, leaving blank pages in the volume. All efforts to find its continuation—if one exists—have so far failed.

There are few, if any, countries in Europe now where a stranger could at short notice hope for a similar welcome. In England de Saussure met with new minds and modes of life as well as fresh landscapes. *Mores hominum multorum novit.*

For the rest of his stay in our country we have to piece together but scanty material. His letters show that he was back in town from his Midland tour on the 21st September, after a visit to Birmingham. On 3rd September he had written from Leeds to the Rector of the Academy at Geneva, begging for an extension of his leave of absence. The reason he gave was that he had been disappointed on his arrival in his hope of mixing in the learned society of London. He continued:

'I expected to find in the capital at least a great number of its literary men, but, to my great disappointment, I found only very few; everyone except those whose business kept them in the City had gone into the country, and the fashionable quarter of London was as deserted as our Grand' Rue during the unhappy Emigration [in 1766]. I was advised to make use of the season to visit some of the English counties which, owing to the mines or other natural curiosities they contain, deserve the attention of Natural Students. The beauty of the weather, and curiosity to see the horse-races at York and the fine company and the splendid entertainments which they are an occasion for, made this plan acceptable to my dear companion.'

He went on to describe how he intended to fill up the time till the beginning of November by a trip to Cornwall and visits to the Universities. Then Parliament would have met, the Royal Society opened its session, and he would be able to encounter the men he most wanted to. He ended by suggesting that if the Rector thought his request for a prolongation of leave to February out of the question, he would say nothing about it, and promising to come back to his duties punctually at any date fixed.

It is amusing to find de Saussure taking steps to have any prolongation of his absence broken gently to his parents and his wife's grandmother, Madame Lullin, who appears to have been an important personage in the family. He proposed to let his relations know of his further stay only when the time drew near, and then by successive suggestions of 'another week!' Heads of a family at Geneva seem to have exercised a control over the younger generation very alien to English custom.

On the 10th October the de Saussures went to a masquerade given for the King of Denmark.

'All the most beautiful and richest ladies in England were there in fancy dress of singular taste and magnificence. Several ladies, and among them Lady Spencer, one of our acquaintances, wore more than a hundred thousand pounds sterling worth of diamonds! My wife was dressed as a Spaniard in pink and silver, which suited her admirably —I have never seen her look better; and all the sensible—or frugal—men were only in dominoes!'

One of de Saussure's correspondents, François Tronchin, pleasantly alludes to 'the King, who was at Madame de Saussure's feet.' It was possibly on this occasion, though he is recorded to have met and danced with her previously at the Hague.

Next day de Saussure, leaving his wife at Putney with her cousins the Boissiers, who had a banking house in London, started at midnight by coach to visit the mines in Cornwall. A letter written immediately after his return describes his experiences:

'The journey was very laborious and fatiguing, but made well worth while by the beauty and singularity of all I saw. The Cornish climate is, I believe, the softest, the pleasantest, and the healthiest in Europe; the land never experiences great heat or great cold; myrtles, pomegranates, laurels, grow in the open air, and hardly ever suffer from frost; provisions cost nothing; fish is so cheap that for two shillings ten people can be fed, and the air is so pure that epidemics are unknown. The only drawback is the absence of trees—at least of large trees; whether from the sea-winds or the character of the soil, they fail to flourish. The crops, however, are successful.'

Senebier in his Memoir asserts that de Saussure contracted in Cornwall a diphtheritic sore throat, the effects of which on his health were lasting. According to his biographer, he was attended by his friend, Dr. Turton, and after suffering a dangerous relapse from a visit to a flint-glass manufactory, was still an invalid when he started homewards at the New Year.[1]

This story is not borne out by any available evidence, and it is difficult to credit it in the face of de Saussure's testimony to

---

[1] Senebier wrote from recollections that were often inaccurate. For instance, he asserts that de Saussure met Banks and Solander on their return from their famous voyage, and was shown 'the curiosities of Otahiti.' In fact, de Saussure supped with Banks the night before his start. There is nothing in the letters written during the last weeks of the de Saussures' stay in England to confirm

the Cornish climate and other facts. We know, for instance, that immediately on his return to London at the end of October he planned and carried out a trip to Cambridge and Oxford, and we have also a letter he wrote two days before starting on it to the Rector of the Academy of Geneva making a second appeal for an extension of his leave of absence (which was granted), and describing his successful visit to the Cornish mines and to the Land's End.

To Cambridge de Saussure took letters of introduction to Dr. Rutherforth, the Regius Professor of Divinity, who was also a F.R.S. One wonders if he called on Gray, whose quiet had just been disturbed by the visit of the King of Denmark, and who was a few months later to be fascinated by de Saussure's and Bonnet's young neighbour and acquaintance, Bonstetten. Of his and his wife's visit to the sister University and Bath, the only record is a bill dated Oxford, 10th November, from one Joshua Platt for a collection of fossils. From its address we learn that the de Saussures were then staying with 'Mr. Hurst opposite Cumberland House, Pall Mall.'

The loss of the diary of de Saussure's last weeks in England is unfortunate, and it is tantalising to read in a letter dated from London, 21st October: 'I have made the complete tour of England, and if I were not afraid that this letter would be drowned with the rest, I would tell you a vast number of things which perhaps might interest you.' It would seem that some catastrophe in the Channel must have occurred to previous letters.

De Saussure was, Senebier tells us, taken sight-seeing in town by Dr. Matey, the Foreign Secretary of the Royal Society and Chief Librarian of the British Museum, whose 'taste, knowledge, and judgment' were commended by Gibbon. Dr. Johnson, however, wroth at some disrespectful comments on his Dictionary, threatened on one occasion to throw him into the Thames! At the house of Sir John Pringle, the President of the Royal Society, de Saussure met many of the men of the day. But there is no record in the books of the Royal Society's Club of his having been,

Senebier's statement as to his health; on the contrary, they show both the de Saussures in active enjoyment of society. De Candolle, in an obituary notice of de Saussure, written immediately after his death (published in the *Décade Philosophique*, vol. iv., June 1799), states explicitly that his illness was caused by his political exertions and anxieties. See also p. 129.

like his son, a guest at any of its dinners. Nor have we any record of his presence at a meeting of the Society. Of the character of its meetings at a somewhat later date, as they appeared to a Genevese savant, a graphic description is given by the botanist de Candolle :

'Meetings of the Royal Society take place in the evening, and are arranged in a way to deprive them of any interest. The papers are read by secretaries in the monotonous voice of people who take no interest in what they are reading ; no discussion on any of them is admitted, no material exhibits serve to awake attention. The Fellows are seated, like schoolboys, on benches facing the President. He wears a large, three-cornered hat on his head, which he lifts from time to time with a solemn air, when he has to announce the election of a new Fellow or to return thanks for the presentation of some work to the Society. . . . Nothing can be more monotonous or lifeless than these meetings, but I took a keen interest in them on account of the number of celebrities assembled, the brilliant series of works of which the Society can boast, and the position that it enjoys in the scientific world.'

In private de Saussure must have met many of the leaders of the London world, both in science and society, but at this period unfortunately his letters are few.

We know that he had congenial converse with Franklin on electrical problems, which he put to practical use on his return home. He frequently met Garrick, then at the height of his fame, and preparing for the Shakespeare festival of the following year. According to Senebier, he 'penetrated the profound philosophy of this unique actor and agreeable poet.' The Dowager Duchess of Portland presented him with a piece of marquetry made of 'all the woods known.' Lord Warwick and Lord Algernon Percy, afterwards Duke of Northumberland, Lord Lyttelton and Horace Walpole were members of the society the Genevese travellers met or were entertained by.

The last glimpse we get of the travellers in town is dining with Lord Warwick on 2nd January 1769. Two days later they left for Dover, and, after waiting for fine weather, crossed happily to Calais on the 7th. On landing de Saussure writes to his sister :

'I confess I am leaving England with regret ; we were so kindly received. I found so much that was of interest for my pursuits, and the life led there suited me so well, that had not a tenderly loved father and mother, a sister, dear children, and a country, which, after all, has its attractions, called me home very strongly, I do not know how I could have returned.'

The preference here expressed by de Saussure for England as a residence was shared by not a few of his countrymen. There were many family and business connections between the two Protestant States: to the serious side of the Genevese character London perhaps proved more congenial than Paris; the Genevese patrician felt at home among the English aristocracy, while the Genevese radical who had reasons for leaving his native city found welcome and congenial employment in many quarters, and might even, like Deluc, the climber of the Buet, aspire to become 'Reader to a Queen,' or with d'Ivernois, to gain the honour of knighthood.

François Tronchin, writing from Paris to de Saussure just before the latter left London, anticipated his friend's favourable opinion of English hospitality:

'The country in which you are is perhaps of all the countries in the world the most attractive. You have not yet told me, but I venture to guess your feeling about it. I should have had more doubts as to Madame de Saussure's, if her letters did not altogether ease my mind as to her life in England. The Paradise of women is not identical with that of every man, and a country where men have the impertinence not to be always at their feet cannot be that which they like best. If you are really enthusiastic about the English we will talk about them as much as you like. Otherwise I shall regret your not having been granted by Heaven a soul of the English stamp and we will avoid the subject.'

Madame de Saussure has answered for us François Tronchin's question. The de Saussures liked England 'prodigiously.'

CHAPTER V

ITALY

ON 1st February 1769 de Saussure returned to Geneva to find his younger sister-in-law, the charming Minette, just married. The bridegroom was a son of the able politician, the Procureur-Général Jean Robert Tronchin, whose memory has survived as the opponent who drew forth Rousseau's famous *Lettres écrites de la Montagne*. The family were on the point of giving a wedding ball in the great house in the Rue de la Cité, where they entertained three hundred guests and the dancing was kept up till eight in the morning. The fact is worth noting as proof that, whatever prejudices might remain against theatres, the austere rules of the city of Calvin had been considerably relaxed in respect of other forms of amusement.

De Saussure found plenty of work awaiting him on his return: his lectures had to be resumed, the store of instruments, books, and objects he had collected abroad to be unpacked and studied. His travels, he tells Haller, in a letter congratulating him on having resisted all temptations from foreign kings and universities to quit Berne, had added to his taste for natural history. Henceforth he intends physics and chemistry, 'with so much literature and society as may keep me from becoming a bear,' to form his main occupation and pleasure. With politics and office, for which he had never felt any attraction, the troubles of the times had, he writes, still further disgusted him. He 'prefers a tranquil independence to a stormy servitude.' In the following year he refused a nomination to the Council of Two Hundred, of which he did not become a member till several years later.

He was more agreeably engaged as a leading figure in the brilliant society that gathered at Geneva during the sixties and seventies of the eighteenth century. Himself a member of an old patrician family, and the husband of the eldest of the

Boissier heiresses, de Saussure was closely connected with three of the most distinguished families in the city, the Tronchins, the Turrettinis, and the de la Rives. As the host and more or less the master of the mansion in the Rue de la Cité and the beautiful country home on the lakeshore at Genthod, the young philosopher was obviously called on to take a conspicuous part in the social life and gaieties of the Upper Town. There was in Geneva at that time, before the troubles of the end of the century, a somewhat exclusive set of the 'best families,' the 'Nobles' and 'Spectables' of the old aristocracy, which was celebrated both for its agreeable and informal character and for its literary culture. It was one of the attractions that drew Voltaire to take up his abode in the neighbourhood. In the letters of the day we read of constant picnics and exchanges of visits between the inmates of the neighbouring country-houses in summer, and of afternoon assemblies and tea-parties in town during the winter.

The long-standing connection between England and Geneva had grown very intimate. A common form of religion, coupled with educational advantages, drew many of our countrymen to the pleasant town on Lake Leman. But the particular magnet that brought some of the first families in France and England about 1760 was Dr. Tronchin. He made Geneva a fashionable health resort, and the 'world' flocked to its favourite doctor as in later years it did to mineral spas—to Homburg, Marienbad, and St. Moritz. So great was the crowd that lodgings were scarce and dear, and the Genevese, when they went out to their country villas for the summer, had no difficulty in letting their town houses. Voltaire and his theatre no doubt added to the double attraction of society and scenery.

All our evidence—and there is a good deal—goes to show that de Saussure thoroughly enjoyed the social atmosphere by which he found himself surrounded. He was himself by all accounts an attractive personality, with a rare power of giving out the best of himself, full of sympathy among his friends and of natural gaiety in general society. In a note in an unusually lively strain written during his stay in England to Haller's son in Holland, he shows an eye keenly observant of personal traits. 'If you meet on your way the wig of M. Biermann, the sword of M. l'Amiral, the wife of M. Van der Meulen, or the eyebrows of

ITALY

M. Fizeau, please offer them my respects.' He goes on : ' I love with passion all ladies who are at once very charming and fond of natural science.'[1] He must have needed an expansive heart, for in the eighteenth century it was as fashionable with the fair sex to set up ' cabinets ' and pretend a taste for shells and fossils as it is in the twentieth to buy vellum-bound volumes of Greek philosophy and discuss psychical problems.

Voltaire more than once expressed his warm esteem for his amiable country neighbour, to whom he gave an introduction to his friend the Cardinal de Bernis, then French Ambassador to the Vatican, for use on de Saussure's visit to Rome. In due course the Cardinal replied congratulating the host of Ferney on living in a society which had such an agreeable member. But the best evidence to de Saussure's talent for friendship is afforded by his private correspondence. From that we learn on what intimate, and often affectionate, terms he was, both with the English nobility and the great French ladies who on their visits to Geneva received the hospitality of the mansion in the Rue de la Cité. The latter in their letters speedily drop the customary formalities and compliments of the time, and in their place end by assuring their ' dear friend ' of a lifelong affection.

The Geneva Visitors' List was a remarkable one. Among the celebrities from Paris were the philosophers Condorcet and d'Alembert ; Madame d'Epinay was Dr. Tronchin's favourite patient, and she delighted in his company as much as she profited by his prescriptions. Other distinguished visitors were the Duchesse d'Enville, ' the Philosophic Duchess,' mother of the young Duc de la Rochefoucauld d'Enville ; Madame de Montesson, the acknowledged wife (though she did not take his name in society) of Louis Philippe, the fourth Duc d'Orléans and father of Philippe Egalité ; the attractive and romantic Duchesse de Bourbon, his daughter and the mother of the Duc d'Enghien ; Madame de Lezay-Marnésia, the wife of a Marquis de Lezay-Marnésia, who travelled in America and wrote *Letters from the Banks of the Ohio*.

With most of these de Saussure was on intimate terms. The Duchesse d'Enville and Madame de Montesson remained his

[1] De Saussure describes in this note the blackballing of Dr. J. Hill at the Royal Society. Hill was a successful producer of quack medicines. Dr. Johnson labelled him an ingenious man who had no veracity.

constant correspondents, and their letters show a warmth of feeling and a certainty of meeting with a corresponding sympathy, both in happiness and sorrow, which is the best proof of true friendship. De Saussure's complete freedom from vanity and pedantry, coupled with his natural gaiety and a quick wit, must have appealed to the visitors from Paris, and doubtless formed a pleasing counterpoise both to the cynical if brilliant atmosphere of Ferney and the more serious tone of the coteries of the Upper Town. From England came Lord Palmerston; Lord and Lady Stanhope, who lived at Geneva for several years for the education of their sons; Lord Algernon Percy, and many others.

De Saussure does not seem to have allowed himself to be distracted by the calls of society, or even by the duties of his professorship, from his life-work, original research. Before setting out (in 1767) on his northern tour he had been at pains to explain to Bonnet his aims and the causes of his delay in publishing his results:

'Various tasks have retarded my Glaciers (*sic*). I am taking your advice, and writing down what I may forget and the points on which my impressions may grow faint. But I shall publish nothing for a long time. I realise that my work can only gain any value by the thoroughness of my investigations. Journeys have been made for more interesting objects, journeys more fatiguing, more dangerous, and more remarkable. What can I have to describe which has not been seen on a greater scale in the Cordilleras [1] and elsewhere? What is wanted is a series of thoroughly carried out investigations into the causes of the low temperatures in the upper layers of the atmosphere, on electricity, on the chemical composition and the formation of mountains, on vapours, meteors, plants, animals.'

In the early summer of 1769 de Saussure paid an unfruitful visit to the neighbourhood of Grenoble and Chambéry and the Grande Chartreuse. He met with a snowstorm and a gale on the heights above the convent. On the Mont Granier (6358 feet), celebrated for a great landslip in 1248, he was more fortunate in his quest for flowering plants. At this period he was still occupying himself a good deal with botany, and going over the different species represented in Haller's great work.

[1] A reference to the recent journeys (*circa* 1740) in the Andes of the French Academician, La Condamine, and his companions.

In 1770 there was a renewal of political disorders in Geneva. Under the Edict of 1768 the unenfranchised 'Natifs' who had taken part with the Représentants in the late disputes had gained relief from some of their disabilities. But their position still left them with many just grievances. The Représentants, on their part, recognised in the growing number and prosperous condition of the 'Natifs' the prospect of a formidable rivalry, commercial as well as political. They showed no disposition to give them the civic vote or to combine with them in opposition to the patrician oligarchy. In a heated atmosphere a trifling incident often leads to serious consequences. In 1770 the Councils seized on the occasion of a riot arising out of the prosecution of an individual for reciting a satirical street ballad to pass an ordinance dissolving the numerous clubs, which had played an important part in the recent struggles. In a city of so few amusements and among a race only too prone to talk and argument these social institutions filled an obvious need. But, as at Paris, they tended to become centres of political excitement and intrigue. The Councils next proceeded to make it penal to propose any further change in the political position of the 'Natifs,' and to banish their leaders. These measures, confirmed by the General Assembly, were for the time successful. The city was now to have some eleven years of relative tranquillity, at any rate on the surface, under its patrician government. But the old feuds were only dormant. The Représentants continued to agitate for the promised Code; the 'Natifs' were still clamorous for the removal of their practical grievances. De Saussure, fully occupied in his own studies and duties at the Academy and divided in his sympathies, held consistently aloof from the politics of the hour.

In 1770 his friend Lord Palmerston begged him to join a party, consisting of himself and two friends, in a visit to the glaciers of Chamonix and Grindelwald. He also asked him to recommend a German translation of Homer. Haller, on being appealed to, replied that he knew of none! He advised de Saussure, apparently on botanical grounds, to prefer the Valais, the Grisons, and Val Tellina to the Bernese Oberland, but the suggestion was not followed. No record of the tour exists, but we learn from incidental allusions that it was carried out successfully. The party visited the Rhône Glacier, and early in August, perhaps on his return, de Saussure ascended the Dent de Jaman behind Montreux. He praises the view and tells an amusing story of a minister from the Pays de Vaud who went with him, but was so terrified on the descent that he had to be carried down by his legs and shoulders like a corpse.[1]

For the following summer (1771) a more ambitious plan was formed, a tour beginning in June with the Simplon, and having for its principal object the flora of the Italian Lakes. De Saussure rowed up Lago Maggiore to Locarno, crossed the Monte Cenere, ascended Monte Brè, visited Como and Pliny's Villa. He went on to Milan. In a long letter to his wife he describes how he was taken round the town by Père Frisi, a Professor of Physics, Science, and Engineering, and introduced to Père Boscovich, celebrated as a philosopher, an astronomer, and an optician. I quote part of the letter as a specimen of de Saussure in his lighter mood:

'Père Frisi took me in a carriage the round of the churches, and then we called together on Père Boscovich, who was out, so we went on to the Corso. I noticed many fair ladies bow and smile to Père Frisi. He told me the names of everyone, but he did not repeat a single scandalous tale of the kind you would have cared for; he seems so good, so upright, that I believe he never thinks any evil. I took him home and had a long talk over physics and natural history; conversation with him is a great pleasure; his gentleness and modesty are charming.

'Next day I visited Père Boscovich. He is in quite a different style to Père Frisi. His style is that of the French savant whose object is to make a great show of his learning and new ideas in your eyes, without thinking much of his visitor. Let me tell you something of his ideas. I am glad to write them down before I forget them. He does not believe that the soul has any fixed seat in the brain, but that it moves about from one place to another, so that if a man survives the loss of a great part of his brain from a wound, it is owing to his luck in the soul having been in the part of the brain that was untouched, while another time a slight wound in the part where the soul is may cause death. He believes that if God created the world He must have created it such as it would have been had it previously existed for millions of years. At the moment of creation—according to him—the rivers filled their beds although the water had not flowed

---

[1] *Voyages*, section 1659.

from the hills, vegetation was complete, the trees as big as if they had grown naturally. The earth, which cannot be fertile unless enriched by animal and vegetable ingredients, contained these ingredients as if it had been from all time. The petrifactions formed on mountains do not prove that the world has undergone revolutions that would require far more than six thousand years, because God, in creating it, created it, petrifactions and all, such as it would have been if it had really undergone these revolutions.

'Here is certainly the most ingenious method ever invented for reconciling the story of Moses with natural history. He thinks that the only explanation of the prodigious disturbances of which continual evidence is found in the mountains is that the subterranean fires have acted as mines and thrown them into the air, and that in falling again they have been heaped up pell-mell in all sorts of irregular situations.

'Père Boscovich then described in detail the construction of a clock he had invented which is not subject to expansion by heat or contraction by cold. At this moment he was summoned to take a class, and I think you won't be sorry, for all this astronomy must have bored you greatly. . . . Up to this point, my dear Albertine, I have told you frankly and honestly all I have done since my departure. But now I have to confess an escapade which I have concealed so as to save you anxiety! You realise that I was very anxious to meet Père Spallanzani, the great observer of animalcules, the reproducer of snails, salamanders, etc. I had hoped to find him at Milan; not at all—he was at Pavia, where he is a Professor. Père Frisi put it into my head to go to Pavia; he made it clear as day that this détour would only lengthen my journey by twenty-four hours, and that by hiring a carriage I could recover the time lost. As soon as it was made plain to me my return would not be put off, I was soon persuaded, but the trouble was to tell you, because had I done so you would have at once believed that from place to place I should go on to Rome, and who knows but that your tender anxiety would not have shortly made you see your husband at Naples and next at Constantinople!

'Two hours after I got to Pavia—seven leagues from Milan—I hastened to the Abbé Spallanzani,[1] who asked me to dinner. I had immense pleasure in talking to him; my unexpected arrival seemed to be a joy and surprise to him, which flattered me greatly. He showed me all his microscopes and his instruments and talked a great deal

---

[1] Spallanzani was chiefly celebrated as a physiologist. His discoveries in the mode of reproduction of minute organisms proved the important fact that animalcules cannot develop in infusions that have been boiled and kept sealed.

of M. Bonnet. I dined with him and some other Professors of Pavia; they all three or four board together. They were very intimate between themselves, and see little of the Pavians, because they are all foreigners. They have succeeded some Pavia Professors who were donkeys; the Emperor dismissed them and appointed the present ones, who are, accordingly, not looked on with too kind eyes at Pavia. One of the Professors, M. Moscati, has an electrical machine, not a very powerful one; he showed me a curious experiment I shall repeat at Geneva. But the best thing Moscati has is a very young and very pretty wife, who had dined in town but came in in the evening. She could not speak French, but I understood her Italian and succeeded in making her understand mine. I addressed to her some gallant speeches, which she took in very good part, but her presence did not prevent us from making experiments with scorpions and salamanders and glow-worms. Her husband, however, complained all the time that she had no taste for such things, and would not attempt to learn about them. I thought to myself I was a far more fortunate husband!

'I amused and at the same time instructed myself. Raspberry syrup was served in place of supper, and at half-past eleven I took leave of this agreeable company, heaped with tokens of friendship, laden with books and a thousand little presents which they bestowed on me; and neither the science and the wit of the Professors nor the beautiful eyes and soft Italian speeches of Madame Moscati could make me promise to put off my departure for a single day!'

It will be noted here, and it holds good of his letters and diaries as a whole, that de Saussure seldom refers to art or architecture. In England, York Cathedral is the only building he mentions; at Milan he passes unnoticed the Duomo, at Pavia the Certosa, at Venice St. Mark's, only at Rome do antiquities attract his notice, and even there the attraction was mainly historical. Next to nature, his interest lay in human beings, and letters such as the one translated above show that he understood and appreciated them. If de Saussure was, as he says, a fortunate husband, Madame de Saussure was a still more fortunate wife, despite such passing infidelities as were caused by the glaciers of Savoy.

From Milan de Saussure returned to Geneva by Novara, Vercelli, Aosta, and the Great St. Bernard.

De Saussure's diary refers to a serious indisposition on the Great St. Bernard from which he suffered on his return from this trip. It may be remembered that Senebier, his biographer, asserts

ITALY

that de Saussure's bad health dated from his visit to the Cornish mines, an assertion that, as I have pointed out, receives no confirmation from the contemporary correspondence that is available. It is further contradicted by the detailed medical report on de Saussure's case made shortly after his death by his physician, Dr. Odier. The doctor's statement is definite and, I think, conclusive.

'Professor de Saussure, accustomed from his childhood to mountain excursions, and in his expeditions to brave rain and snow, heat and cold and fatigue, had enjoyed generally good health, until, after a journey he made to the Borromean Islands in which he ate a quantity of unripe fruit, he was attacked some thirty years ago by a long and serious illness, which ruined his digestion and rendered him subject thenceforth to the most distressing symptoms.'[1]

It was during de Saussure's absence in Italy in 1771 that a fête, famous at the time, was given by Lord and Lady Stanhope on the occasion of their son, Lord Mahon, a youth of eighteen, having won the prize in the annual competition of the Archery Society.[2] The Stanhopes had been living in Geneva for ten years for the education of their boys, the elder of whom had died there in 1763. By their liberal charities and geniality they had made themselves very popular, and they now offered to provide the town not only with a feast, but with a brilliant spectacle. Unfortunately, on the day for which it was first fixed rain fell in torrents, and Madame de Saussure, who writes an account to her husband, tells him how all the gay decorations of the Pré l'Evêque, where tables were to have been spread, were ruined. A week later, however, the fête came off. There was a procession, with a car on which were perched twelve Cupids, children between three and eight, and a Mercury of fifteen. There was an obelisk decorated with the arms of Geneva and the Stanhopes, there were alfresco lunches and military dances, and, needless to add in Geneva, complimentary verses to the newly adopted citizen. According to an English visitor, Dr. Moore,[3] the young nobleman,

[1] Dr. Odier, who made a post-mortem examination, enters into very full medical details of his patient's symptoms and their causes. The reader must marvel at the pluck with which, despite such disqualifications, de Saussure persisted for twenty years in his mountaineering career.

[2] See *L'ancienne Genève*, 1535-1798, L. Dufour Vernes (Geneva, 1909), for a full description of the connection of the Stanhopes with Geneva.

[3] See pp. 44, 135.

I

while at Geneva, took vehemently the part of the Représentants, refusing to associate with the aristocrats, and after the counter-revolution of 1782 resigning his citizenship by way of protest.

In later years Lord Mahon gave proof of the influence his republican upbringing had had on his mind. He was popularly known as 'Citizen Stanhope,' or 'the mad Lord Stanhope.' At that date that an English peer should both profess Radicalism and show marked ability as a scientific inventor was doubtless held sufficient ground for the epithet.

About this time de Saussure made practical use of his frequent talks with Franklin and his own electrical researches by fixing a lightning-conductor, a mast surmounted by an iron spike, said to have been 100 feet above the ground, to his townhouse. This portentous novelty was regarded with much distrust by his neighbours, who threatened a riot, and de Saussure was obliged to write a pamphlet to dissipate their fears.[1] A lightning-conductor still exists on the house.

In the autumn of the next year, 1772, after an unsuccessful visit to the waters of Aix, his general health and his throat gave de Saussure such trouble that he was advised by Dr. Tronchin[2] to pass the winter in the south. He writes to Haller: 'As the cold always disagrees with me, I am determined to spend the next winter in Naples.' He tells him he proposes to describe Italy from the point of view of natural science; of books dealing with art and antiquity, of parleyings over pictures and raptures on ruins, there were already, he held, enough.

Accordingly, in the autumn of 1772 he set out, accompanied by his wife and his daughter, then a child of six. At the start he was so ill that there was some question whether his health would allow him to continue the journey, but once over the Mont Cenis he made rapid improvement, and was able to carry out his intentions very thoroughly.

At Bologna de Saussure met and admired the celebrated lady doctor, Signora Laura Bassi. The party reached Florence at the end of October. There they made the acquaintance of Sir Horace Mann, the correspondent of Walpole. De Saussure

[1] This pamphlet was translated into Italian and reissued at Venice.
[2] So says Senebier. Dr. Tronchin had left Geneva for Paris in 1766. But his biographer indicates that he visited Geneva subsequently. (See *Th. Tronchin*, by H. Tronchin, Geneva, 1900.)

had a long conversation with the Grand Duke, who surprised him by his ability and the extent of his scientific knowledge. They visited Volterra, where de Saussure noted the boracic acid works and the marine shells in the Etruscan walls. From Leghorn he boldly sailed to visit the iron mines in the island of Elba, and then, passing through Pisa and Siena, came to Rome. All he finds to say of Pisa is that, though very decayed, it has a good Museum of Natural History and an Observatory.

Voltaire, as has been recorded, had furnished him with an introduction to the Cardinal de Bernis, the French Ambassador at Rome, who was also a poet, an ex-minister, and a man of the world. Its terms were an honour both to giver and receiver. 'De Saussure,' writes Voltaire, 'is one of the first scientific men in Europe, and his modesty is equal to his knowledge.' The Cardinal secured for him and his brother-in-law, Turrettini, who was of the party, a private audience with the Pope, Clement XIV. They were received, writes de Saussure, ' with the simplicity and cordiality of a good Prior who offers to strangers the hospitality of his convent.' The genial Pope was so charmed with the little Albertine that he not only blessed but kissed her, and then turned to one of his Cardinals with the clerical joke: 'Il faut que je me confesse, parce que je viens d'embrasser une jolie fille.' Her delighted mother wrote home : 'Albertine's story is true. The Pope and the Cardinals talk of nothing but her ; all Rome is enchanted, and I am enchanted with Rome.' On the first visit of the family to Ferney after their return the honour was duly recounted to Voltaire, to whom it had been mainly due. 'Well,' he exclaimed, 'since you have been kissed by the Pope, it is only fair you should be kissed by the Antipope.' This was not the only benediction the little Albertine received on her travels. On their way home her parents stopped at Berne, and she was taken to see 'le grand Haller.' In after years she described her recollection of the scene : 'Haller was very old and enveloped in a great dressing-gown, and I passed under an enormous table at which he was seated, to receive his blessing.'

After three weeks at Rome, where de Saussure made some excursions with an English antiquarian and virtuoso named James Byers, and found the prodigies of art occupied him far more than he had expected, ' since true beauty attracts and transports even the profane,' the party went on by Gaeta and the coast road to the warmer climate of Naples. There de Saussure met with a most congenial companion and guide in the English Minister, Sir William Hamilton, who had already lived at Naples for six years, and had recently published his *Observations on Etna, Vesuvius, and other Volcanoes*.[1] Hamilton was equally keen on natural science and on classical vases. He was delighted to act as de Saussure's guide to Vesuvius. While the philosophers climbed, or wandered over the Phlegraean fields, their wives—the first Lady Hamilton was then alive—made friends. Then the whole company visited the islands, Procida and Ischia, listened to the *improvisatori*, who celebrated their visitors' arrival in appropriate chants, and studied the manners and customs of the peasants, which recalled to de Saussure Greece and Homer. Of this visit to Naples Senebier writes :

'You should have heard de Saussure himself speak ; his enthusiasm returned in thinking of it, and he renewed his happiness in remembrance.'

Here is his own description, written on the spot to Madame Bonnet :

'Oh, my aunt, my good aunt, this is the place, this is the climate you need to restore your health ; this air, pure, lovely, and soft, we breathe, this sun, whose heat is always tempered by a fresh breeze, these magnificent prospects, these woods of oranges and lemons enclosed by hedges of figs and aloes crowned by some great palm-trees !'

and in another letter :

'What an abode for a naturalist ! The earth covered with rare plants, the sea as yet hardly at all investigated by capable observers, ancient and modern volcanoes, and their various products, vapours, baths, mineral springs. To study this land as it deserves, not one man, but a thousand, not a few days, but centuries, would be needed. And imagine there is not a single man—I repeat, not one—to make such a study, I do not say his occupation, but his amusement.'

The last sentence seems a little hard on Sir William Hamilton, who did occupy himself a good deal in a dilettante way at Naples. At any rate, he went up Vesuvius twenty-four times in four

[1] His *Campi Phlegræi*, published in 1779, contains many references to de Saussure.

years, and fifty-eight times in all, and published a work in three volumes on the *Campi Phlegræi*, besides making a collection of Greek and Roman vases which 'forms the groundwork of the present department of Greek and Roman antiquities at the British Museum.'

At the Court the little Albertine repeated her Roman success. She recited fables before the Queen with much applause.

During his stay at Naples de Saussure had an experience singularly appropriate for a practical student of electricity. This happened at an assembly of two or three hundred persons, including the Foreign Ministers and nobility of Naples, held in a palace inhabited by Lord Tilney, an Irish peer:

'The guests, occupied in playing or conversing, were scattered about the six or seven rooms that formed the apartment, when of a sudden the house was struck by lightning. A brilliant flash passed before the eyes of each guest and a noise like the report of a pistol was heard. There was a general panic and a crowd of pale faces, in which one saw depicted fear, superstition, anxiety.'

Some were unhurt, others felt a bruise or a pain in their limbs. Many were sprinkled with a bright dust, of which at first they could not imagine the origin. But they soon found that this dust came from the gilding of the cornices and furniture. Everywhere sofas and ceilings were blackened, burnt, and stript by the flash.

'Though the danger was over,' writes de Saussure, 'knowledge of the risk run seemed only to increase the fright. People recognised on the sofa on which they had been sitting the traces of the flame that had run over it. The sofa most seriously damaged was that on which a Neapolitan princess had been sitting between two of her lovers! It was undoubtedly due to the excessive gilding of the room that we owed our safety. Sir William Hamilton and I went next morning to examine the spot. He wrote an account for the Royal Society, and I one for Paris.'

At Naples the party lingered till the beginning of May, when they sailed for Palermo, where they were entertained by the Viceroy and the local society of Princesses and Duchesses, and drove out to see the neighbouring churches, convents, and country seats. Thence they crossed the island to Catania, where they stayed with the Prince de Biscari, a rich and patriotic Sicilian and a collector of scientific tastes. On 5th June de Saussure ascended and measured the height of Etna, the altitude he obtained being 34 metres (111 feet) more than that now adopted—3304 metres (10,841 feet). The reflections on the greatness of nature and the littleness of man, inspired by the view from the summit, are recorded at some length in a passage of unusual eloquence in the 'Discours Préliminaire' to his *Voyages*.

From Naples the party returned through Rome to North Italy, stopping at Terni to see the waterfall, and then by Ancona, San Marino, Rimini, Ravenna, Bologna, Ferrara, Padua, to Venice. At Padua he renewed his acquaintance with the celebrated Spallanzani, whom he had already met at Pavia in 1771, and at Venice he again met Boscovich, the mathematician and astronomer—who on the suppression of the order of the Jesuits had exchanged his professorship at the Collegio Romano for a chair in the University of Padua. He adds a witty epigram to the description of the latter given to his wife two years previously, and already quoted :

'He delights,' de Saussure says, 'in making a display of systems and new ideas. His talk is a lecture, and he admires the lecturer (*Il professe en causant et s'admire professant*).'

The party returned by Tyrol—that is, no doubt, by the Brenner [1]—and passing through Zurich, Basle, and Berne, reached Geneva in August. It had been de Saussure's intention to publish a 'Naturalist's Tour in Italy,' but his customary diffidence and dislike of literary work led to its indefinite postponement, and the greater part of the letters he wrote to his two chief correspondents, Bonnet and Haller, have perished. The few that have been preserved make us regret their loss. In one of them he speaks of himself as a bad letter-writer ; but bad letter-writers often write the best letters !

The only literary results of his journey were two articles, ' Idée Générale de la Constitution Physique d'Italie,' published

[1] At that date it was for carriage travellers the only alternative to the Mont Cenis. Thus Gibbon, prevented by the war with France from crossing the Mont Cenis to join his friends in Italy, writes to Lady Elizabeth Foster : 'My aged and gouty limbs would have failed me in the bold attempt of scaling St. Bernard, and I wanted patience to undertake the circum-itineration of the Tyrol.' 'Circum-itineration' is appropriately expressive.

in the first volume of the *Voyage en Italie* of Lalande (1786), which, though no doubt valuable at the time, does not now seem more than an average encyclopædia article; and a Letter addressed to Sir William Hamilton on 'La Géographie Physique d'Italie,' published in the seventh volume of the *Journal de Physique*. They were both highly praised by a competent contemporary critic—Romé de l'Isle. He wrote to de Saussure:

'Your learned and luminous description of your Italian journey reveals a profound naturalist. It sweeps away the empty hypotheses of our geological theories as the north wind sweeps away the clouds which the western seas send us.'

The following passage from the Letter may serve as a specimen of de Saussure's clear and complete method of scientific exposition:

'All this vast plain of Lombardy, the greatest and the richest in Europe, which, beginning at Turin, extends to Bologna, Ancona, and Venice, is nothing else than the deposit of the rivers which descend from the Alps and Apennines. These great streams, rapid at their sources, tear up the surface of the ground and carry with them fragments of the rocks; but, gradually slackening their current, they deposit in succession the material with which they are laden; these deposits are governed by the weight and the bulk of the material; the same stream which at Turin carries large stones, lays down on the edge of the sea only sand and a fine and impalpable mud; yet the continual accumulation of this mud extends the borders of the dry land, fills little by little the lagoons of Venice, and will end by one day joining it to the Continent.'

An event of a very serious and distressing character served to hasten the de Saussures' return from Italy. The details given here are borrowed from the work of the doctor who about this date accompanied the Duke of Hamilton to Chamonix and the Mer de Glace.[1]

In 1773 Jean Louis Tronchin, then a young man of twenty-eight, the husband of de Saussure's younger sister-in-law, shot himself in his own house, apparently without any warning. He had been married only four years. Our countryman takes the

[1] His name was John Moore, M.D. He was a prolific writer and the father of Sir John Moore, who died at Corunna. (See *A View of Society and Manners in France, Switzerland, and Germany, by a Gentleman*, London, 1779.) His portrait was included in a group sold in the Hamilton sale at Christie's in November 1919. See also pp. 44, 129.

occasion to moralise on the frequency of suicides at Geneva, of which, he says, there had been a 'multiplicity of instances' during his stay. Having pointed out that the climate and coal fogs, commonly alleged as the causes of suicide in England, cannot here be held responsible, he falls back on the safe conclusion that melancholia is an illness! How far frequent intermarriages and a depressing creed may have been responsible for the tragedies recorded he does not pause to inquire.

During de Saussure's absence in Italy another incident had occurred which is recorded in several of the Memoirs of the time. While he was in England in 1768 his sister Judith, then twenty-three, had sent him a lively account of an agreeable evening with Voltaire. She wrote:

'We have had a very pleasant summer—one of the most brilliant on record in our poor Geneva. Comedies were played at Pregny. The Demoiselles Sales have plenty of talent and are really charming girls, to whom the public, often unfair, has done great injustice. The *Enfant Prodigue* was played. M. de Voltaire came from Ferney to enjoy the success of his piece. I was enchanted to find myself sitting next him. He talked of you, and charged me to write and tell you "he had had the happiness to pass two hours at my side." He asked me to dinner. I think we shall go one of these days. How does your wife amuse herself in London? One hears it is not a place where women much enjoy themselves.'[1]

The two households were already on friendly terms, and the expected invitation soon came and led to others. It is evident that the old wit found the young lady good company, and their acquaintanceship ripened and led to some correspondence, for on Voltaire's death, Judith wrote to ask that the 'one or two letters' she had written to him might, if found, be returned to her.

Four years later her brother, in a letter from Naples, charged his father to transmit through Judith, when next she visited Voltaire, news of the performance of his plays *L'Ecossaise* and *Tancrède*. She was to tell him that they had been played at Naples by a French company, the best ever seen out of Paris, and had had an astonishing success, so that stalls were selling at a louis: the King had sent for the company to Caserta to give the pieces there, and their

[1] Englishmen at this date were generally believed to be too much absorbed in business or sport to pay the other sex the attention they were accustomed to on the Continent.

ITALY

author was as famous and admired at Naples as in Paris. This was written in February 1773. Some weeks previously, probably in December, on a day when Judith had been invited to Ferney, Voltaire, feeling unequal to entertain a large house-party, left, as he frequently did, his niece, Madame Denis, to take his place, while he dined *tête-à-tête* with Judith. The host was seventy-eight; his guest twenty-seven, and there should have been no excuse for scandal. But no doubt the other guests were not dumb in their disappointment, and in a town at that date much addicted to ill-natured gossip, Voltaire afforded a tempting and provoking subject.

A version of the incident, coloured and exaggerated by malicious tongues, was spread abroad and reported in Paris, and even reached the ears of Louis Quinze, who through the Duc de Richelieu sent a ribald message to the Patriarch of Ferney. Voltaire replied—as his years doubly justified him in doing—by a repetition of the Horatian *fuge suspicari* which would have been in better taste had he shown more resentment of an unmannerly insult to his guest. The serious annoyance caused to its victim is shown in the bitter comments on the bad manners of the Genevese we find in letters written by Judith to her brother and sister-in-law many years afterwards.[1] That she had ample grounds for her resentment, one at least of the contemporary journals that has survived offers conclusive evidence. Grimm's comment on the affair is to the point: 'See how calumny with its venomous tongue pursues innocence and beauty!' Since one of the first acts of the de Saussures on their return from Italy was to call on Voltaire to thank him for the introduction to the Vatican he had given them, it is obvious that the family treated the town talk with the contempt it deserved.

It will be convenient to conclude this chapter by the story of the subsequent career of Horace Benedict's only sister, who sympathised with his pursuits and appears to have shared his inherited weakness of constitution.

In 1768 we already hear of her suffering from eye trouble;

---

[1] Judith evidently shared her brother's power of expressing resentment of any groundless and impertinent criticism or comment. She wrote to her brother: 'Nous sommes furieusement méchants dans notre charmante République. Je suis persuadée qu'on pourrait parcourir le monde entier sans trouver une ville où la méchanceté soit poussée aussi loin.'

in 1773 she was in the doctor's hands, and Haller was consulted. Somewhat later she was recommended to seek a warmer climate than that of Geneva in winter, and she consequently took up her abode at Montpellier, which before the French Revolution and the rise of the Riviera was both an important administrative centre and the fashionable resort of invalids from Paris, and even from our own country. Here as a lady of great intelligence, some personal attraction, and an independent fortune she soon found herself welcomed as a member of the best society of the town, and made many friends, English as well as French. Among the latter was Madame Roland, with whom she stayed at her rustic home, 'le Clos en Beaujolais.'[1]

Mlle. de Saussure, though she retained property in the town and from time to time paid visits to her parents at Frontenex and her brother at Genthod, or stayed for a few weeks in summer in one of the smaller towns on the lake, never returned to live at Geneva. In the autumn of 1780, at the conclusion of a tour of the Riviera, de Saussure paid her a brief visit at Montpellier, where she entertained him and introduced him and his companion Pictet to her brilliant circle of friends. Pictet describes her as making an agreeable impression, though her good looks and complexion had suffered from constant ill-health.

On his return to Geneva, de Saussure wrote to his sister expressing his pleasure at having found her in pleasant surroundings and among good friends.

'Yet,' he continues, 'you will leave next spring those amiable inhabitants of Montpellier to return to the bosom of a family which knows how to love you even better than they do. I, and we all of us, look forward to this moment with the greatest impatience. Take care of yourself, and avoid carefully any indisposition that may deprive us of this happiness.'

The Genevese revolution of February 1781, described in letters from de Saussure and his father to Judith, may have put a stop

[1] Madame Roland, in 1787, visited Western Switzerland and Grindelwald (see her *Lettres sur la Suisse*, 1787). For her relations with Geneva and the Gosse family, see *Un Genevois d'autrefois*, par Mlle. Danielle Plan (Geneva, 1909). Monsieur Roland, when appointed a member of the Society of Arts, wrote to 'M. de Saussure' as secretary, thanking him. Théodore de Saussure then held the office.

to this projected visit. A year later Madame de Saussure reports to Judith the state of the family :

'Your mother is always solitary. . . . Your father is always busy with his farm and an antiquated system of physics; even politics are a feeble distraction to him. Your brother is very well and embraces you tenderly. Your niece [Albertine de Saussure] is surrounded by extracts and works of devotion: she is to take her first communion at Easter. I only see my children when they are at their Latin lesson or out walking.'

Mlle. de Saussure kept up a constant correspondence with her family, and such of her letters as have been preserved tell of much social gaiety. More than once she begs her brother to send her one of the famous lake trout from Geneva as a contribution to her or her friends' entertainments. These fish were often dispatched as far as Paris, and we read on one occasion of the Envoy of the Genevese Republic there begging that a particularly fine specimen may be provided as a compliment to the First Consul (Bonaparte), whom at the moment it was very desirable to propitiate. Mlle. de Saussure would sometimes send her brother in return geological specimens collected by the travelled members of the French nobility who frequented her *salon*. From time to time she consulted him as to her treatment of her admirers, or recommended some of her agreeable English acquaintances to his care. But though she paid occasional visits to Genthod, she never showed a disposition to return to Geneva for any length of time. For her summer holidays she preferred the Cévennes, or, if she wished to meet her family, Nyon or one of the smaller Swiss towns on the lake.

In 1785, however, Judith visited her relations at Geneva, and she was there again in 1790. We next hear of her in July 1792, undeterred by the Revolution, staying in Paris with her brother's friend Madame de Montesson. On the 11th she writes to him :

'It is quite true that Paris is very gloomy, and may at any moment become dangerous, but you know my character. When those to whom I am attached are in danger, I suffer more when I am separated from them than when I share the danger, and this was why I was so ill and shaken last year on the 13th February. I was at

Genthod; had I been at Geneva and able to know from moment to moment what was going on and that you were safe, I should not have been the victim of the darkest forebodings.'[1]

She goes on to describe vividly Louis Seize's character:

'He has plenty of physical courage, but no resolution. He yields to the last advice given him, and his feebleness and vacillation endanger the lives not only of those who are attached to him, but of all the people of Paris and France, because, as a Jacobin very truly said the other day, "If there is a revolution, all who have anything to lose will be robbed and murdered!"'

Judith must have kept a home, or at any rate property, in Geneva, for in 1794 the revolutionaries seized in her apartments 895 ounces of silver and 8687 florins. The last letter I have of hers is to her sister-in-law, written in reply to one describing Bonaparte's visit to Madame de Saussure in May 1800 during her early widowhood. Madame de Saussure's letter is unfortunately missing. Judith avows herself one of the warmest admirers of Bonaparte; she sees no one else capable of giving peace and a stable government to France, and her feelings towards him, she writes, are those of devotion and gratitude. Is the rumour true that he is going to take the command of the army in Italy, where he will be proclaimed Emperor? She concludes by expressing her regret that her sister-in-law had not seized the opportunity for obtaining from the First Consul some favours for her family or her friends.

Judith published in 1808 a little volume entitled *Anecdotes extraites de la Volumineuse Histoire de Russie de Le Clerc, par Mlle. de Saussure, auteur de l'éloge de M. le Comte de Périgord.* Its interest for us lies in the preface, in which she states that when at Geneva in 1795 she had tried to distract her brother by reading to him these extracts, as he was too ill to attempt the original work. She now publishes them because 'she loves all that reminds her of her brother,' and adds that she would have dedicated them to his memory had she not desired to pay a compliment to M. Baume, her doctor at Montpellier, to whom she owed much. A copy of the book is preserved in the library at Genthod.

I have put together in these few pages the little we know of

[1] This was the date of the revolt of the peasants led by Grenus. (See p. 359.)

Judith de Saussure. The impression left by the few letters and the scattered references available is that of a woman endowed in youth with good looks and high spirits, and through life possessed of much force and independence of character.[1] That she found the home life at Frontenex with her invalid mother and agricultural father irksome; that she was out of sympathy with the social coteries of Geneva, and never forgave the grievous slight that had been put on her, is obvious. At Montpellier she showed herself ready to take a leading part in society as far as her health allowed her. Though her life as a whole was a detached one, she succeeded in making many friends, both French and English, and in keeping at bay at least one admirer. She sympathised keenly with her brother's scientific pursuits, and was active in taking advantage of any opportunity to help him to add to his collections. She did her best to cheer him in his last illness and to keep alive his memory after his death.

[1] Judith de Saussure is thus described by a contemporary: 'She had a regular profile, with finely modelled features, large deep-coloured eyes which threw up the whiteness of her complexion; brown hair, which she powdered in her youth. She was short, but had a perfect figure, which she retained to an advanced age.' (Kohler's *Madame de Staël et la Suisse*, Lausanne, Paris, 1916.)

CHAPTER VI

TEN YEARS' ALPINE TRAVEL (1774-84)

THE warmth of the south had done its work in restoring de Saussure to health. For a long interval after his return from Italy we hear no more complaints of any serious or prolonged indisposition. Though he was often in doctors' hands and his digestion remained always difficult and precarious, he was able during the next sixteen years, with but one interruption, to lead a life of various activity as a hard-working Professor, a man of science, a citizen, and a mountain traveller.

These were the years of his principal Alpine explorations, which culminated in 1787-88 and 1789 in the ascent of Mont Blanc, the stay on the Col du Géant, and the tour of Monte Rosa. It will be on the whole more convenient at this point to abandon chronological order for a time and to give in the following chapters a consecutive account of de Saussure's career as a scientific mountaineer, reserving for subsequent pages the narrative of his home life and political activities and of the misfortunes that clouded his last years.

The period from 1774 to 1784, covering the middle years of de Saussure's life (thirty-four to forty-four), was one of continual activity in travel and observation. The available record of it is considerable: in addition to the *Voyages*, I have had the advantage of reading several of his private diaries and many intimate letters to his wife and family. The diaries were based on rough notes, made in a pocket-book while on the road, and often in the saddle, which he was in the habit of writing out fair—but in a hand at times almost illegible—every few days. His wife's constant anxiety during his absences, which seems to have diminished but little with years and habit, had this good result. It made her devoted husband an excellent correspondent. His letters not only add to the human incidents recorded in the *Voyages*, but often bring into relief fresh traits in de Saussure's character.

H. B. DE SAUSSURE ABOUT 1777
By Jens Juel

I shall not attempt here to follow in their chronological order the Alpine tours of which we have records. In his *Voyages* de Saussure summarised and combined the results of several tours under three separate headings. The first of these is the tour of Mont Blanc. This, de Saussure, when in 1786 he published the second of his four volumes, had already made four times. He gives as a second 'Voyage' his passage of the Mont Cenis and his visits to the Riviera and Provence.[1] The third 'Voyage' is a very condensed account of his many visits to the Gries, the St. Gotthard, and the Italian lakes.

Further journeys, of which little or no mention is found in the *Voyages*, are that of 1777 to the Bernese Oberland and over the St. Gotthard and Gries to the Lake of Como, returning by the Splügen, Chur, Wallenstadt, and Zurich, and that of 1784, mainly sub-alpine, which included a visit to Engelberg and an ascent of the Graustock (8737 feet) above the Joch Pass.

De Saussure had made his first tour of Mont Blanc in 1767 in company with Jean Louis Pictet, an astronomer and student of physics, and a young friend, Jalabert. On his second tour in 1774 he was alone with his guides. On his third tour, in 1778, he had the company of Jean Trembley, and his pupil and greatest ally, Marc Auguste Pictet. In the published narrative he refers to the advantage and pleasure he derived from their company; but his subsequent practice indicates that there were certain drawbacks. De Saussure found that his observations often took more time than his companions wished to spend. In later Alpine journeys, when not travelling with his wife and family or his son, he, as a rule, went alone, no doubt finding it left his attention more free to keep his notebooks in constant use.

His letters to his wife written during his second journey, in 1774, furnish many picturesque details of Alpine travel in its earlier stages. Here is the description of his quarters at Sallanches:

'The inn has a long gallery, not ornamented with pictures and sculptures like that of the Villa Lullin,[2] but with a view of the course of the Arve through a valley surrounded by mountains of immense height and the strangest forms crowned by Mont Blanc, which nowhere

---
[1] They are dealt with in chapters xiii. and xiv.
[2] The villa at Genthod, which belonged to his wife's family.

looks so majestic as from here. Its head, which pierces above the clouds, resembles a cloud whiter than the rest, so that those who see it for the first time cannot believe it to be a mountain.'

The story is continued in a letter written from Courmayeur a week later :

'On Monday morning the rain prevented me from starting from Sallanches, for I had determined, as much for the sake of my observations as for my own personal comfort, never to travel in the rain. I got up late and spent the morning in putting in order all my luggage, testing its arrangement on the mules, going over my agenda, and such-like jobs. M. Efsancet, my host, who is a young gallant of Sallanches, gave me more of his company than I wanted, and treated me to the sweet melody of a carillon made up of cowbells which he had invented. If he had not put a fancy price on it, I might have bought it for Milord Jack [his seven-year-old son] to meet his taste for good music. He told me news that grieved me—the death of Madame Charlet of Chamonix, the wife of the Châtelain, the lady who thought it such a pity I must be damned. . . . About midday the weather cleared, and I started. Here is the order of march we keep on all the good roads. For we have two orders of battle. One for good roads and one for difficult passes. On the good roads Pierre Simon [his guide] plays the part of Volante, he leads the march on foot with, in place of a banner, his big tin box, and for a staff of command my alpenstock ; next comes your husband, mounted on his mule, looking about him right and left, and noting down all he sees in his red pocket-book ; for my mule has such gentle paces that I can write very legibly while he moves ; I have written as much as eight pages a day in this way. Next comes Charles [his servant], also on his mule, looking at all the mountains with startled eyes, and whenever he sees a specially terrible and needle-like one, inquiring : "Monsieur, shall we ascend that mountain ?" Then comes the baggage mule charged with my basket covered with oil-cloth. Last, Favret, on foot, closes the march. In difficult places the baggage mule goes first and all the rest follow on foot.

'Thus we jog-trotted to St. Gervais, where I halted to make some observations, and then we entered the valley which leads to the Bonhomme. I slept at Contamines, and as the *cabaret* was so bad that Pierre Simon (who also fills the place of *maréchal des logis*, and goes ahead to prepare my lodging when we draw near) thought I should not be comfortable, he went to ask for a bed at the Curé's. The Curé was away from home, but his Vicaire, who is called Monsieur l'Abbé, took on himself to receive us, and since it would have been beneath his dignity to come and tell me so on the public road, he sent one of his *pensionnaires*, a young scholar who puts all the ink of the place on his fingers and on his coat, so as to prevent any mistake as to his being a student. The young ambassador came, with many bows, to tell me I should be welcome, that it was much regretted M. le Curé was away, but that in his absence M. l'Abbé would do his best to receive me properly. I got down, therefore, and found M. l'Abbé on the step of his door. He is a little hump-back who attempts fine language. He conducted me very politely to a rising ground where I wished to make my observations, and gave me his company for the evening.

'He had read the *Voyage Pittoresque* [obviously Bordier's little volume published in the previous year] with the greatest satisfaction, and consequently did me the honour to take me for its author. I, as you may imagine, disowned it, and even ventured such light criticisms as I could without disputing the opinion expressed by M. l'Abbé. "It is true," he said, "that it is not written in that sublime style which, when you have read one page, forces you to read all; one can read it by fits and starts, but that is just what I like." All the same, M. l'Abbé is a great reader; he has poor health, which does not allow him to drink, and books, when he can get them, are his only pleasure. He complained much of the tipsiness and the rough manners of his brethren. We had a specimen that very day. About 10 P.M. we heard a terrible noise: it was a Vicaire, who, having supped two leagues off on the mountains, came to spend the evening with the local Curé. Already almost tipsy, he called for wine, drank three or four glasses, and then went on to continue his round.

'Next day I resumed my march, in spite of the urgent entreaties of M. l'Abbé, who wanted to take me to dine with the Curé of Notre Dame de la Gorge, where all the Curés of the neighbourhood were dining. I was so terrified at the idea of this fête that I even went out of my way so as not to pass Notre Dame!

'From this point one begins to climb by a path very good for foot-travellers, but very laborious for the mules, which delayed us a little; but the greatest hindrance was the rain, which began to fall heavily. We, who are prudence itself, did not think it suitable weather for crossing the Bonhomme, and we halted at the highest inhabited chalets we met with. These, which are only occupied at midsummer, are named the chalets of Nant Borrant. At one of them wine is sold, and it calls itself, consequently, a *cabaret*. We turned our mules to it. Under the eaves was a little girl of the age and height of my dear Albertine, who, when she saw us approach, ran into the house like a mouse into its hole, and shut the door behind her.

K

'It needed long negotiations through the keyhole before she could make up her mind to let us in, as she was alone. At last she opened, and even rendered us all the little services in her power. She is really as pretty as Albertine, and talks Savoyard as well as Albertine does French; she described everything, the farm, the cows, the goats, the names of the mountains; she had been once on a very steep glacier one sees from the chalet. I had time enough to make friends with her, since we were forced to spend the day and sleep there. But you need not be anxious, my dear angel, about my food. I had an excellent stew in a pot which Jeanne had made for me. Charles, who is very good in the kitchen, made me a soup and cooked some eggs. And as to sleeping, I had a good bed and slept better than I have ever slept in my life. The mountain hay has a delicious smell—that of the best tea, and I have been *parfumé au thé* for two days. In the evening the rain stopped, and I took some strolls about the chalet which gave me several interesting observations.

'On Wednesday morning we set out to cross the Bonhomme; it is a mountain-pass closed at its head by a lofty ridge with pointed crags on either side, which look like the horns one makes when playing at horns with the fingers. The local wits say that it is from these horns that the name of Bonhomme comes.

'Our passage was extremely fortunate, the snow, of which we had two leagues,[1] was of exactly the right consistence, neither too soft nor too hard. The weather was beautiful; no sun (which I should have been glad of for observations), and a few clouds on the peaks. But it was excellent weather for travel and for observing rocks. I had a great deal of pleasure and satisfaction; this one day gave me more ideas on the structure of our globe than all the work I did between the College Prize Day and my start. The descent of the mountain is very easy; it is over a pasturage four leagues in extent, on what, for these mountains, is a gentle slope without a single *mauvais pas*. I did it all on foot and without fatigue. From the top of the pass the village where one sleeps is visible at such a depth beneath one's feet that one would say it was at the bottom of hell, and yet when one gets there and consults the barometer, one is surprised to find one is still at the height of the Dôle. It is only inhabited in summer. This place is called Chapieu; it is perhaps of all the inhabited places in the world the most savage and terrible. It consists of a dozen miserable huts

---

[1] Leagues with de Saussure is a vague measure. It appears generally to be equivalent on the mountains to an hour's walk. There must, anyhow, have been a very unusual amount of snow for the middle of July. I have, however found an hour's snow on the pass in August.

built against the hillside, having opposite them the stony bed of the torrent and on all sides mountains of alarming height which offer only snow and barren rocks. In every direction one hears the hideous roar of torrents. A man not accustomed to similar situations might easily contract melancholia. Charles, who was much more tired than I, and perturbed to an indescribable extent by the passage of the mountain, was, as you may imagine, not cheered up; he managed, however, to take great care of my belongings and to cook my supper, and I was better satisfied with him than I could have hoped to be. I had the honour to sleep in a bed, but I regretted my hay of the previous night, for the bed was harder than a plank, while my hay was most luxurious.'

It may be remembered that on de Saussure's first tour of Mont Blanc in 1767, the Genevese servants of the party had been so terrified by the Bonhomme that on being told at Chapieu that the Col de la Seigne was worse, they plotted to force the travellers to go round by the Little St. Bernard :

'It seemed to us amusing,' de Saussure wrote, 'to find ourselves in the position of the navigators who, setting out for great discoveries, have to combat the mutiny of their crews.'

The accommodation at Chapieu remained very much the same for the next eighty years, and de Saussure's description might very well have served as late as 1856, when the writer first visited the spot. Nor does he exaggerate in his denunciation of the landscape. It attains a stony ugliness rare in the Alps, at any rate outside Dauphiné.

At the head of the glen above Chapieu the gorge expands into a pastoral basin, which contains the alp of Les Mottets. De Saussure, always interested in peasant life, describes his reception there :

'A short distance above the hamlet of Glacier is a large chalet inhabited by a family of peasants from St. Maurice in the Tarentaise. All the surrounding pastures belong to this family, and they are extensive enough to feed in summer a herd of cows, of which sixty are their own. This is a considerable and rare fortune in the district; with such resources it would be possible not only to live without working, but even to occupy a good position in a town. Yet these people have lost nothing of the simplicity of their condition: the wife of the head of the family passes the summer at the chalet, and looks after its management, while the husband remains in the plain to see to the field labours. These good people lodged me in their chalet in 1781. They had not much spare room, because their son, who had just married, had come with his wife to pass some days on the mountains with his mother. They found, however, a corner and some dry hay for me, and I had my share of a lamb which had been killed to feast the newly married pair. Although they were of the most perfect straightforwardness, and had an address and manners appropriate to their condition, one saw that they were conscious of their prosperity and the power they had of living in different conditions.' [*Voyages*, 839.]

I return to de Saussure's letter to his wife. It ends thus:

'Next morning I mounted my mule to cross another ridge which has to be passed on the way to Courmayeur. It is called the Col de la Seigne, and is about the same height as the Bonhomme, but much gentler. We crossed it without difficulty or fatigue. I saw the magnificent glaciers at the back of Mont Blanc and the tremendous mountains of snow and granite between which they issue. This route through the Allée Blanche is above all description, so I shall not attempt any, the more as the express messenger I am sending to carry this letter to Martigny is growing impatient. Farewell, my dear angel; rest assured that I shall always take care of myself, and that you will see me return better in health and richer in knowledge than when I set out.'[1]

Of the peasants of Courmayeur de Saussure gives in the *Voyages* the following account:

'The people of Courmayeur are very good folk, and although they talk the Savoyard patois and like to be held Savoyards, they share to some extent the physical and moral qualities of Italians—dark complexions, aquiline noses, black hair and eyes, and something of that tendency to boastfulness and exaggeration which is characteristic of southern races. I may give an instance. Descending alone and on foot by a steep and narrow path above Courmayeur, I overtook a peasant mounted on a mule laden with two great bales of hay, which was going very slowly. It was impossible to pass without his drawing his mule to one side. I very politely begged him to do this, pointing out that the flies attracted by his mule and the heat were

[1] The messenger to whom this missive was entrusted made a mistake which naturally infuriated de Saussure; he brought it back with him from Martigny, leaving there in its place a letter de Saussure was expecting from his wife. The ordinary post at that date between Geneva and the Val d'Aosta by the Mont Cenis and Turin was too slow to be any use to the traveller. It was not till he reached the Great St. Bernard that any home news reached him.

inconveniencing me greatly. This man, who doubtless believed that I only went on foot because I could not afford to ride, answered me with a really comic air of dignity. I ought, he said, "to bear the discomfort patiently, since it was quite right that those on foot should suffer something at the hands of those who were on horseback." Nevertheless, he let me pass, no doubt to make me feel doubly his superiority.' [*Voyages*, 884.]

From Courmayeur de Saussure in 1778 made his second ascent of the Crammont. He writes :

'I felt an inexpressible satisfaction in finding myself on this magnificent belvedere, which had given me so much pleasure four years earlier. The air was perfectly clear, the sun threw a great flood of light on Mont Blanc and all its chain; no vestige of cloud or vapour robbed us of the view of the objects we had come to gaze on, and the certainty of enjoying for several hours this great spectacle gave the mind an assurance which doubled the feeling of enjoyment. My first object was to revise and complete the notes I had taken in 1774, but I soon found this work distasteful ; it seemed to me that it was an insult to the sublimity of the scene to compare it to anything but itself. I began accordingly my observations afresh. . . .'

' It is a law general to all the primitive mountains that the secondary chains which flank them on either side have their strata tilted towards the central range. . . . I saw the primitive chain composed of layers which may be regarded as strata ; these strata are vertical in the central range, while those of the secondary ridges, almost vertical where they abut on the former, become less inclined as they are more distant, and as they recede farther and farther approach gradually to the horizontal.

' I thus recognised that the relations between the primitive and the secondary mountains which I had already noticed in the substances of which they consist extend also to the form and position of their strata, since all the secondary summits in view culminated in pyramidal blades with sharp edges like Mont Blanc and the primitive mountains. I concluded from these characteristics that since the secondary mountains had been formed in the bosom of the waters, the primitive must have had the same origin. Retracing in my brain the succession of the great revolutions which our globe has undergone, I saw the sea, covering the whole surface of the globe, form by successive deposits and crystallisations first the primitive mountains, then the secondary. I saw these deposits arrange themselves symmetrically in concentric beds, and subsequently the fire or other elastic fluids contained in the interior of the globe lift and break up this crust and thus press out the interior and primitive part of this crust, leaving the exterior or secondary portions piled up against the interior beds. I saw next the waters precipitate themselves into the gulfs split open and emptied by the explosion of the elastic fluids [gases ?], and these waters, rushing towards the gulfs, carry with them to great distances the blocks we find on our plains. I saw finally, after the retreat of the waters, the germs of plants and animals, fertilised by the atmosphere newly created, begin to develop on the ground abandoned by the waters and in the waters themselves where they were retained in the hollows of the surface.' [*Voyages*, 909-919.]

The ascent of the Crammont had not been de Saussure's only expedition from Courmayeur on his previous visit in 1774. Having found a chamois-hunter nicknamed Patience [1] who knew the mountains well, he started with him and his servant (de Saussure's valets probably found his service trying—they were, at any rate, frequently changed) to explore the upper part of the Miage Glacier. He was anxious to reconnoitre all the possible approaches to Mont Blanc. Having apparently no rope, the party halted at the point where the crevasses became covered with snow and took to the rocky slopes on the left bank of the glacier. Having reached a height of 8240 feet, further progress was judged impracticable. De Saussure speaks of the head of the Miage as a barrier that would always be impracticable except to chamois. It is obvious, therefore, that no rumours of early passages of the Col de Miage were brought to his ears. Since such rumours subsequently reached Napoleon and caused local inquiry to be made, this must at first sight seem remarkable. But we may surmise that refugees' and smugglers' passes were for good reason apt to be little talked about.

In 1778 de Saussure and his friends rode their mules down the long and hot Val d'Aosta from Courmayeur to Ivrea. His remarks on the road are almost entirely geological. He just notes in passing the snows above the openings of the Val de Rhêmes and Val Savaranche, Mont Emilius, and the valley that leads to Mont Cervin, as he calls the Matterhorn.

From Ivrea, despite the trying heat of midsummer, the company rode out towards the Lake of Vivarone to examine the great banks of transported material which spread out fan-wise, like a

[1] His real name was Jean Laurent Jordanay. He kept an inn at Courmayeur. The fact that he guided de Saussure is mentioned in the entry of his death in the Parish Register.

gigantic rampart, from the mouth of Val d'Aosta. He at once recognised that the character of the boulders showed that they had come from the recesses of the central chain. But as to the mode of their transport, so obvious to our eyes, he remained absolutely blind; he was too firmly imbued with the current belief in the agency of prehistoric floods.

It must be matter of astonishment to every modern mountaineer who reads the *Voyages* that anyone with de Saussure's opportunities of observation should have failed to recognise a connection between the moraines of existing glaciers and these monuments of their great predecessors. But de Saussure passes on, serenely unconscious of the inference that to our eyes seems inevitable. Yet he had noted that in the valley of Chamonix great banks marked former fluctuations of the ice, and that it was the glacier that had brought the Pierre des Anglais to the Montenvers.

But the usually cautious philosopher on this occasion went out of his way to make matters worse. So unsuspicious was he of any possibility of error that he paused to congratulate himself on his demonstration. After reminding his readers that he had pointed out that the erratic blocks on the northern flank of the Alps 'have been carried there by impetuous currents descending from the heights,' he argued that it follows that on the opposite flank a similar agency had produced a similar effect, and that 'in the great flood the waters burst forth with equal fury on both sides of the chain.' He concluded:

'I know not if I am under an illusion, but it appears to me that, short of the evidence of eye-witnesses, it is impossible to imagine monuments that bear witness to and verify a fact with greater force.'

So far as the identity of the active agency on both sides of the Alps was concerned, his argument was sound, but unfortunately he was altogether mistaken as to the nature of that agency.

The Hospice of the St. Bernard was on many occasions used by de Saussure as a centre for excursions. It had the advantage of its great height; he also found there a capable and congenial companion in the Abbé Murith, at one time Prior of the convent, and afterwards Curé of Liddes. This worthy priest was the first climber of the Vélan (12,353 feet), the snowy dome which overlooks the Hospice. He would seem to have had more success on the mountains than in the management of a parish, for his sojourn at Liddes (1778-91) was marked by a succession of lawsuits. It was apparently the custom for the Curé to conduct two processions a week between Easter and Midsummer in return for which he was entitled to receive a cheese from each family of his parishioners. A number having refused their offering, Murith appealed to the law, obtained a judgment in his favour, and proceeded, perhaps rashly, to read it out from the pulpit. The aggrieved parish took its defeat ill, followed their pastor to his home, and turned him out, 'without giving him time to get his dinner, or even his hat.' Ten days later he was reinstated by the 'Baron de Preux, Governor, and the Banneret Barberini of the Dixaine of Sion.' But ecclesiastical discipline having been thus vindicated, the energetic Curé was judiciously promoted to the Priory of Martigny.

In 1779 Murith, then thirty-seven, succeeded in climbing the Vélan. No account of his expedition, except a travestied report by Bourrit, was to hand until Mr. Montagnier lighted on the following letter addressed to de Saussure :

'5th Sept. 1779.

' MONSIEUR,—After great labours, difficulties, and fatigues, I have at last succeeded in transporting myself, with thermometer, barometer, and a compass with level, to the summit of Mont Vélan by a terrible climb.

' Why did I not have you at my side ? You would have enjoyed on the 31st August the finest sight it is possible for an amateur of mountains and glaciers to imagine. You would even have been in a position to compare in a vast circle all the mountains and their different heights, from Turin to the Little St. Bernard, from Mont Blanc to the Lake of Geneva, from Vevey to the St. Gotthard, from the St. Gotthard to Turin—in a word, what would you not have seen ? But I dare not promise to give you the enjoyment of this ravishing spectacle. I had too much difficulty, despite my hardihood, myself to gain this icy colossus. . . .'

In 1781 de Saussure was taken by Murith to the Otemma Glacier in Val de Bagnes. His manuscript journal contains a careful notice, the first on record, of the veined structure of the ice, which is nowhere referred to in the *Voyages*.

In treating of the St. Bernard, de Saussure breaks his usual practice in order to give a historical sketch of the monastery ; to this he adds an account of the rescue work done by the monks and a warm tribute to their arduous and self-sacrificing lives—a tribute which, coming from a Protestant source, no doubt had double weight. It seems to have been at least partly called forth by libellous attacks calculated to interfere with the monks in obtaining the subscriptions on which they in great part depended, since many of the legacies left them by pious donors in return for service rendered had lapsed after the Reformation. Amongst these were lands in diverse countries, including some in England. It is worth note that de Saussure bears explicit witness to the great service rendered by the famous dogs in tracking and discovering travellers lost in the snow, which has been treated as more or less apocryphal by some recent writers.

De Saussure found the Hospice an excellent centre for excursions, and in 1774 climbed the Chenalette and several other panoramic points of about 9000 feet in height in the range between it and the Val Ferret.[1] He also visited, both in 1767 and 1778, the Valsorey Glacier, which lies at the north-east foot of Mont Vélan, and is familiar to modern mountaineers who make use of the so-called high-level route from Chamonix to Zermatt. A basin contained by two of its tributaries was formerly filled by a lake known as the Gouille à Vassu, the waters of which periodically broke loose and caused inundations in the lower valley.

De Saussure suggests that these outbreaks were due to the subglacial streams which drained the lake becoming frozen in winter and their channels blocked, so that the meltings of the upper slopes accumulated in spring in the basin until a fresh issue was suddenly forced.

It must have been on one of the tours summarised in this *Voyage* that de Saussure stayed with another clerical friend, J. M. Clément, the Vicaire of Val d'Illiez, who was, in 1784, the first to climb the Dent du Midi. The worthy Vicaire was not only a mountaineer, but a naturalist and book-collector, and the walls of his guest-chamber were lined with some eight hundred volumes. When during de Saussure's visit a shelf collapsed on his bed, his host excused himself on the ground that since it was the weight of the copy of the *Voyages*, which de Saussure had

[1] During these excursions he observed, and was at a loss to account for, a sheet of highly polished rock marked with striations, mentioned also in King's *Italian Valleys of the Alps*. He also noted the occurrence of veins of limestone cutting at a right angle the strata of quartz.

presented to him in a handsome binding, that had caused the accident, it must be laid to the charge ' of the frightful luxury of you Genevese.' De Saussure comments thus on the scene: ' Comme je fus grondé par ce bon ecclésiastique et quel plaisir me fit cette scène, digne de la plume de Sterne et du pinceau d'Hogarth.'[1] Clément must have been a most attractive character. His friend the Doyen Bridel describes him thus:

'A discreet and modest priest, a benefactor of the poor and the rich, a trusty and disinterested friend, an indefatigable worker, he earned the esteem and regret of all who knew him. His library, the richest in Vallais, specially in natural history and languages, was all he possessed, and his only pleasure.'

The last group of tours—the only one mainly in the Swiss Alps dealt with in the *Voyages*—is introduced by de Saussure in the following terms:[2]

' My third journey, which includes the crossing of the Alps by the Gries, the Grimsel, and the Furca del Bosco, seems to me, I must confess, interesting as a whole, at any rate for those who are in the least curious as to the natural history of mountains.

' These great mountain ranges of granite, whether solid or foliated, of which I have studied the structure with the greatest care, the magnificent horizontal beds of the veined granites of St. Roch, the great and singular exfoliations of these granites, the progressive change in the nature of their upper beds arising from their more recent date, seem to me facts of the greatest importance for the Theory.

' And readers who have no taste for geology will, I trust, read with pleasure of the source of the Rhône, its glacier, that of the Gries, and the other grand and beautiful scenes presented by nature in this savage and little-known region.

' As to the Theory, I have in this volume followed the same method as in the preceding ones: I have laid down principles as I observed the facts which seemed to me to establish them. But of a complete system I suspend any publication. I wait in order to make the observations I have planned and of which I have need in order to decide questions which seem to me still problematic. 20th November 1795.'

In truth, as a careful reader will note, de Saussure thinks as well as observes as he proceeds. He not infrequently makes, almost as an aside, some important scientific induction.

[1] Wolf's *Biographien zur Kulturgeschichte der Schweiz*, vol. iii. (Zurich, 1858).
[2] Preface to vol. iii.

De Saussure, who, in order to verify and complete his observations, was very apt to return to sites already visited in place of breaking new ground, paid repeated visits to the Gries, Grimsel, and St. Gotthard. The fame of this portion of the Alpine range as the source of the great rivers of Central Europe would seem to have drawn him to it and prevented him from turning his steps to other regions, such as the Grisons or the South-western Alps.[1]

There was up to this time a lingering belief—derived from Roman times—that the Summae Alpes of the old writers must deserve their name. As to the relative height of the individual Alpine summits, there was also very considerable doubt. The height of Mont Blanc, it is true, had been ascertained with approximate accuracy, but its supremacy was still vigorously contested. The rivals put forward by Swiss observers were the Schreckhorn (until the superior height of the Finsteraarhorn had been recognised) and certain vaguely indicated summits in the St. Gotthard group.[2]

The claim thus set up gave de Saussure an active interest in investigating this portion of the chain.

In 1775 he wrote to Haller for an itinerary of a tour east of the St. Gotthard among the sources of the Rhine. Haller discouraged any attempt to reach the Hinter Rhein Thal by a more direct route than the San Bernardino. The passage of the 'Monte Avicula,' the Rheinwald group, he wrote, was impracticable; such a short cut would be full of interest, no doubt, but 'you are a citizen and a married man, and mere curiosity ought not to lead you to expose yourself in order to see snow and ice.'

De Saussure acted on this prudent advice, and, in fact, no direct pass from Val Blenio to the Hinter Rhein was made until late in the nineteenth century. De Saussure did not even follow Haller's recommendation to cross the San Bernardino, but in

[1] The Rhône, the Rhine, and the Inn (representing the Danube). By counting the Ticino as a source of the Po, a fourth was added. Orographers were not very particular in early times. See also p. 7.

[2] The observer mainly responsible for this confusion was a Genevese who had a singularly chequered and unfortunate career, by name Micheli du Crest. After serving in his youth in one of the Swiss regiments in France, he was employed on the Committee entrusted with the new fortifications of Geneva. He rashly took the occasion not only to differ from, but to criticise his colleagues, and to accuse them of laying a needless burden of taxation on their fellow-citizens. Despite sundry condemnations, he persisted in his criticisms with so much acerbity that the Senate not only banished him, but condemned him to death in his

1777, when he carried out his project of visiting the Grisons, used the Splügen.

The tour round which he centres his third ' Voyage ' is that of 1783. Crossing the Col de Jaman from Vevey, he passed down the Simmenthal, noting its picturesque wooden cottages and dairy farms. Small properties, he points out, are invariably found to stand in the way of good agriculture. At Spiez, on the Lake of Thun, he embarked on a boat the crew of which was an old woman, a girl, and one man, and landed at the inn at Neuhaus. Interlaken had not yet grown from a convent and a nunnery into a tourist resort. But on the Grimsel track there were plenty of inns, good and indifferent, at Brienz, Meiringen, Guttannen, the Grimsel Hospice, Obergestelen. This is accounted for by the considerable traffic to and from Italy that then followed the Grimsel and the Gries. Most of the villagers at Guttannen spoke Italian, and the innkeeper had cut on his walls an Italian motto : ' Il passato mi castiga, il presente mi dispiace, il futuro mi spaventa,' which, de Saussure remarks, ' might have better suited an Englishman devoured by spleen.' The Handegg chalet served as a restaurant ; but the waterfall, hid in its chasm, escaped the traveller's notice. He observes the polished rocks that make the track dangerous for mules, but again they fail to suggest to him their glacial origin.

At the Grimsel Hospice the accommodation was rough, but the food good, and the innkeeper's family very hospitable. De Saussure found a guide to take him to the Aar Glaciers, the lower ends of which he explored pretty thoroughly. They were already among the recognised sights of the Oberland, and often visited by the early Alpine artists. At Obergestelen de Saussure was taken ill, and the greedy innkeeper tried to turn him out of the house, so as not to lose his Sunday customers, but finally, ' by means of money, which was the real object of this villain, he was persuaded to let me stay.'

absence. Taking refuge in the Bernese territory, he fared little better from the local government, who found an excuse they thought sufficient for interning him in the castle of Aarburg as a political prisoner. Here he sought occupation in drawing a panorama of the portion of the Alps visible from his terrace in fine weather, and endeavouring to identify the summits and ascertain their heights. In neither effort was he very successful. What were the summits he wrongly identified as belonging to the St. Gotthard group, to which he assigned heights of over 16,000 and 17,000 feet, must be left uncertain.

Of the Gries a full topographic account is given, and when de Saussure gets to the Tosa Falls he allows himself a description of that splendid cataract, which, by force of accumulation of precise detail, becomes picturesque :

'This oratory is built on the edge of a cliff of 500 or 600 feet, over which the Tosa throws itself, forming the most beautifully diversified features possible. It starts by falling perpendicularly into a deep horizontal hollow in the rock resembling an immense shell, from which the water rebounds to a great height in jets of admirable beauty and volume. All these streams fall back on to a protruding crag, which they envelope, forming a cylindrical column of water which breaks upon rocks inclined and coloured like those of the Grimsel, and ends by sliding over them in an infinity of diverging and varying sheets.' [*Voyages*, 1742.]

I add another picture from this noble valley :

'The Tosa suddenly throws itself with a terrible roar into a chasm, along which the path follows it. As we approached, a dense mist rose out of the gulf, hiding the path we had to follow and appearing like the smoke of a great caldron, while the falling torrent represented the boiling contents. A pine wood, dark and thick, which clothed the approach to this ravine, rendered its aspect more alarming. It is new and extraordinary spectacles of this sort, such unlooked-for incidents, which lend its indescribable charm to travel among the great mountains and make those who have once enjoyed them unable any longer to endure the monotony of the plains.' [*Voyages*, 1746.]

At Formazza he found

'the inn in the Italian style, rooms crowded with images, but at least well whitewashed, and far more cleanliness and friendliness than in the Upper Vallais. As a rule the houses are larger and better built, and the peasantry appear in much better circumstances.' [*Voyages*, 1744.]

The beauty of the lower Val Formazza made a deep impression on de Saussure, who could appreciate romantic scenery, even though he missed in it the classical grace of a Claude or a Poussin landscape.

'It does not offer, like the Vale of Chamonix, the great spectacle of glaciers, but in its place has a softer and more pastoral air ; its crags, mixed with fields and forests, have no rude or savage features. The valley is sprinkled with hamlets whose neat white houses have a charming effect set in the rich verdure which carpets its slopes, and every here and there little rocky hillocks, covered with branching larches, suggest a sacred grove, in the middle of which one looks for an altar or a statue.'

From Crodo in Val Formazza, de Saussure made in 1775 a plunge across the mountains by an unfrequented track to the head of Lago Maggiore. His route lay over a rough pass known as the Furca del Bosco, and down Val di Bosco, a side glen of Val Maggia. At Cerentino, its principal village, he passed the night, and met with quarters characteristic of this region. The house externally was uninviting, but within he found to his surprise the table laid with silver and his bed provided with damask sheets. The peasants of this region frequently emigrate, make small fortunes abroad, chiefly in South America, and return to live in their native villages, where they build large houses their neighbours call *palazzi*, and find it a pleasant variety to take in the rare passing traveller.

At Cevio, where de Saussure entered the main valley, he records an amusing encounter.

While taking an observation to ascertain the height of the place above the sea, he was greeted and invited to enter by the *bailli* or chief magistrate of Val Maggia. He gives the following account of the interview which followed :

'It being some time,' writes de Saussure, 'since I had had any news from the civilised world, I accepted the invitation, hoping to learn some. What was my surprise when the *bailli* told me that though it was long since he had a letter from the other side of the Alps, he should be happy to give an answer to any inquiry I might wish to make. At the same time he showed me an old black seal, and this was the oracle which answered all his questions. He held in his hand a string, to the end of which the seal was attached, and he dangled the seal thus fastened in the centre of a drinking-glass. Little by little the trembling of the hand communicated to the thread and seal a motion which made the latter strike against the sides of the glass. The number of the blows indicated the answer to the question which the person who held the string had in his mind. He assured me, with the seriousness of profound conviction, that he knew by this means not only everything that was going on at home, but also the elections for the Council of Basle, and the number of votes each candidate had obtained. He questioned me on the object of my travels, and after having learnt it, showed me in his almanac the age which common chronology gives the world, and asked me what I thought about it. I told him that my observations of mountains had led me to look on the world as somewhat older. "Ah," he answered with an air of triumph, "my seal had already told me so, because the other day I had the patience to count the blows while reflecting on the world's age, and I found it was four years older than it is set down in this almanac."' [*Voyages*, 1782]

From Cevio de Saussure took the road through the deep trench of the lower Val Maggia to Locarno, thus missing by a mile or two one of the most exquisite spots in the Italian Alps, Bignasco. This village, a cluster of a few houses, is situated at the junction of the two glens that unite to form the main Val Maggia. One of the happiest of my Alpine memories is of a day spent there in 1864, when there was no regular inn, but guests were received, as in de Saussure's time, in a private house that stands between the two torrents. From its upper windows the eyes look up the long vista of Val Bavona over a foreground of trellised vineyards, through receding distances of granite cliffs and forested bluffs, to the snows of the Basodino. At one's feet arched bridges span two amazingly clear and blue torrents, linking banks draped in chestnut and birch groves and carpeted with bushes of Alpine rhododendron, here growing among the vines and far below its usual level.

On an earlier passage of the Gries de Saussure had descended past Domo d'Ossola to Lago Maggiore. He pronounces what most travellers who do not aim at singularity in taste will consider a just verdict on the Isola Bella. The formal garden, he admits, has gone out of fashion, yet even those who prefer, as a rule, nature less lavishly adorned may, he suggests, here make an exception. He confesses to have found singular pleasure in wandering round the shady laurel groves and statued terraces of oranges and lemons, and enjoying the exquisite views of the lake and mountains that open on all sides of Count Borromeo's superb fantasy.

From Locarno de Saussure took the road of the St. Gotthard through Bellinzona.[1] At Airolo, the village at the southern foot of the pass, he on two occasions made some stay. On his second visit (1783) he was sorry not to find the crystal-hunter who had

[1] On the Grimsel-Gries road there was no lack of inns: on the St. Gotthard, those at Bellinzona, Airolo, and Andermatt are noted as good; at Dazio Grande, Giornico, Göschenen, and Flüelen there was passable accommodation.

served as his guide eight years previously. The poor man, he tells us, had gone out with his children to collect wild hay, and had told them to start home with their burden and that he would soon follow. He failed to do so, and when sought for was found lying dead with his hands crossed on his chest as if in peaceable sleep. De Saussure comments:

'A hard-working and good life ending in so gentle a death, in an attitude which seemed to indicate that, feeling his powers failing, he had addressed to Heaven his last looks and his last thoughts, had inspired in the village a kind of reverence for his memory.' [*Voyages*, 1806.]

De Saussure made it his first business on reaching Airolo to climb to a height on the southern side of Val Leventina whence he would get a general view of the peaks round the St. Gotthard Pass. He recognised at once that there was no peak rivalling Mont Blanc or the Oberland summits, and correctly estimated that the 'Gletscherberg,' north of the Furka (probably the Galenstock), the loftiest, did not reach 12,000 feet. This discovery, de Saussure says, 'somewhat diminished his respect for the St. Gotthard.'

Some letters written to his wife in 1777 and 1783 give a lively picture of travel at that date:

'The situation of Airolo,' de Saussure writes, 'is unique for a naturalist, surrounded by very high mountains, almost all accessible through a smiling valley inhabited by a friendly population which understands rocks, and provided with a very good inn, managed by zealous and polite hosts, excellent air, good water, and delicious salmon trout.

'I am very pleased with Joseph (his servant); he has charming manners and is very attentive. He does not love and climb rocks as well as I do, but it is unreasonable to ask this of a man not born in the Alps; still he is much better in these respects than Charles [his predecessor]. He looks so well in his blue uniform, which we told him to wear on the journey, that yesterday, when I was dining with an Italian shopkeeper, and Joseph at another table at the bottom of the room, the shopkeeper thought he was an officer who was too proud to dine with us, and formed a great respect for me when he learnt he was my servant.'

The Capuchins of the St. Gotthard Hospice de Saussure found hospitable enough, though men of a far less intelligent type than the monks of the St. Bernard. After de Saussure's first visit they told his Bernese friend Wyttenbach that he seemed a worthy man, but that it was a misfortune he should suffer from a ridiculous mania for picking up all the stones he met with, filling his pockets, and loading his mules with them. He describes the Hospice:

'After leaving Airolo I came with much boredom and disgust to sleep at the Hospice of the Capuchins. You know how I hate monks! To make matters worse, two more Capuchins on their travels arrived, with whom we had to sup. We sat down at the same table, four Capuchins, two tailors, a mason, Joseph, and myself. They served us, with many polite speeches, a detestable supper. Next morning (yesterday) I thought I should hang myself when on getting up I saw the mountain covered with snow, and feared I should be forced to spend one or two days in this wretched place, where I had come only to be near the high summits. But at last, about nine, the clouds broke, and I climbed very briskly one of the loftiest peaks on which I have ever been and took my observations in the finest possible weather! I returned to the Capuchins to eat soup made of boiled veal and the veal that had been boiled in the soup, and started at once to descend to Urseren, whence I sent back my mules to Chamonix.'

The summit lying west of the pass reached by de Saussure on this occasion, to which he gives the name of the Fient, was undoubtedly that called in *The Alpine Guide*, La Fibbia, 8997 feet, though de Saussure applies the latter name to a more distant and loftier snow-peak he reckoned some 1500 feet higher. Despite the description given by his guide Lombardo, 'who represented the difficulties and dangers of the ascent with all the emphasis of his mother-tongue,' the climb proved easy enough. On his return to the Hospice, de Saussure found that an unprecedented event had taken place. An English traveller had arrived in his cabriolet. The St. Gotthard track at this time was fairly broad and paved with large slabs, and de Saussure was informed that on an average 1000 laden horses crossed it daily! But it was not held practicable for wheels. The eccentric Englishman was Charles Greville, on his way to visit his uncle, Sir William Hamilton, at Naples. His 'fantasy,' which we learn cost him eighteen louis, was successfully accomplished. Greville in the *Voyages* is politely qualified as a 'celebrated mineralogist,' but in his letters home de Saussure describes him more accurately as an 'amateur of natural history.' He was also an amateur of beauty, and his chief title to fame is having been the protector and educator of the famous lady who became his aunt. De Saussure found him

'ready to talk rocks: at first I was afraid he wanted to get the benefit of my observations, but I found with a pleasure which was perhaps ignoble that he was not a serious student and did not attempt to generalise. He was on the look-out for curious specimens for his collection, without any consideration for grouping them. I recognised that he was in no sense a formidable rival.'

On a second visit to the St. Gotthard, de Saussure climbed the Prosa (8983 feet), a peak east of the Hospice. It was fairly steep and regarded by the Capuchins as inaccessible. He found a dead cow at its foot, and remarks that, though this animal is not 'a symbol of agility, there are few naturalists of the plain who would care to follow wherever an Alpine cow led.' For himself, on this occasion he found no difficulty.

From Andermatt de Saussure visited the lake on the Oberalp Pass, one of the sources of the Vorder Rhein. The fishery of the lake was let to the hotel-keeper at Andermatt for 900 francs for ten years.

The descent to Altdorf interested de Saussure deeply as a geologist. He found on the St. Gotthard far better opportunities of studying the features of granitic rocks than even in the chain of Mont Blanc. He satisfied himself that they were stratified, and that the strata were in many instances vertical. He came to the conclusion that the cause of the dislocation and contortion of the rocks was not internal explosions, but compression. He records his conviction that his observations would be verified even where they were controverted by 'Buffon and other constructors of systems.' In another branch of his work he was less satisfied. Writing to his wife, he regrets that he does not yet get on well with his attempts at sketching:

'It is a terrible task,' he says, 'to draw a mountain in its detail, to make it all come out clearly, so that the beds and the joints do not look flat—that it does not resemble a split board. Oh, this is really difficult! Still, I struggle on, and by degrees I shall end by making intelligible sketches of the St. Gotthard, which is the most important point. For you, my good angel, you always have the same success in making your little ladies who fan themselves at the foot of a tree with a shepherd on his knees, who offers them a nosegay. Such a group would make an agreeable foreground for my mountains, and perhaps I shall ask you to make me one, but you must find something less civilised than a fan, for the shepherdesses of the Grimsel and the Upper Valais are very far from using fans. . . .'

The drawings here referred to must, I think, be the originals of the two illustrations of the gorge of Schöllenen in vol. iv. of the *Voyages,* which have no artist's name attached to them. If this be so, de Saussure was obviously right in recognising that his artistic powers were limited. The rocks represented in these woodcuts are such as we associate with the theatre rather than with nature.

At Altdorf de Saussure was welcomed by M. Müller, a former Landamman of Uri, whose large and luxuriously appointed house seemed to him out of place in the little mountain town. The Genevese traveller's republican sentiment was stirred at finding himself in the cradle of freedom, and he grows eloquent on the virtue of the heroes of the Forest Cantons. Of the Tell legend he expresses no doubt, though it had already been prematurely called in question by an audacious Bernese writer, who had suffered prosecution for his unpatriotic scepticism. The high political morality of the Landesgemeinde, or popular assembly, he illustrates by an entertaining anecdote. The wealthier members of the community were compelled by law to lend a part of their capital at a fixed rate of interest to their less well-to-do neighbours. Some local radicals, quoting Scripture to prove that this was wicked usury, and therefore contrary to sound religion, proposed that the interest hitherto paid should be counted as instalments towards the repayment of the original debt. The popular assembly not only rejected the proposal with scorn, but permanently disenfranchised those who had made themselves responsible for it.

De Saussure rowed in eight hours from Flüelen to Lucerne, but he finds little to say of the scenery of the lake ; the structure of the neighbouring mountains, and particularly of the Rigi (which he did not climb), was what interested him. At Lucerne he was on several occasions the guest of M. Pfyffer, an ex-officer of a Swiss regiment serving in France, who spent most of his leisure in constructing a model on a large scale of this part of the

Central Alps. There were no accurate maps to serve as bases, and the task therefore was one of great difficulty and labour. M. Pfyffer is said, while engaged on it, to have camped out and lived on the milk of goats he took with him. He often, de Saussure tells us, risked being attacked by peasants, suspicious, like all primitive people, that any survey meant interference with their property or their rights. His relief, if technically inexact, must have had considerable merits, since de Saussure goes so far as to say that its inspection gave him pleasure comparable to that he had enjoyed from the panoramas of the Crammont and Mont Blanc.

At a later date (1791) de Saussure travelled to Aarau to inspect another work of the same kind due to the enterprise of M. Meyer, a ribbon manufacturer of that town. It occurred to this enterprising tradesman to produce ribbons on which should be woven the forms of the mountains of his native land. For this purpose he had models made of some parts of the snowy range. Their success encouraged him to attempt to represent 'all the mountains of Switzerland.' He found in M. Weiss a geographer capable of undertaking the task, and de Saussure in his last volume (published 1796) expresses a hope that a model, some 15 feet by 8 feet, of the Alps from the Lake of Constance to Mont Blanc would be completed shortly. It was from M. Pfyffer and M. Weiss that de Saussure first heard the report that the Schreckhorn was possibly higher than Mont Blanc.

In 1784 de Saussure returned to the scene of his early scrambles, the base of the Chamonix Aiguilles, spending three nights in a chalet at the Plan de l'Aiguille in order to explore more fully their cliffs and glaciers. In so doing he met with what seems to have been his nearest approach to a mountaineering accident. His description of it is a good example of direct and simple narrative, stripped of emotion, but not of humour.

De Saussure, accompanied by his favourite, Pierre Balmat, and another guide, had been geologising at the base of the Aiguille du Midi. It was nearly 2 P.M. when they turned, apparently unroped, to descend the glacier, the surface of which was covered with snow, now softened by the midday sunshine.

'Suddenly the snow gave way under both my feet at once; the right, which was behind, rested on nothing, but the left had still some support, and I found myself half seated and half astride on the snow. At the same moment Pierre, who was close behind me, fell also in almost the same position. He at once cried out to me as loudly and imperatively as he could, "Don't stir, Monsieur—don't make the least movement." I recognised that we were over a crevasse, and that any inopportune exertion might break the snow which still supported us. The other guide, who was one or two paces in front, and who had not fallen, remained planted where he stood. Pierre, without himself moving, cried out to him to ascertain the direction of the crevasse and of its least breadth ; interrupting himself at every instant to beg me not to move. I assured him I would remain motionless, that I was quite calm, and that he had nothing to do but to join me in considering with as little emotion as possible the best way to get out of our difficulty. I saw it was needful to give these assurances, because the two guides were in such a state of nervousness that I was afraid they would lose their heads. We came to the conclusion that the line we were taking had been at right angles to the crevasse, and the fact that my left foot had support, while my right found none, confirmed me in this. As for Pierre, his two feet were both in the air, the snow had even given way between his legs, and through the opening he saw beneath himself and me the void and the green depths of the crevasse. Our actual situation made clear, he placed in front of me the two crossed sticks and I threw myself on them, Pierre in turn did the same, and we thus both happily escaped from our "mauvais pas." As for the second guide, he remained where he stood, without holding out a hand to one or other of us ; and it is true we had not asked him. But he told us afterwards very quietly that he had reflected that if Pierre and I fell into the crevasse, it would be as well that he should remain clear of it to get us out.' [*Voyages*, 675.]

We have now run through the mountain tours of the period with which we are dealing (1774-84) that are recorded or summarised in the *Voyages*. The mountaineer of the present day may be struck by the frequent returns to old ground, the absence of any passion for exploration, or any evidence of the pursuit of scenery for its own sake. He will note the lack of any descriptions of the beauties of the Bernese Oberland, the splendour of the Jungfrau seen from the Wengern Alp, the noble landscape of the Vale of Grindelwald, or the woodland glades of Rosenlaui. That in his published works de Saussure makes such scanty reference to his travels in this district may possibly point to a scruple on his part in trespassing on the field of his friends Haller and Wyttenbach. But in other parts of the Alps no such reason can be alleged. In after years we shall find that the Gorner Glacier and the great ring of peaks round Zermatt, the scenery of the Vispthal and of Val d'Aosta call forth no expressions of enthusiasm. The Matterhorn draws but one short descriptive sentence from its literary discoverer. Either de Saussure had little eye for landscape, except as a key to geological problems, or, as is more probable, he deliberately abstained from interrupting his geological notes by picturesque word-pictures. That he was capable of appreciating the more romantic aspects of nature is shown by his description of the sunsets seen on the Col du Géant, and from the base of the Aiguille du Goûter. But such indulgences to his readers were reserved for rare occasions and granted only under extreme provocation.

The *Voyages*, as I have indicated, record only a portion of de Saussure's Alpine experiences. There were other tours, and of one of the most notable, that of 1777, de Saussure's manuscript journal has happily been preserved. It records at some length his excursions in the Bernese Oberland, but is unfortunately meagre as to the return through the Grisons. De Saussure's first object was apparently to investigate the reputed rival of Mont Blanc—the Schreckhorn. He accepted the popular derivation and meaning of its name—the Peak of Terror.[1]

In 1777 de Saussure commenced his tour of the Oberland at Lauterbrunnen. In that village he could get no guide but a lad too young even to act as porter, so he sent his servant with the luggage round by road while he walked over the Wengern Alp.

[1] The occasion tempts me to insert a few lines on the mountain nomenclature of the Bernese Oberland. It is obvious that at least in one group the names attributed to the peaks show an imagination hardly found elsewhere in the Alps. The peasant, as a rule, fixes on some obvious characteristic: colour—the Red Horn or the White Horn; or shape—the Broad Horn, the Upright Needle (the Dru, corrupted at an early date into Aiguille du Dru); or situation—the Aiguille d'Envers (the Needle at the Back), corrupted into Aiguille Verte. Bordier (p. 198) in 1773 wrote of 'le Dru.' This was probably the original local form. The first instance of the substitution of Aiguille Verte for Aiguille d'Argentière that I have come across is in 1786, in the manuscript journal of an Englishman named Brand. See Mr. Coolidge's paper on the peak names in the Mont Blanc district in the *Annuaire du Club Alpin Suisse*, vol. 38. But in the range above the Vale of Lauterbrunnen we find the Jungfrau (the Virgin) supported as in an altar-piece by the Black and White Monks, while the Eiger stands in attendance on them like a giant St. Christopher. These are the summits visible from Interlaken, and there can be little doubt that their names are due to the poetical imagination of the inmates of the two religious houses long established there. The remaining peaks of the Oberland bear names of the usual obvious character— the Wetterhorn (the Peak of Storms), round which the clouds gather, the Finster-

At Grindelwald at this date travellers, as was so often the case in remote parts of the Alps fifty years ago, were still entertained as 'paying guests' by the pastor, or priest. De Saussure found some difficulty in explaining to the guide provided for him that he wanted not 'to visit the glaciers,' as was already the fashion, but to get a near view of the Schreckhorn—the reputed rival of Mont Blanc. The guide led his traveller up the slopes in the direction of the Great Scheideck, whence the top of the Schreckhorn may be seen behind the mass of the Mettenberg. This was not at all what de Saussure wanted, and he insisted on returning. When near the village his guide gave him a choice between the easy path to the foot of the Lower Glacier, used by tourists, and a long and, by his account, perilous one leading to the source of the glacier, whence he asserted the Schreckhorn would not be visible. De Saussure, however, trusting to his map, and distrusting his informant, decided to risk the venture. As usual, he had his servant with him.

I quote extracts from the detailed account of this excursion given in de Saussure's manuscript journal:

'I began to climb through a pine wood up a very steep but perfectly safe path. After ascending through the wood for three-quarters of an hour, we came to the foot of a limestone crag with thick beds and began to turn to the west (the right) and take the traverse on the edge of the precipices. For ten minutes or so one has a pine wood under one's feet, and there is consequently no danger, but beyond the forest one begins to see the great drop there is to the glacier underfoot, whose broken waves seem designed to mutilate the

aarhorn, at the source of the Aar, the Fiescherhörner, the peaks behind which lies Fiesch. I may surprise most of my readers if I add the Schreckhorn to this list; for its name has hitherto been universally interpreted as the Peak of Terror. It had long struck me as curious that a peak which from the basin of Grindelwald is far from a conspicuous object should have acquired such a name from an unimaginative peasantry; so that I was not surprised when in an article describing the Bregenzer Wald I lighted on a sentence which appears to furnish a very plausible alternative derivation. This is the passage:

'Schröchen.—Oh, the lovely village; and how poor the etymological jest which would derive the name of this charming spot from a word meaning terror! In the Bregenzer Wald district Schröchen signifies a rocky bluff, and this is far more likely to be the true derivation.' (*Annuaire du Club Alpin Français*, vol. 29.)

I find that the first author to treat in detail of the mountains of the Bernese Oberland, Thomas Schöpf (*circa* 1570), writes of the 'Schreckshorn (*sic*), quae vox sonaret obliquum cornu, vel terribile cornu. Utrumque verò nomen huic monti convenientissimè quadrat': thus supporting my conjecture. See Coolidge's *Josias Simler*, p. 250*.

unhappy man who should fall on them. Still the path is firm and smooth, and the slope towards the cliff is not so steep but that if unlucky enough to slip one might hope to stop oneself. But here and there the path narrows, passes across rocky slabs, and the abruptness of the slope no longer leaves any hope of recovering a false step. At each bad place of this sort we asked the guide if it was the worst. He answered, "This is nothing; what is to come is a hundred times worse." At this juncture we met an old shepherd who for forty years had guarded the sheep and goats, the only animals which can penetrate into those recesses, forbidden to all creatures which have not good heads and sure feet. I had been told of this shepherd, and as our guide seemed quite a novice, I begged the shepherd to turn back with us and act as leader. He was on his way down to Grindelwald with a load of goats' milk, and he did not like turning back; still he made up his mind to do so, hid his milk behind a rock, and came with us.

'About the middle of the bad path we found in a hollow a small spring which fell from the rocks and had worn itself a basin at their feet, in which the water was so clear and beautiful that the spot tempted us to rest and recover our force. After some twenty minutes we set out and had another three-quarters of an hour on this path, which at times became very risky, but there was always foothold, and the anticipation I had formed made me find the reality quite tolerable. At last we reached the level of the more gently sloping portion of the glacier. It was now necessary to scramble on to it and traverse it to the end of the ice valley where our shepherd's hut was. In order to get on the glacier, we had to climb on to the ridge of an enormous rib of ice which had horribly precipitous sides. The old shepherd seized an axe which he was in the habit of leaving there for the purpose and began cutting steps along the ridge. While waiting I looked to see if there was any way of avoiding this awkward passage, but in vain—everywhere else bottomless crevasses cut us off from the glacier. This isthmus was the only bridge there was between us and the Mer de Glace. I let, therefore, the shepherd finish his staircase. That accomplished, he gallantly offered me his hand, and I marched with firm steps—for in places of this kind one must either not go at all or advance boldly—and so reached the level of the glacier.

'We had still on the ice several places not so bad as this but not quite without risk, then the rest of the way was perfectly easy. The glacier, though steep, had no more crevasses. It was covered with blocks of primitive rocks, among which I did not see a single bit of limestone, but everywhere fragments mixed with *schistes d'amiante*, quartz, etc., none of which approached what I collected on the Glacier de Miage.

'What gave me most pleasure was that, as we advanced on the ice, I began to see behind the Mettenberg a very lofty peak, and it entered my mind that it might be the so-much-sought Schreckhorn. I asked my guide its name, but he could not understand. He thought I was talking all the time of the Mettenberg. He told long stories of sheep lost on the mountains, of shepherds overwhelmed by avalanches; he exhausted my patience, until at last, as the peak gradually revealed itself, he saw what I wanted him to see, and said as if I ought to have known, "That is the Schreckhorn."

'I walked on gaily and as quickly as I could in order to have plenty of time to examine it before the clouds, which I saw gathering behind us on the side of the plains, came up and covered it. Despite my efforts, it took us an hour to cross the glacier, and a quarter of an hour more to the wretched hut of the shepherd, which was opposite the peak and almost as near as it was possible to get.

'Picture to yourself one of the faces of an immense pyramid, of which the top, though more than a league distant, rises 33 degrees above the horizon, and of which the edges fall one to the north-west, reposing on the top of the Mettenberg, itself from the valley of Grindelwald of a prodigious height, another still sharper, on the, south-west, falling towards the Bierselberg and Fiescherberg ridges. These ridges are broken. . . . The summit is not sharp, but blunt, and the face opposite us a precipice of a thousand to fifteen hundred feet. Through glasses the stratification appeared to me to be vertical.

'After having noted what seemed to me most interesting in this noble mountain, I turned to study the other heights by which I was surrounded. The rock called the Zäsenberg, on which I stood, was like an island between two great glaciers. Its base is clothed with pasture which feeds sheep and goats. Behind it and above it rises the Fiescherberg. Its summit is nearly horizontal, a little concave on one side, and covered with snow which juts out like the eaves of a roof.'

De Saussure's return to the valley was hastened by a sign of bad weather he was quick to interpret—a light cloud that, as it passed across the sun, assumed rainbow hues. He got back just in time to escape a violent storm.[1]

[1] This incident is recorded in his volume, *Essais sur l'Hygromètre*, 1783, p. 359. De Saussure further notes in the same connection the beautiful effects caused at sunset (or sunrise) by a wind from behind a mountain, itself in shadow, blowing off it a cloud of frozen snow which crowns the summit ridges with a bright red halo. This is most often seen in winter.

From Grindelwald de Saussure crossed the Great Scheideck and took the now familiar route over the Grimsel and the Gries to the Italian Lakes. After calling on the celebrated electrical inventor Volta at Como, he crossed the Splügen and travelled by the Via Mala, Chur, and Wallenstadt to Zurich and Berne, where he paid a visit to Haller, whose health was fast failing. For the latter part of the tour the journal is little more than a skeleton and contains nothing of interest.

While the first volume of the *Voyages* was going through the press in 1779, de Saussure received from Berne an offer for its translation into German from a man who during most of his life had been the pastor of one of the churches in that city. Jakob Samuel Wyttenbach had been associated with Haller in his publications on the Bernese Oberland, and had already translated and commented on portions of Deluc's Travels. After Haller's death, Wyttenbach, if he had no claim to the European reputation of his predecessor, took his place to a great extent as a source of information for the many travellers who were now turning their minds to the Alps, and as a link between the various observers who were working in various parts of Switzerland to promote a better knowledge of the mountains and their phenomena.[1] Large extracts from his voluminous correspondence have been published by Dr. Dübi, who has shown that Wyttenbach was the channel through which Baron de Gersdorf, the eye-witness of the first ascent of Mont Blanc, mainly carried on his communications with Chamonix and Geneva.

De Saussure, while protesting that Wyttenbach would employ his time to better purpose in composing an original work on the mountains, gratefully accepted the offer of so competent a translator, and the first two volumes of the *Voyages* appeared in four in German, published at Leipzig in 1781 and 1786. It appears, however, that Wyttenbach in the end acted rather as the supervisor than the actual translator,[2] who was probably a lady geologist, a Mlle. Müller, who is mentioned in the correspondence of the time.

It is interesting among Wyttenbach's letters to find several

[1] In 1776 he supplied the text accompanying Wagner's views in the Bernese Oberland. In 1787 he published a small volume entitled, *Instruction pour les Voyageurs qui vont voir les Glaciers et les Alpes du Canton de Berne*.
[2] See de Saussure to Wyttenbach, 9th November 1781. Dübi's *Jakob Samuel Wyttenbach und seine Freunde* (Berne, 1910).

from the worthy monk of Disentis, Placidus a Spescha, who, as has been pointed out, was, next to de Saussure, the most conspicuous figure in the mountaineering annals of the eighteenth century, and as a climber the first man of his time. Tardy justice has lately been done by his fellow-countrymen to one of the most remarkable among Alpine pioneers in a full and handsome biography.[1]

In 1792 Spescha was anxious to learn the result of de Saussure's first visit to Monte Rosa, whether he had proved it to be higher than Mont Blanc, and if he had written anything on the mountains of the Grisons ? As far as we know, de Saussure never heard of his rival's exploits. No mention of Spescha occurs in his works or in any of his papers that have come to my notice. It is a pity the two men never met; for if the good monk had but scanty scientific knowledge, he showed a very considerable talent for orography, and his maps contrast favourably with those constructed for the Genevese savant.

In the summer of 1776 Sir George Shuckburgh, then lately elected a Fellow of the Royal Society, proposed to de Saussure to accompany him in an excursion to the Môle. Shuckburgh was anxious to test previous measurements of the height of Mont Blanc, and specially those of the Delucs, and had brought from England for the purpose a number of the best instruments available. He writes: 'Mr. de Saussure, a very ingenious gentleman of this place, and well skilled in various parts of natural and experimental philosophy, gave me all the information necessary, and obligingly promised to accompany me, as did also Mr. Trembley.'

The party set out from St. Jeoire, a town at the foot of the Môle, with a large company of porters charged with their instruments, but presently lost the way in a mist, even de Saussure, who had been seven or eight times on the mountain, being at a loss. Arrived on the summit, Shuckburgh describes his sensations thus:

'I perceived myself elevated about 6000 feet in the atmosphere, and standing, as it were, on a knife-edge, for such is the figure of the ridge or top of this mountain; length without breadth, or the least appearance of a plain, as I had expected to find. Before me an im-

---

[1] See my article on Spescha (*Alpine Journal*, vol. x.) and the large volume dealing with his life and activities published at Berne in 1913, *Pater Placidus a Spescha, sein Leben und seine Schriften.*

mediate precipice, *à pic*, of above 1000 feet, and behind me the very steep ascent I had just surmounted. I was imprudently the first of the company: the surprise was perfect horror, and two steps further had sent me headlong from the rock.'

In 1777 Shuckburgh published the result of his observations in the *Philosophical Transactions of the Royal Society*. The figure obtained by his triangulation was 4787 metres (15,705 feet). De Saussure, by calculating his barometrical observations by four different methods and taking the mean of them as his result, succeeded, somewhat ingeniously, in arriving at about the same figure, 2450 toises (15,667 feet).

It may be of interest if I run over here some of the earlier endeavours to determine the height of Mont Blanc. The first attempt to measure 'the Hill called Cursed' was made by Nicolas Fatio de Duillier, and is thus recorded by Gilbert Burnet:[2]

'The hill not far from Geneva called Maudit or Cursed, of which one-third is always covered with snow, is two miles of perpendicular height, according to the observation of that incomparable Mathematician and Philosopher, Nicolas Fatio Duillier, who at twenty-two years of age is already one of the greatest men of his age, and seems to be born to carry learning some sizes beyond what it has yet attained.'

Fatio made the height 2000 toises above the Lake of Geneva, or 15,268 feet above sea-level. Nicolas Fatio was a Fellow of the Royal Society. The next reference to hypsometry in its annals is interesting as an indication of the rudimentary state of the science in the earlier part of the eighteenth century. It is in the form of an article by J. D. Scheuchzer, a son of J. J. Scheuchzer, the author of the 'Ουρεσιφοίτης *Helveticus*.'

The writer preludes as follows:[3] 'The height of mountains and their elevation above the sea-level has been at all times thought worthy of the attention of inquisitive philosophers.' He then proceeds to refer to the fact that 'certain Greek philo-

[1] See *Phil. Trans. of the Royal Society*, vol. lxvii. p. 592.

[2] *Letters containing an account of what seemed most remarkable in Italy, Switzerland, etc.* (Rotterdam, 1686). Fatio's measurement is also referred to in a work, *Astro-Theology*, by W. Derham (London, 1715), and in Spon's *History of Geneva*, vol. ii. (Geneva, 1730). The later volume contains an article by N. Fatio's brother, J. C. Fatio, 'Remarques faites sur l'Histoire Naturelle des Environs du Lac de Genève.'

[3] *Phil. Trans. of the Royal Society, Abridgement*, vol. vii. p. 265.

sophers who lived some time before our Saviour's Nativity fixed the perpendicular height of the highest mountains at about 10,000 feet.' Subsequent writers, he regrets, however, to have to point out, have run them up 'to an extravagant and altogether unnatural height,' owing to their preference of a trigonometrical to a barometrical method. Scheuchzer dilates at some length on the disadvantages which he believes to be incident to the former method, and firmly asserts that the mountains of Switzerland, though the highest in Europe, do not rise above 10,000 French feet.

Scheuchzer does not seem to have put his method into practice. The next observer to try his hand on Mont Blanc was Loys de Cheseaux, a Vaudois astronomer, who about 1744 obtained by trigonometry an elevation for the mountain of 2246 toises above the lake, or 15,582 feet above sea-level.[1]

Martel, the engineer, who visited Chamonix in 1742, got for Mont Blanc by a trigonometrical measurement from a base of 1536 feet in the Chamonix valley a height closely corresponding to Fatio de Duillier's. Early in the seventies, Deluc was busy with his barometrical experiments and methods for the ascertainment of heights, and combining these with trigonometrical measurements from Geneva and the Buet he obtained for Mont Blanc the height of about 15,285 feet, or some five hundred feet too low.

Dr. Paccard stated in the *Journal de Lausanne* that in 1786 he consulted his barometer on the top of Mont Blanc, but his results were valueless, and Bonnet mentions that his instrument was damaged. It is probable that some air had got into it.

There have been many slightly varying official determinations of the height of the mountain in recent years. The latest, and probably the most exact, is that of M. Joseph Vallot, based on levelling from the Mediterranean to Geneva and on a most careful triangulation. The result is 807 metres (15,771 feet), or only a few feet higher than Shuckburgh's. The height of the snow-cap probably varies by a few feet in different years and at different seasons. It may therefore fairly be claimed for Shuckburgh

[1] *Traité de la Comète*, Lausanne, 1744.

that he was the first to determine the height of Mont Blanc with approximate accuracy. He was equally fortunate in several other cases in the same neighbourhood.[1]

---

[1] See Whymper's *Guide to Chamonix and the Range of Mont Blanc*, and the *Phil. Trans. of the Royal Society*, vol. lxvii. part ii. In the *Annuaire Météorologique de France*, 1851, an interesting paper will be found, *Notice sur les Altitudes du Mont Blanc et du Mont Rose, par le Commandant Delcroz*. The author devotes several pages to de Saussure's observations. Developed according to the formula of Laplace and Delcroz's own tables, these give an altitude for the mountain of 4817·3 metres. Delcroz, however, prefers a method by which he gets a result of 4808·1 metres, practically identical with that of the Vallot brothers' triangulation.

CHAPTER VII

THE BUET

MOUNTAINEERING in Savoy began, modestly enough, with the ascent of the Buet. The story of that mountain is, in fact, a prelude to that of Mont Blanc, and it brings on the scene two characters who were intimately associated, though in different ways, with de Saussure's activities, Jean André Deluc and Marc Théodore Bourrit.

It was originally proposed that the little 'temple,' the successor to our countryman Blair's cabin on the Montenvers, that was erected in 1795 by Félix Desportes,[1] while he was the French Resident at Geneva, and dedicated by an inscription on its front 'à la Nature,' should bear on its walls the names of a number of men of science of European reputation, and among them of six distinguished Genevese, including de Saussure, Deluc, and Bourrit. It seems to me appropriate, before dealing with the crowning events of de Saussure's life as an Alpine climber, to devote a few pages to sketches of the men who were thus connected with the great naturalist, to allow them to give some account of their exploits, and, in so doing, to throw light on their very diverse characters.

Jean André was the elder son of Jacques François Deluc, by trade a watchmaker and in private life an active member of the popular party in Geneva, and the author of many religious and political tracts. Jacques François was at one time on intimate terms with Rousseau, who has left on record that he found him an intolerable bore. He was, however, held in respect in his native town, and we find him appointed to head the delegation of Représentants which in 1774 congratulated de Saussure on his proposals for educational reform. His two sons, Jean André

[1] Desportes charged Bourrit with the erection of this edifice, and gave him two thousand francs for the purpose. It was furnished with beds, a table, and a visitors' book.

and Guillaume Antoine, inherited their father's political principles, while adding to them scientific pursuits and a taste for climbing which combined to incite the brothers to attempt in 1770 the first ascent of the Buet. Two years later, owing either to his part in the political troubles of the time, or more probably to financial reverses, Jean André found it expedient to leave his native city, and establish himself in England, where he married. His scientific reputation as a meteorologist and inventor led to his being elected a Fellow of the Royal Society, while scruples as to his radical principles did not stand in the way of his accepting an appointment as Reader to Queen Charlotte. We catch a glimpse of the quaint figure of the old republican in Miss Burney's Memoirs, wandering about the Court at Windsor and subject to the gibes, or practical jokes, of the dull royal dukes. Deluc's old age was spent at or near Windsor. The last mention we have of him is a report of his enjoying the descriptions of scenery in Byron's 'Prisoner of Chillon,' and being reminded by them of his own voyage round the lake with Rousseau more than sixty years before.[1] He died in 1817 at the age of ninety, and his tombstone may be found in the churchyard at Clewer.

Jean André Deluc was a very voluminous author; but it was as a physical student and a skilful constructor of instruments that he chiefly deserves respect. Meteorology was his special field, and if he got the worst of his controversy with de Saussure on the merits of their rival hygrometers, he was acknowledged by his contemporaries to have contributed substantially to the progress of the science. But his excursions into geology and cosmology were less fortunate. The full title of his principal work may help to explain this. It states that the treatise has been designed to prove the divine mission of Moses. In short, Deluc may be said to have had Genesis on the brain. In his cosmology he postulated a convulsion in which the old continents had given place to oceans, and the old sea-beds had become dry land. Thus the story of the universal deluge was vindicated and the presence of marine fossils on the high mountains accounted for. His views were in 1778 set forth in a work of six volumes, entitled, *Lettres Physiques et Morales sur les Montagnes et sur l'Histoire de la Terre et de l'Homme*, dedicated to the Queen of Great Britain.

[1] See p. 28.

In 1762 Deluc had submitted in manuscript to the Paris Academy his *Recherches sur les Modifications de l'Atmosphère, ou Théorie des Baromètres et des Thermomètres* (published ten years later), a work which served to establish a method of ascertaining the heights of mountains by barometrical observations, and was recognised at the time as one of the best treatises on the use of instruments in meteorology. Its author claimed more for the Letters; he asserted in the preface that they supplied the outline of a treatise on nature and man's place in it. The text depicts the scenery of the Lake of Geneva and the Bernese Oberland; the descriptions are interspersed with many reflections on the advantages of a pastoral life and the virtue of Swiss peasants, obviously derived for the most part from Rousseau.

If Deluc claims our respect as a scientific worker and an Alpine traveller, he does his best in his writings to make us forget it by his attitude as a universal philosopher and a courtier. The modern reader is amused rather than instructed or edified by his books, particularly when the author is led by 'the ecstasies in which he often finds himself on the mountains' into a long assault on materialism, and then apologises in a proportionately long footnote for introducing 'discussions too far removed from the objects of attention of a Queen.' 'Queen' is in capitals![1]

To return, however, to the Buet. We may best do the Delucs justice as mountaineers by summarising the account of their first climbs which appeared in the English edition of Bourrit's work.[2]

It was in August 1765 that the two brothers started to attempt the Buet for the first time. From the neighbourhood of Geneva, Jean had observed to the north of the 'pikes in the form of obelisks' which rose in a forbidding fence round the mighty dome of Mont Blanc, a mountain whose summit, though always covered with ice, seemed to him accessible and proper for his experiments.

'He endeavoured then to inform himself of the name of this mountain, the place where it was situated, the road necessary to be taken to arrive at it, and whether or not it was to be ascended; but

---

[1] A full and appreciative account of the character and the scientific and religious writings of the brothers Deluc will be found in Sayous' *Le dixhuitième Siècle à l'Etranger*, vol. i. ch. 12.

[2] Bourrit, *Description of the Glaciers of Savoy* (English edition, Norwich, 1775).

no person could be found that knew it, nor could he gain the least intelligence with respect to any of his questions; he was obliged, therefore, at all events, to take a journey in search of it and endeavour to find it himself.'

Such a passage and the following narrative give a curious idea of the state of ignorance in which Geneva lived of objects within its daily horizon, even after 'the discovery' of Chamonix. With many doubts as to the right road, anxiously looking out for any glimpse of the snows, and seriously disquieted when they lost sight of them, the two Delucs arrived late at night at Sixt, where 'their guide gave them no hope of finding any accommodation.' Fortunately, despite the lateness of the hour, the convent opened its gates and received them most hospitably.

The peasants of the village could give no information as to the snow mountain they were in search of, but offered to lead the travellers to some chalets, where a hunter who knew more might possibly be met with.[1] This plan was carried out, the chalets reached, and the hunter secured. But they followed him with uneasy minds, for their frozen summit had entirely disappeared. When, after some rough scrambling, they reached the ridge of rocks known as the Grenier des Communes, which had long formed their skyline, 'they perceived themselves upon the brink of one of the most frightful precipices, which separated them from the summit they came in search of.'

There was nothing for it but to go back, after having gazed 'with admiration as well as horror' at Mont Blanc, which appeared before them in all its majesty. An accident to the most important member of the party, the thermometer, compelled them to return to Geneva.

It was not till 1770 that the Delucs again attempted to carry out their design. Led by an 'apprentice to a hunter,' they climbed 'from one jutting point to another up the clefts of an immense wall of stone which was almost perpendicular,' only to find themselves 'upon the very same precipice they had been on five years before.' They consoled themselves by scrambling to the highest point of the ridge, the Grenairon. In this effort they had to take the lead from their poor-spirited guides. The conduct

---

[1] It appears that the mountain was known as the Mortine in Valorsine, but had no name on the Sixt side. Buet was properly the name of a lower point.

of one of these men was, indeed, most reprehensible. 'Fatigued with the labour he had undergone and in a fit of laughter at the folly of taking all this trouble to boil a little water, he threw himself, unluckily, with all his weight on Jean Deluc's foot and badly sprained it.' The 'author of the misfortune' then abandoned his employers, in order to go down and milk his cows. Jean Deluc was equal to the occasion, both as a philosopher and as a mountaineer. He candidly imputed the man's behaviour to his mistaken sense of duty to his master (the owner of the cows) rather than to want of feeling. Further, he contrived to slide upon his back 'down 1500 perpendicular feet.' Night then came on, and the climbers were compelled to sleep out, making a barricade to prevent themselves from rolling down the steep. Next morning Deluc's foot was less painful, and he was able to descend to Sixt.

On the following day the village fair was held, and the Delucs learnt from some of the assembled peasants that the snowy dome they were in search of was known as the Buet, a name derived, they were told, from Bovet, an upper pasturage, near the snow.

A month later, in company with a hunter, they ascended to the hamlet of Les Fonds, now well known from the description of the late Sir Alfred Wills, who built himself a house in this lovely spot, and wrote of it with an owner's appreciation.[1] No raptures, however, can exceed those of the Delucs on this 'most superb amphitheatre,' 'delightful plain,' 'romantic solitude,' which 'they could not cease admiring.' Rain drove the brothers back to Sixt, but at the instance of the monks they waited until a fine day enabled them to return with better prospects to Les Fonds. Next morning they were off at daybreak, and by 7 A.M. had reached the 'Plain de Léchaud,' where they saw three of the 'native burghers' of the country—that is to say, chamois. 'Proceeding, they enjoyed for two hours the sensible succession of new objects without any other inconvenience than that of walking up an exceeding steep slope, which was nothing to their spirits and resolution.'

In plain language, they were drawing near the snow, and the upper slopes were still hard from the night's frost. Having had experience of the difficulty of using crampons, 'which

[1] See *The Eagle's Nest* (London, 1868).

were apt to turn upon the foot and deceive them,' they had provided themselves with thick woollen socks to put over their shoes, by means of which, and their iron-pointed staves, they 'presumed it possible to step with the utmost security. Their shoes, however, were absolutely improper for such an undertaking.' Happily, the guides had broad soles and hobnails with which they crushed footsteps through the frozen crust. It was about noon when the party gained the summit, 'which commanded in a manner at one view all the straights of the Alps, of whose pikes there were but few which raised their points above them.' The last statement calls for very large qualification. The height of the Buet is only 10,200 feet.

'For long they were absorbed in contemplation of the scene before them. When their attention returned upon themselves, they found that they were standing only upon a mass of congealed snow which jutted over a most frightful precipice. Their first impulse was to retreat with all speed, but soon reflecting that the addition of their weight to this prodigious frozen mass, which had been supported thus for ages, could have no effect to bring it down, they laid aside their fears and went again upon that horrid terrace.' After a halt of three-quarters of an hour, and making two boiling-water observations for height, they retired to some rocks a couple of hundred feet below the top for another hour and a half. During this prolonged stay, 'they were forced, by the absence of any disagreeable sensation, to remark what a wonderfully adaptive machine is the human body, whose equilibrium remains undisturbed within while the atmosphere without is changed in density.'

The descent was easy. The Delucs observed with envy, though they did not venture to imitate, the mode of progression of their guides, who glissaded, as we now say—that is, slid leaning on their poles down the slopes. They found out, however, another method which they thought very agreeable. It consisted in a series of jumps, made 'with regularity and due deliberation,' and would seem to have been modelled on the gait of a kangaroo. At the foot of the snow they were saluted by the whistles of marmots, which suggested to them the signals of banditti. Sixt was regained after nightfall.

A second ascent [1] of the Buet was made in 1772 by J. A. Deluc, his brother, and a young Genevese clergyman named Dentan, from the chalets of Anterne by a different route, recommended by their guides. Deluc's object was to make further observations. Unluckily, at the chalets he again broke his thermometer. His account of the accident is a specimen of the naïve enthusiasm of the early observers: 'I looked with emotion for my thermometer; it was broken. I gave a cry which shook the cabin.' Happily, the hygrometer survived to reach the summit, and afterwards to be honoured with a place in Queen Charlotte's apartments. The climbers took eight hours to reach the top, and on their return they were benighted and caught in a thunderstorm among the cliffs of the mountain. From this unpleasant situation they were rescued by the mistress of the chalet in which they had passed the previous night. Her courageous conduct and refusal to accept any recompense suggest to Deluc some of his usual reflections on the virtues of the mountaineer, and he concludes his story with the exclamation, 'Je me reprocherois toujours si Anterne pouvoit devenir un lieu fréquenté!' Elsewhere, however, with an inconsistency not uncommon among travellers, he pronounces the Buet to be 'the most engaging to a man of taste of all the mountains of the Alps,' and expresses a hope that some of his readers may undertake its ascent.

It is now the turn of Deluc's follower on the Buet, Marc Théodore Bourrit, to be brought on the stage. The faithful historian must feel some diffidence in attempting a sketch of this many-sided and unequal character. Deluc was an enthusiast in his feeling for the mountains, but his enthusiasm was not free from the affectation of the age. Bourrit's love of the Alps was absolutely genuine, and for its sake the critic who shares his passion is disposed to forgive him much and even to feel a touch of compunction when called on to record the too obvious weaknesses which were combined with this sympathetic quality.

We owe the following vivid contemporary sketch of 'the Historiographer of the Alps'—as Bourrit liked to be called—to a Herr Fischer of Berlin, who, having visited Geneva in 1795 and

[1] *Lettres Physiques et Morales sur les Montagnes et sur l'Histoire de la Terre et de l'Homme*, Deluc, 1778, in which a published account of the expedition by M. Dentan is also referred to. The work is in six volumes.

been admitted to Bourrit's studio, succeeded in anticipating the method of the modern interviewer.

He writes :

'Bourrit's figure is long and thin, his complexion dark as a negro's, his eyes burning and full of genius and life, his mouth marked by a touch of mobility and good nature which inspires confidence—such is a rapid sketch of this singular man.

'His description of the Alps, written, if you will, in too poetical and too exalted a style, is a real masterpiece. Bourrit is less exact than Saussure; he paints with a broad brush, and often neglects details, but he makes up for this failing by the colour and vivacity of his pictures. Saussure speaks as a philosopher, Bourrit as a poet; while the former instructs you frigidly, and sometimes sends you to sleep, the latter may bore you by his too frequently repeated exclamations, but his style is fiery, and the perusal of his works excites and draws you on. The talent of Bourrit as an artist is not less distinguished. The style of his composition is characteristic and individual. Many of his pictures, none of which is without merit, have been sold in England and Russia; his house is hung with those that remain. He lives a quiet and retired life. Although he no longer serves in the cathedral choir, the salary attached to the office has been continued to him, as he has lost the pension he had from France.

'He has, besides, many eccentricities in his way of living: he sleeps during eight months in the year under a walnut-tree in his garden, with a fur coat in July, and no greatcoat in January. He talks of Mont Blanc with the most exalted enthusiasm, and when leading travellers to the Montenvers, utters appropriate little prayers while climbing the mountain.

'The companion of his excursions, the faithful Raton, so well known to his readers, has passed away: he carefully preserves his skin: the successor of this cherished companion in his frequent pilgrimages promises to be quite as interesting.

'For the rest, there is not in the world a character more kind or more obliging than Bourrit. It is true he talks too much of the Alps, and, above all, of himself. But who will not pardon this little weakness in a man whose merits are so well known, and who, in the double rôle of painter and author, is an honour to his country?'[1]

Beside this impression of a passing visitor we may put the portrait supplied by Bonnet, whose criticisms were always tempered by his kindness of heart and desire to be just.

[1] See C. A. Fischer, *Ueber Genf und der Genfersee* (Berlin, 1796).

'The Alpine travels of our Bourrit are in reality only descriptive: this man, Precentor in our cathedral, has talent for music and in painting, but he is no physical student or naturalist, and his imagination is always effervescent. Still we must give him due credit for his enthusiasm and his pluck.'

Contrasted with the in every respect wider intellect of de Saussure, the man of philosophic mind, who wrote with the calm and measured precision of a man of science, the aristocrat with the finest house in Geneva for his home and ample means at his disposal, Bourrit makes no imposing figure. He was a *natif*—that is, a plebeian by birth. Gifted by nature with a fine voice and some artistic talent, he obtained at an early age an appointment as Precentor in the cathedral choir. He added to his income by setting up as a painter of miniatures. But when he was twenty-two a visit to Les Voirons, one of the lower heights near Geneva, revealed to him his true vocation. He fell in love with the Alps, and at the same time he made the convenient discovery that there was at Geneva a better market for mountain landscapes than for portraits. Bourrit obviously had in more senses than one the artistic temperament. He is recorded to have been on several occasions reproved for unpunctuality and petty irregularities by the cathedral authorities. We find him often borrowing or asking for payments in advance from de Saussure, whose *Voyages* he helped to illustrate. He even got into needless trouble over the accounts of the subscription he had helped to raise in Germany for Balmat, after the latter's ascent of Mont Blanc. Art, however, soon became with Bourrit only a profitable adjunct to authorship. His mission in life was to be the doorkeeper in the temple of Jupiter Penninus, the showman to introduce the 'visitors to the glaciers' to their 'agreeable horrors.' In the summer months he was always to be found either at his house in Geneva or at hand in his chalet at Chamonix. In the case of any person of distinction he was delighted to furnish an itinerary, or even personally to conduct his tour. In 1773 he wrote to a friend that Lord Chesterfield,[1] 'a Mylord of fine figure and great wealth,' who was studying at Geneva, had offered him fifty louis in advance to accompany him to Chamonix.

[1] The fifth Earl of Chesterfield, the godson and successor of the author of the famous Letters. A supplementary volume of letters addressed to his godson by the fourth Earl was edited by Lord Carnarvon.

In 1777 he applied earnestly—though in vain—to de Saussure to get the Emperor Joseph II. to visit his studio and accept his services as a courier or guide to the glaciers. But in his literary efforts he was more fortunate; they met with all, and perhaps more than all, the success they deserved. He was a ready and successful writer, though he is reported to have needed the help of his friend Jean Pierre Bérenger, the Genevese historian, in putting his manuscript into shape.

His *Description des Glacières*, first published in 1773, was soon (1775) translated into English, and went through three English editions. In the printed list of subscribers we meet with many of the celebrities of the time: Sir Joshua Reynolds, Angelica Kaufman, Horace Walpole, Dr. Johnson, Bartolozzi. Goethe read it and described its author as a 'passionirter Kletterer.' Bourrit's fame spread till it reached even royal ears. In 1775 the King of Sardinia received him at Chambéry and gave him a substantial recompense, a compliment he was never tired of recalling to his visitors' notice. Thus encouraged, Bourrit in 1779-80 took courage to face the ordeal of Paris. Here he was fortunate in finding an influential friend in Buffon. It is, I think, clear that there was little personal sympathy or intellectual fellowship between de Saussure and the author of the *Epoques de la Nature*. The reader will find in an earlier chapter de Saussure's personal impressions of the great scientist. Buffon, on his part, seems to have been annoyed by de Saussure's insistence on the necessity for exact observation, if he did not feel it as an implicit reproach. In his chapter on Glaciers he quotes Bourrit, and Bourrit alone. He was at the pains to read the proofs of Bourrit's later work, *Description des Alpes Pennines et Rhétiennes*, and to acknowledge them in these surprisingly warm terms:

'I have read, too, with great satisfaction, the seven sheets of your second volume which you have been good enough to send me, and which I have the honour to return. It is impossible to praise too highly the courage—or rather the intrepidity—with which you faced the dangers of your difficult travels among the glaciers and the summits of the High Alps, and the description you give of them is the justification of your labours and your exertions. I have been particularly struck by the prodigious glacier at the source of the Rhône, and in general it is impossible not to praise your observations and also your pictures.'

Buffon concluded by asking for an appointment to visit Bourrit's studio.

At Court, thanks largely to his patron's kind offices, Bourrit was presented to Louis Seize, who bought one of his pictures, a view of the Oeschinen See near Kandersteg, and on condition he sent him two pictures every year, granted him a pension of 600 livres, which after the restoration was renewed by Louis Dix-huit. It is little wonder if these successes completely turned Bourrit's head. Henceforth he always signed himself 'Pensionnaire du Roi.' His neighbours might still smile at their Precentor. But his fame increased with distance. He wrote to de Saussure, asking him for copies of his *Voyages*, that he might present them to Necker, Buffon, Le Roi (Director of the Cabinet de Physique), and Marat. Bourrit looked on the future demagogue as a second Newton who had invented a new Theory of the Universe. Frederic the Great wrote to the proud Precentor and dubbed him 'The Historiographer of the Alps.' Prince Henry of Prussia paid a visit to his studio, of which an amusing account is preserved in a volume written by the father of Alfred de Musset:[1]

'From the retreat where M. Senebier is incessantly at work, I went to visit M. Bourrit, the author of the *Voyage des Alpes*. I shall not permit myself any comment, but content myself with giving an exact account of what I saw and what he said to me. On entering the court I saw a sort of framework on which was a wretched mattress; this was the bed of M. Bourrit. He moves about this portable bedstead according to the weather or his whim, placing it sometimes near the wall, sometimes in the middle of his court. He described to us a visit he had received from Prince Henry of Prussia. "At his request," he told us, "I described a sunrise: I pictured to him the orb flinging his rays into the recesses of the Alps till, fired by my description, the Prince cried out, 'Our Lekain[2] was ice compared to this man.'"

'M. Bourrit pointed out to us his little staircase, which, in fact, is very narrow. He said that while going down it Prince Henry had said to his suite, "How many great staircases there are for little men! I am delighted to have found at last a great man with a little staircase." I hope for M. Bourrit's sake that there is a real disproportion between his staircase and himself, and that the prince's antithesis is sound.

---

[1] *Voyage en Suisse et en Italie fait avec l'Armée de Réserve*, par V. A. D. (Paris, An ix).

[2] A famous actor of the time.

'If Bonaparte had consulted M. Bourrit, he would have pointed out to him a route through the Alps shorter, more convenient, and easier than any of those by which he transported the different divisions of his army!

'As we left we saw again the bed on the frame, and my companion whispered to me that M. Bourrit had some resemblance to Diogenes. On looking at him I saw that his sleeve had a hole in it.'

The Bishop of Annecy granted, at Bourrit's request, a dispensation from fasting to the visitors to Chamonix. An extract from his eloquent appeal to the Bishop may serve to show his special regard for our countrymen:

'Curiosity brings to them [the Chamoniards] strangers, men of distinction, above all, Englishmen, who come to admire the spot where Nature reveals her grandeur in its beautiful and its terrible aspects: they arrive tired, exhausted; they are told of the obligation to fast—they soon feel no obligation but that to leave, to get away. The inhabitants appeal in this matter to your indulgence, your kindness; they do not ask to be themselves dispensed from fasting, but they beg you to permit them to feed visitors according to their wishes, and as the fatigues they have undergone and those they still endure in travelling among these mountains demand.'

It was no doubt a small fly in the ointment that Bourrit's fellow-citizens failed to show proper respect for 'notre Bourrit,' that the Genevese literary public smiled at the pretensions of the worthy Precentor, and that the local men of science refused to take his romantic rhapsodies at his own valuation.

Bourrit himself was at no pains to conceal his character: his books and letters are self-revelations. His style is a parody of that of the day, alternately familiar, sentimental, and high-flown. At one moment he is pouring out lengthy confidences about the marvellous intelligence of his dog, Raton; the next he is celebrating the charms of the rustic beauties of the Bernese Oberland, or in incoherent ecstasies over the *belles horreurs* of the mountains, or descanting on the fearful dangers he believes himself to have escaped. His feats, and the perils they lead him into, appear in his eyes prodigiously magnified. His perpetual state of emotion deprives him of any power of accurate observation. As the English translators of his *Journey to the Glaciers of Savoy* naïvely remark: 'In all his descriptions he discovers that luxuriance and enthusiasm of fancy which without instructions have constituted him the painter and the musician of nature.' Forbes puts it more crudely: 'He conveys the simplest facts through a medium of unmixed bombast.'

With his disregard for accuracy, Bourrit combined a boundless vanity. If he loved the Alps well, he loved Bourrit still more. If Mont Blanc was his idol, he looked on himself as its high priest, and was jealous of any intrusion on the shrine. De Saussure wrote, 'M. Bourrit takes even more interest than I do in the conquest of Mont Blanc.' The enthusiastic worshipper would have greatly preferred to have had no rival in his devotion. But for obvious reasons it was needful to treat de Saussure with respect. It was an honour to the Precentor to be associated with the wealthy patrician and man of science, while as a needy artist he found in him a kindly and munificent patron. Bourrit had to be content with doing his best to link himself on to de Saussure in the latter's attacks on the great mountain. But lesser trespassers he could not abide. Had his vanity been harmless, it might have been forgotten, or passed over lightly, but unfortunately it led him into an exhibition of jealousy which, as will be shown in the next chapter, helped for nearly a century to obscure the story of the conquest of Mont Blanc. We have the testimony of one of de Saussure's grandsons that Bourrit was the originator of the legend of Balmat, which many years later was to be adorned by Alexandre Dumas (the elder) with all the romantic detail of which he was a master. Apart from this deplorable episode, it would be possible for mountain-lovers to look with a lenient eye on Bourrit's complacency and self-conceit. De Saussure himself has set us an example.[1] His general attitude towards Bourrit was one of more or less indulgent toleration. In his *Voyages* he praises warmly the artist and refers kindly to the fellow-climber. The letter in which he thanks Bourrit for a copy of his first book is a model of its kind; he gives what praise he can; at the same time he suggests, under cover of a gentle irony, qualifications sufficient to satisfy his own conscience,

[1] Bourrit's relations with de Saussure and his family are best illustrated by de Saussure's journal during his long stay at Chamonix in 1787, and the boy Charles Bourrit's diary during the same period. They remained of a very friendly character despite the Aiguille du Goûter incident to be recounted in the next chapter.

and yet such as Bourrit's vanity might lead him to overlook. He writes :

'The public owes you its thanks for the lively and really picturesque descriptions of objects so interesting and so little known. I also propose myself to publish something on these same mountains—it is with this purpose that I have been studying them for so many years. I shall owe it to your book to have called the attention of the public to these great objects, and to have aroused in it a desire to know more of them.'

In 1780, thanking Bourrit for a later volume, he writes :

'I have just finished reading your work with singular pleasure. One recognises everywhere that picturesque imagination and that lively appreciation of the beauties of nature which are the marked characteristics of your descriptions. I also greatly enjoy the historical details with which you enrich them. There are some points in physics in which I do not share your opinion, but that does not necessarily prove that you are wrong.'

The rest of the note consists of a vigorous correction of Bourrit's hypsometry.

Nothing could be more judicious : the letters might serve as models for that embarrassing branch of correspondence, the acknowledgment of a presentation copy. But when we turn to later letters to Bourrit, we find that he candidly calls him to account for his excess of imagination, whilst in familiar correspondence with friends he was wont to refer to the Precentor's failings in plain language.

Such was the knight who advanced in September 1775 to the attack of the Buet from the side of Valorsine—the first inventor of that lately somewhat hardly pressed resource of modern climbers, the 'new route.' Bourrit was by no means the man to take an easy peak by surprise ; his approaches were always made in due form. In the previous year (1775) he had inspected with de Saussure the Delucs' route from Les Fonds, and been impressed by its formidable aspect. So he now went round to the other side and summoned a council of the inhabitants of Valorsine, which, as they did not know the mountain in question by the name of Buet, naturally led to no result. Vexed at his failure, he rather hastily set off to make the tour by Cluses to Sixt, but meeting at Les Houches the former Curé of Valorsine, he was induced to retrace his steps. Accordingly a second council was held, and a hunter made the brilliant suggestion that possibly the peak Bourrit called the Buet might be that they knew as the Mortine. Accordingly a start was made by the valley of the Eau Noire; but a cloudy day discouraged the climbers and induced them to return. The impulsive Bourrit set off a second time for Geneva, got as far as Sallanches, and then, finding a clear sky irresistible, rushed back to his mountain. This time all went well, and eight hours after leaving Valorsine the party found themselves on the desired summit. Bourrit was not the man to under-estimate the importance of his success: ' From this moment he conceived the greatest hope for the History of the Earth as well as for physical science.' The view he describes with rapture; but the best proof of his enjoyment is the fact that he repeated the expedition no less than six times in subsequent years. His memory still lives in the name of ' La Table du Chantre '—the Precentor's Table—given to a huge slab of rock some distance below the summit on the side of Valorsine on which he rested.

His hopes for physical science were in some measure fulfilled by the ascent of de Saussure, led by Pierre Simon and a local guide named Pierre Boyon in the following year (1776). From the mountaineer's point of view this expedition does not present any features worth record, although it furnished opportunity for a lengthy review of the structure of the granite peaks of the Mont Blanc chain and a dissertation on the rarefaction of the atmosphere.

Bourrit had the satisfaction of supplying the savant's work with a panorama of the view from the summit. It is drawn in the old-fashioned circle, but is fairly correct, though the identification of the peaks is faulty. Bourrit drew in the centre of his illustration the singular icicle-fringed cornice in which the snow dome of the Buet formerly broke away towards the north. De Saussure thereon went out of his way to say in a note that Bourrit was solely responsible for this feature, of which he had no recollection. Either the cornice had broken away in the interval between the two ascents, or the man of science in this instance has proved himself less observant than the artist. I was inclined to think Bourrit might at any rate have exaggerated, but a reference to an old photograph proves that there was in the sixties of the last century a cornice of dimensions equal to that he represents on the mountain.

This is the description Bourrit gave in a letter written to de Saussure of an attempt to sketch the panorama made on his second ascent, a fortnight after the Professor's:

'Next, in order to make good use of my time, I got out my instruments—or rather yours—and set to work to draw: at first the snow came up to my calves, but insensibly I sank up to the belt, while the foot of the quadrant sank also. I tried to change my position, but it was useless, the wind was violent, and so was the cold; my companions beat themselves like madmen to get warm while I felt my powers abandon me and my blood freeze in my veins. One of my companions noticed it and rescued me from my situation. I descended to the first rocks, where I fell senseless on my guides; they placed me in the shelter of some rocks and gave me something to drink, while Favret held me stretched in his arms; this rest and the sun's warmth restored me.'

Bourrit's endeavours as an Alpine artist call for sympathy. He was one of the first draftsmen of his time to try to draw mountains as they are. His predecessors, like the 'æsthetic critics' of the present day, had looked on them as rude masses, whose lines required to be reduced to simplicity and symmetry by the 'man of taste.' Few of Bourrit's paintings still exist;[1] they were numerous. The fourteen sketches intended to have been etched as illustrations to the English edition of the *Journey to the Glaciers* are said to have passed into the hands of a 'gentleman in England.' All we know about them is from Bourrit himself, who, in the preface, tells us how they came to be made. He observes

'that the first time he went into this romantic country the number and immensity of the objects which struck his sight at the same time presented difficulties it was impossible for him then to surmount, not having formed the least idea of them before he set out. His second attempt was more successful, when he not only determined his choice of the prospects, but was enabled to invent a new method of taking them with greater exactness.

---

[1] There are two in the Art Gallery at Geneva—but they are kept in a cupboard—and one in the rooms of the Club Alpin Suisse.

'His end thus answered, he brought back fourteen sketches, which those who are pleased with these subjects, as well foreigners as natives, have judged worthy the attention of the curious.

'He takes upon him to assure the public that not only the larger masses are designed in these views, but that he has made out even the smaller, and that nothing is added from imagination only, as in almost[1] all the drawings of these places he has had an opportunity of seeing. That he had examined the print from a plate of Mr. Vivaré in London, representing the icy valley of Montanvert, of which he affirms there is hardly as much as one stroke taken from nature; and that another of the valley of Chamonix is equally false (he means the thirteenth plate in the account of the glaciers of Switzerland, by Mr. Grouner); all which will not appear extraordinary, when we are informed that those gentlemen who had hitherto gone over the glaciers were rather men of taste than draftsmen. He has experienced besides that one journey is insufficient to render drawings of this sort perfect. That he found it highly necessary to attend to the peculiar state and condition of the air and weather, of which we never can be secure, and which may prove very unfavourable to the designer upon a single visit or in one season only, though the completion of his sketches must depend upon their clearness and serenity. We go to the valleys—are struck with admiration—trace out some loose lines in haste—add a few revising touches by way of memoranda, and at our return imagination does the rest.'

Book illustrations are at the present day the chief material we have from which to judge of Bourrit's art. As might be expected from a miniaturist, the plates of his own book are laboured, and the foreground to the Lac de Chède (beside which he desired to be buried) is beautified in the landscape gardener's style with 'bosquets.' He would seem to have had a failing for painting reflections in water, and in several instances could not refrain from turning the Arve into a glassy stream. But the mountain outlines are, as a rule, firm and fairly correct. For the period this is no slight praise, as may be seen by contrasting Bourrit's plates with the more ambitious illustrations to Albanis Beaumont's folio *The Pennine Alps*. When we turn to the plates which Bourrit furnished to de Saussure we are often agreeably surprised

---

[1] The author has excepted from this censure two views of Chamonix drawn with great care and exactness by Mr. Jalabert. (Original note.) Jalabert was de Saussure's companion in his first tour of Mont Blanc.

at the accuracy of topographical detail attained in such difficult subjects as the chain of Mont Blanc from the Allée Blanche, and still more at the power and vigour shown in many of the blotted-in sketches of individual peaks. The rock structure was all-important for de Saussure's purposes; in the preface to the *Voyages* he tells us how he has insisted on its reproduction. Doubtless the connection between them was most advantageous to Bourrit by necessarily fixing his attention on facts, and forbidding any indulgence in the prettinesses of which he was far too fond. But with every disposition to estimate Bourrit's work as kindly as de Saussure does in the passage referred to, we are forced to admit that, even judged by the standard of his time, it shows little real artistic sense or power. It cannot compare with that of Wolf, the painter who furnished the plates of the Aar glaciers and other scenes in the Bernese Oberland produced at about the same date.

The Buet was not long in becoming a recognised excursion for adventurous tourists, as well as for the men of science who found it a convenient observatory and post for measuring Mont Blanc. The Delucs climbed the mountain twice. So did de Saussure, in 1776 and 1778. He narrates an incident at the chalets above Valorsine which shows that visitors were still a rarity:

'We were conducted by a bevy of young girls, very lively and in high spirits, to whom the object of our journey, our dress, our mode of speech, even our least movements, were matters for immoderate bursts of laughter.[1] They accompanied us as far as La Courterai with unflagging mirth, and even succeeded in communicating to us some of their gaiety.'

Bourrit returned often to a mountain which suited so well his climbing powers. Before the end of the century three English ladies, the Misses Parminter, who, we are told, had already made a long Alpine tour, found their way to the top, escorted by Bourrit's

[1] An account of a similar incident in the same locality in 1780 may be found in the *Alpine Journal*, vol. xxxii. p. 75. These lively damsels were natives of the valley Ruskin selected as an example of 'mountain gloom'! Had he met a similar troop on his own ascent of the Buet (*Alpine Journal*, vol. xxxii. p. 335) we might have lost one of the most eloquent chapters in *Modern Painters*! Bordier also expatiates on the *bonheur* of the inhabitants of the Trient Valley in the eighteenth century as an example of Rousseau's ideal rural happiness.

friend Béranger and the guide known as Le Grand Jorasse. In 1800 a young Dane, attempting to make the ascent from Servoz, lost his life by falling into a crevasse, and his monument was made a tactful use of by the authorities as a means of conveying a suitable warning to future travellers not to fail to follow the advice of their guides.[1]

There remains yet another incident in Bourrit's literary career which calls for a passing reference. Some years before the attacks on Mont Blanc he rushed into a literary squabble with a rival who remains an obscure but interesting figure in the annals of glacier research. In 1773 the Precentor was on the point of publishing his first work on the glaciers of Savoy, when, to his infinite disgust, he found himself anticipated. To add insult to injury, the interloper had on his title-page veiled his identity under the initial 'Mr. B.' Some at least of the public naturally attributed the little book, consisting for the most part of the notes of a lively tourist on the round tour to Martigny, the Col de Balme, and, Chamonix to Bourrit. The author was, in fact, André César Bordier, a minister at Geneva. The first 'B.'s' wrath knew no bounds, but, far from being inarticulate, it found vent in the *Cercles* or clubs of Geneva. Bourrit alleged that Bordier had used as the basis of his work a copy of the manuscript notes he—Bourrit—was accustomed to lend to visitors to Chamonix. That one of Bordier's party had had a copy of these notes in his pocket was not disputed. A critical eye can find, however, little trace in Bordier's book of any substantial use having been made of them. Still Bourrit, whose work was already announced, obviously had a legitimate grievance in the misleading use of the common initial on the title-page. He appears to have made the most of it in the social 'Circles' of the town. The pair rushed into print. Bordier was stimulated into issuing a tedious pamphlet full of minute and captious criticism of Bourrit's book. Bourrit retorted in another written in a similar spirit. It is impossible for a modern reader to peruse with any patience either of these deplorable productions. The whole controversy might, indeed, well be forgotten but for one very remarkable fact. Bordier in his slender and for the most part slight record of a holiday trip inserted a chapter in which

[1] See *Alpine Journal*, vol. xiii. p. 179, for a note as to this accident and Eschen's complicated nationality.

the theory of the structure of glacier ice subsequently propounded by Rendu and Forbes was clearly anticipated. I quote the crucial passage in the original French :

'*Hypothèse sur les différents Phénomènes des Glacières réduits à un seul principe*

'Il est tems maintenant de considérer tous ces objets avec les yeux de la Raison, et d'abord d'étudier la marche et la position des Glacières, et de chercher la solution des principaux Phénomènes qu'elles présentent. Au premier aspect des Monts de glace une observation s'offrit à moi, et elle me parut suffire à tout. C'est que la Masse entière des Glaces est liée ensemble, et pèse l'une sur l'autre de haut en bas à la manière des Fluides. Considérons donc l'assemblage des glaces non point comme une masse entièrement dure et immobile, mais comme un amas de matière coagulée, où comme de la cire amollie, flexible et ductile jusqu'à un certain point ; supposons ensuite que les sommités du Mont Blanc, point le plus élevé des environs, se soyent trouvées couvertes de glace et voyons ce qui aura dû en résulter.'

The suggestion here put forward is remarkable in itself. But what is perhaps still more remarkable is that it attracted no attention at the time, or for ninety years afterwards. The little volume had its short day of popularity—1300 copies were sold in three months—and then it was completely forgotten. It was left to a Bernese professor to call attention to the chapter on glaciers. Bernard Studer, in his *Physiographie der Schweiz* (1863), introduced the passage already quoted in the following words :

'It is wonderful how, under the influence of de Saussure, the views of one of his fellow-citizens, which have of late been recognised as the more accurate, have been so completely forgotten that in the disputes of recent years over the earliest traces of the theory that treats glaciers as viscous masses, his name has never once been mentioned.'

Professor Studer was an early friend and companion of Forbes, who dedicated his travels to him, and must have read his 1863 book. There is perhaps evidence of this in a mention of Bordier in his article published in 1865, two years later, in the *North British Review*, but it is a bare mention, without any reference to his glacier theory.[1] Studer's emphatic claim attracted no notice in scientific circles in this country until Tyndall—his

[1] See Coolidge's edition of Forbes' *Travels through the Alps*, p. 530.

attention having been called to it by the present writer—in 1872 cited it in his *Forms of Water*. The greater portion of Bordier's chapter was subsequently reprinted in the *Alpine Journal* (vol. ix.). A copy of the original volume is in the Alpine Club and Geographical Society's Libraries.

There are two questions which must force themselves on all readers who are at the pains to compare carefully this attempt at a glacier theory with the lively but slight narrative in which it is embedded. Can they possibly both be by the same hand? Can the essay on glaciers be the product of a tourist who spent only a few hours at Chamonix, and, as far as we know, had no scientific training? The suggestions contained in it are acute, and for the most part sound and in advance of their time. They read like the product of a student with a keen eye and an ingenious mind who has studied glaciers carefully and fixed his attention on the problems connected with their motion. Was there anyone among Bordier's acquaintances at Geneva at that date who answers to this description? I am unable to throw any light on the question, and I must leave the inquiry to local historians. I have quoted the opening sentences in Bordier's glacier chapter; the following ones from a later page (276) strengthen my doubts as to the authorship—they could hardly have been written by anyone who did not know well what he was writing about:

'Il serait à souhaiter qu'il y eût à Chamonix quelqu'un qui pût observer les Glacières pendant une suite d'années et comparer leur marche et leurs vicissitudes avec les observations météorologiques ; la position du Bourg seroit extrêmement commode pour cela ; cependant l'on tire peu de lumières des habitants. Il faudroit marquer précisément quelles sont les bornes et l'aspect successif des différents Glaciers, en quel temps ils s'avancent ou rétrogradent et quelles sont les années les plus remarquables à ces deux égards. Il faudroit examiner quand les fentes et les chutes des glaçons sont plus considérables, quelles altérations subissent les rivières qui découlent des Glaciers, quelles sont les différentes hauteurs du Lac de Glace, ce que l'on pourroit observer dans les rochers latéraux. Il faudroit essayer de placer des fardeaux sur les grosses ondes du Glacier des Bossons et voir quand et comment ils seroient renversés. Il faudroit examiner si la glace, étant *idioélectrique*, ces vastes monceaux de glace ne donneroient aucuns phénomènes dans les tempêtes, etc. etc.'

The only clue I can offer is the fact that about this time, at the instigation of M. Hennin, the French Resident at Geneva, steps were being taken to ascertain the rate of movement of the Mer de Glace opposite the Montenvers. This is a sign that a new interest in glacial problems was springing up. Who were the promoters who shared in the undertaking?

If it is difficult to believe that Bordier, who has no known claim to any scientific interests or capacity, should have had the insight shown in this instance, it is certainly remarkable that de Saussure should not have thought the hypothesis thus put forward at some length deserving of his consideration, or even of a passing comment. We know he had seen Bordier's book, for in a letter written from Contamines in 1774 he refers to having felt the reverse of flattered at having the authorship of the *Voyage Pittoresque* attributed to him by the local Vicaire. De Saussure's nature was too generous to allow us to attribute his silence to any feelings of jealousy. The best suggestion I can offer, and I admit it is a poor one, is that he glanced at the comparatively trivial narrative of the early chapters of Bordier's volume and then threw it hastily aside.

MONT BLANC

The Grands Mulets cabin is on the rock partly shown in the left-hand bottom corner. De Saussure's hut was on the higher rock. The snowy shelves under the summit are the two "anciens passages." The "Corridor" and "Mur de la Côte" lie to the left of the picture, the "Bosses" are on the ridge to the right of the picture.

CHAPTER VIII

MONT BLANC

IN 1760 de Saussure, as has already been pointed out, had had posted in every commune of the Chamonix valley a notice promising a handsome reward to the first man to climb Mont Blanc, and also payment to pioneers for time spent in the endeavour. Fifteen years passed without any serious effort being made to take advantage of his offer.

Pierre Simon, de Saussure's first guide, it is true, undertook some sort of reconnaissance of the mountain both from the Tacul and from the Chamonix flank, but in neither case did he push beyond the first difficulties. Yet the Chamoniards were a race accustomed to brave the perils of the peaks and glaciers in search of crystals or in pursuit of chamois. What was the cause of their lack of adventure in this instance? It may probably be attributed in part to the moral effect of a deeply rooted belief in the inaccessibility of the ' Great White Mountain,' in part to the particular character of the perils to be encountered in the attempt. Even practised cragsmen may well have been deterred by the vast extent of the slopes of treacherous snow, seamed with hidden pitfalls, that had to be traversed in order to approach the far-withdrawn summit, and by the knowledge that at least one night would probably have to be spent in the frozen wastes. The Chamoniards, it must be borne in mind, unlike in this respect the natives of Zermatt or Val d'Hérens, had no need to cross glacier passes in ordinary life; they could always get to Italy by going round Mont Blanc, and consequently they were very much behind the Vallaisans in learning the use of the rope. It was not till the latter half of the eighteenth century that Alpine exploration in Savoy made any decisive advance. About 1770 the hitherto rare ' visitors to the glaciers ' became more frequent, and the interest taken in Mont Blanc by the troops of tourists who penetrated to its foot had a stimulating effect on the villagers. They had already found profitable employment as guides, and the more enterprising among them were now excited to attempt higher ventures that might bring higher rewards. The first serious attempt was made in 1775, when four guides attempted the obvious approach by the Montagne de la Côte, the ridge which separates the lower portions of the Glaciers des Bossons and de Taconnaz. The party entered on the ice and advanced as far as the level of the Grands Mulets. There they were stopped, not so much by any difficulties of the ground as by their own sensations of fatigue and nausea. They imputed their failure to the suffocating heat and a total loss of appetite. It probably arose as much from moral as from physical causes. The result, anyhow, was that the discouraging report the adventurers brought back put a stop to any further attempts for another eight years.

The frequent references in almost all early mountaineering records to physical discomforts may largely be accounted for by the low level of the climbers' bivouacs and the late hour at which they were apt to start in the morning, which resulted in the midday sun finding them still toiling uphill in soft snow. They themselves were apt to attribute their sufferings to the stagnation of the air in the snow valley under the Dôme du Goûter. That mountain-sickness is felt less on a windy than on a still day has been proved by many examples. But as the early climbers suffered equally on the topmost ridges and on the summit itself, it is obvious that the main source of their indisposition must be looked for elsewhere.

In 1783 a party of Chamoniards made a fresh attack by the same route with a similar result. They got nearly two thousand feet higher—as far as the Petit Plateau, under 'the arch of ice which crowns the rocks of the Little Mont Blanc' (the Dôme du Goûter). Here one of the party fell ill and his companions abandoned the climb. A stalwart guide, Lombard, known as Le Grand Jorasse, afterwards told de Saussure that it was no use taking provisions, that if called on to try again he should provide himself only with a parasol and a smelling-bottle. De Saussure's comment—written in 1786—was :

'When I try to figure to myself this stout and robust mountaineer climbing the snows with, in one hand, a little parasol, and in the other a flask of Eau Sanspareil, the picture seems so strange and ridiculous that nothing could be a more convincing proof of the difficulties of the enterprise, and consequently its impossibility to those who have not the head or the heels of a good Chamonix guide. For myself, after all I heard from the men who attempted the mountain on that side, I looked on success as absolutely impossible, and this was the opinion of all the wise people of Chamonix.' [*Voyages*, 1104.]

It was a case—not a rare one—in which wisdom was not justified of her children. There was one man at Chamonix who by de Saussure's admission was more eager about the ascent of Mont Blanc than the philosopher himself. The enthusiast Bourrit—it is his chief claim to our respect—would not accept the verdict impossible. It is, I think, probable that he had some part in instigating the second attempt of the guides. No variety of scientific objects and interests distracted Bourrit's mind. He had a single aim before him—to make himself the Hero of Mont Blanc. In 1780 he had returned from a visit to Paris with a new consciousness of his own fame and an added eagerness to extend it. The pension granted to him by the King had relieved him from the money difficulties to which his numerous appeals to de Saussure for help or advances in preceding years bear witness, and had provided him with funds for securing the service of guides. It may, therefore, fairly be put to Louis Seize's credit that he materially assisted in the conquest of Mont Blanc! Bourrit now brought to bear on the guides the influence of his own eagerness and his belief that success was not unobtainable. Instead of acquiescing in this new repulse he persuaded them to join him in a fresh attack by the same route before the autumn snows made it too late. He even disregarded a friendly warning which the event fully justified. De Saussure wrote:

'*August* 23, 1783.

' I wish you, Monsieur, every success in your hazardous undertaking, and I wish it more than I anticipate it. . . . I thank you heartily for your offer to return [to Mont Blanc] with me, but I do not expect to take advantage of it. I certainly shall do nothing to discourage you in this enterprise : since I gather that you have decided and made preparations for it, it would be useless trouble. I cannot, however, refrain from telling you that I do not think you have the necessary health or strength, and I fear lest the attempt, even if it is as fortunate as you hope it may be, may leave you with reason for long regrets.'

The party slept at the usual bivouac on the Montagne de la Côte, but on the following morning the weather broke; Bourrit did not venture on the ice at all, and the others were soon forced to turn back.

On this occasion a new figure appears for the first time in the annals of Mont Blanc. Michel Gabriel Paccard, who joined Bourrit in this expedition, was the son of the Public Notary at Chamonix, a man of sufficient means and intelligence to give his children a good education.

As in most of the Chamonix families—five Dévouassouds and four Balmats went up Mont Blanc with de Saussure—the Paccards formed a clan. One of the doctor's brothers was an Abbé, another an *avocat*.[1]

Sent to the University at Turin, Michel Gabriel had obtained there a medical degree and had subsequently studied in Paris, where he and Bourrit, who was also in his youth in the French capital, had frequently spent their evenings together. On his return to his native valley he set up as a doctor. He had a taste for science and studied botany. He made frequent geological notes on his excursions, and applied to de Saussure for help in securing instruments for the measurement of heights, and he more than once contributed papers to the scientific journals of the day.[2] He was now in the full vigour of manhood, and in the habit of making mountain expeditions. In the year following his attempt with Bourrit he made two serious reconnaissances of the approaches to Mont Blanc. With Pierre Balmat, he slept on the rocks beside the Glacier de Tacul and penetrated its upper basin to a certain distance. The climbers, however, soon got into difficulty in the icefall and, from what they could see of the range beyond, came

[1] Paccard had also a cousin, a guide, François Paccard, whose name appears from time to time in Alpine history. He was for some years banished from Savoy on the ground that he had acted as guide to the famous bandit and smuggler Mandrin, who was executed at Valence in 1755. F. Paccard was allowed to return as a reward for procuring some live *bouquetins* (*Rupicapri*) for the Count de Caylus. Subsequently, in 1786, he got into trouble again with Bourrit, who procured his temporary arrest on a charge of libel and abusive language. The date suggests that the quarrel must have arisen out of the unfortunate part played by Bourrit in the dispute over the first ascent of Mont Blanc.

[2] See the *Journal de Physique*, vol. xviii. 1781, 'Extrait de quelques lettres du Docteur Paccard sur les causes de l'arrangement en arc, en feston, en coin, etc., et de la direction oblique, perpendiculaire, horizontale des couches vraies et apparentes, etc.'

to the sound conclusion that Mont Blanc was less accessible from this quarter than by its Chamonix face. Early in September Paccard was again in the field wandering under the cliffs of the Aiguille du Goûter and reconnoitring their ridges and gullies, without, however, pushing any further attack.

It was at the end of August 1784, between these two expeditions, that the first meeting of Paccard and de Saussure took place. It is recorded in de Saussure's hitherto unpublished diary for that year. Madame Couteran's inn being full, de Saussure found lodging in the house of a member of the Paccard family, where he met the doctor. He describes him as ' a fine fellow (*joli garçon*), full, as it seemed, of intelligence, fond of botany, creating a garden of Alpine plants, wanting to climb Mont Blanc, or at least to attempt it.' A week later he met Paccard again, and invited him to supper, but 'he had an air of being offended, and appeared to take it as a reproach to him for not having asked me first. We parted, however, with offers of mutual service which had a strong air of sincerity.' Paccard, probably, was somewhat sensitive as to his social position, and did not want to be treated on the same footing with the Chamoniards who served as guides.

The persevering Bourrit had let the best of the summer slip away, but news having reached him that two hunters had succeeded in climbing the Aiguille du Goûter and reaching the upper snows, he set out from Geneva on September 11th—as usual, a month too late—and on the 16th and 17th made a serious attempt with six guides to scale the mountain by this route. His powers—as de Saussure had predicted—proved unequal to the task set them, and he broke down on the first rocks at the foot of the Aiguille. Two of his guides, however, persevered, climbed the Aiguille, crossed the Dôme, and reached the rocks below the Bosses, where M. Vallot's observatory now stands (14,312 feet).

This was a very remarkable advance. The outer defences of Mont Blanc were overcome, and only the last citadel, the final 1360 feet, remained to be stormed. De Saussure recognised the importance of the ground gained, and determined to return to the attack next year on the first opportunity. Unfortunately, however, the summer of 1785 was wet (the eighties of the eighteenth century seem to have been a period of abnormal precipitation), and again the start was put off to the shortening days of mid-September. A further handicap to the expedition was its size and the inclusion in it of Bourrit and his elder son, Isaac, a youth of twenty-one. De Saussure's judgment yielded on this occasion to his kindness. Having regard to the fact that Bourrit had made the first serious attempt to open this route, he broke his usual practice of taking no companion except his guides, and acquiesced in the desire of the two Bourrits to be allowed to join the party.

The first night (13th September) was spent in a rough cabin de Saussure had had built on a brow known as the Pierre Ronde at the base of the rocks of the Aiguille du Goûter. The Aiguille de Bionnassay—then called the Rogne—attracted the climbers' attention by its avalanche-swept sides and great height, but the guides asserted—and they were right—that from 'the Dôme de l'Aiguille' they would look down on it.[1] De Saussure busied himself with his experiments. His boiling-point thermometer proved a failure.

'But,' he writes, 'the beauty of the evening and the magnificence of the spectacle presented by the sunset from my observatory consoled me for this disappointment. The evening vapours, like a light gauze, tempered the brilliancy of the sun and half hid the vast expanse under our feet, forming a belt of the most beautiful purple which embraced all the western horizon, while to the east the snows of the base of Mont Blanc, illuminated by the rich glow, offered a singularly magnificent spectacle. As the vapour fell lower and condensed, this belt grew narrower and deeper in colour until it turned blood-red, and at the same moment little clouds which rose above it threw out so vivid a light that they resembled stars or flaming meteors. I returned to the spot after night had completely fallen. The sky was then perfectly pure and cloudless. The mist was confined to the bottom of the valleys; the stars, brilliant but without any trace of sparkle, poured an exceedingly faint, pale light over the tops of the mountains, which yet was sufficient to distinguish their groups and distances. The peace and complete silence which reigned over this vast space, magnified further by the imagination, affected me with a kind of terror. I fancied myself the only survivor of the universe, and that I was gazing on its corpse stretched at my feet. Sad as are ideas of this description, they have a fascination which it is difficult to resist.

---

[1] This is a proof that the guides had, on the previous occasion, really reached the Dôme du Goûter.

I turned my eyes more frequently towards these obscure solitudes than towards Mont Blanc, whose brilliant and seemingly phosphorescent snows still retained the sense of life and movement.' [*Voyages*, 401.]

Next morning, at the unfortunate suggestion of Bourrit, who feared the cold, a start was not made till too late (6.15 A.M.). The party was large, twelve in all, and naturally moved slowly. Fresh snow, fallen two days previously, lay on the steep rocks which form the face of the Aiguille. After five hours' climbing, Pierre Balmat, de Saussure's leading guide, called a halt and went ahead to reconnoitre. At midday he returned to report that there was a great deal more fresh snow on the upper rocks, and a foot and a half on the slopes leading to the Dôme. It was consequently, we are told, unanimously resolved to give up the expedition at a point estimated by de Saussure as between 600 and 700 feet below the top of the Aiguille. During the descent de Saussure lingered to take observations. Arrived at the cabin, he found to his surprise the Bourrits, father and son, preparing to descend to the valley. De Saussure spent a second night comfortably in the cabin. Thus ended an adventure which, he tells us, made him resolve never again to admit companions on a glacier expedition. Some correspondence that has lately come to light more than explains his resolve and supplies a humorous side to the story.

Shortly after his return to Geneva de Saussure learnt that very exaggerated tales as to the perils that had been encountered were running about the town. To him, always anxiously concerned to prevent his wife and family being alarmed by his Alpine travels, this was naturally no slight annoyance. But there was worse behind. The legend ran that the cause of the party turning back had been his own failure as a rock climber. These reports were clearly traced to the Bourrits. De Saussure was not the man to allow any perversion of fact to pass unnoticed. The first letter he wrote to Bourrit has not been preserved, but the rest of the correspondence sufficiently indicates its contents. Bourrit replied with more daring than discretion:

'I could not but notice that the way in which you came down was not the happiest. You might have fallen backwards, you might have been hit by the rocks dislodged by the guides, whom you made keep behind you, and we noticed the trouble they had to take to avoid this. As to my mode of coming down, I followed the advice of Gervais, who saw how impossible it was for me, with ruined boots which had lost their heels, to keep myself from falling. I was forced to put my feet in his footsteps ; and, if I rested on him, I took care to do so as lightly as possible.'

Bourrit, with his usual fear of cold, had attempted to climb the rocks in fur boots!

Having thus far tried to make out a case for himself, Bourrit enclosed as a peace-offering an account of the expedition warmly eulogising de Saussure. To this de Saussure replied as follows :

' My intention, sir, is not to cause you pain, but I was obliged to take steps to put a stop to legends such as your own conversation gave cause to apprehend. No one perhaps believes more than I do in the kindness and honesty of your heart, but I know very well also that your flighty imagination often makes you see things in a false light. If you could put aside this tendency, there is no reason why you should not keep an agreeable recollection of our excursion. I had every reason to be satisfied both with you and your son. The letter, of which you furnished me a copy, seems to be excellent, except that I am too much praised, which is not what I want. I can do very well without praise, and I do not desire to be put in the foreground, but I cannot—however, let us say no more. Do not be vexed, and I beg you to get to work on a fine drawing of the Aiguille du Goûter which may help to explain our expedition and may be engraved in the volume I have in the press.'

Before Bourrit had had time to get this reply, his son Isaac had fired off a long and singularly impertinent letter to de Saussure : ' Sir,' he wrote, ' do you not envy me my twenty-one years ? Who will wonder if a youth of this age, who has nothing to lose, is bolder than a father of a family, a man of forty-six ? '

De Saussure's reply is a model of the retort courteous :

' Monsieur, a moderate amount of boastfulness is no great crime, especially at your age. This is all I charge you with, and your letter is a fresh proof of it. You say you descended agilely. It is true, you descended agilely enough in the easy places, but in the difficult places you were, like your father, resting on the shoulder of one guide in front, and held up behind by another. I don't blame you for these precautions ; they were wise, prudent, even indispensable ; but in no language in the world is that style of progress styled agile climbing.

But enough. I have thought it right to put a stop to stories which might have caused me annoyance, and of which I had heard sufficient to give me reason to anticipate their spread; but there is no call for heroics on your part. One may proclaim oneself a little stronger, a little more active, a little more courageous than one really is, and yet be the most honest fellow in the world. The truth is that though I recognised in you a slight tendency in this direction, I did not fail also to find you very amiable, and I am glad to have made during this excursion a closer and more intimate acquaintance with you than I could have in my lecture-room. If you will not take too tragically the very mild and gentle reproach I have made to you, there is no reason why I may not retain an agreeable recollection of your company, and that we should not be good friends for life. After what I have written to you, sir, I am under no anxiety as to anything that you may say or write, and am very far from asking you to show me your narrative. On the contrary, I desire there may be an end to this discussion.'

Having delivered this adequate reprimand, de Saussure two years later magnanimously referred in his *Voyages* to his companions in the most friendly terms:

'In excursions of this sort I prefer always to be alone with my guides, but M. Bourrit, who had been the first to call attention to this route, having begged we should attempt it together, I consented with pleasure. We even took with us his son, a youth of twenty-one, whose talents promise him a highly successful career, and whose love of botany and of the great objects that the Alps offer for our contemplation have often led him in the footsteps of his father.' [*Voyages*, 1106.]

Further light is thrown on the parts played by the chief actors in this expedition by the account given of it in Dr. Paccard's notebook,[1] which must be taken to represent the story told him by the guides. De Saussure, we learn, was on a rope with a guide in front and two behind; Bourrit *père* leant on the shoulder of one guide and was held up behind by the collar of his coat by another. In ascending, Bourrit *fils* hung on to a guide's coat. Paccard remarks that de Saussure was tied 'like a prisoner' by a rope under his arms. The comment is suggestive, and illustrates the attitude of the Chamoniards to the use of the rope. It was practically ignored in the earlier glacier expeditions in the chain

[1] Now in the possession of the Alpine Club. Extracts from it are printed in Mr. C. E. Mathew's *Annals of Mont Blanc*.

of Mont Blanc, though it had been known and practised for two centuries at Zermatt. On this occasion de Saussure was for once roped in the proper way; on several others the rope was only uncoiled when one of the party was already in a crevasse.

On his return to Geneva de Saussure sent a full account of the expedition to his sympathetic friend the Prince de Ligne. This letter and the Prince's reply may still be read with pleasure:

'*September 26th*, 1785.

'Since your Excellency has shown your interest in attempts on Mont Blanc, I promised you in the last letter I had the honour to write to you that I would send you news of that which I had planned.

'Not to keep you in suspense, I will begin by telling you that its success was not complete, but nevertheless I reached a higher level than any observer before me had in the Alps, and I satisfied myself that in a more favourable season, starting from a higher point, and with the aid of a good head and stout limbs, the top of the mountain might be gained.

'You know, Monsieur, that Mont Blanc rises to about 2400 toises above sea-level, and that at 1400 toises the region of eternal snow and ice is reached. This thousand toises to surmount above the snow-level had repulsed all who had attempted to climb to the summit of the mountain. The brilliancy of the light, the oppression of the air from which they described themselves to have suffered, and possibly moral causes, such as the weariness of a long march on steep snowslopes and the dread of these immense solitudes, served to dishearten them even in the absence of any real and actually insurmountable obstacles.

'M. Bourrit, who has long been eager for the conquest of Mont Blanc, learnt last year that two hunters in the pursuit of chamois had climbed two-thirds of these thousand toises by rocky ridges, which, though above the snow-level, are too steep to remain snow-covered. He wanted to attempt this route, but, since he started from the foot of the mountain, fatigue and cold stopped him at the base of the rocks, while two of his guides climbed to their top, and reported that they had encountered great dangers in the ascent, but had found an easier route on their return, and that with more time and help they could have reached the summit.

'From the moment when this attempt led me to look on the thing as possible I resolved to make another as soon as the season allowed it. Unluckily, the snows accumulated during the hard winter of 1784-85, added to those which fell frequently during the cold and wet summer that succeeded it, put off the undertaking till the middle of September. At last the Chamonix guides, whom I had instructed to keep a watch for the favourable moment, came to tell me that the snows were melted. In consequence I gave M. Bourrit a rendezvous at the foot of the mountain. For though, as a rule, I infinitely prefer to make excursions of the sort alone with my guides, I could not refuse to associate M. Bourrit—who had been the first to make known this route—and his son in the enterprise.

'In order not to have to climb the whole mountain in one day we had had built at the spot where the snows begin, at 1400 toises, a little hut of flat stones. We carried up there straw, wraps, and firewood. The Bourrits were somewhat inconvenienced by the rarity of the air, but for myself, whom this air suits, I passed a delicious night.

'We started next morning in the finest weather possible. It was the 14th of the month. We were accompanied by nine strong, brisk mountaineers, who were as eager as we were for the success of the attempt. Everything seemed to promise well for the result.

'We had, as I have already said, a thousand toises to climb, six hundred of which were up extremely steep rocky ridges, and the rest over fairly gentle slopes of snow and ice. We accomplished easily the first two hundred toises, but as we mounted, the rocks became steeper and less solid. These friable rocks, fractured by weather, now broke away under our feet, now came away in our hands when we tried to cling to them. . . . To add to our trouble, the interstices in the crags were filled by snow that had fallen two days previously and masked the hard snow and ice that were often our footing. Still, after five hours of this arduous march we had gained a height of some five hundred toises along these ridges when the quantity of snow and the increasing declivity drove us to hold a council as to whether we should persevere in our advance. We sent the most active and boldest of our guides to examine what remained to be done to gain the top of the rocks. He brought back word that, having regard to the amount of new snow, we could not reach the crest without danger and extreme fatigue, and that there we should be forced to stop because the upper part of the mountain was entirely covered with a foot and a half of new snow in which it was impossible to advance. His gaiters, covered with snow to above the knees, bore witness to the truth of his story, which the amount of snow round us was enough to prove. In consequence, considering the uselessness of going any higher, we resolved unanimously not to push on.

'I observed the barometer, and the height of 18 inches 1 line ¾ at which it stood proved that we were about 1900 toises above sea-level, and consequently on the level of the Peak of Teneriffe, a height no physical observer had ever obtained on a European mountain.

'I made several observations of the thermometer, the hygrometer, and the electrometer. I collected some interesting specimens, I observed the structure and nature of these elevated crags, and we enjoyed a view of immense extent and beauty, since we looked down on our lake over the high ranges which separated us from it.

'These enjoyments did not, however, give us pure pleasure: our satisfaction was marred by the regret at not getting higher and by some anxiety as to our return. For, as you know, the descent is much more dangerous than the ascent, and we had passed some pretty bad places on the climb. Still, by proceeding cautiously and by making use of the support of our guides, whose strength and courage were really admirable, we returned safe and sound to our cabin, where I passed another excellent night.

'But for the new snow we should certainly have got 100 toises higher—that is, to the top of the rocks which are called the Aiguille du Goûter; but we should have got there after midday, and we should still have had 400 toises on the hard snows—it is true, by no means steep, but of great extent. We could not, therefore, have reached the summit of Mont Blanc even if we had met with no further obstacles. Time would have failed us, because it is impossible to pass the night at these heights, or to traverse in the dark any part of the route we had done in the day.

'To reach this summit, then, it is essential to find some shelter for the night at a higher point than ours, and to select a year when the mountain is entirely stripped of snow [new snow is meant] by the month of July, or at latest by the beginning of August, and even then the enterprise will be pretty dangerous and always infinitely laborious.

'While climbing with so much fatigue these steep rocks I envied the lot of aeronauts who rise to such great heights comfortably seated in their gondolas, and I even speculated on the possibility of using these aerial cars for attaining inaccessible peaks like Mont Blanc. But I believe it would be very dangerous, since on high mountains one is subject to violent and irregular gusts of wind which might break the machine by driving it against the cliffs, and it would further be needful to have very perfect means of control, in order to reach points so precisely determined.'

The Prince de Ligne replied:

'*23rd October* 1785.

'I am greatly interested in Mont Blanc, Monsieur, but not so much as in you! Your loss would be serious at any time. But remember that at the present time above all you are too precious not to be accountable for your life to Europe. We are about to lose M. de Buffon; another reason for taking care of yourself. How will all the academic chairs be filled ? I really fear the Academy will have to be reduced to twenty, for soon it will consist of nothing but Cordons Bleus and Bishops.

'I believe that by dividing your expedition between three days you might succeed, to the great advantage of your pursuits and to the honour of your century. But once more take care lest Nature, to revenge herself on you, does not catch you in the act. I can see M. Bourrit offering to paint the scene ! I had suggested to him previously the second resting-place. Would it not be possible to approach it by military methods ? If your workmen, your hunters, your mountaineers exerted themselves, it seems to me that with spade and axe it would be possible by slow degrees to smooth the rough places, cut down your Aiguilles, destroy your summits, and construct little platforms. If you only advanced ten toises a day, at the end of six weeks you would be able to set out in the fine season and to succeed without as much danger as you have already encountered, and we poor mortals at your feet would pray for you, while you were treating us *de haut en bas*.

'In return for mine, Monsieur, grant me always the honour of your remembrance, which to-day, when I have received your sublime letter, is more precious to me than you can imagine, since the letter is clear and simple like yourself. If one could only trust what the aeronauts tell us (but " a beau mentir qui vient de haut "), you might take advantage of what they say as to the hot and cold temperatures they constantly encounter. But with them it is an affair of minutes, and you would not be able to stop long in these extraordinary altitudes.'

As has been shown, Chamonix men had on two occasions overcome the cliffs of the Aiguille and advanced on the relatively gentle snow slopes that lead towards the final cupola of Mont Blanc. The prize, they must have felt, was almost within their grasp. Accordingly, at the earliest possible moment, June 1786, a well-planned attack on the mountain was made. Its first object was to test the rival routes by the Montagne de la Côte and the Aiguille. The Côte party climbed the Dôme by its northern slopes, thus avoiding the danger of avalanches on the Petit Plateau. This route has never come into common use, yet it is the only one on the northern side of the mountain that is altogether safe from falling snow or stones. The two parties met on some rocks near the top of the Dôme, that from the Côte arriving the earlier. Their united forces advanced to the foot of the *arête* of the Bosses, which joins the summit of Mont Blanc to the Dôme du Goûter. But this crest seemed to them so narrow and so steep that they believed it impossible to follow it. Their decision is a typical instance of the reluctance of the Chamoniards of that date to face the unknown. The ridge of the Bosses, given calm weather and ordinary conditions, affords a comfortable footpath. Mountaineers to-day walk up and run down it with their hands in their pockets. We may, perhaps, assume, though the excuse is not offered, that signs of a change in the weather were already visible and affected the determination to retreat.

It is difficult, no doubt, for the athletic climber of the twentieth century to enter into the attitude of the early mountaineers towards Mont Blanc. The youth who on a fine day walks up the mountain by a trodden track is apt to wonder how the climb can ever have been thought perilous. He may even dare to describe it as ' a dull grind.' This point of view was not shared by the best Chamonix guides I have known in the last generation. Men of the widest experience, such as François Dévouassoud, have confessed in such a phrase as ' One is always content to be back safely from Mont Blanc ' their respect for the monarch of the Alps. It is, of course, true that no climbing is called for on the ordinary route ; a lame man, M. Jansen, was once dragged on a sledge to the top ! But the great mountain has its moods, and it can be terrible, as the list of its victims proves. I shall not forget a morning of storm on the Aiguille du Goûter, when, wrapped in Scotch plaids, W. F. Donkin and I rushed down the cliffs, through mists which, urged by a south-west gale, raced past us in a wild procession. In a similar gale an Italian climber and two guides were blown off the narrow crest of the Aiguille de Bionnassay. Sudden fog and bad weather on Mont Blanc must always be a grave peril; the mountain is so large. In addition to these dangers, the first adventurers, it must be remembered, had no sleeping quarters above the snow level, they took a route up the final slope which was at all times badly exposed to avalanches, and they habitually neglected the proper use of the rope. At one spot on the ordinary route—in crossing the Petit Plateau—there is still a minor but appreciable risk from ice avalanches falling from the Dôme.

At this point another leading character in the drama of Mont Blanc comes on the stage. Jacques Balmat was a young man of twenty-four who owned a cottage near the Glacier des Bossons. He was apparently not on very good terms with the men of the chief hamlet, Le Prieuré, who usually served as guides. He had joined the Côte party uninvited, and his companions looked somewhat askance on the intruder. On the return he separated from them near the Grand Plateau under pretence of looking for crystals. Towards evening clouds and darkness overtook him, and, no longer able to follow his companions' track, he resolved to spend the night as best he could in the snow. Daylight found him not seriously the worse, and, the weather having recovered, he spent the morning in examining the possible accesses to the summit, which rose some 3500 feet immediately above him. Having satisfied himself that he had discovered a possible route, he returned without accident to the valley. His first idea was to keep his discovery secret, probably with the very legitimate intention of entering into communication with de Saussure and selling it in the best market. But circumstances compelled him to a different line of action. De Saussure and Bourrit were not the only competitors in the field. There was another and, inasmuch as he was actually on the spot and a born mountaineer, a more dangerous one. Balmat learned that Dr. Paccard had an early attempt on the mountain in view. He grasped the situation; his object was not only to climb Mont Blanc, but to be able to produce decisive evidence to his success. He recognised that as a companion Paccard would be an excellent witness, while at the same time he might be trusted not to make any claim to a share in the promised reward. Accordingly, Balmat made haste to come to an understanding with the Doctor. Bad weather delayed their start for three weeks, but on the 7th August they slipped away separately from the valley and climbed to the familiar bivouac on the top of the Montagne de la Côte. On the following day, at 6.25 in the evening, after a climb of fourteen and a half hours, they stood together on the top of Mont Blanc. The conquest of the great mountain was achieved. Balmat before starting had asked a friend to look out for him on the snows, and the progress of the climbers during the final ascent was followed and eagerly watched by the whole village.[1] Amongst the watchers was Baron de Gersdorf, a German traveller of scientific reputation, who fortunately happened to be at Chamonix at the moment. Mr. Brand, an English visitor, whose letters have been preserved, tells us the climbers were seen by many people from Chamonix and other parts of the valley with ordinary small telescopes. The Baron de Gersdorf observed them through a good achromatic glass, so as to be able to distinguish the identity of their persons. The Baron made notes and drawings on the spot illustrating the climbers' route. These notes have only recently been made public, and provide very valuable evidence in the case.[2] For, strange as it may seem, no full and satisfactory report of the first ascent of Mont Blanc from either of the two men who took part in it had, until de Saussure's diary came to light, ever appeared. Dr. Paccard shortly after his climb visited Lausanne and issued a printed prospectus asking for subscribers to a narrative of the expedition. A copy of this prospectus has survived and was reproduced in the *Alpine Journal* (vol. xxvi., 1912), but the promised work has of late years been sought for in vain in every library in Europe, and it is now generally assumed that it never reached the printing-press.

The news that Mont Blanc had been climbed was promptly sent down to de Saussure at Geneva by J. P. Tairraz, the Chamonix innkeeper, by a special messenger, while Balmat himself arrived a few days later (13th August) to claim his promised reward and to offer his services for the future. He would appear on this occasion to have placed himself at the disposal of Bourrit as well as of de Saussure, for in June of the following year we find him writing to Bourrit that the mountain is open, and urging him to hasten his arrival. Immediately on receiving the great news de Saussure instructed Tairraz to send a party of guides to build two huts— one at the bivouac on the top of the Montagne de la Côte, the second on the higher of the two Grands Mulets crags—to make smooth the rough places at the entrance to the glacier, and to

[1] On his return Balmat learnt that his infant child had died during his absence. This sad incident, which had escaped notice, is attested by the Register of Le Prieuré.

[2] See Dr. Dübi's work, *Paccard wider Balmat* (Berne, 1913).

arrange with Jacques Balmat to procure a staff of guides for the ascent. De Saussure's name was not to be mentioned in connection with these preparations, which were to be attributed to the orders of an Italian nobleman [1]—a step, doubtless, due to de Saussure's habitual reluctance to arouse the anxiety of his family. No time was lost. On 15th August he left Geneva, by his own account in a state of high nervous excitement. He writes in his diary: 'My head is so full of my project that it is a fatigue, and almost an illness, if I leave off thinking of it for a moment. It affects my brain so as to cause me an emotion that is very distressing. In short, it is a thorn that I must absolutely pluck out of my foot.' On the 18th he was at Chamonix and ready to start. Next day he called at Paccard's, and was disappointed to find that 'ce diable de Docteur!'—as he calls him in his diary—whom he had counted on to take observations in the valley corresponding with his on the mountain, had gone off again in the direction of Mont Blanc. De Saussure at first imagined he might be trying to repeat the ascent. Next day, however, as he was himself starting for the Côte, he learnt that Chamonix gossip had alarmed him needlessly. The Doctor's object had been limited to an endeavour to cross the crevasses of the upper Bossons Glacier from the Montagne de la Côte to the foot of the Aiguille du Midi. It was, in fact, an attempt to open the route now always taken in ascents from Chamonix. For the moment the attempt failed, but the fact that it was made by the Doctor and his brother, a lawyer, *with one guide*, is perhaps the best comment on Bourrit's depreciation of the Doctor's energy and climbing powers. Before his own start de Saussure succeeded in finding Paccard at home and in arranging with him and his brother for the simultaneous observations he wanted being taken at Chamonix during his ascent. In the afternoon the party, de Saussure and his servant, Têtu—de Saussure's unfortunate valet had always to share his adventures—with sixteen guides, set out for the bivouac. At the end of thirty-six hours he was back at Chamonix, driven down by the doubtful weather and the guides' advice.

On the 22nd August, the day after his return, de Saussure again visited the Paccards, in order to give them further instructions in the method of ascertaining heights by the use of the barometer.

[1] The letter was, in fact, taken to Chamonix by an Italian traveller.

On this occasion Paccard *père*, the village notary, invited de Saussure to dine with the family. This dinner is an incident of historical importance in the annals of Mont Blanc, for if we have not Dr. Paccard's printed *Voyage*, we get here a detailed account of his expedition taken down from his own lips by de Saussure, a fortnight after the events took place. De Saussure showed the value he attached to the record by mentioning in his diary that he sat up late in order to put it down in writing the same evening. I give a literal translation of his notes, now published for the first time :

'We discussed at length the Doctor's ascent of Mont Blanc. He says that he found near the top large hailstones embedded in the snow ;[1] that fresh snow is far more fatiguing to the eyes than the old, and that this has been the cause of more than one failure. I grasped his route perfectly. After crossing the glacier he left well to his left the chain of dark rocks [the Grands Mulets], on which is my second cabin, and swerved towards the foot of the Dôme du Goûter, called here the Gros Mont. He kept close to its foot, leaving it always on the right. After a long ascent he found himself on a great plain, or at least a very gently inclined snow-slope, and, turning to the left, reached a kind of snowy bank planted between two lofty and perpendicular rocks, bare of snow. He passed over the top of the left-hand rock,[2] skirting the base of the summit of Mont Blanc and, having thus borne a good deal to the east, turned again southwards to climb the last slope, which is very steep and fairly hard. Still on the top the snow seemed loose (*tendre*). It was easy to plant the barometer as deeply as was desirable.

'From the top it is possible to descend the gentle slope on the Val d'Aosta side and reach some rocks which rise in a sharp crest [the Mont Blanc de Courmayeur]. He looked there for a possible sleeping-place, but the wind was everywhere equally strong and cold. He found at the foot of the last slope some loose stones on the snow and higher up the two little rocks one sees from Chamonix, perhaps some hundred paces below the top.

---

[1] Compare L. da Vinci's note on his ascent of Mon Boso (see p. 7). The occurrence is not uncommon. It is produced by the granular structure of the ice and the melting produced by recent sunshine.

[2] This passage is conclusive as to the point—hitherto, I believe, unnoticed—that in the first ascent Balmat and Paccard passed between the two Rochers Rouges, while in de Saussure's ascent the route taken lay to the right of, and over, both. This was obviously the easier passage Balmat in his letter of June 1787 reported to de Saussure that he had discovered (see p. 219).

'Four times the snow covering crevasses failed under their feet, and they saw the abyss below them, but they escaped a catastrophe by throwing themselves flat on their poles laid horizontally on the snow, and then, placing their two poles side by side, slid along them until they were across the crevasse. He thinks it would be an excellent idea to take a ladder. The place where they met the most crevasses was near the rocks on which my second cabin stands. He told me he owed his success in part to the observations I made on the Buet on the periodicity of fatigue and recovery. When they reached a considerable height he noticed that he was obliged to take breath and allow his strength to recover about every hundred paces, and as they advanced more often, down to every fourteen paces; but after a rest his strength immediately came back, as I have also noted.

'It was midday before they were opposite my second cabin, although they had started at 4 A.M. from the first, so if one starts from the second one would gain greatly, and might reach the summit early in the day. A curious observation on sunburn and snow-blindness is that they did not come on till the next morning. They did not descend without a halt, as has been alleged. They stopped before midnight on the top of the Montagne de la Côte; and up to that point they did not suffer any inconvenience, but next morning, when at dawn they set out to return to the Priory, the Doctor could not see enough to find his path, and had to be led by the guide. He says it may prove one of the inconveniences of sleeping *en route* that it may lead to the eyes being weak on awaking. Anyhow, it is a suggestion that one should take precautions against the brilliancy of the sunshine. He confirmed the statement that the ink in his bottle was frozen in his pocket, and also some meat the guide had in his sack. He thinks his hand was frozen at a relatively moderate temperature because his skin glove had been wetted by his leaning on the ice. His hand became black and insensible. He got rid of the blackness by rubbing it with snow. He adds that his finger-tips are still numb. He changed gloves with Balmat, who had a pair of fur gloves, and the latter then also had his hand frozen; it turned pale and was cured by the same method of rubbing it with snow.

'He agrees with Pierre and Jacques Balmat in thinking that the best time for ascents would be the beginning of June, because the crevasses are choked and the winter snows are firmer than those which fall in the summer months. The long days are another advantage. The distant objects were not clear; the accumulated vapour seemed to form and settle on the horizon. When they reached the plain which I have mentioned at the foot of Mont Blanc, they endured great fatigue from the fact that the surface was covered with a thin crust which alternately bore them and gave way under their steps. The guide told him he could not persevere unless he (Paccard) was prepared to take the lead from time to time and to break the snow, *and he did this all the way to the top.* There they were exposed to a bitterly cold west wind which affected their breathing. They sought for temporary shelter below the final crest, but found the temperature insupportable. They could only withstand the cold by keeping continually in movement. He had a compass, and he believed that on the top its variation was different. I passed the rest of the evening in writing this.'

These are the rough notes jotted down, in no very orderly sequence, by one of the most accurate of men after listening to Paccard's description of the incidents of the ascent, given a fortnight after it took place. They now leap to light to contradict finally the legend that was fabricated by Bourrit and endorsed and embroidered by Alexandre Dumas, that Paccard was an incompetent climber who was dragged to the top by his brave companion. Surely it is time that the Alpine Clubs provided for the erection beside the monument at Chamonix to de Saussure and Balmat of some memorial to the village doctor.[1]

De Saussure lingered another ten days in the mountains, during which time he made an excursion to Martigny and to the foot of the Dent de Morcles. On his return to Chamonix the weather continued broken, his servant fell ill, and with many regrets he gave up the game for the year, venting his feelings, when Mont Blanc shone down on his departure, by quoting in his diary the lines of Horace (*Satires*, book ii. 7):

> ' Poscit te mulier, vexat, foribusque repulsum
> Perfundit gelidâ, rursus vocat.'
> The jade invites you, plagues you, from her door
> Drives with cold douches; then calls back once more.[2]

In the hotel book at St. Martin he added to his name, ' on return from his fourteenth visit to the glaciers.'

De Saussure's friends Pictet and Bonnet quickly spread the

[1] For a full statement of the documentary evidence in this protracted controversy and a fair summing up, readers must turn to Dr. Dübi's able and exhaustive volume, already referred to, *Paccard wider Balmat* (Berne, 1913).

[2] It will be noted that, to fit the quotation better to his own case, de Saussure leaves out the double accusative carried by the words *quinque talenta* in the preceding line.

news of Dr. Paccard's and his companion's success in their private correspondence and in communications to the public journals. It reached England, and de Saussure's old friend, Lord Palmerston, wrote, 'I congratulate you on the conquest of Mont Blanc. I wish you had been the first to set foot on the summit, a distinction to which you are so well entitled. I am convinced, however, that we must wait till you arrive there before our curiosity will be satisfactorily gratified.' It was not long before the officious Bourrit also appeared on the scene as a mischief-maker. It was a bitter blow to him that anyone should have anticipated him in reaching the mountain he had so often attempted; had the conqueror been de Saussure, he might have borne it better, but that an old acquaintance, the village doctor, should have won the race drove him to fury. His vanity, always the predominant trait in his character, was unfortunately in this instance linked with a jealousy which led him to very unworthy action. His first instinct on hearing the news was to endeavour to discredit it. In writing to de Saussure he insinuated that the ascent might not have been complete, that there might well be a higher crest invisible from Chamonix beyond that on which the climbers had been seen.[1] Finding this argument untenable, he set his busy pen to work with a double object—to assert his own claim to be the real explorer of Mont Blanc, and to disparage as far as possible his rival by giving the whole credit for the ascent to the guide Balmat. He wrote a pamphlet which he sent to many of the leading journals of the time. In this he recounted at length his own previous adventures, and went on to represent Paccard as having been led, or rather forcibly dragged, to the top of Mont Blanc by his companion, who, after having himself reached the summit alone, had to return some distance to fetch him. This pamphlet (probably while still in manuscript) was brought to de Saussure's notice shortly after his return to Geneva, and he at once wrote to remonstrate with its author. Bourrit's rejoinder has been preserved, and exhibits a deplorable mixture of obsequiousness and self-assertion. He found it expedient, however, to add a postscript to his pamphlet in which he made a disingenuous apology for the terms in which

[1] Unpublished letter from Bourrit to de Saussure, written from Sallanches on 11th August 1786.

Paccard had been mentioned. De Saussure acknowledged this very inadequate withdrawal in the following note:

'*Geneva, 19th October* 1786.—I thank you a thousand times for the fresh copies of your letter that you have sent me. The postscript you have added will throw some balm on the wound the body of the letter cannot fail to inflict on the Doctor, and if it is at my instigation that you have written it, I am glad that I wrote to you, and thank you for your compliance. The description of the Doctor's journey, whatever form it may take, will be read from one end of Europe to the other, and I should have been sorry to have seen in it what must have caused you pain. No doubt you would have replied, but you would have suffered annoyance, and that is what I wished to avoid.'

De Saussure, whose object obviously was to prevent an unpleasant controversy, had, we learn, written at the same time to Paccard. The latter subsequently dealt with the matter by supplying material for a controversial note in the *Journal de Lausanne* (obviously edited by some ill-informed hand before publication), and subsequently procuring to be published in the same journal duly witnessed affidavits signed by Balmat contradicting the main statements in Bourrit's letter.[1]

With the full facts now disclosed, it is, I fear, beyond doubt that, in the words of de Saussure's grandson, M. Henri de Saussure, Bourrit was the prime author of the legend which was to be given a world-wide circulation by Alexandre Dumas, the elder, on the strength of an interview he had with Balmat over his bottle in a Chamonix hotel forty-six years after the events described.[2] Up to the present moment this legend has been the only account known to exist purporting to be derived from the mouth of one

[1] See *Journal de Lausanne*, 24th February and 12th May 1787. In the earlier note there is a blundering reference to Paccard's explorations under the Aiguille du Goûter and a vague complaint that a rival has tried to obscure the Doctor's exploit by disparaging as well as attempting to repeat it. Dr. Dübi suggests de Saussure was here aimed at. But the relations between de Saussure and Paccard at this moment, as related in de Saussure's diary, are inconsistent with this explanation. Bourrit, who was at Sallanches on 13th August 1786, trying to collect evidence to throw doubt on Paccard's ascent, must be the rival rebuked. The suggestion that Paccard induced Balmat to sign a blank piece of paper, which he filled up afterwards, is sufficiently refuted by the fact that the two witnesses to the document were both men of character and position in the valley, who would have been most unlikely to lend themselves to a patent fraud.

[2] A few months after his conversation with Dumas, J. Balmat met with his death while searching for gold on the slopes of Mont Ruan, above Sixt. The curious circumstances are related by Sir A. Wills in *The Eagle's Nest*.

of the two climbers. After the publication of de Gersdorf's evidence, it became impossible for any competent critic to treat the Bourrit-Dumas legend as a credible narrative. Indeed Bourrit himself in later years (1803) went more than half-way to withdraw his statement.[1] Fortunately, we are now in a position to confront with it the report of the story told by Paccard at the time given by de Saussure in his private diary.

It may be noted that it was fresh from listening to this first-hand narrative, and after entertaining at Genthod Baron de Gersdorf, the eye-witness of the ascent, that de Saussure wrote to rebuke Bourrit for the version he was putting forward.

There was to be another year of impatience for de Saussure and of anxiety for his wife. The winter, as will be related, was shortened by a tour in Dauphiné and Provence. When summer came it was resolved to make the famous expedition the occasion of a prolonged picnic in the mountains. In this way the anxieties of a lengthy absence might be avoided, and the adventure accomplished under the eyes of the assembled family, who could watch every step in the climbers' progress. De Saussure must be allowed to describe the start in the words of his diary:

'On 28th June J. Balmat wrote to me that on the 26th he had made a second attempt, and that despite the quantity of snow he had almost got to the top, and that he would have reached it but for the violence of the wind and an impassable crevasse. He ended by saying he would return to the attack shortly by another and an easier route, and that he would come immediately to bring me the news.[2] He complained of having suffered more than the previous year from the brilliancy of the snow and the keenness of the air; his eyes, he said, were painful, his face swollen, his skin peeling. It was true

---

[1] See the edition of 1803 of his *Guide-book to Chamonix*, in which Bourrit writes of the expedition as one in which Dr. Paccard took part, 'if he was not himself the author of it.' There had been, in the interval, a coldness between Bourrit and Balmat owing to the latter's complaint of delay on Bourrit's part in handing over to him the full amount of the subscription raised in Germany for Balmat's benefit.

[2] Dr. Paccard's statement to de Saussure (p. 214), that in his ascent he passed '*between* two lofty and perpendicular rocks bare of snow and over the top of the left-hand rock,' proves, as I have already shown, that the first climbers passed between the Rochers Rouges. The easier route here referred to, used in the second and third ascents (the three guides' and de Saussure's), was to the right (west) and over the top of both rocks.

that he had taken no precautions, and it was natural that the days being longer and the sun more powerful at this season he had been more affected.

'I waited, then, his arrival with impatience; all my instruments were ready, and I was afraid that while he came to fetch me and I was travelling to Chamonix, the weather might change and that I might lose perhaps my only chance. My wife shared my feelings, and we consequently fixed our start for Saturday, July 7th.

'It is with reason I say *we*, for we are six on this journey: my wife, who imagines she will be less anxious at Chamonix, her sisters, who will not leave her, and my two sons.[1] We came into Geneva [from Genthod] to sleep on Friday, intending to start very early next morning and to get through in the day to Chamonix.

'On Saturday morning it poured; it was late before we could load up, so we did not get off from the town till 6.10 A.M. We took four hours to Bonneville, where we found the fresh horses we had sent on in advance. The weather was too bad when we got to Sallanches to think of going on to Chamonix.'

On Sunday the weather was uncertain, and the party remained at Sallanches, where Jacques Balmat met them, and Bourrit appeared, having closely followed the party from Geneva. Madame de Saussure sent a letter to her daughter by his return driver to reassure her as to their prospects and to explain that their delay was the fault of the weather, and ' not of the three sisters, or of the black and jonquil hat, the most elegant in the world, which is worn by your Aunt Tronchin.'[2]

'*Monday, 8th.*—Left Sallanches in charabancs at 7.10. The rain began as we started, and got worse continually. We went on, however, and it fortunately stopped while we crossed on foot the Nant de Joux, where we lost an hour and a half owing to the road being destroyed by the torrent, and our ladies were obliged to be carried. We lunched at Servoz while our horses baited, and after passing with some difficulty the Nants of the valley, arrived at Chamonix at 3.30. We had for companion on the road Jacques Balmat, who met us on his way to Geneva to bring me the news of his second attempt (this year) on Mont Blanc. He had started on the 4th with

[1] His daughter, Madame Necker-de Saussure, who was in delicate health, expresses in letters which have been preserved, her passionate regret at not being able to be one of the party, and her eagerness for news of her father's success and afe return.

[2] See portrait of Madame Tronchin, p. 256.

Cachat and Alexis Tournier. They slept at my first cabin, started from there at 1.30 A.M., at 5 o'clock were opposite my second cabin, at 10.30 A.M. at the foot of the last and great slope of Mont Blanc, and at 3 P.M. on the summit, where the wind and cold did not allow them to stop long. They were only seven hours in descending, and J. Balmat, to whom I had sent a veil with which he covered his face, did not suffer at all from the snow, while the others were inconvenienced.

'From this account I gathered that my huts were very badly arranged, since I had for the first day only four hours, for the second three hours and a half, and for the third ten hours of climbing.[1] In consequence, after many talks with Jacques and afterwards with Pierre Balmat, I made up my mind to camp the first day on the top of the Montagne de la Côte close to the glacier, which would take me about five hours and a half, from there to the extremity of the last cul-de-sac under the top of Mont Blanc, which would take seven hours and a half, leaving four hours and a half on to the top. It was true this involved sleeping on the snow, but they all think that under the tent one will be well protected from the cold and that the snow will not melt under the rugs and still less under the planks of the bed.'

Bourrit, who, as has been noted, had followed close in de Saussure's footsteps, this time with his younger son, Charles, a boy of fifteen, arrived at Chamonix at the same moment, ready for any chance of accompanying, or following, his patron. But this year he found there was to be no question of a joint expedition. Bourrit might start six hours after de Saussure, twenty-four hours after him, or when he saw his party on the top—he was always changing his plans—but there was to be no companionship above the snow level. In the valley de Saussure and his household were friendly enough with 'the historiographer of the Alps,' and the ladies were kind to his boy, who picked bouquets for them. Bourrit hired a chalet in the meadows behind the church at the foot of the Brévent, where he showed his pictures and sold them, or hand-coloured prints, to the 'visitors to the glaciers.' Of the three weeks of persistently bad or broken weather that ensued we have very full details, owing to the survival not only of de Saussure's diary, but of that of the younger Bourrit. The fine intervals were all too brief for climbing purposes. Mont

[1] Colonel Beaufoy, however, proved the contrary. He climbed Mont Blanc from the second hut, and returned to it the same evening. De Saussure was handicapped by his scientific baggage.

Blanc appeared only in fleeting and splendid visions of sunset rose, soon to wrap himself up again in his mantle of clouds. At night a long mist-banner would float out from the summit, which, when the moon rose behind it and shone through, showed white and transparent in the centre with an orange ring. De Saussure recognised that the particles of this apparently stationary cloud were always changing, that it was formed by the condensation caused by the chill of the snows rendering visible the moisture carried by a warm wind.

Despite the frequent rainstorms which cut short their excursions, the three sisters seem to have behaved bravely. 'Madame de Saussure,' writes Madame Tronchin, 'had never been in such high spirits.' The wet days were lightened by the arrival of interesting travellers, or of parcels of books and delicacies from friends at Geneva, which, de Saussure notes, cheered up 'nos dames.' He could employ his time in testing and improving instruments, or in getting himself into training and ascertaining his pace by assiduously pacing measured distances on the hillside opposite the hotel. He found 1500 feet an hour was the most he could hope to keep up. When it was too wet, which it generally was, he turned to the classics. Here is the entry for one day :

'*Tuesday*, 10*th*.—I start with enthusiasm to read the *Iliad*, which I had never read right through. I run over the Latin translation, and when I come on a fine passage I look it up in the original, copy it out, and even learn it by heart. About 11 I go with my son for a walk under the Brévent to test myself and my boots on some steep slopes, and return pleased with both. After dinner we drive to the source of the Arveyron and find the glacier much advanced and its foot very difficult of access.'

Between the storms de Saussure and his two sisters-in-law would ride to the Glacier des Bossons, or walk to the source of the Arveyron, at that time and up till 1860 an ice-cave on the level floor of the valley. They even, greatly daring, made an expedition to the Montenvers and enjoyed a gay picnic at Blair's cabin, though the ladies could not be induced to go on the ice. They took no less than four and a half hours to descend from the Montenvers to Chamonix, and were terribly tired. But it must be borne in mind that it was not till later that a mule-path was made to the Montenvers. The old track was a very rough one. The ladies made the best use of their stay among the mountains, for which they were greatly pitied by their friends at Geneva. They left, Bourrit records, greatly regretted by the villagers, on many of whom they had bestowed friendly sympathy and substantial kindnesses.

In the fourth week of July the rains were still at their worst, and Dr. Paccard's father, the notary, who was an elderly man, having rashly started alone for Sallanches on official business, fell off the plank over the torrent from the Griaz Glacier near Les Houches and was drowned. The son, Dr. Paccard, was absent at Courmayeur at the time, but hurried back on hearing the news. He had started just before de Saussure's arrival for the Italian side of Mont Blanc. De Saussure in his diary remarks: 'I think he does not want to see me before my expedition,' and on his return adds, 'He seems to have taken pains everywhere to have gone a little further and higher than I have been.' These passing references do not seem to me to have any significance beyond showing that de Saussure was human enough to be at heart a little jealous of his precursor, as well as of the climbing powers of the younger man.

The entries in the diary for the last days of July are as follows:

'29*th*.—In the evening the thermometer at 6 P.M. stands at 23° Centigrade, and stones and dust can be seen blown off the Montagne de la Côte by the violence of the south-west wind.

'30*th*.—Same weather! [He measures the speed of the clouds and finds they move 12 degrees in 68 seconds—that is, about 60 feet a second.]

'31*st*.—The weather at last promises well, and everyone prophesies a fine spell. Mont Blanc at sunset is alternately rose and pale white; it returns, however, to rose, and the quiet clouds which rest on Mont Blanc are also rose. The barometer mounts quickly. I make, therefore, all arrangements for a start, but keep the secret from my wife. I go to see the Intendant and write up this journal.'

The new month brought at length a break in the clouds, and the so much longed-for and dreaded moment arrived. The summits cleared under a bright north-west wind, and on the morning of the 1st August the great procession of eighteen well-laden guides started. No pains had been spared as to equipment, practical as well as scientific; it included what nineteenth-century mountaineers would have considered luxuries: a bed was provided, with 'mattresses, sheets, coverlet, and a green curtain,' amongst the clothes were two green great-coats, two night-shirts, and three pairs of shoes. Between a tent and a ladder in the list of 'requisites' appears a parasol and its case. De Saussure and the faithful Têtu both rode on mule-back for the first two hours. All Chamonix was there to see the party off—with one exception. Who that was we learn from the happy survival of a *billet doux* written by his wife on a thin sheet of rose-coloured paper addressed to 'M. de Saussure at his first bivouac,' and sent after him by a guide who had waited behind to take up a forgotten parcel :

'A Monsieur de Saussure à son premier gîte en me levant à onze heures du matin :

'I, too, *mon cher ami*, am very glad that Balmat stopped behind, not so much for the sake of the pistol as that he may take you this fresh mince-meat. I was really vexed about that you have, which has been made for two days, though Babet assures me it is excellent. But I shall be better satisfied that you have this as a supplement. I thought much about it last night. I did not sleep much; my poor knees feel as if they had climbed the Montenvers from having so often been up and down from my bed. Ah! what a beautiful night it was, what vows I made for this weather to last, you will believe! I assure you I am very well, very reasonable—as well as it is possible to be when all one's happiness is on Mont Blanc. Ask my sisters if they are not pleased with me. I assure you I should have been very sorry had you not profited by this weather, since your heart is set on this expedition. Anyhow, you are off, and in four days we shall all be happy, if you take care of yourself. I count on your promises. I should have liked this morning to have watched you start at the head of your troop. I wanted to throw you kisses, but it seemed to me useless to speak to you of it. I was often behind the green curtain, and yet I managed to miss the moment to see you go off.

'The poor Englishman has a sharp attack of fever. His friend came to consult me. I behaved like the doctor's wife; I told Marian to recommend them to make him drink a great deal, and not to take James's Powders so often.[1]

[1] Dr. Odier was eventually summoned from Geneva to attend to the patient, whose name is not recorded.

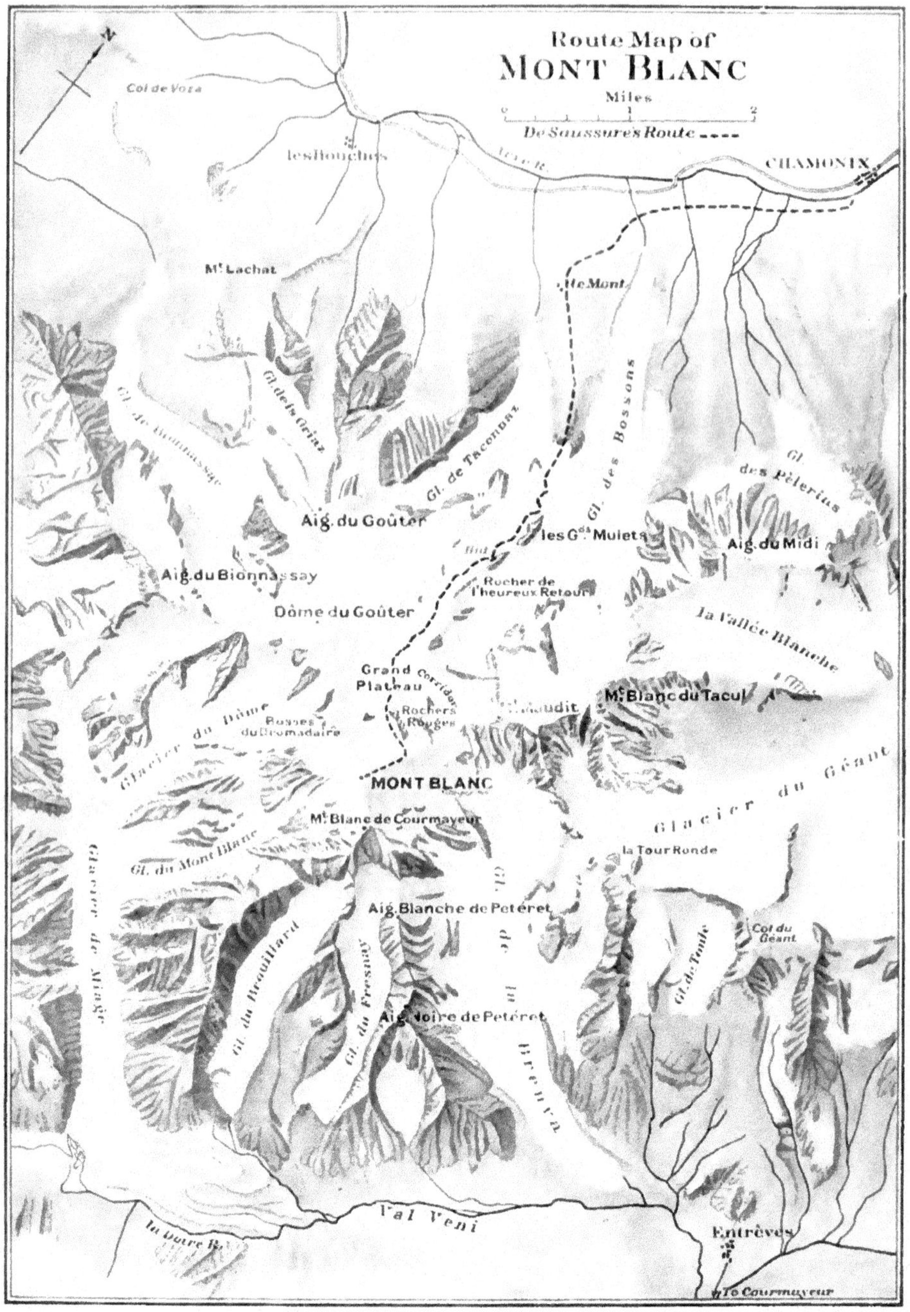
Route Map of
MONT BLANC
Miles
De Saussure's Route
Col de Voza
les Houches
Arve R.
CHAMONIX
Mt Lachat
le Mont
Gl. de Bionnassay
Gl. des Griaz
Gl. de Taconnaz
Gl. des Bossons
Gl. des Pèlerins
Aig. du Goûter
les Gds Mulets
Aig. du Midi
Aig. du Bionnassay
Rocher de l'heureux Retour
Dôme du Goûter
la Vallée Blanche
Grand Plateau
Corridor
Rochers Rouges
Bosses du Dromadaire
Mt Blanc du Tacul
Glacier du Dôme
MONT BLANC
Glacier du Géant
Mt Blanc de Courmayeur
la Tour Ronde
Gl. du Mont Blanc
Glacier de Miage
Aig. Blanche de Peteret
Col du Géant
Gl. de Toule
Gl. du Brouillard
Gl. du Freney
Aig. Noire de Peteret
Gl. de la Brenva
Val Veni
Entrèves
To Courmayeur

'I leave this note open so that Théo may give you the thermometer readings: he is careful in his observations. We looked well to see you had forgotten nothing. Do not forget what you have left at Chamonix, and let the remembrance bind you to take care of yourself. My compliments to your companions. My sisters are out walking; they are very kind.

'I have no mischievous hand near me to fold my note the wrong way in order to tease me about it. I have used rose-coloured paper so that you may have something else than the white of the snows to look at. Will you sleep well under your tent, *mon cher ami*? I trust so.'

Here follow Théodore's meteorological notes.

Madame de Saussure's anxiety during the following days was greatly relieved by the ease with which the expedition's progress could be followed from Chamonix through the telescope. She was able to watch the steady and unbroken advance of the party, to count its number, and to enjoy the emotion, almost too thrilling, of seeing all gathered on the summit. From his bivouac on the descent her husband sent down an express messenger to assure her that all had gone well, and that his scientific objects had been attained.

The *Short Narrative*, published at Geneva immediately after the ascent, has been excellently translated in Whymper's *Guide to Chamonix*. In the *Voyages* de Saussure added many graphic details to it. The following story is compiled from his hitherto unpublished manuscript diary and the *Voyages*:

'*1st August.*—I start at 7.25 on a mule with Têtu and several of the guides; some of them propose to take a short cut by crossing the Bossons.'

De Saussure was able to ride for two hours, but to a height of only some 800 feet above Chamonix. As he climbed the long ridge between the Bossons and the Taconnaz Glaciers he amused himself by watching the little flocks of visitors, timorously clinging to their guides as they crossed the plateau of the Bossons; thus, as he says, qualifying themselves to tell a pompous tale on their return of the dangers they had run and the courage with which they had surmounted them. Higher up the party came to a cave where the guides had left a ladder and a long pole for use on the glacier;

the ladder was there, but the pole had been stolen. De Saussure consoled himself with the jest it could not be called a highway robbery (*vol de grande route*). The whole climb to the top of the Montagne de la Côte took nearly six hours and a half. His tent was pitched against one of the big boulders brought down by the glacier, Whymper thinks from the Rochers Rouges. Three of the guides went off to reconnoitre the entrance on the ice and to cut steps. They came back three hours later to report that the glacier was not too difficult. Marie Couttet, however, had broken though the crust over a hidden crevasse, but as they were luckily roped, Marie was held up between the other two. They told the story very cheerfully, but the news spread gloom over the faces of the other guides, despite some jests which they launched at one another, and which the victims sometimes failed to appreciate.

Next morning (the 2nd August) the start was delayed till 6.30 by disputes among the guides as to the distribution of their loads, a cause of delay only too familiar to the explorers of the Caucasus and the Himalaya of the present day.

'The entry on the glacier proved easy, but soon one plunges into a labyrinth of *séracs* divided by great crevasses, some entirely open, some choked with snow, others crossed by frail arches which are the only safe means of traversing them. In places a narrow ice-ridge serves as a bridge; when the crevasses are absolutely open one is obliged to descend into the bottom and climb the opposite wall by means of steps cut in the hard ice. There are moments when it seems that it must be impossible to find a way out. Yet as long as the ice is bare, however narrow the ridges, however steep the slopes, these brave Chamoniards, whose heads and feet are equally firm, show no sign of fear, or even anxiety—they talk, laugh, joke between themselves; but when the track lies across these vaults hung over hidden abysses one sees them marching without a word, the three in front tied together by ropes at a distance of five or six feet apart, their eyes fixed on their feet, and each placing his foot exactly in the steps of his predecessor. It was above all at the spot where Marie Couttet had broken through that this sort of alarm culminated. The snow had suddenly failed under his feet, leaving a hole six or seven feet in diameter and laying open a chasm of which neither the sides nor the bottom were visible, and that in a place where there was no visible sign to give the slightest warning of danger.' [*Voyages*, 1973.]

Nearly three hours were spent in this formidable icefall. Then steeper but less treacherous slopes of snow led up to the foot of the lowest of the crags since known as the Grands Mulets. After a short rest on the rocks the party, profiting by a snow-bridge which was likely to fall later in the season, swerved to the right and then back again to the higher block of the chain of rocks, that on which a second cabin had been built.

De Saussure's guides now compelled him to a long halt. They were very averse to sleeping on the snow, and their object was to delay him so that they might not get before nightfall into a region where there were no rocks. However, it was only eleven when they started again. De Saussure had spent the time in examining the nature of the rocks and admiring the broken masses of the ice that tumbles from the recess under the Aiguille du Midi. As the climbers advanced, portions of the Lake of Geneva, with the town of Nyon, came into view, and the ranges of Faucigny gradually sank below the horizon, the Aiguille Percée du Reposoir being the last to dip beneath the blue line of the distant Jura. 'Each victory of this sort was a matter of rejoicing to all the caravan, for nothing is so cheering and encouraging as a clear proof of progress.'

De Saussure proceeds in his diary:

'One rests from time to time on one's pole, but a few minutes are enough; the caravan marches slowly because it does not wish to go faster; they rarely make more than thirty steps without halting to take breath; still they only sit down every half-hour.'

They now came to the edge of a vast crevasse.

'Although it was more than a hundred feet in breadth one could nowhere see the bottom. At the moment when we were all collected on its brink admiring its depth and observing the courses of its snowy walls, my servant, from I know not what distraction, let slip the pedestal of my barometer which he had in his hand. It slid with the swiftness of an arrow down the sloping wall of the crevasse and planted itself at a great depth in the opposite side, where it remained fixed and quivering like the lance of Achilles on the bank of the Scamander. I was extremely vexed, for this pedestal served not only for the barometer, but for a compass, a telescope, and several other instruments. But without hesitation several of the guides, seeing my vexation, offered to recover it, and when the fear of imperilling them made me hesitate, protested that there was no risk. In a moment one of them tied the rope under his arms and the others let him down to the pedestal, which he snatched and brought up in triumph. During this operation I was doubly anxious, first for the guide who was roped, next because, being in view of Chamonix, whence with a telescope our movements could be watched, I feared they would have their eyes fixed on us and be sure to imagine it was one of us who was lost in the crevasse whom we were trying to rescue. I learnt afterwards that at that moment they were fortunately not looking at us.' [*Voyages*, 1978.]

Having crossed this obstacle by a perilous bridge, they reached by a steep slope the highest but one of the rocks of the Grands Mulets chain, which on his return de Saussure named the Rocher de l'Heureux Retour. Here they arrived at 1.30 and dined in the sunshine with good appetite. Water was wanting, but the guides, by throwing snowballs against the warm rocks, soon procured an adequate supply.

'This isolated rock surrounded by the snows seemed to the guides a Palace of Delight, a Garden of Calypso; they could not make up their minds to leave it, and were determined to pass the night here. They had only sought it with that object, for it is off the route. They fancied that during the night the cold on these vast snowfields must be absolutely insupportable, and they were seriously afraid that they would perish. I only persuaded them to go on by promising I would dig a large hole in the snow, in which I would set up the tent, and we would all sleep inside it.'

Half an hour later they came to the 'First Plateau' [now known as the Petit Plateau]. On the left de Saussure admired 'the vertical position of the strata in the cliffs of the Aiguille du Midi; on the right, close at hand, the rounded head of the Dôme du Goûter, crowned by a tier of icy cliffs, presented a magnificent spectacle. In front was Mont Blanc.

'The rocks on its left we call [at Geneva] the Staircase of Mont Blanc [the Monts Maudits], supported cliffs of the most brilliant snow. We took twenty minutes to cross this plateau, which seemed to us very long—for since the guides' last ascent it had been swept by two enormous ice-avalanches, and we had to cross their débris in fear of being overtaken by another.[1] I noticed that the lowest portion

---

[1] I have, in three ascents of Mont Blanc, crossed the Petit Plateau, and never without being obliged to traverse the remains of a fairly recent avalanche. This is the chief danger-spot on the ordinary route up Mont Blanc, but accidents have been fortunately rare. In 1891, however, five of a party of seven were

of the ice-cliff next to the rocks is ice, harder and more compact than that of glaciers in ordinary, and I recognised all the gradations between snow and ice, for the top of each block is snow. Some blocks—not less than twelve feet in diameter—had travelled far without breaking up. One cannot but reflect in passing on the danger from these avalanches, a danger one would not naturally anticipate, as the foot of the cliff is at some distance and the slope below it gentle. The violence and mass of the fall must be enormous to carry the blocks so far.'

An hour's march up a slope of 34°, broken by a splendid crevasse, brought the party to the lower verge of the second, now called the Grand Plateau. It was four o'clock, and with many misgivings as to hidden crevasses, they began to look about for a site for a camp. They finally fixed on a spot a hundred yards from the top of the slope.

Directly the guides set to work to dig a platform in the snow they began to suffer from the rarity of the air, and had to rest after every five or six spadefuls had been lifted. De Saussure found himself exhausted by making some barometrical observations. While waiting for the tent to be pitched they were all very wretched: those who worked felt sick, those who rested suffered from the cold. All were exceptionally thirsty, but had to wait till some snow had been melted on the fire that was successfully lit.

The plateau on which they found themselves led to a cul-de-sac. To the east were the rocks passed in the ascent, to the west a gentle slope leading to the Dôme du Goûter. The morrow's route and the very steep slope to be climbed were full in view.[1]

De Saussure describes the scene, the complete environment by dazzling snows, the whiteness of which contrasted with the dark blue of the heavens, the cold and the silence. He takes the occasion to pay a tribute to his predecessors.

'When I pictured to myself Dr. Paccard and Jacques Balmat arriving in the decline of day in this desert without shelter, without hope of succour, without even the assurance that man could live at the height they were aiming at, and yet persevering undaunted in their adventure, I admired their resolution and their courage.'

---

swept by an avalanche into a crevasse, and two of them perished. Whymper's assertion that avalanches seldom, if ever, extend right across the plateau must therefore, not be trusted.

[1] De Saussure writes of three plateaux. Whymper failed to recognise that he divides what is now called the Grand Plateau into a second and a third plateau. There is a rise of some 160 feet in the middle of the Grand Plateau.

After a rest three of the guides went off in the direction of the Dôme du Goûter to collect rocks, and, on their way back, to cut some steps for next day. They found a crevasse which had hindered them on the previous ascent was choked, but reported the slope to be very hard and steep.

The tent once pitched, all the guides crowded in, and after an early supper, 'eaten with appetite but digested with disgust,' de Saussure prepared to endure what proved a 'detestable night—sickness, colic, close atmosphere produced by twenty heated and panting inmates.'

'I was obliged to go out in the middle of the night for fresh air. The magnificent basin, glowing in the light of the moon which shone with the greatest brilliancy in an ebon sky, presented a superb spectacle. Jupiter rose radiant behind the Aiguille du Midi, and the glow reflected from the snows was so brilliant that only stars of the first and second magnitude were visible. After midnight, as we were dropping into sleep, we were awakened by the roar of a great avalanche which covered part of the slope we had to follow on the morrow.'

Daybreak at last brought the long penance of night to a close. The guides as usual were slow in moving, and then water had to be melted, so that it was 6 A.M. before the party set off. Pioneers were again sent in front to prepare a path. De Saussure writes:

'After having crossed the second plateau, at the entry to which we had slept, we mounted on the third, and in half an hour reached the foot of the great slope which runs towards the east over the rock which forms the left shoulder of Mont Blanc.'

De Saussure, whose personal experience of the effect of the rarefied air on Mont Blanc contrasts markedly with his subsequent immunity on the Col du Géant, was already distressed, and had to halt every thirty steps for a few moments to regain breath. After forty minutes' climb the party came on the track of the avalanche that had fallen in the night,

'and each of us made to himself his own reflections. Pierre Balmat said to me very politely that I must recover my breath and try to cross the avalanche track without halting. I, who felt the impossibility of complying, answered him with equal politeness "that the safest spot was where the unstable snows had just fallen"; and we took breath twice in crossing. The slope now became steeper, and we had to cross a crevasse at the corner of a *sérac* which barred the passage. This was one of the worst places ; the slope is 39°, the precipice below is frightful, and the snow, hard on the surface, was flour beneath. Steps were cut, but the legs insecurely placed in this flour rested on a lower crust which was often very thin, and then slipped. Here I found the pole held by two guides as a balustrade for me on the side of the precipice was of great service.' [*Diary*.]

This steep ascent, known henceforth as the 'Ancien Passage,' lasted for two hours before the party gained the little depression or *col* between the eastern shoulder and the final cupola of Mont Blanc.

'Immense view of Italy, but sickness. I eat some bread and frozen beef, raw and nasty, and drink some water which had been carried up for me.' There now remained to climb only some 900 feet up a moderate slope, free from any difficulty or danger. But de Saussure's sufferings from mountain sickness became acute, he felt faint and dizzy, his legs failed under him, between every fifteen or sixteen steps he had to rest on his stick. The only palliative was to face and inhale the fresh northern breeze.[1] The party spent two hours on this last slope, for which Whymper's *Guide* allows fifty minutes.

'Since,' writes de Saussure, 'I had had for the last two hours under my eyes almost all one sees from the summit, the arrival was no *coup de théâtre*—it did not even give me all the pleasure one might have imagined; my most lively and agreeable sensation was to feel myself at the end of my uncertainties; for the length of the struggle, the recollection and the still vivid impression of the exertion it had

---

[1] See sec. 559 in *Voyages*. There de Saussure lays down about 12,000 feet as the height at which he and the majority of dwellers in mountain districts begin to feel the results of the rarity of the air directly they undertake any exertion, mental or physical. It may be worth noting that in the first two ascents of Elbruz, 18,500 feet, one on a windy the other on a still day, both made by mountaineers in good training, no one suffered on the windy day, while all more or less suffered on the still day. In the Alps Mont Blanc is exceptional with regard to mountain sickness. The continuous, monotonous snowy treadmill of the ascent may partly account for this. On Monte Rosa very few cases of sickness are recorded; nor, as a rule, do climbers suffer inconvenience elsewhere in the Alps. It is noteworthy that since fair quarters have been provided on Mont Blanc much less has been heard of serious indisposition on the part of travellers and guides. The men who slept at the Vallot hut, while employed to build Jansen's hut on the top, climbed the last slope at a great pace: *experto crede*. I once tried to keep up with them in order to conceal from too inquisitive telescopes in the Guides' Bureau that in our party of three there was only one guide, a breach of the local regulations.

cost me, caused me a kind of irritation. At the moment that I trod the highest point of the snow that crowned the summit I trampled it with a feeling of anger rather than of pleasure. Besides, my object was not only to reach the highest point, I was bound to make the observations and experiments which alone gave value to my venture, and I was very doubtful of being able to carry out more than a portion of what I had planned.

'Still the grand spectacle I had under my eyes gave me a lively pleasure. A light haze suspended in the lower layers of the atmosphere hid, it is true, the more distant and low-lying objects, such as the plains of France and Lombardy,[1] but I did not greatly regret this loss; that which I came to see, and now recognised with the greatest clearness, was the order of the great ranges of which I had so long desired to ascertain the grouping. I could hardly believe my eyes, it seemed a dream, when I saw under my feet these majestic peaks, these formidable Aiguilles du Midi, d'Argentière [Aiguille Verte], du Géant, of which I had found even the bases so difficult and dangerous of approach. I seized their connections, their relation, their structure, and a single glance cleared away doubts which years of work had not sufficed to remove.' [*Voyages*, 1991.]

It is noteworthy that de Saussure, bent as he was on a crowd of scientific inquiries and hampered by physical discomforts, was yet able to appreciate the splendour of the spectacle. For, despite its frequent disparagement by more or less exhausted tourists, Mont Blanc offers to those who have eyes to see a unique panorama. On the east the great group of the Aiguille Verte and Grandes Jorasses presents in the foreground a noble and imposing sheaf of summits: beyond, the forested slopes and green alps of the Valais separate the peaks of the Oberland from the Pennine snows; to the south the depths of Val d'Aosta, seamed with a thinnest ribbon of straight white road, divide the Grand Combin and Monte Rosa groups from the silver shield of the Ruitor and the sharp spears of the Graians. Away to the south-west the golden cornfields and green meadows of the Val d'Isère above Grenoble bask in the midday sunshine, fenced by the distant crags of Dauphiné. Turning towards the north-west the heights of the Jura lie like a blue ribbon across the landscape, separating the Swiss lakes and

---

[1] No part of the plain of Lombardy or Piedmont is visible from Mont Blanc, nor is Mont Blanc seen from the Piedmontese plain. The Grand Paradis is often taken for it. The mountain is well seen from the railway near Macon.

lowlands from the plains of Burgundy and Franche-Comté, which stretch out in faint amethystine spaces that melt into the far-off horizon. There are doubtless many more picturesque summit-views in the Alps. But for an equally impressive and suggestive panorama the climber must go to the Caucasus or Sikkim.

De Saussure in his manuscript diary gives a prodigious—to use his own favourite adjective—list of the work he accomplished in the four and a half hours he spent on the top of Mont Blanc, and concludes it with the following sentence :

'My work would have been far more complete had I been in any ordinary situation, and I venture to boast that it needed no common effort to accomplish what I did in the condition I was. Despite the delight which this superb spectacle gave me, I felt a painful sense of not being able to draw from it all the profit possible, and that my power of appreciation was limited by my difficulty in breathing. I was like an epicure invited to a splendid festival and prevented from enjoying it by violent nausea.

'At length the clouds which had gathered under my feet about the tops of the lower mountains began to collect round Mont Blanc. The fear of taking as long to go down as I had to mount forced me, at 3.30 P.M., to leave this post which I had so long wished to reach. I went with a regret in my heart at not having got all the advantage I had hoped out of it. For though I had set to work first on what seemed to me of the greatest interest, I counted what I had done but little compared to what I had hoped to do.'

To the top of the Rochers Rouges the party took under an hour :

'Here began the trying part of the descent. The view of the precipices was rendered more alarming by a burning sun which shone in my eyes and softened the surface of the snow which was our support. From the top to the camp took us half the time it had in mounting, and that without any exhaustion, which proves it is the pressure on the chest from lifting the knees which causes the enormous fatigue one feels in going uphill. An hour more brought us to a rock I call the "Rocher de l'Heureux Retour." It was 7.15, and I determined to sleep there. We pitched our tent against the southern end of the rock in a truly singular situation. It was on the snow and at the edge of a great crevasse which cut it off from a very steep slope falling towards the great hollow under the rocks of the Dôme. This rock is opposite what we call from Geneva the third staircase of Mont Blanc [Mont Blanc de Tacul]; it is not the highest of the isolated chain—there is another, reddish in colour, separated from it by the snowfield and half buried. I search for lichens and find some, also some moss, a gramen, and a pretty bunch of *Silene acaulis*.

'The clouds assembled, or rather scattered, in the valleys and on the mountains below us produce the most singular effect; they resemble towers, castles, giants, the strangest shapes in place of the level slabs one sees from the plain. Above these clouds we see the Jura bordered by a red ribbon made up of two bands, the lower the darker, almost blood-colour, while from the upper springs a flame like an aurora, irregular, clear, and mottled. From here the top of the Reposoir (the Aiguille Percée) was just level with that of the Jura.

'Next morning start at 6.15 for the final descent. Pass the cabin built the previous year. Very frail bridge—one of the guides who quits our steps goes through with one leg. Slope of 50° to avoid some crevasses that have opened. Then into the thick of the glacier, difficulties in path-finding, wanderings to and fro, ladder frequently in use. I note on the glacier some traces of red snow, but I saw not the least vestige of it above the upper cabin; the upper snows are of the purest white, and though there is dust in places, it is the grey dust detached by wind from the neighbouring rocks.

'We saw no insects or flies or birds, the last living thing I noticed was a little grey moth on the first plateau. However, one was seen near the top of Mont Blanc. At last, very impatient of the long march on the glacier, we touch land at half-past nine. Slip of one of the guides, who nearly tumbles into a crevasse and loses one of the sticks of my tent. A great icicle falls with a crash into a crevasse, shakes the glacier, and frightens all my troop. I find M. Bourrit, who hoped to make the ascent, but the guides refuse. Sunday mass and weariness call them home.

'I descend to Les Monts, where I meet the mules and ride in an hour and twenty minutes to Le Prieuré. Great emotion and tender embraces with my wife, my sisters-in-law, and Madame Necker de Germagny [his daughter's mother-in-law].

'I am not tired, only a little stiff, and the enormous descent of to-day accounts for that; my eyes are quite right, and I am but little sunburnt, though the bad condition of the Glacier de la Côte forced me to take off my veil in order to see to my footing.'[1]

---

[1] De Saussure paid his guides for the ascent, including J. Balmat, five louis each. In previous years de Saussure in his journal notes that on ordinary tours he paid his guides four *livres de Piémont* a day, without food, which he thought dear.

A day or two later de Saussure's Bernese friend and correspondent Wyttenbach met at Servoz the Happy Warrior on his return. He describes how de Saussure rushed into his arms with the exclamation: 'Congratulate me: I come from the conquest of Mont Blanc.' After all, de Saussure had the feelings of a climber as well as of a philosopher!

It was no doubt on reading the first account of his success that Madame Necker was drawn to address to de Saussure (with whom she had recently become connected by his daughter's marriage to her nephew) her congratulations:

'We have trembled while following you among precipices and perils; you have made us experience all the feelings of hope and fear which render the life of the chamois-hunter at once so delightful and so terrible; we have fancied ourselves enjoying with you the magnificent spectacle with which you were greeted when, a modern Enceladus, you scaled Mont Blanc.

'You have lifted my soul, Monsieur, by showing me these storehouses of the world, and I continually grieve at the weakness which hinders me from following in your footsteps. But my imagination supplies my lack of strength. While I read you I hear the dull roar of avalanches and the palpitations of the electric current. Full of terror and admiration I see at times in the distance the grave of the rash hunter, I watch his shade wandering peacefully in these solitudes, and feel that I envy him. I imagine that I could wish to end my days in these quiet retreats beside M. Necker, so as to render a last homage to Nature and to married love, the only things that remain to us in the wreck of all the illusions of life. We have shuddered together over your dangers while admiring your courage; and, remembering the ties that attach us to you, we feel we have a right to urge you to take care of a life very dear to us.'

Bourrit, who, forced by the guides' refusal, had returned to Chamonix with de Saussure, very pluckily started again next day for the bivouac, but, with his habitual bad luck, met with a break in the weather. His equally habitual impatience again betrayed him. The break was but a passing storm. His guides, he tells us, held a debate about waiting at the bivouac or returning, but what decided the question was his having some dust blown into his eye. His son states that his father's eyes suffered from exposure to the rough weather. This incident is accounted for by Mr. Mark Beaufoy, the young Englishman who on the 8th of

August, only five days after de Saussure's ascent, climbed Mont Blanc. He mentions that he picked up on the mountain Bourrit's blue spectacles and made use of them.

Sleeping at de Saussure's second cabin—which de Saussure had made no use of—Beaufoy reached the top at 10.30 A.M. and stayed there two hours, thus proving that de Saussure's original project for dividing the day's work was a very feasible one. Paccard, in the memoranda relating to ascents of Mont Blanc which he left behind him, remarks that Beaufoy walked like a guide.

Poor Bourrit, who is recorded to have wept on witnessing de Saussure's arrival on the summit, lingered on at Chamonix only to watch and chronicle his rivals' successes, and to prepare ladders for another attempt that never came off. He found some distraction in conversing with Beaufoy's young wife. The help she was able to give her husband in writing out his observations filled Bourrit with admiration for the education of Englishwomen.[1] But Beaufoy himself disappointed the sentimental Precentor. For when on being asked in his wife's presence if his first thought on gaining the summit had been of her, he replied, 'Not at all.' In matters of the heart Englishmen are apt to do themselves injustice in the eyes of members of less reticent nationalities, who do not realise that still waters may run deep.

Beaufoy was a man of scientific tastes and attainments, and a paper on his ascent was read before the Royal Society on the 13th December of the same year.[2] He appears to have been more successful than Sir William Hamilton in calling the attention of the Society to the eminent claims of his predecessor, for in the following year de Saussure was admitted to a seat on its benches. But though Beaufoy himself became a Fellow, his paper on Mont Blanc was not considered worth printing in the *Transactions* of that learned body. Nor did the *Relation Abrégée* receive that honour.

Colonel Beaufoy—as he afterwards became—kept up his interest in science and exploration throughout his life. In 1818

[1] Bourrit asserts that Mrs. Beaufoy was only nineteen. She had, however, been married three years, and had two children.

[2] The paper was reprinted from the original manuscript, in the possession of the Royal Society, in the *Alpine Journal*, vol. xxix. (1915). It had previously appeared in the number for 18th February 1817 of *The Annals of Philosophy*, a scientific magazine.

he published articles on the North-West Passage and on the possibility of reaching the North Pole. He died in 1827, and is buried in Stanmore Church, where an inscription records his services to astronomy and the science of navigation.

We shall meet Bourrit again on the Col du Géant. But his last climb on Mont Blanc calls for an honourable mention here. In the following year, 1788, he renewed his assault as a member of a combined—it may almost be called an international—expedition. His companions were an Englishman named Woodley and a Dutchman named Camper. The weather was broken and the wind high. The Englishman and his guide alone got to the top. Bourrit, whose slow pace soon left him in the rear, gave in, after a plucky struggle, at the last rocks, the Petits Mulets, only 400 feet below the summit. His failure supplied the 'Historiographer' with material for a spirited narrative, in which he almost persuades his readers—and quite persuaded himself—that he had, for all practical purposes, attained the long-sought goal.

De Saussure lost no time on his return in giving to the public an account of his ascent. A brief preliminary note in the second number of the newly-founded *Journal de Genève* was followed within a week by the carefully drawn up *Relation Abrégée*, subsequently incorporated in the *Voyages*. Geneva, which seems to have paid but little attention to the conquest of the mountain by the two Chamoniards in the previous year, was thrilled by the success of its illustrious Professor. Now when the Geneva of the eighteenth century was thrilled, politically or otherwise, it made a practice of bursting into rhymed prose.

By such an event as the conquest of Mont Blanc the local Muse, not, it must be admitted, a frequenter of the heights of Parnassus, was naturally roused to make special efforts. Several of the poems written for the occasion survive, notably a long tribute or *Hommage* to de Saussure composed by a minor playwright of the period named Marignié.[1] For the benefit of the curious I have appended at the end of this chapter extracts from this and other compositions of a like character. In these the reader will find a harrowing description of the terrors of Madame

[1] 'Hommage à M. de Saussure sur son ascension et ses expériences physiques au sommet du Mont Blanc.'

de Saussure and the anxiety of her sisters while they watched the progress of the climbers, a picture, it must be said, hardly borne out by the letters already printed. He will be amused by striking specimens of the passion for puerile allusions to the Classics, which infects the political pamphlets of Geneva, and would seem to have been a principal result of the system of teaching de Saussure tried in vain to reform. In the rival suggestions to attach a personal name to the great mountain he may recognise an echo both of the political controversies of the moment and of the personal jealousies of Bourrit.

NOTE

VERSES ON DE SAUSSURE'S ASCENT OF MONT BLANC

I give here a few short extracts from three of the copies of verses called forth by the early ascents of Mont Blanc. The first of these, Marignié's tribute to de Saussure, extended to 112 lines. The passage describing de Saussure's start and the emotions of his family may serve as a specimen of its style. I leave out five lines devoted to Madame de Saussure's telescope, 'ce tube qu'approche l'objet qu'éloigne la distance':

> 'Il marche ; vingt chasseurs ardens, pleins de courage,
> Guides des curieux dans ce séjour sauvage,
> Partagent avec lui ses travaux périlleux :
> On dirait des Titans escaladant les cieux.
> Son épouse elle est là, mêlée aux spectateurs,
> Sur son époux sans cesse elle a fixé sa vue
> Sa présence soutient son âme suspendue
> Et son éloignement la livre à la terreur. . . .
> Elle le voit, s'écrie, et dans sa joie extrême
> Appelle à l'observer les doux objets qu'elle aime
> Et ses fidèles sœurs et ses fils chéris ;
> Sa fille manque seule à ses sens attendris.'

The conclusion is an appeal to the public of a kind that has been more than once made since by indiscreet climbers, or their admirers, eager to use mountains as personal monuments.

> 'Si, courant à la hâte, entraîné par le zèle,
> Soudain j'ai célébré cette gloire nouvelle
> Je demande pour prix que le nom du vainqueur
> S'attache au mont fameux qu'a franchi son ardeur,
> Que par ma voix il parvienne à la race future
> Paré d'un nom plus beau, du nom de Mont Saussure.'

This foolish, if well-meant, suggestion called forth, as was to be expected, a counterblast. Here was an opportunity for a bard of the popular party, a Représentant, to tune his lyre. One was found in E. S. Reybaz, an eloquent preacher and something of a rhymer, who, concerned in the affair of 1782, had left Geneva for Paris,[1] while we can hardly be wrong in recognising in the background Bourrit, eager to provide material for such a theme. There can be little doubt that he had a finger in the ' Epître à Messieurs Balmat et Pacard (sic) sur leur ascension du Mont Blanc le 8 Août 1786,' which followed promptly on the publication of Marignié's tribute. The internal evidence is strong. Not only is Bourrit mentioned in a footnote on the first page, but on the last page, a couplet, amplified by another footnote, celebrates his art :

' Bourrit par ses pinceaux fait briller ces hauteurs
Où se verse aujourd'hui l'or des admirateurs.'

The writer is at pains to show his erudition and reading. Balmat is compared to Columbus and other discoverers or inventors who were robbed of the fame due to them. He is an athlete ; de Saussure only a philosopher :

' On ne vit jamais chez les Grecs Aristote, ou Platon,
Le disputer encore au terrible Milon.'

The Bourrit version of the ascent is faithfully rendered as follows :

' Toutefois dans son cœur Balmat sent un besoin :
Aux beautés qu'il contemple il faut plus d'un témoin,
Il faut à ses transports un cœur qui les partage :
Il descend : il revoit non loin du pic sauvage
Son ami succombant aux peines, à l'effroi ;
" Compagnon," lui dit-il, " J'ai vaincu sans toi,
Un déplaisir secret attriste ma victoire,
Que tout nous soit commun, le péril est partout,
Mais Balmat te soutient, et l'honneur est au bout ! " '

Growing more eloquent and classical as he draws to a close, the bard apostrophises Balmat :

' Ah ! qu'un riche lettré, noble en ses jouissances
Porte jusqu'au Mont Blanc le luxe des sciences,
Qu'attentifs à ses pas vingt guides éprouvés
Le sauvent des périls qu'ils ont vingt fois bravés,
J'applaudis ; c'est Jason et sa troupe intrépide
Qui s'arment pour dompter l'Hydre de la Colchide ;
Leur victoire me plaît et ne m'étonne pas ;
Mais qu'Hercule tout seul étouffe dans ses bras
Ce monstre rugissant, l'effroi de la Némée,
Hercule est plus qu'un homme et vaut seul une armée.'

---

[1] Reybaz was Minister Resident of the Genevan Republic at Paris from 1794 to 1797.

These were not the only verses dedicated to the climbers. Paccard had his poetess in a Mlle. Chapuis, who in two lines summarised the discussion in his favour :

> 'De Saussure à la cime est arrivé trop tard
> Et déjà le Mont Blanc était le Mont Paccard.'

And she met with a sympathiser in the *Gazette de Lausanne* (August 25, 1787) :

> 'Mortels, ne courez plus après un vain renom,
> L'Erreur et l'Injustice maîtrisent la Nature :
> Vespuce à l'Amérique a su donner son nom
> Et le Mont Paccard est nommé le Mont Saussure.'

There was no limit to the congratulations and poetical tributes showered on the heroes of the hour. One came from a murderer in prison enduring a life sentence, a noble Savoyard of the name of de Coppenex. It was described as by 'Le petit domicilié de l'Hôtel de Patience, le dix-huit du mois d'Auguste et la cent vingt-neuvième lune de sa captivité.'

These effusions, however small their literary claims, seem worth notice, as evidence of the interest created at the time by de Saussure's success, and also as specimens of a class of composition—topical squibs—much in favour in the Geneva of the eighteenth century.

We have an interesting comment on the *Epître* in a manuscript note on the copy of it preserved in the Library of the Geneva branch of the Swiss Alpine Club. Good grounds exist for believing it to be written by the late M. Henri de Saussure, the grandson of Horace Benedict. In any case, the opinion of the character of Jacques Balmat here expressed coincides exactly with that given to me verbally by M. H. de Saussure when I visited him at Genthod in 1891. The note runs :

'The preceding *Epître* must be considered as a disguised diatribe directed against H. B. de Saussure. It appeared at an epoch when the revolutionary agitation in France had begun to spread to Geneva, and when certain parties strove to depreciate everything connected with the old families.

'The following Dialogue set things fairly right. Jacques Balmat was never anything but a hired journeyman (*ouvrier*) of H. B. de Saussure. It was only the prospect of the large reward offered by the latter which ended in drawing Balmat to the top of Mont Blanc. He several times abandoned his attempt on finding himself followed by other guides. Always greedy of gain, his great fear was that of having to share with others, not the glory, but the money. That is, no doubt, what Marignié would have put in Balmat's mouth had he known the facts.

'Balmat presents the most exact specimen of the type of Savoyard with a spirit limited to narrow interests. If he ended by associating himself with Dr. Paccard, it was because the latter sought nothing for himself.

'Balmat the explorer, eager for discovery, striving for fame, who has been depicted by various writers, is a Balmat of legend and pure phantasy.'

The third document, the Dialogue, also by Marignié, to which M. H. de Saussure alludes, survives. It is entitled : 'Scène Dialoguée entre Balmat et l'Auteur de *l'Hommage* à l'occasion de *l'Epître* d'un anonyme à MM. Paccard et Balmat.'

In this somewhat heavy pleasantry Balmat is represented as calling on the author of the *Hommage* and introducing himself as all the characters in turn to whom he has been compared in the *Epître* before he reveals his own identity :

'*L'Auteur.* N'aurez-vous jamais un véritable nom ?
'*Balmat.* O que si, mais, Monsieur, quand on a l'avantage
   De compter pour patrons des gens de haut parage
   On s'en vante un moment. Mais pour ne plus mentir,
   Je suis le Savoyard Balmat à votre service.'

After several pages of rhymes the author sums up the discussion :

'Balmat, votre bon sens me ravit et m'enchante.
 Voilà ce que dans vous vraiment il faut qu'on chante. . . .
 Ici comme partout on manque à l'apropos
 Vous êtes un brave homme, on vous fait un héros :
 Si vous l'étiez, voyez que de votre victoire
 On rehaussirait moins le mérite et la gloire :
 On dirait : " Après tout, il a fait son métier ;
 Ainsi qu'à galoper s'exerce le coursier,
 Le montagnard s'exerce à gravir sur les cimes ;
 Il est fait au danger, il est fait aux abîmes ;
 Et c'est même une honte pour un chasseur savoyard
 De ne s'être là-haut élevé que si tard." '

CHAPTER IX

THE COL DU GÉANT

The concluding sentences of de Saussure's *Short Narrative* indicate that he was already planning a fresh Alpine adventure. As was usual with him, his main object in the proposed expedition was not exploration or cartography, but scientific and, in this instance, more particularly meteorological research. His stay on the top of Mont Blanc had been too short to enable him to carry out the long list of observations and experiments he had tabulated on his agenda, and until the gaps were filled up he could not rest satisfied. An opportunity now presented itself. The summer of 1787 had been marked not only by three ascents of Mont Blanc,[1] but also by the opening of the legendary pass from Chamonix to Courmayeur across the lofty ridge that fronts the traveller's eyes from the head of the Val d'Aosta, and forms part of the watershed at the head of the snowy recess known as the Tacul, the source of the southern feeder of the Mer de Glace.

The climb from the Italian side, though long and steep, offers no serious difficulty, and the crest had doubtless been reached by chamois and bouquetin hunters long before the visit of Patience,[2] the innkeeper and hunter of Courmayeur who had once served de Saussure as guide in his excursion on the Miage Glacier. The main obstacle to the passage of the chain at this point lay, as it still does, in the broken icefall below the upper basin of the Glacier du Tacul, known in after years as Les Séracs du Géant.

The authentic history of the pass begins in 1786. But, like the Fiescher Joch in the Bernese Oberland, it has a legend. The oldest document quoted in its support is an account written by a

[1] Those of (1) the three guides, (2) de Saussure, (3) Colonel Beaufoy.

[2] 'Patience' was the nickname of Jean Laurent Jordanay, who died in 1825, aged eighty-five. He was often employed by de Saussure, and in the Parish Register of Courmayeur his death is entered with a note, 'Guide de M. de Saussure, naturaliste, sur le Mont Blanc.'

Piedmontese official of the name of Arnod of an attempt made by him with three hunters. There existed at Courmayeur, Arnod asserts, a vague tradition handed down from father to son, that a passage to Chamonix over the glaciers of Mont Fréty had once been practicable. He then describes his own attempt in 1689 :

'Je pris trois bons chasseurs avec des grappins aux pieds, des hâchons et des crocs de fer à la main pour se faire pas sur la glace Il n'y eut pourtant jamais moyen de pouvoir monter n'y avancer à cause des grandes crevaces et interruptions qui se sont faits depuis bien d'années.'[1]

Both Windham and Martel, in their respective pamphlets, record a similar tradition as prevalent at Chamonix, and a possible instance of such a passage is referred to in a letter by Gosse published in the *Journal de Genève*.[2] The experience of the last sixty years has shown living mountaineers that the only difficulty of the pass lies in traversing the broken glacier on the Savoyard side, the labyrinth of the Séracs du Géant, and that this varies greatly from year to year, and from month to month. In the late summer of 1863 first-rate guides held the icefall impassable, and led a party of travellers, of whom I was one, along the steep slopes of La Noire on the right of the glacier. On several subsequent occasions I have walked, both up and down, straight through the Séracs. It seems therefore reasonable to suppose that the story is not without foundation, and that from time to time some of the Courmayeur hunters, who, Bourrit tells us in his first book (1773), had gained the ridge from the south-east side, hardier than their comrades, risked the perils of the crevasses, and

[1] *Relation des Passages de tout le circuit du Duché d'Aosta* (1691 and 1692). Edited by Signor Vaccarone, *Boll. del Club Alpino Italiano*, 1880, and reprinted by Mr. Coolidge in his *Josias Simler*.

[2] Quoted in *Alpine Journal*, vol. ix. p. 88. The short time alleged to have been taken is a very uncertain proof. Sallanches might be reached from Courmayeur in less time by the Col des Fours than by the Col du Géant. Ribel, the courier in question, was a German of disreputable connections, whose wife was expelled from Geneva for immorality. On this occasion he was carrying letters from Geneva to Turin. The usual route was the Mont Cenis. The growth of the tradition seems to me very obvious. Bordier's report of a legend that peasants at one time were in the habit of crossing from Chamonix to Courmayeur in six hours or less, and his story of the witty Capuchin who asserted he had walked over the ice from Aosta to Chamonix in fourteen hours, are clearly exaggerations. Nor can the assertion of the Duc de la Rochefoucauld's guide (see *Ann. du Club Alpin Français*, vol. xx. (1893)) be easily fitted to any pass approached by the Mer de Glace. It is possibly a misreported reference to the Col du Tour.

crossed from Chamonix to Courmayeur, or *vice versâ*, by the Mer de Glace.

Whether this putative hunters' pass is referred to by the words 'Col Major' found on old maps is a wholly distinct question. On some of these maps we find 'Col Major ou Cormoyeu,' which suggests a cartographer's or copyist's error. There is no ground whatever for the suggestion that de Saussure had ever heard the pass so designated. In writing to his wife he expressly states that this point in the watershed had been called the Tacul, though nowhere near the spot at the junction of the sources of the Mer de Glace properly so named, and that he had consequently with the approval of his guides named it the Col du Géant after the adjacent Aiguille.

It was not till September 1786 that the first fully recorded attempt to force a pass at the head of the Mer de Glace was made. At that date, M. Exchaquet, the director of the mines at Servoz, a man who knew as much about the mountains of Savoy as anyone then living, and was frequently consulted by de Saussure, resolved to put into execution the project he had long had in his mind of rediscovering the lost pass.

Exchaquet's share in Alpine exploration deserves more notice than it has generally received. His correspondence with de Saussure and Wyttenbach shows him to have been an observer of considerable intelligence, specially in matters connected with meteorology. He had also a talent for topography, which he put to practical and profitable use by constructing and selling relief models of the chain of Mont Blanc, of part of the Valais, and of the St. Gotthard group. The models of Mont Blanc were sold for the high price of thirty louis. They were made of wood, the snows and pastures shown in their natural colours, and the glaciers represented by fragments of spar tinted sky-blue. Their size was about 3 feet 6 inches by 15 inches.[1]

[1] There was at the time a certain demand for reliefs of this kind, resulting from the newly awakened interest in the Alps. The only copy of Exchaquet's relief of Mont Blanc believed to exist is that presented by Baron de Gersdorf to the Museum at Görlitz. In London, thirty years later, J. B. Troye, of Frith Street, Soho, who advertised himself as a pupil of Exchaquet, and had probably been his workman, offered for sale small models of Mont Blanc. One, perhaps of his construction, is in the possession of the Alpine Club. General Pfyffer's and Meyer's models of the Swiss Alps have been noticed elsewhere (see p. 163).

It is recorded that on Napoleon's visit to Chambéry in 1805, a model of

Exchaquet's prolonged residence at Servoz, where he was engaged as 'Directeur-Général of the Mines of Faucigny,' gave him opportunities for mountain excursions by which he fully profited. He went up the Buet five or six times, and at all hours of the day, in order to study the variations in the temperature. He climbed the Pointe de Tanneverge and several summits over the Val d'Illiez. He got very near to the top of one of the Aiguilles des Courtes above the Talèfre Glacier. He explored among the lesser summits of the western wing of the Bernese Oberland round the Sanetsch Pass, and as far east as the Gemmi and the Lötschen Thal. Though he never reached any peak rivalling Mont Blanc or Mont Vélan, his climbs above the snow-level and the extent of his wanderings entitle him to rank high among the early pioneers. By his success in overcoming the famous *séracs* he gave proof of his Alpine qualifications, and by his modesty in describing his adventure he afforded Bourrit an additional reason for ignoring a predecessor who diminished to some extent the exploits of the Precentor.

Exchaquet found a companion for his first attempt in a Mr. Hill, a member of one of several English families then resident at Geneva. They took with them three guides, and slept on the rocks at the Couvercle, the meeting-place of the glaciers that form the Mer de Glace. Next morning, when they assailed the formidable icefall, they found the crevasses numerous and large. 'Mr. Hill,' writes Exchaquet, 'not being accustomed to glaciers, greatly delayed our progress, so, seeing how little advance we had made in two hours, and reckoning that it would take many more to get through the bad part of the glacier, we resolved to return rather than risk having to pass the night among the snows of the Tacul.'

Mr. Hill subsequently went round Mont Blanc by the Col de Bonhomme and Col de la Seigne to Courmayeur. Thence with a friend, the guide Marie Couttet of Chamonix, and a local hunter, he climbed to the top of the pass and returned the same

Mont Blanc, 12 feet long, was placed in his apartment with these lines attached :
'Sur ses bases éternelles
Le Mont Blanc est moins assuré
Que dans nos cœurs fidèles,
De tes lois l'Empire sacré.'
Nothing is reported of what Napoleon thought of this somewhat cumbrous piece of furniture and flattery.

evening to Courmayeur. His object was not to cross the chain, but to ascertain the chances of approach to Mont Blanc from this side. De Saussure, we shall see, refers to this excursion in one of his letters written from the Col. It has been through a confusion, or combination, of these two explorations from opposite sides of the pass that several writers have been led to give our countryman the credit of having been the first traveller to cross it.

Early in the following summer (1787), M. Exchaquet resolved to make a fresh attempt to carry out his project. He told Marie Couttet and Jean Michel Cachat of his plans, and they promised to accompany him. But three days later, on 27th June, he found that Cachat and a comrade, Alexis Tournier, had slipped off—nominally to look for crystals. He lost no time in filling the former's place, and, starting next morning at 2.15 A.M. from Chamonix itself with Marie Couttet and Jean Michel Tournier, reached Courmayeur at 8 P.M. the same day, a very creditable performance for that date. The party had fine weather, and Exchaquet, who was obviously not, like Bourrit, a writer for the press, frankly stated that 'they met with no difficulties' in the passage. On the snowfields above the *séracs* they noticed footsteps, and on their arrival at Courmayeur they found that Cachat and his companion had anticipated them by twenty-four hours, and had been at pains to secure a certificate of their exploit from the local authorities. In the account the two guides gave of the passage they reported that the first shepherds they met on the Italian side fled from them in dismay, and that the villagers of Entrèves were equally astonished at their appearance by a route held from all times *inconnue et impraticable*.

The facts relating to the two earliest crossings of the Col du Géant given above are derived from an anonymous letter from Chamonix in the *Journal de Lausanne* (8th July 1787), and a narrative sent by M. Exchaquet to his friend Henri A. Gosse.[1] They have been frequently distorted. Bourrit appears once more as the principal author of the mischief. In the opening

[1] It was used by Gosse as foundation for a *Précis historique sur le passage de la Vallée de Chamonix à Cormayeur* (sic) *nouvellement retrouvée par les Glaciers des Bois et du Tacul*. It will be printed for the first time by Mr. Montagnier (*Alpine Journal*, vol. xxxiv.), who has also supplied me with the report of the guides.

of the pass he saw an opportunity to cover his repulse on Mont Blanc. If he could manage to cross the Grand Col, as the Chamoniards for the next hundred years called the pass, and write the first account of it, he might proclaim the adventure a mountaineering feat at least comparable to de Saussure's; in his own phrase, 'a discovery equivalent to the ascent of Mont Blanc.' This unworthy idea he proceeded to put into execution. In order to claim for himself the credit of the first passage by a traveller, he boldly omitted all notice of Exchaquet's previous success. We cannot but feel sorry for the vainglorious Precentor when we find him thus doing his best to diminish with posterity the credit his pluck in this instance fairly entitles him to.

Accordingly, on 27th August 1787, two months after Exchaquet's expedition, Bourrit set out with his second son, Charles, a boy of fifteen, and four of the best Chamonix guides, including the two men who had so unscrupulously anticipated Exchaquet. The party spent the night at the Montenvers. For the rest Bourrit must be left to narrate his own exploits. The following account is that which he sent to the Hon. Maria Craven, a daughter of the well-known Lady Craven, who, after being divorced from her English husband, married the Margrave of Anspach.[1] Miss Craven, a girl of seventeen, had, while staying at Vevey, heard of de Saussure's ascent and boldly applied to the 'Historiographer of the Alps' for details. Bourrit, enchanted at an opportunity to pose in that character, readily complied with the request, and characteristically could not resist the opportunity for adding an account of his own recent adventure. It was written, as given here, in the third person.

'On the morning of the 28th the party passed, by moonlight, Les Pontets, rocks many find so difficult that they look on them as an impassable barrier. At daybreak they entered on the ice. At a quarter to seven they reached the base of the Jorasse, and at eight began to climb the slopes of the Glacier du Tacul. They had a ladder twelve and a half feet long for crossing the crevasses, and they soon had occasion to use it. The water in the cracks was frozen, and the glacier covered with new snow. By nine the work of climbing and crossing the crevasses had doubled in difficulty; their position was horrible. They found themselves in cavities so narrow, so deep, and

---

[1] See *Dictionary of National Biography*.

so over-arched that they did not know how to get out of them. They had to climb ridges hollow underneath and encompassed by enormous precipices. The ledges on which they risked themselves were often only three inches wide. The axe for cutting staircases was as useful as the ladder and the rope, to which they had all tied themselves. Between ten and one o'clock the ladder was used thirty-eight times.

'They next reached steep plateaux (*sic*) cut by bottomless crevasses extending the whole breadth of the glacier, which might be a league, and so wide that the ladder scarcely stretched across them. About one clouds began to cover the summits, wind beat on them from every direction, and the cold increased. At two no clear sky was visible, the sea of ice they were traversing seemed boundless, they were like polar travellers, and the mists completed the parallel. The effect was as sublime as it was alarming. Their anxiety was further increased by the vast crevasses concealed under extremely thin snow-arches. They must have perished but for the rope by which they were attached. The guide Charlet broke through one of these fragile bridges, and had he not been carrying the ladder, he would never have been able to emerge from the abyss at his feet. His head, caught between the rungs, gave him the look of a man taken in a snare or a trap. At three their distress grew still greater because they found they had gone past the strait which they ought to take in order to get to Courmayeur, and they thought of returning in their footsteps, already half effaced by the wind and the falling snow. The cold began, too, to be insupportable, and the thermometer was at 6° below zero (Réaumur). Their hair, as well as their veils, were fringed with icicles. Young Bourrit had some half an inch in length. This youth, who had lost sensation in his feet and fingers, bore his sufferings with a courage which drew the admiration of the guides. The cold increased still more. At three their clothes froze, as well as the laces of their boots. The guides, firmly convinced that they had passed the point they had to make for, ran backwards and forwards like men who, after a shipwreck, avoid the waves by scrambling from rock to rock. They sought for some crag or passage by which they might escape from their perilous situation. M. Bourrit and his son, who kept close to him, were already planning to pass the night where they were rather than wander further. They proposed to break up the ladder to provide fuel, put their legs in their sacks, and huddle together. But the guides, who did not believe it possible to resist the cold of the night and the bad weather, were resolved to rescue them at all costs from this dreadful desert. The thermometer marked $7\frac{1}{2}$° below zero. At this moment a gust of wind drove off the mist and revealed some of the peaks. They saw clearly that the field of snow on which they were sloped downwards before them. This raised their hopes, and a second gust, while obscuring the crag they had just noticed, revealed another to their right but a short way off. Cries of joy gave the news to the more distant guides, all ran together, and this rock, which formed the crest of the mountain, was named the Roc Sauveur. It proved so in effect, for from it they had, under their eyes, all the valley of Aosta, and at their feet the village of Courmayeur. The sun shone brightly, throwing shafts of light in every direction, and principally on the summits of the Great and Little St. Bernard. Thus from a situation of the greatest anxiety they passed suddenly to the top of their hopes. They exchanged congratulations, and the youth whose courage had not failed him, who had shared the sufferings of the guides without adding to them by useless complaints, became the object of the tenderest caresses. They had been on the ice for twelve hours.

'By the avowal of the guides, who had all four been on Mont Blanc with M. de Saussure or Mr. Beaufoy,[1] the difficulties of that mountain do not approach those of this expedition. The most dangerous part of Mont Blanc is the Glacier de la Côte, which can be crossed in less than an hour and a half, while the obstacles and difficulties met with by our travellers on the Tacul lasted six hours. The crevasses exceeded those of Mont Blanc in horror as well as in size, and if snow avalanches were to be feared on Mont Blanc, there was no less danger of the fall of the *séracs* of the Tacul, which were like towers, thin and hollow at the base. These towers, these broken walls, often rose to a height of three or four hundred feet. The guides admitted, it is true, that a month earlier the glacier did not present such great horrors.

'The guides further declared that, except for the pleasure of finding oneself on the actual summit of Mont Blanc, the Tacul offered beauties quite as remarkable. The rocks of the Géant, of the Charmoz, of Mont Blanc itself, the glaciers which flowed from it, the icefall of the Tacul, its gigantic towers, its needles, the bridges thrown, as it were, into the air, the frozen vaults, the corridors and labyrinths of the glacier, the boldness of their formation, their superb outline, the play of light across these transparent masses of naked ice, form objects beyond description and surpass all the richest imagination can conceive

'The descent to Courmayeur proved long and difficult. It took them five and a half hours. They followed ridges resembling those of the Aiguille du Goûter. The descent is in part dangerous either

---

[1] Cachat le Géant, Tournier l'Oiseau, Charlet, and one other.

from its steepness or from the looseness of the rocks, which break in the hand or slip from under the feet. They arrived at Courmayeur at half-past nine by clear moonlight. Their day's journey was of seventeen and a half leagues (hours). M. Bourrit praises his guides, but gives the greatest credit to Cachat le Géant, whom he has named Sans Peur. He returned to Geneva bringing back from his memorable expedition the most extraordinary pictures and the honour of having crossed in one day to Piedmont through a thousand dangers—dangers which added to his satisfaction by the proof they afford of what men can do when animated by the love of glory!'

Not a word, it will be noted, as to Exchaquet's previous passage of the Col. Called to account at the time for this omission, Bourrit protested that, having mentioned that two guides had made the first passage, he was not called on to notice any other predecessor. The motive that had led him astray in the case of Paccard and Mont Blanc, his intense jealousy of any climber other than a professional guide, again drew him from the path of truth. In this case he has succeeded in obscuring the facts and misleading the most accurate Alpine chroniclers up to the present day. In Bourrit's account of the perils he went through, we must always make a large allowance for his temperament. We may also admit in his favour that the Géant *séracs* vary greatly in difficulty, and that his passage was made two months later in the year than that of Exchaquet. Nor will any mountaineer rate lightly the terrors of a storm on the high snowfields. But I fear no similar excuses are available for Bourrit's account of the descent to Courmayeur, which urged even de Saussure to critical comment.[1]

We may now turn to de Saussure's admirable narrative of what I am disposed to think was by far his most daring adventure. It was not till nearly forty years afterwards that any camp was pitched in the Alpine snows at so lofty an elevation and then only for a single night. De Saussure points out in his opening sentences the aim he had in view in his long stay on the top of the Col du Géant at a height of nearly 11,000 feet.

'Physical observers who propose to visit the top of some high mountain arrange, as a rule, to reach it about noon, and, having

---

[1] Besides Bourrit's narrative, we have a letter written by his son to a friend describing the great adventure. The lad may be excused if he outdoes his father. His crevasses are a league long, his *séracs* four hundred feet high.

arrived, they hasten to make their observations so as to descend before nightfall. Thus they always reach great heights at about the same time of day, and for a very short stay, and in consequence are unable to form any true notion of the state of the air at other hours, still less during the night. It seemed to me it would be interesting to endeavour to fill up this gap in our meteorological records by making a stay on an elevated spot sufficiently long to enable me to ascertain the daily variations of the various meteorological instruments, and to take advantage of the opportunity of observing the origin of meteorological phenomena such as winds, rain, and storms.' [*Voyages*, 2005.]

De Saussure's remarks on the advantage of prolonged visits to the heights at other than the mid-day hours in which most climbers attain them are, it may be pointed out, as true from the picturesque as from the scientific point of view. Afternoon shadows and evening lights add enormously to the effect of mountain panoramas by lending a variety in colour and detail lost under the equal glow of noon. The summit views that linger most in my memory are those gained from heights reached early or late in the day, either in the dawn or gloaming, or when every lofty ridge and spur throws a long shadow. Prominent among such recollections are the rising of the morning star above the crests of the Caucasus seen from a height of 16,000 feet on the slopes of Elbruz, and the after-glow reflected from the snowy ranges of Tibet viewed from 19,000 feet on one of the spurs of Kangchenjanga.

Before setting out, de Saussure obtained from Exchaquet details as to his excursion which satisfied him that the top of the pass (of which Exchaquet had somewhat over-estimated the height [1]) would afford him the space and solid ground he required for a camp and for setting up his instruments. In order to lose no chances, he set out with his son Théodore early in June for Chamonix, and remained there till the end of the month, perfecting his preparations and waiting for the promise of a spell of fine weather.

It was on the 2nd July that the caravan set out. On the first night they pitched their tents beside the little Lac du Tacul, at the junction of the ice-streams that form the Mer de Glace.

---

[1] Exchaquet made it 1800 toises = 11,511 feet. The accepted height is, according to Vallot, 10,959 feet.

The *séracs*, which had presented no difficulty to Exchaquet a twelvemonth before, were held by the guides to be impassable even thus early in the season, and they preferred to turn them on their south-eastern flank, formed by a crag known as La Noire. These rocks are not difficult, but the route involves some scrambling and the traverse of several steep snow-slopes.[1]

De Saussure comments as follows on his experiences:

'Our guides warned us that this route is much more dangerous than that which had been taken the year before, but I do not lay much stress on their statements, for one reason that present danger always seems greater than that which is past; for another that they think to flatter their employers by telling them they have escaped grave perils. Still, it is true that this passage of La Noire is really dangerous; and, as it had frozen in the night, it would have been impossible for us to cross these steep and hard slopes, had not the guides trampled steps in the snow the evening before, when it was softened by the sun.

'Next, as on Mont Blanc'—continues de Saussure—'we had to meet the danger of crevasses concealed under a thin coating of snow. These crevasses grew fewer and less large as we got higher, and we thought we were almost free of them when we heard a sudden cry of "The ropes, the ropes!" One of our porters, Alexis Balmat, who was about a hundred paces ahead, had disappeared of a sudden from among his comrades, swallowed by a large crevasse, 60 feet deep. Happily, half-way down—that is, at 30 feet—he lighted on a block of snow wedged in the crevasse. He fell on this with no further injury than a few scratches on the face. His greatest friend, P. J. Favret, at once had himself tied to the rope and let down. The porter's burden was first hauled up, then the two men separately. Balmat came out looking a little pale, but showed no emotion; he took on his shoulder our mattresses which formed his load, and continued his march with imperturbable coolness.' [*Voyages*, 2028.]

The incident thus recorded is another example of the carelessness or ignorance of the proper use of the rope shown by the Chamonix guides in most of the early expeditions. Even in the seventies of the nineteenth century, some of the best Engadine guides were equally reckless. The rope is irksome, and a smooth snowfield does not suggest danger to a dull mind.

---

[1] The only danger, even for a novice, is from falling stones. But this is a real risk, if a slight one.

THE ASCENT

The story of the arrival on the Col may best be given in the words of the letter de Saussure hurriedly sent off on the spot to Genthod. De Saussure's care to say nothing to his family about the perils of La Noire or the incident of the crevasse is characteristic. The contrast between his reticence and Bourrit's exaggerations may remind an English reader of Clough's lines in the Bothie of Tober na Vuolich :

'Colouring, he, dilating, magniloquent, glowing in picture,
He to a matter-of-fact, still softening, paring, abating,
He to the great might have been upsoaring, sublime and ideal;
He to the merest it was, restricting, diminishing, dwarfing.'

Here is the account de Saussure wrote to his wife :

'3rd July.

' I am sending Jacques [1] to carry you the news of our happy arrival on the *Col du Géant*, where our hut is in the finest situation in the world. We left Chamonix yesterday morning, passed the Montenvers, and came on to sleep at the end of the glacier. Your sisters saw the place where we slept.[2] We started this morning at 5.30 A.M. and got to the hut at 12.30 P.M. We met with some *mauvais pas*, some steep slopes, but we had no misadventures, and there need be no alarm about our return, as we have decided to come back by Courmayeur; it is a little longer, but not fatiguing, and free from any sort of danger; there are neither snows nor crags—nothing but loose stones. Mr. Hill, the most clumsy of climbers, made this descent by night, tumbling five hundred times, without even giving himself a scratch. So have no fear about our return. I did not deceive you in telling you there was no danger in coming here, but the very light snowfall of last winter forced us to take a different route,[3] which, without being really dangerous, presented some obstacles. These will increase in a week's time, hence my high caution has decided me to come back by Courmayeur. The slight difficulties we met with afforded me a great satisfaction from the way Théodore met them without being in the least affected by the rarity of the air. I am, therefore, as pleased as possible as to these first difficulties we have had to encounter. . . . I ought to tell you also that Etienne [a new servant] walks like a stag, and at least as well as Têtu, and that I am in almost every respect very pleased with him. . . .

---

[1] This 'Jacques' was probably Jacques Balmat, the climber of Mont Blanc (see p. 259).
[2] This refers to their visit to the Montenvers in the previous year.
[3] The implication, of course, is that it had not sufficed to choke the crevasses.

'I have rebaptized this mountain [the Col du Géant]. It has been called the Tacul, which is seven leagues [hours] off, while it is quite close to the splendid Aiguille du Géant, which is visible from Genthod. All the guides approve this change; you must correct Coco [his grandchild] and not let him say any more "Grandpapa is at Tacul."'

The next letter we have was written four days later:

'*July 7th.*

'Neighbour of heaven though I am, I am very far from being detached from earthly objects—that is, if the objects that attach me to life can be reckoned as earthly! When some one said, "Here are our letters," I felt so much emotion that I did not know what I was doing, and ran to meet the "Grand Menton" and the "Chevrier" [nicknames of the guides who brought the post]. Long before they could hear me I began shouting, "Have you good news?" and their silence filled me with fear. At last they came up, and I quickly seized the letter addressed "au Col du Géant," my hands trembled, my eyes filled with tears, to the point of hindering me in reading, and my delight in finding all your good and delightful news affected me almost as painfully as the anxiety in which I had been before reading it. I believe it is this rare atmosphere that increases one's sensibility, or else this absolute separation makes one realise more fully the value of what one loves. The atmosphere, however, causes us absolutely no discomfort, we have the best possible appetites, no feeling of oppression, not the slightest indisposition. But the bad weather pursues us; yesterday was the first fine day. So we are making the best use of it possible, and you must not be surprised if Théo does not write at all and I write you a short letter. Besides, our messengers want to start. [He sent down some of his guides to Courmayeur from time to time to get provisions. The letters were probably forwarded thence by the Col Ferret and Martigny. This, at any rate, was the route used on a previous occasion.] Be content, then, to know we are very well in health and in every way. We have suffered a little from cold, the water froze in our glasses in the hut, while we were supping round our little stove. Still, the thermometer only marked less than four degrees of frost (Réaumur), but then the hut does not shut up like your *salons*, and the fire has the greatest trouble to burn in this rare air; it goes out as soon as you leave off using the bellows. I wanted to see a fine storm, and I have had that satisfaction—thunder, hail, snow, and sleet all at once, and plenty of them; it was on Saturday night and Sunday morning. But it all did us no harm, and as we cannot have anything worse, you must not have any anxiety as to our future, the more so since we have learnt how to procure, if not all the conveniences of life, at any rate preservatives against the worse inconveniences. This bad weather has relieved us of M. Exchaquet, who had the indiscretion to bring with him four guides, or sightseers, and we were at a loss where to put them. He only stayed with us twenty-four hours, and took advantage of an interval of fine weather to go down to Courmayeur.'

Their only other visitors on the heights were three chamois. But there were lesser forms of life in the number of butterflies which were carried up by the wind and took refuge on the sheltered side of the mountain, where they afforded an easy prey to the choughs, whose gambols enlivened the snowy wilderness.

In his *Voyages*, published eight years later, de Saussure gives a more detailed account of the storm than he had thought prudent to send home at the time:

' On the following night [4th-5th July] we were assailed by the most terrible storm I have ever witnessed. It arose an hour after midnight with a south-west wind of such violence that I expected at every instant it would carry away the stone hut in which my son and I were sleeping. The gale had this peculiarity, that it was periodically interrupted by intervals of the most perfect calm. In these intervals we heard the wind howling below us in the depth of the Allée Blanche, while the most absolute tranquillity reigned round our cabin. But these calm moments were succeeded by blasts of an indescribable violence; double blows like discharges of artillery. We felt even the mountain shake under our mattresses; the wind penetrated through the cracks in the walls of the hut, it once lifted my sheets and rugs and froze me from head to foot. At daybreak the gale fell a little, but it soon rose again and came back accompanied by snow, which penetrated on all sides into the hut. We then took refuge in one of the tents, which gave better protection. We found the guides obliged continually to hold up the poles for fear the violence of the gale should upset them and carry them away with the tent.

'About seven continuous hail and thunder were added to the storm; one flash struck so near us that we heard distinctly a spark slide hissing down the wet canvas of the tent just behind the place occupied by my son. The air was so full of electricity that directly I put only the point of my electrometer outside the tent the bubbles separated as far as the threads would allow them, and at almost every explosion of the thunder the electricity changed from positive to negative or *vice versâ*.' [*Voyages*, 2030.]

The following charming letter was addressed to his sisters-in-law :

'11th July.

'While Théo writes to his mother I will write a line to his two aunts, and perhaps there is good reason I should, lest they forget me; for they are giving such a double share of affection to their sister that there may be none left for her vagabond of a husband! My wife in her letters never ceases to extol to me the kindness of her sisters, their indulgence, their attentions, and the charming fête which made her cry with emotion, and made me, too, weep in sympathy amidst the frost that surrounds me. She described to me this fête and the outflow of tenderness that accompanied it in colours so vivid that I vow I fancied myself there, and it was one of the greatest pleasures I have enjoyed since I left Geneva.

'But in truth this tender companionship of the three sisters makes the chief charm of my life; it is my greatest pleasure when I am with them and my dearest recollection when I am absent. And the best proof of my eagerness to return to you is that I am giving up the excursion I meant to make in the Valais. I should have liked to make it; had this part of the journey only taken three weeks, as I hoped, my whole absence would only have been about five weeks, but on no account would I lose eight or nine weeks' of our stay at Genthod, as I must if I carried out my first plan. For I must stay four or five days more here to finish my experiments, which do not advance any too quickly, as the weather is often against us. We have not had any more of those terrible storms like the one you had also at Genthod, but in revenge we have two or three showers every day, with an accompaniment of hail or snow. All the same, we are as well as possible, and Etienne has great difficulty to cook enough to satisfy our appetites. One would think we lived in a forge; as the coke will only burn when blown, our bellows are extremely exhausted and husky. Our guides, who are also ravenous, seize the stove as soon as we have done with it, so that one constantly hears the bellows mixed with the noise of the snow and rock avalanches all round us. We are perfectly sheltered from them; it is one of the chief amusements of Etienne and the guides to set rolling great boulders which, falling on the frozen slopes, produce really magnificent torrents of stones and snow.

'But I am afraid of chilling you by telling of nothing but frost and snow and icy crags, and I would far rather warm your hearts and inspire them with feelings as lively and as tender as those I have for

Mlle. Albertine de Saussure

Mme. Tronchin    Mme. Turrettini

from miniatures

you. A thousand greetings to my wife and children. I hope that in a fortnight we shall all be reunited. I look forward with joy to that moment.'

The next letter was to his wife :

'17th July.

'I never felt in better health. I slept last night in my tent, which had frozen after the rain so that the canvas crackled like a bracelet, yet I have not had the least indisposition or cold. Théodore, too, is very well. We have furious appetites, our days are very pleasant, but the evenings, even when it is fine, are always very trying, and when the weather is bad, naturally still more so. The messenger my daughter sends me wants me to let him go, so I have no time to write you a learned letter for Uncle Bonnet; that must be for next time. Still, you may tell him that the constellations near the zenith—at this moment Lyra and Aquila—do not scintillate at all . . . that the shooting stars appear overhead, and never under my feet, and that they look very small. . . .'[1]

'18th July.

'Do not be alarmed at receiving this little letter dated from a spot so full of terror for your sensitive heart. I am leaving it to-morrow, and certainly for ever. I shall close this letter to-morrow at Courmayeur and send it off at once to announce my happy return to the regions destined for mortals. Yet these heights have tried their best to make us regret them, we have had the most magnificent evening; all these high peaks that surround us and the snows that separate them were coloured with the most beautiful shades of rose and carmine. The Italian horizon was girdled with a broad belt from which the full moon, of a rich vermilion tint, rose with the majesty of a queen. The air was calm and of an admirable purity; the vapours condensed below us in the valleys made them seem an obscure and gloomy dwelling-place compared to the empyrean which we inhabit. . . . I have made a number of fresh important observations on meteorology, electricity, and the winds, but principally on the origin of rain. I have been able to watch its development from the smallest cloud to the most terrible of storms, because Mont Blanc, which we are so near, is the centre round which all the atmospheric changes take place. I always keep watch till midnight, while Théodore goes to bed early, but, on the other hand, he gets up at four and I remain in bed till seven, and though we are both conscious of the rarity of the air, mental effort costs me far less than in the plain. I find much more easily solutions

---

[1] See p. 435.

for the problems that perplex me; my body is susceptible to fatigue, but my head, which so soon grows weary in the plain, is here absolutely indefatigable.[1]

'Here is the little sketch of my labours you asked for. If you see Uncle Bonnet, express to him my affection and respects, and read him as much of this letter as you think may interest him. If you wrote to me in the silence of the morning, I am writing to you in the silence of the night; all my companions are asleep, while I, shut up in my tent, buried in my furs, my feet on a hot stone, and seated beside my compass, anticipate with delight the moment which will bring me back to all that is dearest to me.

'I have just been out to take my observations. What a glorious night! These snows and rocks, of which the brilliancy is unsupportable by sunlight, present a wonderful and delightful spectacle by the soft radiance of the moon. How magnificent is the contrast between these granite crags, shadowed or thrown out with such sharpness and boldness, and the brilliant snows! What a moment for meditation! For how many trials and privations are not such moments a compensation! The soul is uplifted, the powers of the intelligence seem to widen, and in the midst of this majestic silence one seems to hear the voice of Nature and to become the confidant of her most secret workings.[2] Ah! how I should like to let you share this pleasure—you who are so sensitive to all the beauties of nature! For my uncle I should be afraid lest his weak eyes would find even the moon too dazzling—and for my aunt! I cannot even conceive the idea of her exposed to this cold and exciting air: so that when Bourrit wrote to ask me to lend him my *tante* for his ascent of Mont Blanc, I reflected I could easily lend him my tent, but for my *tante*, I very much doubted if she would care to be his companion. But the hour of my watch is over; I must go and lie down in my tent beside Théodore.

'The hut is so small that though our beds are only 3 feet wide they fill it entirely—one cannot put a foot between them—so that I have to get on to my bed and sit up to undress myself. But we sleep excellently, and that is the essential.'

'20th July.

'At last, my dear, here we are, safe and sound, at Courmayeur without the least accident, but a bit tired, as our scamps of guides,

---

[1] This account of the stimulating effect on the brain of a rarefied atmosphere, repeated emphatically in the *Voyages*, contrasts markedly with what de Saussure had previously recorded of his experience on the top of Mont Blanc. But the difference in height is over 4700 feet.

[2] Compare Conrad Gesner's outburst in his *De Montium Admiratione*. (See p. 10.)

in order to make it impossible for us to remain any longer, had destroyed all our provisions, so that we have been forced to make the descent in great haste and some suffering, with nothing to eat from seven in the morning to seven in the evening. And you know I cannot walk unless I have some food. But for this, we should have come down very gallantly. Jacques Balmat du Mont Blanc will bring you this letter; he has taken no part in this proceeding.[1] I am well pleased with him. Good-bye. I am delighted to feel myself once more nearly at your level and out of all the trials of the last enterprise of the kind I shall ever undertake.'

And yet he set off next year to Macugnaga, Val Tournanche, and the St. Théodule! Well might Madame de Saussure distrust her husband's promises and protestations!

In the account in the *Voyages* de Saussure refers to the absence of any difficulties in the descent to Courmayeur, which, he says, ' has been wrongly compared to the rocks of the Aiguille du Goûter.' This is the only reference he makes to Bourrit's bombastic narrative. The rebuke thus given, while complete, is in form characteristic of de Saussure's consideration for his former companion. The party returned by the Col Ferret, Martigny, and the Col de Balme. Charles Bourrit, who was at Chamonix on their return, noticed that they had all grown beards while on the mountain.

A letter to his wife, written from Chamonix on the way home, completes the story:

'*24th July.*

' At last here I am at Chamonix. M. de la Rive, the artist, whom I have had the luck to meet, will bring you my news.

' Arrived here yesterday, I remain two days, sleep Sunday at Sallanches and rejoin you Monday evening. . . . I have completed my journey back with the finest weather in the world. I started so exactly at the right moment that Couttet, who returned to the cabin [on the Col du Géant] to get the planks of my bed, which had been left behind, found it full of snow which had come in through the gaps in the walls and roof. You see I have a happy star, first because you are my wife, next because everything succeeds with me, and I always extricate myself happily. . . . Poor de la Rive is not so fortunate. He came with his wife and the dowager Mme. de Prangins. They were wetted to the skin in coming. As soon as they were dry they

---

[1] The word in the copy of de Saussure's letter which I translate is ' expédition.' But the sentence seems to require the sense given above. See also p. 253.

must start for the Arveyron. Madame de la Rive put her foot on a loose stone and fell into the water without hurting herself, but the alarm caused Mme. de Prangins an attack of nerves. She had to be put to bed, and the only thing to be done was to send her back to her château. Luckily your pretty château is on the road to hers, so this letter is sure to be conveyed to you.

'I expected yesterday evening that rogue (*manant*) Jacques Balmat; he ought to have come back and brought your news, but he has stopped at Sallanches to get painted ! . . .'

It was doubtless on this occasion that the portrait of Jacques Balmat, which was reproduced as a companion to one of Dr. Paccard, was painted. Both were by Louis Albert Guislain Bacler d'Albe (1761-1824), a man who had a singularly varied and distinguished career. He lived at Sallanches from 1786 to 1793, when he enlisted in the French army, made the acquaintance of Napoleon at Toulon, became first Chef du Service Topographique de la République Cisalpine, and later Chef des Ingénieurs Géographes at Paris, Directeur du Cabinet Topographique de l'Empereur, Baron de l'Empire, and Général de Brigade. He accompanied Napoleon on all his campaigns except the Egyptian one.

Before closing the story of the encampment on the Col du Géant, I must mention the still popular coloured prints illustrative of this great adventure. Their printed titles, it is true, in most instances make them refer to the ascent of Mont Blanc. But this appears to have been an afterthought of an enterprising publisher who held it might be profitable to associate the plates with the more spectacular enterprise. There seems no room for doubt that they were all derived from a common source, drawings illustrative of the passage of the Col du Géant, made by Henri l'Evêque, a young Genevese artist who accompanied de Saussure to Chamonix in 1788. The drawings were reproduced at Basle by a well-known engraver of the day, Chrétien de Méchel, who had frequent relations with de Saussure. A conclusive proof that they refer to the passage of the Col is the presence in them of a second and younger traveller—de Saussure's son Théodore.

De Saussure would seem to have supervised their publication with a critical eye from the climber's point of view. In a variant of one of the plates (which is extremely rare) he is represented as being let down with a rope in a sitting posture to the brink of a

THE DESCENT

crevasse. But in the ordinary copies we see him in a less undignified posture, standing upright and leaning on his alpenstock in the ordinary attitude of a glissade.[1]

As we have seen from his correspondence with young Isaac Bourrit about the Goûter expedition, the philosopher did not suffer gladly reflections on the mountaineer.

[1] The drawings were also issued, with slight modifications, as hand-coloured lithographs by Kellner at Geneva, and it is from these that the plates here given have been taken. Copies of the lithographs are at the Royal Geographical Society. For further details the reader may consult Mr. Baillie Grohman's fine work, *Sport in Art* (London, 1913).

CHAPTER X

MONTE ROSA

THE bold and, from the scientific point of view, wonderfully successful adventure on the Col du Géant might well have seemed to de Saussure a fitting conclusion to his Alpine career; and, close on the age of fifty, he might have been content to spend his summers in the society of his family and the modest luxury of Genthod. There were other and more serious reasons which would have sufficiently justified him had he done so. He had public as well as private anxieties. Politics at Geneva had, for the third time in his life, reached a violent crisis—one in which he was to find himself forced to play an active part. Moreover, his fortune was invested in French securities, and France was now on the brink of the Great Revolution.

But the call of the mountains was too strong. Many years before de Saussure had admired and tried to sketch the noble outline of Monte Rosa seen from the Piedmontese plain. It had now been ascertained that it was the only close rival of Mont Blanc among Alpine summits, or, as was then believed, among the mountains of the old world. His correspondent, Count Morozzo of Turin, had brought to his notice the beauty of Val Anzasca and the convenient situation of Macugnaga at the very base of the snows. De Saussure could not desist from his travels until he had endeavoured to accurately measure and make the tour of the mountain. His plan was a comprehensive one—to cross the Simplon, go up to the head of Val Anzasca, and then find a way round to the St. Théodule and Zermatt.

The only criticism we might make nowadays on this programme, which was repeated in the reverse direction by Forbes in 1843, is that de Saussure might better have begun with a visit to Saas and the passage of the Monte Moro, a track known and frequented in early times.[1] Unfortunately, the old paved track over it had for many years been impracticable for beasts of burden, and de Saussure's heavy equipment confined him to mule passes.

The party was thoroughly organised. De Saussure took his son Théodore with him, and through the innkeeper Tairraz, hired Chamonix guides and mules for the whole tour. The price fixed was a louis a day for a driver and five mules. The troop met him at Martigny. The party then rode up the Valais and across the Simplon. This, and not 'Saint Plomb,' de Saussure dryly remarks, is the proper French form of the word, ' as there is no saint named St. Plomb.' At the village of the same name he found even at that date an excellent inn. His notes on the pass deal more with the geology than the scenery. In the gorge of Gondo the old track, before Napoleon made his road, was only four feet wide and paved with smooth and slippery blocks of granite. Yet de Saussure writes, ' The path on the Italian side is as alarming as the torrents, but it is throughout safe and well maintained, partly because it is the way taken by the post to Milan, and partly because, as the road to Lago Maggiore, there is a large traffic in corn, wine, and cheeses carried on the back of mules.' The travellers broke the journey from Domo d'Ossola to Macugnaga at the village of Vanzone, a little above Ponte Grande, where they found reasonable accommodation.

Successive generations of Alpine travellers have expatiated on the beauty of Val Anzasca ; it has been left to Ruskin to proclaim in one of the most perverse pages of his *Præterita* its ' supreme dullness.' He complains of the absence of any level space, or valley-bottom, beside the stream, and of the want of cliffs and defiles such as may be found in the Vispthal or the Haslithal. Monte Rosa is described as ' a white heap with no more form in it than a haycock after a thunder-shower ! ' For a parallel to this inept comparison I may quote a description of the

---

[1] On the legend of the Saracens at Saas see *Alpine Journal*, vol. ix. 208, 254, and x. 269. An origin of the name Monte Moro which seems fairly obvious remains to be suggested. Was it the dark pass as compared with the white pass—the Weiss Thor—which led over the snowfields of the Gorner Glacier ? The Schwarzberg—Weiss Thor perhaps owes its self-contradictory name to being the White Gate nearest the Dark Mountain. Schwarzberg may be intended as the equivalent for Monte Moro.

Matterhorn I heard given to his companion by a tourist—probably an upholsterer—newly arrived at the Riffel: 'just like a roll of stair carpet, set on end.' The passage, as a whole, is interesting from its complete reversal of the earlier attitude of mind which thought the bolder features of mountain landscapes *horrid*. It is quite inconsistent with its author's normal point of view with regard to Alpine scenery. But then, consistency is the last thing one looks for—or desires—in the stimulating paradoxes of Ruskin's thirty-eight volumes.[1]

The lovers of Val Anzasca can well afford to smile at such characteristic petulance. The supreme beauty of the middle portion of the valley lies, it is true, not in the more abrupt incidents of scenery, the crags and the defiles that are the delight of the child and the tourist, but in the association of an Italian foreground with a relatively near view of one of the noblest of Alpine summits. Framed between yet high above the folds of forested hillside, the sloping lawns shaded by gigantic chestnut groves, the terraced vineyards that half bury the white hamlets, and the tall campanili that break through the foliage, shines the silver wall of Monte Rosa. Severed from the spectator by no visible base of rocky desolation, such as is too frequent in views of great mountains, it hangs faint as a celestial city in the golden haze of noon, or flushes rose-red in the full light of dawn above the deep shadows of the valley. In contrast to the great critic's disparagement, I may record a fact not to be found in any of the commentaries on the works of a late Poet Laureate. Tennyson's lines entitled 'The Voice and the Peak' were written in the inn at Ponte Grande. He went there at my suggestion after failing to find any inspiration in the scenery of the Upper Engadine.

De Saussure, if apt to be topographical and little given to fine writing, was not blind to the charm of Val Anzasca. He writes :

'One need not cross the bridge (the Ponte Grande), but it is necessary to walk out on to the bold arch in order to enjoy the view of this beautiful mountain, which presents itself as majestically as Mont Blanc does from Sallanches.' [*Voyages*, 2130.]

---

[1] See vol. 35 of the collected edition of Ruskin's works.

This comparison, coming from de Saussure, is in itself the highest praise, but he goes on :

'Monte Rosa has even the advantage of appearing framed in the verdant slopes of the deep and narrow Val Anzasca, which enhance marvellously the effect of its ice and snow. The valley is remarkable for the beauty and, I venture the phrase, the magnificence of its vegetation; everywhere except in its highest and coldest portion the paths are shaded by vine-trellises that cover them entirely like the pergolas which sheltered the walks of our fathers' gardens. Other trellises in steps, supported by walls, climb the mountain slopes, for in all this district the vines are only grown in this manner. But wherever the hillsides, seamed by torrents, afford retreating angles capable of irrigation, one meets with meadows shaded by chestnut trees of a size and beauty that are really admirable, while the torrent often forms a cascade which adds to the charm of these magnificent groves. Another remarkable feature of this valley is that it has no level bottom: the two opposite slopes join at their base and form an acute angle in which the Anza flows, so that the numerous villages are almost all perched on the steep slopes, or on narrow shelves that interrupt them.' [*Voyages*, 2130.]

The travellers reached Macugnaga—that is, the cluster of houses known as Staffa on the edge of the meadows below the old church —at noon.[1] Their first impression was one of enchantment with the situation of the village. Different in character as the landscape here is to those of the lower valley, it retains gentle features which are relatively rare at a similar altitude (4350 feet).

'The houses, built of mixed wood and stone, but well and solidly constructed, are scattered about in meadows diversified by clumps of larch and ash. These meadows rise in a gentle slope towards the base of the towering crags of Monte Rosa, which form the boundary of this pleasant platform.' [*Voyages*, 2131.]

The travellers' first difficulty was to get housed. De Saussure writes to his wife :

'We were more than five hours trying to find a lodging. Strangers being so rare, there is no proper inn, and quite recently a well-dressed individual, who had been hospitably entertained, had made off without paying his bill and after robbing his host. Consequently, on our arrival, the villagers locked their doors and fled to the mountains.

---

[1] 'Macugnaga' comprehends several hamlets some distance apart.

It occurred to me to have recourse to the Curé, who, luckily, proved a very kindly man, and at once gave us something to eat ; then, on seeing the letters I had for the notables of the village, which I had been unable to present on account of their being either really abroad or in hiding, he wrote a note to a sort of Monsieur with whom we had reckoned on lodging, but who had bolted to an hour's distance on the mountains, and sent it off by a messenger. The " Monsieur," reassured, came back at once and has lodged us very comfortably ; we have each our room ; but we have very poor fare, depending on the powers of Etienne [his servant], whose recipes are very limited. We are greatly bored by the Italian boastfulness and volubility of our host, whom we dare not offend lest he should show us the door.'

At Macugnaga de Saussure spent eleven days, much of the time in broken weather. The wet day following his arrival was devoted to a visit to the gold-mines near Pestarena, a few miles lower down the valley. They had at one time employed a thousand labourers, but there were now not more than half that number. The principal proprietor was a Signor Testoni, whose mines produced the equivalent of 66,560 French livres (£3300) annually, leaving, after paying all expenses and the royalty of a tenth due to Count Borromeo, a net profit of £650 to the proprietor. The product at the date of de Saussure's visit was falling off, and the peasant owners of the smaller mines showed much eagerness to part with their property to the strangers. It is a common experience of early explorers in an out-of-the-way mountain district to be taken for mining prospectors. The first Chamonix ice-axes were picks, and even in 1865 Tyrolese peasants found it difficult to imagine they could have any other use. Twenty-five years later, in the wilds of the Caucasus, the writer was pressed by a Suanetian prince, educated at Odessa, to induce our countrymen to search for the hidden gold in the mountains which feed the sources of the Ingur, the fabled stream of the Golden Fleece. The mines in Val Anzasca were for many years, and possibly still are, worked, though on a very small scale, by an English company.

De Saussure during his stay in this remote spot was not altogether dependent for distraction during wet days on the exciting news of the fall of the Bastille contained in his home letters. The Curé proved to be a man of intelligence ; he had a plausible explanation of the presence on the pastures at the head of the Italian valleys of Monte Rosa of a German-speaking population. He attributed it to their aptitude for pastoral pursuits being greater than that of the neighbouring Piedmontese peasantry. Mr. Coolidge, however, has pointed out that in the thirteenth century the same family, the Counts of Biandrate, became Lords both of Visp and of the southern vales, and took steps to shift the population from one side of the chain to the other in either direction. This may account for the Germans in Val Anzasca, but it is a little difficult to believe that Gressoney and Alagna (Allemagna) as well as Macugnaga could have been colonised by any arbitrary act of authority. The Curé's explanation is plausible, and may be supported by similar instances elsewhere.[1]

In the character of the inhabitants the de Saussures noted many points of interest. Their native tongue being German, the peasantry of Macugnaga found themselves of necessity bilingual, a circumstance which aided them greatly in the wanderings to which the very limited resources of their own district compelled a considerable proportion of the population. On the women left behind was thrown all the labour of cultivation, and even of transport. De Saussure mentions that when, anxious to send down to Vanzone a box of geological specimens, he inquired for a porter, he learnt that there was no man ready to carry it, and that it was at once given to a woman. Most recent travellers have had the same experience. Yet he found the sex more than equal to their tasks. He tells how he met a party of six girls crossing a high pass on their way home from a religious festival:

'Accustomed to cross the mountains loaded with their enormous burdens, it was play for them, unladen, to make the journey twice on the same day. They ran, chased one another, scrambled gaily on the heights beside our path, got every now and then two or three hundred paces in front of us, and amused themselves by picking flowers, or singing under the shadow of a rock, to fly off again like a flock of birds the moment our slow and uniform pace brought us up to them.' [*Voyages*, 2224.]

Plain living was a virtue these simple people carried perhaps to excess. Fresh meat was unknown; this is still the case in winter

[1] See Murray's *Handbook for Switzerland*, 1904, for reference to authorities on this question.

in many Alpine villages. The bread was eaten when it was six months old, first cut with a hatchet, then sopped in skimmed milk. Cheese and 'a bit of cold cow or salt goat' were dainties reserved for feast-days and haytime; as a rule, even the wealthier peasants were content to flavour their bread with a bunch of garlic. Yet those who had been abroad were eager to return to their native valley and diet and loath to leave them again.

'Their greatest fault,' concludes de Saussure, 'is their lack of hospitality: not only are they reluctant to receive strangers, but if they meet them on the road they seek to avoid them, and look on them with an air of dislike and fear. Still the people at Macugnaga, where we stayed ten or twelve days, after they had got accustomed to us, came to greet us with friendliness; we were even told they were pleased at our taking an interest in their mountains. The mercenary hospitality found in countries frequented by foreigners is, no doubt, more convenient to travellers, but is it any proof of a better disposition than the primitive rudeness of the dwellers round Monte Rosa?' [*Voyages*, 2224.]

As soon as fine weather returned, de Saussure put in hand the expedition which was the prime aim of his journey. He had promised his family he would make no attempt on any of the peaks of Monte Rosa itself. His object, he assured his wife—no doubt he had got his information from Count Morozzo—was a safe and commodious mountain about the height of the Buet, the Pizzo Bianco (10,552 feet), which rises in front of the great screen formed by the peaks of Monte Rosa and opposite its south-eastern angle. To make sure of having plenty of time for observations on the top, he took his tents and slept for two nights at the Pedriolo Alp (6733 feet), which occupies a superb position at the very base of the great precipices of the Macugnaga face of Monte Rosa.

'These meadows were bounded by the rocks and glaciers of Monte Rosa, whose lofty peaks stood out magnificently against the deep blue vault of heaven. Close to our tent ran a rivulet of the freshest and clearest water; on the other side was an overhanging boulder in whose shelter we lit a fire of rhododendrons, the only fuel that grows at this height.' [*Voyages*, 2136.]

Up to a few years ago the site of de Saussure's camp was still pointed out to travellers.

De Saussure found the ascent from the alp fatiguing. It presented the ordinary features of rough boulders followed by steep snow-slopes, and ended in a ridge of rocks which gave neither firm foot nor hand hold. At the close of five hours the party found themselves on a point, but not the highest point, of the mountain. This still rose some 250 feet above them, and was cut off by a snowy gap. De Saussure confesses to having been somewhat poor-spirited in resisting his son's desire to complete the ascent. His comments on the view in the *Voyages* are those of an orographer; he confines himself to remarks on the mountain structure, but a letter to his wife shows that he appreciated the wonderful extent and grandeur of the panorama. On his return to camp he wrote home :

'From the Pedriolo Alp—*July* 30, 1789.—We are just back, Théo and I, very well, but a bit tired from an excursion we have been making on one of the lower summits of Monte Rosa. I said nothing to you about this mountain, although the wish to visit it was the chief motive of my journey, because I was afraid that you would imagine that I wanted to reach the highest peak, which is still virgin, and will, I expect, remain so eternally, like your friend Mlle. M. I never thought of it; I did not even attempt another of the accessible summits, higher than that on which I was, because the climb was said to be somewhat risky. I chose a charming peak, not higher than the Buet; we ascended it to-day; we had on one side Italy, Lago Maggiore, Ticino, the Naviglio Grande (a canal), all the kingdoms of the world and the glory of them, but the cities of Milan and Pavia were not visible, on account of the vapour. On the other side we had the circle of Monte Rosa, and by looking at it I have learnt its etymology. It is formed exactly like a single rose; lofty summits ranged round a great space occupied by beautiful pastures.[1] I will not inflict on you more details as to its structure; they interested me deeply, and confirmed entirely the theory I have put forward of the formation of granite. In this sense it is, perhaps, the most instructive excursion I have made.

'We are in our tents, where we slept last night, not, as on the Col du Géant, in a distressful cold-harbour, but among the most delightful meadows, the grass finer and shorter than in the best-kept English garden; but enamelled—literally enamelled—with the most brilliant flowers. Yesterday, when our tents were put up, and before the grass had been trampled, it resembled one of those English carpets with a green ground enlivened with flowers.'

---

[1] De Saussure missed the connection of 'Monte Rosa' with the Monts Roeses of Piedmont and the Ruize de Miage of Courmayeur. Roesa or Ruize is the term for glaciers in the patois of Val d'Aosta.

Before leaving Macugnaga, de Saussure took compass bearings to the Monte Moro and the Weissthor, the positions of which were pointed out to him. These show that the pass correctly indicated to him as the Weissthor was the Schwarzberg Weissthor.[1] On the other hand, the position assigned to the Monte Moro Pass (that of a variation of the Old Weissthor, the gap between Monte Rosa, and the Cima di Jazzi) on Théodore de Saussure's very inaccurate drawing of the view from Macugnaga can only be a blunder. There are not a few in the last volumes of the *Voyages*, which were brought out during de Saussure's illness and carelessly seen through the press by his son, whose sufficient excuse may be found in the disorders and anxieties of the times.

After a stay of eleven days at Macugnaga, the de Saussures pursued their tour of Monte Rosa. They had been able to get information as to the complicated network of passes over the southern spurs of the mountain from two of the travelled inhabitants of Val Anzasca. They did not attempt the Turlo, which was probably thought too difficult for mules. Their first step was to return to Ponte Grande. On a high brow above the bridge south of the Anza, the large village of Banio hides among the chestnut groves. The party arrived on the eve of the annual local *festa*, that of Notre Dame de la Neige, held on 5th August. It is worth noting that a sketch of Leonardo da Vinci's exists bearing the legend ' Madonna della Neve 5 Agosto.' It may well be of some other spot: for ' Our Lady of the Snows ' is a frequent dedication in North Italy. But at any rate the great Milanese painter is more likely to have been in Val Anzasca than, as an eminent French critic has suggested, at the Maria zum Schnee of the Rigi ![2]

The village was so crowded with visitors that the de Saussures were forced to sleep in their tent. Next day they crossed the steep, grassy Col d'Egua (7336 feet), where the baggage mules were in difficulties, and descended Val Sermenza, one of the most romantic of the tributary glens of Val Sesia, to its junction with the main valley. At the village of Buccioletto the Curé was so

---

[1] It should be noted that the word 'Macugnaga' is printed on the 'Siegfried Karte' far below the village of Staffa, where travellers halt. This, of course, must be borne in mind in all dealings with compass bearings.

[2] M. Ravaison. See *Alpine Journal*, vol. x. p. 280.

pertinacious in his questioning of the wonderful invaders of his remote bye-corner that de Saussure lost all patience and sought hospitality farther on.

Of the head of Val Sesia we are told little; the travellers' attention was concentrated on the local copper-mines. They seem to have gone as far as Alagna and the base of the Tagliaferro, but de Saussure fails to notice the splendid aspect of Monte Rosa. On the top of the Col de Val Dobbia (8134 feet) they were surprised to find a substantial shelter in which they could make their observations.

Their next halting-place, where they found good lodging, was one of the hamlets of Gressoney, at the head of Val de Lys, the stream of which flows into the lower Val d'Aosta. The upper portion of the valley contrasts with Val Sesia and Val Anzasca in its more open, pastoral—in a word, Swiss—character. Emigrants from the northern slopes of the Alps found here a landscape that might remind them of the region they had left. The Lyskamm, which, as its name denotes, closes the view, shows as a snowy hummock, with none of the imposing grandeur of the precipices of Monte Rosa. Thence they proceeded to the chalets of Betta in order to climb a summit—one of the many Rothhorns (9834 feet)—on the spur of Monte Rosa west of the Val de Lys, which promised a good view of what de Saussure calls the outside of the *cirque* of Monte Rosa. He was struck by the contrast between the easy snow-slopes above the Lys Glacier and the cliffs of the eastern face opposite the Pedriolo Alp. But his climbing ambition does not seem to have been excited. He listened with critical interest to the legend of the discovery of a lost valley which had reached as far as Turin. A party of peasants had eleven years before (in 1778) claimed to have climbed to a point which is identified as the Lysjoch, and seen beneath them an oasis of green pastures without trees, houses, or cattle. They thus held for some years the record of the highest ascent in the Alps (14,033 feet). On a second occasion they failed in an attempt to descend the glacier on the north side. Had they done so they would undoubtedly have reached the Riffel Alp. The lost valley was obviously the head of the Vispthal. De Saussure, however, supposed it might be the Pedriolo Alp; a conjecture which a better knowledge of the details of the crest of Monte Rosa would have shown him was improbable.

He seems to fall into further confusion in describing the highest peaks of Monte Rosa as ' lying to the left or west of the gap from which the valley is visible.' The Lyskamm is the principal object from Val de Lys, but it is almost incredible that de Saussure should have confused it with the Zumstein Spitze, which an erroneous calculation had led him to take for the culminating summit. Is it possible that he took the Col delle Loccie to have been the point reached by the explorers ?

From St. Jacques d'Ayas, their next stage, the travellers hoped to cross the Cimes Blanches to Zermatt in a day. But being caught in mists on the pass they followed the local guide's advice and descended to Breuil, where they were detained twenty-four hours by bad weather. The only lodging, the house of a peasant named J. B. Hérin (de Saussure calls him Erin), left much to be desired—' a little wretched room without bed or window, a kitchen without a chimney, and all the shortcomings and inconveniences which combined become vexatious.' The son of de Saussure's host, a boy of twelve at the time of his first visit, was alive till after 1855, and remembered well de Saussure's party, and, as a boy would, the great store of provisions they brought with them.[1]

After two nights at Breuil they started for the St. Théodule. Up to the middle of the eighteenth century mules not infrequently crossed the pass, and the de Saussures tried to ride over the glacier. It is not surprising to learn that the animals sank deeply into the snow and had all, including the baggage animals, to be relieved of their burdens. Still they showed signs of exhaustion and suffering, uttering ' plaintive cries ' such as de Saussure had never heard before from mules even on the worst paths. ' It was,' he writes, ' the rarity of the air that affected them as it had us on Mont Blanc.'

On the pass the first object to be noticed was naturally the Mont Cervin or Matterhorn, a ' triangular obelisk of enormous height which looks as if it had been cut out with a chisel. I propose,' says de Saussure, ' to return another year and measure this magnificent rock ! ' For the rest, he refers to the Saasgrat as part of the external *cirque* of Monte Rosa. On the south, he writes,

[1] See *Les Alpes Pennines dans un Jour*, par le Chanoine Carrel (Aosta, 1855). The inn at Breuil was not opened till 1856. I first visited it in 1858.

'is a magnificent chain of high peaks of mingled snow and rock.'[1] In his diary (but not in the *Voyages*) de Saussure mentions, for the only time, the Graian Alps as 'some fine snow-peaks he is told are near Cogne.' It is remarkable that though so often in Val d'Aosta he never noticed the beautiful pyramid of the Grivola, nor, on the descent to Zermatt, the great crests of the Dent Blanche and the Weisshorn. To the early travellers snow-peaks would seem to have been as much alike and indistinguishable as sheep are to everyone but their shepherd.

The descent to Zermatt was without incident. There the Curé, who, as a rule, entertained travellers, refused to receive or to have any dealings with them, 'il disait, qu'il ne voulait rien nous vendre.' This very unusual incident would seem to have been a case of bigotry towards Protestants. The party had to have recourse to the good offices of their Breuil guide to find them lodging at a blacksmith's. No wonder that de Saussure did not linger in the future centre of mountaineering, but rode straight off next morning to St. Niklaus and the Rhône valley. He must have been in a great hurry to get home, for he finds nothing to mention in the remarkable scenery or the geology of the Vispthal. At Loëche, in the Valais, his guides met with another example of churlishness. They were stopped and fined six francs for travelling with mules on Sunday! De Saussure lost little time on the road, but after lodging his complaint at Sion against the local authorities, and calling on Gibbon as he passed through Lausanne, returned to Genthod on 20th August, after a five weeks' absence.

The years following that of his tour of Monte Rosa were for de Saussure a period of much public and private anxiety, and it was not until 1792 that he could find an opportunity to carry out his intention of revisiting the St. Théodule and measuring the Matterhorn.

In August of that year he started with his son Théodore. His experience of Zermatt seems to have discouraged him from taking

[1] It is obvious that by the transposition of a short sentence the following words, 'This chain joins Monte Rosa near the Weissgrat, which leads from Zermatt to Macugnaga,' which should refer to the Saasgrat, have become attached to the chain south of the St. Théodule—that is, the Breithorn and Lyskamm. As I have already had occasion to note, the last two volumes of the *Voyages* show traces of the circumstances under which they were put together and sent to the press.

the obvious route by the Valais, and the party set out once more for the familiar Col de Bonhomme and Val d'Aosta. Instead, however, of taking the Col de la Seigne, they turned off at Chapieu and crossed the Little St. Bernard, which was new to de Saussure, to Pré St. Didier.

The account of this journey, the eighth and last of those recorded in the *Voyages*, contains relatively little of general interest apart from the visit to the St. Théodule and the ascents of the Little Mont Cervin and the Théodulehorn. It is mainly a transcript of a geologist's notebook. There is not much description of scenery, beyond a mention of a 'truly romantic site' in Val Tournanche, and of the view of the Matterhorn from above Breuil. The Gorner Glacier again fails to attract the travellers' attention. Here and there, however, a touch of human interest is thrown in: de Saussure had a taste for homely scenes, such as reminded him of Hogarth's drawings or Dutch pictures. We are introduced to a farmer's family at Chapieu, the mother, a woman 'with a classical figure,' teaching her child to repeat hymns, the grandfather giving its supper to another infant, and both children falling equally fast to sleep. In Val Tournanche he encounters a wealthy peasant, 'a man of very good conversation who seemed to take an interest in my researches and desired to possess a copy of my *Voyages*.' This rare character was claimed as his uncle by the late Chanoine Carrel of Aosta, who was himself a singular instance of what may be done with limited means by a man of intelligence to develop his own district. He corresponded with Forbes on scientific matters, and the early visitors to Cogne owed much to his friendly advice and publications, which included complete panoramas of the Pennine and Graian Alps taken from the Becca di Nona. I possess copies he presented me with in 1860.

One of de Saussure's companions gave him a curious experience. He had brought with him from Geneva a neighbouring peasant who had heard a great deal about glaciers and wanted to see some specimens.

'Knowing him,' writes de Saussure, 'to be handy, robust, and very much in the habit of climbing the mountains near Geneva to collect plants and shrubs for amateurs, we consented without difficulty to his request. He bore the fatigues of the road very well, though burdened with our hammers and the instruments we wanted to have always at hand, and he showed no fear and no regret at having joined our adventure. But when he found himself surrounded by the glaciers of Mont Cervin, and saw the mules wallow to their girths in the snow, in which he himself sank to his knees, and that on the brink of crevasses which he believed ready to engulf him, he was seized with intense terror; he wept, he made vows to all the saints in Paradise, and although he did us the justice to admit that it was he who had begged to be allowed to accompany us, and that he had only his own folly to blame, he poured out the most bitter regrets at having ever embarked on such an enterprise. As the crossing of the glacier took us hours, the time seemed long to him, but he got over safely, and when he reached the tongue of rock on which we were going to camp, he became so wild with joy that it took him some time before he recovered himself enough to be able to assist the guides to finish their hut and level the ground for our tent.' [*Voyages*, 2239.][1]

The first day on the St. Théodule (10,900 feet) was spent in measuring a base on the snowfield on the Zermatt side with a chain on the model of that brought by Sir George Shuckburgh from England to measure Mont Blanc in 1775. De Saussure obtained for the Matterhorn a height 2309·75 toises, or 14,766 feet.[2] This, he believed, entitled it to rank third among Alpine summits. He took no count of its neighbours, the Lyskamm, the Dom, and the Weisshorn. He probably considered them all as part of Monte Rosa. He observed from a distance the structure of the gigantic pyramid and recognised the main features of its geological formation.

This task accomplished, the prospect of an easy climb led the travellers to start for the Breithorn, but on the way their courage or their powers failed them, and they turned aside from the long and somewhat crevassed snow-slopes and contented themselves with the Little Mont Cervin (the Cime Brune du Breithorn, de Saussure calls it), an easy two and a half hours from the pass. On the ascent they remarked the number of dead insects and butterflies on the snow, and ingeniously calculated that in a square of 2000 toises there would be 72 millions! This summit (12,750 feet) was, next to Mont Blanc, by far the highest in the Alps reached by de Saussure.

On the third day of their sojourn on the pass the crags of the

[1] This section is wrongly numbered. I give the correct one.
[2] Federal Survey, 14,705 feet.

Théodulehorn (11,391 feet) were examined in detail. They suggested to de Saussure by their strange juxtapositions of crystalline rocks and micaceous sands and clays reflections on the limitations of scientific inquiry. 'Who,' he asks, 'can by any probable conjectures penetrate the night of Time ? Placed on this planet since yesterday, and that only for a day, we can only aspire to knowledge which in all probability we shall never attain to.'

The same evening they descended to Breuil, and spent a day in further exploring the immediate neighbourhood. De Saussure calls attention to its botanical wealth, and gives a catalogue of Alpine plants found there and in the Vispthal. He adds, 'What makes it delightful to botanise on these mountains is that since they are built of thin horizontal layers, of which the lower protrude farthest, the plants grow as in a stepped rock-garden, within easy reach of the eyes and hand of the collector, and the specimens obtained are of an exceptional growth due to the nature of the soil.' The geologist had not, we note, altogether abandoned his first love.

The caravan next set out—one wonders why—to repeat their passage of the Cimes Blanches (9777 feet) of the previous year. As they mounted the broad pastures they came on several tarns hidden in sheltered hollows, the clear waters of which reflected the crags of the Matterhorn. A crowd of swallows had here found a nesting-place at a very unusual height. A little higher they encountered one of the great flocks of sheep, which, coming up from their winter quarters in Lombardy or Provence, spend the summer on the High Alps, blocking the road for miles in their spring and autumn pilgrimages. Near the top of the pass de Saussure noticed a glacier ending on the summit of a cliff over which the ice fell constantly, forming at its base what has been termed by later glacialists a *glacier remanié*.

This seemed to de Saussure a favourable occasion to deal with a German traveller named Plouquet, who had made a journey into the Alps and written a book with the object of disproving the onward movement of glaciers. Any reply, de Saussure says, he had thought superfluous until one of the most esteemed journals in Germany, the *Literary Gazette of Jena*, had endorsed Plouquet by declaring that he had proved to its critic's satisfaction that the movement of glacier ice was an absolute physical impossibility.

De Saussure had no difficulty in bringing forward facts to prove the contrary. It is interesting to note how nearly he came on this occasion to realising the power of the glacier as an agency of transport. He appeals to the blocks brought down on the ice from its source to the lower ground, and to the moraines which let loose their missiles on the traveller's path, 'not, indeed, at Tübingen, but beneath the Glaciers de Miage and des Pèlerins. There is not a single inhabitant of the Alps who disputes the movement of glacier ice, and the ephemeral doubt raised by this author will pass away as the ice melts when its advance brings it to a temperate climate.' Here we see de Saussure on the brink of a discovery which would have radically affected his Theory. Wise after the event, we wonder how it came to pass that his reason did not carry him on to inquire whether the erratic blocks of the Jura and the moraines of Ivrea, features on a larger scale, but bearing the same general aspect, might not be the result of similar causes, and to recognise that there had been periods of glacial extension in the history of our globe of which they were the authentic and obvious monuments. In patience and accuracy of observation, in honesty and deliberateness in drawing conclusions, de Saussure was supreme. But in readiness to discard the theories of his predecessors, in quickness in drawing novel but legitimate inferences from the facts before his eyes, his intellect, it must be admitted, lacked the illuminating flash we term genius.

The travellers spent two hours in geologising on the rocks near the top of the pass before they pursued the descent in the direction of Val d'Ayas until they came to a spot where their mules could find sufficient pasture. Here they made what de Saussure calls a 'jolie halte.' The phrase may recall to readers of that delightful work, Töpffer's *Voyages en Zigzag*, a passage in which the Genevese schoolmaster dilates on the pleasures of roadside halts in pedestrian tours; of the interludes in which the traveller enjoys momentary release from toil and mingles memories of past pleasures with anticipation of those still to come.

Val d'Ayas did not offer much of interest. At St. Jacques, where they found lodging, they were entertained with tales of recent robberies. The proprietor of a gold-mine which de Saussure had hoped to examine declined to admit visitors. The prevalence of goitres and cretinism among the inhabitants of the lower portion of the valley was very marked. The frequency of these distressing maladies in Val d'Aosta, while they are rare or unknown in most of the valleys of the Italian Alps, has not yet been satisfactorily accounted for. De Saussure devoted a chapter to its discussion. May one of the causes be that the population belong to an old and worn-out stock, in which the *tumidum guttur* of Juvenal has become hereditary?

From Aosta the travellers were taken by their friend M. de St. Réal,[1] whose acquaintance they had made in 1787 in the Maurienne, and who was now the Intendant of the Province, to visit the copper and manganese mines of St. Marcel, situated on the right bank of the Dora Baltea half-way to Châtillon. These mines are reputed to have been worked in Roman times, and traces of the ancient galleries were pointed out. It may be remembered that Strabo asserts that the subjugation of the Salassi was hastened owing to their inconveniencing the inhabitants of the lower valleys by diverting streams for the use of the mines. Even more interesting than the mines was a source of which de Saussure gives a full description:

'A spring large enough to turn a mill, of which the waters, themselves blue, covered all their channel, rocks, stones, wood, and earth, with a substance of every shade between green and blue; what was under the water was deep sky-blue, what was half-wet green, what was dry pale sky-blue. The stream itself, of which the water is perfectly transparent, runs over this painted bed, breaks into spray, and presents by its reflection the most singular effect; it resembles the coloured flames produced by throwing verdigris on burning logs.' [*Voyages*, 2295.]

An analysis showed that the sediment left by the water contained 19 per cent. of copper.

De Saussure lingered so late over this fascinating stream that the party was benighted on the rough mountain path; and de Saussure's mule, which he had luckily got off, put one of its legs through a rotten bridge, and was only saved by breaking up the planks and letting it fall into the torrent. It was midnight when the party got back to St. Marcel, and found the Curé, who was to lodge them, in bed and asleep.

This was to be de Saussure's final adventure in the mountains.

[1] See p. 350.

He returned home from Aosta by the Great St. Bernard, where he was welcomed for the last time by his cordial hosts of the Hospice, with whom he had for so many years been on the best of terms, and whose interests he had at one time promoted by defending them against unfounded aspersions.

Thus ends the record of de Saussure's last journey among his beloved mountains. We belong to a generation which can readily sympathise with him in the summary close to his Alpine travels caused by a political upheaval which convulsed Europe. It was to the civic and domestic anxieties brought on him by the French Revolution, and to its reaction on the ancient Republic of Geneva, that the final breakdown of his always delicate constitution must be mainly attributed. When his concluding volumes were sent to the press in 1796, their author's frame and intellect had been impaired by more than one paralytic stroke. The pages bear signs of careless revision; there is a pathetic incompleteness in the brief 'General View of the Alps,' which follows on the narrative. The writer's failing strength, it is obvious, has not been equal to his intention. We feel pained, as in listening to an orator who is unable to complete his speech. De Saussure lays down his pen, then takes it up again to introduce the Agenda, which he had for years been elaborating, by a quotation from the Preface to the first volume, written seventeen years earlier.

In the present and four preceding chapters I have attempted to tell, or rather to summarise, the story of de Saussure's travels and climbing experiences. This seems to me, therefore, an appropriate place to devote a few pages to a critical estimate of his position as an Alpine explorer and mountaineer. It is a matter on which divergent opinions have been expressed. If his claims have been exaggerated in some quarters, they have been unjustly depreciated in others.

In any fair estimate of de Saussure's Alpine career local conditions and the mental atmosphere of the time must be taken fully into account. The standard of Geneva a hundred and fifty years ago was very different from that of the modern mountaineer. Among its sheltered aristocracy the taste for roughing it was rare, if not altogether absent. It was only natural that a society which habitually wore fine clothes and powdered hair should prefer tea and talk in a lakeside garden to the 'beautiful horrors' of the High Alps, and should look on the Professor's excursions into the mountains as hardy and venturesome, and Madame de Saussure as a wife much to be pitied for her husband's eccentric taste. Alpine travel at the end of the eighteenth century was no doubt rough in a sense, but in the same sense that Dr. Johnson's tour to the Hebrides was rough. When we come to consider the facts in detail, we come to the conclusion that with the resources at de Saussure's disposal, it involved no great privations or real risks. What hardships he encountered in the course of his travels have often been taken too seriously by his early biographers. Apart from his ascent of Mont Blanc and his sojourn on the Col du Géant, which come properly under a different heading—mountaineering—they were in no sense severe tests of endurance, at any rate according to the standard of the latter half of the nineteenth century.

The highlands of Switzerland and Savoy during de Saussure's life were not the unknown, or uncivilised, regions they are sometimes represented. There were frequented mule-tracks over all the great and many of the side passes. The valleys of the Pennine Alps were not untrodden by travellers, or even wholly without accommodation. At most of the places de Saussure visited, Haller's botanical collectors had been before him. One of them had explored the Vispthäler, Saas, and Zermatt, and crossed the St. Théodule into Val Tournanche. Others had been up to the head of the Val d'Hérens and Arolla, recesses which de Saussure himself never penetrated. Laborde's great folio volumes, *Tableaux de la Suisse*, published in 1780, bear witness to the growing knowledge of the Alps. We find plates not only of the Grindelwald and Rosenlaui Glaciers, but also of the Rhône and Aar and Fiesch Glaciers. No one seems to have explored the Aletsch, though it is mentioned in Grüner's second edition. The Linththal and Pantenbruck in Canton Glarus, Lago di Lucendro on the St. Gotthard, Engelberg, and the Gemmi are all pictured. About the same time (1776-86) our worthy countryman, Archdeacon Coxe, was wandering about the Oberland, the Grisons, and the Val Tellina, making the tour of the Bernina by the Muretto Pass, and compiling his three substantial volumes. At many still out-of-the-way places de Saussure met with reasonable accommodation; for instance, in Val d'Ayas, in Val Formazza, at

Cerentino in a side-glen of Val Maggia, at Münster in the Upper Rhône Valley, at St. Remy on the St. Bernard, at Göschenen on the St. Gotthard, he found fair inns. At Courmayeur there was a hotel, and, as now, Italian bathing company. At Chamonix—after 1765—there were 'three large good inns.' Even at Zermatt and Macugnaga there were rough *cabarets* with, it is true, landlords disposed to be churlish and shut the door on unexpected guests. At Chapieu the lodging seems to have been much the same as it was in the fifties of the last century. In short, wherever the valley led to a pass there were wayfarers, though as a rule not of a class to demand much from their hosts. In more remote bye-corners the choice lay between the priest's house and a rough drinking shop. It is all to de Saussure's credit that he took cheerfully what he found in the way of accommodation, that he made little of sleeping in a chalet, or even in his tent, when occasion arose. But the hardships of such rough lodgings must have been sensibly mitigated by the presence of the train of baggage mules and domestics he was in the habit of taking about with him. Moreover his tours were not protracted; his longest journeys were only of a few weeks. In short, he endured cheerfully a considerable amount of discomfort, but little real hardship. The investigation of the Swiss Alps in the eighteenth century was an easy undertaking compared to the task that has faced later explorers in the Himalaya, the Andes, or the Rocky Mountains.

Yet, taking all things into account—and his own uncertain health and frequent indispositions are not to be overlooked—the amount accomplished was considerable. De Saussure probably covered more ground than any other Alpine traveller of his time, except, possibly, Placidus a Spescha. Besides the seven journeys recorded in his book, he went to the Oberland in 1770 and over the Splügen and back by Chur and the Lake of Wallenstadt in 1777. He visited many unfrequented localities in the Jura, Southern and Central France, the Riviera and the Brisgau. If we are tempted to wonder that he did not explore more thoroughly the valleys of the Pennine Alps, we have to remember his family conditions and his unwillingness to put too great a strain on the solicitude of a circle of which he was the adored centre. Bonnet, who himself played at times the part of an anxious uncle, summarises the situation in one of his letters to Haller: 'My nephew has two wives, or rather two mistresses, the mountains and his wife, and I cannot venture to say to which he is the more devoted.' We have also to remember that de Saussure had relatively little of the spirit of an explorer. He was mainly bent on extending his geological observations. Again, the troop with which he travelled confined him to mule-passes, and did not allow of a steeplechase 'over hill, over dale,' such as has been the delight of many simple pedestrians in our times.

Thus far we have confined ourselves to de Saussure's expeditions below the snow-level. We have still to consider his record as a mountaineer. His climbing qualifications would not count for much, perhaps, in the Alpine Clubs of the twentieth century. But it would be a gross injustice to appraise them by the standard of modern peak-hunters. His only serious contemporary rival was Placidus a Spescha, the worthy monk of Disentis, an enthusiast who, with far less means at his disposal, made many first ascents in the Grisons, climbed the Rheinwaldhorn, and almost conquered the Tödi.

De Saussure in his youth was a stout walker according to the standard of the day. When he was twenty, on his first visit to the glaciers, he walked all the way from Geneva to Chamonix. He took considerable pains to keep himself in training for his expeditions. But in his later years he was always ready to avail himself of mules to shorten the day's journey or the proposed climb; he took them even over the St. Théodule, and though he started from his bivouac on the top of the pass, he found the Klein Matterhorn enough and gave up the Breithorn. It is only fair to add, this was when he was fifty-two.

De Saussure was obviously a fair rock-climber, as climbers went in the days before Alpine climbing had become a branch of gymnastics. He makes no great matter of the Aiguille du Goûter cliffs, though in the condition that he found them, covered with fresh snow, they can be unpleasant. Unlike Bourrit, he thought nothing of the steep descent from the Col du Géant to Mont Fréty. In icework he had to begin at the beginning, but he began early. Of his first glacier expedition, the now hackneyed crossing of the Mer de Glace, he gives a somewhat naïve description:

'I cannot recommend it to be attempted from the side of the Montenvers, unless the guides know the actual state of the ice and that it can be crossed without too much difficulty. In my first journey in 1760, I ran some risk, and had difficulty in extricating myself. The glacier at this time was almost impracticable on the side opposite the Montenvers. I jumped the crevices which were not too large, but one met with deep hollows in the ice into which one had to let oneself slide to climb up the other side with extreme fatigue. At other times, in order to cross the large and deep crevices, I had to pass like a rope-dancer along very narrow ice-ridges which reached from one side to the other. Good Pierre Simon, my first guide in the High Alps, regretted much having allowed me to undertake this enterprise; he ran backwards and forwards, searched for the least dangerous places, cut steps in the ice, gave me a hand whenever possible, and, at the same time, taught me the first elements of the art—for it is one—of placing one's feet properly, balancing the body, and using one's stick in difficult places. I escaped, however, without any injury beyond some bruises which I suffered in letting myself slide voluntarily on the very rapid banks of ice we had to descend. Pierre Simon descended sliding upright on his feet, his body bent backwards and resting on his spiked stick. He thus reached the bottom without hurting himself.' [*Voyages*, 616.]

De Saussure goes on to describe the skill with which the guides can glissade on steep slopes, adding, ' This exercise is far more difficult than one would think, and one must have many tumbles before attaining to real proficiency.'

There is, I think, no doubt that the crossing of the Mer de Glace was more formidable at this period than in recent times, and that tourists, in order to avoid the Mauvais Pas, were often taken a longer course over the ice.

It should also be noted that this narrative refers to a date before de Saussure had had any practice on a glacier, and nearly thirty years before his two great expeditions to the Col du Géant and Mont Blanc, and should be taken for what it is, an honest account of a youth's initiation to the mountains. One of de Saussure's most attractive qualities is his absolute honesty and absence of striving after effect. He is always ready to tell a story against himself—as when he records how exhausted he was by being hustled by his guide at a great pace down to Chamonix from the Plan de l'Aiguille.

' I came down too quickly; my guide, fearing we should be benighted in these deserts, made me descend at such a pace that, not being as yet [he was twenty-one] trained for mountaineering, I stumbled at almost every step. I did not get back to Chamonix till late at night, and in a state of fever and fatigue from which it took me some time to recover.' [*Voyages*, 654.]

In later years some of de Saussure's best climbing was done at the base of the Chamonix Aiguilles, where he had at least one narrow escape from falling stones.

In his visit to the Jardin and expeditions on Mont Blanc and the Col du Géant, de Saussure had to deal with formidable icefalls at a date when icecraft at Chamonix was in a very rudimentary condition. Simler two hundred years before had described the proper use of the rope and snow spectacles as practised by travellers on the St. Théodule. But the crystal-hunters employed by de Saussure seem to have neglected the rope, or employed it, if at all, not as a precaution, but as a means of rescue after a comrade had dropped into a crevasse. They carried very long alpenstocks, and stuck short axes, such as they used to extract crystals, in their belts. De Saussure describes how two of his guides held one of these poles, more than 8 feet long, between them horizontally while he or his son leant on the middle. This was the attitude in which he chose to be represented in the plates that served to illustrate his feats. A tourist of the period (Bordier) declared that Alpine peasants were in the habit of holding these long staves in this manner while crossing a glacier, so that in case of a fall the two ends might catch on the side of the crevasse, and the mountaineer seize the moment to spring out. The feat is more easily described than performed !

It has always to be borne in mind that with de Saussure climbing—except perhaps in the case of Mont Blanc, and even with Mont Blanc only in private moments—was considered not as an end in itself, but as a means to scientific research. The Japanese climb with a religious aim, the eighteenth century climbed with scientific objects, the nineteenth and twentieth have done so occasionally, but more often for health or exercise. De Saussure's aim was always serious. He appreciated in his leisure moments— no one more thoroughly—the beauty of the storehouses of snow and the splendours to be seen on the summits. His descriptions of the view from the Crammont and his last sunset on the Col du Géant remain as evidence of his feeling for mountain effects. But scenery was not in his case, as it is with us, a first object. He did not find in it an adequate inducement to face obstacles far more serious in imagination, but also more serious in reality, than those that we encounter to-day. No doubt something must be allowed also both for his deliberate temperament and for the pressure of home influence. We read in his letters how his family—his wife and sons and two devoted sisters-in-law—the whole Genthod household—waited and watched eagerly at Chamonix while the long-contemplated attack on the great mountain was ventured.

What was wanting in de Saussure was the element of rashness that makes a pioneer. It was Bourrit's example that urged him to his first serious attempt and failure on Mont Blanc. It was the success of Paccard and Balmat that spurred him to follow them. It was Exchaquet who induced him to camp on the Col du Géant. He preferred the comparative certainty of reaching a goal already proved attainable to the zest of a new and doubtful adventure. It was in this respect that he differed most from the average modern mountaineer, to whom the climb itself is the main object, and the exertion its own reward.

Before with de Saussure we leave the mountains and turn to trace his share in the troubles and disasters of the revolutionary epoch at Geneva, many of my readers will, I believe, be glad to peruse in his own words the statement of the main aim of his life and travels given at the beginning and end of the *Voyages* by their author. I shall therefore append here a translation of a great part of the Preface, as well as of the Epilogue and Note he supplied at the close of his great work. Their pages set out better than any comment of mine can the spirit in which de Saussure travelled, his genuine love of the Alps, his passion for science, and the strong human sympathies which led him to appreciate so warmly yet with so much discrimination the qualities of the mountain peasantry. The 'Discours Préliminaire' supplies the best portrait, or outline, of the man and the philosopher, while the 'Coup d'Œil Général' and the final Note by their incompleteness bear witness to the physical failure which forced him to leave to others the completion of his life's work.

CHAPTER XI

DISCOURS PRÉLIMINAIRE, ETC.[1]

ALL those who have studied attentively the materials of the earth which we inhabit have been forced to recognise that our globe has suffered great revolutions which must have required for their accomplishment a long series of centuries. Memories of some of these revolutions have even been traced in the traditions of early peoples. The philosophers of antiquity exercised their wits in endeavours to ascertain the order and the causes of these vicissitudes; but, more eager to interpret nature than patient in her study, they relied on inadequate observations and on traditions distorted by poetry and superstition, and thus were led to invent Cosmogonies, or Systems of the Origin of the World, better suited to please the imagination than to satisfy the intellect by a faithful interpretation of nature.

It was long before it was recognised that this branch of Natural Science, like all others, ought to be pursued with the help of observation, and that systems ought never to be put forward except as the results and the consequences of facts.

The science which collects the facts that can alone serve as a basis for the Theory of the Earth, or *Geology*, is Physical Geography, the description of our globe, of its natural divisions, the character, the structure, and the situation of its different parts, of the substances visible on its surface, and of those which it contains in such depths as our feeble resources enable us to penetrate.

But it is above all through the study of mountains that the progress of a Theory of the Earth can be accelerated. Plains are uniform; it is impossible in them to inspect a section of the soil and its different beds except by excavations effected either by water or by the hands of men; and such means are very inadequate, because these excavations are of relatively rare occurrence and extent, and the deepest scarcely descend to 1200 or 1800 feet. High mountains, on the other hand, infinitely various in their material and their form, present to the light of day natural sections of a great extent, in which one can observe with the utmost precision, and embrace in a moment, the order, the situation, the direction, the thickness, and even the nature

---

[1] *Voyages dans les Alpes*, vols. i. and iv.

of the beds of which they are composed and the fractures which traverse them.

It is in vain, however, that mountains offer opportunities for such observations if the student does not know how to look on these great objects as a whole and in their more general relations. The one object of the greater number of the travellers who style themselves Naturalists is to collect curiosities ; they walk, or rather they crawl, their eyes fixed on the ground, picking up little fragments, without making any attempt at generalisation. They resemble the antiquary who, at Rome, would scratch the ground in the middle of the Pantheon or the Coliseum to search for bits of coloured glass without throwing a glance at the architecture of these superb buildings. It is not that I advise neglect of detailed observations ; on the contrary, I regard them as the only base of solid knowledge ; what I ask is that, in observing details, one should never lose sight of the masses as a whole, and that a knowledge of the great objects and their relations should be constantly kept in view in the study of their parts. But in order to obtain these general ideas it is not enough to follow the high-roads, which, as a rule, wind in the bottom of the valleys and cross the mountain chains in their deepest defiles ; one must leave the beaten track and climb the lofty peaks, whence the eyes can embrace at once a multitude of objects. These excursions are, I admit, laborious; one must do without carriages, or even horses, endure great fatigue, and even at times expose oneself to somewhat serious risks. Often the Naturalist on the point of reaching a peak which he eagerly desires to gain is seized with doubt whether his strength will carry him to the top, or whether he can succeed in conquering the cliffs that bar his way ; but the brisk and fresh air he breathes sends through his veins a tonic which restores him, and the hope of the great spectacle he is about to enjoy, and of the new discoveries which he may gain, reanimate his vigour and his courage. He arrives : his eyes, at once dazzled and drawn in every direction, know not at first where to fix themselves ; little by little he accustoms himself to this great light ; he selects the objects which ought principally to occupy him, and he decides on the order in which he should study them. But what language can reproduce the sensations and paint the ideas with which these great spectacles fill the soul of the Philosopher ? He seems to dominate our globe, to discover the sources of its motion, and to recognise at least the principal agents that effect its revolutions.

[A description of the view from Etna is here omitted.]

Thus the view of these grand objects engages the Philosopher to meditate on the past and future revolutions of our globe. But if, in the middle of these meditations, the idea of the little creatures that crawl on its surface crosses his mind ; if he compares their duration to the great epochs of nature, how much must he wonder that, occupying so little space both in place and time, they should have been able to imagine that they were the sole end of the creation of the universe, and when, from the summit of Etna, he sees under his feet two Empires that in other times nourished millions of warriors, how puerile must ambition appear to him ! It is there that the Temple of Wisdom should be built ; in which, to repeat after the bard of nature, 'Suave mari magno.'

The accessible peaks of the Alps present views perhaps not so vast or so brilliant, but even more instructive to the Geologist. It is from them that he sees before him the lofty and ancient mountains, the original and most solid skeleton of our globe, which deserve the name of *primitives* because, disdaining all alien support or extraneous mixture, they invariably repose on homogeneous bases and include in their substance nothing of another nature. He studies their structure, he distinguishes beneath the ravages of time the traces of their original form ; he observes the connection of these ancient mountains with those of more recent formation ; he notices the more recent resting on the older ; he distinguishes the strata, very much disturbed at their contact with the primitives, but more and more horizontal as they are farther from them ; he observes the gradations which nature has followed in passing from one formation to another ; and an acquaintance with these gradations helps him to raise a corner of the veil which covers the mystery of their origin.

The physical student, like the Geologist, finds on the high mountains worthy objects of admiration and study. These great chains, the tops of which pierce into the upper regions of the atmosphere, seem to be the workshop of nature and the reservoirs whence she draws the benefits and the disasters she spreads over our earth, the streams which water it, and the torrents which ravage it, the rains which fertilise it, and the storms which spread desolation. All the phenomena of general physics present themselves with a grandeur and majesty of which the inhabitants of the plains have no idea, the action of the winds and atmospheric electricity assume an astonishing force, the clouds form under the eyes of the observer, and often he watches the tempests which devastate the plains born under his feet, while the sun shines brightly on him, and above his head the sky remains clear and calm. Striking incidents of every kind vary at each moment the scene ; here a torrent flings itself from the rocks, forming jets and cascades which melt into spray and present to the spectator double or triple rainbows which follow him as he shifts his view-point. Then snow avalanches leap down with a rapidity comparable to that of lightning, traverse and cut paths through the forests, breaking short the tallest trees with a noise like that of thunder. Farther distant, great expanses bristling with eternal ice give the idea of a sea suddenly frozen at the moment when the north wind had raised its waves. And beside this ice, in the midst of these terrifying objects, are delicious retreats; smiling meadows, fragrant with the scent of a thousand flowers as rare as they are beautiful and medicinal, present a sweet image of spring in a fortunate clime and offer the botanist the richest harvest.

The human interest in the Alps is no less than the physical. For if mankind are in the main everywhere the same, everywhere the plaything of the same passions produced by the same needs, yet if there is anywhere in Europe where one may hope to find men who have exchanged the savage for the civilised state without losing their natural simplicity, it is in the Alps that one must look for them, in these high valleys where there are no landlords or men of wealth, nor any frequent incursion of strangers. Those who have seen the peasant only in the environs of cities have no idea of the child of nature. Near towns, subject to masters, bound to a humiliating deference, crushed by vain show, corrupted and despised even by those of his fellows who are themselves debased by service, he becomes as abject as his corrupters.

But the peasant of the Alps, seeing none but his equals, forgets the existence of any more powerful class, his soul is ennobled and elevated; the services which he renders, the hospitality which he shows, have in them nothing servile or mercenary, one sees in him sparks of that honourable pride which is the companion and guardian of all the virtues. How often, arriving at nightfall in some remote hamlet where there was no kind of inn, have I knocked at a cottage door, and then, after some inquiry as to the object of my journey, been received with a courtesy, a cordiality, and a disinterestedness of which it would be difficult to find examples elsewhere. And who would believe that in those savage retreats I have come across thinkers, men who, by the unaided strength of their native intelligence, have raised themselves far above the superstitions on which the lower classes in towns feed with avidity?

Such are the pleasures tasted by those who devote themselves to the study of mountains. For myself, I have from childhood felt for them the most positive passion; I still recollect the thrill that I experienced the first time that my hands clasped the rocks of the

Salève and my eyes enjoyed its panorama. At the age of eighteen (in 1758) I had already made several excursions among the mountains nearest Geneva. In the next year I passed a fortnight in one of the highest chalets of the Jura, in order to explore in detail the Dôle and the mountains near it, and in the same year I went up the Môle for the first time. But these relatively low mountains could only imperfectly satisfy my curiosity. I was burning with the desire to see close at hand the High Alps, which from the crest of the lower ranges looked so magnificent. At length, in 1760, I started alone and on foot for the glaciers of Chamonix, then little frequented, and said to be difficult and dangerous of access. I revisited them in the following year, and since that date I have not let a single year pass without making some serious excursions, and even journeys, with the object of studying mountains. In this period (1760-1779) I have crossed the main chain of the Alps fourteen times by eight different passes, and made sixteen other excursions to the centre of the chain. I have explored the Jura, the Vosges, the mountains of Switzerland, those of a part of Germany, of England, of Italy, and Sicily and the adjacent islands. I have visited the extinct volcanoes of Auvergne, part of those of the Vivarais, and several mountains of Forez, Dauphiné, and Burgundy.[1] I made all these journeys, a miner's hammer in my hand, with no aim except that of physical research, climbing all the accessible peaks which promised me interesting observations and always collecting specimens from the mines and the mountains—above all, those which promised to afford some fact useful for the Theory, so that I might examine them at leisure. I also imposed on myself the severe rule of first setting down on the spot the notes of my observations and then writing them out in a fair copy within twenty-four hours, as far as was possible.

One precaution—in my opinion, a very useful one—which I employed, was to prepare in advance for each journey a systematic and detailed agenda of the inquiries to which the journey was dedicated. As a geologist observes and studies, as a rule, on the road, the least distraction may make him miss, perhaps for ever, an interesting observation. Even without distractions, the objects of his study are so varied and so numerous that it is easy to pass over something; often an observation that appears important absorbs all his attention and makes him let slip others. Again, bad weather discourages him, fatigue lessens his power of observation, and the neglected oppor-

---

[1] The eight passes crossed previous to 1779 were the Mont Cenis, the Col Ferret, the Col de la Seigne, the Great St. Bernard, the Simplon, the Gries, the St. Gotthard, and the Splügen. In later years de Saussure added to his list the Col du Géant, St. Théodule, and Little St. Bernard.

tunities that result from all these causes leave behind them bitter regrets, and may even compel him to retrace his steps. But if from time to time he throws a glance at his agenda, he brings back to his recollection all the inquiries which he ought to be occupied with. My list of agenda, limited at first, became enlarged and improved in proportion to the ideas that I had acquired. I propose to publish it in my third volume; it may be of use even to travellers who, without being experts in research, desire to bring back from their travels some notes useful for science. I shall add to these agenda directions for those who propose to undertake a journey among high mountains, and some hints as to the mistakes into which unskilled observers may most easily fall.[1]

Despite all the precautions I take to forget nothing when, in the quiet of my study, I meditate afresh on the objects I have observed during my travels, doubts often arise in my mind which I feel I can only remove by new observations and fresh journeys. It is these doubts, always recurring, which have delayed till now the publication of this work, and which compel me to limit myself to the observations I have made in the last four or five years; those anterior to this date not seeming to me sufficiently complete to be submitted to the eyes of the public. Even these I offer only with extreme diffidence, persuaded that men of science who see after me objects I have described will discover many things which have escaped my examination. . . .

As to my style, I shall make no apology—I know its faults; but more accustomed to climb rocks than to turn and polish phrases, my only object has been to describe clearly what I have seen and felt. If my descriptions give my readers some part of the pleasure I have had myself in my travels—above all, if they serve to incite in some of them a desire to study and to advance a science in the progress of which I take an eager interest, I shall be well pleased and well rewarded for my exertions.—*28th November* 1779.

[The conclusion of the Preface consists mainly of an epitome of the *Voyages* and references to its maps and illustrations.]

GENERAL VIEW OF THE ALPS BETWEEN TYROL AND THE MEDITERRANEAN [2]

I HAVE given in these Travels at the end of each crossing of the Alps a general sketch of the character of the mountains and of the structure they present in each of the passes traversed. I must now furnish a general sketch of the whole range.

---

[1] The agenda here promised were issued in the fourth volume of the *Voyages*, prefaced by the note that follows here.

[2] *Voyages*, vol. iv. 2300, 2303.

In my youth, when I had as yet crossed only a few of the Alpine passes, I imagined myself to have mastered the facts and their general relations. I even delivered, in 1764,[1] a lecture on mountain structure in which I set forth these conclusions. But since repeated journeys in different portions of the chain have furnished me with additional facts, I have recognised that one might almost maintain that the most constant feature of the Alps is their variety.

In fact, if in place of considering my whole Travels, those described in these volumes are alone taken into account, it will be at once noted that the order in which the different rocks are placed is infinitely varied. In one place the outer ranges are limestone, in another magnesian. Here the central and loftiest peaks are solid granite; there they are micaceous limestone schists; in one place we find magnesian rocks, in another gneiss. If one notes the disposition of the strata, they prove to be in one place horizontal, in another vertical, in one place inclined in the same direction as the slope of the mountain, in another in the contrary direction.

Still it will be noted that in general the dip of the strata follows the direction of the longitudinal valleys and of the mountain ridges, and that these valleys, as well as the mountain ranges, have a general direction of east to west or north-east to south-west. It will also be noted that the strata of the more recent formations are, as a rule, inclined towards and resting against the more ancient massifs, except where they are reversed, or inclined in the opposite direction to the mountain slopes.

But a feature which is universal is the mass of debris in the form of blocks, fragments, pudding stone, sandstone, and sand, either piled together and forming mountains or hills, or else scattered on the exterior of the range, or even on the plains lying at the base of the Alps, which bears witness to the violent and sudden retreat of the waters.

We recognise, then, in the Alps the certain proof of the catastrophe, or last scene, in the great drama of the revolutions of the globe. But we see only uncertain and doubtful signs of the preceding events, apart from the proofs of quiet crystallisations in the most remote epochs which preceded the creation of animals, of deposits or sediments in the periods which followed this epoch, and some evidence of violent movements such as the formation of fissures, of pudding stone, the fracture of shells, and the displacement of strata. But I do not propose to enter here into any details of the Theory. I only wish to

---

[1] The date given is 1774. This is obviously one of the many errata in the concluding volumes.—D. W. F.

ascertain if there are any general conclusions which may be put forward by one who has passed his life in visiting the Alps and in studying the character and structure of the ranges which compose them.

The following note, or postscript, occupies a page at the end of the Agenda, and conveys de Saussure's last message to his successors :

The particulars here given may serve to show that Geology is not a study for the idle or the self-indulgent, since a geologist's days are divided between fatiguing and perilous journeys, in which he is cut off from most of the conveniences of life, and complicated and deep studies in his cabinet. But what is rarer and perhaps even more essential than the zeal required to surmount these obstacles is a spirit free from preconceived ideas and intent on truth alone rather than on any desire to create or demolish systems, and capable both of plunging into the details indispensable in exact and reliable observations and of the power to rise to broad views and general conceptions. I would not, however, urge these difficulties as a discouragement. Every traveller can make some useful observations, and bring at least a stone worthy to serve in the construction of the great edifice. Imperfect work may still be of use, for I do not doubt that were one to compare with these Agenda the results of the journeys of mineralogists [1] —even those of the highest reputation (and *a fortiori*, those of the author of the Agenda !)—one would find many gaps, many observations either imperfect or wanting. The reason for this I have given in my Preface. Moreover, many of these ideas have only occurred to me since my travels. This is the reason why I have worked with interest on the Agenda, in the hope of placing young students at the commencement of their career, at the point I have reached after thirty-six years of study and travel.

---

[1] Mineralogy is up to the end of the eighteenth century found in the *Index of the Transactions of the Royal Society*, where Geology would now be the term used.—D. W. F.

CHAPTER XII

POLITICS AT GENEVA

IN the preceding chapters we have been mainly occupied in following de Saussure's scientific career as a physical student and an Alpine explorer. But no portrait of the author of *Voyages dans les Alpes* can pretend to be complete which omits his home life and his services to the Republic.

Whatever criticism the patrician families of Geneva may be liable to as practical politicians, it must be admitted that they were active in fulfilling their public duties. They furnished the State its magistrates, the Academy its professors, and the Church many of its presbyters. They enriched the city by their business enterprise, whether as merchants or bankers. There were few drones in the busy hive planted on the hill above the Rhône. De Saussure was no exception to the general rule. Throughout his life he was engaged in many and very varied occupations, social, civil, and political; he was not only a hard-worked professor and a versatile man of science, he was also an ardent educationalist and, when compelled by occasion, an active legislator. As a young man, during the troubles of 1766-68, he was called on to serve as a political correspondent to his friend Haller, who was at the time engaged officially as an adviser to one of the Mediating Powers, the Canton of Berne. At a later date he was drawn reluctantly into the narrow but turbid stream of Genevese politics in an earnest attempt to save his city from being overrun by the flood of the French Revolution.

Of the difficulties that face a biographer addressing English readers in any attempt to do justice to this hitherto neglected side of de Saussure's character and career I am very conscious. What Sainte-Beuve has written in noticing Sayous' well-known work on French literature outside France,[1] seems to me to apply so exactly to my own case that I am tempted to quote the passage here :

'Why not have put in the front of these volumes a brief account of the constitution and political history of Geneva ? We should have been glad of a summary sketch of the quarrels and the civil wars between the different classes, of the strife between the citizens and the bourgeois, between the members and rulers of the State on the one hand, and on the other the unenfranchised crowd constantly demanding civil rights. These disputes between the High and the Low Town, between patricians and plebeians, reproduced in many of their features those of the Greek and Roman republics. A few pages in which were presented clearly and accurately the vicissitudes of the city-state up to the moment when it was swallowed by the French Revolution, would have informed and relieved our minds.'

Even at the risk of becoming tedious, I feel bound to act on the great critic's suggestion, and to offer such a brief summary of the Genevese Constitution, its origin and growth, as may assist my readers to realise in outline the part played by de Saussure during the revolutionary period. It is not my object to follow closely the kaleidoscopic movements of constantly shifting party combinations, to record in any detail the alternate victories and defeats of the patrician oligarchy in their protracted struggle to keep hold of the reins of government. That task may be left to local historians. My intention is to refer to these events only in so far as they affected the life and fortune of a single actor in them.

In order to understand the successive political episodes in which de Saussure was called on to play a part, it is essential, in the first place, to distinguish the classes into which, about 1760, the inhabitants of Geneva were divided, and to enumerate the various bodies which constituted and controlled the State.

In 1781, according to an official census, the population of the Republic amounted to 24,700, of whom 8000 were adult males. Of these only 3000 were entitled to vote in the General Assembly ; in practice the number voting seems seldom to have exceeded 1600. This enfranchised class was divided into citizens and

[1] *Le Dix-huitième Siècle à l'Etranger : Histoire de la Littérature Française dans les divers pays de l'Europe depuis la mort de Louis XIV. jusqu'à la Révolution Française*, par A. Sayous (Paris, 1861). See vol. i. pp. 400-457.

burghers; the latter section suffered from certain disabilities set out below.

In theory the Geneva of the eighteenth century was a democracy governed by the General Assembly, through four executive officers appointed by it, and known as Syndics. But, as time went on, the power of this body had been gradually limited, or usurped, by two committees distinguished as the Council of Twenty-five, or Small Council, or more generally as the Senate, and the Council of Two Hundred, or Great Council. The Senate was selected from members of the Great Council, for which citizens, amongst whom were included burghers' sons born in the city, were alone eligible. Burghers, though they voted in the General Assembly, could not sit in either of the Councils, or hold any of the higher administrative offices of the State. Families, a member of which had sat in the Senate, or served in one of its chief offices, bore the title of 'Noble,' while doctors, lawyers and ministers were entitled to be addressed as 'Spectable.'

The origin of the Senate, which dates back to the fourteenth century, is somewhat obscure. It would seem to have been at first a committee, with certain special functions, which were enlarged, so that in the course of years it developed into something like a Cabinet. As the affairs of State grew in importance, it delegated a part of its functions to the larger committee known as the Great Council. These bodies were, it appears, originally nominated by the Syndics, and confirmed by the General Assembly. But about the time of the Reformation the Assembly lost its control, and the Councils assumed the right to elect one another. The Senate secured another most important advantage; hitherto the four Syndics had been elected by the free vote of the Assembly, from which they directly derived their authority. Its choice was now limited to four out of eight nominees of the Senate, and the Senate nominated only members of its own body. The combined effect of these changes was to destroy the democratic character of the State: the General Assembly might still be acclaimed as the *Souverain*, but the reins had passed into other hands.

Henceforth all political and judicial power was concentrated in the Senate and Great Council, and these were recruited out of a limited number of closely allied patrician families. As the years went on the powers of the popular body were still further reduced.

No measure could be proposed except in the Senate, and no measure could be brought before the General Assembly until it had been passed both by the Senate and Great Council. The General Assembly might send up remonstrances or petitions to the Councils, but the Councils were not bound to take them into consideration. In the terms in use, the citizens might 'represent,' but the Councils could 'negative.' By the middle of the eighteenth century Geneva had become an oligarchy, controlled by clerics and a group of Noble Families. The General Assembly, however, still met from time to time, if only to give a formal sanction to the enactments of the Councils; and its power of vetoing the Senate's nominations for the chief offices of the State offered an obvious instrument for the expression of the growing discontents.

Outside the enfranchised minority here described lay the bulk of the male population, who were liable to special taxation, and up to 1768 were excluded from public offices, from the liberal professions, and from certain trades. If born in the city they were known as 'Natifs,' if newcomers, as 'Inhabitants.' It was, it is true, possible for individuals of this class to acquire civic rights either by service rendered to the State or by money payment, but after the sixteenth century the process became somewhat costly. In the first seventy years of the eighteenth century some five hundred outsiders were thus admitted as burghers.

Such, in outline, was the Constitution of Geneva in the latter half of the eighteenth century. I have now to indicate the main epochs in its historical development.

For many centuries after Caesar Geneva had remained an obscure provincial town, which won no place in the annals of the later Empire. First Roman and then Burgundian, it shared in the vicissitudes of those dark and troublous times until in the eleventh century it was handed over by the Emperor Conrad II., acting as King of Burgundy, to its Bishop, who was created a Prince of the Holy Roman Empire. The rule of the Prince-Bishops lasted for some five hundred years—until 1535—but it was a perpetual struggle against first the local Counts of the Genevois, and afterwards the House of Savoy. The little city-state found itself surrounded by the dominions of hungry potentates, who, but for the timely aid received from the neighbouring Swiss cantons of Berne and Fribourg, would probably have swallowed it up. The Prince-Bishops' troubles were not only external; they had also to contend with their own subjects within the walls. The Constitution of Geneva was based on the liberties won from one of its sovereigns, embodied and confirmed in 1387 in a document described as the Magna Carta of Genevese history.[1] This definitely recognised the existence and powers of a General Assembly, and provided for the appointment of four Syndics as its executive officers. The Senate, or Council of Twenty-five, is not mentioned in the charter, but independent evidence has been brought to light that it already existed at that date in the form of a committee, with certain well-defined administrative powers.

A hundred and fifty years later, about 1535, the Genevese finally got rid of their Prince-Bishops, and proceeded to develop a constitution by creating in imitation of the neighbouring Swiss cantons the Great Council, and also a Council of Sixty, which dealt with Foreign Affairs, and met only at intervals.

The same date was further marked by the arrival of the reformer Farel and the introduction of the Protestant religion. The Reformation affected the political and social life of the city for evil as well as for good. The old framework of liberty remained, but in place of being adapted to the needs of the time, it was stiffened by Calvin with the spirit of ecclesiastical tyranny.

Recent historians have shown a tendency to exaggerate the services rendered to the cause of popular government by the example and influence of Geneva under its clerical rulers. If the first aim of Calvinism was to be free of the control of princes, it was equally keen to set up a tyranny of its own in some respects even more absolute. Its ideal of liberty was strictly limited by its demand for conformity. It took no account of the claims of the individual conscience; it had no tolerance for those who objected to its creed and doctrine, or its harsh restrictions. When we are invited to regard the little city on Lake Leman as the source from which Hampden and Cromwell drew their energy, and the Pilgrim Fathers their principles, we are tempted to inquire more closely what the extent and nature of the influence

[1] *Coutumes, Ordonnances, Franchises et Libertés de la Ville de Genève.* Recueillies et publiées en l' année 1387, par Adhémar Fabry, Prince et Evêque de l'Eglise et de la dite ville de Genève.

exerted in this country by the Calvinist oligarchy of Geneva really amounted to. Englishmen have at no time needed to go abroad to learn the love of liberty. If the religious refugees who returned to their country from Geneva in the days of Elizabeth brought back with them some fresh experience of a Republic, they brought back also a narrow and ungenial view of life, a bitter sectarianism which infected English Puritanism and hastened the downfall of the Cromwellian government. If the Pilgrim Fathers owed in part their virtues to the teaching of Calvin, their failings —the cruelties and bigotry that marked their early attempts at organising a community—must be laid to the same account.

In 1543 the franchises won by the citizens in 1387 were under Calvin's rule moulded to the purposes of a self-righteous and largely clerical oligarchy, resolute in refusing to suit itself to new conditions and meddlesome to the point of absurdity in matters of dogma and morals. As has already been shown, a committee, under the control of the Venerable Company of Pastors, exercised up to 1770 an intolerably minute supervision over the private lives of the inhabitants. The Genevese citizen could not call his house, his table, or even his clothes, much less his soul, his own. But for the rest the administration under the old aristocracy seems to have been honest, capable, and economical, and every traveller noted the striking contrast between the condition of the inhabitants of the town and its territory and that of the peasantry of Savoy immediately outside the frontier. Education was not altogether neglected, and there were schools—limited to boys—for all classes. Further, to ensure the perpetuation of the order he created, Calvin founded an 'Academy' the studies of which were carefully framed so as to provide a succession of presbyters and pious magistrates imbued with sound doctrines and a proper contempt for free thought and worldly indulgences. The Academy was placed under the control of the Venerable Company of Pastors, the members of which, should occasion arise, were always at hand and ready to advise and admonish their colleagues of the lay Councils.

Meantime, the existence of the Republic, surrounded, as we have seen, by powerful neighbours, was apt to be precarious. In 1602 it was attacked in force by the Duke of Savoy. His assault was repulsed, and the Genevese, proud of the one feat of arms in their city's history, cherished its memory, which is still kept alive in the annual festival of the Escalade. Security was subsequently sought in an alliance with the King of France and the cantons of Berne and Zurich, the latter on the ground of religion taking the place originally held by Fribourg. These States, known in local history as the Mediating Powers, played an important, and in the result a disastrous, part in the history of Geneva. There is no more dangerous defect in a government than a tendency to rely on foreign arms against its own subjects. This blunder the Genevese aristocracy habitually made. In place of strengthening their position by gradually associating the prosperous and growing middle class in the responsibilities of administration and legislation, they persevered in attempts to retain a monopoly of power in their own hands by the aid of alien forces. When France became a Republic the Genevese oligarchy fell pierced by the weapon it had too long relied on.

During the seventeenth century the democratic elements in the ancient constitution were in a state of decay, while the population of the town was increasing in number and prosperity. The General Assembly was reduced to practical impotence and its meetings to empty ceremonies. Public opinion, deprived of any practical mode of expression, took the form of incessant criticism, ever ready to ripen on occasion into serious discontent. In 1707 new duties levied by the Councils on the import of wine and more restrictive game laws were the sparks that served to set a light to the smouldering ashes. A largely signed petition was presented to the Great Council, claiming that votes in the General Assembly should be taken by ballot, that a limit should be put to the number of members of the same family allowed to sit in the Great Council, and that the fundamental laws of the State, the text of which had been untouched for a hundred and fifty years, and was in some points vague, should be revised and reprinted. This was a demand that was repeated over and over again for many years, and met by a series of postponements and evasions on the part of the oligarchy, which largely contributed to its final discomfiture. The petition was contumeliously rejected and ordered to be burnt by the First Syndic. An extraordinary meeting of the Assembly followed, stormy debates were succeeded by riots in the streets, and troops were summoned from Berne. An informer alleged that the democratic party had planned a massacre of the Syndics and the Swiss troops. Several of its leaders, including Pierre Fatio, a lawyer of patrician family and great eloquence, were arrested, condemned, and executed. Thus ended the first of the series of revolutions and counter-revolutions which were to mark the century.

The years 1730-40 may serve as the next point in our summary retrospect. Since the attempted revolution in 1707 had been put down, the patrician oligarchy had further consolidated its power. The Senate and Great Council by a series of ingenious devices had secured to themselves in practice perpetuity of office, the concentration in their own hands of all legislative, executive, and judicial power, the appointment of the four Syndics, and the control of the elections of their own members. The meetings of the General Assembly had become merely formal and fallen largely into disuse. It had to content itself with acting as a Court of Registration for the decrees and nominations of the Councils.

In 1734 the growing discontent was again brought to a head by increased taxation imposed to meet the cost of new fortifications. Either side suspected the other of an intention to resort to violence. Some blood was shed in street riots, but in the end a compromise was arrived at. The British Resident in Switzerland, it is interesting to find, addressed a very sensible and plain-spoken letter to the Syndics and Councils, blaming their conduct and justifying the bourgeoisie in calling in question their claim to the power of imposing taxation. In the result the Assembly was convoked and voted the taxes in question, while the officials who had been concerned in preparing arms for use against the people were dismissed. But the truce proved a hollow one. The Senate condemned Micheli du Crest, an engineer, who on the ground of expense had ventured to criticise and oppose their project of new fortifications; Micheli's adherents were prosecuted without any regard for legal forms; the populace rose in their defence; street-fighting ensued. The Councils by feasts and flattery sought to win over the artisan population to take up arms on their side against the middle-class burghers. In this dilemma recourse was again had to the so-called *Garantie*, the old custom arising out of the need Geneva had experienced in earlier times of protection from the Dukes of Savoy. The King of France and the cantons of Berne and Zurich were invited to exercise their right to intervene in unison as mediators. Delegates were duly appointed by the Powers. After much delay and some bickering between themselves, they drew up a solemn document known as the 'Règlement de l'Illustre Médiation,' designed to put an end to the civic troubles. The Councils were pronounced to be bound to govern according to the established laws of the city, as set out in the Code of 1387, which they were instructed to revise and reissue; on the other hand, they were recognised to possess full executive and judicial powers and the sole right of initiative—that is, of proposing new laws. They were confirmed in the right of nominating the four Syndics and other town officers in the General Assembly, which could, however, reject their nominees. To that body was reserved the power of declaring peace and war, of imposing any fresh taxation, and of enacting such new laws as might be proposed by the Councils, while any of its members—that is, any burgher—was authorised to make from time to time representations to the Councils on matters relating to the interests of the State. It was on the revision and reissue of the laws of the Republic that future trouble was mainly to centre. The burghers continued to 'represent,' but the Councils could not be compelled to act or even to consider. Hence the one party got the name of 'Représentants'—Reformers would in English nearly express their position—the other that of 'Negatifs' or 'Constitutionalists.'

Thus two years before the birth of de Saussure ended the second important act in the long struggle between the patriciate and the democracy. The middle of the eighteenth century was for Geneva a time of material prosperity. Its Academy attracted students from all parts of Europe, its bankers and merchants grew wealthy, its watch-trade flourished. The Senate, it is true, closely allied to the Church by tradition and family ties, continued, though with diminishing zeal and energy, to support the Venerable Company in enforcing sumptuary laws and restrictions on private life, dress, and amusements of a character generally meticulous and often vexatious. On the other hand, it was evasive and dilatory in carrying out one of the most important articles of the Act of Mediation—that which enjoined the publication of a correct text of the ancient laws of the Republic. It preferred to keep their interpretation in its own hands, and this neglect on its part left a legitimate and fruitful ground for future dissensions. Meantime the fatal flaw in the Genevese constitution—the *Garantie*—the power of the Government to appeal for foreign armed aid against its own townspeople—was left untouched.

These political conditions produced frequent contests of a shifting and confused character. At one moment the strife was between the citizens and burghers—the members of the General Assembly—on one side, and their aristocratic rulers—the Senate and the Great Council—on the other, each party constantly striving either to enlarge or to maintain its own powers and privileges. Here the Councils had the advantages that they elected one another, and that the initiative in bringing forward any new proposal rested solely with the Senate. These governing bodies thus formed together an exclusive oligarchy; they were, in fact, a large family party, the composition of which is illustrated by the constant recurrence of the same names in their lists. At another moment the struggle lay between the General Assembly and the unenfranchised classes, who were yearly growing in numbers and prosperity. The latter kept up a perpetual agitation for the removal of their disabilities and for admission to the full rights of citizenship.[1] From time to time the two Councils or the General Assembly made alternate advances towards these outsiders in the hope of strengthening their own hands in the retention or pursuit of power.

The political history of Geneva during de Saussure's lifetime consists therefore in a struggle for supremacy between these warring elements, the aristocracy—the old families of the Upper Town, clinging tenaciously to privileges, thanks to which, they were convinced, the town had enjoyed at their hands for over two hundred years an, on the whole, economical and competent rule; the members of the Assembly, impatient of a control which left them with only a shadow of political power; and a growing class of small tradesmen and artisans, men with specific and very practical grievances of their own.

This political and social unrest was going on and spreading up to the time when, stimulated by the French Revolution, it broke out in the last decade of the eighteenth century in riot and blood-

---

[1] According to the popular leader, Cornuaud, out of 7000 adult males 5000 were without votes. See *Ésaie Gasc, Citoyen de Genève, sa Politique et sa Théologie* (Paris, 1876).

shed, and an end came in the complete sweeping away of the historic constitution of Geneva and its temporary annexation to the French Republic.

From time to time in these recurring contentions the opposing forces came to blows, and even bloodshed. But the Genevese were more handy with the pen than with the sword, and their party spirit found a ready and enjoyable vent in the flights of pamphlets, both in prose and rhyme, which were hurled from side to side with but little intermission. An industrious bibliographer has compiled a catalogue of no fewer than 5885, published between 1735 and 1795!

At intervals variety and relief were sought in formal reconciliations. Church services were held to celebrate the restoration of peace, and Geneva gave itself up to processions, garlands, banquets, and fine sentiments. It would almost seem as if the enforced absence of reasonable amusements had driven the Genevese into a habit of holding these frequent political gambols and junketings, harmless enough in themselves, but sadly incongruous, and even dangerous, when they occurred as interludes in the midst of strife and civil broils. In short, all parties in the State amused themselves by playing with fire until they became finally involved and scorched in the great European conflagration.

The reader may now, I trust, be able to follow the course of events in Geneva from the date when de Saussure first took any active interest in its political struggles.

For over twenty years, however, during the whole of de Saussure's youth, there had been relative peace within the city walls. The Government was economical, free from corruption, and, on the whole, benevolent. The territory of Geneva offered in the condition of its inhabitants a pleasing contrast to the adjacent kingdoms. Trade flourished, work was plentiful, and large fortunes were accumulated by the Genevese merchants and bankers. The growing prosperity led to a gradual relaxation of the more austere features of Calvinism—its control became less arbitrary both in matters of dress and dogma. In 1770 there was a two days' debate in the Senate on the sumptuary regulations, which ended in their substantial modification. The humours and discontents of democracy found a safety-valve in a profusion of pamphlets and squibs of a relatively harmless character. It was not until the dangerous eloquence of Rousseau sounded in their ears that the Councils had resort to an active policy of suppression. In 1763 the long-gathering storm broke out with the condemnation of the *Contrat Social* and *Emile* and the banishment of their author. A band of burghers 'represented'—that is, protested—to the Senate against this 'condemnation' in very strong terms. Their action seems to have been both politically expedient and legally sound; the main point they urged was that, under an article of the Ecclesiastical Ordinances of 1576, the author of any alleged attack on the Established Religion could not be condemned unheard or without previous admonishment.[1] The Senate firmly 'negatived'—that is, refused to receive—their protest. Public interest was aroused; the contest grew wordy, pamphlets flew about on all sides—the Genevese were always ready to rush to the printing-press. The Procureur Général—Jean Robert Tronchin—in an able tract, entitled *Lettres écrites de la Campagne*, stated in moderate terms and with much use of historical parallels the case for the Government; Rousseau fulminated on the other side in the far more famous *Lettres écrites de la Montagne*. The popular party, greatly encouraged and incited by their eloquent supporter, became turbulent. The Senate grew alarmed; it first threatened to resign, and then gave signs of a readiness to compromise. Voltaire, who preferred to live among quiet neighbours, seems on this occasion to have done his best, but in vain, to convert the temporary truce into a more permanent arrangement.

In the following year the quarrel was renewed. The Assembly was obstinate in exercising the one power left it—that of rejecting the candidates for the magistracy nominated by the Councils. The latter replied by throwing themselves into the hands of the Mediating Powers. There were now three main matters in dispute between them and the Assembly. The Councils claimed (1) judicial powers, (2) the right to interpret the ancient laws, and (3) to refuse to entertain any proposal or remonstrance of the citizens. In the absence of any published code the effect of this claim was to make the Councils practically supreme and omni-

[1] 'Art. 88. S'il y a quelqu'un qui dogmatise contre la doctrine resçue qu'il soit appelé pour conférer avec luy : s'il se range, qu'on le supporte sans scandale ni difame : s'il est opiniâtre qu'on l'admoneste par quelques fois pour essayer à le réduire : si on voit enfin qu'il soit métier de plus grande sévérité qu'on lui interdise la Sainte Cène et qu'on en avertisse le magistrat afin d'y pourvoir.'

potent. On the other hand, the Assembly could assert its privilege of rejecting all or any of the candidates for the post of Syndic or other office nominated by the two Councils. It did so on more than one occasion, and with effect. By the use of this weapon the whole administration could be brought to a standstill. The power in some measure took the place held in our own constitution by the financial control of the Lower House.

The result of the appeal to the Mediating Powers was the presentation by them to the Genevese of a projected constitution, known as The Pronouncement, which conformed in almost every respect to the views of the aristocracy. No efforts were spared to ensure its acceptance, yet it was rejected (1st December 1766) by a majority of two to one in the General Assembly.

The French Agent on the spot—France kept a Resident in permanence at Geneva—stormed, but the Swiss cantons, and Zurich in particular, were half-hearted, and the Protecting Powers hesitated to enforce their edict. Meantime, the rest of Europe woke up to what was going on. England, mindful of its many links with the citizens of Geneva, expressed an interest in the liberties of a small Protestant State. Some of the wiser heads among the aristocrats realised the perils of the situation, which were urged on them by a large body of citizens in an eloquent Remonstrance (16th October 1767). It was clear that the 'Pronouncement,' put forth by the Mediators, was unacceptable. At last the Councils gave way so far as to accept a working compromise, and the Représentants smoothed their path by various concessions. The following were the principal changes made in the constitution by the so-called Edict of Pacification (11th March 1768). It was agreed that the Assembly's right of rejecting candidates for the chief offices should be limited to a single ballot, but that in return it should elect every five years half the new members necessary to fill vacancies in the Great Council and four members of the Senate. It was further enacted that a code should be drawn up and printed, including all existing edicts and ordinances. A truce having been concluded on these terms, the Assembly ordered a Day of Prayer and Humiliation. The citizens abounded in virtuous resolves. 'Our prayers,' they proclaimed, 'are at last granted; firmly determined to keep our promises, let us go into the temple of the Most High to offer Him the sacrifice of our hates, our animosities, and our passions.' It was a good resolve, and one they often repeated in the following thirty years, but, unhappily, never proved capable of carrying into effect.

But for the survival of Haller's correspondence we should know nothing of de Saussure's attitude in the struggle here indicated. For local politics he had at this time obviously little bent; all his interests lay in a different direction, and his leisure was fully occupied. Born a patrician, his sympathy was naturally on the side of the established order, and, with his uncle Bonnet, he looked on Rousseau's influence in politics as that of a dangerous agitator. But he shows a more or less open mind and a good deal of sympathy with some of the ideas of the author of *Emile*, on whose famous letter resigning his citizenship after the condemnation of that work he writes (18th May 1763): 'You will find in it all his sentiments, good and bad, and, above all, his self-conceit, developed with much skill, force, and clearness.'

If in the protracted controversy and disorders of 1766-68, de Saussure, happy in his home circle and full of his own affairs, had no inclination to take any prominent part, he could not refuse to act as Haller's correspondent in supplying him with information as to the progress of events in Geneva. Haller was in a position to exercise at this period considerable influence on the Bernese Government, which, of the three Mediating Powers whose intervention had been called for to settle the domestic troubles of Geneva, was the most sympathetic and disinterested. Of the others, Zurich was distant and indifferent, while France under the ' ancien régime ' had small sympathy with a republic, and was entirely opposed to any measures likely to extend its franchise and render it more democratic. Berne, itself a paternal oligarchy, was anxious that Geneva should retain the same form of government, even at the cost of moderate concessions. At this moment Albrecht von Haller held a very high position in his own canton, and though not a member of the Great Council (or inner cabinet) had the ear of its leading politicians.[1] He was recognised throughout Switzerland as the acknowledged champion of religion and order against the subversive doctrines of Voltaire and Rousseau. He had formed a strong affection for the young botanist who was so eager in the pursuit of science, the nephew of his great friend

[1] See chap. xvi.

Bonnet. He now called on him to act as a confidential correspondent by keeping him fully informed as to the position of parties in Geneva, so that he might be able to bring a more effective influence to bear on the Bernese Government, and encourage it in its efforts at mediation.

Many more of Haller's than of de Saussure's letters have come down to us. Haller was very persistent in his demand for information. In 1766 he addressed thirty-one letters, the bulk of them on politics, to Geneva, and the stream ran on well into the next year. However excellent as a companion, he must have been somewhat exacting as a correspondent! Indeed de Saussure on one occasion entreats his illustrious friend not to agitate himself so much. And Haller himself confesses, 'I rush, perhaps with excessive vivacity, into everything I undertake. I am too keen on my job. . . . Any disorder infuriates me, every resistance to law, every individual who prefers the evil and the false raises my wrath.' We learn, moreover, that his letters were not easy to decipher; in 1775 Bonnet complains: 'Your handwriting gets worse and worse, the letters are often unfinished; there are even some which your pen skips. I have gone back five or six times to the same word without being able to make it out. What makes it more annoying for me is that I value highly the least thing that comes from your pen.' Bonnet's letters have a frank spontaneousness and reveal the amiable qualities of a man no one ever quarrelled with, and everybody, even Voltaire, who laughed at his psycho-physical theories, liked.

The position of the writers in the correspondence, much of which is preserved at Berne, is made fairly clear. De Saussure, a member of the patriciate, the grandson of a Syndic, and the son of a member of the Two Hundred, belonged by birth and association to the ruling caste, and to a large extent accepted its point of view. By temper a practical man and a cautious philosopher, he was naturally averse to rash generalisations and sudden changes. The constitution which had given Geneva two hundred years of prosperity was in his judgment not a thing lightly to be thrown aside or tampered with. To transfer the reins of government from a body composed of men of experience and high character to a popular assembly liable to be swayed by sudden and ignorant impulses, seemed to him a dangerous experiment.

The existing Government, whatever its faults, was honest, cheap, and fairly efficient, and had brought prosperity to its subjects. He did not believe that the mere fact of being born in a State gave a man any title to a share in ruling it. Education was, he held, an indispensable condition to the exercise of civic rights. He had a deep distrust of the vague and subversive doctrines preached by Rousseau and embodied in the *Lettres écrites de la Montagne*— which had just come out. He dreaded their effect on an excitable populace. He believed that behind the proposals of the more moderate Représentants lurked projects for the overthrow of the constitution, that the ultimate aim of the popular leaders was to do away altogether with the Councils, and to put all power in the hands of the Assembly, acting through the Syndics. He dreaded a raw and flighty democracy suddenly taking the place of an honest and capable, if obstinate, oligarchy. If I appreciate his position rightly, he stood for Reform, not Revolution; he was the equivalent of an English Whig.

From Haller's letters we may glean a sufficient idea of what was the solution present in his mind. It was to meet the demands of the Représentants by such moderate concessions as were consistent with leaving the reins of government in the hands of the Councils. Haller, who was a sound Tory, prophesied that bad times might be trusted to tranquillise the popular party, and that Geneva might hope for twenty years of relative quiet. But he shrewdly enough added, in a moment of exceptional frankness and foresight, the following warning:

'It will not last; your constitution is vicious, your Council [the Senate] has too much power given it by the law, together with the weakness of not being self-electing. There will always be restless spirits ready from time to time to make use of the control of elections in order to impair the authority of the Council. There has never been an orderly democracy. This is an inevitable misfortune for which there is no cure.'

Haller acknowledged that it was to the interest of the rulers that the people should be granted a legal status for putting forward their complaints. It would, he thought, serve to prove that the magistrates did not aim at tyranny. At one moment he was indignant at the evasions of the Senate, and their failure to show any sort of readiness for concessions. But he was apparently inconsistent when, on the acceptance of the Edict of Pacification in March 1768, he accused the patricians of selling the constitution in a cheap pursuit of popularity. He appears to have thought that in place of repealing minor class restrictions they had given away too many constitutional safeguards. He recommends his friend to 'Despair with patience'; it was a quality he often failed to exhibit in his own case.

De Saussure seems not to have been content to take the advice thus given him without some further independent effort. From a letter written to him at this time by the Duchesse d'Enville from Paris we gather that the young Professor had prepared and submitted to the French mediator, M. de Beauteville, a sketch of a project of reform. The Duchesse refers rather despondently to the difficulty of finding a solution that will satisfy both the Government and the people, 'whose interests are so different,' but assures him of the goodwill of the Resident. Of the details of de Saussure's proposals no record seems to exist. It is, I think, clear that they failed to bear fruit. It may fairly be inferred from his subsequent action that they lay in the direction of a gradual development in a democratic sense of the constitution as opposed to any violent changes which might put control of the administration of the State into the hands of the populace. He foresaw the trend of events and the trouble that was to come, and his remedy for it was an attempt—if the crowd was to rule—to educate it first. Throughout his life popular education was his political watchword.

CHAPTER XIII

EDUCATION AND THE RIVIERA (1772-81)

In the last chapter we have seen how de Saussure, through his correspondence with Haller, was called on to follow and take an interest in the political troubles of Geneva in 1767-8.

On his return from the Grand Tour in January 1769 he found the internal situation relatively tranquil. Geneva was about to enjoy some thirteen years of material prosperity and social brilliance. The young Professor's time was amply occupied. He held the double Chair of Physics and Metaphysics, which entailed lecturing frequently either in French or Latin during many months of the year. He was actively engaged in research in several branches of physical science. Besides these more serious occupations, he was, as the master of the finest house in Geneva, and of a country place on the lake shore, called on to play a leading part in the society of the Upper Town. When it is added that after 1770 he became subject to attacks of a violent form of indigestion, and that his health gave cause for serious anxiety, it will be clear that no apology is needed for his resolve to keep clear of politics, and his consequent refusal of a seat on the Great Council; he had other work in hand.

The part played by de Saussure as a pioneer of educational reform, though his efforts failed to produce any good effect at the time, was a remarkable one, and deserves far more attention than it has hitherto received. The shape in which his suggestions were put forward has been in part accountable for their neglect. Had he, in place of drawing up a scheme for the public school of his own city, embodied them in a treatise or volume addressed to the European public, they would not have been overlooked in the subsequent literature of the subject. Popular education held a place, beside the mountains and geology, as one of the chief and most constant interests in de Saussure's life. The warmth, both of feeling and of expression, shown in his response to the criticisms showered on his 'Project' by his colleagues of the Academy sufficiently indicates how deeply he was in earnest. Conscious of the social ferment which preceded the French Revolution, this Genevese patrician was firmly convinced that the first necessity for the orderly development of a democratic State was the civilisation through education of the demos. In the principles laid down and the practical details set out in his proposals we shall find that he often struck a surprisingly modern note. Many of them have had to wait more than a hundred years for their practical application. Some are still waiting—at any rate, in this country. If in his own lifetime his arguments fell on deaf ears, they were destined, repeated by his talented daughter, to attract and impress the critics, both French and Swiss, of succeeding generations.

De Saussure on his return from Italy in August 1773, with repaired health and renewed energies, resolved to make use of them, not only in the fulfilment of his professorial duties and the prosecution of his scientific studies, but in such action for the advancement of the public welfare as lay to his hand. His appointment as Rector of the Academy (1774-76) gave him an opportunity to bring forward proposals on a matter he had long had at heart, the reform of the system of education in the Collège.

Eleven years previously he had taken education as the subject of his inaugural lecture as a Professor, and had denounced the undue predominance given to the dead languages. He now devoted his energies to a vigorous effort to reconstruct the whole scheme of instruction in the Collège. This was, in fact, a public school for the children between the ages of six and fourteen of the upper classes, and de Saussure's own experience of it had been such that he refused to send his sons to be educated there. They were brought up at home, and had for a time for their tutor an uncle of the historian, Merle d'Aubigné. He now proposed to use the influence and position he had acquired in an endeavour to remodel the school system. He was ready to fight the battle for which his inaugural lecture had been only the preliminary skirmish. His attack was direct and vigorous.

'There is,' he wrote, 'a father of a family who, in common with many others, feels it his duty to refuse to send his children to the Collège so long as it remains in the state in which ours now is, but who would feel he was giving them the best education possible in sending them were the Collège reformed on the principles which form the base of the present proposal.'[1]

De Saussure had small sympathy with the view that looks on education not as a method for forming a mind, but as a means of making a livelihood. In a State where the majority rule, ought, he asked, that majority to be ignorant ? Rousseau's theory of the rights of man had little charm for his ears. He held that men should be taught how to use a vote before they were trusted with one. To hand over political control to an uneducated crowd went, he urged, against common sense. He and his circle of the Upper Town —the governing classes—looked on the author of the *Lettres écrites de la Montagne* as in local politics a disturber of his city's peace. Yet on educational topics de Saussure was affected by the eloquence and adopted not a few of the suggestions of *Emile*. In elementary education he advocated a system of object-lessons such as he had found serve with his own children ; he proposed to teach natural science with the aid of specimens suited to the age of the learner, to link and give life to history and geography by the aid of maps and pictures, to supply models to illustrate lessons in the industrial arts. For older pupils he recommended a mixture of scientific teaching and classical literature. He claimed for an association in secondary instruction between letters and science. The children destined to manufactures and commerce—the greater proportion of the townspeople—got, he held, under the existing system little advantage from their school years.

Early in 1774 he brought out his *Projet de Réforme pour le Collège de Genève*. In a short preface he tells us that it was the result of a series of discussions in a Literary Society to which he belonged, and that it embodied the view of many of its members. He adds, surely superfluously, to the avowal of the public purpose he has at heart a vigorous assertion that he has no personal end to serve, since it would give him far less trouble to bring up his own children privately than to undertake the thorny task of an educational reformer.

The first sentences of the pamphlet sufficiently indicate the

---

[1] *Avertissement* to the *Projet de Réforme pour le Collège de Genève*.

social unrest of Geneva at that date, and the political purpose that was underlying de Saussure's action. He writes:

' If there is a State that more than others needs to attend to education, it is that in which the opinions and the way of living of a considerable portion of its members are opposed to the spirit of its Government. Such an opposition must always produce discontents, public and private quarrels, general distrust, difficulties and shocks dangerous to the State; and it is to education alone that we can look for the removal of these abuses. In a Republic such as ours, therefore, an education is called for which will inspire in the young of all classes the love of country, the sense of common interests, and that spirit of equality which the character of our Government implies and demands.'

He goes on to insist on the advantages a public school has in this and other respects over home education. The Collège, he admits, was originally founded as a seminary for ecclesiastics and civil servants; but the time has come, he urges, when it should be converted to more general uses. He points out unsparingly the defects of a system that had driven from the Collège all the children whose parents could afford to give them a better education. The middle-class pupils, he declares,

' get nothing but some notions, and those imperfect, of religion; the etymology of a few words derived from Greek or Latin, and some scattered scraps of history and mythology; those of the upper class, for whom the curriculum was planned, bring nothing away but some bad Latin and the rudiments of Greek. For all other branches of knowledge they have, on leaving the Collège, to take them up at their A B C as if they had never heard them mentioned.'

De Saussure proceeds to set out in detail his scheme of instruction. It is interesting to note that he cites as a model for imitation Zurich, celebrated at the present day for having some of the best-provided primary schools, attended by all classes, in Europe. The daily school-hours were not to exceed six; of these two were to be given to the dead languages, and two to Science and History, two to Moral Instruction (under which were included Christian doctrine and French poetry!). De Saussure subsequently cut down Morals to one hour. To suit parents who did not want classics, the hours for Latin and Greek were to be so arranged that the pupils could easily absent themselves. For the rest, we find many sensible and essentially modern recommendations. Classes on the same subject are not to be too long, the lessons are as far as possible to be illustrated, the relations of history and geography are to be insisted on, in classical studies composition is in the upper forms to be limited in Latin and altogether suppressed in Greek, while more attention is to be given to translations. De Saussure ends with an earnest appeal which indicates a mind alive to the dangers looming in the near future. ' Our State is but a little island situated between broad, deep, and rapid currents, and our internal divisions, if radical and frequent, may open . . . but I turn my eyes from this terrifying prospect.' Therefore, he urges, let all recognise that a public and common education is the most effectual means to ensure the safety of the Republic.

De Saussure's forcible utterance for the moment caught the public ear, and was eagerly discussed by partisans on both sides ; Condorcet wrote to him from Paris, sending him several pages of sympathetic comment. But at Geneva the novelty of the ideas seems to have created some misunderstanding and much criticism. In patrician circles they excited warm hostility. As has often been the case elsewhere, educational progress was hindered by political prejudices. The clerics and the class they influenced—the Negatives of the Upper Town—were violent in their opposition. De Saussure's colleague, Bertrand, who as a mathematician might have been expected to take a more liberal view, proved a leading opponent. He quoted an Ordinance according to which ' the Collège was founded to educate young men for the Ministry and Magistracy,' and urged that for 'lawyers and theologians, to whom he would add doctors,' any course of instruction not exclusively classical was ill-suited ! If any teaching for artists and artisans was needed, it must, he contended, be given in a wholly separate institution. The public became interested and began to take sides. Tracts and squibs, after the Genevese fashion, filled the air, while a mock protest from the women of Geneva, complaining that they would no longer be fit companions for their over-educated husbands, amused the town.[1] On the other hand, the Représentants, the heads of the popular party, warmly supported the *Projet*. Jacques

---

[1] There were no primary public schools for girls at Geneva before 1804, and no secondary schools before 1836.

François Deluc (the father of Jean Antoine, the meteorologist, and one of the climbers of the Buet) took the lead at the head of a deputation of fifty in presenting an address of thanks to its author. Another deputation, also from the Natifs, was led by the Alpine enthusiast Bourrit. The dispute had become political. De Saussure was regarded by his own party as more or less of a renegade. But in the Radical camp he was hailed with enthusiasm. He delighted his unenfranchised visitors by greeting them as fellow-citizens. D'Ivernois, a Genevese democrat, who spent ten years in exile in England, where he was knighted, writes in the warmest terms of de Saussure's efforts to break down social prejudices and barriers and to promote close and friendly relations between all classes in the State. In these efforts he was, d'Ivernois tells us, ably seconded by young Lord Mahon, who did his best to encourage games and manly exercises among the youth of the aristocracy, who appear to have fallen into sadly effeminate habits.[1]

Meantime, de Saussure was surprised, and not a little indignant, at the hostile attitude of many of his friends and colleagues. He sent out an answer to objectors, *Eclaircissements sur le Projet de Réforme pour le Collège de Genève*. He had, it is clear, been accused of scheming, on the one hand, for his own, the leisured class ; on the other, of attempting to substitute for solid learning a culture extensive but superficial ; to abolish a sound liberal and classical education in favour of an inadequate technical one. He retaliated warmly :

'Even in this century, called "The Century of Facts," it is phrases that govern. Society is divided into little cabals, each of which has its catchword. That which rallies the greatest number is any attack on "the upper class"—*les Gens du Monde*. At its sound all who count as their chief quality misanthropy, all the envious, gather and are ready to tear in pieces those thus presented to them.'

He set aside brusquely an alternative proposal for separate technical schools for the working-man. He refuted vehemently the contention of those who looked on the education of the people as dangerous to society. He treated with scorn the economical objectors who were frightened at the probable cost of carrying out his scheme. The world is divided into two sections—those whose minds instinctively turn first to the objections to any change

[1] See *Tableau historique et politique des Révolutions de Genève dans le dix-huitième Siècle* (Geneva, 1782), and p. 318.

and those who are ready to appreciate fairly the arguments on both sides. De Saussure was born and bred a Negative, but in intellect he showed himself very much the contrary.

De Saussure was obviously before his time, while the Venerable Company was as hopelessly conservative as most clerical Convocations. Moreover, the tincture in de Saussure's eloquence of the doctrines of the recently condemned *Emile* was not likely to recommend his proposals to its friendly consideration. The principles de Saussure propounded, that a nation gets the Government it deserves, that there is no tyranny so vicious as that of an ignorant democracy, that liberty without law spells licence, might be sound, but his application of them was well outside the scope of the Genevese patricians' vision. Since their oligarchy was a Republic in name, they were satisfied to drive on in the old track till the events of the last decade of the eighteenth century threw them into the ditch.

What would appear to be the habitual result of educational discussions followed. De Saussure's proposals were referred to a committee. In due course the committee made some practical suggestions towards carrying them out; it framed a scheme for a system of secondary education. This would have involved the postponement of classical and literary instruction to advanced classes consisting of youths whose abilities gave promise that they would be able to profit by it. The proposals were formally referred back for further consideration and practically shelved.

Some changes for the better were made in 1790, but it was not till sixty-two years later that the education of the Collège was, after continual contests, reformed on modern lines. Latin and Greek were then made optional subjects. Grammar was to be taught through the French language. Geography and history were given an important place. Modern languages, arithmetic, practical geometry, and drawing were dealt with in special classes. 'Thus,' writes the historian of the Collège, 'the adoption of the law of 1836 realised in part the proposals made by de Saussure in 1774, which the Councils of the revolutionary epoch had attempted to carry out in an exaggerated shape, and which the Society of Arts had in 1821 tried without success to revive in their original form.' The variations from de Saussure's scheme lay chiefly in the absence of any recognition of natural science and in the relegation of moral or religious teaching to a comparatively secondary place.

We have been led on in order to complete the story of de Saussure's educational activity. I return to 1774 to record the fact that he was in that year proposed by Lord Mahon and elected a member of a newly founded English Club, which met every Saturday for discussions carried on in our language.

Next year (1775), undeterred by his repulse, de Saussure again attacked the education in vogue. In his capacity of Rector he gave at the Annual 'Promotions,' or prize-day of the Collège, a lecture 'On the Neglect of Athletics and the pampered Bringing-up of the Young.'[1] He wrote to Haller that he had also furnished a programme of the proceedings in verse! This has not survived. The only other occasion on which there is any record of his having yielded to the Genevese habit of rhyming is in some playful lines written in the previous year (1774) for his elder son's seventh birthday. They prove him a wise father, if but an indifferent poet.

At this date de Saussure was acting as Curator of the Town Library, and we find him thanking Lord Stanhope for a handsome present of books. Throughout his career he was continually being called on to take up posts demanding a certain amount of practical ability and sacrifice of time, and he seems readily to have responded to the claims made on him.

Thwarted in his effort to improve and enlarge at its source the public education of Geneva, de Saussure turned his mind and energy to a more indirect method which might serve the double object of bringing the different classes and avocations, men of science and artists, employers and workmen, into closer relation, and at the same time of raising the general intellectual and artistic level. He conceived the plan of a popular Society of Arts, that should combine the efforts of the more enlightened members of every class in the community in a general endeavour to set before their fellows a high standard in all things, and more particularly to promote the application of science to industry, and of art to manufactures and daily life. He was fortunate in securing at the

[1] Rousseau, in his *Lettre à d'Alembert*, insists on this defect in the training of the youth of Geneva. 'Boys are brought up like women: they are guarded from the sun, the wind, the rain, and dust, so that they lose all power of endurance. They are forbidden any exercise, etc.' (See also d'Ivernois, *Révolutions de Genève*.)

start the support and sympathy of an intelligent watchmaker, Louis Faizan, who has been held by some to share with him the credit of the Society's foundation. The project was, no doubt, fully discussed in the hall or on the terrace of de Saussure's townhouse overlooking the Corraterie, before, in April 1776, a solemn assembly of three hundred persons was held in the 'Salle du Magnifique Conseil des Deux Cents,' by the permission of Messieurs les Syndics, in order to found the new 'Société des Arts.' The next step was to form committees. One was charged with the crafts of the watchmakers and jewellers and silversmiths and the like, another with rural and domestic economy and their branches, including machinery. Three lecturers were appointed, with the title of demonstrators. A number of prizes, medals of the substantial value of twenty louis, were offered for essays on subjects, all practical but very diverse—for instance, 'How to Improve the Fertility of the Genevese Territory'; 'How best to Employ Paupers, should a Workhouse be established'; 'How to Improve the Manufacture of Steel'; 'For an Elementary Work on Watchmaking.' 'Virtue,' in the Roman sense of the word, bravery resulting in the saving of human life, was also rewarded in the case of rescues from fire or drowning.

De Saussure, who from the start threw himself with all his energy into the undertaking, was the first President of the Society. He looked forward to the practical results to be obtained in many directions by applying scientific knowledge to industry and the daily affairs of life. But it was also his particular desire to promote an artistic and imaginative sense among his neighbours in Geneva. The fine arts had too long, he thought, lain under the ban of Calvinism; the town record was rich in theologians and men of science, but poor in painters and poets.

The Society had some years of moderately successful existence before it fell under the blight of the political reaction of 1781-2. Under the restrictions enforced by the victorious patricians, its meetings were for a time forbidden, but after an interval, and when political passions had to some extent subsided, de Saussure, naturally unwilling to see his efforts brought to nothing, approached the Government, and in 1786 the Society was reconstituted under its protection on a new basis, and granted an official home, where it could extend its schools of design. De Saussure did not content himself with securing official support. His social and practical spirit was shown not only in inviting ladies to become patronesses and attend the meetings, but also in arranging for more friendly and informal gatherings, which were cheered by tea and coffee and enlightened by the first appearance of the once famous Argand lamp.

In the next year (1787) the original *Journal de Genève* made its appearance as the organ of the Society. It announced as its object the publication of whatever local news might be useful to its readers. Births, deaths, and marriages, elections, new laws and regulations, prices in the market, fill its columns. There is a whole front page (here we note the hand of de Saussure) of meteorological observations. The first number appeared on the day of his return to Chamonix from Mont Blanc; the second contained a short account of his ascent. In the following issues we find it acting as the Journal of the 'Société des Arts' in the stricter sense of the word, reporting its proceedings and the papers read before it. It died after five years, in the troublous days of the Revolution, to be definitely born again as a newspaper in the modern sense in 1830. It has flourished ever since, and is now one of the best daily papers on the Continent.

The 'Société des Arts' survived and still prospers. The story of its achievements and the list of its possessions, its benefactors, and its officers have been recently issued in a handsome volume.[1] Its rooms contain considerable collections, among which is the official portrait of de Saussure, painted a few years before his death by Saint-Ours.

We have transgressed chronological order in order to complete the story of de Saussure's connection with the 'Société des Arts' and the *Journal de Genève*.

In 1775 health was again a matter of anxiety with de Saussure, and he was prescribed for by Dr. Tronchin.

'One word more,' the genial doctor writes, 'to you whose health is so precious to us. Use moderation in drugs. Moderate also your activity and your zeal in all you undertake. Add to your virtues that of bearing contradiction, even where you have least reason to expect it. This virtue is far more necessary in republics than in monarchies; it is the safeguard of peace of soul and tranquillity of mind—conditions which perhaps are not held at their proper value in republics.'

[1] *La Société des Arts et ses Collections*, par J. Crosnier (Geneva, 1910).

This sound advice did not lead to any restriction in the excursions that de Saussure undertook in the following year in the interest of his scientific studies. In 1776, in the early summer, he accompanied his friend Sir William Hamilton to Chamonix. In August he made another dash to Chamonix and climbed the Buet, and later took his wife, children, and servants with him for an extensive family tour through southern France in a berlin with four horses. He went up the Puy de Dôme on 13th October; drove on through the hills of Auvergne to Nîmes, Avignon, Vaucluse, Orange, and Grenoble. On the 12th November he was at Lyons, whence the party made another round by Dijon, Semur, Besançon, and Pontarlier. In the Jura they suffered from the weather, which was not surprising, since they did not return to Genthod till 30th November.

Sir William Hamilton in the same year writes to de Saussure from Paris to report a death in his family. His comments indicate the philosophic mind he was later in life to have occasion to exhibit:

'As for me, I take events for which there is no remedy as best I can, and I confess that since I have learnt to look on nature as a whole, and discovered that what we call ancient is comparatively very modern, and that the longest life of man is little more than that of the insect which is born in the morning and dies in the evening, the saddest events no longer produce the same effect on me. I shall fight vigorously to ward off misfortune; but when there is no remedy one must console oneself. I enjoy as well as I can the present moment.'

At the end of the year we find him proposing de Saussure for the Fellowship of the Royal Society. He writes that he has no doubt de Saussure will be elected without any opposition. For some technical reason—different ones are alleged in the correspondence—either lack of a seconder with personal knowledge, or that de Saussure had not contributed a paper to the *Transactions* of the Society—nothing came of the proposal at the time. It was not till 1788, after de Saussure had established a popular reputation by his ascent of Mont Blanc, that his scientific claims were recognised. The delay contrasts oddly with the Society's relative eagerness to receive de Saussure's far less distinguished townsman,

Jean Antoine Deluc. But Deluc was on the spot and 'Reader to the Queen'!

In July 1777 de Saussure was called on by the Emperor Joseph II. of Austria, who passed through Geneva on his way home from Paris. The prospect of receiving an imperial guest had greatly fluttered the local authorities. They appointed a Committee of Reception; they arranged for his lodging in the house of a wealthy citizen, and resolved to send a distinguished and discreet deputation to welcome him. On the 15th July the Register of the Senate records that the Count de Falkenstein (the Emperor's incognito) had arrived on the previous day at the hotel at Sécheron, that two of the Syndics had gone there and, through one of the Emperor's bankers, had conveyed a message that they desired to pay their respects to him, but that the Emperor had replied that while thanking them he must decline all formal and complimentary visits. The Syndics further reported that the Emperor had that morning driven into Geneva in a hired carriage, visited the Public Library and M. de Saussure's cabinet, and returned by boat, and that he proposed to leave next day.

The dry official record can be supplemented by letters of the date. They tell us that the Emperor had ordered rooms at the Hôtel des Balances in the town, but changed his intention on finding the crowd that had collected, and drove on to the inn at Sécheron,[1] which had the advantage of being outside the gates. Even at Sécheron the road and adjoining terraces that commanded any view of his apartment were thronged with a crowd in carriages and on foot.

De Saussure's friend, Trembley, describes the Emperor's appearance:

'I saw the Emperor; he has, in my opinion, a mediocre figure which indicates a mediocre man. He seemed somewhat cold and unappreciative. He would not see our Syndics. We must find out what M. de Saussure, who had a talk with him, thinks of him.'

Unfortunately, de Saussure's impression is not on record, but we find an account—a remarkable one for a child of eleven—in his daughter Albertine's diary:

'At last he has come! He is a little man, well made, with a somewhat lofty air, a small face, a large aquiline nose, and extraordinarily

---

[1] This was the inn where Byron and Shelley afterwards stayed. Turner made a drawing of Geneva and the lake from a spot near it.

lively, clear blue eyes. He was dressed extremely simply in a short brown coat of Silesian cloth and a white waistcoat and trousers. He looked for a long time at M. Bourrit's pictures of the glaciers. . . . Papa showed him his museum and electrical machine, to which he did not give much attention. On leaving he paid fine compliments to several ladies who had gathered on the great staircase to see him pass.'

De Saussure had been warned that the Emperor might ask to be taken to the glaciers, and Bourrit had written him a letter imploring that the job of acting as local cicerone might, if not wanted by de Saussure, be passed on to the 'Historiographer of the Alps.' But the Emperor was in a hurry, and there was no question of a trip to Chamonix.

Next day he set out on the road to Lausanne and Berne. We owe to Bonnet, who lived not far from Ferney, an amusing, and, for his kindly bent, somewhat malicious, account of what happened :

'The Emperor,' he writes, 'left Sécheron between four and five in the afternoon ; he passed through Ferney like an arrow. The old gentleman [Voltaire], with all his household in full dress, was waiting for him [at the cross-roads where the road to Ferney branches off from the Route de Suisse]. He had got up early and worn his best wig since eight o'clock in the morning, made great preparations for a dinner, and pushed his attention to the sovereign so far as to have all the stones cleared off the road to his house—that is for more than half a league. Nevertheless, the traveller gave him the mortification of not halting for a single instant, and even when the postilion indicated Ferney, the Emperor only shouted twice over, "Fouette, cocher!" It is clear from all his behaviour that he intended to mortify the old pamphleteer, who, I assure you, felt it deeply.'

Bonnet's version of the story was not universally accepted. Voltaire, at any rate, had another tale to tell. He asserted that two men leapt on the steps of the Emperor's carriage and asked him if he was not going to see Voltaire, and that Joseph II., irritated at the impertinence, gave the order to drive on ; that his conduct, therefore, was the result not of any deliberate resolve, but of a sudden pique. Another version is that the Emperor's mother, the Empress Maria Theresa, had instructed her son to avoid Voltaire and visit Haller.

So the Emperor went on his way to call on Haller, then almost on his death-bed at Berne. On his return to Vienna he sent to the invalid 'hampers of the finest wine and quinine,' but they arrived too late, for Haller died in December. Joseph II. bought his library, with many of his manuscripts, and presented them to the University of Pavia. They are now stored in the Biblioteca Ambrosiana at Milan.

A few days later de Saussure found himself at the Baths of Loëche, at the foot of the Gemmi, whence he wrote to his wife a lively description of the bathers. He was fortunate in being welcomed by the talented Dutchwoman married to a Neuchâtelois, Madame de Charrière, to whom Sainte-Beuve has dedicated many pages.[1] She had already been a guest at the house in the Rue de la Cité, where her presence at a dinner party is recorded in Albertine's diary.

De Saussure anticipates and confirms the verdict of the great critic on the author of *Caliste* and the *Lettres Neuchâteloises*. He speaks warmly of her 'gaiety and real wit,' and takes credit to himself with his wife for resisting her invitation to prolong his stay. In the woman who wrote, 'Sitting at my window and looking out on the lake, I thank you, mountains, snow, and sun, for all the pleasure you give me,' he must have found a congenial spirit. She introduced him to the Assembly, where the beauties of Lausanne outshone the Valaisannes, who wore their local costume. De Saussure writes :

'If not very elegant, it was all very singular ; the most singular thing is to see them all *en chemise*, men and women, in the same bath. It is most entertaining, when this circle of people has been formed, to witness new arrivals make their entry and their bows in this comical crowd.'

The custom survived till the middle of the last century, when on the entry of English visitors the bathers were wont to strike up 'God Save the Queen!' De Saussure dined and supped with Madame de Charrière, who held him in conversation, much to the disappointment of the ladies from Lausanne, who were eager for a card party.

The year 1779 was marked by the death of de Saussure's second brother-in-law, Turrettini, a loss by which the whole family

[1] See Sainte-Beuve, *Portraits Littéraires*, vol. iii., and *Portraits de Femmes*, and Sayous, *Le dix-huitième Siècle à l'Etranger*, vol. ii.

was very much affected. De Saussure was now left the only man in the villa at Genthod. At the end of October an interesting visitor presented himself there. Goethe, who was travelling with a German prince on his way to Italy, arrived at Geneva, and at once called on de Saussure to ask for advice on the possibility so late in the year of an Alpine tour. Encouraged to risk a visit to the glaciers, he set out for Chamonix and the Mer de Glace, crossed the Col de Balme to Martigny, and then, favoured by an exceptional season, ventured up the Rhône valley to the Furka and St. Gotthard, arriving at the hospice on the latter on 15th November.

Goethe's letters on his Alpine tour are among the signs of the arrival of a new phase in the attitude of travellers towards mountain scenery. During the previous century their records had been mostly topographical, matter-of-fact observations of natural features, or accounts of the difficulties and incidents of the road. It had been the fashion to look on nature with curious rather than with artistic eyes. In de Saussure's *Voyages* the former point of view still predominates, though from time to time he yields to more personal and romantic impressions. But these are rather the exception than the rule. Too often he neglects to make any attempt to bring before his readers' eyes the distinctive features of the scenery he passes through. For instance, we find in his pages no mention of two of the finest landscapes in the Alps—the glorious view of Mont Blanc from the head of Val d'Aosta or that of the Jungfrau from the Wengern Alp. The beauty of the Lake of Lucerne gets no tribute from his pen. He seems to take pains to justify his own confession that he has no natural talent or taste for fine writing. It requires some very exceptional occasion to draw from him the eloquence of his descriptions of the view from the Crammont, or of his last sunset on the Col du Géant.

In Goethe's case the poet's mind and pen dwell not only on the permanent outline of the landscape before him, but on its shifting aspects under the changes of cloud and sunshine, of dawn and twilight. He sets himself down to compose a picture of passing effects. Such are the descriptions of the first glimpse of Mont Blanc seen in the gloaming on issuing from the defile of Les Montets, and of the peaks and glaciers appearing between two cloud-belts from the Col de Balme. I quote the former:

'It grew darker as we drew near and at last entered the Vale of Chamonix. Only the great masses were visible. The stars shone out one by one, and we noticed over the summits of the range immediately in front of us a light that we could not account for. Clear without sparkle, like the Milky Way, but denser, almost like the Pleiades only larger, it held us long in wonderment, until at last, as we changed our position, like a pyramid illumined by an internal mysterious light that may best be compared to that of a glow-worm, it rose supreme over all the other mountains and we recognised Mont Blanc.

'The scene was of extraordinary beauty; since the mountain shone not with the same vivid light as the stars that surrounded it, but as a broad, single mass which appeared to the eyes to belong to a higher sphere; it was difficult for the mind to realise that it had its roots in the earth.'

Goethe was doubtless the most famous of the early visitors to Chamonix, but he was only one of a number, many of whom shared his appreciation of mountain scenery. Our countryman, Mr. Brand, who was tutor to Sir James Graham, the father of the statesman, may be taken as a typical specimen of the average traveller of his day. Writing in 1786, he tells his sister:

'During the whole summer one is sure to find Englishmen here [that is, on the road to Chamonix] at every stage, some with their wives and daughters, others with their mistresses, but the most part like ourselves, raw youth and sedater manhood.'

In the previous year there had been fifteen hundred 'visitors to the glaciers.' Mr. Brand's enthusiasm for Alpine scenery is not less than the poet's, if it is less eloquently expressed. Here is his description of the view from Sallanches:

'We returned to our inn just as the moon was rising behind the chain of Mont Blanc. Sometimes it was entirely eclipsed by one of those pyramidal summits which they call Aiguilles or Needles, at other times the sharp point of an aiguille passed across its surface, and the outline was marked with all the exactness of one of Mr. Harrington's profiles. Once we saw only two small points of the moon's disk at about two inches asunder, and they shone with a brilliant light like two new splendid planets, till at length she rose above the peaks and tinged the summits of Mont Blanc (which was now uncovered) with a beautiful silver tint reflected by some thin, vapoury clouds that hovered in the atmosphere above. Among the rich pictures which moonlight affords, I never saw any to equal this. We hardly knew how to leave it.'

I might quote further from Mr. Brand's manuscript journal. His taste for scenery is not confined to romantic incidents, such as moonlight on Mont Blanc. He fully appreciates and describes the noble gorges of the lower Val d'Aosta and the beauties of the descent into Italy.

Next year de Saussure's first family excursion to Chamonix was undertaken with his wife, his three children, and an English lady, a Miss Craft.[1] It was quite an expedition. The party drove in three carriages to Sallanches, where twenty-four mules were ordered to be in readiness. Théodore and his mother went to the Montenvers, and de Saussure took the boy (aged thirteen) for a walk on the Mer de Glace, and records that ' he is pleased with the quickness and force he shows in his first lesson in mountain-climbing.'

De Saussure left the party at Sallanches on the way back, and, despite feeling out of sorts, went up to sleep at some chalets on the west side of the Col de Voza above Bionnassay. On the following morning he got as far as the Mont Lachat (6937 feet), the grassy spur below the Aiguille du Goûter. There he was taken ill with a serious feverish attack which cut short his mountaineering for the season. For the moment he turned to an endeavour to complete his book on hygrometry, but by September found himself well enough to set out with his friend M. A. Pictet for a tour in North Italy and along the Riviera, the principal object of which was to embark on a new series of investigations.

De Saussure was a precursor in an inquiry which has since been pursued with great assiduity, that into the temperature of the sea at various depths. For this purpose he devised a form of thermometer, capable of resisting subaqueous pressure, which is still in use.[2] Of

---

[1] Miss Craft went on to Montpellier with an introduction from de Saussure to his sister, and is mentioned in Judith de Saussure's letters as preferring a livelier circle to that in which she lived.

[2] The scientific value of the work accomplished is dealt with separately by Dr. H. R. Mill on pp. 462-5.

the details of the tour we have some account in the *Voyages*. This can be supplemented by extracts from de Saussure's letters home and the unpublished diary of his companion. In his first note, written to his wife from his house in the Rue de la Cité (he had left her at Genthod), he takes his leave for a five weeks' tour with as much emotion as if he were starting for the North Pole. His reference to the tears of the parting scene help us to understand why on other occasions he was apt to slip away at dawn, or even earlier. Three years later, he records that he left home for a visit to the Gries and the St. Gotthard at 4.22 A.M., 'concealing from my wife and children my start, which always causes them acute distress and by its anticipation poisons our last moments.' He seldom set out on any considerable expedition without resorting to some similar subterfuge. Madame de Saussure's 'sensibility' was obviously, even for that date, above the average. Good as well as bad news was a trial to her nerves. It is recorded that on one occasion her sister, Madame Tronchin, thought it well to break to her the fact of her wanderer's return rather than to let it be announced by a servant.

The chief interest of de Saussure's companion's diary lies in the picture it gives of the difficulties of post-travel in a wet autumn. Again and again, first in the Maurienne and then on the plain of Piedmont, the travellers had to take their carriage to pieces and pack it on mules, or to cross flooded rivers in ferry-boats. An enforced halt at Vercelli gave de Saussure opportunity to attempt a sketch. The object which interested him was the beautiful outline of Monte Rosa. But it was not till nine years later that he first made a closer acquaintance with the rival of Mont Blanc. At Milan de Saussure went to the opera, and reports that the ladies were beautiful, but seemed dull. At Genoa he and Pictet hired a boat and, sailing eastward, took soundings and temperatures of the sea-bottom off Porto Fino, despite their sufferings from sea-sickness. These seem to have affected de Saussure's temper. On his return he wrote home :

'I am worn out with boredom and visits, first a certain Dr. Pratolungo, longer in his calls than the meadow from which he takes his name, and next some dear fellow-countrymen, very good people, but thinking one can have nothing better to do than entertain them. Then Pictet has a cold, so I have to go alone to pay return calls, and I find Madame de la Rue at home, and she insists on showing me her apartment, her pictures, her cat, and her dogs, and all with a flow of words and a shrill voice which made me feel sea-sick over again. Impatient to get back and write to you I find the house full of people: but at last I am left free.'

De Saussure had a fall on the marble staircase of his hotel and hurt his leg. Bad weather came to add to his vexations. The long-suffering of his companion, who would have preferred to wait for sunshine, was a further trial. 'Pictet puts up with anything, nothing makes him impatient; his patience makes me impatient.' However, de Saussure had his way, and the travellers rode off in rain and waterproofs and were at once rewarded by the return of sunshine.

At this date, before the road was made, a trip along the Riviera di Ponente was no light matter even in fine weather. This is how de Saussure prefaces his account of the journey:[1]

'Few travellers make the transit by land; it is only practicable on foot or on horseback, and even on horseback it is dangerous in many places, where the only track is a narrow and slippery ledge cut in terraces overhanging the sea.' [*Voyages*, 1355.]

Dante's reference to the villainous character of the old horse-track has often been quoted. But it is perhaps not generally realised that the poet's description held good till the beginning of the nineteenth century, when the great road Napoleon had begun was at last finished. In 1780 the carriage road ceased a few miles beyond Genoa. The travellers accordingly started on horseback, leaving their luggage to follow them by sea in a felucca. They were often forced to dismount and lead their horses, the party got separated, one of the horses was for a time lost, the inns were abominable, and they often preferred a mattress on the floor to venturing in the beds. De Saussure gives a lifelike sketch of the inn at Spiotorno:

'I went down by chance into the kitchen, where I saw a picture in the style of Teniers: our old and hideous hostess, who, by the light of a small lamp with untidy hair and black and wrinkled hands, was pounding on a block the scraps of meat which were to form our supper.'

At last the party reached Nice, found their felucca arrived, and embarked to make a fresh set of deep-sea temperature observations.

Safely landed, de Saussure congratulates himself on having accomplished his task; he was obviously no sailor. Perils by water, however, were not over. The Var at that date was still unbridged, and the travellers' carriage was conducted through the stream by bare-legged men called *égayeurs*, who held it up on either side. The next adventure was the passage of the Esterels, the miniature mountain range the outline at least of which is familiar to visitors to Cannes. Its dangers are depicted in a paragraph of the *Voyages* that agreeably interrupts much geological detail.

'It is on the bit of road immediately below the highest point on the Antibes side that travellers are most frequently held up by highwaymen.

'A long stretch of road is visible in its entirety, shut in between two projecting heights; it is on these that the robbers place their sentinels. They let the travellers advance to about half-way between the two points, and then the robbers ambuscaded in the wood fall on them and strip them, while the sentinels keep watch that they are not surprised by the coastguards. In this case, warned by a whistle or some such signal, they escape into the forest. It is impossible to catch them, for not only is the bush very thick, but the ground beneath it consists of broken blocks, there is neither road nor path, and unless a man knows the locality as well as the robbers do, he can only penetrate with great difficulty and extreme slowness. When M. Pictet and I passed this way the courier from Rome, who travelled with us, pointed out the remains of the carriage of the preceding courier, who had been robbed a few days previously. This forest, which the frequency of accidents of this sort has made so dreaded, is composed of pines and evergreen oaks, under which grow arbutus, cistuses, heaths, etc. It extends to the sea, and has an area of three to four leagues in length by two in breadth. All this region, entirely savage, is the refuge of the prisoners who escape from the galleys of Toulon, the nursery of all the brigands of the country.' [*Voyages*, 1440.]

Seven years later de Saussure explored on foot the recesses of this fascinating range of porphyry and climbed its seaward summit, the Cap Roux. Now he and his companion hastened on to Fréjus, where Pictet tells us the population appeared fever-stricken owing to the marshes in the neighbourhood. In Roman times the town was a health resort. Pliny the younger mentions sending one of his freedmen who had delicate lungs there for the benefit of the climate. Its suburb of St. Raphael is now again frequented by visitors.

Passing through Toulon, Marseilles, and Aix, the travellers found the roads still bad as far as Nîmes, and met with further misadventures from lack of post-horses and broken wheels. In consequence of one of these accidents, they were forced to lodge with a village curé, who had a collection of prints valued at 20,000 francs. He had been a captain of dragoons, 'but an unfortunate affair had forced him to leave the army and take orders!'

At Nîmes the interior of the amphitheatre was at that date filled with mean houses. The charming temple of Diana struck Pictet as 'assez peu de chose.' Architecture was not our travellers' strong point—the Maison Carrée they do not mention. Thence an afternoon's drive brought them to Montpellier, with the object of paying a visit to de Saussure's sister Judith, by whom, as already related, they were entertained and introduced to her circle of distinguished friends. Well satisfied with his sister's situation and surroundings, de Saussure, as usual in a hurry to return to his home, after two days' stay started at midnight for Pont Saint Esprit. Halting at Lyons only long enough to make propitiatory purchases for their female relations, birds for de Saussure's mother and a gown for his wife, the two travellers reached Geneva on the 3rd November.

CHAPTER XIV

POLITICS AND HOME LIFE (1781-92)

The famous Act of Mediation of 1768 gave a respite to the patrician Government that, wisely taken advantage of, might have saved the constitution. But the Councils were blind to the signs of the times. They had before them a double task, to meet the growth of the city by setting up a system of gradual enfranchisement for the class without civic rights, and to satisfy the General Assembly by keeping their promise to codify the laws of the State. They did nothing to extend the franchise on the one hand; on the other they put off the publication of a code by a series of equivocations. Recognising that there was no hope of forcing the Councils to act, the General Assembly in 1777 proposed that a joint Commission should be appointed and charged to report within two years. This limit was taken advantage of by the Negatives, or Constitutionals, as they called themselves, and the Councils on its expiration refused to extend the time, although the Commission had not been able to conclude its task. The two parties were now actively opposed, and during 1779 and 1780 the situation grew from month to month more embittered.

In the following year (1781) the political storm which had been slowly gathering broke out. The situation was complicated by the triangular nature of the contest. It was no longer a duel. On one side were the Negatives, a patrician oligarchy striving to maintain itself by an alliance with the populace, and relying in the last resort on foreign support; on the other the Représentants, citizens torn between their anxiety to preserve the powers of a popular assembly and jealousy of their still unenfranchised fellow-townsmen. But distinct from the two chief combatants were the so-called Natifs, composed of a large proportion of the growing middle class and the artisans, who were ready to join whichever side held out the best offer. After a time their leaders, finding the Représentants but a broken reed, turned for aid to the patricians. Cornuaud, an able demagogue, offered the latter the support of his party in return for the abolition of the restrictions which forbade the Natifs free access to various crafts and professions. Political rights he for the present made no claim to. The French Resident supported the demands of this strange alliance, but the two Swiss cantons—the co-Mediators—declined to follow him.

In February 1781 de Saussure wrote to tell his sister at Montpellier the local news. There had been an unfortunate affair in which some Natifs had fired on their allies the Negatives by mistake, and his friend Trembley had had his left hand badly damaged. Disorder had broken out in the city, the Représentants had seized the occasion to assert that the State was in danger. Cannon had been brought into the streets and the town gates closed. De Saussure had had great difficulty in obtaining permission for his father to return to his country home at Frontenex.

For the moment the popular party held the upper hand. They hastened to outbid their opponents by promising to the Natifs all they asked. The Negatives, surprised and alarmed, gave way, and a few days later the so-called *Edit Bienfaisant* (10th February 1781) was passed, which granted the Natifs freedom from civil disabilities and a prospect of gradual enfranchisement. This might have been the first step towards a real democracy. But in May the Councils, recovered from their panic and relying as before on the support of the Mediators, disavowed their recent action on the plea that they had acted under duress. They declined to carry out the *Edit Bienfaisant* and formally declared that the General Assembly was only one of the several estates of the Commonwealth, and had no claim to the title generally accorded it of 'Le Souverain.' They adjured the citizens of every degree to recognise that the only way to restore peace to the Republic was to await such measures as the Mediators might recommend. The patricians, preferring foreign support to any concession to the bourgeoisie, marched to their doom.

Party feeling ran high, but de Saussure went on undisturbed with his professorial and scientific work, and felt able to leave his wife in order to make a short trip to Chamonix and Chanrion, at the head of the Val de Bagnes, and view the glaciers Bourrit had been enlarging on in his books. Even in the mountains he found traces of the quarrels he had left behind. At 'Blair's Hospital,' the hut erected on the Montenvers two years previously, some Représentants had been at the pains to efface the names of a party of their political opponents.

In Desportes' Temple de la Nature, which was erected in 1795, a Visitors' Book, a 'Livre des Amis,' received the effusions of visitors, but it is unlikely that the earlier hut was similarly provided. A passage in one of the unpublished letters of Mr. Brand (1786) serves, however, to explain the allusion. Our countryman refers to the infinite number of names that were cut or written in the stone walls or on the wooden roof of the building. Mr. Brand adds some details as to Blair. He was a *bon vivant* who had been compelled to leave his home in Dorsetshire and live abroad ' by the costs of his cellar and hunting,' and wanted some place to lunch comfortably in when he visited the Montenvers. His ' Château ' or ' Hospital,' as the guides mockingly called it, was but a rude affair. A few years later, in 1795, Desportes entrusted Bourrit with two thousand francs to erect its successor, the Temple de la Nature, which was decorated with the names of Genevese and foreign savants, and had some furniture and a looking-glass besides its ' Livre des Amis.' The furniture was a few years later wrecked and the Visitors' Book disappeared, but a new one was provided in 1810, which contained an entry made in 1812 by the Empress Josephine.

For a year the Councils persisted in their uncompromising attitude. The result was the popular revolution of April 1782. There was some street fighting and bloodshed. The Représentants and the populace, once more reunited and masters of the situation, demanded the total abolition of the Senate and Great Council. They took steps for the defence of the city from external attack. They appointed a small executive committee, named the Constitutionale, to deal with the political crisis. De Saussure, who had so far succeeded in keeping out of any active share in politics, was one of the members of the patrician party who hurried to the Town Hall on the news that it had been seized by the mob, and he acted as the spokesman of his colleagues in refusing to sit as Magistrates at its bidding. He consequently became one of a small group of patricians who were held as hostages and confined for forty-eight hours at the Hôtel des Balances.

De Saussure's attitude on this occasion may seem to call for some explanation. This may best be found in a letter of Jean Marc Roget, a Genevese pastor, at one time in charge of the Huguenot church in Soho, to Sir Samuel Romilly, whose sister he had married, in which he gives a general view of the political catastrophe of 1782 in Geneva.[1]

Roget, who describes himself as an ardent Représentant, condemns strongly the obstinacy of the more violent Negatives, who had succeeded in controlling the Councils and inducing them to reject the popular demand. But at the same time he expresses his disapproval of the action of the Natifs. He writes ' the kind of fury they exhibit towards some of our opponents disquiets and disgusts me.' The picture he draws is of a revolt of the rabble, with which Représentants like himself were forced to show sympathy in the hope of retaining some control over events. He adds that in the Councils there were many moderate men, whom he terms Constitutionals, who asked for nothing better than a reformed government, but were thwarted and even insulted by their colleagues. It is, I think, clear that de Saussure and Roget were both actuated by a similar motive, to save the State by the formation of a middle party of Moderates.

A few days after his own release de Saussure thought it well to place his children in safety. His daughter Albertine's journal furnishes details of their escape. In the first attempt they were arrested at the gates, though disguised as peasants, Albertine with a basket and Théodore with a *hotte*.

'Papa was very sorry to see us come back. Next Tuesday we were again disguised, I as a lady's maid of Mlle. de Lalgas, who had leave to drive out with two maids, Théodore as a workman, and Alphonse as a ragamuffin. I got to Chambésy to Madame Fabri's in a plight which would have been laughable had one been able to laugh.'

A few weeks later de Saussure's anticipations were justified, and he had an opportunity to show that his courage and energy were not confined to mountain-climbing. On the 23rd June, French troops, acting in their function as agents of one of the Mediating Powers, invaded Genevese territory; the alarm of an attack spread through the town, and five thousand citizens rushed

[1] *Lettres de Jean Roget* (Geneva and Paris, 1911), p. 185-90.

to arms. A rumour spread that the leaders of the Negatives were prepared to open the gates. Orders were given by the revolutionary authorities to search their houses and seize their arms. All patricians were suspected, and one of the houses ordered to be visited was de Saussure's. It was alleged that suspicious groups, amongst them an officer in French uniform, had been seen on his terrace, and that the cellars had been converted into an arsenal. The supposed officer turned out to be a pure Genevese, a man of science and philosopher, de Saussure's friend, Jean Trembley.

De Saussure, forewarned, was also forearmed. He assembled his family, including his two sisters-in-law, laid in provisions, procured some helpers in the defence, and barricaded the doors and windows. A very full account of the affair exists in some letters written by one of his near neighbours, living on the opposite side of the Rue de la Cité, who was an anxious eye-witness, and had her own house twice ransacked by the amateur grenadiers of the town. I must abridge the good lady's graphic report, but its details are many of them too picturesque to be lost.[1]

Two summonses to surrender were disregarded by de Saussure and his little garrison. These were followed by a close investment. Guards were posted on neighbouring points of vantage with orders to prevent all egress or ingress. A whole day was spent in fruitless parleying. Our eye-witness writes:

'I do not know if you have noticed a little iron grille in the door [it is still there] used by people who want to communicate with any of the household. Yesterday all the afternoon his friends kept coming to the grille to try to persuade M. de Saussure to open. It was amusing to watch all the great people of the town ringing the bell and then putting their eyes or their ears to the grille while the master of the house came to speak to them and the sergeant of the guard listened with all his ears and at the same time kept back the crowd. At last the Premier Syndic with his attendant came like the others to the grille and asked for admission. He was let in, and the door closed again, to the great disappointment of the crowd, firmly persuaded that the house was crowded with men and arms.'

Among these would-be peacemakers were Pictet, Tingry, a distinguished chemist belonging to the popular party, Bonnet, who, too infirm to come himself, wrote twice to implore his

[1] The manuscript is in the Public Library at Geneva.

The Town house from the Corraterie

nephew to capitulate, and the Venerable Company of Pastors, who sent their Moderator to do his best. The Syndics used what influence they had with the bourgeois Committee at the Hôtel de Ville to induce them to put off the threatened recourse to violent measures. But the defence showed no signs of yielding. On the contrary, according to family tradition, the few servants in the house were ordered to tramp up and down the stairs and show themselves armed at different windows, while the master shouted martial orders in a loud voice. On their side the bourgeois Committee ordered six companies of grenadiers to advance with their muskets primed. Bombs, and even mines and saps, were also threatened, but still no action followed. There was at all times some prudence, if not timidity, among Genevese revolutionaries, who were more fond of posing as Romans and talking of imitating the example of Saguntum than of facing fire-arms. Moreover, they might well reflect, even if they did not receive specific warning, that any attack on a citizen of the European reputation of de Saussure was not an adventure likely to be without serious consequences. There were 12,000 French and Swiss and Sardinian troops outside the walls, and any crime was likely to meet with speedy punishment. Terms were offered; the besiegers undertook, if allowed to search the house, to leave the inhabitants unmolested and to give any strangers found a safe conduct out of the city. Still the little garrison held out against both menaces and entreaties. They threatened to fire on anyone who approached the walls, they were deaf to the appeals of neighbours who feared their own houses might suffer, and of the twelve members of their own party who were hostages in the hands of the revolutionaries. Duroveray, the Procureur Général, one of the leaders of the Représentants, did his best to calm the mob, who with axes and planks in their hands clamoured for an assault. Fresh parleyings began with the Committee at the Town Hall. Through a hot June afternoon the crowd waited impatiently, not, however, without occasional incidents that helped to pass the hours. They are thus related for us by the eye-witness who lived opposite. Her simple story, written at the moment, brings the scene vividly before us in all its serio-comic aspects:

'The third floor [of the Maison de Saussure], as you know, is occupied by a widow, Madame Rilliet, the mother of M. Rilliet-Fatio, one of the hostages, and mother-in-law of M. Prévost-Lullin, the Syndic. M. Lullin presented himself at the wicket, and as a magistrate summoned the master of the house to open to him. He was refused. He insisted that, as a son-in-law, and a Syndic, it was essential that he should be allowed to talk to his mother-in-law. He had no better success. Loath to give up his attempt, he sat down near the house to write a note, and then presenting himself once more, demanded the delivery of his mother-in-law, with her servants and property. The venerable lady was brought downstairs, and we heard her sobs and her feeble, cracked voice telling her son-in-law she would not leave the house in which she had lived for so many years. M. Lullin insisted, " Madame, in God's name, do this for me, for your son-in-law ; it is your duty—do not refuse me. If the house were on fire would you not leave it ? Well, it is worse. How can I leave you exposed to all these dangers ? Madame, you refuse me ! In God's name, you will be as much at home with me as here ! " All the reply we could hear was the sobs and broken voice of this courageous and resolute woman. At last M. de Saussure was appealed to. " Monsieur, force her to come out ! Drag her out ! " The answer was, " She is in her own house and free : we cannot compel her." M. Lullin got nothing except the squeeze of one of the old lady's fingers through the wicket. " I leave you, then, Madame, with tears in my eyes and distressed by your refusal. But you have still till four o'clock to decide."

' Then there came to our house a poor mother whose daughter was a housemaid at M. de Saussure's. She called out from the fourth floor: " My daughter, come out if you can—come out, I pray you. In God's name, don't stop." When the officials cruelly silenced her, she came down in despair, crying, " O my daughter, my poor daughter, I shall see her no more. I want to get away. Who knows what may happen to her. They say they have so many engines for blowing up the house ! " [There had, in fact, been talk of a mine.] " My God, take me away." And despite all we could do or say to her, she had to be taken home.'

At last, after a siege of six days, terms were agreed on, and a formal capitulation, in no less than seven articles, duly signed, under which the house was allowed to be visited, but no arrests were to be made or arms confiscated. The result of the visit was to prove that the garrison of the fortress that had given cause to so much emotion consisted of eighteen men and twenty guns. De Saussure clearly secured all the honours of war. His wife wrote to their daughter, ' All is ended in the happiest way possible ;

our liveliest hopes could not have foreseen so favourable a surrender. I can still hardly believe it. I am overwhelmed with visits and congratulations on the success of our particular siege. We passed some odd moments.' All this time, we are told, de Saussure's guides were waiting for him at Chamonix; but there was to be no Alpine travel that summer.

A few days later the allied troops entered the town, and the revolution was thus brought to a violent end by the action of two of the Protecting Powers, France and Berne, supported on this occasion by the King of Sardinia. Zurich, already radical, had refused to join in this forcible intervention. The Genevese, very brave in their preparations and professions, prudently succumbed at the sight of hostile batteries planted before their gates and the threat of bombardment. Their leaders made haste to capitulate. The aristocratic Councils, reinstated and strong in the support of the allied troops, remained complete masters of the situation. Geneva fell again under the rule of the patrician oligarchy, which was now not only released from the restrictions imposed on it fourteen years previously, but had gained additional power.

Some six hundred of the popular party left the city. On d'Ivernois' and Lord Mahon's representations, the English Government was induced to assist in founding for the exiles a 'New Geneva' near Waterford in Ireland, and to obtain a grant from Parliament of £50,000 in furtherance of the scheme. The site selected had already, since the close of the seventeenth century, harboured a colony of French exiles. But difficulties soon arose, and after two years the settlement was definitely abandoned by its promoters, and the exiles took refuge elsewhere, many at Constance and in other parts of Germany.

The next seven years were a period of commercial and general prosperity in Geneva; but to a populace growing in numbers and intelligence, the reactionary Government forced on the city by foreign intervention became constantly more and more irksome. The recent home of Voltaire and the birthplace of Rousseau was little likely to escape the influence of the new ideas that were in the air, while the passing of the old order in France could not fail to affect a Republic on its immediate frontier. Bonnet anticipated justly what was to come when he wrote to a Swedish correspondent:

'Our little Republic is but a boat attached to a vessel of the first class. You realise all that is implied in the comparison.'

From this moment, according to Senebier, 'de Saussure put aside science for politics.' The phrase does not fit closely with the facts. Bonnet expresses the situation far more accurately when he tells us that his nephew 'was very much distracted between politics and Alpine travel.' But it is true that henceforth de Saussure was never free to give himself entirely to science. His sense of duty compelled him to conquer his inclination to decline public office. He was already a member of the Council of Two Hundred. As soon as the old order had been re-established by the Mediating Powers, he was appointed to serve on Committees for the revision of the Code and for framing modifications in the form of government. He was also elected a member of the Military Council, which controlled the garrison of the city, a force of under a thousand men.

In the following year (1783) de Saussure was called on to aid in entertaining the Archduke Ferdinand, the Austrian Governor of Lombardy.

The Professor was at this time troubled by a weak throat, which hampered him in lecturing, and busy with bringing out a volume embodying the results of his researches in hygrometry. In its preface he explains that he was led to resume his studies on the subject by the indisposition on Mont Lachat, that had interrupted his mountain excursions in 1780. Five years later he published a reply to his critics, of whom the principal was J. A. Deluc.

Montgolfier was about this time (January 1784) exhibiting his balloon inflated with heated air, and de Saussure went to Lyons to witness the ascent, had long talks with Montgolfier, and subsequently made experiments on his own account to prove what had not previously been recognised, that the ascending power was due solely to the lightness of heated air compared to that of air at a lower temperature.[1] Among his papers is preserved a draft of a letter to an unknown correspondent—probably Faujas de Saint-Fond—in which he describes in detail the Montgolfier machine, and compares the relative powers and uses of fire and gas balloons.[2]

[1] See *Encyclopædia Britannica*, 13th edition, 'Aerostatics.'
[2] In Faujas de Saint-Fond's *Description des Expériences de la Machine Aérostatique de M. M. de Montgolfier* (2 vols, Paris, 1783-84), there is a letter of sixteen pages from de Saussure to the author. It is dated March 20, 1784.

The former, he believes, will be found most suited for carrying weights and for such purposes as revictualling besieged cities, while the latter will serve better for meteorological and electrical investigations. His correspondent had suggested to de Saussure that he should undertake a treatise on aerostatics. He replied that it would be too great an interruption to his geological pursuits, and that, far from wishing to sacrifice mountains to balloons, he hoped to make balloons help him in his mountain researches, not, 'at any rate, for the present,' in gaining inaccessible heights, but in ascertaining the constitution of the upper layers of the atmosphere.

After his return to Geneva, de Saussure entertained his uncle and aunt, the Bonnets, by sending up a balloon from their terrace at Genthod. His experiments were not always successful. We hear from some visitors at Conches of an attempt which, 'with all the science possible,' ended in failure. 'The illustrious Professor was in a terrible temper; he scolded his sons and several savants who, with folded arms, were looking on in silence, or asking questions which did not make him any happier. The rest of us laughed at the whole scene.' [1]

In a letter (13th February 1784) to the *Journal de Paris*, de Saussure replies to some statements as to the effects on the human frame of the rarity of the air at great heights made by M. de Lamanon on the strength of the ascent of a ridge of about 10,500 feet near the Mont Cenis. He begins thus:

'The works of M. de Lamanon would not contribute much to the progress of physical inquiry did he not observe nature with greater accuracy than he reads and quotes the writings of those who have observed it before him. Permit me, sirs, to use the channel of your *Journal* to protest against the absurdities which this naturalist attributes to me despite the fact that my statements are of a diametrically opposite character.'

The points chiefly insisted on by de Saussure are that he had never asserted that there is any difficulty in the act of respiration at great heights, or that the languor and discomfort experienced by some individuals in such situations are universal and unavoidable. The former statement seems at first sight a paradox, and inconsistent with his own view and personal experience as recorded in the *Voyages*. His point, I take it, was that altitude does not

[1] *Rosalie de Constant, sa Famille et ses Amis*, par Mlle. L. Achard (1902).

in itself produce the form of exhaustion known as mountain-sickness, but that this is the result of altitude coupled with the muscular exertion of walking uphill, and that its symptoms cease in repose or during a descent. Rest, he insists, even for a few minutes, removes every trace of discomfort.

The whole question has of late years been most carefully and lengthily discussed by eminent physiologists and mountaineers, and de Saussure's limited observations have been largely superseded. Experience has shown that the susceptibility to the effect of rarefied air varies in individuals as much as the susceptibility to sea-sickness does. It also varies at different periods in the same individual on the same mountain—*e.g.* Mont Blanc ; while the relatively small proportion of the climbers of that mountain seriously affected in recent years may suggest that coarse food and rough lodging, and perhaps also strained nerves, had something to do with the frequent sufferings of mountaineers, guides as well as tourists, in the days before the Grands Mulets boasted a ' hôtel ' and the refuge near the Bosses served as a coffee-stall. A further observation I have not yet seen recorded may perhaps be added. Inconvenience is far more commonly experienced on snow-slopes than on rocks. It would seem that the monotonous exertion of tramping uphill in snow causes a greater muscular strain than the more varied gymnastics of a rock climb. That any prolonged stay at high altitudes or any sudden transference to them sensibly affects the human frame is beyond question. But so far as Alpine heights are concerned, de Saussure's statement is sustainable. It is possible to spend several hours on the top of Mont Blanc or Monte Rosa without experiencing any of the symptoms of mountain-sickness, *experto crede.* I have slept not uncomfortably 5000 feet higher.

In the early summer of 1784 de Saussure started on a family tour through the Swiss lowlands with his wife, sister, daughter, his sister-in-law Madame Tronchin, and his friend Trembley. From Lucerne he made an excursion to Engelberg and the Joch Pass, with which he combined an ascent of the Ochsenstock (9883 feet). The party drove on to Zurich, St. Gall, Constance, and Basle ; it must have been on this occasion that he took measurements of depths in the Lake of Constance. At Zurich he called on 'Monsieur Gesner, the poet.' This was Solomon Gesner, the author of a series of conventional idylls which had an amazing success in their day. Archdeacon Coxe, who visited him, rashly prophesied, 'His writings will be admired by future ages as long as there remains a relish for true pictorial simplicity or taste for original composition.' It is almost impossible to us to believe that our ancestors can have found pleasure in these sham eclogues—insipid tales of ideal peasants with classical names. Yet they were translated into most European languages, and the translator and publisher of an English edition (1775) congratulated himself on presenting readers with a work ' he thinks equal in the beauty of composition (allowance made for the difference of language) to the idylls of Theocritus or Virgil, and far superior in benevolent and pathetic sentiments.' He adds, ' The historical plates and vignettes with which this work is embellished were all designed and drawn by Gesner himself.' De Saussure thus describes the bookseller-poet-painter :

'He is small and ugly, but his face has a great deal of character. He speaks French with difficulty; is very modest about his work. He showed us his pictures with much politeness, and seemed to value them more than his verses. He told us that he had entirely given up painting; that all his thoughts, all his aims, were centred on poetry.'

His pictures, judging from the illustrations, were worthy of his poetry. Each age throws off a quantity of such stuff for the rubbish-heap, and the contemporaries of Cubism and Vorticism are not perhaps in a position to cast the first stone.

Later in the same summer de Saussure made a twelve days' trip to Chamonix, meeting at Servoz Exchaquet, at that date employed as Inspector of the mines of Faucigny, and at Le Prieuré making the acquaintance of Dr. Paccard. It is further recorded that he took tea with the Blairs. Mr. Blair, then a resident at Geneva, has been already mentioned as the Englishman who built and gave his name to the first cabin at the Montenvers.

About this date de Saussure found matter for passing irritation in a reference made to him by a German professor from Göttingen, named Meiners, in a description of a tour in Switzerland in 1782. The passage ran as follows :

' Among the busiest of the Negatives one must give the first place to M. de Saussure, who had recently on several occasions declined the visit of one of my friends, and who, therefore, did not make me desirous to form his acquaintance. The work of this savant has not had in Switzerland as much success as in Germany; not only is it thought too diffuse, but also the accuracy of many of the observations is questioned. In general, people are surprised that a disciple of Bonnet, one who formerly supported the Représentants, should not only suddenly fight on the other side, but should have become one of the most ardent Negatives.'[1]

De Saussure tells Bonnet that the German's bad temper was produced by his not having been sufficiently lionised when he visited Geneva. Consequently he had vented his vanity in abuse. Bonnet writes:

'He pushes it to the point of finding our landscapes insipid. The Lake near Geneva has, he says, the air of an artificial pool, our country estates are all on the same plan, two avenues which, in crossing, divide the whole property, our manners hopeless from every point of view, our wealthy class misers and pitiless to the poor. Our faces are all formed on the same model—forehead, prominent and narrow; nose, sharp and thin; something pinched in all our figures, and a yellow complexion.'

The amiable Bonnet, greatly hurt at this libel on his city and his friends, suggested to our countryman, Archdeacon Coxe, that he might insert a reply to it in the next edition of his very successful *Letters on Switzerland*. Coxe, however, prudently answered that as the object of his work was to give the result of his own travels rather than to correct the misrepresentations of others, he did not see his way to comply, at the same time assuring his correspondent that his and de Saussure's reputations stood in no need of any foreign support.

De Saussure was contented to bide his time; but when, some years later—in 1788—Meiners, again at Geneva, asked to see his geological collection, the German Professor was sharply informed that for a libeller of Geneva there could be no admittance.

Meiners seems to have made himself equally unpleasant on his later visit to Berne, for Wyttenbach in a letter to de Gersdorf of February 1791 refers to him in strong terms: 'Professor Meiners by his clumsy arrogance has made himself generally obnoxious.'[2]

Count Grégoire de Razumouski is another of the small band of

[1] *Briefe über die Schweiz*, Christophe Meiners (Berlin, 1784).
[2] 'Stinkend' is the word used (see Dübi's *Wyttenbach und seine Freunde*).

victims who fell under de Saussure's cudgel. He had remarked veins of quartz traversed by threads of green amianthe. De Saussure's comment is, 'He calls it a transition between amianthe and quartz; he might as well say that a goose on the spit was a transition between the goose and the spit.' On a further occasion the Count is told that ' he obviously considers the limit of his own understanding to be that of the possible, and that what he cannot comprehend nature cannot perform.'

Later in the year (1785) de Saussure's only daughter, Albertine, married Jacques Necker, a nephew of the financier. Madame Necker, whose acquaintance the de Saussures had made in Paris, thus became a near connection of the family.[1]

In January 1786 de Saussure found himself obliged to resign on the ground of ill-health the professorship which he had held for twenty-four years. Some of his biographers, confronted with the fact that in the preceding summer he had attacked Mont Blanc, and that the next four years are the period of his greatest mountaineering activity, have not unnaturally suggested that health was more or less of a pretext. The records before us, however, show that the plea was a true one.

In the previous December he had been forced by throat trouble, following on a severe attack of whooping-cough, to apply for temporary leave to break off his lectures. He now represented

[1] She wrote to de Saussure in June 1786 to describe a visit from Archdeacon Coxe, who had consulted her about getting a fresh translator for his book in the place of M. Ramond, of Pyrenean fame. Coxe thought Ramond too prone to enthusiasm and exaggeration. Madame Necker's comment was very much to the point:

'It is to these faults in his translator that M. Coxe owes in part his success at Paris, for we are still far from that love of nature which recognises perfection in just proportions, in the correspondence of its effects with our taste rather than in the astonishment that they cause us.'

Madame Necker's opinion was fully endorsed by the editor of *Ebel's Guide*, who wrote: 'This work has gained much in the translation, and the notes and additions with which M. Ramond has enriched it amount to 223 pages, and are in many respects more interesting than the original work.'

Madame Necker added:

'I only got the letter of introduction you gave Mr. Coxe after he had left; he never spoke of it—the trait is quaintly English. I received him on his reputation as a person of distinction; on your letter I should have welcomed him as an old friend. I reproach myself for all the marks of attention I did not pay to him, and I cannot forgive him.'

The solid, self-satisfied Archdeacon evidently considered that he stood in no need of any introduction.

that he was forbidden on medical advice to resume them, since his continual throat delicacy did not allow him to give them without risk.[1] He added, it is true, that he was also anxious to make progress with his book, of which only one volume had yet been published. His resignation was doubtless made easier to him by the promise that his friend and disciple, M. A. Pictet, should, without any competition, succeed him in the professorship. Of the character of his teaching and the appreciation of it by his contemporaries, the reader will find an account later on.

In the winter of 1786 an interesting discovery was made by peasants in the bed of the Rhône near Geneva of two elephant's tusks, some five feet in length. One of the discoverers stated they had found many large bones in the same place. De Saussure acquired the tusks for his cabinet, and they are now in the Museum at Geneva. I understand that experts are not disposed to consider them of prehistoric date, and it may therefore be still open—as Ebel long ago suggested—for one of the many intrepid scholars who have plunged into the interminable controversy as to Hannibal's passage of the Alps to cite them as evidence that the Carthaginian general came this way.

We have now reached the years in which de Saussure's mountaineering career culminated: the attempt on the Aiguille du Goûter in 1785, the ascent of Mont Blanc in 1787, the sojourn on the Col du Géant in 1788, and the visits to Monte Rosa in 1789 and 1792. The story of these adventures has been told already.[2] In December of 1786 Bonnet reports that his nephew is keeping himself in training for Mont Blanc by climbing the stairs of his tall city house eight or nine times a day. His newly married daughter wrote from Paris to urge him to come and enjoy the social success ensured by his scientific reputation, from the reflection of which she was profiting. But he was much too occupied and too intent on accomplishing his lifelong ambition to set his feet on the snows that he had always before his eyes when he looked across the lake from the garden at Genthod.

In the spring of 1787—partly, perhaps, to distract his wife's thoughts from the preparations for his great adventure, but also

[1] See de Saussure's letter of January 12, 1786, to the Rector of the Academy (de Saussure MSS.).
[2] See chapters viii., ix., x., xi.

THE STAIRCASE THE INNER COURT

THE TOWN HOUSE

in order to take barometrical observations at sea-level for the purpose of comparison with those he hoped to obtain on the summit of Mont Blanc—he started early in April for a journey in the south of France in company with his wife. On the way de Saussure indulged her desire to make a pilgrimage to the home of Madame de Sévigné's daughter. They accordingly drove from Montélimar, with the aid of two mules to draw their carriage over atrocious roads, to Grignan. Madame de Saussure describes the excursion to her daughter :

'It is not easy to get to Grignan. We took a guide, not that he was much use, as the leader of the two mules we added to our team knew the road much better than the guide, who had only passed it on horseback. At last we set off, but slowly ; the roads were often broken, the ruts deep. We had frequently to get down in the bad places, and to be content with two fresh eggs we swallowed in our carriage, as no room not full of noisy drinkers was to be found in the village of Vallaurie. We laughed a great deal. At last we came in sight of Grignan. It is a vast building ; all its balustraded terraces, beaten by the winds of which Madame de Sévigné speaks, produce a noble effect. Grignan is set on a rock in the middle of a lofty, arid slope ; a little town of about a thousand inhabitants, fairly well built, lies in an amphitheatre below.'

The agent of the owner received the visitors, and Madame de Saussure was lodged in Madame de Sévigné's room, which had her portrait over the chimney-piece, but none of the old furniture. The agent could only talk of the present occupiers. Next morning the de Saussures visited and admired the Rochers de La Rochecourbière, where Madame de Sévigné used to picnic. She describes it as a piece of Switzerland in Provence.

Having now no motive, as in 1780, to hurry home, de Saussure made a detailed examination of the coast of Provence, visiting Toulon, Hyères, and Fréjus. Undeterred by the memory of past sufferings, he even ventured out to sea, in order to explore the Iles d'Hyères.

He climbed several of the coast hills. An excursion he describes at some length is the ascent of the seaward crest of the Esterels, on which he bestowed the name it still bears, the Montagne du Cap Roux. He had some difficulty in finding and then in climbing the highest point of the rocky ridge so familiar as an object on the horizon to visitors to Cannes. He sought the services of the hermit of the Sainte Baume as a guide. Of his home he gives a pleasant description:

'I was agreeably surprised to find two beautiful fountains which throw out full jets of a clear and cool water under the shade of a group of fine trees—chestnuts, nuts, cherries, and figs. The gardens gave me no less pleasure, and though modern taste despises all that is formal, yet a little art and symmetry make an agreeable contrast with the wild and melancholy aspect of these mountains, and the straight alleys of the gardens laid out in terraces covered with trellises of vines and ended by niches cut in the rock created in me a most agreeable impression. The last hermit but one had by his labour brought his little property into the most flourishing condition. The grapes and fruit which he gathered served not only for his own needs, but also by exchange to procure him all he wanted.' [*Voyages*, 1456.]

The garden, when I visited the spot in 1877, had disappeared, and I experienced the same difficulty as de Saussure in finding and forcing a way through the thick scrub of southern growths to the highest crest of the porphyry crags, whence the view extends over the coast lands to the snowy peaks of the Maritime Alps.

From Toulon de Saussure made another excursion to the Montagne de Caume (2856 feet) to ascertain if M. de Lamanon, the geologist, whose manifold mistakes he was often called on to correct, had any grounds for thinking the rocks volcanic. They proved to be limestone. Apart from its technical interest, de Saussure's account of his day's walk may serve as a specimen of the human side of his character.

He drove out from Toulon as far as the village of Revest.

'I had need of a guide. The open door of a cottage showed me a family of peasants at their breakfast. I entered and told them what I wanted. My air of a foreigner and my plan of going over the mountains instead of along the high road, my curiosity about worthless stones, all seemed to them suspicious. All the same, the master of the house, an honest labourer, said, "Sit down, eat a bit of haddock with us, after that we will see what we can do." I accepted his offer, we had a friendly conversation, and he ended by saying he knew the country very well, and even something about stones, and though he had at first thought of finding me another guide, he would come with me himself. This was a most lucky meeting, for I found him an excellent guide.' [*Voyages*, 1486.]

De Saussure comments on the bareness of the surrounding region, caused by the destruction of the forests, and he is at pains to argue that this has produced, on the one hand, a failure in the average rainfall, and, on the other, from time to time violent floods. It is only of recent years that any practical steps have been taken in this region in the direction he pointed out. He was delighted with the view of the coast, its capes, bays, and shores, and the town of Toulon at his feet. He must have been wrong, however, in fancying he identified Mont Blanc. The peaks of Dauphiné stand in the way, and one of these may have caught his eyes.

On the descent he came, hungry and thirsty, to a farm. His guide assured him that their only chance of finding food or drink was to appeal for it either for payment or in charity.

'We knocked, a young and good-looking woman came to the window, and, in answer to our humble petition, said she would willingly give us what she had, eggs, bread, and wine, if we would give our word of honour not to set foot in the house, but to eat in the shade of a mulberry close by what she sent out by the servant. We gave our word and she kept hers, and came to her doorstep and entertained us with lively conversation while we drank her health in the wine she provided. We separated with an air of mutual satisfaction, but without any question of breaking the restraint imposed.' [*Voyages*, 1494.]

On the return journey the future home of Tartarin did not fail to attract the de Saussures by its southern gaiety. Their visit was on a Sunday:

'The little town of Tarascon, or at least the faubourg, was charmingly gay; despite the violent mistral, a crowd was dancing in the middle of a square to the sound of the fife and the tambourine. All the women in red corsets, short petticoats, with red stockings and polished shoes, and kerchiefs of coloured muslin on their heads and necks, with blue eyes and very lively countenances, formed a charming spectacle. We stayed a long time to watch them, and the pleasure we had in doing so seemed to add to theirs.' [*Voyages*, 1603.]

At Châteaubourg, on the Rhône, de Saussure had a curious encounter.[1] He went down to the river bank to test the temperature at which water would boil for the purpose of comparison with

[1] The date is given in the *Voyages* as 1781, but de Saussure was not in the south of France in that year, and the reference to what might have been the issue two years later shows that 1787 must be the true date.

the experiments he proposed to make on Mont Blanc. The villagers gathered round him with many expressions of curiosity, which he satisfied, until a somewhat better-dressed man appeared and told de Saussure in a threatening tone that he—the speaker—was not such a fool as he was taken for, and that he knew perfectly well that de Saussure was making a survey. At the same time he seized the stick de Saussure had laid on the ground. De Saussure snatched it back and used vigorous language, and while the villagers were hesitating which side to take, finished his experiment and got back to the inn. 'This quarrel,' he adds, 'had no further result; two years later, it might have been fatal.'

This was a year of frequent absences from home. In July, as has already been told, the whole party, de Saussure and his family, went to Chamonix to lay siege to Mont Blanc. After his victorious return he and his son Théodore, now twenty, started for Turin, apparently on an invitation from the Court. At St. Jean de Maurienne they encountered the Intendant of the Province, M. de Saint-Réal, who had undertaken a study of the Mont Cenis district, had spent six weeks in the past summer in a tent on the mountains and climbed several summits, including the Rochemelon, on which he had slept in the little chapel half full of snow. He could not conceal that he was far from pleased at the prospect of his particular field being attacked and his observations anticipated by so famous a rival, but de Saussure was able to convince him that their work need not clash, and that they might even be of some mutual service.

'We ended by becoming very good friends. He gave me his own room, which was a Noah's Ark. A huge eagle with open wings, badly stuffed, hung from the ceiling by a slender cord—any movement made it turn and gave it a ghostly air, the tables were littered with books, papers, stones, instruments, all dirty and in the most horrible confusion.'

On the Mont Cenis they lodged at the inn in preference to the hospice. They found guides of a sort. They are summarily sketched as follows : ' Horot, bon enfant, bon muletier, mais pas bien fort. Tours, grand causeur, mais vigoureux et hardi dans la montagne.' Their services were not, however, seriously called upon, for the 'Fraise' of M. de Lamanon proved a very simple matter. 'There was no snow, no ice, not a single "mauvais pas " ; pastures and easy rocks, child's play. Mistouflet [his grandchild] would have got up if I had been on the top with my box of sweetmeats.' De Saussure went on to a loftier summit, the Roche Michel (11,437 feet), whence he enjoyed a fine panorama and took observations. Several of the guides are reported to have suffered from the rarity of the air—but there seems good reason for suspecting that the cold blast on the summit which forced de Saussure to seek a more sheltered spot for his experiments had much to do with their alleged sufferings.

Arrived at Turin, de Saussure found himself the lion of the day, and seems to have enjoyed the position. He writes home :

'My *Voyage* [on Mont Blanc] has made a great impression here; an amiable Marquis [the Marquis de Brézé] has translated it very well into Italian, and everyone, down to the hotel waiters, is reading and talking about it. We went yesterday to the Casino of the Nobility, where we met two nieces of my protector, the Marquis de Brézé, pretty, but loud.'

He was presented to the King at Moncalieri, and sends his wife a long account of the King's clothes and his own and Théodore's. This new experience of a Court and its etiquette seems to have given him a great deal of amusement. The King was gracious, and promised to have the roads to Chamonix seen to. After the fatigues of the royal reception the father and son sought for refreshment at the Opéra Bouffe :

'We went two or three times for our 25 soldi. Théodore was immensely entertained by the ballets, which are charming. The theatre, which is extremely pretty, was quite full of ladies, very much dressed with unbelievable feathers on the back of their heads ; when they turned them they entirely blocked the front of the box. Théo and I were in the box of the Corps Diplomatique and in the two best places—highly honourable, but one sees much better in the pit.'

Some more royal visits and an excursion to the Superga, where de Saussure admired greatly the new tombs of the Kings of Sardinia, filled up the rest of the stay. Then they 'put off their beautiful lace, packed up their beautiful swords and their beautiful buttons, and put on their mountain clothes.' During this visit to the Court Madame de Saussure, we may fancy, got more entertainment from her husband's lively letters than on any of his mountain tours. She in return was able to send him an account of a dinner at La Boissière, where the 'charmante Minette' was staying with her father-in-law, Jean Robert Tronchin. She had sat next Sir Samuel Romilly and found him very agreeable: 'un mélange du ton de Paris avec d'anciennes phrases Genevoises, ce qui fait une conversation assez piquante. Comme il a beaucoup vécu avec Diderot, avec Rousseau, il a des anecdotes intéressantes à raconter.'

It was in the following winter that de Saussure issued his strenuous reply to Deluc's attack on his hygrometer. There appears to be no doubt that he was in the right, though some of his contemporaries thought his tone too severe. He certainly did not spare his opponent's feelings. He told Deluc that 'in his *Recherches sur les Modifications de l'Atmosphère,*' he had given 'none but false or confused ideas of all that has to do with the theory of evaporation.' He continued: 'What he calls *his* theory is nothing but my own. I shall proceed to show on similar evidence that the theories that are really M. Deluc's are worth no more than his hygrometer. Let me not, however, be thought to be an enemy of contradiction; on the contrary, I welcome objections to my opinions when they are proposed with the object of proving or discovering the truth. But when one recognises an obvious intention to disparage a work, when one finds a writer hunting for mistakes for the sole pleasure of exposing them, playing on words in an attempt to involve the author in a contradiction, attributing to himself or others the author's merits, attacking him on generally accepted opinions as if they were peculiar to him, presenting his views in the most unfavourable light, and finally assuming the tone of a schoolmaster who is correcting his pupil's theme and distributing impartial blame and praise, one is equally disgusted at the criticism and the commendation.'[1]

Three months later (April 1788) de Saussure's claims to membership of the Royal Society were at last admitted. That body, which, despite the recommendation of Sir William Hamilton twelve years before, had failed to accept de Saussure's candidature, now opened to the conqueror of Mont Blanc a gate not so narrow

[1] See for a further consideration of de Saussure's meteorological work, Dr. Mill's comments in the Appendix.

as it has since become. This feat, however, was not mentioned in his diploma, which somewhat quaintly specified the grounds of election as 'his services to literature and solid philosophy.' One would like to think that Sir Joseph Banks, while signing it, was led to remember—not without remorse—his last supper with de Saussure and Miss Harriet Blosset before sailing for Otahiti, twenty years earlier!

At the end of June de Saussure started with his son for the Col du Géant. They arrived at Chamonix on the same day as the Duke of Kent, the future father of Queen Victoria, who had been staying in Geneva since the previous year, and remained till January 1790, when, says the official register, he left 'sans avoir pris congé de personne.' The Duke had some excuse. He was a youth at the time, and fled home without leave in order to escape from the control of a severe tutor.

The winter of 1788 was marked by the renewal, after seven years of commercial prosperity but political discontent, of the constitutional struggle within the walls of Geneva. There were adequate causes for an outbreak in the continued reluctance of the Negatives to make any concessions to their opponents by widening the franchise or removing the disabilities that still pressed on the bulk of the growing industrial population. To these specific grievances must be added the unrest that prevailed across the French border and the influence of Rousseau on the Genevese populace. A frivolous dispute about the expulsion of an actress caused the first commotion. But the immediate spark that set light to the highly combustible material ready at hand was an injudicious act on the part of the Government. Owing to a severe frost, ice interfered with the action of the watermills on the Rhône, and the authorities raised the price of bread. Their action produced street rioting; barricades were erected; there was some loss of life. The Government was not in a position to take prompt and vigorous action. Conscious of its weakness and unpopularity, it was reluctant to use against its own citizens the small mercenary force at its disposal. In January 1789 the Councils capitulated without a struggle; they yielded to the demand for a general revision of the constitution and a reversal of the reactionary settlement of 1782. The mercenaries were dismissed, the Clubs re-established, the exiles recalled. Amongst the changes enacted was the abolition of the Military Committee which controlled the garrison of the town, of which de Saussure had ceased to be a member two years previously. In this year he was put on the Council of Sixty, which met occasionally for the management of foreign affairs. No doubt his position and family connection with Necker were thought likely to be of service in the negotiations on hand for obtaining the approval by the guaranteeing Powers of the constitutional reforms.

The Edit de Réconciliation, carried in the General Assembly by an immense majority, was celebrated in the traditional Genevese fashion. There were processions with bands, rows of youths dressed in scarlet scarves, embraces and salutations, and the inevitable poetical effusions, of which the following couplets may serve as a favourable specimen:

> 'Tout change ; un subit orage
> Au lieu de foudre a jeté
> Sur les fers de l'esclavage,
> Les fleurs de la liberté.'

> All passes ; sudden showers
> In place of lightning stroke
> With piles of Freedom's flowers
> Have buried Slavery's yoke.

Geneva, singularly poor in poets, has always been rich in rhymers. Unhappily, in 1789, men's minds were not in a state to be permanently soothed by feeble rhymes and sham sentiment. The disquiet instigated by emissaries from Paris spread from the streets to the villages of the little State, and the peasants, keen to be relieved, like those of France, from the feudal burdens of their tenures, eagerly joined the agitators of the town. Liberal reforms were enacted, but it was too late. Equality was in the air and anarchy at the gates. The revolutionaries of Paris regarded Geneva as 'a nest of aristocrats'; the proletariat of Geneva looked on Paris as Utopia.

De Saussure, we are at first surprised to learn, was one of the relatively small group by whom the Edict was opposed in the Assembly. The reason for his action is, I think, not hard of discovery, although it has hitherto been generally overlooked. The celebrated Edict has been described by a Genevese historian, M. Fazy, as a mediocre piece of patchwork, in many respects

A PROCESSION IN 1789

POLITICS AND HOME LIFE (1781-92)

imperfect and calculated to be a starting-point for fresh disputes![1] On this ground, we learn from the same authority, a group, belonging to the party of the Représentants, voted against it in the Assembly.[2] Now the best a contemporary apologist could find to say for the Edict was, 'Nous avons fait un arrangement aussi passable en soi que l'urgence des temps et la disposition des esprits nous le permettaient.'[3] It is surely reasonable to assume that de Saussure's vote in the Great Council was influenced by reasons similar to those ascribed by M. Fazy to the group of Représentants in the Assembly; and his action a year later in proposing a revision of the Edict appears to afford convincing proof of the truth of this assumption.

M. Fazy's violent outburst on a previous page of his work with respect to de Saussure's attitude on this occasion would seem therefore to be not only inconsistent but unjustifiable. I quote it below with regret, but it is impossible for a biographer of de Saussure to leave unnoticed language which obviously calls for explanation.[4]

For the present the political crisis did not interfere with de Saussure's usual summer visit to the mountains. On this occasion he broke new ground, and at last approached Monte Rosa, the great mountain he had nine years previously tried to sketch the outline of from Vercelli. His diary of the tour and some of his letters to his wife bearing directly on it have already been quoted. Others have an interest, however, apart from mountain exploration, which makes me return to them here.

It was at Macugnaga that de Saussure heard of the fall of the Bastille, and his comment on it proves his liberal sympathies and how far he was from being the obstinate oligarch he has been sometimes represented. The entry in his diary shows that he

---

[1] *Genève de 1788 à 1792: La Fin d'un Régime*, par M. Henri Fazy, Genève, 1917, p. 71.

[2] 'Dans le nombre des 52 rejetants, il y eut, dit-on, autant de Représentants que de Négatifs,' p. 61 of same work.

[3] D'Ivernois, *Révolutions de Genève*, vol. iii. p. 301.

[4] 'Il y eut cependant de l'opposition. Le croirait-on ? le célèbre naturaliste de Saussure fut au nombre de ceux qui se prononcèrent contre le projet. Il arrive fréquemment que des savants du plus grand mérite témoignent d'une complète incompétence, lorsqu'ils sont appelés à se prononcer sur des questions d'ordre politique. En cette occasion de Saussure manqua de la clairvoyance la plus élémentaire.' *Genève de 1788 à 1792*, p. 58.

fully shared the enthusiasm with which Fox is recorded to have greeted the great news :

'*July* 27.—My letters bring very good news from home, and of the happy revolution at Paris and Versailles. This brings balm to my soul.'

In his reply to his wife's letters he comments more fully

'on all these strange events, which you describe to me better and more clearly than [François] Tronchin does in the long bulletin Déjean sends me. Ah! how fine and good it all is; but this wicked Queen and all the authors of this odious plot, will they escape unpunished ? What unheard-of horrors! And this King, said to be good, to have taken part in the assassinations![1] If they had accomplished their crime they would not have been more advanced, for I am convinced they would have had their throats cut by the people. I hope the Queen will be so mortified, will find herself fallen under such opprobrium, that she will be obliged to go back to her own country. Adieu; had you received my two letters you would have seen that I have never had the least doubt as to the happy issue of this business. Still, I am glad to know it is over and how it ended. So I shall not be reduced to become a miner at Macugnaga; in that case I should have brought you here and built you a nice warm house! The place is charming, there are no such fine glaciers anywhere but at Chamonix, and here there is more plain, the most beautiful meadows, delicious woods, the houses all standing separate and surrounded by grass, to the point that one cannot go out without getting one's feet wet. This is a bit too like England!'

A few days before he had written cheerfully to his wife on the effect that the troubles in Paris were likely to have on the French *rentes*, in which, as was general in Geneva, his father's fortune was, in great part, invested. He mentions that there were at Macugnaga several 'merchants' who had connections with France and shared his optimism as to the results of the Revolution.

'The news,' he writes, 'anxious as it is, does not alarm me greatly for our fortunes, since, after all, if neither the King nor the nation desire to be bankrupt, the victor will pay us. Besides, it is possible that in the end these events will produce a more stable situation and give a wholesome warning to the disturbers of the public peace.

'What appears to me doubtful is whether M. Necker will return,

---

[1] The rumours which reached Geneva from Paris as to the action of the Court at this moment would seem to have been very exaggerated.

even if the King begs him, but if the Etats Généraux win, as they certainly will, they are sure to prevent a financial disaster, and force the minister, whoever he may be, to pay the creditors of the State.'

Necker had just retired to Basle on his dismissal from office, and was, it seems, expected at Geneva, and de Saussure, after sending messages to him, goes on :

'You are very kind to assure me you would not complain of being reduced to eat the Conches potatoes, if we shared them. For my part, I protest I should mind reduced circumstances much more for you than myself; but then I should make no more long journeys, we should cultivate our cabbages together, and our affection would supply the dressing. But once more, I am really not at all anxious about our fortunes.'

Towards the end of the year domestic trouble was added to de Saussure's political embarrassments. His wife suffered from a serious attack of fever, and recovered only after a long convalescence, during which he is reported to have watched over her with ceaseless anxiety.

The political situation in Geneva in the winter 1789-90 was still anxious but hopeful. The Powers had more or less reluctantly given their sanction to the proposed reforms. There was an opportunity for a wise and moderate statesman to bring in and carry measures that might have made Geneva a democratic Republic, and have united all the sound elements in the city in resistance to the extreme demagogues, the so-called 'Egaliseurs,' whose object was to make a clean sweep of the old institutions and to start afresh from a dead level of perfect equality. If the little State was to escape foundering in the stormy seas of the French Revolution, strong statesmanship was essential.

On the 1st February 1790, de Saussure brought forward in the Great Council a motion to the following effect :

'That a Committee be constituted of Members of the Senate and Great Council which should carefully take into consideration the changes called for in the Edict of 1789, with the help of the advice of all citizens willing to offer it, so that the result may be brought before the General Assembly on May 1st, since, in view of the new ideas set afloat by the French Revolution, and the political ferment resulting from them, it is impossible not to realise that we have need of a Constitution carefully framed and acceptable to the commonalty.'

This statesmanlike proposal, according to a contemporary chronicler, 'gave pain to many of the patricians, coming as it did from one of their own body.' De Saussure's action on this occasion is correctly appreciated by M. Fazy, the historian quoted above. He writes: 'The Professor showed a wise and far-seeing mind: he heard the storm grumbling in France, and he recognised that the repercussion would soon be felt. His aim was to forestall by opportune measures the revolution of which he recognised the premonitory symptoms. But the Great Council was incapable of any energetic action in the sense of reform.' De Saussure's proposal was two months later politely shelved, though a majority of the members was in favour of it. The Syndics were charged not to suggest improvements on the Edict of the previous year, but to prepare a new code. The result of their labours proved so unpopular, that in November 1790 a committee of twelve, of which de Saussure was a member, was, after all, appointed.

I must interrupt here the political story for a moment to note that in January 1791 de Saussure, after delays caused by the strained relations between the King and the academical authorities, was elected one of the eight Foreign Members of the French Academy of Sciences. His friend and enthusiastic admirer, Madame de Montesson, the widow of the scientific Duc d'Orléans, the father of Philippe Egalité, interested herself deeply in his candidature, and wrote agitated letters telling him of the various obstacles that had to be surmounted.

In the course of the summer de Saussure paid a short visit to the Brisgau, which furnished material for a geological pamphlet.

The next four years were to be a period of continual broils. An improvised administration with no force at its disposal capable of enforcing law and order was confronted by irresponsible bodies, the so-called Clubs, which had sprung into renewed life, while the 'Egaliseurs,' or anarchists, of Geneva were bent on imitating on a small scale the excesses of the rabble of Paris—apes imitating tigers, Madame de Staël called them. Madame Necker expressed, less epigrammatically, the same opinion: 'We have left Geneva; this little city follows in everything in the footsteps of France, and pygmies excite only contempt when they imitate the terrible gestures of Briarean giants. This criminal parody is destroying, perhaps for ever, a city once so flourishing; fortunes are being brought to an equality by perpetual levies, as they are in France by confiscation.'

The report of the Committee on Reform was not presented to the General Assembly until the 15th February 1791. On the same day the town was in uproar and the peasantry of the surrounding villages threatened to break through the gates. Finally, on 22nd March, the report, greatly revised, passed the Assembly in the form of an Edict, and the Committee which had prepared it was called on to codify the laws of the Republic. At this point de Saussure and two other members retired. On the 14th November 1791, the new code was accepted by the General Assembly. In the opinion of competent chroniclers of the time it removed all the more substantial grievances and was a compromise which, loyally carried out, might have made Geneva a prosperous self-governing democracy. But it was exposed to the danger fatal to so many compromises, that it satisfied the partisans on neither side. The extreme party, the ' Egaliseurs,' true to their name, were eager to level to the ground the ancient institutions of the Republic. Meantime, the state of affairs in France gave warning of the troubles to come, and might well have urged the Genevese to set their own house in order.

As the present generation has learnt, ordinary life goes on even in the darkest days. In March 1792 de Saussure found time to lecture at the Society of Arts ' On the Lack of any Expression of the Sentiment of Gratitude in Greek Literature.' Gibbon, who was at the time staying with the Neckers, attended the lecture, and sent through M. Necker de Germagny, the brother of the financier and the father-in-law of de Saussure's daughter, a criticism to be read before the Society. Its point, apparently, was a reproach to de Saussure for having questioned, not the expression, but the *existence* of any sense of gratitude among the Greeks. De Saussure's reply to Gibbon is characteristic of his impatience of any criticism he thought misplaced, and of his vigour in controversy. I quote a portion of it :

' Monsieur—I listened yesterday with much interest to your letter to M. de Germagny which was read to our Society. But I was grieved to find that you seemed to attribute to me a desire to establish that the sentiment of gratitude was unknown to the ancient Greeks. I spoke of the word, of the act of giving thanks, the form which expresses them, but I was very far from questioning the feeling. I said this expressly. I added that this feeling being shown even by animals, it was impossible to suppose that man had ever been without it. I employed further to prove the existence of the feeling and the duty of gratitude the argument which you employ yourself, Monsieur; I said that anyone who asks a service of another would always begin by reminding him of the services previously rendered to him.

'Doubtless, Monsieur, you were distracted during part of this lecture, and when, like you, one has a brain full of great and beautiful thoughts, it is permissible to follow them and neglect those of others. But since the idea you attribute to me is at once infinitely absurd and immoral, it is impossible for me to leave you to believe I ever entertained it. . . .

'I will not further insist on the literary side of this question, and if you persist in maintaining that the Greeks gave thanks and expressed gratitude as the modern Greeks and the Latins and we have since done, I shall not be ashamed if I have been mistaken in opposing you. But what would make me blush perpetually is to have thought that the feeling of gratitude is a modern invention and almost a matter of fashion. This would really be worthy of a tiger or a Jacobin, to use, Monsieur, the ingenious combination you employ in your letter. . . . I seize with eagerness, Monsieur, this opportunity to prove to you how much I value your good opinion, and how charmed I and my family have been to make our acquaintance more intimate, and how much we all hope to be in a better position to cultivate it.'[1]

During the summer of 1792 there was a period of temporary tranquillity at Geneva, a calm before the storm, and de Saussure, freed from his committees, seized the occasion to renew his acquaintance with the Monte Rosa group by a second visit to the St. Théodule Pass. It would seem, however, that he left home with even more than his usual fear of a parting scene, for his diary particularly notes that he slipped off unnoticed at early dawn, and in a letter to his wife from Breuil he expresses his remorse for his conduct:

'I curse,' he writes, 'this passion for the mountains which causes such torments to a soul so sweet, so tender, whose happiness is my most ardent desire. I have bitterly regretted the farewell kiss which I might have given you before starting, but then, how could I disturb your tranquil slumber by causing a flood of tears?'

---

[1] Gibbon's *Miscellaneous Works*, vol. ii. p. 436. Edition of 1814.

His wife's letters to him during his absence show that if she was apt to break down at partings, her courage and high spirits soon returned. If, as she tells him, 'I wept as only I can weep,' she soon dried her tears and turned to household cares. At the farm at Conches, to which she had retired, these were more varied than in town or at the villa at Genthod. She is at pains to reassure him as to her welfare :

'I find I live too little at Conches; to tell the truth, it is the place where I am happiest. . . . I shall be very happy when I get you back, and meantime I assure you I am not sad; yesterday at La Boissière they said I laughed as in old days.'

Madame de Saussure gives details of all the terrible things that are passing in France, the massacre of the Swiss Guard, the King's removal to the Temple. She tells how Paris is the only topic of conversation; how one of their friends in the Swiss Guard has escaped to England after leaving his sword and uniform in a cellar. All amusements had ceased at Lausanne. At Geneva, however, there was still society; at Evian there were even dances. Necker had gone to refresh himself by a trip to Chamonix; an Englishman had failed to get up Mont Blanc,[1] and there had been an accident to his guides. Lord and Lady Palmerston, with a number of English ladies, had called on her. She had refused an afternoon party at the du Pans—preferring to remain at home 'with her book, her bull, and her donkey—I don't mean Alphonse, but the bull's doctor, for the poor beast languishes and makes no progress.' She completes elsewhere the portrait of the incompetent veterinary :

'What an imposing figure the doctor of Carouge makes, with his glass in his hand! He arrives mounted on his donkey. He has fought at Fontenoy and studied in the veterinary schools; he went into the garden to pick herbs, of which he made a potion, promising me a second much more carefully prepared. In fact, I am so much persuaded

---

[1] *Ebel's Guide* adds further and more exact details of this accident. The party consisted of four Englishmen with guides. Their attempt came to a premature and unfortunate end. One of the travellers slipped in traversing some loose rocks at the top of the Montagne de la Côte, and they all fell. Two of the travellers were seriously injured, the guides were more or less bruised. No names are supplied.

of his skill by the stories he tells of the number of beasts he has cured that should I fall ill—which, please God, may not happen—I should send for him sooner than for Dr. Odier!'

On another day, after saying they get no Paris newspapers, she sends her *Gazette de Conches* :

'The Court has gone into deep crape mourning for the noble Bull. The Queen of Conches has been the more affected since the Grand Médecin of Carouge had promised his recovery. There is a gala dinner to-day. Mme. Hubert and Mme. Necker and all the princes of the blood. Mme. de Saussure is very pleased to offer this fête before the return of her dear Seigneur, for it would have bored him. The dogs Loup and Le Bleu send their greeting.'

Loup was de Saussure's companion on at least one of his tours.

And so on, through pages of local gossip and affectionate outpourings, with several pleasant allusions to de Saussure having in some remote Alpine village been taken for Rousseau (who had been dead fourteen years). There is no reference in the letters of this date to the loss of fortune caused by the troubles in France, which was, no doubt, the reason why Madame de Saussure had gone to Conches instead of Genthod for the summer. But we learn that at this time de Saussure borrowed from Necker thirty thousand livres. The debt was after his death released by Madame de Staël, as Necker's heir, transferring the security to her cousin, Madame Necker-de Saussure.

Shortly after de Saussure's return, we find the Marquis de Grouchy (a name Waterloo makes familiar to English readers) writing to thank de Saussure for a copy of his *Voyages*, and for the pleasure he has had from a visit to Chamonix. Grouchy was a brother-in-law of de Saussure's friend, Condorcet, and his wife had literary tastes. On his return he offered de Saussure in exchange some geological specimens.

In the autumn of 1792 the popular party was again turbulent and little disposed to accept the settlement of the previous year, while the Government, alarmed of enemies both without and within the gates, could think of nothing better than to invite a Bernese garrison to protect it. With the chief of the Mediating Powers, France, no longer on their side, this was an act of suicidal folly. The Convention naturally replied by threatening, unless the Swiss troops were dismissed, an occupation of the city. The Government yielded. Bereft of its only support and left face to face with an angry populace, it hastily proposed to offer still larger concessions. Before these could be discussed it was no longer in power; the time for reform had passed and revolution was within the gates. The old constitution of Geneva, its Syndics with their wigs and silk coats and staves of office, its 'Spectables' and 'Nobles' and 'Vénérable Compagnie,' had all passed away, or were to linger only as ineffectual shades. The revolutionary Clubs now became masters of the situation.

In the last days of December 1792, a Committee of forty members was charged to devise a new form of government. A month later the task was transferred to a Constituent Assembly of one hundred and twenty members. Meantime, two Provisional Committees, one of Public Order, one of Administration, were created to carry on affairs. At this crisis de Saussure acted with noteworthy public spirit and courage. Many of the patrician families had already left Geneva; he remained in order to make a gallant effort to act as a check upon the anarchist group who, excited by the events in France, had lost whatever heads they once possessed, and, aided by the French Resident, Soulavie, were now threatening by their excesses to bring the ancient Republic to ruin.

On the Civil Committee de Saussure and his fellow-professor, Bertrand, were at once nominated, and 'through excess of patriotism and at the request of the true friends of liberty,' consented to act as members, while the Military Committee begged the two professors to serve as captains of companies of the Citizen Militia. Yet this patriotic effort did not escape malicious criticism. De Saussure thought it right to bring before the Civil Committee an anonymous letter in which he was informed that his presence and that of other aristocrats impeded the work of their colleagues, and that steps, possibly involving bloodshed, might shortly be taken 'to sweep them out of the Council Chamber.' He added that he was firm in his wish to serve his country in any way practicable, but that he thought it right to consult his colleagues as to what course it seemed to them best for him to take in the public interest. The Committee unanimously assured the members impugned of their appreciation of 'the wisdom, moderation, and true patriotism' which they had displayed, and of their desire to retain their service. In conjunction with his friend Trembley, who was also a member of the Civil Committee, de Saussure lost no time in presenting to his colleagues an address urging the Government to take measures 'for the maintenance of order and of brotherly feeling under the rule of Liberty and Equality.'

Meantime, the victorious 'Egaliseurs' did their best on a small scale to imitate Paris. They planted Trees of Liberty; they organised, in honour of Jean Jacques Rousseau, a theatrical out-of-doors fête of the kind dear to the local mind; they wreathed his bust with flowers and danced and embraced round it; they feasted in the streets, singing:

> 'Oui, désormais libre et tranquille,
> Le Genevois en paix vivra,
> Tous ne feront qu'un dans la ville,
> Le bonheur y résidera.'

These pleasant anticipations were not to be realised.

CHAPTER XV

THE LAST YEARS

IN January 1793 de Saussure, as a member of the Civil or Administrative Committee, was busy in preparing a scheme for establishing the Constituent Assembly. In combination with Etienne Dumont, a moderate Radical, who was a friend of Mirabeau and had spent some time in England, he sent to one of the Genevese Clubs an argumentative letter, urging that in the proposals to be laid before the citizens for the election of the Constituent Assembly the number of members should be fixed, or at any rate only a limited choice between two or three alternative figures offered. He was at pains to point out that unless this course was followed, the result was likely to be a prolonged series of meetings and debates and a consequent delay which might prove a serious danger to the State. The suggestion was obviously a practical one, and it was acted on. De Saussure's action in this instance fully bears out Dumont's expressions in a letter written probably a year earlier to Reybaz, the Genevese Agent at Paris. 'Messieurs de Saussure and Bertrand rally to the democracy and to all it involves for the sake of the independence [of Geneva], and out of weariness of a system which has harassed them.'

Early in the same month we find de Saussure, acting as a member of the Provisional Committee, adding his signature to a despatch to Lord Granville, the British Minister for Foreign Affairs, in which, after an allusion to the close ties that united England and the Genevese Republic, the writers declare that the recent troubles in the State have resulted in the formation of a Committee charged to draw up and promulgate a constitution, which it is hoped may satisfy all parties and lead to a permanent settlement. A month later the Committee nominated a list of 240 names for a Constituent Assembly, from which, according to the old Genevese custom, the General Assembly was invited to select half.

At the end of January the esteem in which de Saussure was held by his fellow-citizens was shown by his selection as one of the delegates to receive General Kellermann, who came on behalf of the French Republic to admonish the Genevese not to look too much towards Switzerland for aid in their troubles. A banquet in honour of the General was held on the day on which the news of the execution of Louis the Sixteenth reached Geneva.

In March de Saussure was put on a small Committee of eleven charged to frame the articles of a new constitution, and in April was further nominated one of three members of a Diplomatic Committee.

In the Constituent Assembly, which was now sitting, we find de Saussure taking the Presidency, which was a frequently shifting office, for a short term. His family, his wife writes, liked him better in his professor's robes than in his presidential garment. In the Assembly he had as a colleague his old acquaintance and companion, Bourrit, the cathedral Precentor. Born a Natif, and never admitted into the society of the Upper Town, 'notre Bourrit,' as his townsfolk called him, now found himself exalted to a share in public life. His two sons, whose Alpine performances we have recorded, had both become pastors and popular preachers. It is to Bourrit's credit that in the present crisis his lifelong connection with the Church proved stronger than his political associations. He stood up manfully for the clergy when it was proposed to exclude them from any part in the control of popular education. Nor was this the only occasion on which he showed the courage of his convictions. Of another debate in the Assembly we have a satirical report from Desonnaz, one of the more violent of the demagogues:

'Nothing could be more entertaining than the sitting of the National Assembly to-day. The subject was the renaming of the churches. A citizen proposed, reasonably enough, names connected with some event, or some particular connection, for each of these houses of God. What greatly amused me was to hear a philosopher (de Saussure) praising the Saints, while a simple artisan (Fol) denounced them. The former maintained that to dedicate a church to Reason was to personify an ideal metaphysical abstraction. Fol replied, "That is true; I agree, one cannot dedicate a church to Reason." Bourrit, *l'homme des Alpes*, judiciously argued that what Calvin had not reformed ought to be let alone. And you will tell me that man has not wit for four! No doubt it was on Mont Blanc that he acquired it. The Assembly decided nothing, but referred the matter to a Committee to report.'[1]

This is Bourrit's last appearance in connection with de Saussure. The Precentor was to live on to the age of eighty; he died in 1819. His French pension was renewed after the Restoration, and when he could no longer conduct his patrons to the glaciers, he continued to issue his Guide-books to Chamonix. It is pleasant to leave him engaged in proving his loyalty to his old church associations and showing the courage of his opinions. For, despite his too many and obvious foibles and failings, the old Precentor keeps a certain hold on our affections. His enthusiasm for the mountains, the pluck and pertinacity with which he tried to be a climber, even his naïve exaggerations, which were to some extent illusions, recommend him to our kindly recollection and go far to make us forget the mischief he wrought. It was not malice so much as vanity that constantly led him astray. Bourrit was not only an honest lover of the Alps, but the author of the first volume in our language of Alpine literature in the modern sense of the words, and we wave a friendly farewell to his fading figure.

Cornuaud, the busy pamphleteer and political agitator already mentioned, bore in a Journal that has only recently been published, the following emphatic testimony to de Saussure's wise counsels during this period :

'Professor Prévost was the most brilliant and subtle of the orators on the side of the ancient constitution, but Professor de Saussure was the most adroit. The latter had a great influence over the debates of the Assembly, and was the last of the men of importance of his party to remain in it. The Republic owed him much ; he diminished the harm that would have been done in his absence. A happy mixture of flexibility and firmness which formed the base of his character— though he could be reserved and haughty in ordinary life—procured for him in the Assembly an influence which was valuable to the

[1] *Correspondance de Grenus et Desonnaz, ou Etat Politique et Moral de la République de Genève*, Genève, 1794, vol. i. p. 65.

Commonwealth. He recognised from the first that the situation was one in which it was not possible to resist the destructive torrent, but rather expedient to appear to follow it, so as to obtain means to check its speed and, when possible, to divert it. He enjoyed, moreover, in the esteem of his fellow-citizens, a well-deserved respect independent of the reputation given him by his position in the scientific world. As a citizen they had seen him show himself a brave and honest aristocrat in the sort of blockade to which his house had been subjected in 1782, a serious and resolute character in 1789, an excellent and serviceable Genevese when the French threatened a siege of the city, and he was gladly recognised as a reasonable and moderate citizen in the National Assembly. To sum up, Professor de Saussure was the citizen of his class who knew best in each change of the political situation to adapt himself with straightforwardness and dignity to the spirit of the time.'[1]

Higher praise could hardly be given.

In May 1793 de Saussure lost his beloved neighbour, friend, and master, Bonnet. Despite his many infirmities, Bonnet had lived to be seventy-three. Even the disturbed state of local politics did not prevent his fellow-citizens from desiring to do honour to his memory. It was resolved to place on his house the tablet which may still be seen opposite the Place du Molard in the Rues Basses. After delay caused by one of the many political riots of the period, de Saussure delivered in the church of St. Germain a funeral oration, which is of interest not only for its eloquent appreciation of his uncle's qualities of head and heart, but also as an indication of his own standpoint in religious matters. The service was attended by all the authorities of the city, who marched in procession from the Town Hall through the crowded streets. The band, it is recorded, played the Marseillaise 'even in church.'

We have an account from the pen of Madame de Saussure of Geneva as it appeared on the day on which it had been first intended de Saussure should deliver his eulogy of his uncle:

'Yesterday I passed one of those days of emotion of which the habit we have acquired does not diminish the impression. There was a call to arms at the orders of the Committees, or the Clubs. The gates were shut, cannon rumbled, women, weeping and screaming, hung out of the windows, in the evening the town had the martial appear-

[1] *Mémoires d'Isaac Cornuaud sur Genève et la Révolution de 1770 à 1795*, publiées par Mlle. E. Cherbuliez (Genève, 1912).

ance you know—the streets full of armed citizens, lit torches, and challenges. All this hubbub went on till two or three o'clock this morning, and then to-day everyone is back in his shop, his café, or his office. . . . This stormy day had been destined for the celebration of a very quiet citizen, your uncle Charles Bonnet. We were thinking only of securing places for the ceremony. The country folk, even the timid ones, had all come into Geneva attracted by the show : they have firmly vowed not to put their feet in town again. . . . Your sister called for a moment to find if I was dying of fear. We have shown the world, we old ladies of Geneva, that we are not to be killed in that way.'

In the following June the 'Egaliseurs' proposed that the citizens should be invited to take a voluntary oath of allegiance to Liberty, Equality, and Fraternity. The object was transparent—to provide a black list of abstainers. De Saussure, anxious in every way in his power to promote unity, took the oath, but both his sons refused.

His multiplied political functions did not deter de Saussure from making yet another effort in the cause which from his youth he had had deeply at heart. In August, returning to the field of his first endeavours, he put forward a scheme for free national education. It is interesting to note that his collaborator was Isaac Bourrit. The pert youth of the Aiguille du Goûter had now developed into a sober minister and administrator.

The primary schools were to serve for boys and girls up to the age of ten. The subjects taught were to be reading, writing, arithmetic, the principles of religion and morals, the rights and duties of citizens, and a summary of the laws. Country children were to be instructed in rural economy and domestic and veterinary medicine, which were to be put in the hands of the local pastors ! Girls were to learn needlework.

De Saussure would have wished to add geography, general history, and elementary science to his scheme. 'But,' he writes, 'my colleagues, less ambitious, and perhaps knowing better than I do what is practicable in existing conditions, have persuaded me that it is better to class these subjects as voluntary studies.' There were to be three divisions : primary, secondary, and final classes. The secondary classes were not to be compulsory. Advanced students were to have the opportunity of learning Latin, Greek, and music. Popular concerts were to be provided. The final classes, destined for pupils over fifteen, were to be given in French, instead of Latin as hitherto. Swimming, gymnastics, and riding were to be encouraged. The pupils were all to wear a simple black uniform. Three annual fêtes were provided for, with, of course, a procession, and a good-conduct prize, to be determined by the pupils' votes. There was to be in addition an Administrative Council, which would exercise paternal discipline, and also look after orphans and illegitimate children. Calvin would seem not to have altogether expelled Cupid! Indeed, the police records provide a good deal of evidence that, despite sumptuary laws and the vigilance of the Consistory, the morals of the town had never been beyond reproach.

Like other political schemes of the date, de Saussure's was swept aside by the French annexation in 1798.

Meantime, de Saussure's elder son, Théodore, unconscious of the disasters impending on his family and country, was absent in England, investigating the manufacturing districts, and greatly enjoying himself in visits to the Isle of Wight, Stow, and Derbyshire in company with Sir John Swinburne and his wife. Lady Swinburne, the daughter of Mr. Bennet, his mother's cousin, who lived at Beckenham, was a distant relation, and Théodore in his letters home expresses the warmest admiration of her wit, talent, and charm. Passing through Oxford, he records that he dined, probably in one of the College Halls, with 'twenty doctors in square caps.' In London he attended the meetings of the Royal Society, of which he was at a later date to become a Foreign Member, and his name is found in the list of guests at the Society's Dining Club.

Madame de Saussure's letters written to her son whilst he was in England throw much light on the situation, political and personal. In the summer of 1793 she describes the terrible heat, 'which drove everyone into the lake,' while her husband and Alphonse, her younger son, as members of the local militia, had to perform their military duties. The city had been scandalised by a masquerade—a mock procession of figures burlesquing the Syndics, dressed in their time-honoured costume, crowned by immense wigs, holding their staves of office, and preceded by ushers in the traditional blue and purple mantles, which went round the town and levied contributions from the butchers and bakers.

In September 1793 Madame de Saussure throws out a first hint that her son's stay in England may have to be cut short on the ground of expense. In December she has to tell him that all the Genevese, her husband among them, have lost their fortunes :

'The only reproach,' she writes, 'that can be brought against your father is that he was too hasty in coming to the help of a friend he believed to be prudent and trustworthy. I am only too glad that my fortune has so far prevented a crash we all dread, but it can no longer, my children, provide you a brilliant existence or even the ease to which we have all been accustomed. If nothing fortunate happens for him, you must look out for a travelling tutorship, or a wealthy bride ; if these fail we shall have to live in our old stuffs and our old green tapestries, with a little maid in a black cap.

'But we must be contented, and think it is our own choice, and not be making comparisons with what we have seen and been accustomed to. You have the opportunity, my friend—see if you can accustom yourself to the simple life, at least for a long time. Perhaps we shall not be less happy.'

The practical position was that the de Saussure fortune was lost, at any rate as far as any present income was concerned, and Madame de Saussure's very seriously impaired. Investments paid no interest, rents could not be collected, very heavy taxation was supplemented by levies on capital. As a last blow, a certain Déjean, an ' agent de change,' or stockbroker, who had acted for de Saussure, had become bankrupt. The Neckers had, as has been already mentioned, come to his help with a substantial loan.

The letter ends with a description of yet another of the inevitable processions in which the Genevese were wont to express their feelings and forget, for a time, their quarrels. This time, however, it was the annual and time-honoured one in celebration of the 'Escalade,' the famous repulse of the Duke of Savoy from the walls in 1602.

Théodore, who was very happy in England, failed at first to realise the gravity of the situation. He evidently thought his mother was needlessly alarmed, and it was not until he received confirmation from his father of the state of affairs that he took matters at all seriously. Then he at once expressed his anxiety to find some occupation which would give him an independent income. To his father's suggestion that he might take a tutorship, he replied that owing to the war the English were not travelling, and that the bent of his studies—scientific rather than classical—was little likely to recommend him to an English patron.

About this time Madame de Saussure mentions a startling visit:

'At supper your father was asked for. The caller was brought into the *salon*, and Têtu [the domestic who climbed Mont Blanc with de Saussure] lit one of the candles on the mantelpiece, which gave but a dim light. Your father left the joint, and saw before him a dark man, who exclaimed, "I am Marat." At the first moment he was tempted to think it was a ghost! It was Marat's brother, of whom we had never heard.'[1]

It was towards the end of 1793, we learn from the report of Dr. Odier already mentioned, that de Saussure's health, always uncertain, for his digestive troubles had never been wholly overcome, gave cause for serious anxiety. Dr. Odier's account (greatly abbreviated) is as follows:

'To de Saussure's long and painful efforts to arrest or direct the torrent of our political revolutions were now added the anxieties caused by the grievous inroads on a fortune already seriously reduced. Similar losses befell most of our capitalists, but in his case the noble use he had always made of his wealth gave him a better right than others to view its loss with bitterness. These mental troubles reacted on his health, and he was attacked by frequent fits of giddiness, followed by a feeling of stiffness in the left arm and the left side of his face, which no remedy could overcome.'

In the following February (1794) de Saussure was invited to stand for election as one of the four Syndics.

'We might,' writes Madame de Saussure, 'have had the honour of being wife and daughter of a Syndic. Your father yesterday declined the prospect of this elevation, to the great content of the Syndic Dentand, who assured him he did well, because his health would have suffered. Your father retorted that it was because he thought he would have obtained a large number of votes that he did not care to take the risk. This conversation between the two candidates made the hearers, who were far from agreeing with Dentand, laugh.'

---

[1] The Marats came from Neuchâtel; but Marat's father, a doctor, had at one time lived in Geneva.

THE LAST YEARS

In a letter of 18th March 1794 we get the first definite warning of the greater misfortune of which Dr. Odier described the first symptoms. Madame de Saussure writes to her son :

'Your poor father—I say your poor father, for he has given me a great fright—at the Assembly ten days ago had a seizure which deprived him of any sense of touch in his arms and fingers, but not of the power of movement. A plaster has lessened, but not yet cured, his stiffness. He calls himself, in joke, the Paralytic ! But I cannot play with this suggestion; it makes me tremble, though I have long foreseen it. Our paralyses do not attack the heart ; you will see.'

From this time forward de Saussure was not only a ruined man constantly engaged in anxious inquiries for some honourable post which would supply an adequate income, but also an invalid driven from time to time to have recourse to Baths in the hope of restoring his health. His position in these respects may recall the last days of Sir Walter Scott. He showed an at least equal courage and energy in the protracted struggle of the following five years.

We next hear of him congratulating—it must have been satirically—the renegade priest Soulavie, who was the French Resident at Geneva, on the recognition by Robespierre of the existence of a Deity shown in the Fête de l'Etre Suprême held at Paris, and receiving the reply : 'Robespierre mocks at *le bon Dieu* as much as I do.'

The troubles of all sorts in which he was now involved produced in de Saussure, never too patient towards scientific dabblers and impostors, a marked increase of irritability. An unfortunate ' Citoyen Boissel ' had floated down the part of the Rhône between the Jura and Lyons and published a *Voyage Pittoresque*, to which the French National Convention was pleased to accord an honourable mention. In the course of his narrative he attributed to de Saussure a statement which drew forth this crushing reprimand :

'I thank you, sir, a thousand times for sending me your *Voyage Pittoresque.*

'But I cannot thank you for the compliments contained in your letter. I should have preferred that, in place of flattering me in private, you had refrained from attributing to me in public an opinion which I never held. You suggest that I believe that the Rhône swallows light bodies thrown into it where it emerges [from the Perte du Rhône]. Now, I have never spoken of what is thrown in at its emergence—that is too obviously stupid and absurd; the question was as to bodies thrown in where it disappears which are not seen to emerge again where it comes out. It is very strange that it should be possible to attribute a blunder of this sort to a creature that walks on two feet. I should have thought that all the details proved that I had never spoken of bits of wood thrown in at the emergence, but of those thrown in at the engulfment. Allow me to tell you, sir, that the very fact that an opinion appears to one absurd ought to make one more careful, before attributing it to an author, to assure oneself he has really held it. Now the word *reappear* which I used in itself proves that I was not talking of a body which one launches at the point of emergence, as one might a boat.'

As a rule, de Saussure's letters follow scrupulously the elaborately polite forms of the period. But when the occasion seemed to him one in which to dispense with them—as in this case, and several previously cited—he could be more than blunt.

The close of the year 1793 had been marked by frequent disorders fomented by the French Resident. On 5th February 1794 a radical constitution, formulated by the Constituent Assembly, was accepted by a popular vote.

On receipt of this news the British Minister at Berne, Lord Robert Fitzgerald, promptly appealed to the Governments of Berne and Zurich to refuse to recognise the new democratic régime of Geneva, which he denounced as 'founded on the same system as that which had already in France produced so many crimes and calamities,' and as 'the fruit of intrigues and acts of violence instigated by the agents of enemies of His Majesty,' adding that 'it had allowed the partisans of anarchy to insult the Allied Powers by permitting public rejoicings over defeats suffered by the armies which were fighting for the preservation and the civilisation of all the States of Europe.'[1]

Little effect seems to have been produced by this forcible remonstrance. At Geneva there was a relative calm for a few months; the annual 'Promotions,' or School Speech-day, was celebrated as usual. But the city was still divided against itself, and the midsummer heat was to prove deadly to the new-born constitution.

[1] Archives Cantonales de Berne, *Acten Geheimen Raths: Genfer Unruhen*, vol. xix. No. 23.

For the three years following (1794-6) a private diary written by de Saussure, mostly in Greek, with occasional lapses into Latin, has been preserved and kindly put in my hands by M. Henri Necker. The handwriting is that of a scholar, small and fairly clear, but varies greatly with the state of the writer's health, and towards the close (November 1796) becomes in places almost illegible.

Unfortunately the contents are in the main medical. De Saussure recorded his daily actions and his own symptoms with singular and curt preciseness. Each day's entry begins with an account of the past night, of the baths, the exercise, and medicine taken. From time to time there are pathetic notes, such as 'weaker and thinner,' 'legs giving way,' 'writing difficult.' He was obviously ordered gentle exercise, and records his daily 'walks in the house' or out of doors, always with his devoted wife or daughter. In the earlier portion he records the public committees he was still attending. But the political entries are very few and brief; for example, 'Murder of the Seven,' 'Murder of Baudit and Pradier' are the only record of the two most tragic moments in Genevese history. For the rest we find notes of incidents of daily life, his visitors' calls, and his correspondence. His literary occupation is carefully set out, and the reader can follow week by week the composition of the two latter volumes of the *Voyages*, through the chapters on Mont Blanc, the Col du Géant, Monte Rosa, and Mont Cervin, to the Agenda and Index. A trip to Neuchâtel, probably to see his publisher, in the spring of 1795 is mentioned. At the same time he was writing to a de Saussure at Charleston, South Carolina, and seeing a good deal of his brother geologist Dolomieu.

The diary gives details as to his daily strolls from Conches, such as 'under the oaks to the weir,' 'through the island to the river,' and 'to the bridge.' Since he was too much of an invalid to go more than a few hundred yards, these entries may serve to identify the exact site of the old farmhouse where his earliest and last days were passed.

One entry runs: 'The Neckers [his daughter and son-in-law] leave, tears of my wife.' It is not the only occasion on which Madame de Saussure's famous tears figure in the diary. Every page of it bears witness to the devotion of a wife who idolised him, and of a daughter who understood and entered into his interests and lightened his last days by her affectionate and untiring care.

In May 1794 Madame Necker, the wife of the financier, died, and in her the de Saussures lost a true and valuable friend.

In the summer of that year Théodore returned to Geneva. His parents, in order to reduce their expenses, had retired to their farm at Conches, while Frontenex, the home of de Saussure's childhood, was sold. We also hear of the sale, through a Frankfort bookseller, of part of his library.

The first waters de Saussure visited in search of health were those of Aix in Savoy, where we find him in May 1794. His wife did not accompany him. The explanation is contained in a letter from which we learn that the de Saussures hesitated both to leave Geneva at the same time on account of the risk of their properties being confiscated as those of emigrants. Empty houses were the first to be seized by the Revolutionary Government.

On the 28th June Madame de Saussure wrote from Conches to her husband at Aix. As usual there had been a festival, the second in twelve months, in honour of Rousseau.

'A great deal of powder was burnt to-day. I am told it was very successful; a procession of girls, some crowned, others half veiled, all carrying garlands they piled on the monument; another of old men leaning on sticks and supported by boys; then the crowd and bands. As there was no rain and no feasting, the festival went off better than that of last year!'

A week later Madame de Saussure was recording the departure for America of several of their friends. The coming storm was throwing its shadow in advance. Before it broke de Saussure had returned to his family at Conches.

A city distracted by civil broils, in the course of which all its ancient institutions had been thrown into the melting-pot, was in no condition to resist the contagion on its borders. The Revolution in France had excited class hostility and suggested the spoliation of the well-to-do; the fumes of the Terror had infected the brains of the Genevese rabble, and made it eager to emulate the crimes of Paris on the peaceful shore of Lake Leman. There was no leader and no force at hand capable of controlling the situation. On the evening of July 19th the town was in the hands of the mob. The Government temporised, the Clubs—always to the front in times of disorder—were invited to send delegates to the Hôtel de Ville. To this irregular meeting was left the appointment of a Revolutionary Committee. A number of prominent citizens were hastily arrested and brought before an improvised tribunal.

The 24th July 1794 remains marked with a black stone in the annals of Geneva as the date of the Massacre on the Bastions. I give Théodore de Saussure's account, written to his sister three days later, of the events that led up to it, and of his own and his brother's escape from the distracted city :

'ROLLE, 27th July 1794.

'The presentiment which led us to pass the summer outside Geneva was not ill-founded. The political situation in the city offered no stable base for any long continuance of tranquillity. It seems as if France had not lost sight of us, and that the misfortunes which afflict us are brought about by her, so that we may be driven to seek happiness by throwing ourselves into her arms. For some time the Egaliseurs have affected to be dissatisfied with the Government. The French Resident instigated them. He gave at Monty a splendid party to the more violent of them who took the name of Montagnards : there were about eighty. He advised them to work for their own ends and to start a second revolution. For that it was necessary to have a riot, and a pretext was soon found. It was reported at the Great Club on Friday evening, 17th July, that a plot in which several Genevese were implicated had been started in Switzerland, to raise the neighbouring French Departments. At the word "Plot" several individuals proposed to take up arms and seize the conspirators, whose names were not even mentioned. The minority persisted, announced that it would take up arms, and rushed tumultuously out of the Club with shouts of "To Arms." All the Genevese then in Geneva flew to arms. But the *honnêtes gens* were at once disarmed. The Montagnards proceeded, without order or distinction, to seize by night the greater number of the so-called Aristocrats and shut up more than six hundred in the Granges and the Granary. At the same time they broke open bureaux, seized papers, money, and in some cases plate. My father's house was respected, as well as those of a very small number of others, without any known reason. Neither he nor Alphonse nor I were arrested. Probably our father covered us with his wings, for, as you know, we had not taken the famous oath, which was quite a good enough reason at the moment for imprisonment.

'The Montagnards asked for a revolutionary tribunal of twenty-one judges to try the prisoners. All Genevese citizens were summoned to attend in arms on the bastions in order to proceed to their election. All came, but the Egaliseurs arrived first, and disarmed, or sent home, those whom they recognised as anti-revolutionaries. Despite this exclusion the voting, according to some, was less bad than might have been expected, and among the judges whose names excited no fear, were Déonna, Flournois, de l'Isle, Lissignol, Bourdillon, Dieday, Romilly, Argand, Bousquet, and others who were held good Genevese, if violent democrats. Events proved the contrary. The judgments had to be confirmed by the people. De Rochemont, the son, was examined. He replied with so much eloquence, firmness, grace, and wit that his speech was drowned in applause. The judges and the audience were touched and satisfied, so that they refused to examine his papers. One heard nothing but voices which exclaimed that the people were being deceived, that it was unworthy to make arrests on such pretexts. M. le Syndic also satisfied his judges. Still the Montagnards declared that victims were necessary to establish the revolution; as, if the revolutionary tribunal did not satisfy the people, it would act for itself. Others suggested that the accused in obtaining their pardon from the people would be more secure than if acquitted by the tribunal. Others that a victim was needed to save the lives of the six hundred prisoners who without this would be in danger. On these considerations the tribunal out of the fourteen it had examined during the day condemned seven to death.

'The people were called together next day, 24th July, on the bastions to confirm the sentence. No one doubted of a pardon; the Montagnards, however, again excluded all the moderate revolutionaries. Despite this, the majority was still for a pardon. Counting the votes began at five in the afternoon. At nine it was still incomplete. Then the scrutineers announced that the counting was sufficiently advanced to show that five were pardoned and that only two remained in doubt. At the word Pardon, Le Clair, a locksmith, a member of the revolutionary tribunal, drew his sword and cried out, "No pardon, they must die!" The Montagnards at once started for the prisons: the partisans of pardon got before them and guarded the doors. The prisoners might have been saved, but the Montagnards came up and threatened attack, the others yielded like cowards, the doors were opened and the seven prisoners were led behind the Montagne des Bastions. The garrison was ordered to fire on them; it refused. The Montagnards themselves did so and the seven unfortunate men lost their lives at ten o'clock with the greatest courage. Nothing was seen in Geneva but tears and consternation. The Montagnards said they had only made a beginning of purging Geneva of its enemies. This unhappy city is a desert, all the honest people have fled or are in prison. Arrests continue. Alphonse and I were warned that we were being looked for and that we might expect to be arrested. Our father urged us to fly immediately.[1] You will realise how difficult it was for us to seek safety while leaving our friends in prison and our parents in danger; that if we could have seen any probability of a rally or resistance we should never have consented. But the case was hopeless, we were useless and a burden to our parents who desired to remain to protect their property, which is almost their only source of income.

'We gained at night by bye-paths the shores of the lake. The Montagnards had already seized all the boats. We crossed the French frontier, found a boat, and landed at Rolle at my aunt Tronchin's, where we are lodging. The two Calandrini are in prison as well as Pasteur and the Pictets, Marcet also. My other friends have escaped. Diodati, the Major, escaped by swimming from "Behind the Rhône," to Sécheron, whence he got into Switzerland. Yesterday and to-day they have released one hundred and fifty prisoners. Some have been completely acquitted, others have been condemned to confiscations, fines, and banishment. Six Montagnards, who called themselves French, have been arrested. Anxiety is now felt only for Duroveray and Bellamy among those under arrest.'

Théodore concludes :

'The moment may come when my parents will be obliged to abandon their property. The confiscation of that of emigrants is already proposed. The wish to be some help to them is the only link that attaches me to life. This idea puts aside all my tastes and all personal considerations. I eagerly desire a post as a tutor or travelling companion. It is the only thing I can do. Geneva is marked with a stain that can never be effaced, it is for me an accursed spot, which I shall never see without horror; I am ashamed of it. I should like to deliver my friends and then burn the town. Let it be no more mentioned.'

Several of the letters written by Madame de Saussure during this brief Reign of Terror have been preserved. They show very remarkable calmness and courage in the terrible circumstances of the moment. The husbands of her friends Mesdames Cayla and

[1] Πορεία τῶν υἱῶν is the concise entry in de Saussure's Greek diary for the day before the murders. It follows on the words 'very bad news of the seven.'

Naville had been murdered by the Revolutionaries. M. Necker de Germagny, her daughter's father-in-law, was held a prisoner for a few days, but 'his charity, his kindness, and his patriotism' led to his speedy release. She adds: 'Your father's courage, his fine spirit have supported mine, and the tendency to resignation which I am supposed to inherit from my grandfather Lullin has been, he says, of use to him.'

On the last day of July, a week after the massacre on the bastion, de Saussure writes to his daughter:

'I am remaining quietly at Conches. I went, however, once into town, the day before this terrible trial; it seemed to me that to remain inactive at such a moment would have shown blameworthy indifference or cowardice. I was well received by those I called on, and returned full of hope and without having suffered any personal annoyance, but I was strongly recommended not to come back before either order was completely restored or I was summoned—which has not happened!'

His wife, he adds, is wonderfully calm, and he is providing her with occupation in copying his *Voyages*. The third volume was already finished and the fourth in hand. Fauche of Neuchâtel was to be the publisher. He has sent a memoir on the Extinct Volcanoes of the Brisgau to the *Journal de Physique* at Paris.

'Thus between my work and the dear society of your mother I find some relief from the troubles and the anxieties which desolate at this moment almost the whole world.'

De Saussure's sons thought it better for the time to follow their parents' earnest wish and not to return to Geneva. The mob, now masters of the city and impatient of their leaders' delays in confiscating and distributing the property of the well-to-do, seized control and appointed fresh committees and tribunals. Four hundred prisoners were held at their mercy. The aspect of these tribunals is thus described in a popular history for school use published in Geneva:

'The tribunal presented a hideous aspect. The judges, for the most part workmen, affected a sullen air and coarse manners, they were in turned-up shirt-sleeves, bare-breasted, wearing red bonnets, from which escaped dishevelled locks, bearded, with pipes in their mouths, and often pistols in their belts, bottles and glasses between their legs, swords and pistols on the table.'[1]

Other executions, or rather murders, quickly followed on the crime of the bastions. The gang who were responsible for them sat for eighteen days, during which they pronounced 500 sentences, 37 of death (of which, fortunately, 26 were on absentees) and 98 of exile. Meantime a second tribunal occupied itself in organising pillage by confiscating the property of the rich and distributing daily allowances to the insurgents and their families, a welcome boon to those who having ceased to be workers learnt that idleness has its drawbacks. The activity of this body produced a fund of five millions of francs—the undistributed residue of which was subsequently declared to be national property. Idleness was encouraged and trade lost, the watchmakers and shawl producers ceased to work, the upper class left the town, or if forced to stay did their best to avoid attracting attention.

It must be put to the credit of the Genevese, always emotional, that their brief Reign of Terror left behind it some feelings of remorse in the hearts of the mass of citizens. But these did not result in any practical effort to put an end to disorder or a curb on cruelty.

Up to this moment de Saussure had grudged no expense of energy or time in the attempt to save his country from the destruction to which it was being brought by the folly of its own children and the intrigues of French anarchists. But the murders of 1794 drove him finally out of politics. He refused to be associated with an administration stained by the blood of its fellow-citizens. Called on to give his reasons for his retirement, he explained that the events of the last summer had made on him an impression which time only deepened. He would, he added, have left his unhappy country had he not the hope that the day would come when the punishment of the guilty would be demanded by those who had had no share in their crimes. Until that day came he could take no part in public affairs.

[1] *Histoire de Genève racontée aux jeunes Genevois*, Jullien, 1863. I quote from a school-book which attempts to be impartial. The picture of the tribunal drawn by Cornuaud, the leader of the 'Natifs,' who successfully defended himself before it, is even more revolting.

In July 1795 the state of his health again gave alarm to his friends, and he visited with his wife the baths of Bourbon l'Archambault, near Moulins, whence he went on to those of Royat, close to Clermont-Ferrand. His son, writing from Rolle, sent him an account of a relatively insignificant riot between Terrorists and Stalwarts ('Englués' is the term Théodore employs), which was followed by a more than usually effusive reconciliation with banquets in the streets, where passers-by were stopped and made to drink to Oblivion and to stick a patch, called an 'oubli,' on their faces. A pastor even preached a sermon with one of these red patches on his forehead. This 'paix plâtrée' Théodore expected to last two months! He mentions that he is busy correcting the proofs of the third volume of the *Voyages*.

From Bourbon l'Archambault de Saussure writes to condole with Pictet on the proposal of the Revolutionary Government to do away with the philosophy professorship at the Academy and to encourage him to protest against so illiberal a proceeding. He also writes to Madame de Staël to clear up a misunderstanding with respect to a suggestion she had made to his daughter of being able to procure for him a chair in the French Académie des Sciences, together with an official post at a handsome salary under the French Republic as an Inspector of Mines.[1] In a second letter Madame de Staël had expressed her surprise that he had not accepted her proposal that he should be 'Directeur en Chef' of the Academy. He replied that as to the Presidency of the Academy (which she had not, he tells her, previously mentioned) it seemed to him obvious that a post that had always been elective was not likely to be conferred on a foreigner. For the rest, having his *Voyages* to finish he would not for some months have the time to take up an Inspectorship of Mines. Madame de Staël's energy, however, was not to be put off! She applied to Göttingen and Berlin, to Sweden and St. Petersburg. In November we find de Saussure writing to his daughter about his plans.

'I see,' he says, 'that your adorable cousin has really done the impossible, that she has knocked at every door. Assure her of my

---

[1] A similar post was held at this time by another geologist, Dolomieu.

lively and deep gratitude. Your mother and I agree with you, and we prefer beyond comparison the post at Göttingen to Berlin or St. Petersburg. My only fear is lest the work should be too fatiguing for my state of health. I must find out for how many lectures a week I should be called on, and how long they would be; if one would have to talk loud and in what language. I believe and hope Latin, because though I read German easily enough I don't talk it easily, and I know enough of the difficulties of the language to be sure that I should never master them.

'I have passed, my dear child, the age of ambition; you are assured if not of being rich, of having enough to live on. So I shall take quite contentedly the part of ending my days with your mother in the strict economy to which we are reduced. But the idea of a bankruptcy is one to which I cannot accustom myself, and unless the French funds recover their value, or I succeed in finding some means of adding to my income, it is almost impossible for me to escape this misfortune. But if I could find a post which would allow me to put aside some five or six hundred louis a year, I should be almost certain to avoid it. This is the object of my ambition. As to personal security I trust we shall enjoy it at Geneva, and I should be tranquil and without anxiety if I had no other cares. The horrible intoxication which caused the crimes which disgraced the last revolution has entirely passed and given place to repentance and remorse. A revolutionary club has proposed that a monument should be erected to the innocent victims of this insurrection It is an idea which I have planted in some warm and honest hearts, and I see with great pleasure that it is spreading and makes progress, but its origin must not be suspected. I cited the sorrow and tears of Alexander on the death of Clitus. Such a monument might give occasion for the finest efforts of oratory and is the only way to wash out the shame of these crimes and prevent their repetition.'

In another letter of about the same date de Saussure goes in fuller detail into the Göttingen project, and points out that he would prefer a post which gave him greater leisure for independent research.

Meantime the news of his difficult circumstances had been widely spread. A Paris newspaper in February 1795 had put in a paragraph: 'Poor Professor Saussure is reduced to such poverty that he is soliciting a post in Germany.' This crude announcement was copied in Italian journals and drew forth the following letter from Lord Bristol, the eccentric and picturesque Bishop of

Derry,[1] then travelling in Italy, to the Genevese bankers Delarue at Genoa :

'SIRS,—Having read this morning in a foreign newspaper that the famous M. de Saussure, the intimate friend of my brother, General Harvey, *era redotto alla povertà*, I beg you to write to him on my behalf and offer him an annuity of fifty louis d'or. And should he find it agreeable to pass the rest of his life as my guest he would receive the same sum paid half-yearly, his board, etc. etc., and might travel at my cost in a country the most rich in the world in natural history, a virgin country, untouched by naturalists, Ireland.'

De Saussure's answer was as follows :

'MY LORD,—I have been moved to tears by the proof of interest and esteem with which you have honoured me, when, on reading in a newspaper that I was reduced to poverty, you at once ordered your bankers to assure me an annual income of fifty louis.

'Certainly, were I in actual want I should not blush to accept the help of a man, my lord, who from love of those who devote their lives to the study of science, and from attachment to an old friend of his brother, desired to protect me from the pangs of extreme misery; but my situation is not yet of this kind. It is true, I have nothing left, but my wife is able to supply the wants if not lavishly at least adequately of myself and my family. So, my lord, I shall not take advantage, at any rate for the present, of the generous offer you make me of an annuity, an offer for which I shall none the less retain the most lively and profound gratitude. As to the further proposal which is equally the result of your kind consideration for me and your love of science, that I should come and study at your home and with means furnished by you the Natural History of Ireland, I should be extremely tempted were I not absolutely inseparable from my wife, not because I live upon her fortune, but because I have for her an attachment of thirty years founded on all the links which can be formed by mind, virtue, and character. . . . Whatever lot Providence has in store for me, your kindness, my lord, will remain engraved in my heart to my last breath.'

The Revolutionary Authorities were now taking steps to put in force an elaborate scheme of taxation on the wealthier class of citizens. On his return to Geneva de Saussure wrote a sharp note to the tax-collector, pointing out that the arrangement he had

[1] See *Dictionary of National Biography.*

been recommended to offer with regard to his liability having been rejected, he should find himself compelled to suspend payments—that is, to acknowledge bankruptcy.[1]

Throughout that year (1795) de Saussure was still looking anxiously for some scientific employment either abroad or in France. He consulted with his daughter as to Göttingen, suggesting that she and her husband should accompany him there, as he could ill endure the parting with his beloved family. He also wrote a letter of remonstrance to St. Petersburg complaining that the proposal put before him through his friend Tingry had not been followed by the definite offer promised. Meantime an invitation came from across the Atlantic. Jefferson was at the time looking for a Faculty to occupy the quaintly Georgian halls and colonnades of his new University at Charlotteville, Virginia. He wrote to Washington from his home at Montecello suggesting that some of the professors of the Genevese Academy might be glad to find a refuge and employment in the States, and among the names he put forward were those of de Saussure and of his friends Pictet and Senebier. The offer was made and repeated in a definite form through d'Ivernois in the same autumn, but nothing came of it.[2]

In his negotiation with Paris, the new French Resident Desportes, the builder of the Temple at the Montenvers, a man of some cultivation, whose frequent and friendly relations with an aristocrat became matter of suspicion to the Genevese Terrorists, was very helpful. De Saussure's Journal shows that frequent visits were exchanged between Desportes and de Saussure. A letter from the latter to Desportes thanking him

[1] For the purposes of this tax or rather levy on capital the citizens were divided into three classes—Aristocrats, Englués, and Patriots. Aristocrats had to pay most, 5 per cent. on the first 12,000 livres and 5·12 extra on every thousand livres in excess of 12,000. The total tax was not to exceed 90 per cent. De Saussure's liability amounted to 25,652 florins.

[2] Sparks' *Correspondence of Washington*, vol. ii. (Boston, 1839): 'The colleges of Geneva and Edinburgh were considered as the two eyes of Europe in matters of science insomuch that no other pretended to any rivalry with either. Edinburgh has been the most famous in medicine since the time of Cullen, but Geneva most so for other branches of science, and much the most resorted to from the Continent of Europe because the French language is that used. M. d'Ivernois of Geneva, and a man of science known as the author of a history of the Republic, has proposed the transplanting of that college as a body to America.'

for a passport is written in very cordial and complimentary terms. In April 1796 he forwarded to Paris de Saussure's acceptance of the position of teacher of Chemistry and Physics in the Ecole Centrale. De Saussure, while pointing out that he had to finish the proofs of his fourth volume, which was already in the press, asked for adequate notice of the date at which he would have to be in Paris, and also for his travelling expenses. He wrote:

'I am in despair at having to make this request, but my father, having the most complete trust in France, placed there all his and my mother's fortunes, so that I have found myself fallen from a handsome income, such as the expenses incident to my travels and researches called for, to a state of penury which makes it impossible for me to provide the cost of the journey.'

A correspondence ensued, in which the Department concerned exhibited a dilatoriness and pettiness combined with a self-complacent pomposity frequently met with in the dealings of similar bodies, whatever the form of government. A year later we find it regretting that it cannot afford the money for de Saussure's travelling expenses. A letter from Dolomieu, the geologist, whose name lives in one of the most romantic districts of the Alps, lets us into the bare facts of the situation. It is dated 1st November 1796:

'I had cherished the hope, Monsieur, of having you this winter in Paris up to the moment when I saw M. Ginguené, but I had to abandon it entirely when the Director of Public Instruction told me that he had never, despite his most earnest entreaties, been able to obtain from the Government the small sum needed for your travelling expenses, and that he could not even offer you lodging as the house he had meant for you was no longer at his disposal. He is even glad that you did not yield to the first proposals made to you and come at once to Paris; the salary promised you would not have been paid and your embarrassments in a new household might have been extreme. The Government does not pay even the most urgent claims, and those relating to Public Education are far from being held of any urgency.'

Simultaneously with this negotiation the educational authorities of the Department of the Puy de Dôme were pressing in their invitation to de Saussure to accept a Chair of Natural

H. B. DE SAUSSURE
From a Portrait by Saint Ours

History at Clermont-Ferrand, an offer which he naturally postponed to his prospects at Paris.

After another twelve months 'François de Neufchâteau de l'Académie Française,' then Minister of the Interior, in a pompous letter offered to put de Saussure on a Pension List for the paltry sum of 200 livres (about £8) a month ! It would appear that a nominal Professorship at Lausanne, the duties of which he was incapable of fulfilling, was attached to this tardy gift, which never took effect.

At this date the only oil portrait of de Saussure in existence was one painted by the Danish painter Juel some eighteen years earlier. In 1796 the Society of Arts expressed a desire to possess before it was too late a portrait of its founder, and after some persuasion de Saussure was persuaded to sit to Saint-Ours, the celebrated portrait painter of the day.

Madame de Saussure describes the many discussions that took place as to the accessories. De Saussure insisted on Mont Blanc being brought in. He wanted to be painted in the act of climbing the mountain, or at any rate gazing at it. The painter objected it would be difficult to manage, and suggested the snows might be shown through the window of de Saussure's study. Every one, Madame de Saussure complains, brought forward a different idea. The result was a compromise. De Saussure is represented sitting under a pine tree with his geologist's hammer in his hand and a theodolite beside him, while a very conventional Mont Blanc towers in the background. In the finished picture, which has been frequently reproduced, the painter's skill has tried in vain to conceal the ravages of illness, the eyes, always described as prominent, have become painfully bulging, while the expression lacks animation. The sketch on the other hand has an air of absolute fidelity, and is a lifelike if pathetic memorial of the great naturalist in his latter days.[1]

The official correspondence relative to the commission has been preserved in the annals of the Society of Arts. A deputation of its members visited Saint-Ours' studio and expressed their satisfaction with the likeness and the composition, and the Society subsequently ordered its secretary to convey to the painter

[1] Now in the collection of Dr. Maillart-Gosse of Geneva, who kindly allows me to reproduce it as the frontispiece to this volume.

its regret that owing to the hard times it could not afford to pay him more than twenty louis for the work.

At the close of 1796 the third and fourth volumes of the *Voyages* were published. The proofs were mainly corrected by Théodore, who must be held responsible for the frequent lapses found in them.

In the previous year de Saussure in order to test his mental powers had compiled a paper on 'The Use of the Blowpipe in geological research.' He was again to return to his first pursuit, botany, in one of his last publications,[1] a little tract, ' Conjectures on the cause of the constant direction of the stalk and the root at the moment of Germination ' (1798). But his working days were over. The concluding volume which was to have summed up his conclusions on the problems of geology was never written. Senebier tells us he had examined two schemes for a system of geology or Theory of the Earth set down by de Saussure in 1794 and 1796, and that they 'indicated generalisations on various branches of the science without putting forward any trace of a general conception which might bind together all the others by submitting them as part of a theory, which might have added one more to the theories invented and abandoned on this vast subject.' But Professor Favre cites a fragmentary MS. dated 7th August 1796, which appears to have been a sketch for the theory that was never written.[2] Some imperfect Memoranda and the Agenda at the end of the *Voyages* are all that we have to indicate what might have been its contents. Even de Saussure's private diary ends at the close of 1796. A second seizure left him from that time forward physically and mentally a wreck. He was unable to attend to his own affairs, and his wife in writing for him constantly speaks of her husband's feebleness. But he was still to live on for a little over two years, which were spent mostly at Conches. In a letter of the time we get a pathetic picture of him while staying with the young Neckers, his daughter and son-in-law, during the winter of 1796 :

'Madame Necker [-de Saussure] has her father and mother with her for the winter. It is a sad sight to see this poor M. de Saussure, his

[1] A paper on the fluctuations and temperature of the Arve was also published in 1796.
[2] See Chapter XVII, on De Saussure in Science and Literature, p. 425.

eyes starting, his walk tottering, and hardly able to speak intelligibly. His mind has not suffered. He is conscious of his condition and yet feels the need of society and distraction. Madame Necker is very interesting between her father and her children.'

Another intimate sketch, from Mlle. de Constant, helps us to realise the domestic situation, and the bravery of the wife and daughter in attempting to furnish some interest to pass the hours of the sorely stricken invalid :

'We often see my neighbours ; Madame de Saussure, the mother, has written a romance and we meet to hear it read, which provides pleasant evenings. The good lady is quite ashamed of her effort, she apologises for it as a folly, assuring us that it was the result of a convalescence [Madame de Saussure had been seriously ill in 1790] that had reduced her to writing it, and that she wondered how she could have the courage to read it in company. "It passes my understanding," she says, "how in this country people set up without scruple as *beaux esprits.*" In effect to write romances is to be in the local fashion. There is no one who cannot draw from his or her pocket a manuscript sufficient to meet the occasion. M. de Saussure takes so much interest in his wife's production that directly the story becomes at all moving it is interrupted by his sobs.' [1]

Madame Necker-de Saussure herself has completed the picture :

'What a sad return for his noble and useful labours. If old age in itself commands respect, what sentiment ought to be excited by this premature decay, this voluntary sacrifice. How much more ought we to reverence the victim of science than the victim of years. His mind has preserved all its energy as his works prove, but if he still lives for his own reputation and the progress of science he no longer lives for happiness. These are the limits on every side set round the destiny of man ; the devouring activity which raises him is fated to consume him, for thought as for the summits of the Alps there is an elevation where it is no longer possible to breathe.'

The great botanist de Candolle records visits about the same date, and the singular advice de Saussure gave him ; advice interesting, as it shows how completely geology had absorbed his attention, and leads us to believe that if his last publication was a

[1] MSS. letters from Rosalie de Constant to her brother. One of these letters is quoted in a volume, *Rosalie de Constant, sa famille et ses amis,* par Mlle. L. Achard (Genève, 1902).

botanical tract this was a concession to his physical weakness rather than a willing return to his first pursuit.

'It was about this time (1796) that I was introduced to the celebrated de Saussure; he had already been attacked by the singular sort of partial paralysis which brought him to his grave, but his expression was still that of a man of intellect, and so long as he was allowed time, his conversation was full of interest. He seemed to attach some kind of importance to enlisting us in the sciences he loved and in deterring me from botanical studies. Each time I saw him he repeatedly assured me that this study promised no success and was not worth pursuing except as a recreation.'

In July 1797 a final resort was had to the waters of Plombières of which no details are at hand. This was the last time the traveller was to leave his home.

Before we come to the final scene, the political events of the last years of de Saussure's life, after the destruction of the Genevese constitution, must be briefly summarised.

In September 1796 the anarchists again broke loose; two more victims were seized, and after some delay and a futile trial allowed to be massacred by the mob. The incident did not lead to an immediate crisis. For another eighteen months the feeble Revolutionary Government continued to exist. But by this time the French Directoire was getting tired of the disorderly travesty of a republic on its borders and alive to the advantage of annexing Geneva as the natural capital of its newly acquired Département du Léman. Napoleon, it is true, passing through on his way to Rastadt in November 1797, felt able to repeat the assurances given four years before by Kellermann and to promise his hosts that their independence should always be respected. He even added that France would like to be surrounded by fifty Genevas! He spent a morning in visiting the Collège and the Society of Arts and held conversations with the leading men of science. His visit was not without result. When he founded an Imperial University of France, the Academy of Calvin alone of provincial institutions preserved its ancient constitution. But his promise was soon broken. Four months later the adroit Desportes, the French Resident, was instructed to inform the Genevese Government that they would do well to prepare to accept quietly and gratefully the honour of becoming the *chef-lieu* of a French

Department.[1] The people of Geneva, whatever their faults, clung to the independence their petulance had endangered and showed no disposition to abandon it voluntarily. Appropriate pressure was accordingly brought to bear on them. The old fable of the Wolf and the Lamb was repeated. The French Resident remonstrated again and again with regard to the smuggling that went on across the frontier; he complained of petty, or invented, discourtesies, he imposed a sort of blockade on the town. A Commission was appointed, at his instigation, to consider the situation. While, torn by divided counsels, it hesitated and delayed, French troops entered the city. On the 15th April 1798 the independence of Geneva came to an end. When it was too late the Genevese realised the result of their civil brawls and dissensions. Not only their independence but their commerce was lost. Distress was prevalent, the Society of Arts was reduced to founding a soup kitchen!

The political story extending over nearly a hundred years I have here tried to summarise is surely a lamentable one. The whole of the eighteenth century at Geneva was marked by a series of popular outbreaks and fictitious and short-lived reconciliations brought about mainly by foreign interference. The patrician oligarchy, honest but slow and obstinate, proved to the end lacking in the political intelligence that might have led it to adapt itself to changing conditions, while the populace recognised only when it was too late that by indulging the passions they had imbibed from France they had wrecked their country's independence. A constitution no longer adapted to the times could not resist the external pressure of the French Revolution.

The charming Genevese writer, Amiel, has pictured his native city as she appeared in his patriotic eyes:

'Geneva is a caldron always boiling over, a furnace of which the fires are never extinguished. Vulcan had more than one forge. Geneva is certainly one of the anvils on which most projects have been hammered out. When one reflects that the proscripts of every kind of cause have harboured here, the mystery is partially explained;

---

[1] See *Félix Desportes et l'annexion de Genève* (F. Barbey, Paris, 1916). It appears that Napoleon was not wilfully deceitful in promising the Genevese that their independence should be respected. The annexation was the work of the Directory in his absence, and contrary to his wish. But he subsequently endorsed it in 1800.

but the better explanation is that republican, protestant, democratic, learned and enterprising, Geneva has through the centuries shown an aptitude to work out her own salvation. Since the days of the Reformation she has been on the alert and marches on, a lantern in her right hand and a sword in her left.'

A caldron and a forge—we may agree—but the heroic attitude of the figure in which Amiel personifies his city must to the foreign observer seem scarcely the most appropriate! In the annals of Geneva the sword has in truth played no conspicuous part. Setting aside domestic brawls, her weapon has been habitually a pen.

The Geneva of the eighteenth century, the historian must admit, earned her fate—or rather her lesson, for sixteen years was the moderate term of her punishment. Her 'salvation' was won, less by her own exertions than by the victories of the Allies in 1813. It consisted in being permanently attached as a self-governing canton to that remarkable association of peoples of different races and languages, the Swiss Confederation. Politically, this decision was probably the best possible; and it may be held to have proved, on the whole, successful. But from the intellectual and literary point of view, the sympathies of Geneva turn naturally to the great nation whose language and civilisation she shares. It is from contact with French, not with Teutonic, influences that her literature has been at all times most benefited. Quickness and lightness of imagination and touch are the ingredients of which it has had most need, and these are nowhere to be found of such quality as on the banks of the Seine.

To summarise: the three main dates to remember in Genevese politics as they affect the life of de Saussure are 1763-6, the period of the protracted struggle of the democratic Assembly against the aristocratic Councils, ending in some advantages for the former; 1782, the oligarchic reaction, when the Councils, by the aid of the Mediating Powers, recovered more than they had lost; and 1789-94, the years of revolution, culminating in the abolition of the old constitution of the State, and finally in 1798 in the annexation of Geneva by the French Directory.

De Saussure did not long survive the fall of the Republic he had done his best to save. In the first days of January 1799 he was known to be dying in his townhouse. The Society of Arts charged his lifelong friend Pictet to express its sympathy to his relatives. On the morning of the 22nd January the end came; after a restless night de Saussure passed away peacefully in his son Théodore's arms before his wife and daughter could be summoned to his bedside. A letter from Madame Necker-de Saussure to her husband gives touching details of the scene, and of her own despair at not having been able to be present at her father's last moments, 'a privilege,' she wrote, 'I had surely earned.'[1] Both his sisters-in-law joined the mourners on the next day. Five deputations from public bodies paid visits of condolence. On the 24th he was buried in the cemetery of Plainpalais outside the walls. The funeral was public. The Professors of the Academy and the Collège walked on either side of the coffin; it was followed by officers of the municipality in their robes, by the French general in command and his staff, by the members of the Societies of Arts and of Natural History, by a crowd of the students whose interests de Saussure had always had at heart. The drums beat as it passed the Hôtel de Ville and the city gates. No ceremonial honour was lacking. Geneva realised, if only for a few hours, that she had lost the most distinguished of her sons and the most loyal of her citizens.

Three months later Tingry, an eminent man of science who has already been mentioned in these pages, suggested that a suitable slab should be placed over de Saussure's grave to mark its position. This proposal, strange to say, was never carried out, and the exact spot is now unknown, though it is believed to be close to the grave of Sir Humphry Davy, who died at Geneva in 1829. It must surely be a matter of lasting regret to the inhabitants of Geneva that the resting-place of one of their most famous fellow-citizens should thus remain uncertain and without record. It may perhaps be urged in extenuation of a contemporary neglect which seems strangely inconsistent with the honours of a public funeral that tombstones were among the 'articles of luxury' long denied to the inhabitants of Geneva by their Calvinistic legislators.

In the year before his death de Saussure had come to an arrangement with the fiscal authorities with regard to the tax on

[1] Madame Necker-de Saussure's account of the death-bed scene obviously supersedes that derived by Professor Naville from a journal of the time. See *Bibl. Universelle*, tome xvii., No. 51, mars 1883.

capital levied by the Terrorist Government. But he died practically insolvent, and his sons were advised to refuse to take up the succession. His wife's income, however, would seem to have recovered to some extent after the annexation of Geneva by France, and we find her property at her death eighteen years later, when it had no doubt further regained in value, estimated at a very considerable sum. She was apparently able next year to reside in the townhouse, for we hear of her receiving a visit from Napoleon on his way to the war in Italy in May 1800. From a letter written by her sister-in-law, Mlle. de Saussure, we gather that the First Consul had been cordial and sympathetic, and had expressed his readiness to grant any personal requests she might wish to put forward.[1]

Madame de Saussure gives the following account of herself at a later date:

'I, my good sister, go out where I shall meet my sisters and my husband's old friends, but I prefer solitude. My sorrow is always there as lively and as deep as last year, every day that passes and adds to the length of this terrible loss makes me feel the weight of it more. In the evening I can sometimes pass a few hours in society: but as I recall having blamed those who bring their own sorrows into the hours devoted to the distractions of which every one has need at the present moment, I remain by my chimney corner when I cannot conceal mine.'

Madame de Saussure died in 1817, at the age of seventy-two. Her younger sisters both survived her. The last glimpse we have of them is as two old ladies with kindly, smiling faces starting in their landau from the portal of the great house in the Rue de

[1] On this occasion Napoleon stayed three days at Geneva with his staff. In order to conceal his intention of passing the Alps by the Great St. Bernard, he had hired a villa, and expressed his intention of taking a cure of asses' milk. He was at pains to explain to the Genevese the advantages they would gain by annexation to France. He gave a dinner and held a reception at the Préfet's house, at which he entertained the local savants and asked to be shown the Genevese ladies, fifty of whom were presented to him. This is the description of the scene given by an eye-witness: 'Il se fait un grand silence à son entrée; il fixe les femmes sans leur parler et reçoit ensuite la cour que les hommes s'empressent de lui faire . . . il est petit, habillé en général de division, cheveux noirs sans poudre et ne frisant point, teint jaune, maladif, figure expressive, regard terrible; il reste deux heures debout au milieu de la salle causant chimie, mathématiques et autres sciences avec les hommes qui l'abordent.' *Papiers de Picot*, quoted in Borgeaud's *L'Académie de Calvin*.

NICOLAS THÉODORE DE SAUSSURE

la Cité for their afternoon drive. Madame Tronchin died in 1824, aged seventy-six, and Madame Turrettini in 1838, when ninety-two. She is described as 'the prettiest and most attractive old lady it is possible to see, a specimen of the best and most elegant type of the old Genevese society. She had visited Voltaire and assisted at his theatrical performances, of which she had many entertaining recollections.'[1]

It only remains to add some brief notice of de Saussure's immediate descendants. His resolve to bring up his children at home in place of sending them to the Collège met with considerable success. He took himself a constant interest and a principal part in their education. His elder son, Nicolas Théodore, after passing with credit through the Academy, adopted his father's pursuits. He was, as we have seen, his companion in his later Alpine journeys and his competent assistant in his scientific work. When forced to leave Geneva by the revolution he went to England with Dr. Marcet, who became physician to Guy's Hospital. In 1796 Théodore was again at Geneva, and married Mlle. Renée Fabri. At a later date he spent several years in Great Britain, where he earned for himself an independent reputation as a man of science and an agriculturist. On his return to Geneva in 1802 he was appointed and held for many years Honorary Professorships of Geology and Mineralogy in the Academy. His chief efforts, however, were devoted to the study of the physiology of plants, and their results were embodied in an important work, *Recherches chimiques sur la Végétation*, which led to his becoming a Correspondent of the Paris Institute. It was frequently referred to by Sir Humphry Davy, who endorsed many of his conclusions, and his name is still quoted with respect in current text-books on Farming. In 1820 he was elected a Foreign Member of the Royal Society. He died in 1845 at the age of seventy-eight.

Of his younger brother Alphonse but little is recorded. The brief references to him in his mother's letters suggest that he was socially inclined, and did not share to any considerable extent in the scientific interests and pursuits of his family. His son, M. Henri de Saussure, to whom I owed some valuable help when

[1] See Madame Rigaud-Picot's Souvenirs, *La Maison Picot et la Rue des Granges* (Geneva, 1913, privately printed).

first contemplating his grandfather's biography, was a distinguished traveller and biologist. He died in 1902.

De Saussure's only daughter and eldest child, Albertine Andrienne, demands fuller mention. Born in 1766, she inherited a large share of her father's intellectual energy as well as of his enthusiasm for educational reform. She records that her father took great pains to help her in her studies and to explain her difficulties. We have read of her social successes as a child of six while travelling with her parents in Italy. At a later age she repaid her father's constant and affectionate interest by a passionate devotion. In her diaries she dwells frequently on his fairness of mind, his sense of justice and his charm of manner. She delighted in his companionship and shared largely in his interests. Her own qualities of mind were derived from him rather than from her mother, whose heart was, as she herself confessed, the strongest— or weakest—point in her character.[1] Albertine's letters to her future husband show her to have been a girl of deep feeling and with a high ideal of woman's rôle in life. As a thinker and a writer of exceptional force and ability she left her mark on her generation. The talent for social observation and shrewd appreciation of character indicated in de Saussure's correspondence was transmitted to her in a marked degree. At nineteen she married a son of M. Necker de Germagny and nephew of M. Necker, the financier, who had served as a captain in the French army, but on his marriage returned to Geneva, and for some years took an active part in public affairs. During the revolutionary period he turned to the study of botany and chemistry, but after the restoration of the Republic he resumed his place in politics and served twice (in 1817 and 1819) as Syndic. He died in 1825. By this marriage Albertine became the first cousin of Madame de Staël. The two young women were the same age, and the friendship that had already sprung up between them became a very close one; they were attracted to one another by their dissimilarities. Madame de Staël felt the warmest admiration for Madame Necker-de Saussure's gifts, her beauty, and her talents, and she fully appre-

---

[1] A recent author, however, writes: 'An interest in education was a tradition in the family of Mme. H. B. de Saussure. Her mother, Mme. Boissier-Lullin, occupied herself ably with education, and her father, Ami Lullin, had the same taste.' (See P. Kohler's *Mme. de Staël et la Suisse*, p. 441. Paris, 1916.)

ciated a steadfastness of character and outlook on life that contrasted markedly with her own impulsiveness. In the *salon* at Coppet Madame de Staël's brilliant paradoxes formed a stimulant to her friend's quick and ready appeals to reason. 'My cousin,' she wrote, ' has all the wit I am given credit for, and all the virtues I lack.' And again, ' I would willingly give half my wit for half your beauty.' Madame Necker-de Saussure's portrait is thus drawn: ' She had regular and finely modelled features, her eyes, large and dark, threw up the whiteness of her complexion; her hair, which was brown, she wore powdered in her youth; she was short, but with a perfect figure, which she preserved to an advanced age.' Nor was it only on the surface of social life that the tie of friendship held fast; Madame de Staël, when forced to quit Switzerland, left her father to die in Madame Necker-de Saussure's arms. On the other hand, Madame Necker-de Saussure delighted in a spontaneity and brilliancy of wit rare in the conversations of what she calls ' our regular Genevese set,' whom, it may be remembered, Gibbon found dull compared to the literary ladies of Lausanne. Her affection for Madame de Staël had a depth that enabled it to overlook her friend's occasional whims and frequent caprices. She easily pardoned the self-absorption that at times drew from her a passing complaint; she made the largest allowances for irregularities of conduct resulting from a mind and a nature touched with genius and incapable of any repose. Yet her admiration was by no means blind, she understood her cousin thoroughly, and in minor matters watched her with the critical eye of an elder sister.

Thus she writes, ' My cousin could not believe for a moment that I was ill. She thought it very odd that I did not want to receive visitors, or to have a little dinner party round my bed. In short, I have fallen greatly in her estimation.' At another moment she protests after some recital, ' Why do you say I felt less than my cousin ? Have you forgotten that she was there, and that her prerogative of taking the lead in appreciation and praise, and also her certainty—well founded, no doubt—that she is the one person appealed to, take away from others all power of utterance—and possibly of more than utterance ? ' The relations of the two ladies are perhaps best illustrated in a vivid picture of the *salon* at Coppet and of the parts played by its hostess and her friend in the social tournaments of which it was the scene given in an article by a shrewd contemporary observer, Pictet de Rochemont, a brother of de Saussure's friend and successor in his Chair of Philosophy.

'In the presence of Mme. de Staël, Mme. Necker showed no inferiority. Their styles were different, their force equal. Nothing could be more admirable or more piquant for those who had the good luck to be admitted than the conversations in which the two cousins each displayed in turn her own skill and showed off the other's wit in the discussion of the most interesting topics.

'Mme. de Staël was generally the assailant, and always without plan, never knowing what she was going to say, but always saying it in the best way possible, and growing the more vivacious as the argument, the calm force, and the perfect fairness of Mme. Necker drove her more and more to the use of all her weapons. Then Mme. Necker also got animated, and called on the resources of close reasoning and her superior judgment. It was a hand-to-hand fight, where shrewd and rapid blows followed one another without a pause. If on one side the fire of eloquence flashed out more freely, on the other a more compact argument resisted its onset. As a rule, the serious yet lively debate ended in an unexpected jest. So in the tricks with light we call fireworks, when the dazzled eyes begin to weary of a revolving sun, a brilliant jet suddenly shoots up and loses itself in a shower of sparks.'[1]

Mme. de Staël died in 1817. In 1820 Mme. Necker-de Saussure wrote a notice, *Sur le Caractère et les Ecrits de Mme. de Staël*, which was admittedly the work of a friend, and rather an apology than an impartial biography. The author was at pains to analyse Mme. de Staël's natural gifts and impulsive character, rather than to explain or apologise for the vagaries of conduct into which they led her. She told the truth, but not the whole truth. Yet her portrait satisfied contemporary critics. One of them wrote to her, 'We have lived with Mme. de Staël for several days; the book is herself.'

The best part of life for Madame Necker-de Saussure was over with her friend's death. In later years deafness gradually cut her off from the pleasures of society and drove her to find a resource in literature. But her loss was, as far as posterity is concerned, her gain. She had already in 1814 translated J. E. Schlegel on Dramatic Literature. Between 1828 and 1838 she composed *L'Education*

[1] See *Mme. de Staël et la Suisse*, p. 452.

Progressive, a work in three volumes, two dealing with the management and education of infancy and childhood, the third with that of girls. We have to picture the brilliant young star of the Coppet *salon* as a stately grandmother, seated at her writing-table and rounding her full and smoothly flowing sentences with a careful touch. Her style is leisurely, laboured, at times didactic; the periods run on with little variety or interruption, the reader's attention may slacken under a monotony of polished exposition, and he may find a multitude of what seem to him somewhat obvious recommendations set out with needless diffuseness. But, as he reads on, he recognises that from her own point of view Madame Necker-de Saussure is sensible and understanding. Novels she holds dangerous—they put romantic ideas into young people's heads. Sir Walter Scott is only grudgingly admitted for the sake of his history. Like her contemporary, Miss Edgeworth, Madame Necker-de Saussure is of her age. The two authoresses met in Pictet de Rochemont's *salon* when Miss Edgeworth was in Geneva in 1820. This was a place of reunion where various circles, philosophers and professors, literary celebrities and politicians encountered one another. Pictet de Rochemont was himself a distinguished diplomatist, and in this capacity represented Switzerland at the Congress of Vienna. He was also a scientific farmer and sheep-breeder. His contributions to literature ranged from papers on potatoes and treatises on merino sheep to translations from Byron, Moore, and Walter Scott, and included one of a work of Miss Edgeworth's on education. The Englishwoman in her diary gives her first impression of her fellow-authoress.

'Met Madame Necker-de Saussure—much more agreeable than her books. Her manner and figure reminded me of our beloved Mrs. Moutray: she, too, is deaf and has the same resignation void of mistrust in her expression when she is not speaking, and the same gracious attention to the person who is speaking to her.'[1]

There is interest in the view Madame Necker-de Saussure puts forward that the study of the grammar of a dead language affords the best elementary discipline for the mind, that it is the nearest road to clearness in thought and accuracy in expression, qualities

[1] *Life and Letters of Maria Edgeworth*, edited by A. C. Hare (Arnold, London, 1894).

nowhere more essential than in science. In support of this now much contested position she was able to quote her father's precepts and example. She could herself read Greek and Latin, as well as English, German, and Italian. As was to be expected, Madame Necker-de Saussure is at her best in her last volume, which deals with the education of her own sex. Here she offers a discriminating analysis of the weaknesses to which the female mind is most inclined, and a judicious criticism of the lack of any adequate attempt to control or combat them in the home circles of her time. With advancing years she insists more and more on the part of religion in life.

I have done my best to set down the impression made on a foreign reader of our own day by *L'Education Progressive*. In doing so I have perhaps failed to do justice to Madame Necker-de Saussure's volumes. Let me in fairness conclude by quoting the high eulogy passed on them by a distinguished critic, her fellow-countryman Amiel, in one of the last pages of his Journal (vol. ii. p. 288):

'Je relis Mme. Necker-de Saussure; *L'Education Progressive* est un œuvre admirable. Quelle mesure, quelle justesse, quelle raison, quelle gravité! Que cela est bien observé, bien pensé, et bien écrit. Ce livre est un beau livre, un traité classique, et Genève peut être fière d'une production qui résume une si haute culture et une si solide sagesse. Voilà la vraie littérature genevoise, la tradition centrale du pays.

'Achevé le troisième volume de Mme. Necker. C'est beau, grave, sensé, délicat, parfait. Quelques aspérités ou incorrections de langage ne comptent pas. On éprouve pour l'auteur un respect mêlé d'attendrissement et l'on s'écrie, "Livre rare où tout est sincère et où tout est vrai!"'

M. Ernest Naville, formerly Professor of Philosophy at Geneva, who knew Madame Necker-de Saussure well, bears equally strong testimony to her merits, declaring that in her great book 'she left a luminous trace of her passage through life.'

Madame Necker-de Saussure had four children, two sons and two daughters. Her elder son inherited the tastes of his maternal grandfather. He was introduced to the glaciers at an early age. There was an entry in the old book of the Montenvers:

'Louis Necker, agé de douze ans et demi, et petit-fils de M. de Saussure, accompagné de sa sœur agée de onze ans, est monté au

Montenvers, Vendredi 20 Juillet, 1798, sous la conduite de son père, et il a vu avec beaucoup de regret ces montagnes que son grand-père ne pourra plus revoir.'

The youth completed his education at Edinburgh.

In after life Louis Necker served for a time as a Professor at Geneva. He was an extensive Alpine traveller. In a Preface to the first volume (the only one published) of a work entitled *Etudes Géologiques dans les Alpes* he mentions that he had crossed the Mont Cenis, the Grimsel, the Splügen, and St. Gotthard, and visited not only Zermatt and Grindelwald, but also the Alps of the Tarentaise, the Maurienne and Carniola. He afterwards returned to Scotland and published three volumes of his travels in that country (Geneva, 1821). Three years later he published in the *Bibliothèque Universelle* (vol. xxiii.) an article on the History of Geology, in which he paid a tribute to the part played in it by his grandfather. In his old age he settled in Edinburgh and became the friend of Professor Forbes, who refers to his geological work on the Alps as rich in observation but wanting in the liveliness of his grandfather's *Voyages*. Professor Bonney quotes from his pages a very minute and closely observed description of a sunset on Mont Blanc as seen from the Lake of Geneva.[1] Forbes contributed an obituary notice of him to the *Proceedings of the Edinburgh Royal Society* (vol. v. p. 53). Louis Necker died and was buried at Portree in the Isle of Skye, in 1861, at the age of seventy-seven.

[1] *The Alpine Regions*, by T. G. Bonney (London and Cambridge, 1868).

CHAPTER XVI

BONNET AND HALLER

IN the opening chapter Albrecht von Haller was spoken of as the last link in the chain of writers connected with Alpine subjects who preceded de Saussure. I there pointed out that it was to his uncle, Charles Bonnet, that the young Professor owed his early introduction to the famous Bernese physician and botanist. These two men were destined to influence him through life, to give a direction and encouragement to his travels and scientific pursuits. His name was fated to be coupled with theirs in the minds and mouths of the next generation of his fellow-citizens:

> 'Émules et jamais rivaux
> Ne cherchons que vérités sûres,
> Rassemblons dans nos travaux
> Plus de faits que conjectures :
> Ayons toujours devant les yeux
> Haller, Bonnet et de Saussure,
> Nous saurons nous montrer comme eux
> Les vrais amis de la Nature.'

Thus chanted, a few months after Waterloo, the guests at a banquet held at Geneva to inaugurate a Helvetic Society of Science. In the course of more than a century the fame of the two elder philosophers has grown somewhat dim, but as the chief formative influences on the character and career of de Saussure they seem to claim a more particular notice, which may conveniently find a place here before we attempt a final summary and estimate of the scientific achievements of their more illustrious disciple.

Charles Bonnet (1720-1793) belonged by birth to the aristocracy of the Upper Town. His father owned a country-house and property at Thonex, a few miles out of Geneva, on the Savoy side. Here the boy was mainly brought up. He was backward for his age in his lessons, and was also hampered by a deafness which exposed him to the gibes of his playfellows. Removed consequently from school, he underwent a course of private tuition, and was then sent to the Academy at Geneva. But his inclination did not lie in the direction of literature. 'Nature,' he writes, 'did not intend me for a man of letters. I was born to be an observer.' At the age of sixteen a work on natural history of some reputation and influence at that time, the *Spectacle de la Nature* (1732, nine volumes) of the Abbé Pluche fell into his hands. It revealed to him his proper pursuit, the minute observation of the lower forms of life. He succeeded with some difficulty in inducing one of his teachers to lend him Réaumur's work on Insects. His next step was to capture some caterpillars and to send the observations he had made on them to that eminent man of science. To the boy's intense joy, his bold step was rewarded by a highly complimentary letter. Bonnet's vocation was sealed. But he had first to obtain degrees in Law and Philosophy. He would seem also to have studied the Classics to some purpose, for the page in his reminiscences in which he describes this ordeal of university examinations is a specimen of an unhappy passion for classical allusions which pursued him through life. Law after Philosophy, he says, is Tartarus after Elysium; Roman Law is the hydra of the Lernean march, and he no Hercules.

Once free from legal toils, Bonnet returned to his researches in Natural History. In these he had an ultimate and philosophical aim, the investigation of the origin of life and of the connection between mind and matter. But the inquiry into these deep subjects began with an attack on a minute question left unsolved by Réaumur: Do woodlice breed without coupling? In order to decide this problem, he kept watch over his insects for five weeks. He compared himself to Argus, or Acrisius, guarding Danae! He had his reward. A letter came from Réaumur telling him that his communication had been read to the Paris Academy, that its great importance was fully recognised, and that its author had been at once nominated a correspondent of the illustrious body. 'You can imagine,' wrote Bonnet, 'what ambition so premature an honour aroused in the soul of a youth of twenty. I came very near to believing myself already on the road to immortality.' His hopes must have been strengthened when three years later he was elected a Fellow of our own Royal

Society. But it was not till 1783, after an interval of forty years, that he received the crowning honour, that of being nominated one of the eight Foreign Members of the Paris Academy.

The young student continued to devote himself to further research among the lower forms of life and into their modes of reproduction. But the continual use of the microscope began to affect his general health and eyesight, and he was forced to turn to less exacting inquiries. He took up the investigation of the nature and development of plant-life. His *Recherches sur l'usage des Feuilles dans les Plantes* (1754) represented the labour of twelve years, and was perhaps his most important contribution to Natural Science. In his observations on the functions of leaves, on their powers of sensation, discernment, and adaptation, he led the way in an obscure branch of investigation that has been successfully pursued since by Charles Darwin and his son, Sir Francis Darwin. Bonnet's work—as de Saussure was at pains to point out—may on one point serve as an illustration of the connection between science and practical results. It is owing to their power of inhaling nourishment through their leaves that broad-leaved vegetables need to draw less from the soil than corn does. The fact is a reason for the rotation of crops.

Bonnet had a speculative mind as well as an observant eye. As a youth philosophical studies had seemed to him 'Elysium.' He now resumed them and combined his natural history with psychological and metaphysical speculations. It was a time when Buffon had set men thinking on the origin and transmission of life, on the distinctions between men and animals, the limits between the animal and the vegetable world, the connection between nerves and sensations. Buffon was maintaining stoutly his theory of organic molecules. Bonnet asserted the conservation of pre-existing germs. It was a struggle between Buffon's theory of a continuous process directed by an immanent Creator and Bonnet's of a single act of creation. Buffon denounced Bonnet's hypothesis as an absurdity and ridiculed his minute observations, declaring that the microscope had produced more blunders than truths. Bonnet on his part repeated the current criticism of Buffon's excessive love of generalisations that had no adequate foundation in observed facts.

Bonnet was at heart a firm Christian, though he could smile

kindly at the more dogmatic orthodoxy of Haller. He was bent on reconciling Science and Metaphysics, Philosophy and Religion. He succeeded in doing so to his own satisfaction ; for his wishes often controlled his thoughts. Starting from the conviction that the world and life are the result of a single act of creation, that matter and spirit, though separate, are susceptible of the most intimate connection, capable of infinite development, and both indestructible, he believed in an advance of the whole creation towards perfection. Assuming a supreme and benevolent power outside and above phenomena, he argued that the universe moves onwards by a continual progression of innumerable germs in ever-varying and developing combinations in which nothing perishes, but every germ passes on to a higher degree of consciousness. He recognised in man a spiritual energy, a soul, incorporated in the human body and working through it, which survives its temporary frame and passes on to higher forms of existence. But while professedly an idealist, he assigned so large a part in the formation of ideas to sensation, to the action of the nerves and tissues of the physical frame, that he fell under some suspicion of materialism.

Bonnet's physiology may seem to modern students in parts faulty, his metaphysics vague, many of his assumptions questionable. Yet his teaching supplied a want in his generation. It served more or less as a buffer between the orthodox creeds of Geneva and Rome and the negative dogmatism of the Encyclopaedists. 'Bonnet,' writes Sayous, a competent and impartial critic, 'is met with everywhere in the moral and philosophic literature of the eighteenth century. There was hardly a country where he did not find admirers, he had correspondents in Sweden, Denmark, and Russia, at the Hague, Berlin, and Hamburg.' London might have been added. Yet so persuasively did he put forward his theories that he never came into any serious controversy with the rigid Protestantism of Geneva. This was no doubt in part due to the personal charm, the charity and modesty, which his contemporaries vie in recognising.

Cuvier, in a passage in the eulogy he pronounced on Bonnet some years after his death, while summing up the argument of Bonnet's last and chief work, the *Palingénésie Philosophique* (1769), pays a singular tribute to his character and its influence on his opinions. 'It is in this work,' Cuvier writes, 'that he paints best the kindness of his soul. The evils of this world and the irregularity of their distribution made another life too necessary a complement of divine justice for him to admit of the existence of the one without the other. He had seen too often in all moving things pain as an accompaniment of sensation to be willing to deprive any of them of this consolation. He admitted, therefore, for animals the upward progress which seemed to him their due, and for human beings a proportionate advance, which would be our principal recompense. Thus every being would mount in the scale of intelligence, and happiness would consist in increase of knowledge. The works of God seemed to Bonnet so excellent that he identified knowledge with love.' His attitude towards science is perhaps best summarised in a single sentence addressed to his nephew: 'The world was not made for observers so like moles as we are. Let us console ourselves and profit gratefully by the portion of the works of the Creator which it is permitted us to examine, trusting that His goodness will one day introduce us to the supreme light.'

Yet Bonnet's fame did not long survive him, and his books have fallen into complete oblivion. Bonstetten, the friend of Gray, visiting Bonnet's old home at Thonex, twenty years after his death, exclaims: 'How he is forgotten; his name is as dead as himself!' This neglect is largely due to his style. It was, it is true, praised by de Saussure and Cuvier, but the judgment of posterity has revised their partial verdict. Bonnet, we learn, composed in his head and dictated; the results inherent to this method, in the lack of close revision, followed—prolixity and repetition. To these faults must be added an excess of the ornate sensibility which was congenial to an age of which Rousseau was the accredited mouthpiece, and Jean Antoine Deluc a warning example.

For sixteen years in his middle life (1752-68) Bonnet was a member of the Council of Two Hundred; in the latter year he was elected a member of the Council of Sixty, which met occasionally to discuss foreign affairs. But he never seems to have taken any active part in politics. At the age of thirty-six, by his marriage with Mlle. Jeanne Marie de la Rive, de Saussure's maternal aunt, he became the fortunate inhabitant of a beautiful country-house at Genthod, on the slope above and within a few hundred yards of the Lullin property which was subsequently the country residence of de Saussure. Here he spent a life of comparative seclusion, content to be an interested and at times agitated spectator of the political storms that raged in the neighbouring city, and unmoved by any curiosity to explore the hills that looked down on his home, or the greater world beyond. His only reported excursion was a visit to Haller at Roche, at the other end of the lake. But he was no recluse, and was always ready to receive and hold interesting converse with the visitors his fame brought to him. We get a glimpse of him in the travels of Sir J. Edward Smith, the founder of the Linnæan Society. After recording a visit of a few minutes only to de Saussure, who had just returned from Mont Blanc, our countryman goes on, 'But the most illustrious philosopher of Geneva, Mr. Bonnet, must not be forgotten. He received me with the greatest kindness, and although almost deprived of sight and hearing, he conversed long and most instructively on his favourite subjects.'

Bonnet was frank and incapable of taking offence, modest in putting forward his own views, and patient in listening to those of others. Trembley, the mathematician, his friend as well as de Saussure's, thus describes him : 'The works of celebrated men are often the best parts of them ; those who knew M. Bonnet felt how much superior he was to his works. His conversation was as agreeable as it was instructive. His memory recalled at the right moment whatever was pertinent to the subject under discussion, and he elucidated it without pretence or display. He knew how to make himself understood by the young, to seize the general ideas that might be serviceable to them, to direct their activity without controlling it ; he made them feel their failings without humiliation, and encouraged them without making them conceited.'

Another witness to Bonnet's kindness of heart is the historian, Jean de Müller, a friend of Bonstetten. At a time when he had fallen out of his post as a tutor in the Tronchin family, and was at a loss for a home, he was received as a guest by Bonnet at Genthod. After describing at length his relations with his host, de Müller concludes in the following terms : 'Bonnet seemed to me almost divine. I have never met either in life or in history a truer philosopher or a nobler or more amiable character, and what makes him the more admirable is that he owes what he is not to nature, but to his philosophy.' Bonnet's letter of invitation to de Müller has been preserved, and is a perfect model of delicate consideration for the recipient of a substantial benefit whom it is desired may feel himself a welcome guest.

For his physical inertia the infirmities which grew with years gave Bonnet sufficient excuse, apart from the fact that his wife, soon after their marriage, was permanently injured in a carriage accident, and became an invalid. Easy-going, too kind-hearted to cherish a grudge against his opponents, though not at all incapable on occasion of a smart retort, such is the picture we get of this amiable philosopher. If Voltaire jeers at his dullness, if he calls him a dreamer and his *Palingénésie* a collection of idle pleasantries, Bonnet is not slow to reply by labelling his assailant as 'the shop-boy of science, who treats the outside world as he does his Bible,' and telling him that he criticises 'Locke, whom he has never read, and Leibnitz, whom he cannot understand.' Yet Bonnet's resentment was apt to be short-lived. On another occasion he writes : 'An unlooked-for chance brought Voltaire to my country home. I had not seen him for six years. He came to talk to one of my neighbours about the unhappy affair of the Calas. There is no denying he has done a number of humane acts, and this one ought to make me forgive him many extravagances.' Bonnet shows the same charity towards Rousseau, whom he looked on as a dangerous demagogue. He dismisses him in a sentence of singular generosity : 'If all those who have played a part on the theatre of life were to make confessions as frank, should we find them less guilty or less degraded than Jean Jacques? How many would there be who would be found lighter in the scales of Eternal Justice ? '

This is the uncle whom de Saussure gained at the age of sixteen. With so many points of sympathy, there was one of marked difference between them. They approached nature from a very different angle. The uncle's pursuits lay in the minute and animate ; the nephew's in the opposite direction. Bonnet never took any account of mountains, and only showed an amused interest in de Saussure's studies and exploits. De Saussure ventured on occasion to write very lightly to his uncle about some of Bonnet's particular theories. The one was a chamber philosopher, the other an out-of-door man of science. But the best evidence of the influence Bonnet had on his nephew's life is contained in the *Eloge* that de Saussure pronounced after Bonnet's death. It is doubly interesting as one of the last public utterances of de Saussure before his own final bodily and mental breakdown. I must quote one sentence here : ' Bonnet was made happy through the source of the greatest good fortune of which man is susceptible—that of loving and being loved. There never was a more loving heart than his ; the friends of his childhood were those of his old age ; never did any cloud or any difference cast a shadow on his friendships or his family life.' [1]

Bonnet was responsible for encouraging the young de Saussure to enter on an active scientific career. But it was under another influence that the lad was led to concentrate himself on the study of the Alps. In 1758, two years after his aunt's marriage to Bonnet, de Saussure came in contact with an intellect which had a greater effect even than Bonnet's on his after-life. His uncle, as has already been mentioned, introduced him to the leading man of science in Switzerland, Dr. Albrecht von Haller of Berne. ' The great Haller,' as his contemporaries liked to call him, partly perhaps on account of his physical stature—he was tall and large-framed, and his presence was imposing and somewhat formidable—was one of Bonnet's closest friends and most frequent correspondents. In Protestant Switzerland their names were constantly coupled together as the chief opponents of the revolutionary and irreligious doctrines of Rousseau and Voltaire.

Albrecht von Haller was at this time just fifty. His interests and activities were manifold. He was a sturdy Protestant, an active conservative politician, a well-known medical writer and physiologist, a botanist responsible for a splendid work on the Alpine flora, a poet whose verses on the Alps went through thirty editions, and lastly, the author of three tales with a political purpose, two of which were translated into English. He was compared to Buffon, and hailed as the Pliny of Switzerland. Sainte-Beuve describes him as ' the Hercules of Physiology, a robust and athletic savant, opinionated, active, ambitious, and versatile.' This remarkable man seems to have made an impression on his

[1] Sayous' *Dix-huitième siècle à l'Etranger*, vol. i., contains an excellent appreciation of Bonnet's character and writings.

generation out of proportion to the value of his literary or scientific remains, solid as these are. His celebrity during his lifetime and for some years after his death in 1777 was European. According to his son, nineteen separate lives and panegyrics of him appeared before 1784. Archdeacon Coxe, in the standard English work on Switzerland of the eighteenth century, devotes no less than forty-five pages to 'Anecdotes of Haller.'

Haller's father was a citizen of Berne and a lawyer. As a boy Albrecht had delicate health but a precocious intellect. To this he added prodigious power of work. Before he was ten he is said to have produced an excellent piece of Greek prose; at thirteen he was studying the metaphysics of Descartes. At the same age he employed his leisure in the dangerous pursuit of composing a satirical Latin poem on his schoolmaster! He also dabbled deeply in verse, completing an epic of four thousand lines on the Rise of the Swiss Republic. It is reported that in an alarm of fire he seized the MSS. in his arms before he fled for safety. But six years later, when twenty-four, he showed more judgment and a rarer courage by committing to the flames his youthful effusions. In after-life his memory and his facility in languages were alike prodigious. He is said to have been able to run off without notes the names of the Emperors of China. He wrote and conversed in English, French, and Italian like a native, his Latin was modelled on Tacitus, he had studied Greek, Hebrew, and Chaldaic, and could read almost any European tongue. This abnormal activity of brain gave no satisfaction to worthy parents who destined the fourth son in a large family for the Church. On his father's death his relatives seem to have had no hesitation in letting him go off at the early age of fifteen to study medicine at Tübingen. Discontented with the lectures at that University, the youth soon wandered on to Leyden, where, at the age of nineteen, he took a doctor's degree.

He next visited London, and was introduced by J. K. Scheuchzer, a son of the author of *Itinera Helvetica* and the translator of Kaempfer's work on Japan, to Sir Hans Sloane, the President of the Royal Society, and to Dr. Pringle, who was soon to be his successor. After spending a few weeks in this country he passed on to Basle, whence in 1728 he made with his friend Johann Gesner a fairly extensive botanical tour in the Alps, crossing the Gemmi and Joch Passes. The return to his native mountains after five years' absence awoke his muse, and he composed the poem on *The Alps*, which, published in 1732, was to give the youth a European reputation. It is somewhat difficult now to appreciate the qualities that caught the public ear. A prose translation can do little justice to poetry. But the following paraphrase may serve to give some idea of Haller's descriptive method (stanzas 34-5) :

'A medley of mountains, lakes, and rocks presents itself clearly to view, clad in colours which fade gradually as the distance grows. On the horizon shines a crown of gleaming summits ; the nearer heights are covered with dark forests. A neighbouring hill stretches out gentle terraces on which feed flocks whose lowings wake the dales. Here a lake spreads its beautiful mirror in the depths of a valley and gives back the quivering light which the sun throws on its ripples. There valleys, carpeted with verdure, open before the eyes and form folds which grow closer as they recede. Elsewhere a bare mountain displays its steep and smooth flanks, while it lifts to the skies the eternal ice, which, like crystal, throws back the sun's rays and dares the attack of the dog-days. Near it a vast and fertile alp supplies abundant pasturages ; its gentler slopes glow with the sheen of ripening crops and its hillocks are covered with herds. Climates so opposite are separated only by a narrow vale, where the shade is always fresh.'

I add a passage from one of his prose works in which, after enumerating the hardships that the botanist has to encounter in the mountains, he exclaims :

'But he has his recompense, the aspect of this majestic nature, these eternal ice-fields, these rocky pyramids, always white with snow, these dark valleys where the impetuous torrents precipitate themselves in a hundred cascades, these silvery lakes, these deserts where no song of birds breaks the silence and solitude ; all these in combination produce a landscape at once moving, magnificent, and sublime, which one recalls with a secret delight and a ceaseless longing to return to it.'

Haller's verse, despite its vigour, may not reach the higher levels of poetry, but there can be no question as to the poetical feeling shown in his prose. The secret of the immense popularity of his poem is obvious. The author struck and gave forcible expression to a new vein of sentiment which was in the air. The age was getting tired of formality and affectation ; the Swiss doctor's verses might be prolix, his descriptions of scenery obvious, but they were genuine and they expressed what the average man was beginning to feel. Touches like the 'secret delight' in recalling mountain landscapes and the longing to return to them ring true. Haller dates the commencement of a transition, the approach of a new era. Snowy mountains had hitherto been looked on by the crowd as blots on the face of creation. At best they had been tolerated, at a distance, for their practical uses in acting as frontiers, feeding rivers, and providing dairy produce. There was already, doubtless, no lack of sham sentiment. A rustic glade might serve as a background for amateur shepherdesses *à la Watteau*, or as a framework for a tableau of idealised pastoral life. But nature in her more austere moods was still repellent to the orthodox taste of the day, and was consequently neglected both in its literature and art. Haller anticipated Rousseau and de Saussure in celebrating the mountains as the cradle of an uncorrupted peasantry, of a race who had exchanged the savage for a civilised state, without having lost its primitive simplicity.[1] But he went beyond Rousseau when he proclaimed the picturesque charm of the scenery of the Bernese Oberland, and dwelt on the feelings snowy mountains excite in a mind sensitive to their appeal. In recognising in his poem on *The Alps*, the snowy wastes as 'the palaces of nature,' he prepared the way for Byron.

Haller gave out that one of his objects in writing poetry was to prove to the European public that the German language was not inferior to the English as a vehicle for serious verse. His success was amazing, and extended far beyond his own country and Germany. In forty-five years his poem had run through thirty editions, and been translated into French, English, Italian, and Latin. It brought to the young poet at least one startling honour. Prince Radziwill sent him a commission as major-general in the Polish army. 'Habent sua fata libelli,' a single edition of a thousand copies of Wordsworth's *Excursion* sufficed the British public for thirteen years.

In 1728 Haller returned to his native city and set up in practice as a surgeon and physician. His leisure was devoted to the study of botany, which was to be the chief occupation of his life. His 'sincere but heavy' fellow-citizens—the epithets are Addison's

[1] 'Hommes assez civilisés pour n'être pas féroces et assez naturels pour n'être pas corrompus.'—De Saussure in Preface to *Voyages*.

—were probably not favourably impressed by such versatility in a family doctor. The publication of his verses, including a local satire, can hardly have conduced to his professional prospects. He had, however, won reputation outside his own town and country. In 1736 he made a second tour in the Alps, which included the more famous sites of the Bernese Oberland. An unexpected *Deus ex machinâ* now appeared in George the Second, King of Hanover and Great Britain. The young University of Göttingen needed a Professor of Botany, Medicine, and Anatomy. They asked much of professors in the eighteenth century ! Haller was offered and accepted the post. Misfortune at first attended his change of residence—his wife died from the effects of a carriage accident in the ill-paved streets of Göttingen. She was the first of three wives to two of whom he wrote memorial verses shortly after their death ; the third evaded this tribute by surviving him. But the success of his teaching was great, and his many scientific treatises earned him a widespread reputation. The learned societies of Europe hurried to enrol him in their lists. The Royal Society elected him in 1751, and three years later he won the blue ribbon of science by becoming one of the Foreign Members of the French Academy. Kings competed for his services ; Frederick the Great clamoured for him. He wrote in 1749 to the president of the Berlin Academy : ' Haller is the best physiologist in Europe, the greatest botanist in Germany, and at the same time a man of genius. I give you *carte blanche* for Haller. Kings are too happy when they can get for a little money what all the diamonds in the world cannot purchase.'

Berne had now, after nine years, begun to realise the merits of her absent son, and Haller was no longer without honour in his own country. In 1745 he was given a seat on the local Council of Two Hundred, and eight years later a magistracy falling to him by lot, and his health somewhat failing, he could not resist the impulse to return to his native air and surroundings. At Berne he found administrative and political employment of various kinds. Ill-luck, coupled with some party prejudice, still hindered him from obtaining the rank of senator. But he received the agreeable post of Director of the salt mines of Bex, which he held for six years, adding to it for two years that of Bailli of Aigle, near the mouth of the Rhône valley. It was here that in 1758, while residing at the Château of Roche, near Villeneuve, a modest country-house that now serves as the vicarage, he made acquaintance with de Saussure and his mother, through an introduction from Bonnet, his friendship for whom dated from earlier meetings at Lausanne. A little later, in 1766-7, he was elected assessor on the Secret Commission that had to deal with the disorders at Geneva, in which Berne was concerned as one of the three mediating Powers.[1] But though kings were again begging him to accept chancellorships of universities, local difficulties prevailed, and he was repeatedly unlucky in the lottery which determined the elections to the Supreme Council. In the end, however, his fellow-townsmen, seriously alarmed at the temptations offered by London and Berlin, created for Haller a special appointment with a salary of fourteen hundred francs a year. 'This small sum,' Haller says, 'was sufficient, coupled with his other emoluments and the state of his health, to make him content to spend the remainder of his life in his own country.'[2]

At Berne he was fully occupied by his public duties and scientific pursuits. He wrote many tracts on surgical and medical topics; he revised his poems. Among the mountains he naturally took up with renewed zest his botanical studies. His great work in three folio volumes, provided with many admirably engraved illustrations, *Historia stirpium Helvetiae indigenarum inchoata*, was dedicated in the most effusive terms to his patron, George III. The preface includes a summary of his own excursions and of those of the collectors who travelled for him, and is a valuable piece of autobiography. Haller tells us that his disposition was all towards a sedentary life, to the study of medicine and books; but that, recognising that his health, never very robust, would suffer, he looked about for some pursuit that might serve as a stimulant and a remedy for his lack of physical energy. He could think of nothing better than botanical studies; these he hoped might compel him to walking exercise. At the start he tells us, 'rupes et horrida saepè praecipitia perreptavi.' 'I often scrambled over rocks and horrid precipices; for at that date I could climb the most difficult rocks without any fear of giddiness.' But his Alpine

[1] See chapter xii.
[2] Condorcet points out that Haller, Jussieu, Linnæus, Voltaire, and Rousseau all died within eight months of each other.

adventures extended hardly, if at all, beyond the 'alps' in the original and local sense of the word—the cow-pastures where the Alpine flora is richest. The recesses of the Pennine Alps were to him 'terrible solitudes.' The Stockhorn and Niesen, the Gemmi, the Grimsel, the Furka and the Joch Pass, the Scheideck, the Upper Steinberg and Tschingeltritt, the heights above Aigle— these were the scenes of his botanical raids.

It is true that in a letter written in 1760 he asserts that he has recently been 'half a league above the snow level in a horrible place surrounded by rocks, snow, and ice,' but a league in those days usually meant an hour's walk. He had to struggle in middle life against physical disability. In the same year he reports that he was very much fatigued by an ascent of the Chamossaire (6950 feet), a grassy viewpoint behind Villars, and next summer, at the very moderate age of fifty-three, he discovered that his own legs were no longer capable of carrying him uphill, and that no horse could be found equal to his weight, so that he had to confine himself to the lower slopes and leave the heights to his numerous band of assistants. But if Haller did not come up to the modern definition of a mountaineer, he was for many years a persistent Alpine traveller. In this respect his record compares very favourably with that of Rousseau, who never crossed a pass or climbed a single summit for pleasure. That Haller looked on mountain landscapes with appreciative discernment is proved not only by his successful poem, but also by passages in some of his minor works, as where he describes the Wetterhorn 'raising its unconquered peak lit by the russet glow through a dark crown of clouds above the blue ridges of the lower hills.' When in 1776 he exclaims, 'What a poor observer is this Bourrit! And what a misfortune that so much exertion and danger should be undergone for the sake of a view, beautiful or frightful,' we must put down the outburst against view-hunters to petulance excited by Bourrit's lack of botanical observation and exuberant style rather than to any indifference on Haller's part to the scenery he had sung the praises of with so much success. Haller was unquestionably irritable. An engraving of a portrait of himself, which he thought 'abominable,' made him vow to tear it out of all the copies of his book he could lay hands on.

The extent of the travels of Haller's swarm of young botanists is noteworthy, and goes far to show that there were no serious difficulties for hardy pedestrians at that date in wandering through the more remote valleys of the High Alps. The Zermatt and Saas valleys were entered, the St. Théodule crossed and Val Tournanche and Courmayeur visited. The Val de Bagnes, Chermontane, Arolla, Ferpècle were explored. In the Bernese Oberland the collectors penetrated, besides more familiar sites, the Gasteren Thal and Kien Thal. In the Grisons they visited the Albula, Maloya, Septimer, Bernina, Scaletta, Val di Fraele; in Canton Ticino, Monte Generoso.

Haller expresses the hope that his high flora may be nearly complete, but recommends a serious student to spend two or three months at the Baths of St. Moritz, or at one of the highest villages in the Rhaetian Alps, or at the hospice on the Simplon. ' Thus he would not pay a mere passing and breathless visit to the highest crests, but be able as a neighbour to despoil them at his leisure of their riches.' The choice of localities could hardly be improved on, and testifies to Haller's local knowledge of the High Alps from a botanist's point of view.

Haller's duties and pursuits did not prevent him from keeping up an immense correspondence, much of which has been preserved. His letters, on the whole, are disappointing. Largely occupied with commissions, botanical exchanges, and political details, they are only occasionally lightened by sententious apophthegms. He was constitutionally something of a pessimist and given to be troubled about many things. In politics and religion he was uncompromisingly conservative and orthodox. He looked on his dearest friend Bonnet as a dangerous freethinker, and on democratic Geneva as a city on the path to perdition. He stood as the champion of the Reformed Church, of establishments civil and religious; he was as a rock of refuge to men perturbed by the waves of revolution and scepticism that were fast rising on all sides. A mind so constituted and so active might have been expected to escape the morbid religious terrors fostered by the stricter forms of Protestantism. That Haller fell a victim to them in his later years must be attributed mainly to an overtaxed brain and an anxious temperament. His correspondence with Bonnet, which fills seven volumes of manuscript, deals largely with religion and dogma: he is dissatisfied with his old friend's laxity and his too great readiness to set up private judgment against authority. Bonnet tells de Saussure of Haller's agitation, and of his resolve not to aggravate it by carrying the argument any further. He writes: 'You know the sort of orthodoxy our excellent friend held—it resembled that of his equal, the great Pascal, and it is astonishing that the genius of these two men, unique in their kind, was not crushed under the overpowering weight of such a creed.' Haller complains in 1766: 'I recognise with pain that I grow heavy with age and incapable of taking exercise from lack of energy. Then I have no one to encourage or aid me. Thus our field of action contracts—once it was the world, to-day it is the town, soon it will be the house, the room, the bed, and the tomb.' These moods were, however, only a passing cloud. He retained to the end his mental qualities; memory and industry coupled with a sound judgment of men as well as of things. He could criticise a nation or an individual with equal trenchancy and shrewdness. Thus of Germany he said: 'Science is a chest full of coin; nothing is added by counting a hoard already in existence. The German man of science is only a cashier.' Again to de Saussure he wrote: 'I hold you happy to have devoted to nature time which more studious youth is apt to devote to books. I felt myself instinctively the disadvantage of this and drew myself close to nature, contrary to the custom of the Germans.' He could frame epigrams on politics: 'Tender hearts must not love. If one loves one's country dearly one must not serve it. A paradox, but unluckily true.' Again, 'Public calamities are the only remedies to check the progress of luxury and irreligion. From this point of view public misfortunes may be presents from Providence more precious even than peace and abundance.' In personal criticism of his contemporaries he could be caustic and uncompromising. Buffon he dismissed as too pretentious, Réaumur as too popular, Duhamel as too dry.

Haller's character and learning were such that he obtained a certain respect even from Voltaire, who on occasion was very polite to his stalwart adversary. Haller seems to have amused rather than annoyed the old cynic. For instance, Voltaire wrote: 'I shall always find time to assure you of my esteem, and even of my love, for I should like you to realise that you are very lovable,'

Haller in response is far less cordial. 'I do not care,' he replied, 'for tolerance as Voltaire offers it me. These philosophers, no sooner tolerated, would become our persecutors.' In formal communications he could sermonise his rival with a pulpit air: 'Providence is bound to keep an equal balance for all mortals. It has heaped you with benefits, it has crowned you with glory. You needed misfortune, it has found a compensation in making you sensitive. Had wishes any power, I would add one more to your gifts. I would give you peace of mind, which flies before genius, which as far as society goes is no match for it, but which is worth far more to the owner; granted this, the most famous man in Europe would also be the happiest.' In private talk Haller was wont to denounce the arch-heretic more roundly. Voltaire, in fact, became a red rag to him. He writes to de Saussure in 1765: 'He is born and will die a mischief-maker; he cares for nothing but his own glory. Vanity will lead him to anything. I view with horror men who employ their talent for the destruction of their country and society in general. At one instant he is working for Servin and benefiting a family; at the next he is troubling a whole city, or vexing right-thinking folk by the shocking impiety of his writings.' There remained for Haller a consolatory reflection; he finds relief in an exclamation, which is very like swearing writ large—'What a moment will be that of his arrival before the Judge; and that moment will be eternal!' But if Haller's temperament and his language were at times ecclesiastic, his rage did not last long. The patriarch of Ferney is condemned one day as a 'mischief-maker, vindictive and false,' but the next Haller writes: 'I do not want to vex Voltaire; I detest his passion for maligning Jesus, and even God, but he remains a man, and as such my brother.'

To Haller's qualities of heart, and also to the charm of his conversation, we have the strongest contemporary evidence. De Saussure may not be an impartial witness, but he is one it is difficult to question when he writes:

'It is impossible to express the admiration, the respect, I had almost said the sentiment of adoration, which were inspired in me by this great man. What variety, what richness, what depth, what clearness were in his ideas! His conversation was animated, not with the spurious fire which at once dazzles and fatigues, but with the gentle and deep glow which penetrates and warms you and seems to lift you to the level of the speaker. If he felt his superiority—and how could he not be conscious of it ?—at least he never asserted it offensively; he listened to objections with the greatest patience, cleared up ambiguities, and never assumed a trenchant and dictatorial air, unless on any question which touched on morals or religion. The week I passed with him [in 1764] left on my mind ineffaceable impressions; his conversation fired me with the love of study and of all that is good and honest; I passed the nights in thinking over and committing to paper what he had said during the day. I separated from him with the deepest regret, and our intimate relations ended only with his premature death.' [*Voyages*, 1094.]

Haller's summary comment on this visit was conveyed in a letter to Bonnet : 'I talked too much to your nephew.' Was there not a touch of Dr. Johnson in the Swiss philosopher ?

De Saussure's impression was shared by other visitors. Haller's fellow-countryman, Bonstetten, wrote : 'Haller was tall, well made, and, despite his stoutness, had dignity. Nothing could be finer than his glance, which was at once penetrating and sympathetic. Genius shone in his fine eyes. Of all the men I have known he was the most intellectual and the most amiable ; his vast knowledge had the charm of impromptu. He spent his time, as a rule, in his large library, where he was always to be found alone and writing.' Haller had many children, with whom he seems to have occupied himself but little. In Bonstetten's *Souvenirs* there is an amusing reference to the tall girls with holes in their stockings, whom as a boy he used frequently to see climbing on the rocks like chamois and darting in and out of the Château at Roche, but never succeeded in making friends with.

Similar tributes might be quoted from other contemporaries ; but I cannot omit the remarkable one paid by Gibbon in his Journal : 'I am little interested in a work on botany, but very much in Mr. Haller. This universal genius unites the fire of poetry with the sagacity and discernment of the philosopher : his natural abilities are equal to his acquired knowledge. His memory is retentive to a degree almost miraculous.' He goes on, however, 'With all his admirers, Haller has few friends. Where-ever he has happened to reside, at Göttingen, Berne, or in the Pays de Vaud, his harsh, haughty, and ambitious character has offended all his acquaintances.' I suspect that there were two Hallers, the devoted friend, and the formidable and, at times, truculent professor; the combination is far from rare. I feel sure Voltaire's acuteness did not fail him when he told his Swiss rival, ' you are very lovable.'[1]

[1] For a full notice of A. von Haller see Wolf's *Biographien zur Kulturgeschichte der Schweiz*, vol. iii. (Zurich, 1859), and Sayous' *Le Dix-huitième Siècle à l'Etranger*, vol. ii.

CHAPTER XVII

DE SAUSSURE IN SCIENCE AND LITERATURE

To the Genevese patrician of whose life some account has been given in these pages, the branch of physical inquiry which deals with the structure and story of our globe owes not only its name, but also the earliest serious attempt at a definition of its scope and method. Two years before the publication of the first volume of the *Voyages*, Deluc had hesitated to employ the term Geology. It was de Saussure who gave it official sanction and currency. It was under his auspices that the science made its first steps forward in the right path.

Before de Saussure's day an imperfect study of the earth's crust had, it is true, given rise from time to time to hazardous speculations on the part of 'natural philosophers' whose theories now survive mainly as historical curiosities. But his predecessors had been either mineralogists who pondered over fossils, which they surmised to be 'lusus naturæ'—freaks of nature—or possibly proofs supplied by Providence to confirm Holy Writ and confute unbelievers in a universal deluge ; or else ' cosmogonists,' who propounded such vague Theories of the Earth as could be brought into some sort of harmony with the tenets of the Church. When observation failed them, imagination was ever at hand to fill the gap. On such vague imaginings de Saussure put a check. He led inquirers back to the true path by insisting, both by his precept and example, that the history of the earth in its past ages was only to be elucidated by a sedulous examination of the substances composing its crust, and that this could nowhere be carried on so effectually as among mountains, in whose cliffs and defiles the successive formations and strata lie exposed to the eyes of the intelligent student.

While de Saussure was writing—the publication of his *Voyages*[1]

[1] Vol. i. of *Voyages* was published 1779 ; vol. ii. 1784 ; vols. iii. and iv. 1796.

extended over seventeen years—his contemporaries, A. G. Werner and Buffon, held the field and were busy in Germany and France in propounding so-called 'Theories of the Earth.'

The 'Geognosy' of Werner (1750-1817), to which de Saussure often refers, in so far as it was founded on observation was an inquiry into the nature of the materials constituting the present crust of the globe without any reference to their bearing on its past history. It made no attempt to read the record of the rocks. For the rest, it mostly veiled its limitations in a cloak of fantastic speculation. Its *deus ex machinâ* was a series of floods and deluges caused by the sudden retreat of a universal ocean.[1] Buffon's imagination took a more definite scope. He based a large superstructure of fancy on scanty foundations in fact. He was ready to offer a 'Story of the Earth' divided into seven chapters, or epochs. Yet, despite the eloquence of his style and his widespread reputation with the European public, his lucubrations inspired little confidence among his own countrymen. He shared the proverbial fate of prophets.[2]

While in Paris in 1768 de Saussure was brought into relations with two notable geologists of that day, Desmarets (1725-1815) and Guettard (1715-86). Both were concerned in the discovery of the volcanoes of Auvergne and the consequent argument on the character of basalt, in which de Saussure subsequently took part. Desmarets visited 'the glaciers of Savoy' in 1765, and published a paper on the progressive movement of glaciers.[3] Guettard compiled a Mineralogy of Dauphiné, and visited Geneva on his way

[1] Werner published in 1774 a *Traité des Caractères des Minéraux*. His *Classification et Description des Montagnes* did not appear until 1787. De Saussure's diary shows that he was reading the latter in the nineties. De Saussure, in his Index, mentions that he had not seen, in 1786, Werner's earlier work.

[2] The chapter on 'Glaciers' in Buffon's *Natural History* (English edition, 1785) is vague and full of inaccurate statements, which is less surprising since the authority he cites is Bourrit, on whose evidence he expresses himself convinced that 'the glaciers must always continue to have a progressive increase.' His omission to refer to de Saussure, with whom, as has been previously shown, he had been in friendly relations, is curious. Their minds were more or less antagonistic and their methods opposed. Buffon patronised Bourrit on his visit to Paris and introduced him to Louis XVI. (See p. 184.)

[3] 'Précis d'un Mémoire sur le Mouvement progressif des Glaces dans les Glaciers et sur les Phénomènes qui dépendent de ce Déplacement successif,' par M. Desmarets, *Journal de Physique*, vol. 13, 1779. See for further mention of Desmaret's treatment of glaciers, p. 431.

to Chamonix in 1772. De Saussure records that he liked him very much, 'though he had compared Switzerland to Canada.'[1]

Another contemporary geologist who carried on work of a wider scope and significance was Pallas, a German of encyclopædic mental activity who was sent as a member of a scientific mission to Siberia by the Empress Catherine. After six years of sedulous travel and toil he returned to St. Petersburg in 1774. The results of his journeys—several ponderous volumes dealing with various branches of natural history—were first issued in German. A French edition in five volumes, published at Paris, did not appear till 1788. De Saussure, writing in 1779, must have had before him at least Pallas's treatise on *The Formation of Mountains*, published in 1777. He writes in the Preface to the *Voyages*: 'Pallas's work is possibly the greatest and best model of its class; he has collected out of the vast treasury of his observations what seemed to him most valuable with regard to the formation of mountains.' Taking the Ural chain as a type of mountain structure, Pallas proposed to recognise in it primary, secondary, and tertiary formations, the first forming the centre of the range. 'These geological terms,' writes Sir A. Geikie, 'were not used by him in their more precise modern definition . . . the main value of his observations lies in his clear recognition of a geological sequence in passing from the centre to the outside. He saw that the oldest portions were to be found along the axis of the chain; the youngest on the lower ground on either side.' With this praise we may compare Cuvier's verdict in his *Eloge* of Pallas. He points out that Pallas's experiences in Siberia led him to the conclusion that 'as a rule mountain chains consist of a granite core flanked by successive zones of schistose and calcareous rocks. This great fact which he records gave birth to modern geology. De Saussure, Deluc, and Werner make it the foundation of a true knowledge of the structure of the earth, as distinguished from the fantastic notions of their predecessors.' It must not, however, be inferred from Cuvier's language that it was wholly due to Pallas that this succession of formations was pointed out. De Saussure had observed it independently, if he was not the first to give it publicity.

The work of another contemporary, the Scotsman Hutton,

[1] See for an account of Guettard's work, Sir A. Geikie's *Founders of Geology*.

one of the most eminent founders of current geology, and the chief of the early advocates of the Plutonic theory, was not brought clearly and prominently before the world until de Saussure's career was near its close, and there is no trace of his having profited by it.

In the building up of a new branch of scientific inquiry there must always be room for various types of intellect. There is need for both the flash of intuition and the more steady light thrown by the collection, collation, and classification of field observations. The former may often seize on a hypothesis which bears successfully the test of further inquiry. But though genius may thus aid and shorten the task of research, it can never dispense with it. It fell to de Saussure in an age too much given to theorise to assert the prominent part that fieldwork must play in all geological investigation, to recognise and enforce the lesson that the story of the earth was not to be revealed by flights of poetical imagination, but unravelled by laborious examination of the nature and origin of the materials of which our globe is composed, of the sequence of the different formations and of their relations to one another. His distinguishing claim to be a precursor is that he was the first in his century to recognise and insist that a great mountain chain such as the Alps, where the successive strata have been twisted, broken, and exposed, affords the geologist the most favourable opportunity for pursuing this inquiry. 'It is,' he wrote, 'the study of mountains which above all else can quicken the study of the earth, or geology.' I write, 'in his century,' for it must never be forgotten that Leonardo da Vinci, who, had he not been a supreme artist, might have been famous as one of the greatest as well as one of the most versatile of scientific inquirers, had two hundred years earlier touched in his Notes on many of the problems of mountain structure and valley formation.

'Il ne concluait pas assez,' said Buffon of his Genevese visitor. The criticism was not without some foundation, if the retort was obvious. But it was de Saussure's highest title to praise that he declined to submit his conclusions to the world until he had secured a sufficient base for them. He was content to be a quarrier, to provide material for the future use of himself and others. I say of himself, for Cuvier in his *Eloge* must have been under a misapprehension when he praised de Saussure for a deliberate purpose to refrain from basing any theory on his observations. It is clear from the concluding words of the 'Avertissement' in the third volume of the *Voyages*,[1] from passages in the fourth volume of the *Voyages*, and also from de Saussure's private letters and memoranda about 1796, that in his intention it was only a postponement. Had his labours not been interrupted by political troubles, or had his life attained its full span, he would have carried out, in part at any rate, his scheme, and have put forward as an outline of a History of the Earth conclusions drawn from his accumulated facts. In any criticism of his work it has to be borne in mind that at fifty-four, when he might have hoped for twenty, or at least ten, years of leisure to arrange and consider his material, he was struck down by successive strokes of paralysis. The last two volumes of his *Voyages* were issued after a second and more severe seizure, and after his fortune as well as his health had been shattered by the great convulsion of the French Revolution and the consequences it brought on Geneva. There is, therefore, a pathetic interest in the sixty pages of 'Agenda, ou Tableau Général des Observations et des Recherches dont les résultats doivent servir de base à la Théorie de la Terre,' appended to the last volume of the *Voyages*.[2] They form de Saussure's bequest to posterity, and it is a bequest which posterity is far from having exhausted. Of the problems he presented many doubtless have long ago received their solution, but there are still not a few which await a further and conclusive investigation. Nor were these Agenda his only effort in the direction of making use of his material. In 1796 he wrote to the astronomer La Place: 'I am going to work at a Theory of the Earth now that I have ended my travels. Well satisfied if I can explain the physical story of our globe, I shall leave the problem of its formation to those, like yourself, whose genius embraces the plan of the universe.' A memorandum of the same date which has been preserved and quoted by

[1] 'As to the theory, I have in this volume followed the same method as in the preceding ones. I have set down principles in so far as I have found facts on which to base them. But for the scheme I put off publication. I wait for the completion of observations I have in contemplation, which I need in order to enable me to decide on questions that appear to me still doubtful.'

[2] Published also in the *Journal des Mines*, iv. (No. 20), in 1796, pp. 1-20, and in the *Philosophical Magazine* for 1799, iii. pp. 33-41, 147-156; iv. pp. 188-190, 259-263, 351 and 359; v. pp. 24-29, 135-140, 217-221. It was also published separately at Geneva.

Professor Alphonse Favre probably contains the germs of what de Saussure had in his mind. The Theory of the Earth, de Saussure writes, 'is the science which explains the causes of the modifications which the earth has undergone since its first formation up to our own days, and aids us to foresee those it will undergo in the future. Our only means of arriving at a knowledge of these modifications and their causes is by studying the present state of the globe in order to remount gradually to its preceding states, and to arrive at probable conjectures as to its future. The actual condition of the earth is the only solid base on which it is possible to theorise. Reason therefore requires that we should begin by giving a description of the terrestrial globe. This description, in order to be methodical, must start from general features and come afterwards to details which should be gone into in proportion as they seem more important and less known.'[1]

Unhappily, all that survives of this proposed statement of the Theory is its skeleton. It was to have been divided into three parts. The first would have comprised the general results obtained by workers in natural science. De Saussure's intention was to describe the various characters of the rocks that compose the mountain ranges, and to deal more fully than he had hitherto done with the conclusions to be drawn from the fossils found in them. Since the earth's surface is profoundly modified by its outer envelope, the effects of air, moisture, heat, light, and electricity were to have been treated. The second part was to have been an exposition of physical and chemical laws, including that of gravitation; in the third part he proposed to arrange the facts set forth in the first section under the laws laid down in the second.

Had this programme been carried out we should doubtless have had a work of great interest, and one full of suggestions for de Saussure's immediate followers. In a sense it might have been only a temporary stepping-stone. For de Saussure, if prudent in advancing any new hypothesis of his own, was also cautious in dismissing those of his predecessors. Brought up to accept the theory insisted on by Werner and known as the Neptunian, he remained to the end of his life more or less under its influence.

[1] 'H. B. de Saussure et les Alpes,' *Bibl. Univ.* 1870. Read before the Swiss Alpine Club at Geneva, 1869.

Its author maintained that the solid materials of the globe had been formed under a primeval ocean, the withdrawal of which in some unaccountable manner into the bowels of the earth had led to a series of catastrophic floods.

It is obvious that, given such an agency, the physicist was spared much trouble in ascertaining causes for any unusual phenomena he might meet with. They could conveniently be put down to the deluge, or one of the deluges, caused by the retreating waters. Erratic blocks and moraines were accepted as among the quite minor monuments of Neptune!

The theory in its more extreme form has long since fallen into discredit, so much so that it was dismissed by Sedgwick as 'Wernerian nonsense,' or 'water on the brain'; but in its day it held the field, or was at least treated with respect by competent investigators.

Under its influence de Saussure was disposed to look on all strata as marine sediments; the differences between stratified and unstratified rocks he attributed to the state of the waters in which they were deposited. The conception of a slowly contracting globe the surface of which as it shrank wrinkled into bosses and ridges, hollows and clefts, which were left as raw material for the great sculptors, heat and cold, water and ice, had not yet fully dawned on his generation. The violence of the forces resulting from this contraction—upthrusts which bent one rock over another, removed some strata and forced others out of their place—was still wholly unrealised. It is true that towards the end of de Saussure's career we find in his Agenda traces of a growing disposition to question how far the theory fitted the facts, to look outside it for possible explanations of natural phenomena. But it remained to the end more or less of a stumbling-block in his investigation of Alpine features.

The most remarkable instance of how slow a scientific eye and mind may be to recognise for the first time facts that, once pointed out, become obvious to every tourist, may be found in de Saussure's treatment of glaciers. The 'Glaciers of Savoy' had been the prime motive of his travels. Before starting for his fourth trip to Chamonix in 1767, he had consulted Haller as to whether he could profitably write a supplement to what was then the standard work dealing with them—Grüner's *Eisgebirge* (1760). He might, therefore, have been expected to treat glacial phenomena with particular care and insight. Yet his contributions to the better understanding of the movements and action of the ice-stream are relatively incomplete and unsatisfactory.

With regard to the advance of glaciers valleywards, he recognised that the frozen mass was pushed down the mountain slope by its weight, and by the pressure of the snows in the upper basins, while he suggested that the natural heat of the earth, of which he exaggerated the effect, assisted the process by melting the ice where it touched the ground.[1]

He insisted on the main fact that the substance of glaciers, *névé* or ice, moves continually downwards from the heights towards the valleys. He was ready to hurl sarcasm at a foolish professor of Tübingen, who had confidently asserted 'that any forward movement of ice was a physical impossibility.' But here he stopped; he took no practical steps to ascertain the nature of glacier movement, or to measure its rate. This is the more surprising since the need of such measurements was already being insisted on. In the chapter on 'Natural History' in Laborde's monumental work on Switzerland [2]—published about 1780—the writer says: 'We have proposed to plant stakes on the glaciers, and to arrange them in a line with trees or other recognisable objects, so that the rate of movement of the ice may be ascertained.... We have urged this on priests and presbyters; will it be done? We doubt it.' He goes on in a footnote to tell us that Monsieur Hennin, while acting as the French Resident at Geneva, had seven years before persuaded the Vicaire of Chamonix to have three stakes set up on the Mer de Glace opposite the Pierre des Anglais, and that in the first year they had advanced fourteen French

[1] It may be interesting to set beside de Saussure's statement the concluding sentence of M. Vallot's *Annales de l'Observatoire du Mont Blanc*, vol. iv., 1900: 'The conclusion of this work is that the advance of glaciers is caused by the sliding of the mass caused by the slope of their beds, and aided by the thrust of the upper portions. Weight appears to be the only agent, to the exclusion of any action of heat.'

[2] *Tableaux Topographiques, Pittoresques, Physiques, Historiques, Moraux, Politiques, et Littéraires de la Suisse*, 4 vols., Paris, 1780. Owing probably to its unwieldy dimensions, the amount of information, both topographic and scientific, contained in this work has been generally overlooked. It was published only a year after the first volume of the *Voyages*. The plates (in some copies coloured) of the principal Swiss ice-streams are excellent, but there are none of the glaciers of Savoy.

(about fifteen English) feet. He adds that some Englishmen had applied the same test with heaps of stones and had got a like result. These rough attempts probably formed the basis of a corresponding statement in Ebel's Guide (1793), severely commented on by Forbes, whose own observations gave the yearly motion at the same spot as 482 feet! It is curious to find that Forbes' measurement had been anticipated by an observation recorded in the work of a Genevese pastor published in 1817.[1] A boulder that had fallen from the Dru on to the glacier had moved eighty and a half toises in eleven months—at a rate, that is, of about 520 feet in the year.[2] Again, it is strange to find that de Saussure believed that the middle of the glacial surface advances more slowly than its sides; although the dirt-bands, visibly convex towards the lower end of the glacier, serve to prove the contrary. Once more, the origin of medial moraines from the meeting of inner lateral moraines where two ice-streams join is nowadays generally recognised even by an average peasant. I can only endorse with regret the comment of Forbes on de Saussure's treatment of this feature: 'There is nothing more surprising to be found in his writings than the most unsatisfactory explanation which he gives of medial moraines.' It is fair to quote the passage (*Voyages*, 537) which called forth this severe comment. I have slightly abbreviated it:

'In the heat of summer, streams, formed by the melting of the ice, flow on the surface of the glacier and crevasses open, and as the trough of the glacier has the form of a cradle, the ice in the middle shrinks and falls, while the stones on the sides of the glacier [the outer lateral moraines] slide away from the mountain towards its centre. The accuracy of this statement is shown by the fact that towards the end of summer one sees frequently, and particularly in the larger valleys, a considerable gap between the foot of the mountain and the edge of the glacier, and these gaps arise not only from the melting of the glacier's edges, but also from their having shrunk away from the mountain in falling towards the centre of the glacial trough.

---

[1] *Promenades Philosophiques et Religieuses aux Environs du Mont-Blanc*, Geneva and Paris, 1817.

[2] In the eighties of the eighteenth century the Chamonix glaciers were on the increase. Of the Glacier des Bois Mr. Brand, in a manuscript diary of a tour in 1786, writes: 'It was really curious to see the green tops of larches which the glacier had borne down by its pressure showing themselves amongst the fragments of ice and granite.'

During the following winter these gaps fill with snow; this snow, saturated with water, turns into ice; the edges of the new ice next the mountain are covered with fresh debris; these covered banks move in succession towards the middle of the glacier, and it is thus that are formed the parallel ridges that move obliquely with a composite movement resulting from the slope of the trough towards the middle of the glacier and the slope of the same trough towards the lower valley.'

De Saussure's observation is here singularly at fault. Glaciers are not in the habit of waxing laterally by the help of plasters of winter snow locally applied, nor do they at any time of the year slope downwards to their centre, though, where the glacier has shrunk, old lateral moraines may occasionally rise above it.

Again, of the surprising abilities of the ice-stream as a sledge, or carrier, de Saussure had a very inadequate idea. He mentions here and there that boulders have been brought to their present site by the advancing ice, but this fact never suggested to him that a former extension of the ice might be the key to many of his perplexities. The idea of a glacial epoch, or of several, never occurred to him. The great belt of granite boulders that girds the wooded slopes of the vale of Sallanches below Combloux, the erratic granite blocks near Monthey and on the Jura, the vast series of moraines that encircle the mouth of the valley of Aosta below Ivrea, failed to tell him their story. He was too entirely convinced that all such phenomena owed their origin to gigantic catastrophes, or floods, to look for any less heroic agency. 'The explanation,' he writes, ' I have given of the origin of these fragments of primitive rocks ought to be sufficient for naturalists. They are aware that granite boulders do not spring up in the earth like truffles, or grow like pines on limestone. So the only possible difference of opinion on the matter is whether the transporting force was a catastrophe or a deluge.' [*Voyages*, 209.]

Controversy still smoulders over the exact constitution of the substance of the glacier. Students may argue or quibble over terms, but no one at the present day will deny that glacier ice possesses qualities which, whether we call it viscous, or plastic, or, with Heim, 'thick-flowing' (*dickflüssige*), assimilate it rather to a semi-fluid than to a solid body. Of the inner structure of the ice, of the character of its particles, matters recently minutely investigated, de Saussure took small account.[1] Assuming it to be a solid and rigid mass, he paid little attention to the features inconsistent with this theory which were subsequently pointed out by Rendu and Forbes, and were in his own day indicated—in a casual fashion, it is true—by an obscure 'Visitor to the Glaciers,' one of his fellow-citizens.[2]

That de Saussure, always suspicious of theories without facts, should have paid no attention to an ingenious speculation introduced casually into the narrative of a slender volume entitled a *Voyage Pittoresque*, is surprising, but explicable. In his own mind and writings the picturesque was always kept in strict subordination. But a paper on glaciers by a geologist of repute, read before the Académie des Sciences at Paris, and published to the world, could not fail to call for notice on his part. His comments were contained in the chapter on glaciers in the *Voyages* (section 528). Elsewhere in the work, and in connection with other subjects, Desmarets is mentioned by name, but here, for some unknown reason, the paper criticised is referred to only as by a 'very capable modern author.'

Desmarets' article, as published in the *Journal de Physique*, in May 1779, appears to be an abstract of a lecture he gave before the Paris Academy three years previously, in which he described the results of a visit to Chamonix in August 1765, made with the object of studying the glacial problem.

Desmarets examined most of the glaciers of the valley, paying particular attention to the Glacier des Bossons and the Mer de Glace. He noticed with a careful eye their less obvious features as well as those that strike every traveller. Thus he called attention not only to the moraines, séracs, and crevasses, but also to the structure of the ice, its layers, or bands, its blue veins and opaque white patches. He pointed out that the nature of the rocks carried and deposited by the ice showed that they had been brought from the centre of the range. But when Desmarets

[1] De Saussure, as has been pointed out (p. 152), observed and recorded in 1781 in his manuscript diary the veined structure of the ice; but, since he was unable to discover a satisfactory explanation of it, never troubled himself to call attention to a feature which, recognised by Forbes, led in after years to prolonged discussions.

[2] See chapter viii. for an account of the remarkable anticipation of the views of Rendu and Forbes on glacier motion contained in Bordier's *Voyage Pittoresque aux Glacières*, 1773.

turned from observation to theory, and attempted to account for the formation and movement of glaciers, his intelligence failed him. He had visited the Alps only at midsummer, when much melting goes on in the day and some freezing at night. He came to the conclusion that the upper snowfields were converted into ice by these daily alternations of temperature during the warm months. De Saussure, on the contrary, asserted that it was the cold of winter acting on the mass saturated by the summer heats that affected the transformation. Neither of the savants made due allowance for the results of pressure; Desmarets altogether ignored it. As for motion, Desmarets' idea was crude in the extreme. He argued that the diurnal melting and freezing, having produced blocks of ice, soon proceeds to undermine them, until the fall of one block leads to that of the next to it, and then of others, so that the whole glacier, like a bank of loose stones, cascades valleywards. De Saussure had little difficulty in dealing with so simple a solution of glacial advance, the main causes of which—mass, pressure, and gravity—he had firmly grasped.

De Saussure, if in glacier problems he made a less advance than might have been looked for, at least provided the technical terms in which we discuss them to-day. He was the first to substitute definitely 'glacier' for 'glacière,'[1] to give the Savoyard words 'moraine' and 'sérac' literary sanction. He invented for the ice-rubbed rocks the phrase *moutonnées*, which had previously been applied, he tells us, to a smooth, curly variety of the wigs then in common use. He divided glaciers into two orders—primary glaciers, that fill trenches in the mountains, and secondary, that rest on their slopes. It is to de Saussure also that we owe the first authoritative contradiction of the myth promulgated by Bourrit, of several continuous longitudinal troughs, or 'valleys of ice,' extending between the highest ridges of the Alps, and forming a common reservoir for their glaciers. He refers to the Chermontane Glacier as the only instance he knows of such a trough. In the still undecided controversy that throughout the

[1] Bordier suggests that 'glacière' is properly used for the upper basins, the 'névé'(?), and 'glacier' for the snout protruding below the summer snow-level. But this use, if it ever prevailed, was soon dropped. The form 'Glassier' is found in a document of 1605 preserved in the Chamonix Archives and cited in *La Géographie. Bull. de la Section de Géographie, Ministère de l'Instruction publique*, vol. xxviii. nos. 1 and 2, 1913.

last fifty years has raged with regard to the action of glaciers on the beds they flow over, whether they serve as an erosive, or as an abrasive, or as a protective agency, de Saussure took no part. That the ice rubbed off corners, scoured hard surfaces, and moved soft material, he could scarcely fail to notice. But since the records of the extension of the ice in past ages escaped him, he was never tempted to anticipate the rash speculations of the modern geologists who have attempted to credit glaciers with the excavation of the great valleys and sub-alpine lake-basins.

It is impossible, in an attempt to deal more or less comprehensively with de Saussure's scientific work as an Alpine explorer, to pass over the weak points in his contribution to our knowledge of glaciers. But it would be unjust to him to let them affect seriously our estimate of his general work among the mountains. The glaciers—those 'miracles of nature,' as the old Swiss writers liked to call them—had first attracted his youthful enthusiasm. But his frequent visits to Chamonix and his further travels had imbued him with the consciousness of larger problems waiting to be solved. He recognised that in the crags of the Alps the skeleton of the earth was, as it were, displayed to the scientific eye, and that there, if anywhere, was to be found the key to its past history. His leading object came to be the investigation of the great processes of world-building. Absorbed in this inquiry, the glaciers appeared to him as little more than decorative details in the work of the great architect, Nature. He found no time to give their phenomena the close study that was essential to their elucidation, and as a consequence he failed to realise that in former ages ice as well as water had played an important part in shaping the surface of our globe as we now see it.

In other inquiries open to the geologist and mountaineer de Saussure was more successful. If his modesty and caution in speculation had not equalled his energy and industry in research, if his reluctance to theorise had not been accompanied by an equal hesitation to discard the theories of others, he might have done even more than he did to advance the progress of geology. Yet the list of Agenda at the close of his work proves that his observations were leading him to question many of the received beliefs of his forerunners. For example, he realised the importance of a close study of the succession and juxtaposition of strata as a clue to the story of the evolution of our planet. In this connection he insisted on the value of the examination and comparison of fossils, about which the old naturalists had frequently made absurd blunders. He recognised in the Alps the typical structure that is repeated in so many great ranges, a core of granite and crystalline schists forming the central axis, flanked on either side by limestones showing a writing-desk formation—that is, dipping steeply on the flanks of the central crystalline core while their slope declines gradually towards the outer foot-hills, which are composed of more recent beds of softer material. He showed that the base of the secondary rocks in the Alps is formed of a conglomerate, marking a pause between the formation of the primary and secondary mountain chains, and that this phenomenon is again met with at the base of the tertiary range. Though at first reluctant to recognise any upthrust capable of raising the mountains and dislocating their materials, he was gradually led to admit that the stratified rocks had been originally deposited in a horizontal position, and as a consequence that the dip of the strata must be accounted for by the action of forces subsequent to the formation of the earth's solid crust. Wherever he found that joints, perpendicular to the stratification, were inclined at a sharp angle to the horizon, he accepted the fact as conclusive evidence that the mass of the mountain had shifted from its original position.

Conscious as he was of the great influence of atmospheric conditions in moulding the earth's surface, de Saussure did not limit his investigations to its solid crust. He was equally interested in the conditions of its outer envelope.

To the advance of the kindred science of meteorology he made very important contributions. It is true that he took up and pursued its study rather for its bearing on other branches of inquiry than for its own sake, and that his attention was mainly concentrated on the comparison of meteorological phenomena at different altitudes and the practical application of them in the measurement of heights. But his patience and accuracy in observation, coupled with his very exceptional ingenuity and adroitness in inventing and constructing instruments, made him the leading meteorologist of the Alps, and set an example to be followed by many observers to whom a wider field of observation has since been open. On so technical a subject only an expert can speak with confidence, and I am glad to be able to refer readers to the critical remarks on de Saussure's meteorological work with which my friend, Dr. H. R. Mill, has kindly furnished me.[1]

Professor Raoul Gautier, Professor of Astronomy, and now Rector of the University of Geneva, has called my attention to a particular observation made on the Col du Géant. He writes: 'At this date the question of the atmospheric or cosmic origin of shooting stars was still under discussion, and they were commonly held to be produced in the lower regions of our atmosphere. The great good sense and shrewdness of de Saussure led him to make two crucial remarks: "I have observed," he says, "all these stars above the horizon, and none below; this seems to me to prove that these meteors are only formed in extremely lofty regions of the atmosphere." He goes on: "The cause of these phenomena, though they are so frequent and remarkable, appears to be still unknown. Even the upper limit of their range is uncertain. It could, however, easily be determined. In order to do this it would be enough for two observers, placed at stations the distance between which was known, to arrange to take simultaneous observations of all that appeared on the same night, comparing them with known stars and noting their characteristics and the precise moment of their appearance. Their parallax would give their elevation and their distance." This is precisely the method which some years later was employed by Benzenberg and Brandes at Göttingen to determine the height of the appearance of shooting stars (about one hundred kilomètres) and their velocity.'

In his meteorological work de Saussure found frequent occasion to display his ability as an inventor. Among the instruments he constructed was the Hygrometer, with which he settled the problem of moisture in the atmosphere. He also contrived a Diaphanometer and a Cyanometer to test the relative transparency of the air, and an Anemometer to ascertain the force of the wind. He invented an apparatus for testing the sun's heat; he even attempted to apply 'bottled sunshine' to heating purposes. He devised a practical instrument for the study of the evaporation of water and ice, and applied his

[1] See Dr. Mill's Note.

experimental observations to the phenomena of respiration on the High Alps and on the plains.

De Saussure was also a pioneer in several branches of electrical research, and in 1766 in his *Dissertatio physica de electricitate* he strongly supported Franklin's views. Two years later he made his acquaintance in England. In 1784 de Saussure perfected a portable Electrometer with which he studied atmospheric electricity and that produced by the evaporation of heated water under various conditions. He communicated to Spallanzani, who was investigating the animalcules of infusoria, a method of killing them by electricity. The concluding sentences of his chapter on the 'Electricity of the Atmosphere' are characteristic of his mental attitude : 'Do not the investigations here described show by their very imperfection how imperfect is our knowledge of the action and force of electricity, and in particular of atmospheric electricity, its causes and relations with other variations of the atmosphere ? Happy will be the student who finds the time and the means to cultivate this fruitful field and to develop the truths of which it holds the germs.'

Again, de Saussure was one of the earliest observers to insist on the very important work water, by means of streams and rivers, has done as an agent in moulding the details of the earth's surface, in deepening valleys and forming estuaries.

While living on his estate at Conches, if deprived of a view of Mont Blanc, he could still feel a link with the glaciers in the Arve, along whose banks, as Senebier tells us, he loved to stray. He found occupation in observing the variations in the volume and the temperature of its waters. At the time the stream was highest the temperature was lowest. He accounted for this fact by showing that the rise of the river resulted from the diurnal melting of the glaciers, which increased the proportion of ice-water in the stream. A calculation of the hours the flood would take in reaching the environs of Geneva showed that the previous day's melting passed Conches early the next morning.[1]

It is also to his credit that he introduced new methods of

[1] See 'Mémoire sur les variations de hauteur et de température de l'Arve,' par M. Desaussure, *Journal de Physique*, vi. 1798. Observe the revolutionary spelling of the author's name! This was, I think, de Saussure's last literary output.

experimental geology, devising an elaborate series of chemical experiments in order to ascertain the composition of different rocks, and whether one variety could by fusion be transmuted into another.

Having been initiated by Monget, the explorer of the South Seas, into the art of using the blowpipe, de Saussure employed it extensively in mineralogy. He invented a method of soldering fragments of rock to small glass tubes for the purpose of submitting them to intense heat and decomposing their constituents. He thus ascertained the fusibility of one hundred and thirty minerals, and divided them into six classes, forming a scale of fusibility. His results were published in a treatise, *Sur l'usage du Chalumeau*.

De Saussure was not content with determining heights. He was very active in taking observations of the temperatures and depths of ten of the Swiss lakes, and on two occasions (in 1780 and 1787) proceeded to do the same in the sea deeps off the Mediterranean coast. For this purpose he devised a special form of thermometer capable of resisting the pressure at great depths, constructed on a principle which is still in use.[1]

During the last five years of his life de Saussure made several attempts to determine the temperature of the earth at different depths, a matter which has since his time been made the subject of more detailed observations.

Much interested by the efforts of Montgolfier at Lyons for the raising of balloons by means of heated air, he made experiments on his own account. He ventured a prophecy, the fulfilment of which seems close at hand, that aeronautics would one day play a part in mountain exploration. He introduced, not without considerable opposition, the use of lightning conductors at Geneva and in Italy; he also invented a self-adjusting windmill, with vanes that opened or closed according to the strength of the wind, the construction of which, according to the Report of a Committee of the Genevese Society of Arts, 'involved difficult and curious physico-mathematical problems.'

The desire to collect flowers for his invalid mother, the object of de Saussure's boyish rambles, had been the origin of his earliest vocation, botany. Under Haller's influence, it developed into a

[1] See Dr. Mill's Note.

scientific pursuit. As early as 1762 he published his *Observations sur l'Ecorce des Feuilles et des Pétales*, in which he was the first to distinguish between the cortex and the epidermis of plants. He dedicated the little work to his Bernese friend. The treatise, writes Senebier, himself a botanist, shows great patience and accuracy. He continued to the end of his travels to take a keen interest in the Alpine flora, but botany was before long relegated to a secondary place in favour of geology. In his last days we find him urging the future great botanist, de Candolle, not to spend energy on a branch of science he held relatively unimportant! If in his last publication he reverted to the pursuit of his youth, it was probably as a relaxation from the more exacting brainwork of his geological speculations.

This brief catalogue may give some idea of the activity of de Saussure's mind, the multiplicity of his studies, the ingenuity of his constructive talent, and his power of applying it to practical ends. 'He had,' writes Dr. Mill, 'such a gift of planning observations and devising instruments, that it comes as a shock every now and then to realise that a hundred and fifty years ago no one knew many of the facts that are now the basis of all our ideas of natural processes.' This reflection, I must remind the reader, applies equally to de Saussure's geological work; it is difficult for the student of the present day to put himself back mentally to the standpoint of the latter half of the eighteenth century, and we are apt to forget that the discoveries of one age—or even its undiscovered facts—may well be the commonplaces of the next. If de Saussure, for instance, failed to elucidate glacial phenomena, we have to bear in mind that it took the concentration of many scientific intellects to collect the facts and formulate the theories which are now in every text-book. If the earliest mountain explorers failed to realise the nature and extent of glacial action, their successors in many cases—notably in those of Tyndall and Ramsay—have greatly exaggerated it. Even now we are in the presence of conflicting schools whose respective dogmas, however confidently formulated, fail to produce any lasting impression on their opponents. In Germany and beyond the Atlantic professors and students of high reputation still advance theories that to many of those who know mountains best seem

Installation au pied du Mont Blanc d'un Successeur à M. de Saussure dans la charge d'Historien des Alpes.

DOLOMIEU AS SUCCESSOR TO DE SAUSSURE

incapable of reconciliation with the facts that nature puts before our eyes.[1]

A biographer without special qualifications in natural research may well hesitate before venturing on any final estimate of de Saussure's position in the annals of science. He will prefer to place before his readers the verdict of the Genevese Professor's most eminent followers and successors.[2]

In his own generation de Saussure's services to the advance of knowledge were universally recognised. My first quotation may well come from his contemporary Dolomieu; it is taken from an official report presented by him to the Institut National, under which he served as an Inspector of Mines:

'I feel proud when I am able to quote some of these great and beautiful observations of de Saussure, of whom I hold it an honour to declare myself the pupil, since his works have been almost invariably my guide, since it is from him I learnt how to reason on the great problems of geology, and the use to make of them in constructing a system, since he is one of the first and best of the men of science who treat of the formation of our continents.'[3]

A pen-sketch by Saint-Ours made after de Saussure's death still exists at Geneva, which shows M. d'Eymar, the French Préfet of the Département du Léman after the temporary annexation of the city, attaching to Dolomieu's shoulders a scarf lettered, 'L'historiographe des Alpes,' in front of a pyramid inscribed with the name of de Saussure. D'Eymar, an ardent admirer of

[1] The arguments of those—mostly practical mountaineers—who maintain the protective action of ice may be found in Dr. Bonney's numerous works, in my paper on 'The Conservative Action of Ice,' *Proceedings of the Royal Geographical Society*, vol. x., 1888, Professor Garwood's 'Hanging Valleys,' etc., *Quarterly Journal Geological Society*, vol. lxviii., 1902, 'Tarns of Canton Ticino,' vol. lxii., 1906, and 'Features of Alpine Scenery due to Glacial Protection,' *Geographical Journal*, vol. xxxiii., 1910. For the opposite view see Penck and Brückner's 'Die Alpen in Eiszeitalter,' 1909, and papers by Professor Davis in *Quarterly Journal Geological Society*, vol. lxv., 1909, in *Geological Journal*, vol. xxxiv., 1909, and the *Scottish Geographical Magazine*, vol. xxii., and elsewhere.

[2] Professor Zittel's *History of Geology and Palæontology* (English edition, 1901) is recommended by Sir A. Geikie as ' a work of extraordinary labour, fullness, and accuracy.' It is therefore needful to point out to students that the references in it to de Saussure (pp. 52-5 and 221), while as a whole appreciative, embody many inaccuracies. These affect mainly the field of de Saussure's labour, his mountaineering feats, and the titles and dates of his works.

[3] 'Rapport fait à l'Institut National par le Citoyen Dolomieu, Ingénieur des Mines, sur ses Voyages de l'An v. et de l'An vi.' (*Journal des Mines*).

Rousseau, was interested in the Alps, and it was he who erected at Servoz the monument to Eschen, the young traveller who perished on the Buet in 1800. Dolomieu's own memory is preserved in the title of one of the loveliest districts in the Italian Alps. He endeavoured to pay his master a similar compliment by naming a mineral Saussurite. After having been imprisoned in Naples on his return from Egypt and released through the intervention of the Royal Society, Dolomieu died only a year after de Saussure of a fever said to have been caught in Dauphiné.

Both Humboldt and Alphonse Favre similarly acknowledged de Saussure as their master. The former, who called on de Saussure at Geneva in the autumn of 1795, has recorded that his chief ambition was to imitate a predecessor whom he regarded as his model.[1] It was the perusal of Humboldt's works which awoke in the young Charles Darwin the passion for travel and discovery. Thus is the torch handed on by kindred spirits. Alphonse Favre (1815-90), in his *Recherches Géologiques*, attempted successfully to carry on de Saussure's work in his own field and by his own method of observation.

In Sir Humphry Davy's works we find this striking testimony to the method and talents of the author of the *Voyages*.

'Of a kindred character [to the writings of Dolomieu] are the descriptions of M. de Saussure. Educated amidst the magnificent scenery of the Alps, this illustrious person felt in his earliest days the warmest passion for the study [geology], and his whole life was more or less devoted to it. Possessing from nature a penetrating genius, he assisted its efforts by all the refinements and resources of science. In his researches he spared no labour and yielded nothing to the common sentiment of self-love. A constant inhabitant of the mountains, he has exceeded all other writers in his description of them. His delineations are equally vivid and correct, and as far as mere language is capable, they awake pictures in the mind. De Saussure has presented the rare instance of a powerful imagination associated with the coolest judgment, of the brilliancy of the ideas and feelings of the poet connected with the minute research and deep sagacity of the philosopher.' [*Lectures on Geology*.]

---

[1] 'Dites au vénérable de Saussure que j'ai relu cet hiver mot pour mot tous ses ouvrages, et que je me suis marqué toutes les expériences qu'il désire qu'on fasse. J'aime de marcher sur les traces d'un grand homme' (Humboldt to M. Pictet, January 1798).

Still more striking and weighty—coming as it does from a fellow-worker in the same field, one who, in bent of intellect, bore in some respects a singular resemblance to de Saussure, and who also imitated him in the literary form he gave to the record of his travels and researches by combining both in a consecutive narrative—is the warm recognition of the Genevese philosopher's merits which prefaces Forbes's work on the Alps, published in 1843. I give a few of the crucial sentences :

'Where,' asks Forbes, 'where are we to look for travels like de Saussure's, and why are comprehensive works adapted for the general reader and student of nature to be replaced entirely by studied monographs connected with some single science in some single district ? ' These are questions echo may still repeat with advantage. Again—' There is scarcely one of the modern authors with whom I am acquainted . . . whose writings can be compared with those of the great historian of the Alps.' Forbes resolved to travel, he tells us, 'not as an amusement, but as a serious occupation,' with de Saussure before him as a model.[1]

We turn to a leading geologist of our own day, Sir Archibald Geikie. The oracle may seem at first to speak with no certain voice. Sir Archibald indicates that it is difficult from de Saussure's works to ascertain definitely what were his views on many fundamental questions. In Sir Archibald's article on 'Geology' in the *Encyclopædia Britannica,* we are surprised to find no mention of de Saussure in the list of those to whom a direct advance in the progress of the science is attributable. Yet elsewhere, in his *Founders of Geology,* the omission is explained, and de Saussure's claims are summed up and appreciated as follows :

'The labours of de Saussure mark an epoch in the investigation of the history of the globe. De Saussure was the first and most illustrious of that distinguished band of geologists which Switzerland has furnished to the ranks of science. . . . His descriptions of a great mountain-chain form admirable models of careful observation and luminous narrative. Though he did not add much to the advancement of geological theory, he contributed largely to the stock of ascertained fact, which was so needful as a basis for theoretical specu-

---

[1] One of de Saussure's guides, J. M. Cachat, called 'le Géant,' accompanied Professor Forbes to the Mer de Glace in 1829, forty-two years after his ascent of Mont Blanc with the Genevese savant.

lations. The data which he collected became thus of the utmost service to those who had to work out the principles of geology. To Hutton, for example, they supplied many admirable illustrations of the geological processes on which he based his *Theory of the Earth*. It was under the guidance of the Swiss observer that the Scottish philosopher stood in imagination on the summit of the Alps and watched from that high tower of observation the ceaseless decay of the mountains, the never-ending erosion of the valleys, and that majestic evolution of topography which he so clearly portrayed. Among the illustrious men who contributed to plant the foundations of geology an honoured place must always be assigned to de Saussure.

'To him,' continues Sir Archibald Geikie, 'we owe the first adoption of the terms geology and geologist. This science had formed a part of mineralogy, and subsequently of physical geography. The earliest writer who dignified it with the name it now bears was the first great explorer of the Alps. We are able to fix the exact date. In 1778 J. A. Deluc apologises for not adopting the term because "it was not a word in use." In 1779 de Saussure uses geology and geologist as accepted terms.'

To de Saussure's position as a founder, if not the founder, of modern geology I have perhaps cited sufficient evidence. We must admit that he lacked the highest form of genius, the flash that reveals the causes and connections that govern the workings of nature. Where he relatively failed it was on account of caution, from a dread of premature guesses, from a reluctance to cast aside theories or explanations that had got the sanction of time. His endeavour was not to propound ingenious speculations, but to place on a sound basis of observation the two new sciences, Geology and Meteorology, to set an example to his successors both of the spirit and the method in which these studies should be carried on. He did this with a combination of perseverance and patience, and an indifference to personal fame, which have been rarely equalled.

De Saussure not only stamped with his authority the word Geology, he constituted the science as a distinct branch of geophysics, or what was then called Physical Geography. He made it the study that does for the past history of the globe what geography does for its present condition. Both by his precept and example he helped to start and direct his successors on the right track. He was the first to give the science a method as well as a name;

he taught its students not to make random and romantic guesses, but to collect, and reason from, carefully observed facts. He demonstrated that it was their business to use the picture of the earth presented by the geographer, and the particulars as to the composition of its surface supplied by the mineralogist, as a starting-point for ascertaining, as far as possible, the manner and dates of its structural changes. Geologists had, he argued, to pursue their task by close investigation of the material at hand, by examining carefully the relative situations of the rocks and their strata, and finally by testing their chemical composition.

To de Saussure's merits as a writer, apart from his qualifications as a man of science, many excellent critics have borne testimony. First of these in order of time (1810) comes Cuvier [1] in the official *Eloge* I have already quoted. De Candolle, Töpffer, Alphonse Favre, Sainte-Beuve, Sayous, have all paid their tribute to the charm to be found in the *Voyages* by the persevering reader.

Ruskin throughout his life was enthusiastic in his appreciation; he chose, he tells us, for his present on his fifteenth birthday a copy of the *Voyages*, and in his works he frequently refers to de Saussure in enthusiastic terms.[2] Yet in this country the *Voyages* are little read, and, despite the fashion for Alpine literature, command but a low price.

What are the grounds of this relative neglect? In his own day de Saussure was criticised for carelessness and a certain provincialism in his style, for the absence of the ornamental phraseology customary in works of that date, and for a homeliness alleged to be beneath the dignity of so great a subject. The public missed the sounding phrases of Buffon, the sentimentality of Rousseau and Bonnet, even, perhaps, the stilted and clumsy rhapsodies of J. A. Deluc, Senebier, and Bourrit. The modern reader will base his criticism on different grounds. His first and most obvious objection will be that the great work has no unity, that it is made up of various ingredients, which have not been sufficiently fused. Many of its chapters, he finds, are mixtures of a geologist's notebook and a traveller's impressions. Others are

[1] Mr. C. E. Mathews was inexact in writing of biographies by Cuvier and de Candolle. Their notices are not more than short articles.

[2] In *Præterita* he hails him as 'Papa Saussure.' Mr. Mumm has recently pointed out that Ruskin followed in de Saussure's footsteps by climbing the Buet. (*Alpine Journal*, vol. xxxii. p. 328.)

independent treatises on very diverse scientific and miscellaneous subjects, such as Glaciers, Hypsometry, Electricity, Meteorology, Subterranean and Submarine Temperatures, even Crétins and Albinos. The literary critic may further complain that there is no attempt at arrangement or effect, that the descriptions of landscapes are, with certain noble exceptions, apt to be colourless and baldly topographical, while even a geologist may find too many details of day by day observations, which might have been further condensed and better arranged.

The *Voyages*, it must be admitted, is not in its original form a book for the general reader. Any judicious publisher nowadays would advise the author to divide the material between three separate works—a volume of Alpine Travels, another of Geological Observations, and a third of miscellaneous Scientific Essays. French readers owe a debt to M. Sayous for having shown how easy it was to separate the travel from the geology and the science, and to present the former to the public in a convenient form. Except in the omission of the Preface, a valuable autobiographical document, M. Sayous performed his task with excellent judgment, though the reader may regret the absence of some of de Saussure's lighter incidents, such as the story of the 'Baillif' of Val Maggia.[1]

De Saussure's reason for publishing his *Voyages* in the ponderous form he did is intelligible. He did not write for the general public, or for the reader in search of amusement. The *Voyages* were to him his monument, the record of his life's work, put forth in order to aid men of similar pursuits to follow in his footsteps and carry on his investigations. He regarded his travels as a part and incident of his scientific career. Even the conquest of Mont Blanc, though to himself it might be a matter of intense personal interest,[2] he treated as a means to a scientific end, a subject for a chapter rather than a volume. Mont Blanc, he writes, 'is one of the mountains of Europe the exploration of which would help to throw light on the theory of the earth.'[3]

[1] An eight-volume octavo edition was published contemporaneously with the quarto volumes, between 1780 and 1796. It was reissued complete in 1803. M. Sayous' abridgment in one volume of the *Partie Pittoresque* has been frequently reproduced in France.

[2] Note his desire that Mont Blanc should be conspicuously introduced in his official portrait by Saint-Ours, p. 387.

[3] *Voyages*, vol. i., Introduction to 'Tour of Mont Blanc.'

What would his friend and successor in the Chair of Philosophy, Marc Pictet, have thought of his master had he committed such an indiscretion as to publish a work of Alpine adventure ? 'How little merit and glory there is,' wrote the worthy Professor, 'in risking one's life in feats of prowess in which the most ordinary rope-dancer will always excel the traveller who thinks to give proof of his steady head, or of his agility, in these dangerous *tours de force*!'[1] Such apparently was the view a citizen at Geneva, who was himself one of the few Alpine travellers at the time, took of mountain-climbing for its own sake. De Saussure was fortunate in having 'a serious aim' to justify and even ennoble his adventure in the eyes of his colleagues and contemporaries. A week after his return from Mont Blanc the Moderator of the Venerable Company of Pastors and Professors was empowered to present their late Secretary with the compliments of the Company on his success in 'carrying out a project formed for the advance of science.'

In the concluding sentences of his Preface de Saussure tells us that style and literary success were very secondary considerations with him. It is obvious that he makes no endeavour for artistic effect or arrangement; his one aim is to give as simply and directly as possible all the facts bearing on his subject, great or little, that he possesses. He does not overlook the incidents of the road and the humours of its chance encounters, or eschew practical matters, such as clothes, equipment, or even details such as the proper length of an alpenstock—de Saussure's was eight feet long!—or the best form of crampons. Above all, he is never on literary stilts; in the age of sensibility he stands for sense; though no one can read his pages, or, still better, his private letters carefully, without recognising that he was a man of sentiment. But he was averse to its public display; he was constitutionally opposed to exaggeration of any kind. In all he writes there is an obvious accuracy of observation and language, a mixture of frankness and restraint, an unselfish and impartial attitude that win our absolute confidence. He is not only a man

[1] See some very sensible practical hints as to the use of guides, costume, and nailed boots, published by Professor Pictet in 1800 in the *Bibliothèque Britannique*, vol. xiv., and reprinted in Leschevin's *Voyage à Genève et dans la Vallée de Chamouni*, 1812. These show that the amiable Professor was an Alpine traveller, if not a climber.

of science, but a great gentleman and a pleasant companion. An aristocrat who dreaded Rousseau's influence on Genevese politics, he had assimilated some of Rousseau's more generous ideas (it is recorded that Bonnet read *Emile* out loud to his family), and he had a very warm sympathy for the mountain people as well as a love for the mountains. This appears throughout his pages, but particularly in the chapter given to the Chamoniards, which is full of charming touches. He was obviously a shrewd judge of character, but he is never unkindly, though apt to be severe to anyone who trespasses on his forbearance in scientific matters. His reserve or self-restraint is sometimes suggestive, notably in his treatment of Bourrit, who must at times have been extremely tiresome.

The illustrations and maps in the *Voyages* are, I must confess, inadequate and disappointing. De Saussure's appreciation of art was, he says himself, limited, and his journals prove it. His taste for painting, so far as he had any, would seem to have lain in the direction of genre pictures. He refers once or twice to Teniers, and he had some drawings by Hogarth in his possession at the time of his death. He was certainly unfortunate in his choice of artists to illustrate his great work. All that can be said for the plates is that they are better than Grüner's deplorable travesties. Nor can it fairly be urged that there were no better artists available. In 1780 the first volume of Laborde's lavishly illustrated work, already referred to, was issued.[1] Between that date and 1785 the long list of craftsmen catalogued in Ebel's Guide were most of them at work. Linck, Hackert, Wolf, Lory, Bacler d'Albe, our countryman William Pars, and others were producing the innumerable prints, both plain and coloured, of mountain landscapes which still attract connoisseurs and are seen at sales. Unfortunately, de Saussure was content to go to the man who was nearest at hand. Bourrit, on whom he most relied, was meant for a miniaturist; he had all the prettinesses and pettinesses of the craft. He drew mountains, as it were, under protest; he was always doing his best to soften their 'horrors,' he was delighted whenever possible to introduce

[1] It is curious that in the long list of subscribers to these volumes there is not one from Geneva. There are over ninety from England, among them de Saussure's relative and correspondent, R. H. A. Bennet.

a *bosquet* or to turn a glacier torrent into a tranquil trout stream. In the little headpieces and in the illustrations to his own books we meet Bourrit in his natural style. At de Saussure's instance, and no doubt under his eyes, he made an effort to adopt a bolder method in order to show rock structure. But his plates are poor things compared with the better art of his day. Théodore de Saussure's sketches from the Col du Géant have some vigour, and for the date are creditable. But his attempt to draw Monte Rosa from Macugnaga is a sad failure. The most impressive illustration in the *Voyages*, perhaps, is one of Mont Blanc from Val Ferret by Bartolozzi, a Florentine artist, not to be confused with the famous engraver, or his son. De Saussure himself did not add any artistic talent to his many accomplishments, though he once tried to sketch Monte Rosa from Vercelli, and made some rough diagrams near the Devil's Bridge on the St. Gotthard. He missed the chance of giving the world the first outline of the stupendous obelisk of the Matterhorn. The Mont Cervin, as it was then called, seems to have failed to make the unique impression on the early travellers that it did on all nineteenth-century visitors to Zermatt.

The illustrations to the *Voyages*, however, if of little artistic value, have, as de Saussure himself urges, at least the merit of an attempt, occasionally successful, at fidelity and of an obvious desire to avoid exaggeration. But of the maps, though again de Saussure writes of them with respect, it is impossible not to endorse the severe comment of Forbes—' Of these it is hardly possible to speak too disparagingly.' After making due allowance for the date and the state of Alpine cartography, they are sadly wanting, even as eye-sketches. De Saussure must surely have been influenced by friendship when he gave the map of the chain of Mont Blanc provided by Jean L. Pictet credit for accuracy. The area of the sources of the Mer de Glace, it is true, is approximately indicated, but no attempt is made to separate the basins of the glaciers at either end of the range. Anyone who had climbed the Buet ought to have learned more of their relations. De Saussure, on the whole, contributed singularly little to Alpine cartography. It is, I think, evident that he had a geologic rather than an orographic eye.

The modern mountaineer is apt to think he has tendered his

mite to knowledge when he has put for the first time the peaks and passes and glacier basins of the district he is exploring in their proper places on the map. The modern geologist can ill afford to neglect the details of orography, but at the date of de Saussure's labours, to a mind full of the deepest problems of geology and absorbed in abstruse investigations into the past story of the earth, the exact relations to one another of a particular group of mountains may have seemed matters of secondary interest. The fact remains that de Saussure made little use of his opportunities to improve the maps of either the Mont Blanc or the Monte Rosa groups. The identifications in Bourrit's panorama from the top of the Buet, which with two exceptions de Saussure specifically endorses, are many of them fantastic. Bourrit's Furka is apparently the Bietschhorn, and his 'St. Plomb' (*sic*) the Monte Leone, unhappy illustrations of de Saussure's remark that passes being depressions in a chain, and inconspicuous in distant views, their name is often applied to—more or less—adjacent summits.

Finally, in all our criticism, literary or artistic, of the *Voyages*, we must continually remind ourselves that de Saussure's fixed purpose was to produce not an attractive volume of Travel, but a solid contribution to Natural Science, and that he subordinated all else to this intention. We must further endeavour to realise to what an extent he had to find his own way and clear a path for others in his scientific researches. In estimating the importance of his lifework we must compare it, not with our knowledge to-day, but with the work of those who went before him. There were some brave men at Berne and Zurich, but de Saussure was the Agamemnon of Alpine science.

Besides being a traveller and an author, de Saussure was a Professor of Metaphysics. In the eighteenth century Philosophy covered a multitude of subjects. The double duties of its two Professors in the Academy of Geneva[1] were set out in a scheme very alien to our modern ideas. They were expected to lecture alternately, one year on Physics, that is, Natural Science, in French, the next on Metaphysics in Latin. De Saussure was therefore

[1] The Academy in the eighteenth century had no local habitation. The 'Auditoire de Philosophie' was in the Chapelle des Maccabées, adjacent to the Cathedral.

compelled to devote much of his time and mind, and to neglect his special pursuits, in order to prepare discourses on a subject for which, it may without injustice be said, he had no particular vocation, while his life-study was dealt with by a clerical Latinist. It is significant that beyond the lecture-room he never took any steps to put his philosophic tenets before the public. Had not one of his successors in the University, himself a distinguished metaphysician, the late Ernest Naville, discovered the notebooks of some members of his own family who were among de Saussure's pupils, this branch of his work might have passed into oblivion, and posterity would have had to be content with the official testimony borne to de Saussure's success by his colleagues. This was of no doubtful warmth. The following is a minute of the meeting of the senate of the Academy on the 23rd January 1799, a few days after de Saussure's death :

'Readiness of speech, clearness in arrangement, choice and wealth of observed facts, judgment and wisdom in the consequences he drew from them, profundity in his views; these were the distinguishing qualities in his lectures, of which his numerous pupils in this Company will never lose the memory. He did not separate Physics and Philosophy from those great conceptions without which Nature, restricted to Matter, would present an inexplicable enigma. Natural Theology, coupled with the doctrine of the independent existence and immortality of the soul, formed an essential portion of his teaching.'

It would appear from the terms of this tribute that de Saussure had been fully successful in dissipating the fears expressed by the Venerable Company at the date of his election, that the preponderance physical studies were everywhere attaining might be detrimental to the interests of religion and the higher philosophy as taught in the Academy; while it may well be, as Professor Borgeaud suggests, that the obligation laid on him by the double lectureship helped to broaden his views and extend his intellectual horizon. In 1762, the moment was, no doubt, an anxious one for all established modes of thought, whether in politics or religion. In that year Rousseau's *Emile* and *Contrat Social* were burnt by the public executioner at Geneva. At Paris the great Encyclopædia was in course of publication. The philosophy in vogue was materialism; the doctrines of Hobbes, of Voltaire, and of Holbach. In his youth de Saussure's mind had been formed under the influence of two men who were both strongly opposed to this tendency of the age, and who clung to idealism, coupled, in Bonnet's case, with a broad Christianity, and in Haller's with a morbid form of Protestantism. There was, I imagine, little that was original in de Saussure's philosophical lectures, and their chief importance for us is as further indications of the bent of his intellect, and of the cautious, if open-minded, attitude which characterised him in all matters, both of research and speculation. It may be interesting if, without attempting to follow in any detail de Saussure's expositions as reproduced by Naville, I attempt briefly to indicate his general line of thought.

In the fundamental controversy that divided the philosophic world in the years preceding the French Revolution de Saussure was not on the side of Voltaire and the Encyclopædists. He was frankly opposed to the wave of materialism that was spreading from France over Western Europe. He affirmed strenuously the existence of spirit, and that the connection with matter, in which alone we know it, is temporary and unessential; he regarded body and soul as concomitants capable of action on each other. He believed in free will, without which there can be, he argued, no morality. He postulated the existence of a supreme energy or Being outside creation, who not only sets it going but keeps it running, who, in philosophical language, is not only transcendent but also immanent. To this Being, whom he designated God, he attributed a benevolence which calls for the worship and gratitude of mankind. He affirmed the survival of the human soul on the ground that, unlike the body, it is one and indivisible, and incapable, therefore, of dissolution, and he held that a future life is postulated as a sanction for morality in the present. He urged that the desire for immortality implanted in mankind may be taken as an argument in its favour, and that the creative will would appear to have endowed the soul with a tendency to progress towards its own ultimate perfection. He was careful to separate philosophy from religion—at any rate, from its established forms. But he avoided in any way committing himself to a positive attitude towards current creeds; he goes no further than the negative statement that there is nothing in philosophy to make a special intervention of God in the world incredible, and that we ought to receive with respect any alleged revelation that recommends itself to our intellects as coming from a benevolent Creator.

I quote a portion of the summary given by Naville of the scientific method adopted by de Saussure:

'While maintaining very firmly the distinction between philosophy and traditional religion, de Saussure did not regard this distinction as an opposition, and he was careful to admit the possibility of a special revelation of the Divinity.

'Science thus established in absolute freedom, what are the methods she should use in the construction of her theories ? This question brings to the front the secular dispute between Empiricism and Rationalism, between the pretension to construct a system *a priori* and the affirmation that it is by the observation of facts that we can discover the laws that govern them. De Saussure evades both these dangers. He makes a firm stand against rationalism, and his reputation, as is well known, rests in great part on his having proved himself an observer of the first rank without ever committing himself to a system. He was in the habit of telling his class : "We are not the schoolmasters of Nature, but the scholars of Experience." Following in the steps of Galileo, he urged not only observation, but that it should be conducted with the utmost precision. To count, to weigh, to measure, such is the task of the Natural Student. His feelings on this subject drew from him the impatient exclamation : "Some fool has said that accuracy is the virtue of fools," and he went on—" Yet it is the fact that no trustworthy results were acquired in Physical Research until men had learnt to give up flights of imagination for the rule and the compass of the mathematician, and to study nature in detail with the aid of the barometer, the thermometer, the hydrometer, the pluviometer, etc." [1]

'If de Saussure is very far from rationalism, he does not allow himself to be drawn by a blind reaction into the waters of empiricism. He recognises that observation is the essential condition of serious science, but he also recognises that observation, though the basis and controller of theories, is not by itself capable of their invention, and he asserts the place of hypothesis. "Analogy and hypothesis, in accordance with the use that is made of them, are fruitful sources of truth and error." It was in this sense he expressed himself in the essays which he was called on to produce in the contest for the Chair

---

[1] De Saussure leaves out the fact, well known to the historians of science, that he had himself invented or perfected many of the instruments essential to exact observations.—D. W. F.

of Philosophy, which was awarded him. "Geology," which at a later date became his favourite study, was well suited to confirm his views in this respect. . . . The geologist less than any other man of science can doubt the place and the need for hypothesis in the pursuit of his study. In the *salon* of the Society of Arts at Geneva there is a fine portrait of de Saussure by Saint-Ours. The geologist holds in one of his hands a hammer resting on the native rock; the other grasps a fragment of stone, but his look is upward and seeks the idea. The idea discovered, he must turn to the hammer and the stone to verify it, but the idea does not mount from the ground, it must descend from the heights of the intellect. This portrait is a speaking symbol of the true scientific method—observation, theory, verification.'[1]

The general impression derived from Naville's essay is that de Saussure's metaphysics were very largely mixed, as might be expected, with physics. While a man of a deeply religious mind, he shows very little sympathy with dogmatism. In this attitude he was the inheritor of Chouet and Turrettini, whose influence had done much to soften Genevese Calvinism. His attempted harmonising of physiology and psychology seems to have been very largely derived from Bonnet, who was far from a clear thinker, and by modern lights much of it must be judged obsolete. De Saussure took pains to keep his philosophy—he did not pretend that it was original, or endeavour to perpetuate it apart from his pupils' notebooks—distinct from his religion, and his religion almost entirely to himself. He was, however, a resolute opponent of the fashionable materialism of the century, and more than once gave forcible expression to his deep sense of the value of a religious faith in meeting the troubles of life.

Even in his course of Metaphysics the practical man and the scientist in de Saussure at times crop up curiously. Under the head of Logic he treats of Physiology, and in describing the functions of the senses, he deals with the means of keeping them in good order. He recommends out-of-door exercise, temperance in drink, and abstinence from tobacco, the solace of so many modern philosophers. He even makes an excursion into

[1] E. Naville, 'La Philosophie d'Horace Benedict de Saussure,' *Séances et Travaux de l'Académie des Sciences morales et politiques*, vol. cxx. pp. 92, 350; and 'Horace Benedict de Saussure et sa Philosophie d'après des documents inédits' (*Bibliothèque Universelle*, Mars-Mai, 1883). The passages quoted above are given by Professor Borgeaud in his *Histoire de l'Université de Genève*, 1900.

Eugenics. Here we recognise the influence of Tronchin, as elsewhere that of Bonnet.

De Saussure was not only a man of science and a Professor of Philosophy, he also to the end of his life remained a scholar. On the title-page of his *Voyages* he quotes two lines from Ovid, which might equally have served Darwin :

'Nec species sua cuique manet, rerumque novatrix
 Ex aliis alias reparat natura figuras.'[1]

On the first page of the last volume he cites Homer, and elsewhere Lucretius. During his long detention at Chamonix by bad weather in 1787 he diverted his thoughts by reading the *Iliad*, and a copy of Horace figures among the 'requisites' for his 'Voyage au Mont Blanc.' In his later years he wrote a confidential diary in Greek. In 1792 he gave the lecture already referred to at the Society of Arts, 'On the Lack of any Expression of the Sentiment of Gratitude in Greek Literature,' at which Gibbon was one of the audience.[2]

In the preceding pages I have endeavoured, to the best of my ability, to set out and estimate de Saussure's qualities and activities in the various stations of life which he was called on to occupy ; to present him as the centre of a family and a member of a brilliant society, as a citizen, as a professor and practical educational reformer, as an observer and experimentalist in many branches of science, and last, but not least, from the point of view in which he has been most generally regarded, as an Alpine traveller and author.

In so doing I have watched, forming itself slowly before my eyes, the picture of a very definite and distinguished personality. If I can to any extent succeed in transmitting it to my readers I shall have attained my object. To me the great geologist and the conqueror of Mont Blanc stands revealed in his published works, and still more in the diaries and intimate correspondence which I have been allowed to handle, as a singularly attractive figure. As a son, a husband, and a father, in every family relation, he showed a warmth of affection which happily met with a full

[1] *Metamorphoses*, bk. xv., line 252. The following lines run :
'Nec perit in tanto quicquam, mihi credite, mundo,
 Sed variat, faciemque novat, nascique vocatur.'
[2] See p. 359.

return. His letters to his wife remained love-letters even after their silver-wedding day; he was adored by his children, two of whom were inspired by his example. He made friends wherever he went, in Paris and England as well as at Geneva. He was, it is obvious, fond of society and played a prominent part in it. Full of human sympathies, an interested spectator of the game of life, he was himself an interesting member of whatever circle he found himself in, whether the *salons* of Paris, or the country houses of England, or the cottages of the peasantry of the Alps.

The Upper Town of Geneva at that date was, as we have seen, much divided into clubs and coteries, and its social habits and bent of mind were apt to be found formal and stiff by visitors from the Seine. De Saussure was free from this provincialism—still less had he of the proverbial dryness of a professor; his science was happily mixed with sentiment. He enjoyed conversation, and seems soon to have overcome his youthful shyness. I have quoted (p. 103) his avowal of 'a passion for all ladies at once charming and interested in natural science,' and the great ladies, attracted and perhaps a little piqued by the agreeable young philosopher, protested in their letters that they returned a sentiment which in his case seems never to have gone beyond friendship. Perhaps the most vivid sketch of de Saussure in society is one given in a note written to him about 1790 by Madame Necker:

'It is not without real regret that I give up the hope of seeing you this evening. You must be conscious of the charm which you carry with you in our circle; everyone feels its influence, but no one perhaps as much as I do. Often while listening to you and letting myself be carried away by the gentle gaiety which graces all you say, I forget Paris, or rather I feel I have found a reflection of it which is better than the original.'

At the same time, like most people who enjoy social intercourse, he had a considerable capacity for social suffering, and he did not suffer boredom gladly. He was constitutionally impatient of irrelevant or unsound criticism, whether in speech or writing. When he was really annoyed he drew off the gloves and hit out straight at any unlucky opponent, such as J. A. Deluc, or the German who asserted glacier movement to be an impossibility. Companionable as he seems to have been, he made many of his journeys without a fellow-traveller. He accounts for this in a letter describing his 1767 tour of Mont Blanc, where he says that his friends hurried him on from Courmayeur before he had completed his work. On the road also he was doubtless kept fully occupied with his notes, and gained by the absence of any distraction. In his dealings with that flighty enthusiast, Bourrit, he was called on for considerable forbearance, which (if he had sometimes to administer private rebukes) he never failed to show in his published writings. Young Bourrit's diary at Chamonix in 1787 shows that, short of letting them join in his expedition, de Saussure was willing to treat the worthy but vainglorious Precentor and his progeny with much kindliness.

In Genevese politics de Saussure's position was remarkable. Born in and closely allied to the old patrician families, he from his youth up clearly foresaw that a great popular movement was approaching throughout Europe, though he probably failed to anticipate how soon the storm would break. An aristocrat by birth and association, he was at heart a liberal, ready to work for the education of the democracy of the future. His inclinations did not draw him towards taking a part in the day by day politics of the town, in the constantly recurring struggles between the stubbornness of the Councils and the insistent claims of the burghers and newcomers. Separated though he was both by birth and by mental habit from Rousseau, whom his circle, and Charles Bonnet in particular, denounced as a rash and dangerous agitator, there was a fundamental sympathy in politics between the two men. Rousseau's dictum, 'An aristocracy is the best form of government (*i.e.* administration), but the worst of sovereignty,' comes near to expressing the ultimate object of de Saussure's efforts during his last years, when he took an active part in the attempt to remodel the constitution of Geneva.

Early in life, as soon as he was in a position to make his influence felt, he had come forward with a forcible appeal to his fellow-citizens to prepare for the new order by educating their future masters. At the time he was recognised by the unenfranchised classes of the town as their champion, and looked on with grave suspicion by his associates of the Venerable Company. The opposition, apparently unexpected, he met with on this question roused him for the moment to vigorous controversy, and left him permanently disheartened at his colleagues' narrowness of outlook. For some years he remained aloof from political affairs, until the times grew critical, when he gave his best energies to a most gallant attempt to save the Republic. He failed, and may, I think, truly be said to have killed himself in the attempt. For it seems certain that it was not so much the hardships of the Col du Géant in 1788 as the disorders which culminated in the murders on the bastion in 1794, which led to the succession of paralytic strokes that brought his life to a premature close.[1]

De Saussure's mind was singularly exempt from the foibles that beset so many investigators. Well content if he could succeed in laying solid foundations for others to build on, he was loath to waste time in disputes over claims to priority in discovery. His main object was to give his successors an example of the plan and method by which the new science of geology might best be advanced. The record of travel and research embodied in the four volumes of the *Voyages* remains as his legacy to posterity and his best monument. His fellow-citizens have held it a sufficient one, and it has been left to others to preserve his memory with the crowd by the erection at Chamonix of the picturesque group (representing Jacques Balmat pointing out to de Saussure the way up Mont Blanc) which records the most striking incident in a career full of the very varied activities to which in the preceding pages I have endeavoured to do some tardy justice.

[1] See on de Saussure's constitution and illness the medical report of his physician, Dr. Odier, p. 129, and de Candolle's obituary notice.

A NOTE ON

THE METEOROLOGICAL WORK AND OBSERVATIONS ON DEEP TEMPERATURES OF H. B. DE SAUSSURE

By H. R. MILL, D.Sc., LL.D.

In the second half of the eighteenth century the observational sciences were only beginning to differentiate themselves from the general study of Natural History and Natural Philosophy. Meteorology was recognised as including observations of atmospheric phenomena, but it was neither defined nor formulated. Observations of the barometer, the thermometer, and the rain gauge had been kept up intermittently for many years at a few observatories and by a few travellers in distant parts of the earth; but with the exception of Halley's Theory of the Trade Winds, these had led to no broad generalisations. Rapid progress was taking place in the construction of instruments. The barometer had been made sufficiently portable to be used for determining the height of mountains; the horrible diversity of thermometer scales had been so far overcome that three amongst the dozens which had been put forward had attained definite prominence and that of Réaumur was fairly established on the Continent. Hygroscopes, mostly based on the 'weather-house' principle of changes in the length of a piece of cat-gut by absorbing moisture, were common; but these were useless for comparative purposes owing to the want of any consistent method of graduating the scale. As to the measurement of other meteorological conditions each observer devised his own instruments, and the methods of using the instruments varied according to the fancy or the intelligence of the observer.

While the barometer was in principle perfect from its invention by Torricelli, its use was hampered in de Saussure's time by the clumsiness of the subdivisions of units of measurement. His observations were made in inches, lines (12 to an inch), sixteenths of lines, and finally tenths of sixteenths, the task of adding up and averaging a series of observations being thus a formidable piece of compound addition and division.

De Saussure was not so much concerned with the advancement

of meteorology as with the application of meteorological methods to the measurement of heights and to the explanation of the differences between atmospheric phenomena at different altitudes. So far as I have been able to ascertain he never proposed a system of national observations, nor attempted to map any of the elements of climate, an advance which was reserved for Humboldt in the next generation. Like Franklin, he was inclined to attribute more importance to electricity than to heat in controlling meteorological phenomena, though he did recognise the vital relation of heat to evaporation and condensation of water vapour as fully as was possible before the foundations of thermodynamics had been laid.

The most striking characteristics of de Saussure as a meteorological observer were his extraordinary skill in manipulating delicate instruments in almost impossible conditions and his accuracy in reading and recording. He differed from the majority of his contemporaries also in not making observations for their own sake. He always had some definite problem in mind, and the ingenuity with which he planned and executed his experiments was matched by the lucidity of his reasoning on the results. He had the mind of a true experimental philosopher, being singularly free from prepossessions and apparently quite without prejudices. He had the advantage of living at a period when no standards of scientific orthodoxy had been set up, and there were no recognised authorities whose views, in so far as they were erroneous, an investigator had to contend against. As yet such authorities had not arisen, and the field was free from all obstructions.

Chemists had already demonstrated the fact that atmospheric air consisted of a mixture of oxygen and nitrogen with a small proportion of carbonic acid, but the proportion of oxygen or vital air was believed to vary considerably from place to place, hence it was assumed that the healthiness of a district depended on a larger proportion of oxygen being present in the air, and the use of the eudiometer for measuring this proportion was popular with scientific travellers. The methods of determination were crude and the results obtained are now known to be fallacious. However, de Saussure and his son believed that they found indications of a reduced proportion of oxygen at high mountain stations, and this is in accordance with modern theory. The facts, however, lie outside meteorology.

The finest piece of pure meteorological observation which de Saussure carried out was on the Col du Géant at an altitude of 11,030 feet above sea-level from the 5th to the 18th July 1788. This may indeed be looked on as the first establishment of a mountain meteorological station, and showed that de Saussure had a very sound knowledge of what should be done at such an observatory. In those days there were no self-recording instruments, and de Saussure did his best to secure readings at uniform intervals throughout the whole period, arranging for simultaneous observations to be made at Chamonix (3445 feet) and Geneva (1230 feet). A full transcript of the whole of the observations from de Saussure's original copy was published by his grandson in 1891 in the *Mémoires* of the Geneva Physical and Natural History Society on the occasion of its centenary. Only a summary of the results appears in the *Voyages dans les Alpes*. Observations of a very accurate mercurial barometer which required much care were made as far as possible every two hours from 4 A.M. to midnight, with the definite object of ascertaining the daily range in order to find the best hour of the day for the barometric determination of height. From various causes, more often affecting the low-level observations than those on the mountain, a detailed comparison could only be made for the period of twelve hours from 8 A.M. to 8 P.M., but these gave results of great interest and value. It is certainly remarkable that observations extending over only half the day and continued for a single fortnight, should have revealed the order of diurnal range which has been confirmed by years of continuous observation at high and low level observatories a hundred years after his time.

He showed clearly that the hour of the two daily maxima and minima of barometric pressure differed with altitude. Hence he deduced the practical conclusion that observations of the barometer for measuring heights are best made about noon, when both high and low levels have nearly their mean daily pressure. In the morning and evening the range at high and low levels is at opposite extremes, hence at those times the risk of error in height determinations is at its maximum.

Temperature observations were made also at two-hourly intervals from 4 A.M. to midnight and compared with those at lower stations. These showed a diminution of temperature on the average of 1° Réaumur for 100 toises, or 1° Fahrenheit for 282 feet, an extremely close approximation to the value now generally accepted.

Recognising that there was a greater range of temperature between day and night and between summer and winter near sea-level than at higher altitudes, he calculated that at heights of between 7000 and 8000 toises (say 40,000 feet) the temperature of the air would be uniform at all hours and at all seasons—in other words, that the air at such a height would neither be warmed nor cooled by radiation. He also reasoned from the diminution of temperature by arithmetical progression as the height increased that reduction of temperature would go on increasingly until it reached the uniform condition of interplanetary space. Modern researches on the upper air show that this is not the case, but that the rate of diminution of temperature decreases as the height increases, until at about 40,000 feet the fall of temperature practically ceases and the stratosphere or portion of the atmosphere above that level remains throughout at a uniform low temperature, far higher however than the absolute zero which may be supposed to prevail in interplanetary space.

De Saussure took occasion to make a careful comparison between the readings of a thermometer freely exposed to the sun's rays and that of a similar instrument equally open to the air but shaded from the sun. He found that the difference between the readings was greatest in the morning and evening and least at noon. This he believed to be due to the fact that wind was usually strongest in the middle of the day, and the excess of heat was then more rapidly carried off from the exposed bulb. He rightly grasped the importance of using shade temperatures as the true temperature of the air, and also of securing a strong current of air across the thermometer bulb to ensure full contact. For this purpose he devised the sling thermometer, the instrument being suspended by a string which was whirled rapidly through the air.

Deluc had advised the use of temperature in the sun for reducing barometric heights, and loosely explained the variations in the readings of sun-thermometers as due to 'local causes.' De Saussure, however, showed in a convincing way that it was due to an inherent vice in the thermometer itself, the upper part of the bulb being thicker than the lower and thus opposing a greater resistance to heating when the rays fell at a high angle than when they fell at a low angle. This, rather than the stronger winds at noon, should probably also be held to account for the difference in the diurnal variations in the sun and shade thermometers.

De Saussure devoted much time to observations on the electrification and the transparency of the air, on the colour of the sky, and on the rate of various chemical reactions at different levels. Into these we cannot enter in detail, as they were all of minor importance compared with his researches on evaporation and atmospheric humidity.

De Saussure's name lives in Meteorology as the father of Hygrometry. His *Essai sur l'Hygrométrie*, published in 1783, may still be read as a model of scientific experiment and reasoning. He discussed the whole question of moisture in the atmosphere, including evaporation and condensation, and although the state of physical science was not then advanced enough to allow him to perfect a theory, he made very important practical advances. He showed that temperature was the governing condition of humidity, that for every temperature there was a certain amount of water vapour which could be held in the air; when that amount was reached, evaporation stopped, and if the temperature fell, condensation took place, or if the temperature rose, evaporation could be resumed. The higher the temperature, the greater is the amount of vapour which can be taken up. These facts were proved by experiments of the utmost simplicity and completeness, skilfully devised so as to eliminate disturbing causes and described with admirable precision. There are practically only two principles on which a hygrometer can be constructed for measuring the humidity of the atmosphere—(1) the variation in volume or weight of a hygroscopic substance which absorbs moisture from the atmosphere, and (2) the fall of temperature produced by evaporation. De Saussure experimented with both methods, but unfortunately he decided that the hygroscopic was the better. Meteorologists of the next generation reverted to the temperature method, and thus it came about that the dew-point hygrometer and the wet and dry bulb thermometers came into use for the determination both of absolute and relative humidity. The great disadvantage of these is that somewhat elaborate tables have to be used in order to convert the thermometer readings into percentage of relative humidity or absolute humidity, as the case may be. De Saussure adopted as his hygrometer a single human hair fixed at one end and attached at the other to an index finger which moved along a graduated arc as the hair lengthened by absorbing or shortened by losing moisture. The graduations represented relative humidities directly; but each instrument required to be graduated by direct experiment. The single-hair hygrometer in its original form gave good results in the hands of its inventor, but it was very delicate, required careful handling, and in the course of time the indications became less sensitive. Since the introduction of self-recording instruments the use of the hair hygrometer has revived, and it is now employed in the hygrograph, utilising a number of hairs instead of one, and acting on a lever carrying a pen which records the relative humidity on a moving drum. Thus, after more than a century of neglect, the principle which was so dear to de Saussure has again been adopted, and is likely to continue in use.

De Saussure used his hygrometer as frequently as he did the barometer and the thermometer, and by its means he discovered that the atmosphere was subject to great variations of humidity by night as well as by day. These he was unable to explain, but they were probably associated with *Föhn* (a phenomenon which, so far as I have been able to ascertain from studying the index to the *Voyages dans les Alpes*, de Saussure did not investigate). One interesting point noted was that at night the lowest humidities on the Col du Géant occurred when the humidity at Chamonix was relatively high. Dealing with the question of the rate of evaporation, he showed that on the Col du Géant a given rise of temperature evaporated three times the weight of water that it did at low levels, a well-known fact associated with diminution of pressure now used commercially in the vacuum pans for concentrating sugar solutions and the like.

De Saussure was unable to deal fully with the temperature relations of evaporation, because, as he regretfully acknowledged, there was no method of determining the absolute zero of temperature. The advancement of science has found such a method, and meteorologists are now beginning to reckon temperature from the absolute zero on account of the facility it gives to thermodynamic calculations.

The innumerable observations on storms, mist, and haze made by de Saussure in the course of his wanderings are full of interest, and he often detected facts the full explanation of which was beyond the reach of the science of his day. His observations on the formation of cloud were particularly interesting, and their value is not much affected by the assumption he made that the hypothesis of the time was correct which attributed the maintenance of a cloud in the air to the hollow vesicles of which it was believed to consist. He showed in a very convincing way that the cloud banners which are often seen streaming from a mountain are not at rest, but are continually forming where the moisture-laden air encounters the chill of the peak and evaporating as it passes beyond its influence.

The many lakes of the Alps received the attention of de Saussure less from the point of view of a geographer than from that of a natural philosopher intent upon establishing a theory of the earth. Thus he makes no suggestion of a systematic survey of lake-basins, but contents himself in most cases by ascertaining the depth of the part reputed locally to be deepest. This found, he devoted much ingenuity to ascertaining the temperature of the water at the bottom, also noting that at the surface. The temperature at the bottom he measured by means of a slow-action thermometer the construction of which was simple and efficient and the results obtained by its use extremely accurate. For use in lakes he had a thermometer provided with a thick bulb covered with non-conducting material and entirely enclosed in a clear glass bottle full of water. This was lowered to the bottom and left for several hours so that the whole should have acquired the temperature of the lake water. Then it was rapidly raised to the surface and the thermometer read through the sides of the bottle without opening it. Except for the slowness of the process, it is perfect and could not be improved upon.

De Saussure found that however high the surface temperature might be in summer, the temperature at the bottom of the deep lakes was always within a degree or so of 4° R. (5° C.). The cause of this low temperature puzzled him completely. If he had taken temperature observations at intermediate depths and at different seasons of the year, he would almost certainly have discovered the cause, which is the cooling action at the surface in winter until the temperature there falls to about 4° C., the temperature of maximum density of water. Down to that temperature the surface water sinks, carrying the low temperature to the bottom, but further cooling makes the cold water lighter, and it remains at the surface until it freezes. This normal process is of course subject to variations on account of the mixture of the water by currents due to wind. De Saussure appears to have been ignorant of the fact that water had a maximum density temperature, and the only cause he could assign for the cold deep water was the inflow below the surface of streams fed by melting snow. This explanation he could not accept, but gave it up reluctantly, bringing forward all the arguments against it in great detail, and concluding the whole matter with : ' En attendant, je crois pouvoir affirmer qu'il n'y a aucun principe généralement reconnu qui puisse rendre une raison satisfaisante du froid de nos lacs.'

Perhaps de Saussure was hindered in his reasoning by including in the same discussion the phenomena of cold air issuing from the ground in certain localities even in summer. This he accounted for by the cooling by evaporation of water in the passages by which air stored in caverns found its way to the surface. This explanation he confirmed by experiment ; but, curiously enough, he imagined that the cooling from this cause could not lower the temperature of air by more than 3° R., one of the few instances of failure to interpret aright the results of his experiments. In this case I am inclined to attribute the cold air to the downward flow of air chilled by radiation or by contact with snow on mountain slopes through scree material which prevents free mixture with the atmosphere ; but I am not familiar with recent work on this phenomenon, which may have another explanation.

De Saussure also linked his observations on the temperature of deep lakes with those on the temperature of the soil. He made experiments for three years with thermometers at depths of two to six feet, and also with similar thermometers at the bottom of a pit about thirty feet deep. He found that the seasonal range of temperature decreased and the period was retarded as the depth increased, but on the average the deeper he went the colder it was. He was aware of the fact that deep-seated springs were usually warm and that in deep mines the heat became very great ; but he attributed this heat to chemical action, or, as he put it, 'fermentation,' and supposed it to be a mere local disturbance of the normal fall of temperature towards the centre of the Earth. He allowed, however, that more observations were necessary to settle the question. He understood that at a certain depth in the ground the effect of the seasons disappeared ; but he did not see that, in order to ascertain the real temperature of the Earth's crust, the observations must be continued far beyond this depth. Had he known that the depth to which the mean annual temperature of the soil continues to diminish is greater in polar climates than in temperate, and in temperate climates than in tropical, he might have been less confident as to the probability of a cool interior. Throughout his researches he seems to have missed the powerful effect of winter cold alternating with summer heat.

One obstacle to belief in the general fall of temperature with depth below the surface was Donati's observation that the temperature of the deep parts of the Mediterranean was 10° R. at the bottom. De Saussure had a special slow-action thermometer made to test this statement. It had a thick glass bulb an inch in diameter, was filled with spirits of wine, and the bulb was embedded in a ball of soft wax more than six inches in diameter, and the whole enclosed in an iron-bound wooden box. This instrument required many hours before it took the temperature of its surroundings ; but once it did so a long time elapsed before the temperature changed by a perceptible fraction of a degree. On two occasions off the coast of the Riviera this instrument was anchored out for a night, once in 886, and once in 1800 feet of water. Each time the temperature was found to be 10·6° R. De Saussure could not doubt the accuracy of his observations, which have, indeed, been fully confirmed by subsequent work, but he could not reconcile them with the low temperature of the Swiss lakes. He did indeed suggest the possibility of a rise of temperature in the deep sea due to fermentation; but he did not lay much stress on this, and looked on the matter as one only to be settled by future observations. Had he only known that the high temperature at great depths is confined to tropical and warm temperate seas shut off by barriers from the ocean (in which the bottom temperature rarely rises more than a degree above 0° R.), he would doubtless have elaborated a theory of the Earth with a cold centre to which so many of his imperfect observations pointed. As it was, however, he took the Mediterranean as 'the sea,' and wisely turned his thoughts to more profitable channels.

The inventive power and the ingenious devices to avoid error are as obvious in the work on deep temperature as on hygrometry, but the latter subject was free from the disturbing causes which baffled all eighteenth-century observers of the physical conditions of lakes and seas.

Erratum

Graustock, p. 143. De Saussure did not climb this summit but the Ochsenstock, or Kopf (see p. 342).

LIST OF THE PRINCIPAL PUBLISHED WORKS AND SCIENTIFIC PAPERS OF HORACE BENEDICT DE SAUSSURE [1]

Dissertatio Physica de Igne. 4to, pp. 36. Genevae, 1758.

Observations sur l'Ecorce des Feuilles et des Pétales des Plantes. 12mo, pp. xxiii+102. Genève, 1762.

Exposition abrégée de l'Utilité des Conducteurs Electriques. 4to, pp. 9. Genève, 1771.

Description des Effets du Tonnerre, observés à Naples dans la Maison de Mylord Tylney. In *Observations sur la Physique*, etc., vol. ii. pp. 442-450. Paris, 1773.

Projet de Réforme pour le Collège de Genève. 8vo, pp. 74. Genève, 1774.

Eclaircissemens sur le Projet de Réforme pour le Collège de Genève. 8vo, pp. ix+134. Genève, 1774.

Voyages dans les Alpes, précédés d'un Essai sur l'Histoire Naturelle des Environs de Genève. 4 vols, 4to, Neuchâtel, 1779, 1786, 1796, 1796. Also printed in 8 vols. 8vo, Neuchâtel, 1780-1796.

Voyages dans les Alpes. Partie Pittoresque des Ouvrages de H. B. de Saussure. 12mo, pp. xxvii+396. Genève et Paris, 1834. (With an introduction by A. Sayous.)

Essais sur l'Hygrométrie. 4to, pp. xiv+367. Neuchâtel, 1783. Also printed in an 8vo edition, pp. xii+524. Neuchâtel, 1783.

Lettre à Son Excellence M. le Chevalier Hamilton . . . sur la Géographie de l'Italie. In *Observations sur la Physique*, etc., vol. vii. pp. 19-38. Paris, 1784.

Lettre de M. de Saussure à M. Faujas de Saint-Fond. In *Description des Expériences Aérostatiques de MM. de Montgolfier, par Faujas de Saint-Fond*, vol. ii. pp. 112-27. Paris 1784.

Lettre de M. de Saussure à M. l'Abbé Monget le jeune sur l'Usage du Chalumeau. In *Observations sur la Physique*, etc., vol. xxvi. pp. 409-13. Paris 1785.

---

[1] This list is probably incomplete, and may be added to by a more thorough search in periodicals of the date, *e.g.* the *Journal des Mines*, the *Journal de Paris*, *Observations sur la Physique*, and the *Mémoires de l'Académie Royale de Turin*.

Défense de l'Hygromètre à Cheveu. [In *Observations sur la Physique*, etc. vol. xxxi. pp. 24-45, 98-107. Paris, 1787. Reprinted as a separate volume]. 12mo, pp. 82. Genève, 1788.

Relation abrégée d'un Voyage à la Cime du Mont-Blanc. 8vo, p. 32. Genève, 1787.

Description d'un Diaphanomètre ou d'un Appareil destiné à mesurer l'intensité de la Couleur bleue du Ciel. In the *Mémoires de l'Académie Royale de Turin*, vol. iv. pp. 425-53. Turin, 1788-1789.

Description d'un Cyanomètre ou d'un Appareil destiné à mesurer la Transparence de l'Air. In the *Mémoires de l'Académie Royale de Turin*, vol. iv. pp. 409-24. Turin, 1788-1789.

De la Constitution Physique de l'Italie. In *Voyage en Italie, par M. de la Lande*, vol. i. pp. 45-48. Genève, 1790.

Description de deux Nouvelles Espèces de Trémelles douées d'un mouvement spontané. In *Observations sur la Physique*, etc., vol. xxxvi. pp. 401-9. Paris, 1791.

Sur les Collines Volcaniques du Brisgau. In the *Journal de Physique*, vol. i. pp. 325-62. Paris, An II. (1793).

Eloge Historique de Charles Bonnet. 12mo, pp. vii+32. Genève, 1793.

Notice sur la Mine de Fer de Saint-George en Maurienne. In the *Journal des Mines*, vol. i. pp. 56-61. Paris, An III. (1794).

Agenda ou Tableau Général des Observations et des Recherches dont les Résultats doivent servir de base à la Théorie de la Terre. In the *Journal des Mines*, vol. iv. pp. 2-70. Reprinted in *Voyages dans les Alpes*, vol. iv. (vol. viii. of the 8vo edition), and as a separate volume, 12mo, pp. iv+56. Genève, 1796.

Rapport et projet de Loi du Comité d'Instruction Publique. Lu à l'Assemblée Nationale le 9e Août 1793 par les Citoyens Desaussure et Bourrit fils. 8vo, pp. 91. Genève, 1793.

Mémoire sur les Variations de Hauteur et de Température de l'Arve. In the *Journal de Physique*, vol iv. pp. 50-55. Paris, An VI (1797).

INDEX

AAR GLACIERS, 17, 156, 192, 280.
Aarburg Castle, 156 n.
Academy, French, of Letters, 24, 209.
—— —— of Sciences, 358, 382, 403, 404, 413, 431.
—— of Sciences of Berlin, 74, 413.
—— Genevese. See Geneva.
Addison, Joseph, 21, 28, 58, 412.
Aeronautics, 413, 437.
Aigle, 413, 415.
Airolo, 159-61.
Aix (Provence), 331.
—— (Savoy), 130, 376.
Alagna, 8, 267, 271.
Albula Pass, 416.
Alembert, Jean Le Rond d', 123.
Aletsch Glacier, 18 n., 280.
Allée Blanche, 148, 192, 255.
Alps, Graian, 232, 273, 274, 278, 440.
—— Italian, 232, 273, 274.
—— Maritime, 348, 440.
—— Pennine, 32, 274, 280.
—— Rhaetian, 15, 184, 416.
Altdorf, 162, 163.
Altmann, J. G., 17.
Amiel, H. F., 391, 400.
Amsterdam, 99-102.
Annecy, 54.
Antibes, 330.
Antoine, Duke of Lorraine, 47.
Anzasca, Val, 262-7.
Aosta, 128, 274, 279.
—— Val d', 150, 232, 242, 249, 271, 273, 274, 278, 325, 327, 430.
Apennines, 4, 135.
Arathon d'Alex, Bishop Jean d', 62
Argentière, 73.
—— Aiguille d', 52, 166, 232.
Arnod, P. A., 243.
Arolla, 280, 416.
Auvergne, 96, 290, 321.
—— volcanoes of, 422.
Avienus. See Vogel.
Ayas, Val d', 277, 280.
Aymon, Count of Geneva, 61.

BACLER D'ALBE, 260, 446.
Baden, 5.
Bagnes, Val de, 280, 333, 416.

Balloons, 208, 209, 340, 341, 437.
Balmat, Alexis, 252.
—— Jacques (du Mont Blanc), 71, 183, 211-21, 229, 234, 239-41, 253, 259, 260, 285.
—— Pierre, 164, 200, 203, 215, 221, 230.
Banio, 270.
Banks, Sir Joseph, 105, 106, 108, 117 n., 353.
Barberini, Banneret, 152.
Bartolozzi, 447.
Basle, 134, 342, 357, 410.
Basodino, 159.
Bassi, Dr. Laura, 130.
Bastille, fall of, 266, 355.
Baume, Antoine, 96.
Baume, Dr., 140.
Bavona, Val, 159.
Beauclerk, Lady Diana, 107.
—— Topham, 107.
Beaufoy, Colonel Mark, 221 n., 235, 237, 249.
Beaumont, Albanis, 191.
Beauteville, M. de, 310.
Becca di Nona, 274.
Beckford, William, 25, 45.
Bellinzona, 159.
Bennet, R. H. A., 370, 446 n.
Benningborough Hall, 107, 110.
Béranger, J. P., 184, 193.
Berlin, 382, 383, 414.
Bernard, Great Saint, Pass, 61, 90, 128, 151, 279.
—— Little Saint, Pass, 274.
Berne, 19, 63, 121, 131, 134, 170, 344, 374.
—— Canton of, 294, 297, 300, 301, 307, 339.
Bernina, 280, 416.
Bernis, Cardinal de, 123, 131.
Bertrand, Prof. Louis, 74, 315, 363, 365.
Bex, 59.
Bignasco, 159.
Blosset, Miss H., 105-8.
Boissier, Albertine Amélie. See Saussure, Mme. H. B. de.
—— Anne Caroline (Minette). See Tronchin, Mme. J. L.

Boissier, Jean Jacques André, 77, 85.
—— Jeanne Françoise. *See* Turrettini, Mme. J. A.
Boissière, La, 352, 361.
Bologna, 130.
Bonhomme, Col du, 89, 146, 274.
Bonnet, Charles, 21, 52, 57-9, 66, 84, 182, 257, 258, 281, 308, 323, 336, 341, 344, 368, 402-9, 446, 450, 453, 455.
—— Mme., 57, 132, 258, 341, 406.
Bonneville, 60, 220.
Bonney, Prof. T. G., 401.
Bonstetten, C. V. de, 79, 118, 406, 419.
Bordier, A. C., 145, 192, 194-6.
Borgeaud, Prof. Charles, 2, 449.
Bormio, Baths of, 5, 7.
Borromean Islands, 129, 159.
—— Count, 159, 266.
Bosco, Val di, 158.
Boscowitz, Père R. J., 126, 134.
Bosses du Dromodaire, 201, 210, 342.
Bossons, Glacier des, 68, 195, 198, 211, 221, 225, 431.
Bourbon, Duchess of, 123.
—— l'Archambault, 382.
Bourrit, Charles, 221, 235, 247, 248, 259, 366, 455.
—— Isaac, 202-5, 207, 261, 366, 369.
—— Marc Théodore, 26, 27, 71, 175, 181-93, 207, 209, 211-13, 223, 234-9, 243, 245, 250, 257, 258, 259, 285, 316, 323, 334, 366, 367, 446-8, 455.
Boyon, Pierre, 189.
Brand, Mr., 166 *n.*, 212, 326, 327, 334, 429 *n.*
Brandes, 435.
Breithorn, 282.
—— Cime Brune du. *See* Klein Matterhorn.
Brenner Pass, 29, 134.
Brenva Glacier, 90.
Breuil, 272, 274, 276, 360.
Brévent, 68, 87, 221.
Brézé, Marquis de, 351.
Bridel, Doyen, 154.
Bridgewater Canal, 114.
Brienz, 156.
Brigue, 5.
Brisgau, 281, 358, 380.
Bristol, Frederick Augustus, fourth Earl of, and Lord Bishop of Derry, 383.
British Museum, 118, 133.
Buccioletto, 270.
Buet, 173, 175-96, 215, 245, 321, 440, 447, 448.
Buffon, 92, 93, 162, 184, 209, 404, 417, 422, 424.
Burghley, 109.
Burnet, Gilbert, 15, 172.

Burnet, William, 16.
Burney, Miss, 176.
Buxton, 115.
Byers, James, 131.
Byron, Lord, 24, 28, 43, 98, 176, 399, 412.

Cachat, Jean Michel ('le Géant'), 221, 246, 249 *n.*, 250, 441 *n.*
Caenwood House, 109.
Calvin, John. 19, 34, 36, 99, 298, 299, 370.
Cambridge, 118.
Candolle, A. P. de, 49, 50, 53, 60, 119, 389, 438, 443.
Cannes, 330, 348.
Canterbury, 104.
Cap Roux, 330, 347.
Carrel, Chanoine, 274.
Cartography, Alpine, 447.
Castle Howard, 110.
Catania, 133.
Catherine I, Empress of Russia, 50, 423.
Caucasus, 36, 72, 104, 226, 233, 251, 266.
Caume, Montagne de, 348.
Cavendish, Lord John, 107, 109, 114.
Cerentino, 158, 281.
Cervin, Mont. *See* Matterhorn.
—— Petit Mont. *See* Klein Matterhorn.
Cevennes, 139.
Cevio, 153, 159.
Chambéry, 24, 124, 184.
Chambésy, 335.
Chamonix, 2, 13; early history of, 61-66; de Saussure's first visits to, 66-74; in winter 80; de Saussure's visit to, in 1767, 87-89, 96, 103, 125, 135, 173, 183; English visitors at, 186; 191, 193, 195-201, 209, 212, 220-5, 235, 236, 242-6, 251, 259, 260, 281, 290, 321, 325-7, 333, 350, 351, 353, 356, 361, 362, 367, 428, 429, 433, 459, 462.
Chamonix, Aiguilles of, 164, 284, 326.
—— guides, 210, 247, 252.
—— Vale of, 61 *n.*, 157, 326.
Chamossaire, 415.
Chanrion, 333.
Chapieu, 90, 146-7, 274, 281.
Chapuis, Mlle., 240.
Charleston, U.S.A., 375.
Charlet, 248, 249.
—— Mme., 144.
Charlotte, Queen, 176, 181.
Charlotteville, U.S.A., 385.
Charrière, Mme. de, 324.
Chartreuse, Grande, 5, 124.
Châteaubourg, 349.
Chateaubriand, 23.
Châtillon, 278.
Chatsworth, 114.

INDEX

Chêde, Lac de, 191.
Chenalette, 153.
Chermontane, 416, 432.
Chesterfield, Lord, 183.
Choisy le Roy, 96.
Chouet, J. R., 19, 452.
Christine, Duchess of Lorraine, 48.
Chur, 143, 170, 281.
Cime Brune. *See* Klein Matterhorn.
Cimes Blanches, 272, 276.
Clairon, Mlle., 45, 97-9.
Clarens, 21.
Clement XIV., Pope, 131.
—— Vicaire, J. M., 153.
Clermont-Ferrand, 382, 387.
Clewer, 28 *n.*, 176, 177.
Cogne, 273, 274.
Coke, Lady Mary, 108.
Combin, Grand, 232.
Combloux, 430.
Como, 126, 170.
—— Lake of, 6, 143.
Conches, 47, 49, 51, 357, 361, 375, 376, 380, 436.
Condorcet, 123, 315, 362.
Conrad II., Emperor, 297.
Constance, 339, 342.
—— Lake of, 164, 342.
Contamines, 144, 196.
Conway, General H. S., 114.
Coolidge, Rev. W. A. B., 30 *n.*, 267.
Coppet, 397, 399.
Coppenex, 240.
Cornuaud, Isaac, 333, 367.
Cornwall, 116, 118.
Coste, 96.
Côte, Glacier de la, 234, 249.
—— Montagne de la, 198, 200, 209-13, 215, 221, 223, 226, 361 *n.*
Courmayeur, 90, 148-50, 242, 246, 248-250, 253-5, 259, 281, 416.
Courterai, 192.
Couteran, M., 201.
Couttet, Joseph Marie, 71.
—— Marie, 71, 226, 245, 246, 259.
—— Michel Alphonse, 71.
Couvercle, 245.
Cowper, William, 28, 29.
Coxe, Archdeacon, 26, 45, 280, 343, 344, 345 *n.*, 410.
Craft, Miss, 327.
Crammont, 149-50, 164, 284, 325.
Craven, Hon. Maria, 247.
—— Lady (Margravine of Anspach), 247.
Crodo (Val Formazza), 158.
Crommelin, M., 97, 99.
Curchod, Mlle. Susanne. *See* Necker, Mme. Jacques.
Cuvier, 8, 48, 58, 74, 405, 406, 423, 424, 443.

DARWIN, Charles, 404, 440, 453.
—— Sir Francis, 404.
Dauphiné, 219, 232, 422, 440.
Davy, Sir Humphry, 393, 395, 440.
Déjean, 356.
Delcroz, Commandant, 174.
Délices de la Suisse, 16.
Deluc, G. A. and J. A., 28, 171; the ascent of the Buet, 175-81; 188, 192, 316, 322, 340, 352, 406, 421, 423, 442, 443, 454, 460.
—— J. F., 28, 175, 316.
Denmark, King of, 117.
Dentan, Pasteur, 181.
—— Julien, Syndic, 372.
Dent Blanche, 273.
—— du Midi, 153.
—— de Jaman, 126.
Derbyshire, 370.
Derry, Bishop of. *See* Bristol.
Descartes, 75, 410.
Desmarets, Nicolas, 96, 422, 431-2.
Desonnaz, 366-7.
Desportes, Félix, 175, 334, 385, 390, 391.
Dévouassoud, family, 200.
—— François, 70, 72, 210.
—— Jean Louis, 72.
Diderot, 352.
Dijon, 321.
Diodati, 48, 379.
Directoire, French, 390, 392.
Disentis, 5, 171, 282.
Dobson, Austin, 109.
Dôle, 55, 290.
Dolomieu, 375, 386, 439, 440.
Domo d'Ossola, 159, 263.
Donati, 465.
Dora Baltea, 278.
Dover, 104, 119.
Dübi, Dr. H., 170, 218 *n.*
Dumas, Alexandre, *père*, 187, 216, 218, 219.
Dumont, Etienne, 365.
Duncombe Park, 111.
Duroveray, J. A., 337, 379.

EARLE, Mr. and Mrs., 107, 110.
Eaton Hall, 115.
Eau Noire Valley, 189.
Ebel, J. G., 26, 346, 361, 429, 446.
Edgeworth, Maria, 399.
Edinburgh, 33, 385, 401.
Egalité, Philippe, 358.
Elba, 131.
Elbruz, 36, 231, 251.
Engadine, 5, 64, 252, 264.
Engelberg, 5, 143, 280, 342.
Enghien, Duc d', 123.

England, 97, 101, 103, 120, 128, 136, 176, 217, 306, 316, 356, 365, 370, 371, 395, 436, 446, 454.
Entrèves, 246.
Enville, Duchesse d', 94, 96, 123, 310.
Epinay, Mme. d', 41, 59, 97, 123.
Eschen, M., 193, 440.
Espinasse, M. l', 106-8.
Estérel, 330, 347, 432.
Etna, 134, 287.
Evelyn, John, his *Diary*, 20, 63 *n*.
Exchaquet, C. F., 244, 247, 250-2, 255, 285, 343.
Eymar, Comte d', 439.

FABRI, Mme., 335.
—— Mlle. Renée. *See* Mme. Nicolas Théodore de Saussure.
Faizan, Louis, 319.
Falkenstein, Count. *See* Joseph II.
Farel, Guillaume, 48, 298.
Fatio de Duillier, J. C., 172.
—— —— Nicolas, 15, 16, 63, 172, 173.
—— Pierre, 301.
Fauche-Borel, 380.
Faucigny, 64, 81, 227.
—— Alps of, 170.
—— Glaciers of, 16, 18, 64.
—— mines, 245, 343.
Faujas de Saint-Fond, 340.
Favre, Prof. Alphonse, 388, 426, 440, 443.
Fazy, M. Henri, 355, 358.
Ferdinand of Austria, Archduke, 340.
Ferney, 39, 98, 123, 124, 131, 137, 323, 418.
Ferpècle, 416.
Ferrand, M. Henri, 81.
Fibbia, la, 161.
Fiesch, 167.
—— Glaciers of, 280.
Fiescherberg, 169.
Fiescher Joch, 242.
Fiescherhörner, 167.
Finsteraarhorn, 15, 155, 166.
Fischer, C. A., 181, 182.
Fitzgerald, Lord Robert, 374.
Florence, 130.
Flushing, 104.
Fol, 366.
Fonds, les, 179, 188.
Fontainebleau, 20.
Forbes, Prof. D. J., 187, 194, 262, 274, 401, 429, 431, 441, 447.
Forclaz (St. Gervais), 61.
Formazza, Val, 157, 158, 280.
Fountains Abbey, 111.
Fraele, Val di, 416.
France, 7, 20, 34, 38, 91-9, 108, 109, 140, 281, 295, 301, 306, 307, 339, 347- 350, 358, 359, 361, 376, 386, 390, 391, 450.
Franche-Comté, 233.
Frederick the Great, 114, 185, 413.
Franklin, Benjamin, 119, 130, 436, 458.
Fréjus, 330, 347.
Fribourg, 297, 300.
—— Canton of, 56.
Frisi, Père, 126, 127.
Frontenex, 48, 50-2, 103, 138, 141, 333, 376.

GALENSTOCK, 160.
Galiani, Abbé, 96.
Garda, Lake of, 38.
Gardens, English and foreign, compared, 21.
Garrick, David, 103, 106, 107, 119.
Garwood, Prof. E., 439.
Gautier, Prof. Raoul, 435.
Gawthorpe, 112.
Géant, Col du, 71, 143, 262, 435, 447, 456, 458, 462.
Geikie, Sir Archibald, 423, 434, 439, 441, 442.
Geneva, *passim*; in the eighteenth century, 31-46; its Society, 35-9; sumptuary rules, 36-7; theatricals, 45; the Academy, 44; Collège, 312-18; foreign students, 44; political events, 294-310, 332-401.
Genève, Journal de, 237, 243, 246, 320.
Genevois, Counts of, 297.
Genoa, 328, 329, 363, 384, 440.
Genthod, 21, 52, 82, 138-40, 143, 240, 254, 325, 341.
Geology, 8, 286-8, 292-3, 421-4.
George II., 413.
Gersdorf, Baron de, 170, 212, 219, 244, 344.
Gesner, Conrad, 5, 8-13, 29.
—— Johann, 410.
—— Solomon, 342, 343.
Gibbon, Edward, 63, 97, 118, 134, 273, 359, 397, 419, 453.
Gilpin, 109.
Giornico, 159.
Glaciers, 14, 17, 151, 276; observations and theories concerning, 427-33; rate of movement, 428.
Godet, Prof. Philippe, 24.
Goethe, 184, 325, 326.
Goldsmith, Oliver, 108.
Gondo, 263.
Gordon, Duke of, 51.
Görlitz, 244.
Gosse, Edmund, 29.
—— Henri Albert, 138, 243, 246.
Gotthard, Saint, Pass, 7, 155, 160-2.
Göttingen, 382, 383, 385, 413.

Gouille à Vassu, 153.
Graham, Sir James, 326.
Graian Alps, 232, 273, 274.
Granville, Lord, 365.
Graubünden. *See* Grisons.
Gray, Thomas, 29, 36, 79, 406.
Grenairon, 178.
Grenier des Communes (Sixt), 178.
Grenoble, 62, 124, 232, 321.
Grenus, Jacques, 140, 367.
Gressoney, 8, 267, 271.
Greville, Charles, 161.
Griaz, Glacier of, 223.
Gribble, Francis, 30 n.
Gries Pass, 143, 154, 157, 159, 170, 290, 323.
Grigna, 6.
Grignan, 347.
Grimm, Baron de, 58, 59, 97, 99, 137.
Grimsel Pass, 154-7, 159, 163, 170, 401, 415.
Grindelwald, 17, 70, 125, 138, 165, 166, 168, 169, 170, 401.
—— Glaciers of, 14, 16, 63, 280.
Grisons, 14, 15, 125, 155, 166, 171, 280, 282, 416.
Grivola, 273.
Grouchy, Marquis de, 362.
Grüner, G. S., 16, 17, 18, 19, 87, 191, 280, 427, 446.
Guettard, 433.
Guttannen, 156.

HAARLEM, 395.
Hackfall, 111.
Hague, the, 101, 117, 405.
Haller, A. von, 2, 19, 22, 26, 29, 58-60, 64, 66, 74-8, 81, 85-8, 92, 101, 121, 122, 124, 131, 134, 138, 155, 165, 170, 280, 281, 294, 307-9, 311, 318, 323, 324, 402-20 ; his son, 122, 454.
Halley, Edmund, 457.
Hamilton, Duke of, 44, 135.
—— Sir William, 132, 133, 135, 161, 236, 321, 352.
Handegg, 156.
Harcourt, Duc d', 96.
—— Marquis d', 96.
Haslithal, 70, 263.
Heim, Prof., 430.
Helmsley, 111.
Helvoetsluys, 103.
Hennin, 196, 428.
Henry, Prince, of Prussia, 185.
Hérens, Val d', 197.
Hérin (or Erin), J. B., 272.
Hill, Mr., 245, 253.
—— Dr. J., 123.
Himalaya, 226, 281.

Hobbes, Thomas, 449.
Hogarth, W., 154, 274, 446.
Holbach, Baron d', 97, 449.
Holland, 99-105.
Homer, 453.
Horace, 3, 216, 224, 453.
Horngacher, 99.
Hottinger, 18.
Houches, les, 68, 188, 223.
Humboldt, Alexander von, 34, 440, 458.
Hutton, James, 423, 442.
Hyères, 347.

ILLIEZ, Val d', 153, 245.
Inns, Alpine, 69, 280.
Institut de France, 58, 395, 439.
Interlaken, 166.
Ireland, 339, 384.
Ischia, 132.
Iseo, Lake of, 38.
Iséran, Col d', 87.
Isère, Val d', 232.
Italy, 121-41, 327.
—— Lakes of, 126, 143, 170.
Ivrea, 150, 277, 430.
Ivernois, Sir Francis d', 316, 339, 385.

JALABERT, François, 54, 86, 87, 103, 143, 191.
Jaman, Col de, 156.
—— Dent de, 126.
Jansen, M., 210, 231.
Jardin, le, 91.
Jazzi, Cima di, 270.
Jebb, Sir Richard, 72.
Jefferson, Thomas, 385.
Jena, Literary Gazette of, 276.
Joch Pass, 143, 342, 410, 415.
Johnson, Dr. Samuel, 107, 111, 118, 123, 184, 280, 419.
Jorasse, le Grand. *See* Lombard.
Jorasses, les Grandes, 52, 232, 247.
Jordanay, J. L., 150, 242.
Joseph II., 184, 322-24.
Josephine, Empress, 334.
Joux, Nant de, 220.
Judith. *See* de Saussure.
Juel, Jens, 387.
Jullien, J., 381.
Jungfrau, 165, 166, 325.
Jura, 24, 54, 55, 57, 78, 277, 290, 321.
Jussieu, Bernard de, 91, 94, 414.
Justel, Henri, 15.

KELLERMANN, General, 366, 390.
Kent, Duke of, 353.
Kien Thal, 416.
Knaresborough, 112.

LABORDE, 42, 280, 428, 446.
La Condamine, C. M. de, 124.
Lake depths and temperatures, 463-5.
Lalande, J. J. de, 135.
Lamanon, M. de, 341, 348.
Land's End, 118.
La Place, Marquis de, 425.
La Rochefoucauld d'Enville, Duc de, 16, 66, 96, 123, 243.
Lassels, 38.
Lausanne, 26, 47, 48, 63, 173, 212, 273, 323, 324, 361, 387, 397, 414.
—— Journal de, 173, 218, 246.
Lauterbrunnen, 166.
Léchaud, Plain de, 179.
Leeds, 112, 114.
Leghorn, 131.
Leibnitz, 75, 408.
Léman, Département du, 390.
—— Lake, 1, 22, 28, 31, 56, 66, 122, 152, 172, 177, 227, 298, 344, 376.
Le Pays, M., 62.
Lescarbot, M., 14.
L'Espinasse, M., 106-8.
Le Roy, M., 185.
Leukerbad. See Loëche.
Levantina, Val, 83, 160.
L'Evêque, Henri, 260.
Lever, Sir Ashton, 114.
Lezay-Marnésia, Marquis de, 123.
—— —— Marquise de, 123.
Liddes, 152.
Ligne, Prince de, 206-09.
Linck, J. A., 446.
Lincoln, 110.
Linththal, 280.
Locarno, 126, 159.
Loccie, Col delle, 272.
Loëche, 5, 273, 324.
Loiseau de Mauléon, 95.
Lombard, Jean Baptiste, dit le Grand Jorasse, 161, 193, 198.
Lombardy, 8, 135, 232, 276, 340.
London, 77, 105-8, 116-19, 136, 410, 414.
Lorraine, 47.
—— Duke of, 47.
Lotschen Thal, 245.
Louis XIV., 3.
—— XV., 21, 137.
—— XVI., 49, 99, 140, 185, 199, 356-8, 361, 422.
—— XVIII., 185.
Louis-Philippe, Duke of Orleans, 123.
Lucendro, Lago di, 280.
Lucerne, 11, 163, 342.
—— Lake of, 325.
Lullin, Ami, 77, 380, 386.
—— —— Mme., 104, 116.
—— Jean Antoine, 77, 78.

Lyons, 321, 331, 340, 373, 437.
Lys Glacier, 271.
—— Val de, 7, 271, 272.
Lyskamm, 271, 272, 273.

MACUGNAGA, 265-8, 270, 273, 281, 355, 356, 447.
Maggia, Val, 158, 159, 281, 444.
Mahon, Lord, 129, 130, 316, 318, 339.
Maggiore, Lago, 38, 126, 158, 159, 263, 269.
Maillart-Gosse, Dr. H., 387.
Maladetta, La, 69.
Maloya, 416.
Manchester, 114.
Mann, Sir Horace, 130.
Mansfield, Lord, 109.
Marat, Jean Paul, 185, 372.
Maresfield Park, 43.
Maria Theresa, Empress, 323.
Marignié, L. E. F., 237, 238, 240, 241.
Marmontel, J. F., 99.
Marseilles, 331.
Martel, Pierre, 1, 63, 66, 173, 243.
Marti, Benoit, 11, 12.
Martigny, 90, 148, 152, 193, 216, 254, 259, 263, 325.
Masino, Baths of, 5.
Matey, Dr., 106, 108.
Matlock, 114.
Mathews, C. E., 205.
Matterhorn, 150, 166, 264, 272, 276, 447.
—— Klein, 282.
Maurienne, 328, 401.
Méchel, Chrétien de, 260.
Mediating Powers, 294, 300, 305-7, 335, 339, 340, 362, 391, 392, 414.
Mediterranean, 173, 291, 437, 465.
Meiners, Prof., 343, 344.
Meiringen, 156.
Mercier, François, 76.
Mer de Glace, 44, 70, 88, 103, 135, 168, 196, 242-5, 251, 282, 283, 325, 327, 428, 431, 441, 447.
Merian, 14, 18.
Merle d'Aubigné, 312.
Metaphysics, 448-52.
Meteorology, 242, 434, 435, 457-62.
Mettenberg, 167, 169.
Metz, 47.
Meyer, 164, 244.
Miage, Col de, 150.
—— Glacier de, 150, 242, 269, 277.
Micheli du Crest, J. B., 155, 301.
Midi, Aiguille du, 75, 164, 227, 228, 230.
—— Dent du, 153.
Milan, 126-8, 263, 269, 328.

Mill, Dr. H. R., 327, 352, 435, 438, 457-65.
Milton, John, 3.
Mineralogy, 437.
Minette. See Tronchin, Mme. J. L.
Mirabeau, Comte de, 365.
—— Marquis de, 99.
Mönch, 166.
Môle, 60, 171, 290.
Mon Boso, 7, 214.
Moncalieri, 351.
Monget, 437.
Montagnes Maudites, Les, 65.
Montagnier, H. F., 152, 246.
Mont Blanc, passim; early attempts on, 197-9, 209; Paccard and Balmat's success, 211-19; de Saussure's ascent, 197-238; verses on, 238-41.
Montecello, 385.
Montélimar, 347.
Monte Moro, 262, 270.
Montenvers, 63, 68, 70, 151, 175, 196, 222, 247, 327, 334, 343, 385, 400.
Monte Rosa, 7, 171, 262-77.
Montesquieu, 42.
Montesson, Mme. de, 123, 139, 358.
Montets, Les, 61, 67, 68, 325.
Monteuil, 47.
Montgolfier, 340, 437.
Monthey, 430.
Montjoie, Valley of, 56.
Montpellier, 138, 140, 141, 327, 331, 333.
Montreux, 126.
Monts, Les, 234.
Monts Maudits, 35, 69, 82, 172, 228.
Monty, 377.
Moraines, 151; de Saussure's theory of, 429-30.
Moore, Dr. John, 42, 44, 129, 135, 399.
—— Sir John, 135.
Morat, Lake of, 38.
Morellet, Abbé, 97.
Morley, Lord, 23, 24, 96.
Morozzo, Count, 262, 268.
Morrice, Mr., 108.
Mortine, La, 178, 189.
Moscati, Prof., 128.
Mottets, Les, 147.
Mountain sickness, 230-1, 341-2.
Moutray, Mrs., 399.
Mowbray Point, 111.
Müller, J. de, 407, 408.
—— Mlle., 170.
—— M., 163.
Mumm, A. L., 443.
Munster, Sebastian, 64.
Muraltus, Mr., 281.
Muretto Pass, 280.
Murith, Abbé, 151, 152.

NANT BORRANT, 145.
Naples, 127, 130, 132-4, 136, 161, 440.
Napoleon, 42, 139, 140, 186, 245, 260, 263, 329, 390, 391, 394.
Naviglio, Grande, 269.
Naville, Ernest, 400, 449, 450, 451.
Necker, Henri M., 375.
—— de Germagny, 359, 380, 396.
—— Jacques, 354, 356, 357, 362, 371, 396, 397.
—— Mme. (Susanne Curchod), 97, 98, 235, 345, 358, 371, 376, 454.
—— de Saussure, Jacques, 345, 375, 388, 393, 396.
—— —— Mme., 85, 97, 98, 145, 146, 345, 387, 393.
—— Louis, 400, 401.
Neuchâtel, 24, 48, 372, 375.
Neuhaus, 156.
Neville, Mr., 45.
Newton, Sir Isaac, 15, 42, 185.
Nice, 329.
Niesen, 3, 12, 415.
Nîmes, 321, 331.
Noire, La, 243, 252, 253.
Nomenclature, Alpine, 166.
Northumberland, Duke of, 119.
Novalesa, 5.
Novara, 128.
Noyon, 99.
Nyon, 139, 227.

OBERALP PASS, 162.
Oberemps, 27.
Obergestelen, 156.
Oberland, Bernese, 11, 13-15, 70, 143, 156, 165, 170, 186, 192, 245, 280, 281, 412, 413, 416.
—— Bündner, 5.
Ochsenstock, 342.
Odier, Dr. Louis, 129, 224, 362, 372, 373.
Oeschinen See, 185.
Orbe, source of, 57.
Orleans, Duke of, 59, 358.
—— Louis-Philippe, Duke of, 123, 358.
Ostend, 101, 104.
Otahiti, 117, 353.
Otemma Glacier, 152.
Ovid, quoted, 453.
Oxford, 103, 118, 317, 370.

PACCARD, François, 200.
—— Dr. Michel Gabriel, 43, 173, 200, 201, 205, 217, 218, 219, 223, 229, 236, 239-41, 250, 260, 285, 343.
—— père, 214, 223.
Palais Royal, 96.
Pallas, 423.

Palmerston, Lord, 103, 106, 107, 115, 119, 124, 125, 217, 361.
Pantenbruck, 280.
Paris, 42, 91-9, 139-40, 356, 358, 361, 376, 385, 386.
—— Journal de, 341.
Parminter, the Misses, 192.
Pars, William, 103, 446.
Passy, 61, 89.
Patience. See Jordanay, J. L.
Pavia, 127, 324.
—— Certosa di, 128.
Peak Cavern, 114.
Pedriolo Alp, 268-71.
Pèlerins, Glacier des, 277.
Penck, Prof., 439.
Pennant, Mr., 111.
Périgord, Comte de, 140.
Pestarena, 266.
Petit, Pierre, 91.
Petrarch, 8, 57.
Pfäffers, 5.
Physiology, 452.
Pfyffer, General, 163, 164, 244.
Pictet, J. L., 54, 86, 87, 143, 447.
—— M. A., 54, 138, 143, 216, 327, 328, 336, 346, 382, 385, 392, 445.
—— de Rochemont, Charles, 398, 399.
Piedmont, 328.
Pierre Ronde, 202.
Pilatus, 9, 10, 11.
Pisa, 131.
Pizzo Bianco, 268-9.
Plan de l'Aiguille, 283.
Planpraz, 87.
Plateau, Grand, 211, 229.
—— Petit, 198, 209, 210, 228.
Platt, Joshua, 117.
Pliny, the Younger, 3, 330, 409; his villa, 126.
Plouquet, 276.
Pluche, Abbé, 403.
Pococke, 16, 63, 65, 68.
Pointe Percée, 64, 227.
Ponte Grande, 264.
Pope, Alexander, 21, 58, 109.
Portland, Duchess of, 119.
Porto Fino, 401.
Portree, 401.
Poussin, N., 157.
Praborgne. See Zermatt.
Pradier, 375.
Prangins, Mme. de, 259, 260.
Pratolungo, Dr., 328.
Pré-St. Didier, 274.
Preux, Baron de, 152.
Prévost, Pierre, 367.
Prévost-Lullin, 338.
Pringle, Sir John, 118, 410.
Procida, 132.

Prosa, La, 162.
Provence, 219, 347-9.
Pugnani, 113.
Puy de Dôme, 321, 387.
Pyrenees, 4, 69.

RADZIWILL, Prince, 412.
Ramond, 26, 345.
Ramsay, 438.
Ravenna, 134.
Rawlins, F. H., 72.
Razumouski, Count, 344, 345.
Réaumur, R. A., 403, 417, 457, 459.
Rebmann, 3.
Récamier, Mme., 40, 41.
Reformation, the, 19, 34, 62, 153, 296, 298.
Remiremont, 47.
Renaissance, the, 8, 12, 13, 19, 33.
Rendu, Bishop, 194, 431.
René II., Duke of Lorraine, 47.
Reposoir, 111, 227, 234.
—— Aiguille Percée du, 227, 234.
—— Chartreuse du, 64.
Reybaz, E. S., 239, 366.
Reynolds, Sir Joshua, 103, 108, 184.
Rhine, 7, 32, 37, 156.
—— Hinter, 155.
—— Vorder, 162.
Rheinthal, 155.
Rheinwald, 155.
Rheinwaldhorn, 17, 282.
Rhêmes, Val de, 150.
Rhône Glacier, 125, 280.
—— Valley, 27, 78, 281, 374.
Ribel, 243 n.
Richelieu, Duc de, 137.
Richmond Park, 107.
Riffel Alp, 264, 271.
Rigi, 163, 270.
Rilliet-Fatio, 337.
Rilliet, Mme., 337.
Rive, Mme. de la, 260.
—— Jeanne Marie de la. See Bonnet, Mme. Charles.
—— Pierre Louis de la, 49.
—— Renée de la. See de Saussure, Mme. Nicolas.
—— Porte de, 33.
Riviera, 138, 143, 281, 311, 327, 329.
Roche, 59, 78, 407, 414, 419.
Rochecourbière, Rochers de la, 347.
Rochemelon, 350.
Roche Michel, 351.
Rochemont, de, 378.
Rochers Rouges, 214, 219, 226, 233.
Rochester, 105.
Roche-sur-Foron, La, 82.
Rockingham, Lady, 109-10, 114.
—— Lord, 107, 109, 113.

INDEX

Roget, J. M., 335.
Roland, J. M., 138.
—— Mme., 138.
Rolle, 377, 379, 382.
Rome, 4, 55, 123, 127, 134, 287, 330, 405.
Romé de l'Isle, 135.
Romilly, Sir Samuel, 53, 335, 352, 378.
Rosenlaui, 165, 280.
Rosslyn, Lord. *See* Wedderburn, Alexander.
Rothhorn, 271.
Rotterdam, 99, 103, 172.
Rouelle, G., 91.
Rousseau, J. J., 2, 19, 21, 22 ; his *Nouvelle Héloïse*, 23, 25, 27, 29, 31, 38, 39, 43, 56, 114 ; his *Lettres écrites de la Montagne*, 121, 175-7, 192, 304 ; his *Contrat Social*, 305, 307, 309, 313 ; his *Emile*, 317, 440 ; his *Lettre à d'Alembert*, 318 ; condemnation of *Emile* and the *Contrat Social*, 449.
Royal Society, 14, 116, 118, 119, 123, 133, 171, 172, 176, 236, 293, 321, 352, 370, 395, 403, 410, 413, 440.
Royat, 382.
Rue, Mme. de la, 329.
Ruitor, 232.
Ruskin, John, 57, 70, 71, 192, 263, 264, 443.

Saas, 262, 263, 280.
Saas-Grat, 273.
Sainte-Beuve, 24, 49, 58, 324, 409, 443.
Saint-Ours, J. P., 320, 387, 439, 444, 452.
St. Marcel, mines at, 278.
St. Moritz, 5, 416.
Saint-Réal, M. de, 278, 350.
Sales, Mlles., 136.
Salève, 25, 30, 34, 45, 54, 64, 290.
Sallanches, 35, 62, 65, 68, 89, 143, 220, 264, 326, 327, 430.
Samoens, 86.
Sanetsch Pass, 245.
Sardinia, King of, 36, 184, 339.
Sassina, Val, 6.
Saulxures, 47.
Saussure, Albertine Andrienne. *See* Necker, Mme. Jacques.
—— Alphonse de, 220, 335, 361, 370, 377, 379, 395.
—— Anne de, 49.
—— Antoine de, 47, 48.
—— César de, 48.
—— Elie de, 48.
—— Henri de, 35, 72, 218, 241, 395.
—— H. B. de, *passim* ; ancestry, 47 ; homes, 51 ; early life and visits to Chamonix, 53-90 ; Professor, 75 ; marriage, 78 ; grand tour, 91-120 ; visits Italy, 120-35 ; Alpine travels, 142-196, 279-85 ; ascends Mont Blanc, 223-34 ; observations on Col du Géant, 242-61 ; tour of Monte Rosa, 264-85 ; home life, 332-45 ; educational efforts, 310-18 ; founds Société des Arts, 318 ; visits Riviera, 328-31 ; political activity, 382-92 ; house besieged, 326-38 ; loss of fortune, 371, 383 ; illness and death, 372-93 ; place in science, 421-443, 457-64 ; in literature, 443-8 ; in philosophy, 448-52 ; inventor of scientific instruments, 435 ; his character, 454 ; list of publications, 467 ; his 'Discours Préliminaire,' 286-93.
—— Mme. H. B. de (*née* Albertine Amélie Boissier), 39, 40, 77-9, 84, 88, 95, 99, 100, 115-17, 120, 129, 140, 142, 220, 222, 224, 225, 280, 282, 327, 328, 342, 347, 351, 361, 366, 368, 370-3, 375, 376, 379, 387, 389, 394, 396.
—— Jean Baptiste de, 48.
—— Judith de, 29, 136-9, 140, 141, 327, 331, 342, 346, 394.
—— Mongin de, 48.
—— Nicolas de, 48, 49, 59, 138.
—— Mme. Nicolas de, 40, 49, 52, 58, 59, 77, 94, 331.
—— Nicolas Théodore de, 43, 90, 138, 225, 251, 253, 258, 260, 263, 269, 273, 335, 350, 351, 370, 376, 377, 379, 388, 393, 395, 447.
—— Mme. Nicolas Théodore (*née* Renée Fabri), 395.
—— Théodore, Syndic, 48, 49.
Savannah, 48.
Savile, Sir George, 107, 109, 110, 114.
Savoy, Duke of, 20, 32, 299, 371, 301.
—— Glaciers of, 1, 63, 177, 186, 193, 422, 427.
Sayous, P. A., 294, 324, 405, 443, 444.
Scenery, Alpine, early appreciation of, 1-30, 35.
Scheideck, Great, 167, 170, 415.
Scheldt, 104.
Scheuchzer, J. D., 172, 173.
—— J. J., 14, 15, 16, 18, 63, 172, 410.
Schlegel, J. E., 398.
Schöllenen Gorge, 163.
Schöpf, Thomas, 167 *n*.
Schreckhorn, 15, 155, 164, 167, 169.
Schwarzberg, 263.
Scotland, 29, 109, 401.
Sécheron, 49, 322, 323, 399.
Seigne, Col de la, 90, 147, 148, 245, 274, 290.
Senebier, J., 1, 42, 49, 50, 53, 60, 64, 65, 77, 82, 91, 101, 117, 119, 128, 130, 132, 185, 340, 385, 388, 438, 443.

Septimer Pass, 416.
Sermenza, Val, 270.
Servoz, 61, 68, 89, 193, 200, 235, 244, 343, 440.
Sesia, Val, 7, 270, 271.
Sévigné, Mme. de, 347.
Shakespeare, 45, 74, 119.
Sheffield, 114.
Shelley, Lady, 42, 43.
—— Sir John, 42, 43.
—— Percy Bysshe, 10, 28, 322.
Shuckburgh, Sir George, 275.
Sicily, 290.
Siegfried Map, 27, 270.
Simler, Josias, 13, 14, 18, 284.
Simmenthal, 156.
Simon, Pierre, 68, 71, 144, 189, 197, 283.
Simplon Pass, 27, 28, 126, 262, 263, 290, 416.
Sion, 273.
Sismondi, 43, 53.
Sixt, 86, 178, 179, 180, 188, 218.
Skye, Isle of, 401.
Sloane, Sir Hans, 16, 410.
Smith, Sir J. E., 407.
Solander, Dr., 106.
Soulavie, 363, 373.
Spa, 100.
Spallanzani, 85, 127, 134, 436.
Spencer, Lady, 117.
Spescha, Placidus a, 171, 281, 282.
Spiez, 156.
Splugen Pass, 6, 143, 156, 170, 281, 290, 401.
Spon, J., 32, 172.
Staël, Mme. de, 26, 42, 85, 141, 358, 362, 371, 382, 396, 397, 398.
Staffa, 265, 270.
Stamford, 109.
Stanhope, Lady, 124, 129.
—— Lord, 43, 87, 124, 129, 130, 318.
Stanmore Church, 237.
Steinberg, 415.
Stephen, Sir Leslie, 23.
Stern, Lawrence, 154.
Stockhorn, 3, 12, 415.
Stow, 370.
Studer, Bernard, 17, 194.
Studley, 111.
Suanetia, 63.
—— Prince of, 36.
Sulmo (Solmona), 3.
Sulzbach, Prince of, 63.
Superga, 351.
Susa, 61.
Susten Pass, 17.
Swinburne, Lady, 370.
—— Sir John, 370.

TACONNAZ, Glacier de, 67, 189, 225.
Tacul, 52, 242, 244, 249, 254.
—— Glacier du, 200, 242, 246, 247.
—— Lac du, 251.
Tagliaferro, 271.
Tairraz, J. P., 212, 263.
Tanneverge, Pointe de, 245.
Tarascon, 349.
Tarentaise, 147, 401.
Temperatures, deep sea, 328, 329, 463-465; lake, 463-5.
Terni, 134.
Teneriffe, Peak of, 208.
Teniers, David, 329, 446.
Tennyson, Lord, 9, 112, 264.
Testoni, Sig., 266.
Theodulehorn, 273, 276.
—— Pass, 272, 275.
Thirsk, 111.
Thonez, 402, 406.
Thonon, 28, 50.
Thrale, Mrs., 29.
Thun, 12.
—— Lake of, 156.
Ticino, Canton, 155, 269, 416.
Tilney, Lord, 133.
Tingry, P. F., 336, 385, 393.
Tödi, 282.
Töpffer, Rodolphe, 277, 443.
Torricelli, 457.
Tosa Falls, 157.
Toulon, 260, 330, 331, 347-9.
Tour, Col du, 243.
Tournanche, Val, 259, 274, 280, 416.
Tournier, Alexis, 221, 246, 249.
—— Jean Michel, 246.
Travel, Alpine, 280.
Trembley, Jean, 143, 171, 322, 323, 336, 342, 407.
Trient Valley, 192.
Tronchin, François, 91.
—— Henri, 91, 130.
—— Jean Louis, 135.
—— Mme. J. L. (Minette), 84, 91, 95, 99-101, 121, 220, 222, 256, 328, 342, 352, 379, 393, 395.
—— Jean Robert, 95, 122, 123, 130, 320, 453.
—— Dr. Theodore, 41, 58, 59, 74, 77, 85, 95, 122, 123, 130, 320, 453.
—— François (son of Dr. Tronchin), 91, 117, 120, 356.
—— Mlle., 95, 96.
Troublet, Abbé, 99.
Troye, J. B. N., 244.
Tübingen, 277, 410, 428.
Turin, 135, 200, 243, 262, 271, 350, 351.
Turlo Pass, 270.
Turrettini, Jean Alphonse, 19, 82, 99, 131, 324, 452.

INDEX

Turrettini, Mme. Jean Alphonse (*née* Boissier), 81, 91, 95, 99, 100, 220, 256, 336, 393, 395.
Turtmann, 27.
Turton, Dr., 85, 103, 105, 108, 117.
Tyndall, John, 134, 291.

UNTERBECK, 27.
Unteremps, 27.
Ural, 423.
Urseren, 161.
Uzielli, Sig. F., 7.

VACCARONE, Sig., 243.
Valence, 200.
Valais, 7, 9, 13, 14, 27, 125, 256, 263.
Val d'Ayas, 277.
Vallaurie, 347.
Vallette, Gaspard, 347.
Vallorbes, 57.
Vallot, Joseph, 173, 201, 251, 428.
—— Cabane, 231.
Valmont de Bomare, J. C., 94, 96.
—— —— Mme., 94, 96.
Valorsine, 178, 188, 189, 192.
Valsorey, Glacier de, 153.
Val Tellina, 5, 6, 125, 280.
Vanzone, 263, 267.
Var, 330.
Varallo, 5.
Varens, Aiguille de, 89.
Vaucluse, 57, 231.
Vaud, Alps of, 59.
—— Pays de, 47, 55, 126, 420.
Vélan, Mont, 151-3, 245.
Venice, 27, 128, 130, 134, 135.
Vercelli, 128, 328, 355, 447.
Versailles, 84, 356.
Vesuvius, 152, 156, 247.
Via Mala, 170.
Vienna, 323.
—— Congress of, 399.
Villars, 415.
Villeneuve, 414.
Vinci, Leonardo da, 5-8, 214, 270, 424.
Viscari, Prince de, 133.
Visp, 27, 267.
Vispthal, 166, 263, 271, 273, 276, 280.
Vivaré, Mr., 191.
Vivarone, Lake of, 150.
Vogel (Avienus), 183.
Voirons, Les, 54, 183.
Volta, Alexander, 170.
Voltaire, 38, 39, 43, 45, 59, 98, 122, 123, 131, 136, 137, 305, 307, 323, 408, 409, 417, 418, 420, 450.
Volterra, 131.
Vosges, 47, 290.
Voza, Col de, 327.

WALLENSTADT, 38, 143, 170, 201.
Walpole, Horace, 1, 107, 114, 119, 130, 184.
Warwick, Lord, 119.
Washington, George, 385.
Waterford, 339.
Waterloo, 362, 402.
Wedderburn, Alexander (Lord Rosslyn), 112, 113.
Weiss, M., 164.
Weisshorn, 273, 275.
Weissthor, 263, 270.
—— Schwartzberg, 270.
Wengern Alp, 17, 165, 166, 325.
Wentworth House, 113, 114.
Werner, A. G., 96, 422, 423, 426.
Wetterhorn, 166, 415.
Whymper, Edward, 61, 225, 228, 229, 231.
Wills, Sir Alfred, 179.
Windham, William, of Felbrigg, 1, 16, 45, 63, 68, 243.
Windsor, 28, 176, 177.
Witt, John de, 58.
Wolf, 192, 420, 446.
Woodley, 237.
Woollett, 103.
Wordsworth, William, 28, 29, 30, 412.
Wynn, Sir W. W., 113.
—— Captain, 113.
Wynnstay, 113.
Wyttenbach, J. S., 18, 161, 165, 170, 235, 244, 344.

YORK, 107-10, 112, 114, 116.
Yorkshire, 21, 52, 106, 107, 110, 112.

ZASENBERG, 169
Zermatt, 61, 166, 197, 206, 262, 272, 273, 275, 280, 281, 401, 416, 447.
Zittel, 439.
Zumstein Spitze, 272.
Zurich, 8, 19, 134, 143, 170, 314, 374, 448.
—— Canton of, 300, 301, 306, 307, 339, 374.
—— Lake of, 300, 301, 306, 307, 339, 374.
Zurlauben, Baron de, 42.

BOOKS BY MR. DOUGLAS FRESHFIELD

THE EXPLORATION OF THE CAUCASUS

In two volumes, Imperial 8vo, £3, 3s. net

Illustrated by over 70 Full-page Photogravures and several Mountain Panoramas, chiefly from Photographs by Signor Vittorio Sella, and by more than 100 Illustrations in the Text, of the Scenery, People, and Buildings of the Mountain Region of the Caucasus, from Photographs by Signor Sella, M. de Déchy, Mr. H. Woolley, and Mr. W. F. Donkin.

'Mr. Freshfield has chosen a great subject, and has produced a work in every way worthy of it.'—*The Times.*

'No record of exploration has ever been published in this country in so splendid a material form.'—*Daily Chronicle.*

ROUND KANGCHENJUNGA

With Maps and 42 Illustrations, Royal 8vo, 18s. net

The magnificent range of Kangchenjunga is familiar to visitors to Darjiling, but the complete circuit of the great mountain had never been made until it was achieved by Mr. Freshfield's expedition. Its record, the value of which is enhanced by Signor Sella's splendid photographs, must greatly interest all lovers of mountain scenery and adventure.

'The book is one of the best that has been published on mountain exploration.'—*Sir Martin Conway.*

HANNIBAL ONCE MORE

With Illustrations and Maps, 8vo, 5s. net

'The vexed question of the pass by which Hannibal entered Italy is one of those problems on the border-line of history and geography which are equally fascinating and insoluble. . . . It is enough to say that Mr. Freshfield's discussion of the question, if not decisive, is very interesting, and will appeal to all who care to study the problem of mountain traffic in all ages and countries.'—*The Times.*

UNTO THE HILLS

Foolscap 8vo, 5s. net

'It might have been predicted beforehand that if Mr. Douglas Freshfield wrote poetry, it would be about the hills and valleys. The volume will stir many memories in the old friends of the author, and recall to those who have read his books many a scene on which their imagination has delighted to linger.'—*Country Life.*

LONDON: EDWARD ARNOLD

CPSIA information can be obtained
at www.ICGtesting.com
Printed in the USA
LVHW061954151120
671765LV00009B/145

9 789354 189739